PSYCHOLOGICAL STUDIES of
HUMAN DEVELOPMENT

THE CENTURY PSYCHOLOGY SERIES

Richard M. Elliott, Kenneth MacCorquodale,
Gardner Lindzey, and Kenneth E. Clark

EDITORS

PSYCHOLOGICAL STUDIES of HUMAN DEVELOPMENT

THIRD EDITION

EDITED BY

RAYMOND G. KUHLEN

late of Syracuse University

GEORGE G. THOMPSON

The Ohio State University

APPLETON-CENTURY-CROFTS

EDUCATIONAL DIVISION

New York   MEREDITH CORPORATION

PRINTED IN THE UNITED STATES OF AMERICA
390-52875-7

Preface

When Raymond G. Kuhlen, my close friend and longtime professional colleague, was informed by his physician that he had a limited amount of time to live, he started to put his personal and professional affairs in order. These activities raised the question of what should be done about our jointly edited book, *Psychological Studies of Human Development*. Neither of us had ever been too happy about the coverage of late adolescence, early maturity, and the aged in the second edition, so it seemed a good idea, in both our judgments, to correct this situation while we could still confer on selecting the most appropriate and representative papers. As the first step, we came to an agreement on the new papers that should be included for an up-to-date and well-balanced presentation of developmental changes over the *total* life span. Then came the always difficult decisions about papers which could be deleted in order to keep the new edition from becoming too bulky for a paper-bound volume. We became convinced, although reluctantly, that some of the old landmarks, such as the pioneer papers by Miles, Ruch, Terman and Oden, Jones and Conrad, and others, would have to go. Newer studies that had been built on their initial excellence were available, and we decided that they should be brought to the attention of students who might some day extend these advancements even farther.

Soon after we had agreed on plans for the new edition and after Dr. Kuhlen had abridged and adapted the new papers, he entered the terminal stage of his illness. After his death, our close friend Eric F. Gardner gave unstintingly of his time to send me the materials on which Dr. Kuhlen was working until just a few days before he died. Although I take full responsibility for the introductions to the papers and the final organization of the volume, I have in all instances tried to guess at what my co-editor's suggestions and criticisms would have been had he been available to offer them. I like to believe that Dr. Kuhlen would have approved of the present volume. We agreed on nearly all the major values of life, such as the priorities of family, friends, science-making, teaching, and personal integrity, so I am inclined to believe that again we would have been of a common mind on the outcome of this project.

Dr. Kuhlen and I were always proud of this co-edited volume. It had been unusually well received in its first two editions, and we had persuaded ourselves that this favorable reception was due in some measure to the time and energy we had given to preparing the abridgments and writing the introductory and integrative sections. We were convinced that there is a firm and useful place for such collected papers in modern education. The following observations, taken from the preface to the second edition, summarize our many discussions on this point of view.

Almost every college or university professor has felt the need, at one time or another, to have his students read primary research and theoretical reports. This need is often frustrated. It is unrealistic and grossly unfair to ask a class of thirty or forty students to read a journal article or a monograph when the library has only one available copy. The instructor further realizes that the wear and tear of much handling will soon reduce expensive, and in some instances irreplaceable, journals to illegible shreds, useless for the scholarly pursuits of other students and investigators. One answer to this common dilemma in college teaching is the source book of original writings, long popular in the humanities and becoming increasingly standard practice in the sciences. There seems to be little doubt that books of "readings" in psychology can serve as useful teaching resources supplementing other instructional devices. It is well known that a book in the student's hands has a better chance of being read than a book in the library.

The research and theoretical papers included in this third edition provide convenient access to some of the more interesting studies of psychological growth trends over the life span. Encompassing as they do the developmental period from infancy to senescence, they encourage a broad perspective of the effects of aging on psychological adjustment within a cultural context. Dr. Kuhlen and I always believed that such psychological studies of human development could be convenient and useful teaching aids in several areas of collegiate instruction: courses in developmental psychology, including courses in child psychology, the psychology of adolescence, the psychology of maturity and old age, or a course utilizing a life-span approach; courses in human growth and development especially designed for teachers-in-training; introductory courses in general psychology which seek to promote an understanding of self and others through consideration of the adjustment difficulties of people of all ages; courses in social psychology which consider as primary data the individual's potentialities for social interaction and growth.

What have been the bases of the selection of *particular* papers? Why this particular set of papers rather than another made up of different ones on the same topics? To a degree, any collection of papers reflects the biases of the collector. The present papers have been selected to provide a sampling both with respect to important areas of research in the psychology of human development and with respect to broad age bands of the life span. An effort has been made to present papers which utilize a great variety of research procedures, including studies of individual cases, or which summarize a group of studies as a means of arriving at broader generalizations which may help to extend theory. The papers included are admittedly of uneven scientific quality—this is partly because of the complexity of the problems studied in some areas—but that circumstance should provide students and instructors opportunity for critical class discussion of scientific procedures. It is believed, however, that each paper possesses intrinsic interest value, will prove provocative of thought and discussion, and will illustrate or document significant points.

In this revision the editors have retained forty-eight of the fifty-nine papers presented in the second edition. This third edition presents twelve new additions that report notable advances in our understanding of psychological development during adolescence, maturity, and senescence.

Some of the papers presented in this book have been adapted and abridged in order to conserve space and thereby permit the inclusion of a larger number of reports. These adaptations have taken several forms: omission of some secondary findings which are not vital to the principal hypothesis being tested, abridgment of extended discussions of background literature and experimental methodology, and deletion of interesting but expendable portions of the discussion, such as plans for further research. In each adaption we made a conscientious effort to retain the flavor and style of the original report by using the author's exact wording wherever possible, with only occasional transitional paragraphs inserted to maintain the essential unity and developmental sequence of the investigator's exposition. Needless to say, the surviving editor assumes full responsibility for any distortions of meaning which may have crept into the adapted reports. I can only hope that careful reading and rereading of the original papers and the abridgments have kept such possible distortions at a minimal level. Again, I feel encouraged that our efforts have met with some success since those original writers who have seen our versions have been unanimous in their approval. In a few instances original writers added new material which extended or updated the discussion. I am appreciative of their interest and effort.

In the first edition we largely deleted references to other research and writing that appeared in the selected papers. But we began to feel that this practice limited the potential usefulness of the collected papers. Therefore in this third edition, as in the second, we have retained many of the references, and the titles and publication information of the works referred to in the text appear in alphabetical order at the end of the book. This practice does appear to enhance the usefulness of the book, especially to the graduate student and the dedicated undergraduate major in psychology.

We have always attempted more than a mere "scissors-and-paste" job in editing this collection of psychological studies. The reports are grouped into parts, and each part is introduced by a foreword pointing up the significance of the area under consideration and the specific contribution of each of the selected papers of this area. In addition, each paper is given a brief introduction in an effort to orient the reader and to whet his appetite for the reading before him. It is hoped that the fair degree of continuity and integration provided by the Introduction, the part forewords, and the introductions to the sixty papers will make this volume more usable in undergraduate classes in psychology where a maximum of orientation and guidance sometimes seems desirable.

I am much indebted to the several authors, without whose full cooperation such a source book could not be published, who granted permission not only to use their papers but also to abridge and adapt them to serve the purposes of this volume. Whatever contribution this volume may make to a better understanding of human behavior must, of course, be credited to the original investigators. Publication in the present form merely makes their findings more generally available. Acknowledgment to the publishers of each paper is made in footnote form throughout the book. They were more than generous in permitting us to reproduce their publications, especially where books and monographs were involved.

This third edition is dedicated to Mary Margaret Kuhlen and Evelyn Thompson, our wives, who helped to make our friendship something of far greater value than might have resulted from common professional interests alone. This is a very small token, indeed, of our appreciation; however, it may help to make manifest a sentiment that doesn't get expressed often enough in such relationships. Again, I like to believe that Dr. Kuhlen would have approved of this gesture.

G. G. T.

Contents

PSYCHOLOGICAL STUDIES of
HUMAN DEVELOPMENT

INTRODUCTION

THIS BOOK is concerned with the psychological aspects of human growth and development—with those psychological changes that occur with increasing age and with the many conditions that influence the course of human development and behavior. Developmental psychology is concerned not only with emerging capacities and expanding behavior but also with declining abilities and behavior restrictions in old age. The contents of this volume thus deal with the total life span: childhood, adolescence, maturity, and old age.

As a subject for study, developmental psychology has much to offer every person seeking to understand himself and others.

But since the life span is extensive, those interested in one age group may well ask: Why study such a broad sweep to understand children? Or, why study children in order to understand adults? The answers to these questions lie in the fact that adults were once children and that children will someday become adolescents, adults, and the aged. Different generations intermingle with, influence, and are influenced by one another. An understanding of those of a particular age is achieved in part by understanding the ways in which that age group differs from one's own and from other age groups. Life cannot satisfactorily be categorized into discrete age sections. Although one's interest in life is largely concerned with the present and the years of life that lie ahead, it must be recognized that the past has contributed to present growth and adjustment if maximum understanding of the present is desired, and, in turn, that the future is, psychologically speaking, not something remote and divorced from present adjustment and experience but instead is built upon and derives from the present. There is a basic continuity in the individual patterns of growth and aging, and any phase of life can best be understood and appreciated when seen in the context of a broad developmental sweep.

THE PURPOSES OF THE VOLUME

This book is not a systematic integration of the literature on developmental psychology. Rather it is a series of sixty papers (research and theoretical reports) selected from scientific journals. As a book of readings it has as its primary purpose the provision of a convenient and ready access to descriptive, research, and theoretical reports.

The contents of this volume should add interest to the study of psychological development. In the editors' experience, students seem to enjoy and appreciate first-hand contacts with the raw material from which a science is constructed. Opportunity to read original scientific reports should, then, make the study of human development and behavior more interesting, especially when the papers presented are the original reports of widely known authorities in the field—vigorous, readable, first-hand accounts of research efforts. It is hoped that the student will find these papers stimulating to thought, provocative of discussion, and a stimulus to further informed reading.

It is intended that these studies shall promote a better understanding of the research basis of developmental psychology and of some of the limitations which apply to generalizations commonly presented in textbooks. The task of integrating in a single textbook the total field of child psychology, or the psychology of adolescence, or the psychology of maturity and old age is so complicated an undertaking that it is not always possible to qualify statements and generalizations to the degree that they should be qualified or to discuss in detail the procedures by which the relevant data were obtained. The original research reports do both of these things more effectively. Strengths and weaknesses of experimental procedure become more evident. Points which may have impressed a particular textbook writer as deserving of extensive comment may be found on inspection of the original report to have been minor aspects of the study. Or a paper cited briefly in a textbook discussion may be found upon fuller acquaintance to contain much more related data and an extensive discussion of special interest to the reader. Papers such as those included in this book offer the student an opportunity to examine at first hand some of the primary data on which the science of human development is based.

Another purpose of the present collection of papers is to promote the reader's understanding of basic research methods. A science can be better appreciated when the particular procedures which are used to obtain the facts are understood, their strengths and weaknesses evaluated. Such understanding will result not only in a richer appreciation of the discipline itself but also in a more critical evaluation of new materials as they are encountered.

It is also hoped that the contents of this volume will foster the development of attitudes of objective thinking and critical evaluation. We recognize that many students of developmental psychology will not become professionals in the field or even "consumers" of the technical reports. However, they will probably encounter much related material. Much is written in popular magazines and books on human problems and adjustment, much of potential usefulness in dealing with concrete problems of child rearing, marital adjustments, care of the aged. If an individual is to read these reports intelligently, he must be in a position to separate the wheat from the chaff, to identify the good and reasonably valid, to discount the invalid. The investigators whose work is reported in this book have been unwilling to accept as necessarily sound the prejudiced views, the common-sense conclusions, the opinions that fill popular magazines and books. Instead, these investigators have set themselves the task of systematically collecting evidence to establish facts and answers to questions that they and others have felt the need to inquire into. It is hoped that intimate glimpses into the means by which valid facts about human behavior and adjustment are collected will aid the reader in developing critical attitudes toward the "new discoveries" we hear so much of under the label "psychology."

THE SELECTION OF PAPERS

Since there are many research reports on the psychology of human growth and behavior, the reader may well ask the question, "Why were certain papers included and others omitted?" The editors had in mind several criteria, related to the purposes set forth in the preceding paragraphs, as they went about the task of selecting the investigations to be included in this volume. A breadth of coverage was desired both in diversity of psychological processes and of age-groups within the life span. Studies related to the more modifiable factors in human growth and behavior were generally preferred. However, a substantial number of papers on the maturational components in human growth and behavior were also selected in order that the reader might appreciate the significance of these less modifiable factors. It was felt that investigations designed to relate manipulatable environmental variables to a diversity of human adjustment situations would be more representative of current research efforts in psychology and most helpful to the majority of readers whose study of psychology is usually restricted to two or three college courses.

The editors also attempted to choose studies that would give a fair coverage of the different methods of investigation most commonly used in psychology. Thus, generalizations based on data obtained from case studies, ratings, direct observations, standardized psychological scales, laboratory experiments, and the like will be found in this volume. It is well known that some of these research procedures yield relatively more reliable and valid information than others. The editors are of the opinion that the average reader will be able to detect the scientific deficiencies of these several research methods by a careful study of these more-or-less representative investigations.

In addition to the criteria mentioned above, the editors selected studies which they believe have a strong interest-appeal to college students. For example, case studies are interesting because they reflect the "flavor" of real life situations. It has been the editors' experience in teaching courses in developmental psychology for more than two decades that college students are usually most interested in those research projects that have a direct bearing on their present adjustment problems or on the problems they expect to face in the future—as teachers, husbands or wives, parents, professional psychologists, providers for aged parents, and the like. The studies reported in this book are relevant to such psychological problems.

EVALUATING A RESEARCH REPORT

The research studies included in this volume are of unequal scientific value. There are several relatively neglected areas in the psychology of human development. In such cases the editors selected the "best" (other things being equal) of the investigations that were available. In some instances these reports do little more than pose a series of psychological problems whose clarification and eventual solution is important to the welfare of man. These exploratory studies exemplify, however, the first stage in any fruitful scientific inquiry, the posing of significant problems that give some promise of being amenable to scientific study. As several philosophers of science have noted, the search for "intelligent" questions is sometimes the most difficult task confronting the scientist.

The next requirement in scientific inquiry is that the investigator have the ability, and the imagination, to cast this "intelligent" problem in the form of a testable hypothesis. In order that it be a fruitful hypothesis, it must provide the investigator a definite answer, at least in part, to his original question. An hypothesis which yields an indefinite or ambiguous answer is either poorly cast or unsuitable for rigorous testing by the available data-gathering procedures. In either case, the use of such an hypothesis fails to contribute to scientific knowledge. The sophisticated scientist is well aware that he must either conduct his investigations according to the designs of available research methodology (logic and measuring instruments) or he must invent new research procedures of acceptable reliability and validity.

Once a fruitful and "reasonable" hypothesis has been developed, the scientist's next task is to gather relevant data on the basis of which he can test his hypothetical question. In the area of developmental psychology the scientist must be concerned with problems of the following types: (1) The representativeness of his experimental subjects. Is the particular selection of subjects employed in his investigation chosen without bias and known to be a sample which is representative of the population concerning which he wishes to generalize? (2) The numerical adequacy of his experimental population. Is he including enough individuals to answer his question in a definite, unambiguous way—considering the errors of measurement inherent in his research procedure? (3) The appropriateness of his investigating techniques and procedures. Has he selected the most appropriate scientific tools with which to test the hypothesis under consideration? (4) The adequacy of his experimental controls. Are his controls sufficient so that he can attribute experimentally obtained differences to the systematic variation of factors related to his hypothesis? (5) The amenability of the obtained data to logical, mathematical, or statistical ordering and evaluation. Can he use the obtained data to refute the hypothesis being tested or to produce a definite increment of confidence in it? Just what has been proved in the experiment? What is its outcome?

The last point in the above paragraph, on ordering and evaluating what has been learned from the experiment, deserves special attention because of the particular characteristics of most psychological data. Since human behavior is influenced by a great many variables difficult to control, or in some cases whose existence is completely unknown to the experimenter, the data obtained in most investigations lend themselves best to statistical analysis and interpretation, *and this is often the only adequate way in which the results of the experiment can be stated.* The serious student of the psychology of human development should have a fair grasp of the statistical approach to scientific inference in order to understand the logical framework of the majority of psychological investigations.[1]

The next step in scientific inquiry comes when the experimenter draws general conclusions from his analysis and evaluation of the obtained data. His generalizations should flow directly from his findings. Any extrapolations of results or sheer speculations based on the analysis of the findings should be clearly designated as such in the final reporting—the latter being the point at which he makes the fruits of his research efforts generally available. This final report should be sufficiently precise and detailed that it clearly conveys the several steps in the scientific inquiry. Clarity of reporting tends to prevent misinterpretation, and makes it easier for other investigators either to repeat the study or to extend the research endeavor in the form of related experiments.

Although the foregoing is a highly condensed version of the scientific procedures that characterize valid research, it may serve as a useful guide in evaluating the studies reported in this volume. As noted in the section dealing with purposes, the editors hope that a careful study of these research papers will, among other things, help the reader to become better acquainted with some of the more fruitful and valid research procedures in the psychology of human development.

---

[1] For elementary approaches to the logical procedures in statistical analysis and inference, the reader may wish to consult one or more of the following books: E. C. Bryant, *Statistical Analysis* (N. Y.: McGraw-Hill, 1960). Helen M. Walker and Joseph Lev, *Elementary Statistical Methods* (Revised Edition) (N. Y.: Holt, Rinehart and Winston, 1958). Helen M. Walker and Joseph Lev, *Statistical Inference* (N. Y.: Holt, Rinehart and Winston, 1953). J. E. Wert, C. O. Neidt, and J. S. Ahmann, *Statistical Methods in Educational and Psychological Research* (N. Y.: Appleton-Century-Crofts, 1954).

Part I

THEORIES CONCERNING
PSYCHOLOGICAL GROWTH

SCIENTISTS aim to construct their theories in whatever ways seem best to rationalize and explain the covariations and antecedent-consequent relationships that they have discovered in nature. Theories also do much to stimulate and sustain the scientist's curiosity. They guide his observations, suggest new procedures and instruments for producing and recording variations in natural phenomena, and provide models for relating new findings to the general stream of existing knowledge. Fruitful theories permit the integration and generalization of many diverse empirical relationships, but even more importantly they direct the investigator toward the most promising next steps in scientific inquiry. The most fruitful, or useful, theories are characteristically rigorous in specifying the fundamental properties or features of the system, powerful in relating those properties to observables, provocative in suggesting new antecedent-consequent relationships, and parsimonious in the number of assumptions that are necessary to undergird the model or theoretical construction. Judging from what has gone before in the history of science, it appears that all theories, *without exception,* are doomed either to become subordinate to more embracing conceptions or to be replaced by more useful constructions. Indeed, several philosophers of science have aptly commented that the most fruitful theories specify the means for their own destruction. In this sense currently accepted and established models and theories must be regarded as nothing more than useful devices with an at present largely unknown potential for promoting further contributions to scientific knowledge and understanding.

In the present part, "Theories Concerning Psychological Growth," the reader will encounter nothing of the usual rigor, scope, and power of the theories with which he may be familiar in the physical sciences. Rather he will find a number of rather loosely related guide lines for the interpretation of presently available data and broad programmatic suggestions for further research. In the paper by Inhelder the reader will have the interesting experience of eavesdropping on a group of eminent scientists as they discuss selected theoretical problems in contemporary developmental psychology. Lachman skillfully analyzes the potential fruitfulness of models and theories in the advancement of science. This clarification is especially useful in developmental psychology, where so many models have been borrowed from biology and neurophysiology. Inner "releasing mechanisms" are proposed and emphasized in the papers by Hess and Stendler. Hess reviews the research evidence on imprinting and describes what is known of the necessary conditions for this interesting phenomenon. Stendler then employs imprinting as a model for explaining certain variations in human behavior during the preschool years. She draws on clinical observations in further support of the model.

We close this part on theories with the paper by Hill. In an original and ingenious manner he draws parallels between modern learning theory and the psychoanalytic model as ways of rationalizing major dimensions in the acquisition of values. His cogently reasoned essay should stimulate further scientific inquiry in this vital dimension of human development and environmental response.

1

Theories and Conceptual Models*

Roy Lachman

The scientist constructs theories for a number of different reasons: to integrate known empirical relationships, to open paths to the discovery of new knowledge, and to gratify an apparently insatiable desire for predicting and controlling the forces of nature. Theorizing involves the scientist in efforts to construct language systems and conceptual models that will "explain" the unknown in terms of that which is already known. The history of science records many instances of the scientist's borrowing explanatory models from mathematics in an effort to integrate and extend meaningful relationships in his own area of inquiry. On numerous occasions within its relatively short history psychology has borrowed conceptual models from mathematics, biology, physiology, and other disciplines. In their attempts to describe and integrate the complex behavior patterns of living organisms, psychologists have at various times likened the organism to an

* From Roy Lachman, "The Model in Theory Construction," *Psychological Review*, 1960, Vol. 67, pp. 113-129. (With permission of the author and the American Psychological Association.)

intricate and delicately balanced machine, an electronic data-process-
ing device, a probability-contingency system, and so on. Although
each of these models, or analogies, has proved inadequate to capture
all of the subtleties of behavioral process and change, it cannot be
doubted that the general scientific movement in psychology has been
substantially advanced by the suggestive influence of these models
and associated theories. In his thoughtful analysis of the propaedeutic
function of the model in theory construction, Dr. Lachman makes clear
one of the ways by which the scientist inches his way up the ladder of
knowledge.

The scientific enterprise as here conceived consists of two related but dis-
criminatively different activities. One is the observation of objects and
events, both experimentally and less formally. The other involves the use
of mathematical and natural linguistic symbols, along with the rules for
their manipulation, to represent these sensory experiences, to organize what
is observed into some comprehensible order, and by proper symbolic
manipulation to arrive at a representation of what has not yet been observed. The commentary that accompanies these latter theoretical undertakings frequently includes the term "model," the meaning of which can,
at best, be imperfectly ascertained from the context. It has been claimed,
not infrequently, that while some distinct referent can be delineated in
physics, the term "model" has lost all semblance of meaning in psychology
(e.g., Underwood, 1957, p. 257). Actually, the physical scientist has permitted himself wide latitude in the use of the term "model" and the
psychologist has followed suit.

The plan of this paper is to analyze certain meanings and functions of
the concept of a model; distinctions made will then be exemplified in some
actual theories from contemporary psychology and classical physics. Implications of the properties of models for theory construction will then
be examined in a systematic fashion. The consequences of this analysis for
a sample of methodological problems currently at issue will be explored.

Two properties of the analysis to follow should be noted. First, although
the profusion of ideas referred to by the term model is often interrelated and
compounded, it will be necessary for analytic purposes to separate the
various meanings and functions into discrete categories. With this exception, the explication of the concept of the model will follow as closely as
possible the actual scientific usage. Secondly, while the symbolic form of
conveying the ideas of a model may take the form of a word, sentence,
diagram, or mathematical calculus, the distinctions to be made concern the
meanings of the concept of model and its functional properties within a
theoretical system.

Since model has been used interchangeably with or in reference to various parts of a theory, it is necessary to distinguish such theoretical struc-

tures, if only crudely. For our present purpose, it will suffice to differentiate among the parts of certain theories: (*a*) the principles, postulates, or hypothetical ideas, including the relations among them; (*b*) the sentences, equations, or theorems, derived therefrom; (*c*) the coordinating definitions relating theoretical terms to the observational sentences. The textual commentary accompanying the type of theory with which we are concerned may not explicitly designate all the parts of such a structure. It is part of the task of methodological analysis to isolate this structure. Finally, it will be useful to distinguish the formal theory from the *separate system* which is the model. This meaning of model may refer to, but need not necessarily refer to, what is frequently called the analogy. A model as an order structurally independent of the theory is the prominent notion. Equally important, more than one model generally functions for a theory. The model, consisting of a separate system, brings to bear an external organization of ideas, laws, or relationships upon the hypothetical propositions of a theory or the phenomena it encompasses. This external organization or model contributes to the construction, application, and interpretation of the theory. Precisely how this is accomplished can be clarified by analyzing the meanings and functions of the model concept.

FUNCTIONS OF MODELS

I. Models Providing Modes of Representation. Empirical elements and relationships which constitute the phenomena to be organized by a theory are known to us by the symbolic system or language that designates these data. By introducing a model constituting a separately organized system, we are providing an additional system of representation for the phenomena and a suitable way of speaking about them. An essential characteristic of "modular"[1] representation constitutes the furnishing of *new* ways of regarding or thinking about the empirical objects and events. Attributes and meanings of the model are transferred from their initial context of usage to the new setting. This application of unprecedented modes of representation can be executed on two levels. Objects and events formulated directly from observation are thought about in the new and unusual fashion prescribed by the model.

At another level, a model may provide novel modes for conceiving the hypothetical ideas and postulates of a theory. Consider the conditioning model: applied to perceptual phenomena, it illustrates the first or empirical level of application. If perception is *regarded* as though it were a conditioned response, to some *determinable* degree perceptual behavior should be capable of treatment in accordance with the laws of conditioning: frequency, stimulation interval, etc.; if so, the relationships and language of conditioning may be fruitfully applied. Howes and Solomon's (1951)

---

[1] Hereinafter the word "modular" is intended to pertain to a "model," not a mode.

findings may be so regarded. In this example, some such analogy with conditioning is said to provide an empirical or pretheoretical model (Koch, 1954). In contrast, the fractional anticipatory response mechanism— r_g theory—(Amsel, 1958; Kendler and Levine, 1951; Moltz, 1957; Spence, 1951a, 1951b; etc.) illustrates the second level of representative functioning for the conditioning model. Here, the postulated nonobservable fractional antedating response is conceived of as operating according to conditioning principles to *whatever* degree desirable. We assign any individual or combination of properties from the model to the theoretical construct guided by pragmatic considerations of predictive fertility and consistency of usage required for the integration of diverse areas. To reiterate this important point, a model may be applied to directly accessible (empirical) objects and events or to inaccessible and imaginary concepts of a theory. Though the levels of modular application considered are not discrete but represent extremes of a continuum, an important distinction should not be overlooked: while theoretical entities can be said to be anything we want them to be, this is not so for categories close to observation. The latter are spoken of only in an *as if* fashion. By invoking the conditioning model, perception, meaning, and verbal behavior are not said to be conditioned responses; it is only claimed that if represented and spoken of in such a fashion, important empirical consequences can be obtained. This point is well illustrated by Toulmin's analysis of the rectilinear propagation model of geometrical optics, "We do not *find* light atomized into individual rays: we *represent* it as consisting of such rays" (Toulmin, 1953, p. 29).

II. Models Functioning as Rules of Inference. Given the assumptions of some theory along with the experimental arrangements, a train of reasoning leads to the prediction sentences. From what source do the rules for such inference arise?

In the language used to talk about a theory, the term model may refer directly to a mathematical calculus or to a system of relationships from some other source such as electronic computers, the classical laws of motion, the laws of conditioning, etc. Any one of these separate systems in conjunction with the initial conditions of a given experiment may permit the predicton of what is to be observed. Here, model signifies *the rules* by which the theoretical symbols (some, at least, having been empirically coordinated) are manipulated to arrive at new relations; the rules by which one sentence is inferred from another or the theorems are derived. The probability calculus utilized in statistical learning theory (Estes, 1959) exemplifies such a mathematical model, while some of the relations holding among electronic communication systems play a role in providing the inference rules or calculus for information theory (Grant, 1954). Another example is the laws of classical conditioning which, alone or supplemented, are the means by which inferences are drawn in application of r_g theory to a given experiment (Kendler and Levine, 1951; Moltz and Maddi, 1956).

Calculational rules of mathematical systems and the semantic principles of natural language are themselves rules of inference for the symbolism involved. In contrast to this mode of derivation, Munitz (1957a, p. 42) recognizes the necessity for distinguishing a more specific set of inference rules provided by certain equations and supplementary textual commentary which prescribe the precise manner in which the theoretical terms and symbols are to be connected; these occasionally are termed "implicit definitions." Although some models may imply how assumptions and implicit definitions are to be formulated, the terms "mathematical model" and "conditioning model" apparently refer to the general inference principles employed in the first sense rather than to the implicit definitions. This is illustrated in r_g theory by the relation or implicit definition $r_g \rightarrow s_g$, for there is nothing in the laws of classical conditioning that requires the hypothetical response to have a hypothetical response-produced cue. But it is precisely the laws of classical conditioning that function as the basis for the rules by which we arrive at the consequences of the several implicit definitions. An additional illustration is provided by statistical learning theory's operator or difference equations, the specific choice of which is in no way dictated by the rules of mathematics, although the operators may be suggested by some second model. While the operator equations determine the form of the learning function to be derived, it is only by the mathematical rules that the derivation itself is executed. It immediately follows that in the expressions mathematical model and conditioning model, the adjectives preceding the term model describe the *source* of the general inference principles. In both cases, this is a separate system external to the structure of the theory. The major source of statistical learning theory's inference rules are to be found in the texts on probability theory and the types of mathematics involved. The rules of inference for r_g can be found in the experimental literature on classical conditioning. For precision in derivation, it is obvious that the rules of mathematics are to be preferred. Furthermore, if it is not yet apparent, later analysis of specific theories will show that these modes of inference drawing do not follow the logic-book deduction of which some scientists and philosophers are so fond.

III. Interpretational Function of Models. The inference rules or calculus of r_g theory is formulated by amending and adapting the rules contained in the conditioning model; the model serves the additional function of interpreting the calculus. This is not the case for theories with inference rules primarily adopted from a mathematical calculus; the mathematical model may be supplemented with one or more additional models which serve to interpret and make intelligible the inference rules employed. Estes' statistical learning theory (1959), for example, makes use of a stimulus-sampling model; this second model provides a mode of representation functioning as a coherent way of speaking about the theory. Moreover, it functions as one possible interpretation of the theoretical terms. Formulae and symbols are rendered intelligible by the modular interpretation which also shows how to apply the theory and suggests procedures for extending the use of individual parameters and the theory as a whole. Thus, the stimulus-sampling model would tend to suggest that in extending the scope of statistical learning theory to include motivational phenomena, deprivational states would be conceptualized as producing differential configurations of the stimulus set available for sampling; this is precisely what Estes (1958) has done.

Some applications of the conditioning model suggest, in addition to inference principles, the rules for their application to the phenomena involved, the interpretation of the inference principles. Here, the modular interpretation produces propositions such as: the strength of r_g increases to some asymptote as a function of the quantity, time, and magnitude of consummatory experience in the goal box. In psychology such symptom relations are generally termed "coordinating definitions" which designate the class of propositions tying together theoretical terms with their associated empirical sentences. The model as an interpretation of a theory guides the formulating of coordinating definitions. Hutten (1956, p. 87) adds saliently, "The model so becomes a *link* between theory and experiment. We explain and test the theory in terms of the model."

IV. Models Providing Pictorial Visualization. Probably the most common meaning employed and service rendered by a model consist of the reproduction of the theoretical prototype in terms of mental pictures or images. Agents mediating this function range from a rigorously integrated separate system to a loose analogy with familiar sensory experience. The popularity of this modular activity follows from the ubiquitous desire for an intuitively satisfying account of any theory. Preoccupation of classical physicists with model building of this limited pictorial type initiated the counter-view that model construction was a disreputable enterprise. Duhem (1954), for one, considered model construction to be both superfluous and the refuge of weak minds. Residual forms of this position are in evidence today; Carnap (1955, p. 209), while recognizing esthetic, didactic, and heuristic value, finds models nonessential for successful application of theory. Although this may be true of some theoretical activity, as a generalization it is deficient on several grounds and it neglects certain essential aspects of the behavior of a good number of scientists. In modern physics, although visual representation is no longer a prerequisite for the acceptance of a theory, the pictorial model may serve decisively in the initial phase of theory construction. While contemporary quantum theory cannot provide coherent visualization, it did develop from "Bohr's atom" which was associated with a pictorial model. Moreover, some current theoretical efforts concerning the atomic nucleus utilize the shell and water drop models. Axiomatization of a theory, or the attempts to do so, does not compromise this argument. Construction of an axiomatic system, apparently, is not attempted until theory construction is well under way, usually with the aid of some model. It is necessary, therefore, to carefully distinguish simple pictorial functions from the less trivial enterprises described in the previous sections. A model providing satisfying intuitive pictures may also serve one or more of the functions enumerated above, with influence upon theory construction and application that cannot easily be overrated. Conversely, a model providing *only* visual representation serves, at best, didactically; even then, it probably does more to mislead the student than to teach him. Consider Lewin's (1951) topological and field-theoretical models. Following Braithwaite (1953, p. 366n) we must agree that the essence of a calculus is not its symbolism but its inference rules, whereas Lewin's model functions as "a calculus that doesn't calculate." In contrast, the conditioning model, while possibly providing some S-R theorists with all the beautiful imagery associated with salivating dogs, also contributes the essential inference rules. The work of Staats and Staats (1957, 1958) provides an admirable illustration by their demonstrations that verbal meaning and attitudes may be treated as analogous to a conventional conditioned response whose laws furnish the calculus employed.

ILLUSTRATIONS OF MODELS

Although the functions enumerated here have been illustrated by examples from contemporary psychological research and theory, for some readers the distinctions made may still be rather vague. The situation may be remedied by analyzing different models and noting their functions in specific theories within cultivated areas of science. Certain theories of classical physics provide an excellent opportunity for comparative analysis with current theoretical efforts in psychology. Additional functions will be served by such an analysis in at once demonstrating the initial contention that models are utilized in an essentially similar fashion in both classical physics and psychology. At the same time, some light may be cast upon a question that has elicited a good deal of polemic: the problem of the emulation of physics by psychologists. The r_g theory, statistical learning theory, and the classical kinetic theory of gases have been selected to illustrate the role of the model in a theory. The rigorous methodological analysis to which the latter theory has previously been subjected is the basis for its selection. The language to be employed in this illustration will be accessible to almost every student of psychology; we turn, now, to that task.

The Kinetic Theory of Gases. Let us first observe the pictorial model of the kinetic theory in its most limited form. A gas is represented by this initial model as consisting of minute invisible particles (molecules or atoms) in incessant motion, colliding with one another and with the walls of any restricting container; at a given instant, most of the particles are separated by vacant space. Consider, now, the interpretation by means of the pictorial model of the known properties of a gas residing in a container composed of rigid walls, one of which is movable in the manner of a piston. The adjustable wall may be moved inward; this is interpreted as a reduction in the available space between the particles and accounts for the property of compressibility of a gas. While pushing in the wall we experience resistance against our efforts. As we continue to reduce the space, the resistance increases ever more. The model attributes this to an increase in the number of collisions following from a reduction in volume and resulting in an increase in the velocity of the gas particles. Boyle's Law, which states the relationship between volume and pressure, thus is attributed to an increase in the rate of impact between the particles and the wall of the container, which is part of the general picture of increment in the number of collisions among the particles produced by the decrement in the space between them. But the diminution in volume has increased not only the pressure but also the temperature. This is accounted for by the increased velocity of the particles adding to their kinetic energy. Thus, the law relating temperature to pressure is acknowledged. While the presentation, thus far, is not dissimilar to D. Bernoulli's original hypothesis (D'Abro, 1951, p. 381) we have proceeded somewhat beyond the initial model which essentially involves a picture of mass-points in motion functioning as a representation for and way of talking about the hypothetical ideas and postulates of the initial theory.

Introducing additional models or the amendment of the original provides the inference rules. The first addition involves the well developed laws governing a separate phenomenon which are applied to the ideas of the pictorial model. This may be termed the dynamical Model II[2] for the theory under consideration. Here, the gas particles are conceived as behaving analogously to medium sized bodies such as billiard balls, rocks, or planets: the laws of classical mechanics governing the motions of the latter and the principles of dynamics describing their energy states are ascribed, approximately, to the motions and energy states of the imaginary gas particles pictured by the Model IV. The laws provided by the dynamical model are in mathematical form and are themselves supplemented by an additional Model II, the calculus of probabilities. Thereby, the rules of reasoning or calculus of the theory are formulated, by means of which consequences are derived from the initial theoretical terms. But the combining of Models II cannot, itself, be given any rules, for the essential ingredient is the creative imagination of the scientist.

Following Campbell's (1920) detailed analysis, let us schematically describe one of the more elementary derivations in a suitably idealized and

[2] A Roman numeral designating the specific type of model will be affixed where this may be in doubt.

simplified fashion. The postulates of the theory may be represented by terms which include the symbols: $t, m, v, l, n,$ and (x, y, z). The postulates, which we need not reproduce, consist of several implicit definitions in the form of equations relating these theoretical variables and associated textual commentary. Now, (x, y, z) may be pictured by the Model IV as rectangular coordinates for the position of each of the imaginary particles: m their mass, v their mean velocity, n their number, t as time, and l as the length of an edge of the hypothetical container. The implicit definitions relating the postulated variables *are approximate in form to the laws which would govern the motions of such an isolated system of entities pictured by the model.* From the initial terms and their postulated interrelationships, the expression,

$$p = \frac{n \, m \, v^2}{3 l^3} \qquad\qquad [1]$$

is derived in accordance with the mathematical rules involved.[3] For *some* of the individual theoretical terms and several combinations of them, co-ordinating definitions are stated relating them to the appropriate empirical terms. The coordinating propositions are suggested by the pictorial model in its interpretative function. Thus, coordinating l with the length of a cubical container holding a real gas, it follows that l^3 is the volume V of the gas. Likewise, p is coordinated with the pressure P on a wall of the vessel, and mv^2/a with the absolute temperature T of the gas.[4] Substituting the empirical terms P, V, T in the theoretically derived Expression 1, the term $a \, n/3$ remains, which is a constant k, and we have,

$$P \, V = k \, T, \qquad\qquad [2]$$

the familiar gas law relating temperature pressure, and volume, which is applicable over an empirically determined range for a given type of gas.

Returning to the derivation of Expression 1, application of the in-

---

[3] The term "p" is a compact way of writing a more complex arrangement of the above symbols involved in the postulates. The actual derivation is frequently performed in the Gibbsian manner of treating a gas particle's three components of position and three of momentum as the coordinates of a single "phase point" located in a "phase space" of six dimensions or $6N$ dimensions for N particles (Jeans, 1940, p. 17 ff). For the present considerations, this illustrates the not infrequent situation of identical consequences being derived from somewhat different assumptions.

The distinction usually made between an ideal gas and a real gas will be avoided. Instead, the propositions concerning a real gas will be amended with a statement concerning their range of validity. This alternative method will be employed in accordance with the view that a scientific law cannot be regarded as a universal proposition both on empirical and logical grounds. With respect to the hypothetical ideas of a theory, as here viewed, these are always ideal situations, since they are creations of the imagination directed toward executing derivations in agreement with experiment and the achievement of mathematical simplicity.

[4] For a definition and analysis of the term a, consult the work of Campbell (1920, p. 127).

ference rules provided by the laws of dynamics requires certain assumptions concerning properties of the modular particles; namely, they are infinitesimal, so that their diameters and orientation in space may be ignored. In addition, they are assumed to be perfectly elastic. Nonelastic particles would suffer a reduction in velocity with each impact upon the container wall and eventually their motion would cease entirely, precluding the derivation of consequences in agreement with observation. The critics of certain theoretical assumptions in psychology would do well to ponder the implications of the assumptions of an *infinitesimal* and *perfectly elastic* particle, properties that it is impossible to assign to observable objects.

Campbell (1920) discriminates two processes for extending a theory. It will be recalled that only some of the postulated variables were coordinated with empirical terms. The formulation of additional coordinating definitions for the uncoordinated terms illustrates the first method of theoretical extension. A second method of theoretical development involves making amendments to the postulated terms and the equations expressing their interrelationships. This second method proceeds as follows: the previous assumptions are modified or amended and new theoretical terms are introduced into the postulates corresponding to the additional assumptions. The pictorial model may prescribe this extension. Thus, viscosity relations of a gas may be derived by altering the previous postulates with a term suggested by the pictorial-dynamical model corresponding to a diameter for the hypothetical particles. Consideration of the space occupied by the modular particles and their mutual attractions leads to other derivations. This accumulation of assumptions following from the extension of ideas contained in the model has been termed "modular deployment" by Toulmin (1953). In the present theory, experimental agreement breaks down when the model is deployed to include internal rotations of the imaginary particles. General failure of observational agreement also occurs with the attempted extension of the theoretical *scope* to extreme ranges of temperature and pressure. In both instances, quantum mechanics supersedes the classical kinetic theory.

r_g **Theory.** Turning to r_g theory, let us first examine the pictorial model involved. A rat is placed in a T maze, one arm of which is baited with food; the second is empty. A noncorrection procedure of training is employed. On the trials during which the correct goal box is entered, the animal executes unconditioned responses (UR) of approach movements, chewing, salivating, etc., to the unconditioned stimulus (US), food. On subsequent trials, stimulus objects and patterns of the choice-point and starting arm are encountered at a point in space prior to the food, or US. Since these choice-point stimuli are located spatially antecedent to the US, they are, therefore, encountered at some temporal interval prior to the food or US, depending on the animal's rate of locomotion. The antecedent stimulus patterns come to elicit imaginary or invisible conditioned responses (CR), such as chewing and salivating, which logically consist of components of the empirical UR to food. These invisible antedating conditioned responses (r_g) are acquired in a fashion exactly analogous to Pavlovian conditioning of observable responses. The unobservable r_g in turn, produces a hypothetical proprioceptive response-produced stimulus (s_g), which likewise functions in the fashion of an overt and observable stimulus.

Cues at the choice-point may consist of different visual texture or brightness patterns for each of the maze arms, as well as proprioceptive consequences of locomotion and receptor orientation toward the left or right end box. One and only one of these choice-point stimulus patterns is consistently followed by the US, food. Thus, only this specific set of stimuli will selectively begin to act as a CS and elicit the hypothetical conditioned response, r_g. Evocation of r_g will occur with increased frequency and amplitude, the greater the spatial proximity between the set of cues and the goal object, or the greater the similarity between the choice-point cues and the goal box stimuli. This, of course, follows from classical conditioning laws dealing with CS-US interval and generalization. It is possible to imagine a sequence of events occurring during a trial early in training which is terminated by the rewarded or correct response: S locomotes to the choice-point where VTE behavior occurs, after which S orients its musculature and receptors toward the cues of the rewarded end box. Since only a moderate amount of training has preceded, the correct cues elicit r_g with low frequency and minimum amplitude. Orienting responses are followed by penetration into the correct end box which terminates with the consummatory or goal response. Notice what is imagined to occur: since the correct choice-point stimuli have been followed by the US of food, these choice-point cues have increased their strength of evocation of the conditioned response, (r_g). At the same time s_g, which is available only when r_g occurs, would be selectively present prior to the performance of the correct instrumental response. With prolonged training, the strength and probability of r_g elicitation by the correct cues are continuously enhanced via classical conditioning. A concomitant increment in frequency of occurrence of s_g takes place. Likewise, by means of S-R contiguity, s_g elicits the appropriate selective-learning response with greater frequency. In this fashion, the frequency of the correct response approaches some asymptote, which for the present experimental conditions is unity.

A basic form of selective-learning has been accounted for by the model without appealing to some special mechanism of reinforcement; the changes in behavior are mediated solely by classical conditioning and S-R contiguity. It might be questioned: why not explain the behavior by molar S-R contiguity alone and not introduce invisible events? As we shall see, this non-observable system of events mediates other predictions for several different initial conditions, most of which cannot be derived and integrated by molar principles alone. An exactly analogous situation exists between thermodynamics and the kinetic gas theory.

Deployment of the model has made the picture more complex: a class of events has been introduced into the negative end box. Frustration and avoidance responses are assumed also to "move forward" by means of classical conditioning to the incorrect cues at the choice-point. To pursue this phase of modular deployment is not necessary for our purposes. Let us instead examine that which has already been presented. We have proceeded beyond the pictorial model and described the inference techniques of the theory. The pictorial model itself essentially involves the idea or picture of objects and events occurring at the terminal portion of a behavioral chain influencing prior events. Terminal goal box events function as US's whose appropriate CR's "move forward" to determine and mediate events occurring earlier in the behavioral sequence. Serving as a representation for and manner of talking about the ideas of r_g theory, the pictorial model provides a seemingly necessary service.

The model of classical conditioning also provides the inference rules or calculus of r_g theory, which for the most part is the product of Spence's (1951a, 1951b) creative theorizing. Nonobservable r_g is conceived as behaving analogously to observable conditioning: the acquisition and extinction laws of the latter are ascribed, approximately, to the former. In conjunction with the initial conditions of a given experiment, the conditioning laws mediate the derivation of specific predictions, as has been demonstrated. Utilizing one of the many examples available (Amsel, 1958; Kendler and Levine, 1951; Moltz, 1957; Spence, 1956), let us again examine the manner in which the laws of conditioning serve as the model and provide the inference rules. Moltz (1957) has demonstrated that the observations concerning latent or nonresponse extinction may be derived by the calculus of r_g. Modified only slightly, Moltz's derivation proceeds as follows. Placing an animal in a previously rewarded but now empty goal box results in the repeated evocation of r_g by the cues that were in close proximity to the now absent goal object. Since the CS (goal box cues) eliciting r_g is no longer followed by the US (food), the extinction laws of classical conditioning would require that the hypothetical CR (r_g) should suffer a reduction in strength. Invoking the generalization of extinction laws, it can be reasoned that the frequency of r_g evocation at the choice-point is reduced and that the reduction is a function of the degree of similarity between choice-point and goal box cues. Since a concomitant reduction in s_g occurs, it follows that a decrement in the probability of the observable choice behavior must occur. Such a reduction in choice behavior as a consequence of latent extinction had been previously observed. But once again utilizing the inference rules provided by the model, consequences not yet observed were derived. Moltz selected two conditioning laws as inference rules: (*a*) the rate of evocation of an observable conditioned response covaries with relevant drive during extinction, and (*b*) the reduction in response strength during extinction is a monotonic increasing function of the number of response evocations in the absence of the *US*. Notice that the logical status of the two conditioning laws has now changed from empirical propositions to inference rules. The initial conditions of an experiment must now be stated in order to derive the prediction sentences. Training may first be administered in a T maze. The animals must then be divided into a number of groups with different drive schedules and placed in the empty goal box. In accordance with the drive law (*a*), the animals with the highest motivation should produce the greatest emission rate of the imaginary response, r_g. These subjects, according to the extinction law (*b*), should show the greatest reduction in the strength of r_g. Thus, the decrement in choice behavior on subsequent test trials should covary with the drive level present during placement in the empty goal box. Experimental verification for this prediction was obtained (Moltz and Maddi, 1956).

Having demonstrated that the conditioning model of r_g theory provides in addition to pictorial and representational function the rules of reasoning, we need only consider the model's interpretative function. Although coordinating definitions were systematically formulated during the derivation of observable consequences, they were not explicitly denoted. Examining first the empirical antecedent variables, coordinating definitions may be formulated by imagining that r_g is an ordinary conditioned response. This is an alternate way of stating that the conditioning model is being utilized. Thus, the strength of r_g is a negatively accelerated increasing function of the number of trials that the eliciting stimulus of r_g is followed by the reward or *US*. The strength of r_g is a decreasing function of the temporal interval between its eliciting stimulus and the *US*. In this fashion, the various relationships between an observable *CR* and the variables of which the *CR* is a function define the empirical coordinates of r_g. The term "define" in this last statement must be qualified. It will be recalled that in the analysis of the kinetic theory of gases, one method of developing the theory involved the formulation and revision of coordinating definitions. Thus, coordinating propositions are to be understood as hypotheses rather than conventions: those that prove fruitful are retained, the useless coordinates are discarded. Finally, considering the consequent empirical variables, the probability of the correct response in selective learning is coordinated with the availability of s_g at the choice-point.

Having demonstrated the role of the model in r_g theory, an evaluation of the system might be in order. Aside from its apparent promising potential, the primitive state of the theory precludes any definitive judgment. However, the conditioning model of r_g theory does appear to function in a fashion quite similar to the mechanical model of the prequantitative

(Bernoulli's) kinetic theory. Accordingly, one wonders if the conditioning model is destined to play the same role in psychology that the mechanical model served in physics.

Statistical Learning Theory. We shift now to an examination of a multiple model system. Estes' probability learning theory (1959) offers some interesting contrasts to r_g theory. As we shall see, the pictorial model of Estes' theory invokes nonobservable stimulus occurrences while r_g theory appealed essentially to nonobservable response events.

If a T-maze experiment with a correction procedure is employed for the purpose of illustration, then an analysis may be rendered that is suitably simplified for the present purpose of studying the functions of the several types of scientific models. Let us, therefore, consider such an experiment. Over a large number of trials the reward is randomly placed in the left arm 70 per cent of the time; on the remaining 30 per cent of the trials, the reward is in the right arm. When an animal selects a nonrewarded arm, it is permitted to retrace. In this fashion, each trial terminates with reinforcement. The initial right or left turn is defined as the response for that trial. These two response classes are mutually exclusive and exhaustive.

The pictorial model associated with Estes' theory permits us to imagine the external environment of the maze and the internal environment of the animal as consisting of a very large but finite number of invisible stimulus elements. On any given trial, a sample of these stimulus elements is available. Each element has an equal probability of being included in the sample (this is assumed for the present type of experimental situation). At any specific moment, a given stimulus element is in an associative state with (conditioned to) one and only one response. In addition, the probability of a given response is dependent upon the number of stimulus elements conditioned to it. The sum of the probabilities of the available, mutually exclusive, and exhaustive response classes equals unity: one of them must occur.

During the initial trials in the T maze, the two alternative responses may sometimes occur with equal frequency and it is possible to imagine that an equivalent number of elements of the stimulus set are conditioned to the two response classes at the start of training. With continued training, the ratio of stimulus elements conditioned to each of the response classes undergoes a change. When the rewarded arm is ultimately selected on each trial, all the stimulus elements in the sample available during that trial are conditioned to the reinforced alternative. It will be recalled that a response to the left arm was assigned a reinforcement schedule of 70 per cent. Regardless of the initial response executed, and as a result of retracing, 70 per cent of a large series of training trials will terminate with a response to the left arm. Likewise, 30 per cent of the trials terminate in the right end box. Thus, as training progresses, the stimulus set tends to approach a composition of 70 per cent of the elements conditioned to the left response and 30 per cent associated with the alternative response. Since the content of the subset of stimulus elements sampled on any trial approximates the composition of the total set, an initial response to the left arm will approach a probability of .7 with continued training. Thus, 70 per cent of the initial responses to the left end box will be observed over a long series of trials.

So much for the pictorial model which represents the experimental situation as a series of imaginary stimulus events, the composite set of which undergoes a cumulative change in associative connection. Unavoidably, other matters such as the assumptions or postulates of the theory were included. To these and to the rules of inference or mathematical model we now direct our attention.

Following the thorough presentation of Estes (1959), and Estes and Straughn (1954) and introducing some modifications for expository purposes, let us partially describe the derivations for the previously portrayed T-maze conditions. The theoretical postulates involve combinations of such symbols as, $F_{(n)}$, θ', π', A_1, A_2, n, etc., and the related textual commentary. Interpreting these symbols in a strict theoretical language by means of the pictorial model, A_1 and A_2 may be imagined as the two theoretical response classes available, n as the number of theoretical trials, π' as the probability of the hypothetical reinforcing event following the occurrence of A_1. In addition, θ' may be conceived of as the probability of any single stimulus element being included in the sample available on a given theoretical trial, and $F_{(n)}$ as the probability that a given stimulus element is connected to imaginary response A_1 after trial n.

A few examples from Estes' postulate set will be helpful. One axiom previously indicated in the discussion of the pictorial model is expressed by the following proposition:

$$\text{``}F_{(n)} = (1-\theta')F_{(n-1)} \tag{3}$$

when response A_2 is reinforced on trial n." Interpreted by the pictorial model the equation states: after a reinforcement of response A_2 on trial n, the probability or proportion $F_{(n)}$ of the elements conditioned to response A_1 equals the proportion of stimulus elements *not* sampled $(1-\theta')$ on trial n that were already conditioned to the A_1 response ($F_{(n-1)}$) at the end of the previous trial. This is a consequence of the terminal response A_2 on trial n during which all the elements sampled were conditioned to A_2. The postulate for the consequences of reinforcement of response A_1 during these imaginary events is given by the equation,

$$F_{(n)} = (1-\theta')F_{(n-1)} + \theta'. \tag{4}$$

Expressing it in an algebraically equivalent form,

$$F_{(n)} = \theta'(1 - F_{(n-1)}) + F_{(n-1)},\qquad\qquad [5]$$

may facilitate the interpretation of the postulate. Thus, the term '$(1 - F_{(n-1)})$' may be described as the probability that an element was *not* conditioned to response A_1 at the end of the previous trial $(n-1)$, since the probabilities sum to unity. Thus, loosely interpreted by the pictorial model, the proposition reads: after a reinforcement on trial n, the probability or proportion of the element $F_{(n)}$ conditioned to A_1 after trial n is equal to that proportion of the elements sampled (θ') which were not previously conditioned $(1 - F_{(n-1)})$, plus that proportion of stimulus elements $(F_{(n-1)})$ already conditioned to response A_1. In this fashion, the postulates and hypothetical ideas of the theory may be interpreted by means of the pictorial model.

Starting with the theory's set of postulates, parts of which are expressed in the difference equations 3 and 4, derivations are made by means of the inference rules or mathematical models which include the separate systems of the calculus of probabilities, the rules of algebra, and the methods of mathematical induction. Among the theorems derived (Estes, 1959; Estes and Straughn, 1954) is the function

$$F_{(n)} = \pi' - (\pi' - F_{(1)}) (1 - \theta')^{n-1},\qquad\qquad [6]$$

which expresses the acquisition curve for the imaginary events.

Once again guided by the pictorial model, coordinating definitions are formulated. For the empirical counterpart of the T-maze situation previously described, $F_{(n)}$ is coordinated with $P_{(n)}$, the average probability of an A_1 response for a group of subjects. The A_1 response is coordinated with that class of empirical responses involving an initial selection of the left end box. Coordinating π' with π, the latter term is defined as the empirical ratio of reinforcement for the response coordinated with A_1. In the T-maze situation exemplified, the reinforcement schedule for the left response is 70 per cent or .7; in this situation $\pi = .7$ by definition. Finally, n is coordinated with N, the number of empirical trials, one of which is defined as the sequence of events initiating in the start box and terminating in the rewarded end box. The concept 'θ',' let us simply say, is coordinated with the empirical acquisition rate, θ. Substituting these terms in equation (6), we have the empirical learning function for the T-maze situation previously portrayed,

$$P_{(N)} = \pi - (\pi - P_{(1)}) (1 - \theta)^{n-1},\qquad\qquad [7]$$

which is stated in terms of the data language. When N is large, the extreme right-hand term approaches zero, since $(1 - \theta)$ is less than unity. The function, therefore, reduces to $P_{(N)} = \pi$. This agrees with the observation that asymptotic response frequency for a correction procedure T-maze habit approaches the reinforcement ratio when frequency of reinforcement is set at π and $(1-\pi)$ for the two alternative responses. The empirical scope of this law has not been determined. That is, the sets of initial conditions (experimental arrangements) within which the law is correct await empirical demonstration.

The several meanings and functions of scientific models have been demonstrated in statistical learning theory. A characteristic feature of Estes' theory obviously is that the rules of inference employed are entirely mathematical in form. As recently as the late 19th century, a good number of experimental physicists were openly expressing their distaste for mathematics in their science. Consequently, it would be surprising not to hear the same sort of thing from some contemporary psychologists. Perspective gained with passage of time as well as the fantastic success of mathematical physics silenced the critics. A good case is yet to be made against the expectation that the same might occur in psychology. Be that as it may, a cogent point is often made: fancy mathematics is no substitute for creative imagination. It would appear, however, that Estes' theory contains a good deal of both.

CRITERIA FOR EVALUATING A MODEL

The modes of operation of several models within their respective theories have been demonstrated. It becomes necessary now to formulate criteria for evaluating a given model. Following Toulmin's (1953) analysis of science, which was influenced by Wittgenstein's (1922) views, several grounds for judging a model may be stated.

Deployability. The degree to which the terms in the model in their primary context of usage can successfully be brought to the new setting. In r_g theory, deployability means the extent to which the nonobservable r_g can be assigned the properties of its observable counterpart, the conditioned response. As additional properties and laws of the separate system are assigned to r_g, the conditioning model is being deployed.

Scope. The range of phenomena to which the model is applicable. This means the number or extent of facts and data that may be derived by use of the model. According to this view, a theory does *not* contain formal limits; instead, the scope of applicability is empirically determined.

Delineation of the scope of a theory provides the guides and incentives for subsequent theorizing. This may take the form of changes in the initial theory or the construction of a more comprehensive system. In the latter case, the original theory frequently becomes a first approximation or a special instance of the general theory: the equations of the comprehensive theory reduce to the equations of the limited system for the special cases involved. The efforts of Estes and other mathematical model builders make it possible to envisage this future state of affairs in psychology.

While "scope" refers to the *empirical* derivatives of a theory which are generated with the aid of a model, "deployability" is an attribute of the set of relationships or meanings contained in the model that are employed in formulating the *logical* propositions of the theory. Generally, the more a model is deployed the greater will be the scope of the theory; the reverse, however, is not true.

Precision. For psychology, this in the present paper refers to the degree to which the consequences of a theory are unequivocally derived through application of the inference rules provided by the model. This feature is of special importance since the prequantitative character of most models in psychology often permits contradictory derivations.

Several implications of the viewpoint that generated these criteria merit specific consideration. A fundamental point concerns the criterion of truth. Although the terms true and false are applicable to empirical sentences, these adjectives are devoid of meaning when applied to a model or the theory the model serves. A model has lesser or greater deployability and scope and a certain degree of precision, but not truth or falsity.

An adjunct to the three judgmental criteria is the dichotomy between models providing calculi, coordinating definitions, and related functions and those yielding *only* pictorial imagery. The latter, in psychology, have taken the form of cognitive maps, S-R switchboards, behavioral fields, and a variety of peculiar things in the nervous system. When mistaken for more serious instruments, the *exclusively* pictorial model can generate a good deal of useless experimental labor, a point eloquently presented by Kendler (1952). Where the inferential or interpretative function is sacrificed for the best intuitive picture such as a model reflecting, "the existential richness of human life . . ." (Allport, 1955, p. 11), the scientist usurps the poet's function.

One consequence of confusing modular terms with empirical sentences is the variety of cases continuously made against one or another model. For example, Harlow (1953) contends that simple behavior has explanatory value only for simpler phenomena and provides no information concerning complex behavior. This view loses all urgency when one seeks the basis for the distinction between simple and complex. Occasionally, the distinction is held to be self-evident. However, this cannot be seriously regarded, as that which is considered self-evident for one generation of science is frequently believed to be absurd by some other generation. More often, the distinction between simple and complex phenomena is predicated upon the more extensive knowledge accumulated concerning the former: what is relatively well understood is simple; that which is less well known is complex. Harlow (1953) and Asch (1952) have been most critical of the "simplicity" involved in the conditioning model. We may look forward to the day when the research being done by these scientists transforms "complex" incentive-motivational, exploratory and social behaviors into "simple" phenomena.

THE ROLE OF ANALOGY

There are no sufficient a priori grounds for determining how well some separate system will function as a theoretical model for another realm of phenomena. The successful theorist's imagination does, initially, grasp an analogy between the data of interest and the separate system. As the basis for selecting some model, recognition of a critical analogy has sometimes produced the most incredible accomplishments: de Broglie's wave mechanics and Einstein's relativity are two instances. Successful apprehension of analogy is not limited to the most illustrious examples, for as Munitz (1957b) has demonstrated, analogy has served a core function in man's interpretation of his environment from Babylonian mythology to modern science. Consequently, the logician has exerted some effort in the attempt to torture the notion of analogy into a neat classificatory scheme. With the exception of the recent heroic efforts of Braithwaite (1953), the basis for the analogical relationship between a model's separate system and the ideas of the theory it serves has not been explicated.

MODULAR THEORIES AND MODULAR CONSTRUCTS

One corollary of the methodological position outlined is the required distinction between constructs introduced by a model and those defined immediately in terms of observables. Stimulus elements and r_g are *theoretical or modular constructs,* whereas drive, defined in terms of the known laws concerning the energizing and facilitative effects of deprivation, might be termed an *empirical construct.* An essentially similar distinction has recently been made by Ginsberg (1954), so we need not pursue it further except for one additional consideration. Dichotomizing constructs along the lines suggested might provide one basis for categorizing scientific theories. Borrowing the classification of *empirical construct theory* and *axiomatic-model theory* from Spence (1957), we would suggest that whereas the former class of theory employs empirical constructs, the latter utilizes modular or theoretical constructs. Examples of axiomatic-model theories have been analyzed here; there are no examples of relatively pure empirical construct theory in psychology. Interestingly enough, Spence's (1956) theory might be considered a mixed type, as he employs empirical constructs such as drive and habit and theoretical constructs such as r_g and s_g.

In the course of the last century, theories of the axiomatic-model type were considered extremely objectionable to a number of scientists and philosophers such as Mach, Duhem, and Ostwald. Characteristic objections concerned the employment of concepts at another level of discourse, that is, the appeal to suprasensible occurrences. The great success of the axiomatic-model type of theory in classical physics eventually silenced the positivistic critics. In contemporary psychology, however, this viewpoint has sired the school of radical empiricism. Although the ingenuity and imagination of Skinner's experimentation are probably unequaled, his views on theory (Skinner, 1950) should be severely questioned.

THE MODEL AND REALITY

On pragmatic grounds, most scientists find it necessary to acknowledge an external world independent of the observer. As a consequence, discourse is generated concerning the relationship between the models and constructs of science and the phenomena these represent. Since a successful model enables us to predict the future outcome of sets of events, the model is sometimes assumed to be a literal description of reality. For example, it might be argued that the kinetic theory predicts the behavior of gases and since a gas must be composed of something, why not the molecules pictured by the model? Such an assumption in no way interferes with the scientists' activity and may be disregarded. However, one consequence of that view is not so harmless. Occasionally it is argued that if there is a reality, then one and only one model can provide the best description of it. This last proposition and the assumption of reality correspondence upon which it is based are seriously discredited by the very content of physics and psychology. Numerous examples are available of several models serving the same class of events. Conversely, a single model can function in behalf of independent classes of phenomena. Whittaker provides an admirable illustration of the latter state of affairs:

. . . it happens very often that different physical systems are represented by identical mathematical description. For example, the vibrations of a membrane which has the shape of an ellipse can be calculated by means of a differential equation known as Mathieu's equation: but this same equation is also arrived at when we study the dynamics of a circus performer, who holds an assistant balanced on a pole while he himself stands on a spherical ball rolling on the ground. If we now imagine an observer who discovers that the future course of a certain phenomenon can be predicted by Mathieu's equation, but who is unable for some reason to perceive the system which generates the phenomenon, then evidently he would be unable to tell whether the system in question is an elliptic membrane or a variety artiste (Whittaker, 1942, p. 17).

SUMMARY

The functions of models in theory construction were analytically categorized as (a) representational, (b) inferential, (c) interpretational, and (d) pictorial. Distinctions introduced were exemplified in the kinetic theory of gases, r_g theory, and statistical learning theory. Implications of the analysis for current methodological problems in psychology were examined.

2

Criteria of the Stages of Mental Development*

Bärbel Inhelder

The following report is unusually interesting from several points of view. It presents some of the most important features of Piaget's seminal thinking on the criteria for identifying stages in mental development. It also reflects the extreme casualness of a conference of scholars discussing their topic. Such a conference is a currently popular method of communication among scholars. In her introduction, Dr. Inhelder, professor of child psychology at the University of Geneva, gives us an interesting sidelight on the report, when she states "I have been asked to expound Piaget's conception in front of Piaget himself."

After listening to Dr. Inhelder, Dr. Piaget joined in the discussion with the other notable American and European scientists who were present at this section of the conference: Drs. Fremont-Smith, Lorenz, Mead, Rémond, Tanner, Walter, and Zazzo. The comments made by the contributors during the discussion catch a good deal of the flavor of scientists in the process of thinking out a problem as contrasted with the more formal summing up after they have done some research or

* From Bärbel Inhelder, "Criteria of the Stages of Mental Development," In J. M. Tanner and B. Inhelder (Eds.) *Discussions on Child Development: A Consideration of the Biological, Psychological, and Cultural Approaches to the Understanding of Human Development and Behavior.* Vol. 1 of the Proceedings of the First Meeting of the World Health Organization Study Group on the Psychological Development of the Child, Geneva, 1953. New York: International Universities Press, 1953. (pp. 75-96). (With permission of author, editors, and Tavistock Publications.)

formulated a hypothesis they favor. Reflection on a problem, in the course of this discussion, tends to ramble, get out of focus, arouse strong feelings, and finally fade away when no satisfactory solution is apparent. All in all, an enjoyable experience.

INHELDER: I find myself in a most unenviable position. To begin with, I have been asked to expound Piaget's conception in front of Piaget himself. The conception of mental development as it appears in the works of M. Piaget is somewhat disconcerting, not because of the facts but because of the terminology. M. Piaget, who is a zoologist by training, an epistemologist by vocation and a logician by method, employs a terminology as yet not much used in psychology (Piaget, 1951a, 1951b, 1952). He expresses himself mainly in terms of *structures,* which by definition are systems of mental operations obeying definite laws of composition such as, for example, the mathematical laws of group and lattice. According to a number of cyberneticists structures are as much physiological as mental. It seems to me necessary to keep in mind this triple orientation—biological, epistemological and logico-mathematical—which is continually reflected in Piaget's vocabulary, in order to find one's way easily among the Geneva studies. But once these characteristics are appreciated the data and laws deriving from them become clear and are easily verified.

The general subject of this meeting is a determination of the criteria of the stages of development. How can we define a stage of development from the psychological point of view? The schools of Freud, Wallon, and Piaget have adopted different but complementary points of view. I should like to expound briefly that of M. Piaget.

The stages are defined by two main criteria:
(*a*) the process of formation or genesis;
(*b*) the complete form or final equilibrium.

The equilibrium of a stage while marking the completion of one period marks at the same time the beginning of a new period of transformation.

STRUCTURES

M. Piaget has been able to demonstrate three types of structures:
(1) sensori-motor "group" structures;
(2) concrete operation *"groupement"* structures;
(3) combined "group" and "lattice" formal structures.

I will define each of these structures while describing them.

1. The structure consisting of a group of sensori-motor operations appears in the period of infancy and prepares for the stage of childhood. It is achieved at about one and a half years and is characterized by a system or group of reversible actions. The term "reversible" is taken not in its medical but in its mathematical sense. Thus at one and a half years the

baby is usually capable of making detours and of retracing his steps: in other words, of carrying out what Poincaré has called a "group of displacements." However, these actions are carried out by successive movements and not yet with the help of simultaneous representation.

2. The structure of concrete groupement begins in early childhood and reaches its equilibrium during later childhood. Actually it comes to full achievement between seven and eleven years. The concrete groupements which are carried out mentally permit the simultaneous, and not merely successive, evocation of a displacement or transformation and its inverse. Thus, for example, when a child transforms a ball of plasticine into a sausage or a cake (Figure 1)[1] he can from seven years onwards mentally cancel this transformation and thus arrive at the conservation of matter. At about ten years he shows himself capable of carrying out the same reversible reasoning in connexion with conservation of weight and at about eleven years with conservation of volume. In each of these reasonings an actual transformation is cancelled by an inverse mental operation, thus leading to conservation. However, the child, unlike the adolescent, can only carry out one operative groupement after the other, not two simultaneously.

3. The structure of combined groups and lattices of formal thought marks the peak of adolescence. This structure develops between eleven and fourteen years and reaches its equilibrium at about fifteen years. The

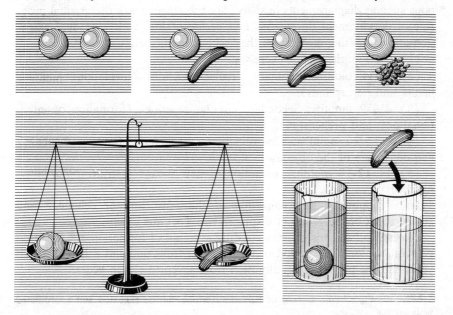

FIGURE 1. Conservation of Matter

[1] I wish to thank Mr. Vinh Bang for the accompanying illustrations.

groups of formal operations integrate the partial groupements in a structured whole. The adolescent carries out a group of formal operations of the lattice type when he makes combinatorial analyses. At about fifteen years adolescents can make up a mixture of a number of chemical solutions not merely by chance but through combinations, associating each of the elements with all the others of the system. This reveals a new structure. Similarly, the adolescent can carry out a number of formal operations with a reciprocal and a negative corresponding to each, thus showing a group structure. The concept of proportion which the adolescent applies in the field of geometry and physics depends also on the group. The structure of formal operations thus shows an unlimited degree of reversibility and mobility.

GENESIS

Having defined the structures we can now describe the stages of development as processes of formation leading to structures of equilibrium. I will limit myself to giving a few brief indications and examples.

The first stage stretches from zero to one and a half years approximately. This first period of life can be characterized by the genesis of the sensori-motor stage of intelligence and is achieved with the formation of the sensori-motor group. This consists of a combination of reversible actions such as displacements in space. Six sub-stages mark the gradual progress of development during this first period of life, with a gradual extension and increasing mobility of the "schemata" of behaviour.[2]

(1) 0-1 month: Reflex exercises.

(2) 1-4½ months: Primary circular reactions (formation of motor habits and perceptions).

(3) 4½-9 months: Secondary circular reactions (formation of intentional acts and prehension).

(4) 9-11/12 months: Co-ordination of schemata (ends and means) and constancy of the object.

(5) 11/12-18 months: Invention of new means (sensori-motor intelligence).

(6) 18 months:- Internalization of the sensori-motor schemata and achievement of the group of displacements (detours).

The second stage is characterized by a period of formation and a period of equilibration. The period of formation is from one and a half to seven years and the period of equilibration from seven to eleven years.[3]

---

[2] Piaget calls schema a piece of behaviour which can be repeated and coordinated with others.

[3] Since every equilibration phase is at the same time (in respect of the later phase) a preparatory phase, the phase seven to eleven years can be considered equally well as the phase of equilibration of the structures prepared between two

The formation period is characterized by the genesis of representative intelligence. Within this long period of formation can be distinguished two phases without clear demarcation.

The first is determined by the formation of symbolic thought leading to representation. Actually the change from sensori-motor action in the infant to mental representation in the child is due to the symbolic function which differentiates the significant from the significate. Everyone knows of the child's first attempt to represent events by symbolic play, drawing, and language.

The second phase is determined by the formation of concrete operations. Mental actions (internalized actions accompanied by representation) are irreversible before being grouped in reversible systems. Up to the age of six years the whole intellectual behaviour of the child is still determined by the irreversibility of mental actions.

I will quote as an example the behaviour of two boys, Vincent and Marco, who at regular six-monthly intervals were willing to undergo a psychological combined with an electro-encephalographic examination. We wished to complement our cross-sectional studies undertaken upon a large number of subjects by some longitudinal studies. The psychological behaviour of Marco at the age of five years six months and of Vincent at the age of six years is in fact marked by irreversibility in their reasoning. Here is a sample of the experiments which the two boys were submitted to.

For the first test (Piaget and Szeminska, 1941) a certain number of egg-cups and eggs are used (Figure 2). The two boys had not the slightest difficulty in choosing from a basket as many eggs as there were egg-cups on the table. By means of an operation of a one-to-one and reciprocal correspondence they were able to place an egg each time opposite an egg-cup and so on. However, when the experimenter destroyed this perceptual correspondence by spacing out the eggs and putting the egg-cups close together or vice versa the children denied the existence of conservation of number and estimated the number of eggs as a function of the space occupied.

---

and seven years and as the preparatory phase for the structures which are completed between eleven and fifteen years. Therefore we should speak of the stage from two to eleven years and another from seven to fifteen years, because structures follow each other with no definite break, since each new structure integrates the preceding ones and is prepared by them. The break at seven or eleven years is simply a question of convention or convenience. Here we use the following convention: stage I from zero to one and a half year; stage II from one and a half to eleven years with formation or genesis from one and a half to seven years and equilibration from seven to eleven years; stage III from eleven to fifteen years with final equilibrium reached at about fourteen to fifteen years. The levels of equilibration for concrete operations (particularly at seven years and eight to ten years) are numerous precisely because these operations are not yet formal, that is to say they are not yet entirely detached from their contents but constitute a progressive structuration of these various contents.

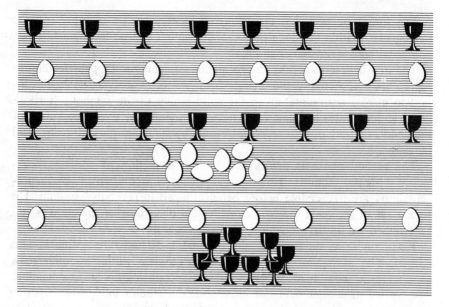

FIGURE 2. Numerical Correspondence

In a second test (Piaget and Szeminska, 1941) a liquid has to be poured from a tall, narrow glass into a low, wide one or else from a big glass into several little ones (Figure 3) (for children we make believe it is a fruit juice we want to pour). Although they had themselves poured the liquid, the two boys believed that its quantity increased or decreased. The direct action of pouring could not be reversed mentally. In the same way the two boys were incapable of understanding the reciprocal compensation of dimensions (tall x narrow=wide x low).

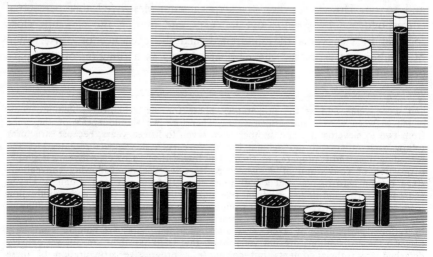

FIGURE 3. Conservation of Liquids

FIGURE 4. Conservation of Length

For the third test (Piaget, Inhelder and Szeminska, 1948) two rods of the same length are used. One of them is displaced parallel to the other (Figure 4). Once again the two boys, centering their attention on the displacement of the rod, through lack of reversibility, thought it became first longer and then shorter than the other.

In the fourth test (Piaget, Inhelder and Szeminska, 1948) two surfaces are used which represent fields on which two cows are pasturing (Figure 5). On each of the fields simultaneously we put a first house, then a second house and so on up to fourteen; only on one of the fields the houses are put touching each other whereas on the other the houses are spread out over the whole field. Now the problem is: Are the unoccupied areas of equal size. In the language of the child we ask: "Have the two cows still got the same amount of grass to eat?" Here again it is because of lack of reversibility in their mental actions that the children are incapable of seeing the equality of the remaining surfaces.

For the fifth test (Piaget, Inhelder and Szeminska, 1948) a lake is represented with islands of different sizes on which the child has to build houses of the same volume "with the same space inside" (Figure 6). For the young children there is no question yet of making three-dimensional

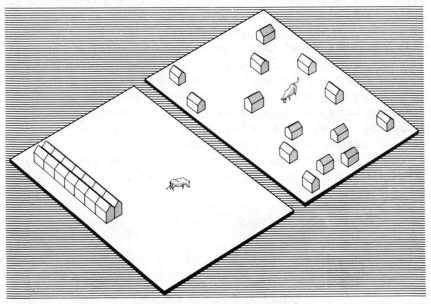

FIGURE 5. Conservation of Surface

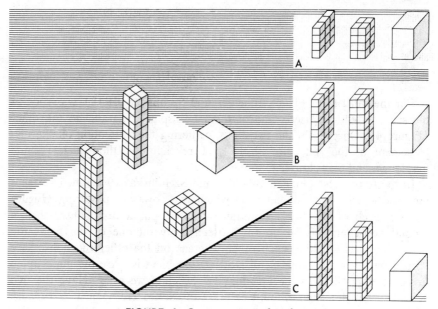

FIGURE 6. Conservation of Volume

measurements. What interests us is to know whether or not they can think of compensating unequal dimensions. The two boys invariably constructed all the houses of the same height whatever the area of the base.

An absence of reversibility goes along with a certain rigidity in the systems of reference. This is why during the sixth test (Piaget and Inhelder, 1948) Vincent and Marco were not yet able to imagine the water level as being horizontal in inclined flasks (Figure 7).

In respect of a seventh test (Piaget and Inhelder, 1941), and an eighth (Inhelder, unpublished), the two children had difficulty, which is characteristic for their age, in arranging objects in series according to their size, or in classifying them according to two or three criteria at once.

In short, in these few tests, and in others, the two children were capable of carrying out mental actions but not yet mental operations, operations being by definition reversible mental actions.

After a slow continuous evolution the change from irreversibility to reversibility often occurs abruptly for a particular problem. Concrete

FIGURE 7. System of Reference

operations as a whole, however, only very gradually impinge upon reality; the age of seven years marks only the beginning of reversibility.

The change from irreversibility to the first forms of reversibility occurred quite suddenly in Marco. After an interval of six months, that is to say between six years and six-and-a-half years, Marco's behaviour when confronted with the same experiments was completely altered. By means of a system of reversible operations he was able at six and a half years to understand certain invariances which he had denied at the age of six years. In the same way he was able to carry out operations of arrangement in series and of classification. The same change was more gradual but not less striking in Vincent's case.

The balanced structure consisting of a groupement of concrete operations not only marks the conclusion of early childhood but serves as a basis for further development. Here can be distinguished different substages. At the age of seven years on the average the child is able to carry out logico-arithmetical operations (classifications, arrangements in series, and one-to-one correspondences) but it is a year later that the time-space operations are achieved (Euclidean co-ordinates, projective concepts and simultaneity). Thus up to about eleven years there develops gradually a system of concrete operations which will later serve as a basis for formal operations.

The third stage is characterized by the formation of formal operations which reach their state of equilibrium at about fourteen to fifteen years. At eleven years the pre-adolescent is already capable of deducing by means of hypotheses and not simply from concrete facts. His reasoning frees itself from the concrete. But only at about fourteen to fifteen years does this new form of intelligence attain a balanced structure governed by laws of groups and lattices.

In fact two boys, Philippe at the age of fourteen, and Udrea at the age of fifteen and a half, showed themselves capable of carrying out combinatorial and proportional operations, whereas a year earlier confronted with the same experiment they only proceeded by trial and error without reaching an exact solution to the problems. In the experiment mentioned earlier, developed with the help of Dr. G. Noelting (Inhelder, unpublished) on colouring obtained by mixture of different chemical solutions, the two boys proceeded through a systematic combination of the elements presented. They combined the five colourless solutions in different orders: $1 + 2, 1 + 3, 1 + 4, 1 + 5$; then $1 + 2 + 3$ and so on, with two, three, four, and five elements until they were able not only to obtain the colouring asked for but to discover the part played by a neutral and a reversing element.

In the projection experiment developed with the help of Mr. Vinh Bang (Inhelder, unpublished) (Figure 8) the two boys managed, at fourteen and fifteen years but not earlier, to produce a single shadow on the

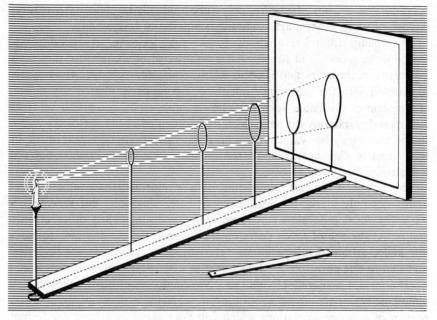

FIGURE 8. Light Projection

screen by means of a series of rings of different sizes placed at different distances, discovering, without previous teaching at school, that the size of the shadow is proportional to the diameters of the rings and inversely proportional to the distances from the source of light.

The formal type of reasoning of adolescents is thus disclosed, not only through verbal expression, but also by the way they organize an experiment and furnish a proof. The age of fourteen to fifteen years seems characteristic of this last form of equilibrium which brings about the completion of formal operations.

CRITERIA OF STAGES

In conclusion I would like to specify the criteria of the stages.

1. *The stages of development are defined by structured wholes* and not by any isolated pieces of behaviour.

The concrete groupement structure allows not only the solution of particular concrete problems but all the elementary types of classification, arrangement in series, and conservation of number. The appearance of a structured whole allows us to generalize from one particular piece of behaviour to others of the same type. Unlike the tests modelled on the Binet-Simon tests which do not allow of any generalization since they proceed by summation of successes and failures, the appearance of an operational groupement allows us to identify a mental structure.

But there is more than that: structured wholes go beyond the operations actually carried out and are the base for a whole system of possible operations. We have seen that when confronted with the problem of combining chemical solutions the adolescent at a fifteen-year level proceeds to use a combinatorial method without any previous teaching. Thus not only does he recall the operations already carried out but he can construct a system of possible operations.

2. *The passage from an inferior stage to a superior stage is equivalent to an integration:* the inferior becomes part of a superior. It is easy to show that concrete operations serve as a base for the formal operations of which they are part. The combinatorial method, for example, is based on changes of order which are possible during childhood and later develop into combinatorial operations. Proportions themselves are operations applied to operations, or operations to the power two.

3. *The order of succession of stages is constant* but the age at which the structures appear is relative to the environment, which can either provoke or impede their appearance. The genetic development seems to follow a general law of the same type as the laws of organic growth. However, may I emphasize this: the age of realization cannot be fixed absolutely; it is always relative to the environment. The influence of the environment can act in many ways—at one time through the content to be constructed, at another by the possibilities of learning, or again by the social interchange itself.

The content to be structured: a group of objects may be more or less easy to classify according to their particular perceptual qualities.

Learning: it has been found that certain spatial representations are made easier by sensori-motor explorations.

Social interchange: certain comparative studies have shown that in an environment of free interchange and discussion magical representations decline rapidly in favour of rational representations, whereas they persist much longer in an authoritative environment.

These observations as a whole show the age margin which must be allowed for in our stages. Even if the intellectual development follows a constant order its manifestations are subject to fluctuation.

In summary we could say that the criteria of stages as shown by M. Piaget are based on structured wholes which follow one another in a constant order according to a law of integration.

The genetic conception of M. Piaget opens a number of new perspectives:

(1) The operational pattern of psychological structures may perhaps facilitate correlation with the neurological (cybernetic) patterns.

(2) Since the development of cognitive functions cannot be dissociated from that of affective functions, it will perhaps be possible to demonstrate their parallelism. M. Piaget has already shown the relation

between the intellectual operation and social co-operation, as well as the interdependence of the pre-logic of childhood and moral realism.

(3) The establishment of a scale of development based on balanced structures will enable us to identify the level of operations in a child and not only individual successes and failures.

(4) The study of structured wholes is, however, insufficient if it is not complemented by research in differential psychology (sex, race, social environment).

FREMONT-SMITH: Thank you very much. I watched Professor Piaget's face very carefully and he seemed calm and peaceful and at times even delighted. Mlle Inhelder's presentation is now open to discussion.

GREY WALTER: I have been, in England and in my particular milieu, one of the most enthusiastic proponents of M. Piaget. I have tried to convey the ideas which have been developed here to my colleagues in physiology, with varying success, and I should like to put to you directly a question which is always put to me when I am trying to convince my colleagues that this type of behavioural analysis has validity in connexion with physiological problems. It is this: could you tell us very roughly how many children you studied, from what groups they were drawn, and whether you have subjected your quantitative results to any of the standard statistical analyses?

INHELDER: I am not able to quote from memory the exact number of subjects examined in each of our studies. For the studies dealing with experimental reasoning in children and adolescents we examined individually more than 1,500 subjects from five to sixteen years. In some studies the examination of 100 children was enough to give us interesting indications, whereas for others 200 to 500 were necessary.

Moreover we are now taking up again with our students those studies which gave us the most significant results for the diagnosis of mental development. We are working on a large scale and trying to study for particular age-groups the relations between our various results.

GREY WALTER: What I would like to have is, for example, a set of distribution curves showing the range of the variation of these various behaviour standards with age, comparable with the curves for reading ability or arithmetical ability or the other factors which more conventional psychologists are accustomed to plot.

INHELDER: One of our students is now preparing a thesis for a doctorate on this subject and he is studying the distribution of the results as a function of age.

TANNER: All this work reminds me very much of the sequence of ossification occurring in children. Obviously, this is a large jump in analogy. Nevertheless, something similar does happen. The sequences of ossification are held to even if the child's development is slowed up. If I understand Mlle Inhelder and Professor Piaget correctly, one of the most cogent arguments for the existence of their developmental stages is that the sequence of them remains the same even if as a whole they are retarded or advanced. This is exactly the same with ossification centres, and this seems to me a powerful argument in favour of the existence of the mental stages, and of their neurological bases.

I want also to ask a question. Some children are advanced physically during the period of growth, and we have several ways of measuring the degree of advancement, of which two, I think, are of chief interest in this context. One is the state of the ossification centres—the "bone age," and the other is the state of development of the teeth. At the present time my colleagues and I are doing a study in which we hope to relate these two things—to discover whether a child that is dentally advanced is also skeletally advanced. In general I am fairly sure that the two measures are not related to the same thing, though there may be a small correlation between them. The head grows rather differently from the rest of the skeleton, and the teeth are part of the head. Now does advancement or retardation in the sequence of mental tests relate to advancement or retardation in the teeth, or in the skeleton, or in neither?

INHELDER: In the present state of our research I am unable to reply to that.

ZAZZO: It seems to me that the main interest of the Geneva work lies in the establishment of the sequence and the explanation of the passage from one stage to another. This is a contribution of considerable importance to psychology. However, one problem arises, that of the curve of growth, and of the significance of the more or less rapid passages from one stage to another. Mlle Inhelder moreover stated the problem very clearly in her work on mental deficiency and she has already formulated several hypotheses. The problem I should like to underline is one of method. You said that the age at which the structures are realized is very variable and you give as the main reason the influence of environment. This is obviously one of the causes. I wonder, however, if there are not others. It has been noted for a long time that tests of mosaic or multiple-variety type enable us to determine the mental level with greater precision. One wonders whether Piaget tests should not be used in conjunction with other tests dealing only with an isolated aspect of behaviour. In all these tests one notes a surprising unrepeatability of results which arises, no doubt, from the

educational conditions, diversity of environment and perhaps also from
the conditions of the experiment. There are extraordinary variations related
to the test situation, the experimental situation, and, in a general way, affective conditions. There is no doubt that this type of test is the most
subject to affective fluctuations linked with experience. I think, therefore,
that the difficulty of establishing a precise age for your stages comes not
only from the fact that there is a wide dispersion but also in certain cases
that an isolated activity does not enable us to obtain the same results as
when a mosaic-type test is used. I should like to know what Mlle Inhelder and Professor Piaget think on this last point.

INHELDER: I agree with M. Zazzo that there is a certain dispersion and
even a certain lability in intellectual behaviour. Nevertheless, I am always struck by the fact that among developing children the dispersion
within a stage is relatively small compared with the wide differences between behaviour in one stage or another, between one mental structure
and another.

I am not so pessimistic as you as regards the unreliability of the results due to fluctuations in affectivity. It is above all important to encourage each child to do his very best by creating an atmosphere favourable
to the examination.

ZAZZO: It seems that with these two types of test, the mosaic test and the
Piaget test, we have this alternative: with the first type, we may determine a
very precise age, within three or four months, but without knowing anything that lies behind it from the point of view of intellectual mechanism;
with the second type of test, we may understand the intellectual mechanisms very well but not be able to fix an intellectual level. In the present
state of affairs it does not seem possible by means of your tests to establish
any kind of prognosis of development.

INHELDER: I am entirely in agreement with you. In the present state of
our research we are not able to say: "such and such a child is exactly at
the level of six years nine months." However, I wonder if the compensations operating in mosaic-type tests are any more than compensations of
a statistical order and whether they reveal the essential characteristics of
an age level? That is another question.

PIAGET: I should like to make a remark to the two previous speakers. The
object of these studies, initially, was not to establish a scale of development and to obtain precise determinations of age as regards stages. It
was a question of trying to understand the intellectual mechanism used in
the solution of problems and of determining the mechanism of reasoning.
For that we used a method which is not standardized, a clinical method,

a method of free conversation with the child. We encouraged each child, as far as possible, in a way which was not comparable to that used with the preceding child. That is why, personally, I am always very suspicious of statistics on our results. Not that I dislike statistics; I worked on biometrics enthusiastically when I was a zoologist, but to make statistical tables on children when each was questioned differently appears to me very much open to criticism as regards the results of the dispersion. It would be very easy to make all this into a test-scale, but it would not have the value of a standardized piece of work like that which Mlle Inhelder's co-workers are undertaking now, for example. In reply to M. Zazzo, I think that by taking the operatorial mechanism for a particular level one attains something more general than the mechanism of compensations in a mosaic test. I think that Mlle Inhelder has somewhat exaggerated the differences of age, the variations with environment in order to be the "Devil's advocate." In actual fact, I have personally been quite surprised by the first results of Mlle Inhelder's students who are now carrying out a standardization in the form of tests. The regularity is greater than I should have thought judging by my clinical conversations with the children. I do not despair of obtaining a scale which will perhaps not be exact within three months but which, from the very fact that it will give a structured whole, will reveal more than would a system of compensations such as the mosaic-tests.

RÉMOND: I should like to know if you have attempted to check the validity of your deductions by the "educational artefact." I will explain what I mean. A child from a known environment who has received the instruction normal to this environment is submitted to a course of training which might facilitate for him the acquisition of these stages. Have you tried to put yourself in conditions which are different from those of the children who are usually around you? In this connexion perhaps Dr. Mead could tell us if among children of a so-called primitive population, that is at least not having had a Western education, one would find the same stages and the same ages defined by these stages. Taking the case of Negroes, for example, should we not find that the acquisition of these stages in American Negroes receiving the same education as the white people was normal, whereas on the contrary there would be a marked retardation among certain African peoples who have a very different educational system?

INHELDER: I have not been able to experiment by varying systematically the educational factor or going so far as to carry out the experiment in a different cultural environment. My personal experience, apart from work on normal children, is confined solely to children whose schooling has been irregular, children who were refugees in Switzerland during the war. I noted that certain of these children at first contact gave a response which seemed to be at a level inferior to that which one could expect from them. However, after a quarter of an hour of experimenting and conversation these same children reached a higher level. In a certain sense they had caught up on their pedagogic retardation whereas the true mentally defective are never able to do this. Therefore it does not seem to me impossible that in our cultural environment the method of clinical interrogation by means of concrete experiments should enable us to disclose the potential level of an individual. But I base this on only a few observations and cannot draw any generalization from it.

PIAGET: I would like to give a second reply to Dr. Rémond. Let us take the last of the stages mentioned, the attainment of the formal level. There we have a whole structure which is characterized at first by the appearance of the logic of propositions, and if we study the lattices intervening in these propositional operations we find a correlation with proportions and combinatorial operations. From the point of view of the educational artefact it is surprising to note that proportions are taught, but combinatorial operations, at least in Geneva, are never taught in school. However, children invent these combinations by themselves. They find out not the formula, of course, but a complete method giving all the combinations for a certain number of variables. Here there are two operations which derive from the same structured whole, one of which is taught in school and the other not. They are, however, contemporaneous. It is striking that the school should have to wait till the age of fifteen before teaching proportions. I am certain that if teachers had been able to appreciate the concept of proportion in a more concrete manner they would have taught it already at eight years. If teachers have delayed this teaching until twelve years they have done so with good reason.

MEAD: Before I can answer Dr. Rémond's question, I should like to ask Mlle Inhelder if I understood two or three of the points. Do I understand that you were working here only with sequences? Surely you have a lower limit below which you do not expect a given stage to appear? I would like to know how much possible spread you think occurs in development; do you conceive of some children reaching the six-year-old expectation at two, or at three or at five? Do you think of others not reaching it until ten?

The other question is the relationship to what we usually call intelligence. Do you expect a child with an IQ of 70 to show these stages in a rudimentary form, or do you assume that it will not reach stage 2 or stage 3 at all?

INHELDER: As to the first question, I can only reply in a superficial way, letting you see later, perhaps, the necessary documents. In one of the experiments on conservation solved by 75 per cent of the children at the age of six and a half, I did not find a single success until exactly five years and no failure after seven and a half. I was dealing, of course, with "normal" children examined in day nurseries and in infant and primary schools of the town of Geneva. For other experiments the dispersion may be slightly greater or slightly less.

As to the second question, I have had the opportunity of examining retarded children and mentally defective children with IQ's of 70 and less. Among these children the true mental defectives, after a period of slow development, were able, at the age of physiological maturity, to pass the threshold of concrete operation structures (seven to ten years) but were never able to attain even the lower threshold of formal structures (eleven to twelve years). The imbeciles never reached the threshold of concrete operations. However, the IQ of 70 obtained by means of mosaic-type tests does not appear to me to be an absolute norm. I have found a few rare children who, despite an IQ of 70, were able to catch up on their retardation and to give in our tests results of a higher level. The IQ of 70 can in certain cases mask either a normal process unfolding slowly or a pathological process tending towards an early halt.

MEAD: I am going to have to answer Dr. Rémond first on theoretical grounds rather than from observations. Stated as Mlle Inhelder stated it, this framework of stages seems to me to be at such a level of abstraction that it will probably be applicable to every people we know anything about. The sort of cultural variations that one would expect to find would be of this order. The Arapesh, a tribe in New Guinea, are people who only count to twenty-four, and after that say "a lot"—they say one, two, two and one, one dog, one dog and one, one dog and two, one dog and two and one, two dogs—after six dogs they get bored. Now among such a people only the very brilliant are likely to use the same thinking as Piaget stage 3, and it would take a considerable amount of extra education, and we don't know how much, to elicit from the average the same amount of facility in stage 3 that one would find here in this country. On the other hand, in another people not a hundred miles away in New Guinea and of the same general racial type who can count to thousands in their heads, can do the most complicated mathematical arrangements, and are exceedingly interested in adjustment to reality, I would expect many more individuals of average intelligence able to function as in stage 3. Now, when I tried to apply Professor Piaget's formulation of twenty-five years ago, it did not work because the formulation was far more concretely expressed than this formulation now. And when I tried to take magical thinking, the kind of animistic thought imputed to young children, and test it out among my second New Guinea tribe, then I found no correspondence. They were a tribe that had emphasized relationship to reality and factual reporting so intensively that the other type of thinking did not appear in children.

I think we need to distinguish between the cultural evocation of the lines of thought called primary process and secondary process thinking, and the way in which the sequence of development of these types of thinking is correlated with growth. I expect to find such an investigation cross-culturally useful, though at times it may be very difficult for a European to recognize the forms of thinking found in these different cultures.

The thing I don't quite understand, though, is the relationship of this formulation to the formulation of the child's relationship to reality, and the attribution of magical and animistic thinking to young children. That is, how do the two aspects of culture integrate or criss-cross?

INHELDER: I can only make a statement concerning the environment in which I have worked. In fact we observe an inter-penetration of the pre-logical structures on the one hand with the animistic and realistic forms of childhood beliefs on the other hand. The appearance of the first structures of logical thought coincides with that of rational causality in the child. In our environment it seems that there is synchronism between these two processes.

PIAGET: I think that in order to make comparisons between very different social environments, as Dr. Mead has done, it is necessary to find a system of tests as far as possible independent of language. All the tests which I used formerly had the drawback of being essentially connected with language. This is what I would call my pre-operational period. But if you take our tests on space, here is a field where one can find all the operations which can be presented relatively independently of language by a system of drawings, by comparison between a given concrete situation and drawings among which the subject can choose the true and the false. One should find something in common between different civilizations or cultures in the spatial field. These spatial operations are not, however, separate operations: one can find a whole series of groupements and other operations applied to space. As long as no systematic comparison has been made between different cultural environments with these spatial tests one has great difficulty in separating the part played by language, with all its cultural significance, and the part played by operations. It seems to me this still remains to be done.

GREY WALTER: We had an interesting experience with the application of the Piaget methods in the clinic. It is an anecdote rather than a report of the experiment, but it is of interest in relation to whether or not certain stages of development can be concealed or evoked by treatment or circumstance. We had some adult psychiatric patients who displayed extreme immaturity, with retardation in their E.E.G.'s and other physiological peculiarities, and we attempted to relate this finding with the stage of

thinking. We did a series of tests which we based entirely on Piaget principles, and found, in fact, that patients who were in a severely disturbed
psychopathic state had "retarded" E.E.G.'s, and were very primitive in
their behaviour, were not in stage three as they should have been, being
adults, but in stage two of their development.

FREMONT-SMITH: Had they never been normal?

GREY WALTER: Yes, they had been normal people. They were aged between twenty-five and thirty and they had been perfectly capable up to a
certain point, but they had regressed apparently back to a state where they
could not do tests equivalent to simultaneous equations; they couldn't
make reciprocal reversible relationships even in very simple tests. Some
of them were treated and some got better and we could observe, in fact, a
correspondence between the electroencephalographic changes and re-
maturation and reacquisition of the capacity for formal reciprocal thought
for the solution of simultaneous equations. Now we have just applied
exactly the same test to a population of delinquent children. The application of Piaget-type tests to a delinquent population aroused such an
intense emotional response in the subjects that the people responsible for
the children suggested we should abandon the tests forthwith.

RÉMOND: What were these tests?

GREY WALTER: They were very much the same as those Mlle Inhelder
was describing. We put water in glasses, we dropped a stone in the water,
and so on. A particular study was made of the question of causality—we
said, Why do you think the stone sinks?—and they said, "Good God, if
you think I'm such a fool as that . . ."—but they didn't answer.

ZAZZO: As regards the question put by Dr. Mead, I think it is extremely
difficult to separate the parts played by education and by heredity in development because the comparisons that we can make must always be
carried out, even in primitive societies, in a human environment where
there is language. Moreover, it appears that cultural and genetic factors
are not additive. Their relationships are certainly much more complex.
When reading M. Piaget's works I always wondered to what extent evolution and culture derive by a kind of maieutic process from hidden
psychological aptitudes. In this respect, I would recall certain current
jokes or certain well-established facts. It is said that the child of eighteen
months is at the chimpanzee age and that at seven or nine he is at the
Aristotle age.
    You know of certain cases of wild children brought up by animals,
notably the famous case of the wolf-child studied by Gesell (1941). The

report published on the story of little Kamala is very interesting. At the time she entered the orphanage Kamala, who seemed to be about six or seven years, showed no human behaviour. She was re-educated under fairly strict control and at fourteen years, when she died from a uraemic crisis, she had reached the stage of language. This is a fascinating problem. It is obvious that when she was discovered in the jungle Kamala had not reached Piaget's second stage and yet other examinations showed that neurologically she was normal.

LORENZ: I am sorry but I must lodge a passionate resistance against Amala and Kamala. I'll take my oath, and I want to drop dead this minute, if these children have really been raised by animals, and if you try to get hold of Gesell—as I did—he doesn't want to talk about it. Mr. Singh and Mr. Zingg, I am sorry to say, are people to whom the German saying applies, 'Wer einmal lügt, dem glaubt man nicht, und wenn er auch die Wahrheit spricht'.

If somebody assures me that a child raised by wolves has green luminous eyes, then I don't believe a word he says any more. A friend of mine has caught them out in another untruthfulness. In Zingg's book (1941) he proudly refers to an English scientist who, according to him, also refused to believe at first, but later humbly apologized. My friend, Dr. W. H. Thorpe, F.R.S., sought out that man, whose name I have forgotten, to ask him why he apologized and what had made him change his opinion. That poor fellow went wild with passion; it turned out that he had never apologized at all and did not believe a word of the whole story.

Now let me put before you a few of my arguments why I don't believe it. Supposing you have a wolf bitch who has lost her litter—if she had lost her litter there would be some chance of her caring for a child. She will grab that child and carry it to her lair, and then she will throw herself down and make herself ready to be sucked. That is all she does. She has no possibility of helping the child to find her teats. The child must be at an age where it doesn't yet grasp, because Amala and Kamala are reported to have eaten from the earth without using their hands (which a dog *does* by the way, it *does* use its hands in gnawing the bone, which Amala and Kamala surprisingly didn't, because neither Zingg nor Singh knew that dogs did). Then supposing that that child, by some incredible accident, happens by rolling about to find the teats, or that the she-wolf, by rolling about also, happens to bring her teats in contact with the child and raise that child, the she-wolf would suckle that child for two months, and then cease suckling it and feed it on regurgitated carrion. You must remember that she has to start at an age when the child still does not grasp or walk. And now I ask the paediatricians who are here what child taken by the she-wolf—let's be very generous and say at four months of age— suckled two months, and then fed by bitch-vomited carrion—what child would stand that?

MEAD: Are all these details on the behaviour of wolves based on Indian wolves?

LORENZ: Well, those are slightly shorter than the European ones, but otherwise they are the same.

MEAD: And we have well authenticated details on their nursing and feeding?

LORENZ: Oh, yes.

3

Imprinting: An Effect of Early Experience*

Eckhard H. Hess

Man has long believed that the experiences that come earliest in life have the most pervasive and enduring effects on later psychological growth and character development. Imprinting is probably the most dramatic of all evidence supporting this supposition. Husbandmen have known for centuries that the young of certain animals deprived of their natural mothers in earliest life will reject these mothers when they are restored to them at a later time. They have also observed that infant animals tend to become attached to whatever stimuli are present in their environment immediately after birth or hatching. Lorenz, the great European naturalist and ethologist, studied this phenomenon of imprinting in graylag geese who were exposed to his care immediately after hatching. He has written engagingly of the strong attachment of these fowl to their human caretaker. In the following report, Dr. Hess, professor of psychology at the University of Chicago, reviews the research and theoretical literature on imprinting and shows how this phenomenon has been brought into the laboratory for systematic study. There is reason to believe that something like imprinting may also occur in the human organism, as noted in the subsequent paper

* From Eckhard H. Hess, "Imprinting: An Effect of Early Experience, Imprinting Determines Later Social Behavior in Animals." *Science*, 1959, Vol. 130, pp. 133-141. (With permission of the author and the American Association for the Advancement of Science.)

by Dr. Stendler. Much of psychoanalytic theory on character development can be interpreted as imprinting during critical stages of psychosexual development.

Students of behavior generally agree that the early experiences of animals (including man) have a profound effect on their adult behavior. Some psychologists go so far as to state that the effect of early experience upon adult behavior is inversely correlated with age. This may be an oversimplification, but in general it appears to hold true. Thus, the problem of the investigator is not so much to find out *whether* early experience determines adult behavior as to discover *how* it determines adult behavior.

Three statements are usually made about the effects of early experience. The first is that early habits are very persistent and may prevent the formation of new ones. This, of course, refers not only to the experimental study of animals but also to the rearing of children. The second statement is that early perceptions deeply affect all future learning. This concept leads to the difficult question whether basic perceptions—the way we have of seeing the world about us—are inherited or acquired. The third statement is simply that early social contacts determine the character of adult social behavior. This is the phenomenon of imprinting.

At the turn of the century, Craig (1908), experimenting with wild pigeons, found that in order to cross two different species it was first necessary to rear the young of one species under the adults of the other. Upon reaching maturity the birds so reared preferred mates of the same species as their foster parents. Other interspecies sexual fixations have been observed in birds and fishes.

Heinroth (1912; 1924-33) and his wife successfully reared by hand the young of almost every species of European birds. They found that many of the social responses of these birds were transferred to their human caretaker. Lorenz (1935) extended these experiments, dealing especially with graylag geese.

Lorenz was the first to call this phenomenon "imprinting," although earlier workers had observed this effect. He was also the first to point out that it appeared to occur at a critical period early in the life of an animal. He postulated that the first object to elicit a social response later released not only that response but also related responses such as sexual behavior. Imprinting, then, was related not only to the problem of behavior but also to the general biological problem of evolution and speciation.

Although imprinting has been studied mainly in birds, it also has been observed to occur in other animals. Instances of imprinting have been reported in insects, in fish, and in some mammals. Those mammals in which the phenomenon has been found—sheep, deer, and buffalo (Grabowski,

1941; Darling, 1938; Hediger, 1938)—are all animals in which the young are mobile almost immediately after birth. Controlled experimental work with mammals, however, has just begun.

The first systematic investigations of imprinting were published in 1951. Simultaneously in this country and in Europe, the work of Ramsay (1951) and Fabricius (1951) gave the first indication of some of the important variables of the process. Ramsay worked with several species of ducks and a variety of breeds of chickens. He noticed the importance of the auditory component in the imprinting experiment and the effect of changes in coloring on parental recognition as well as on recognition of the parents by the young. His findings also showed that color is an essential element in recognition, while size or form seemed to be of less importance. Most of Ramsay's experiments dealt with exchange of parents and young and did not involve the use of models or decoys as imprinting objects, although he also imprinted some waterfowl on such objects as a football or a green box.

Fabricius carried on experiments with several species of ducklings and was able to determine approximately the critical age at which imprinting was most successful in several species of ducks. In some laboratory experiments he found it impossible to do imprinting in ducklings with a silent decoy—something which my coworkers and I were easily able to do a few years later in our Maryland laboratory. After the appearance of this pioneer work by Ramsay and by Fabricius, no relevant papers appeared until 1954. At that time Ramsay and Hess (1954) published a paper on a laboratory approach to the study of imprinting. The basic technique was modified slightly the following year and then was continued in the form described below. Papers in 1956 by Margaret Nice (1953) and by Hinde, Thorpe, and Vince (1956) include most of the pertinent materials published up to 1956 since Lorenz's classic statement of the problem.

Since 1956, however, there has been an increasing number of papers on imprinting in a variety of journals. However, most investigators report experiments which are primarily designed to look for ways in which imprinting can be likened to associative learning and are not primarily carried out to investigate the phenomenon itself. Later we shall return to a consideration of these experiments; for the present we shall concern ourselves mainly with the program carried out since 1951 at McDonogh and at Lake Farm Laboratory, Maryland, and at our laboratories at the University of Chicago.

EXPERIMENTAL STUDIES

Our laboratory in Maryland had access to a small duck pond in which we kept relatively wild mallards. The birds laid their eggs in nesting boxes, so the eggs could be collected regularly. After storage for a few days, the eggs were incubated in a dark, forced-air incubator. About two days before hatching, the eggs were transferred to a hatching incubator. Precautions were taken to place the newly hatched bird into a small cardboard box (5 by 4 by 4 inches) in such a way that it could see very little in the dim light used to carry out the procedure.

Each bird was given a number, which was recorded on the box itself as well as in our permanent records. The box containing the bird was then placed in a still-air incubator, used as a brooder, and kept there until the bird was to be imprinted. After the young bird had undergone the imprinting procedure, it was automatically returned to the box, and the box was then transferred to a fourth incubator, also used as a brooder, and kept there until the bird was to be tested. Only after testing was completed was the duckling placed in daylight and given food and water.

The apparatus we constructed to be used in the imprinting procedure consisted of a circular runway about 5 feet in diameter. This runway was 12 inches wide and 12½ feet in circumference at the center. Boundaries were formed by walls of Plexiglas 12 inches high. A mallard duck decoy, suspended from an elevated arm radiating from the center of the apparatus, was fitted internally with a loud-speaker and a heating element. It was held about 2 inches above the center of the runway. The arms suspending the decoy could be rotated by either of two variable-speed motors. The speed of rotating and intermittent movement could be regulated from the control panel located behind a one-way screen about 5 feet from the apparatus. The number of rotations of both the decoy and the animal were recorded automatically. Tape recorders with continuous tapes provided the sound that was played through the speaker inside the decoy. A trap door in the runway, operated from the control panel, returned the duckling to its box.

Imprinting Procedure. The young mallard, at a certain number of hours after hatching, was taken in its box from the incubator and placed in the runway of the apparatus (Figure 1). The decoy at this time was situated about 1 foot away. By means of a cord, pulley, and clip arrangement, the observer released the bird and removed the box. As the bird was released, the sound was turned on in the decoy model, and after a short interval the decoy began to move about the circular runway. The sound we used in the imprinting of the mallard ducklings was an arbitrarily chosen human rendition of "*gock,* gock, gock, gock, gock." The decoy emitted this call continually during the imprinting process. The duckling was allowed to remain in the apparatus for a specified amount of time while making a certain number of turns in the runway. At the end of the imprinting period, which was usually less than 1 hour, the duckling was automatically

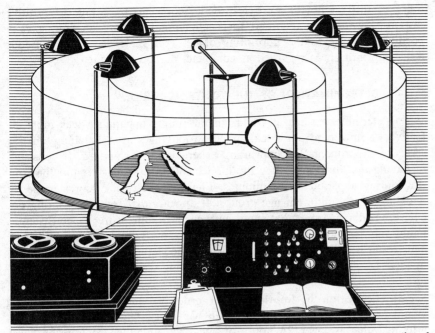

FIGURE 1. The Apparatus Used in the Study of Imprinting Consists Primarily of a Circular Runway Around Which a Decoy Duck Can be Moved. In this drawing a duckling follows the decoy. The controls of the appartus are in the foreground.

returned to its box and placed in an incubator until it was tested for imprinting strength at a later hour.

Testing for Imprinting. Each duckling to be tested was mechanically released from its box halfway between two duck models placed 4 feet apart. One of these was the male mallard model upon which it had been imprinted; the other was a female model which differed from the male only in its coloration. One minute was allowed for the duckling to make a decisive response to the silent models. At the end of this time, regardless of the nature of the duckling's response, sound was turned on simultaneously for each of the models. The male model made the "gock" call upon which the duckling had been imprinted, while the female model gave the call of a real mallard female calling her young.

Four test conditions followed each other in immediate succession in the testing procedure. They were: (1) both models stationary and silent; (2) both models stationary and calling; (3) the male stationary and the female calling; (4) the male stationary and silent and the female moving and calling. We estimated these four tests to be in order of increasing difficulty. The time of response and the character of the call note (pleasure tones or distress notes) were recorded. Scores in percentage of positive responses were then recorded for each animal. If the duckling gave a positive response to the imprinting object (the male decoy) in all four tests, imprinting was regarded as complete, or 100 per cent.

DETERMINATION OF THE "CRITICAL PERIOD"

To determine the age at which an imprinting experience was most effective we imprinted our ducklings at various ages after hatching. In this series of experiments the imprinting experience was standard. It consisted in having the duckling follow the model 150 to 200 feet around the runway during a period of 10 minutes. Figure 2 shows the scores made by ducklings in the different age groups. It appears that some imprinting occurs immediately after hatching, but a maximum score is consistently made only by those ducklings imprinted in the 13- to 16-hour-old group. This result is indicated in Figure 3, which shows the percentage of animals in each age group that made perfect imprinting scores.

Social Facilitation in Imprinting. In order to find whether imprinting would occur in those ducklings which were past the critical age for imprinting—that is, over 24 hours of age—we attempted to imprint these older ducklings in the presence of another duckling which had received an intensive imprinting experience. Ducklings ranging in age from 24 to

FIGURE 2. The Critical Age at Which Ducklings are Most Effectively Imprinted is Depicted by This Curve, Which Shows the Average Test Score of Ducklings Imprinted at Each Age Group.

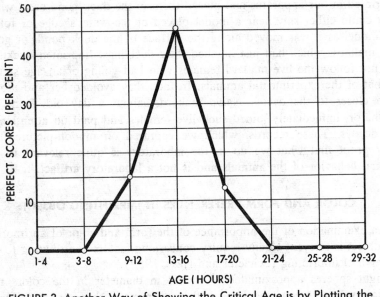

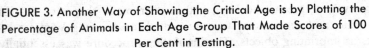

FIGURE 3. Another Way of Showing the Critical Age is by Plotting the Percentage of Animals in Each Age Group That Made Scores of 100 Per Cent in Testing.

52 hours were given 100 feet of following experience during a period of 30 minutes. The average score for the ducklings was 50 per cent; this shows that some imprinting can occur as a result of social facilitation. Two conclusions can be drawn. (1) Social facilitation will extend the critical age for imprinting. (2) The strength of imprinting in these older ducklings is significantly less than that when the animal is imprinted alone at the critical age under the same time and distance conditions; under the latter circumstances the average score made is between 80 and 90 per cent. A further indication of this dissipation of imprintability with increasing age is obtained when we average the scores for those animals which were between 24 and 32 hours old. The average score for these animals was 60 per cent, while the score made by older animals ranging in age from 36 to 52 hours was 43 per cent. One last item points to the difference; even when the time and distance were increased during imprinting of the older ducklings there were no perfect scores. With such a large amount of distance to travel during the imprinting period, approximately 40 per cent of the animals would be expected to make perfect scores if they were imprinted during the critical period.

FIELD TESTS OF IMPRINTING

In this same exploratory vein we have also carried out some studies under more normal environmental conditions. To do this we took animals imprinted in our apparatus and placed them in the duck pond area, where they could either stay near a model placed at the water's edge or follow the model as it was moved along the surface of the duck pond, or go to real mallards which had just hatched their ducklings. Imprinted ducklings did not follow the live mallard females who had young of an age similar to that of the experimental animals. In fact, they avoided her and moved even closer to the decoy. Naive mallards, about a day old, from our incubator, immediately joined such live females and paid no attention to the decoys. These records, which we captured on motion-picture film, offer proof that what we do in the laboratory is quite relevant to the normal behavior of the animals and is not a laboratory artifact.

COLOR AND FORM PREFERENCES IN IMPRINTING OBJECTS

An examination of the importance of the form and color of an imprinting object is relevant to any inquiry concerning factors contributing to the strength of imprinting (Schaefer and Hess, 1959).

Eight spheres approximately 7 inches in diameter in the colors red, orange, yellow, green, and blue, and in achromatic shades of near-black, near-white, and neutral grey were presented to 95 young Vantress broiler chicks as imprinting objects. The imprinting procedure was essentially the same as that described above in the duckling experiments. All the animals were exposed to one of the spheres during the critical period. Each imprinting experience lasted for a total of 17 minutes, during which time the imprinting object moved a distance of 40 feet.

Twenty-four hours after imprinting, each animal was tested in a situation where the object to which it had been imprinted was presented, together with the remaining four colored spheres if the animal had been imprinted to a colored sphere, or with the remaining two achromatic spheres, if the animal had been imprinted to one of the achromatic spheres.

It was found that the stimuli differed significantly in the degree to which they elicited the following-reaction. The stimuli, ranked in their effectiveness for eliciting following during imprinting, from the highest to the lowest, are: blue, red, green, orange, grey, black, yellow, white. These colors, in the same order, were increasingly less effective in terms of the scores made during the testing period. We concluded from this that the coloring of a stimulus is more important than its reflectance.

In order to determine also form preferences in imprinting objects, we took the same spheres we used in determining color preferences and added superstructures of the same coloring, so that the spheres had heads, wings, and tails (Figures 4 and 5).

The addition of superstructures had a definite effect on the ease with which the following reaction could be elicited: the plain ball was found to be the most efficient; the ball with wing and tail-like superstructures, less so; and the ball to which wings, tail, and head had been added, least

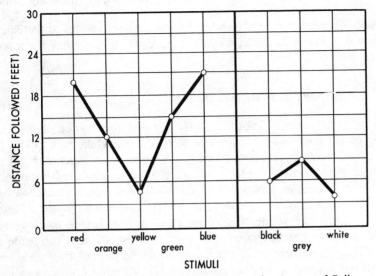

FIGURE 4. Mean Distance, in Feet, Traveled in the Course of Follow-
ing-response, by Eight Groups of Animals, to Eight Stimuli Differing
in Color or Reflectance

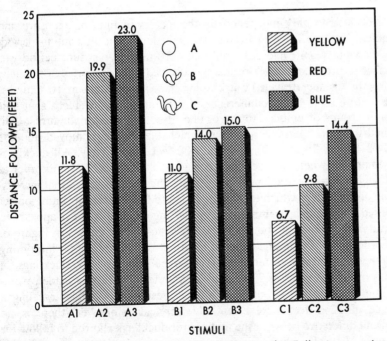

FIGURE 5. Effectiveness of Models in Eliciting the Following-reaction,
Expressed as a Function of Stimulus Complexity and Color

efficient. We even presented a stuffed brown Leghorn rooster to the chicks, and it was found to be the least efficient model of all in eliciting the following response.

AUDITORY IMPRINTING IN THE EGG

Some investigators of imprinting have felt that vocalization of the incubating parent might cause imprinting to that vocalization even before the young fowl hatched. This seemed a likely hypothesis, so we carried out the following experiment. About 30 mallard eggs were incubated in an incubator with a built-in loud-speaker. For 48 hours before hatching these mallards were exposed to a constantly played taped recording of a female mallard calling her young. Eggs were removed just before hatching and placed in a different incubator. Later, when tested, these young made no significantly greater choice of this source of sound than of the "gock" call used in our normal imprinting procedure. [A preliminary experiment was reported earlier (Ramsay and Hess, 1954).] Auditory imprinting, while the mallard is still in the egg, is therefore considered to be unlikely.

LAW OF EFFORT

We decided to vary independently the factors of time of exposure and the actual distance traveled by the duckling during the imprinting period. Since previous results had indicated that a 10-minute exposure period was sufficient to produce testable results, we decided to run a series of animals, varying the distance traveled but keeping the time constant at 10 minutes. We therefore used one circumference of the runway (12½ feet) as a unit and ran groups of animals for zero, one, two, four, and eight turns. This resulted in imprinting experiences in which the ducklings moved about 1 foot, 12½ feet, 25 feet, 50 feet, and 100 feet, respectively. All ducklings were imprinted when they were between 12 and 17 hours of age, in order to keep the variable of critical period constant. The results showed that increasing the distance over which the duckling had to follow the imprinting object increased the strength of imprinting. A leveling-off of this effect appears to occur after a distance of about 50 feet. These results are shown in Figure 6.

In order to determine the effect of length of exposure time on imprinting strength, we chose a distance that could be traversed by ducklings in periods of time as short as 2, 10, and 30 minutes. The scores made by animals imprinted for 2, 10, and 30 minutes, respectively, while traveling a distance of 12½ feet were essentially identical. Moreover, there is no significant difference between the findings for ducklings allowed to follow for a distance of 100 feet during a 10-minute period and those allowed 30 minutes to cover the same distance. These results are shown in Figure 7.

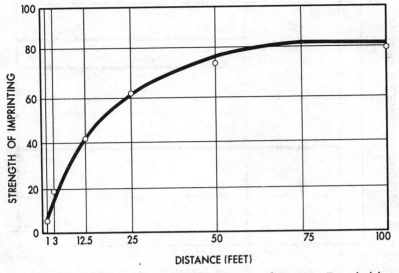

FIGURE 6. Strength of Imprinting as a Function of Distance Traveled by
Ducklings, with Exposure Time Held Constant

The strength of imprinting appeared to be dependent not on the duration of the imprinting period but on the effort exerted by the duckling in
following the imprinting object. To confirm this notion we tried two supplementary experiments (Hess, 1958). In the first, we placed 4-inch hurdles
in the runway so that the ducklings not only had to follow the model but
also had to clear the obstacles. As we suspected, the birds which had to
climb the hurdles, and thus expend more effort, made higher imprinting
scores than those which traveled the same distance without obstacles. In
the second experiment we allowed the duckling to follow the decoy up an
inclined plane, with similar results. After further experiments we came to
the conclusion that we could write a formula for imprinting: the strength
of imprinting equals the logarithm of the effort expended by the animal
to get to the imprinting object during the imprinting period, or $I_s = \log E$.

Previous accounts in the literature on imprinting have made the following of a moving object a necessary condition of imprinting. Our results, as
formulated in the law of effort, indicate that the amount of walking done
by the animal during the imprinting period is of primary significance. The
following experiment was therefore carried out. Two identical decoys were
spaced 3 feet apart. A light over each decoy could be turned on and off so
that only the model giving the "gock" call was illuminated in the darkened
experimental apparatus, and the illumination was made to coincide with
the call. When the duckling reached the lighted and calling model, the light
and sound were turned off in that model and turned on in the other, which
was 3 feet away. In this manner we could shuttle the animal back and forth

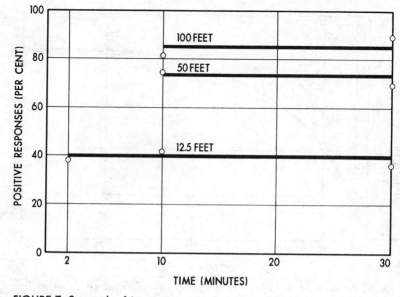

FIGURE 7. Strength of Imprinting as a Function of Duration and Exposure in Minutes. Time had little effect on the test scores of the ducklings when the distance traveled was held constant.

and have it cover a distance similar to that used in the normal imprinting situation, where it walks behind a moving object.

Animals were run at four shuttles and 16 shuttles. The results show scores similar to those obtained previously for the 12½-foot and 50-foot distances (see Figure 6). They indicate, again, that imprinting strength is a function of the distance walked by the duckling, regardless of whether or not the more complex perception of *following* a moving object is involved.

FEAR BEHAVIOR AND LOCOMOTORY ABILITY

In the light of the "critical period" results, the question arises as to what developmental changes might be taking place that would account for the limits of the critical period.

During the very early hours of their lives, animals show no fear. We conducted an experiment with 137 White Rock chicks of different ages (Hess, 1959) and found that there is no fear up to 13 to 16 hours after hatching. Afterwards, the proportion of animals from age group to age group begins gradually to increase up to the age of 33 to 36 hours, when all animals show fear. Fear responses will prevent an animal from engaging in the kind of social behavior necessary for imprinting to take place, since a fearful animal will avoid rather than follow a potential imprinting object.

On the other hand, fear behavior cannot account for the limitation of imprinting before the peak of maximum effectiveness. Since the strength of imprinting is dependent on locomotor activity, we postulated that the ability to move about might thus be an important factor. The ability to move about is a growth function and would limit the onset of the critical period. Hence, we tested 60 Vantress broiler chicks of White Rock stock of different ages to determine the development of increasing locomotor ability.

The two curves we obtained from these two experimental studies—one for increasing locomotor ability and one for increasing incidence of fear behavior with increasing age—were found to be in substantial agreement with the limits of the critical period. In fact, in plotting these two curves together, we obtained a hypothetical "critical period" for imprinting which strongly resembled the empirical one obtained for that breed.

It seems likely that all animals showing the phenomenon of imprinting will have a critical period which ends with the onset of fear. Thus, we can predict in a series of animals, knowing only the time of onset of fear, the end of imprintability for that species. Even in the human being one could thus theoretically place the end of maximum imprinting at about 5½ months, since observers have placed the onset of fear at about that time (Bridges, 1932; Spitz and Wolf, 1946).

INNATE BEHAVIOR PATTERNS AND IMPRINTING

Most commonly the following-reaction to a certain model has been taken as a means of observing the progress of imprinting during the first exposure to the imprinting object and also as an indicator of the effectiveness of this exposure. However, the following-reaction is always accompanied by other innate behaviors which may also be observed and recorded. For the present purpose, the emission of "distress notes" or "contentment tones," maintenance of silence, and fixation of an object were checked for individual animals for a 2-minute period at the beginning of an imprinting session (Hess and Schaefer, 1959).

To differentiate between the "distress notes" and the "contentment tones" of chickens is comparatively easy, even for the layman who has never become familiar with them. "Distress notes" are a series of high-intensity, medium-pitch tones of approximately ¼-second duration in bursts of five to ten. Little pitch modulation occurs in this kind of call. "Contentment tones," on the other hand, are a series of high-pitch, low-intensity notes emitted in bursts of three to eight and with considerable pitch modulation during emission. The duration of the individual tones is much shorter, $\frac{1}{12}$ of a second or less. During distress notes the animal usually holds its head high; during contentment tones it holds its head and beak down. The designations *distress notes* and *contentment tones* are merely labels and should not necessarily be taken literally.

The subjects were 124 Vantress broiler chicks which had never experienced light until the time of the experiment. The experimental situation was much like the first 2 minutes of an imprinting experiment.

We found that the behavior of the animals changed markedly with age. The younger the animals were, the more pronounced was their striving to move under the cover of the nearby model. Figure 8 reflects the way in which this behavior diminished with age. Figure 9 shows that the proportion of animals fixating, or orienting toward, the model also diminished with increasing age. Although it was considerably more difficult for the younger animals to cover even the short distance between their original location and the model because of their poor locomotor ability, the time it took these younger animals to reach the model was much shorter than the time it took the older animals. However, the mode of locomotion for these younger animals was not walking but, rather, a kind of tumbling; they used both feet and wings as supports, and this left them exhausted after reaching the model a few inches away.

These results concerning behavior patterns during imprinting offer still further corroborating evidence for the location of the critical period as empirically determined. The emission of distress notes by animals older than 17 hours, even in the presence of an object that offers warmth and shelter, may be taken as an indication that a new phase of the animals' perception of their environment has set in. This behavior obstructs imprinting under the conditions of our laboratory arrangement. The high incidence of animals emitting contentment tones in the presence of the model is gradually replaced by an increasing number of animals emitting distress

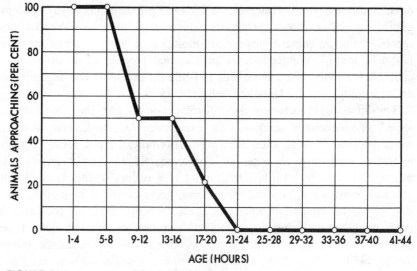

FIGURE 8. Percentage of 124 Chicks That Approached the Stimulus Objects at Different Ages

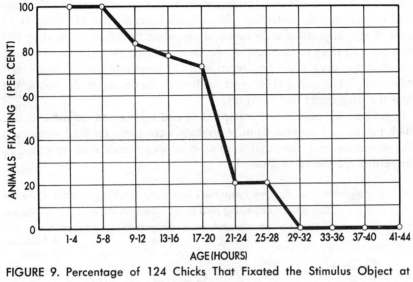

FIGURE 9. Percentage of 124 Chicks That Fixated the Stimulus Object at Different Ages

notes. No similar displacement occurs in animals remaining silent. The emission of contentment tones decreased as the animals became older, and the emission of distress notes increased at the same time.

The most important interpretation of these findings is that elicitation of following behavior by various means after the critical period may not touch upon imprinting phenomena at all. Conventional training methods may be employed to overcome the fear response which the animals show after 17 hours, and it is not impossible to induce them, for example, to follow human beings. However, during the critical period, habituation or learning proper need not be considered as far as lowering of fear behavior is concerned, since at that time there is little or no fear present in the animals.

DRUG STUDIES

The rapid drop in imprinting, then, appears to be coupled with the developing emotional response of fear—a response that makes imprinting impossible. To examine this aspect of imprinting, reduction of the emotional response by means of a tranquilizing drug (Hess, 1957) seemed a logical step. Meprobamate was chosen because of evidence that it would reduce emotionality without markedly influencing motility or coordination. Preliminary experiments with dosages of meprobamate showed clearly that the emotionality of the ducklings was markedly reduced. In fact, the ducklings showed no fear of strange objects or persons, even though they were at an age where marked fear is normally a certainty.

To obtain the maximal information from this experiment, we then decided to test animals under the following four conditions: (1) drug at 12 hours of age, imprinting at 24 hours of age when the effect of the drug had worn off; (2) drug at 12 hours of age, imprinting at 14 to 16 hours of age, test when the drug effect had worn off; (3) imprinting at 16 hours, test under drug later; and (4) drug at 24 hours, imprinting at 26 hours, test when the drug effect had worn off.

In general, the procedure for imprinting and testing was the same as that which has been described. Control animals were given distilled water, and chlorpromazine and Nembutal were used to obtain additional information. The results are shown in Table 1.

TABLE 1. Percentage of Positive Responses Made by Ducklings Under Different Conditions of Testing and Drug Administration

Conditions	Control H_2O	Meprobamate (25 mg/kg)	Nembutal (5 mg/kg)	Chlorpromazine (15 mg/kg)
Drug at 12 hr, imprinting at 24 hr	14	54	31	57
Drug at 12 hr, imprinting at 14-16 hr	62	8	28	63
Imprinting without drug at 16 hr, test under drug	61	65	61	58
Drug at 24 hr, imprinting at 26 hr	19	17	16	59

It is obvious that, while meprobamate reduces fear or emotional behavior, it also makes imprinting almost impossible. It does not, however, interfere with the effects of imprinting. This is clear from the results of test 3. Chlorpromazine allows a high degree of imprinting under all conditions, whereas Nembutal reduces imprintability at all points except under the conditions of test 3.

From the data, it appears that we might interpret the action of the drugs as follows. If we assume that meprobamate and chlorpromazine reduce metabolism, then we could expect the high imprinting scores found at 24 hours of age [test 1], because metabolism had been slowed and we had thus stretched out the imprinting or sensitive period. This did not occur when we used Nembutal or distilled water. The second point deals with the reduction of emotionality. In test 4 we had little evidence of emotionality in the meprobamate and the chlorpromazine groups. Emotionality did occur in the control and in the Nembutal group. Thus far, the only way we can interpret this former result is to consider the law of effort.

Here we had found that the strength of imprinting was a function of effort or of distance traveled. It may be that, since meprobamate is a muscle relaxant, these effects of meprobamate cut into the muscular tension or other afferent consequences and thus nullify the effectiveness of the imprinting experience. Since, under the same circumstances, we attain perfectly good imprinting in all cases with chlorpromazine, this notion becomes even more tenable.

CEREBRAL LESIONS

In addition to drug effects we also studied the results of cerebral lesions on the imprinting behavior of chicks. This was done partly because we had noticed a loss of the fear response in some chicks that had undergone operations—chicks which were old enough to have this response fully developed.

Chicks with a type 1 lesion showed good imprinting at the age of 3 days. This is considerably better than the finding for the control chicks, which only occasionally show this behavior so late in their first few days. Even with this lesion, chicks at 5 and at 7 days showed no imprinting.

Chicks with type 2 lesion showed no imprinting, although some that had been prepared earlier gave no evidence of fear responses to strange objects.

Completely decerebrate animals were run only at 2 days of age, and they followed well, but the tests were inconclusive insofar as imprinting strength was concerned. Diagrams of the various lesions are shown in Figure 10.

Although the number of animals used in this study is still small, this seems to be a fruitful avenue of approach. Control animals that have had sham operations act essentially like normal chicks. Other experiments involving electrical stimulation are being undertaken, since such stimulation may reinforce imprinting behavior.

GENETIC STUDIES

We have also considered the genetic side of imprinting. We kept ducklings which were highly imprintable and bred them separately from ducklings which showed very little imprinting response. We thus had two groups of offspring, those produced by "imprinters" and those produced by "non-imprinters." There was a clear and significant difference in the imprinting behavior of the two groups, even in the first generation. The offspring of imprintable parents were easily imprinted; those of less imprintable parents were difficult to imprint. The "imprinter" ducklings had imprinting test scores more than three times better than those of the "non-

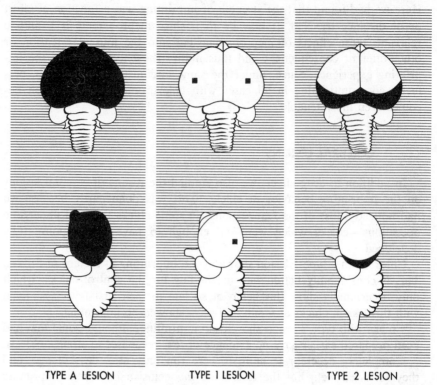

TYPE A LESION   TYPE 1 LESION   TYPE 2 LESION

FIGURE 10. Three Types of Lesions in the Chick Brain, Used to Study the Effect
of Extirpation on Imprintability

imprinter" ducklings. Similar results were also obtained in a study of ban-
tam chicks. We are also following up those animals which have had experimental imprinting experiences to determine what influence, if any,
these experiences have on their behavior as adults. So far the results are inconclusive, but they do suggest that experimental imprinting of mallards
affects their behavior as adults, particularly with respect to courtship
patterns.

Birds of various species show differing degrees of imprintability. Domestic fowl do show imprinting responses, but the results are not as clear as
for wild birds. We have had good success in imprinting some breeds of
chicks, and the best imprinters among them are the Vantress broilers. Leg-
horns, on the other hand, appear to be too highly domesticated to give
clear results. Other animals we have used in our experimentation are two
kinds of geese, black ducks, wood ducks, turkeys, pheasants, quail, Peking
ducks, and Rouens. The various breeds we have so far used in our work
and the degree of imprintability found in each are shown in Table 2.

TABLE 2. Number and Imprintability of Different Experimental Animals. Most of the animals were imprinted in runway and mallard decoy situations. Some of the Vantress broilers were imprinted on colored spheres, and the sheep were imprinted on human beings.

Animal	Number*	Imprintability**
Ducks		
Wild mallard	3500	E+
Domesticated mallard	150	E
Peking	200	G
Rouen	100	F
Wood	50	P
Black	50	G
Total	4050	
Geese		
Canada	30	E+
Pilgrim	50	G
Total	80	
Chickens		
Jungle fowl	100	G
Cochin bantam	300	G
New Hampshire Red	100	G
Rhode Island Red	100	G
Barred Rock	200	G
Vantress broiler	500	G+
White Rock	100	F
Leghorn	200	P
Total	1600	
Other Fowl		
Pheasant	100	P
Eastern bobwhite quail	50	G
California valley quail	20	E
Turkey	30	F
Total	200	
Mammals		
Sheep	2	G
Guinea pig	12	G
Total	14	
Total	5944	

* Estimated for fowl, actual for mammals.
** E, excellent; G, good; F, fair; P, poor.

IMPRINTING IN MAMMALS

The guinea pig is similar to the chick and the duckling in that it is mobile and reasonably self-sufficient soon after birth. For this reason we used it in exploratory work. We first developed a method of obtaining the young from the mother with minimal parental contact. This was done by Caesarean section. However, further work showed that it was sufficient to obtain the young within an hour after they were born, and for the moment we are doing this. Guinea pigs imprint on human beings and follow them about as do the fowl with which we have been working. The maximum effectiveness of the imprinting experience seems to be over by the second day. So far, in using our imprinting apparatus with our usual duck decoy we have obtained best results sometime before the end of the first day of age. Work is being continued so that we can have a more standardized procedure before beginning a major program in this area.

IMPRINTING AND LEARNING

The supposed irreversibility of imprinting has been particularly singled out by some investigators to show that imprinting is nothing but "simple learning"—whatever that is. We do have some isolated instances which point to a long-range effect, but systematic work is just now beginning in our laboratories. Canada goslings, imprinted on human beings for a period of a week or two, will from that time on respond to their former caretaker with the typical "greeting ceremony," as well as accept food out of his hand. This occurs in spite of the fact that they normally associate entirely with the Canada geese on our duck pond. A more striking case is that of a jungle fowl cock which was imprinted by me and kept away from his own species for the first month. This animal, even after 5 years—much of that time in association with his own species—courts human beings with typical behavior, but not females of his own species. This certainly is a far-reaching effect and is similar to the finding of Räber (1948), who reported on a male turkey whose behavior toward human beings was similar. An increased amount of homosexual courtship in mallards has been observed with some of our laboratory imprinted animals, which, while not a statistically valuable finding, perhaps points also to long-range, irreversible effects.

Imprinting is currently receiving much attention, and papers on the subject are being published at an impressive rate. Unfortunately, most experimenters appear to be certain that imprinting is identical with simple association learning and design their experiments as studies in association learning. In many instances the animals are too old when used in the experiments to fall within the critical age for imprinting, with the result that only association learning can occur. Papers falling into this category are those of Jaynes (1956; 1957; 1958), Moltz (1958), and James (1959).

Our own experiments on the relation between association learning with food as a reward and imprinting during the critical period show four distinct differences.

In the first place, learning a visual discrimination problem is quicker and more stable when practice trials are spaced by interspersing time periods between trials than when practice trials are massed by omitting such intervening time periods. With imprinting, however, massed practice is more effective than spaced practice, as shown by our law of effort. Secondly, *recency* in experience is maximally effective in learning a discrimination; in imprinting, *primacy* of experience is the maximally effective factor. The second difference is illustrated by the following experiment. Two groups of 11 ducklings each were imprinted on two different imprinting objects. Group 1 was first imprinted on a male mallard model and then on a female model. Group 2, on the other hand, was first imprinted on a female model and subsequently on a male model. Fourteen of the 22 ducklings, when tested with both models present, preferred the model to which they first had been imprinted, showing primacy. Only five preferred the model to which they had been imprinted last, showing recency, and three showed no preference at all.

In addition, it has been found that the administration of punishment or painful stimulation increases the effectiveness of the imprinting experience, whereas such aversive stimulation results in avoidance of the associated stimulus in the case of visual discrimination learning.

Finally, chicks and ducklings under the influence of meprobamate are able to learn a color discrimination problem just as well as, or better than, they normally do, whereas the administration of this drug reduces imprintability to almost zero.

Imprinting, then, is an obviously interesting phenomenon, and the proper way to approach it is to make no assumptions. To find out its characteristics, to explore its occurrence in different organisms, and to follow its effects would seem a worth-while program of study.

4

Critical Periods in Socialization*

Celia B. Stendler

Imprinting, as discussed in the preceding paper by Dr. Hess, is only one instance of the importance of timing in the developmental-learning interaction. Psychologists now propose that there are probably many critical periods for maximal behavior change during the life history of an organism. Environmental impacts experienced before or after such a critical period are hypothesized to be less effective in modifying or extending the affected behavioral skills. Curriculum planning in our schools may be regarded from this point of view as a search for important critical periods in the learner's psychological growth as well as for the most appropriate teaching materials and methods for increasing the learner's skills and understanding. McGraw has presented convincing evidence that there is a critical period during infancy (latter half of the second year of life) during which training for toilet routines may be most easily and successfully accomplished. In this report, Dr. Stendler suggests that there may be two critical periods in the early socialization process during which excessive frustrations will result in overdependence on the parents. It is further suggested that such overdependent children will have extreme difficulty in making satisfactory adjustments to some of the demands imposed by the culture in their later development.

The process of socialization during the child's early years has been described by many writers. They usually agree that during the first months of an infant's life there are few demands made upon him. The infant leads an irresponsible kind of life where his every whim is gratified and where he need do nothing in return—except grow and develop as a normal healthy baby. He cries and sooner or later he is fed, he sleeps when he is sleepy, evacuates at will, and is indulged and waited upon by loving relatives who make him the center of the household. As a result the child's first concept of himself is not that of a helpless infant, but rather of an omnipotent being

* From Celia B. Stendler, "Critical Periods in Socialization and Overdependency," *Child Development,* 1952, Vol. 23, pp. 3-12. (With permission of the author and the Society for Research in Child Development.)

whose mother and others are at his beck and call. Freud has described this period as one of "infantile omnipotence."

But although from the infant's standpoint this period may be referred to as one of infantile omnipotence, actually during this period the infant is learning, not to be all-powerful, but to be dependent. He is not born with dependency needs, but acquires them, if we follow learning theory, in accordance with certain known principles. The baby is hungry or is in pain; he cries and his mother (or other socializing agent) helps him. Soon he learns to depend upon his mother for reduction of his hunger drive or for alleviation of his pain. Whiting (1944) describes how dependency learning occurs in Kwoma society:

Kwoma infants are cared for almost exclusively by their mothers. For approximately the first three years of his life a Kwoma infant sits in the lap of his mother during the day and lies by her side at night. It is the Kwoma mother's duty to care for all the needs of her child during this period. When, despite this constant care, Kwoma infants suffer frustration, crying is the response which becomes most firmly fixed. A Kwoma mother, whenever her infant cries, does her best to comfort him. If he is hungry she feeds him; if he is cold she warms him; if he is sick or in pain she tries to soothe him. Thus by removing the source of frustration or pain the Kwoma mother rewards crying as a response to these conditions. Toward the end of infancy, when the child begins to talk, he responds to frustration or pain by asking for help, and his mother complies with his request whenever it is possible for her to do so. Thus during infancy a frustration-dependence sequence is established.[1]

Actually, it may not be necessary for frustration (defined as interference with a habit) to occur for the child to learn to be dependent upon the mother. The mother can acquire secondary reward value simply because she becomes associated with the reduction of the hunger drive and the elimination of pain. Gradually the child builds up an association of mother as the giver of love and approval and comes to be dependent upon her for emotional succorance as well as for satisfaction of physical needs (Sears, 1950a).

Five aspects of the socializing agent come to have reward value for the child (Beller, 1948). Perhaps the first aspect of the parent that acquires such value is that of physical contact; the infant learns to associate being picked up with reduction of the hunger drive, or being burped with reduction of pain. Thus the three-months-old baby can be soothed by being picked up and will stop his crying momentarily even though hunger or pain

---

[1] Dr. Whiting has indicated in correspondence a modification of his theory of dependency. He now makes what seems to this writer to be a helpful distinction between dependency as a habit and dependency as a drive. I interpret the above quotation as a description of the learning of a dependency habit. Whether a dependency habit develops depends upon the mother's rewarding or punishing the child's demands. The drive which is behind the habit comes about as a result of the child's learning to associate reduction of the hunger drive and elimination of pain with one person.

still persist. Next, proximity of the parent may become reinforced as the infant comes to associate the mere presence of the socializing agent with drive reduction. This may come at the point when the child actually recognizes the mother and distinguishes her from other adults in his environment. Now the mother does not have to pick the baby up; she merely has to enter the room to stop his flow of tears, while leaving the room may be enough to induce crying or a fear reaction.

Two other aspects of the parent that come to be rewarding to the child are paying attention and verbal praise or approval. Actually these represent a lessening of dependency; they come at a time when independence is on the rise. As the child comes to do more and more things by himself, he depends upon his parent not so much for help as for attention to what he is doing, or for verbal praise and approval.

A fifth aspect of the parent, the helping aspect, also comes when independence is on the rise. As the word "helping" implies, the parent no longer does everything for the child but now only "helps" when the child has begun a task and has encountered difficulties in completing it. Thus the three-year-old may put on his own shoes but his mother helps by pointing out which shoe goes on which foot and by tying the laces.

Dependency needs build up first and fast while independency training begins later and proceeds at a much slower tempo. Nevertheless some six-months-old babies hold their own bottles and are rewarded by being able to regulate the intake of milk to their own liking. The nine-months-old baby may get satisfaction from finger-feeding because his hunger drive can be more readily appeased in that fashion. And as the proud mother exclaims over the baby's achievement he eventually finds enough reward in her approval to want to repeat his independent behavior. Paradoxically, he learns to be independent because he has learned to be dependent upon his mother for acceptance and approval. It is only when he is sufficiently dependent to be pleased at parental approbation that he can make rapid strides in independence.

Independence, like dependence, must be culturally trained, however. It is not enough for the child to be independent in those areas he chooses for himself; he must learn to be independent and dependent in ways of which the culture approves. Therefore the early period of indulgence must end and child training begin. Typically parents in our society begin to make demands upon the child when he is old enough to be dangerous to himself or destructive to objects in his environment. The nine-months infant is restrained from standing in his carriage, the fourteen-months toddler is not permitted to climb stairs by himself but only when accompanied by an adult, the eighteen-months baby must eat with his spoon and not with his fingers, the two-year-old must tell his mother when he needs the bathroom. Over and over again, former habits are interfered with. As one group of writers has put it:

It must learn to walk where it has formerly been carried; . . . it learns not to be picked up when it has experienced some small disaster. It must give up much of the cuddling, holding and petting which is the prerogative of the smallest darling. Childish approximations of table manners and etiquette must be altered in favor of the customs preferred by adults. The child must learn to wait for its food, to keep its face clean, to submit to having its hair combed, to eat in the regular stages designated by our table techniques. At some time or another all of these lengthened sequences invoke frustrations and elicit protest from the child (Dollard, *et al.,* 1939, pp. 64-65).

During this early period of child training, considerable resistant or negative behavior appears. Various psychological explanations of negativism have been advanced (Ausubel, 1950). From one standpoint the period may be viewed as one where the child is learning culturally accepted ways of being dependent and independent, where dependent behavior begins to wane and independent behavior is on the rise. At this point conflicts may arise because the child's conception of independent behavior is at variance with the parent's; that is, the child wants to be independent in ways of which the parent does not or cannot approve. Or conflicts may arise because the parent wants the child to give up his dependence in certain areas, and the child rebels. A satisfactory resolution of the crisis results when the child has learned those areas in which he is expected to be dependent and those in which he is to be independent.

Not all children arrive at a satisfactory dependency-independence ratio, however. Some children become overdependent, some too independent. It is with the overdependent child that we are concerned in this paper.

Reinforcement theory lends itself very well to an explanation of how *over*dependency may originate with some children. Where the child from birth is consistently rewarded for being dependent and non-rewarded or punished for being independent, he becomes a dependent, submissive individual. This kind of treatment is typically afforded the child by overprotecting mothers. Levy (1943) has described extreme cases where this development has taken place. His overprotected children had excessive contact with the mother; they were still being indulged and waited upon as if they were babies; their attempts at independent behavior were discouraged. Such children may be said to be overdependent because of a deficiency in independence training and because dependent behavior is constantly rewarded.

Not all children who are overdependent conform to Levy's description, however. Some overdependent children have mothers who are not overprotecting, as were the mothers Levy described. Levy's parents might be said to be the instigators of the overdependency. In some parent-child relationships, however, the mother *unwillingly* accedes to the child's excessive dependency demands and because of her unwillingness is inconsistent in her treatment of the child. The child is the instigator of extreme dependency demands. Also, the child's overdependency does not extend to all areas but is limited to selected ones. Thus the child of the non-overprotecting mother may insist upon his mother's accompanying him back and forth to school but accomplish such tasks as tying shoe laces at six years of age without demanding help.

It is necessary to elaborate on reinforcement theory to explain how this type of overdependency begins. In a study of ordinal position in the family as a psychological variable, Sears (1950a) found among other things that the oldest child in the family was more likely to have experienced anxiety in the nursing and weaning situations, and at the same time more nurturance at bedtime and more cautioning about sickness and danger than second and later children. Older children were also rated as the more dependent. Sears suggests that the anxiety produced in the nursing and weaning frustration would serve as the facilitating instigator to whatever behavior had been predominant in those infant situations in which the anxiety was aroused. Thus, since dependency behavior is likely to be predominant at the time of nursing and weaning, anxiety produced in nursing and weaning situations will strengthen the dependency needs.

Extending Sears' hypothesis, we might suggest certain critical periods in the socialization process for the formation of *over*dependency. These are the periods when shifts in awareness of his position in relationship to the socializing agent occur in the child. A child builds up a set of expectations with regard to how his dependency needs are to be met. From time to time these expectations change as the child matures in his perceptions and as his culture makes demands upon him. If there is a disturbance during one of these times of change, of such a nature that the child must quickly and radically change his expectations, anxiety will arise. The child will attempt to resolve the anxiety by the method he has learned to resolve anxiety, i.e., demands upon the mother for nurturance.

In order to produce overdependency, however, the anxiety must occur not when one goal response is interfered with, but when whole sets that seriously threaten dependency needs are disturbed. Thus a baby may seem "anxious" if the living room furniture is changed around but he does not become overdependent as a result. But consider a baby whose grandmother has been the important gratifier of his dependency needs and whose mother has been the reinforcing agent for any independence training. If grandmother dies during this critical period in socialization, the child's expectancy of how his dependency needs are to be filled is forced to change. Or an absent father may return, with the result that a mother now plays the role of wife as well as mother, whereas the child had learned to expect her to act only as mother. Or a mother may take on the role of wage-earner and a new socializing agent be introduced. Or the physical environment may be changed by moving about; one's favorite toys, crib, blankets, eating utensils may disappear and only the one stable figure of mother be left. In such cases as these anxiety results in increasing the strength of the already established dependency drive.

Two critical periods for the formation of overdependency are proposed. The first critical period begins when the child begins to test out the mother to see if he can depend upon her. For most children this occurs toward the end of the first year of life. Earlier the infant has been learning to be dependent upon the mother. Now he shows his sudden recognition of the importance of his mother by his demands upon her and especially for his mother's proximity. In effect, he tests out his mother, to see if he really can depend upon her and to see if he can control her. He cries when she leaves his presence and demands that she be in sight or readily available when he needs help. Gesell (1943) reports that as early as 28 weeks the baby "demands more of the one who feeds him." Bowlby (1950, p. 122) suggests that the most critical time for the production of anxiety concerning the mother is after eight months, "when the child's first object relationship (to his mother) is developing in a specific way."

Severe traumatic experiences involving separation from the socializing agent are important to consider, then, during this period when the child has become aware of his dependency upon the mother and is testing his control of her. During this critical period it is necessary that the infant have his dependency needs met in the manner to which he has become accustomed. As Bowlby (1950, p. 122) says, "Once a clearly differentiated relationship with the mother has developed at about nine months, mothering from anyone will not do and it is imperative that the child have an opportunity of forming a continuous affectional attachment to one person." If proximity of the socializing agent is denied the infant at this time for long periods of his waking hours (i.e., if the child is hospitalized, or if the mother becomes ill, or goes back to work), anxiety will be aroused which the child will attempt to resolve by excessive demands upon the mother when he does have her. His dependency drive will be strengthened by the anxiety and overdependency may result.

The next critical period for the formation of overdependency comes during the two- to three-year-old period. As we have already indicated, this is the time in our society when demands upon the child to change his old ways of doing things increase tremendously. Now the child must give up his control of his mother and come to accept his dependence upon her, yet at the same time learn to be independent in culturally approved ways. Again, anxiety arises because important goal responses are being interfered with. In normal socialization the anxiety generated produces the right amount of dependency. But where disturbances of a traumatic nature occur so that important habits must be suddenly and drastically changed, so much anxiety may be generated that overdependency will result.

A case where a break in continuity with regard to dependency needs occurred at this critical period is described below:

Randy was the first child of a young mother and father, born while the father was overseas. His mother had moved back with her own folks while her husband was away and Randy's first two years were spent in an environment where he was the stellar attraction. He was the first grandchild on both sides of the family; paternal grandparents lived in the same community and vied with maternal grandparents in lavishing love and material things upon Randy. The mother had little to do in the household and so she was free to devote herself almost exclusively to Randy. Her major role in the household was that of daughter, however, rather than mother.

At the age of two Randy's father was returned to the States but was hospitalized for a year, during which time he was able to visit his family on a few occasions. Just before Randy's third birthday, a baby brother was born, the father was discharged and the reunited family left the grandparents' roof to set up a home of their own.

In the two years that followed, Randy had several serious accidents. He caught his arm in the wringer of the washing machine; he overturned a pan of boiling water on himself; he was run over by a car. The mother reported that during this period he was continually demanding of her time and attention. "He wouldn't let me leave him, even to go to the store," she said.

When Randy entered school, he made a scene each morning over leaving home. His parents insisted that he go, whereupon he developed stomach aches and vomited each day after breakfast. His mother found it hard to send him off following these spells, but his father broke the cycle one day by carting him off, still retching, to school, where the father requested the teacher to keep Randy even though he continued to vomit. Randy next developed ear aches but again the father firmly but kindly drove him to school in the car when the mother would have permitted him to stay home. It was not until Randy's second year in school that he became resigned to leaving his mother each day.

Randy's case illustrates how a combination of circumstances during a critical period in his socialization prevented the development of certain habits of independence and strengthened habits of dependence. In his early life Randy had learned an expectancy of how his dependency needs would be satisfied. Then Randy lost: 1) the love and affection his grandparents had showered upon him; 2) almost exclusive possession of his mother who took on additional roles as wife, mother of a new baby, and homemaker; 3) a familiar physical setting. At the same time his mother and a stranger called father began to make demands upon him to be a big boy. Randy's reaction was to demand harder than ever what he had once had and was now being denied, and to refuse to grow in independence.

What we have been saying is that there are critical periods in the child's life for the formation of overdependent behavior. These critical periods are normally anxiety-producing for all children because they involve interference with goal responses; disturbances which occur during one of these periods and which arouse excessive anxiety may so strengthen the dependency drive that overdependency will result.

We would like to hypothesize further that the timing of disturbances which affect the dependency drive will also be a factor in determining how other aspects of personality will be affected. That is, the dependency drive is so related to other aspects of personality that a disturbance during one of the critical periods will affect other aspects of personality and that the effects will differ according to the timing of the disturbance. A disturbance during the first critical period will have a different impact upon personality development than will a disturbance during the second critical period.

To clarify our hypothesis we might draw an analogy to what happens in prenatal development. There is a special time in the prenatal timetable for the development of each organ. If an organ does not develop at the proper time "it will never be able to express itself fully, since the moment for the rapid outgrowth of some other part will have arrived" (Stockard, 1931). Thus if something occurs in the prenatal environment at the time when the skull is being formed, then humans with incompletely formed skulls will result. Disturbances of the prenatal environment are tremendously significant and the *timing* of disturbances is the crucial factor.

While we cannot push our analogy too far (for we cannot postulate a timetable of personality development after birth on the basis of any innate factor alone), nevertheless what is proposed here is that disturbances with regard to dependency needs at a particular time will have particular effects upon personality development.

During the first eight or nine months of life the child is building up a set of expectations with regard to how his needs will be met; he is learning dependency. Translated into Erikson's (1950) language, he is learning basic trust in another human being. He learns to depend upon others, as we have pointed out, by having his physical needs met consistently by one person. If he does not learn that he can depend upon others, however, serious personality difficulties arise. Lauretta Bender (1950) has described children who have not had continuous affectionate care of one person up to the age of nine months:

These children impress us with their diffusely impulsive unpatterned behavior. At all levels the behavior is unorganized and remains unorganized. It is exceedingly difficult to find any educational or psychotherapeutic method whereby it can be modified into organized or patterned behavior. The child is driven by inner impulses which demand immediate satisfaction; these impulses or needs show the usual changes with physical and chronological growth of the child, but even this does not add much pattern to the behavior. Motivation, discipline, punishment and insight therapy have little effect.

The behavior remains always infantile. It is true that there are some differences as to the level of the infantile fixation, but it is always pre-oedipal and pre-superego. It is as though a newborn infant had urgent needs which must be satisfied. Screaming, kicking or temper tantrums or disturbed behavior of which the larger child is capable continue when frustration occurs, as it must a good deal of the time. All kinds of oral activity, clinging, wetting, soiling, senseless motor activity, genital manipulation may be observed. These are not neurotic traits and do not indicate regression but retardation in personality development. Psychopathic behavior-disordered children are often attention-seeking, clinging, passively dependent, seductive and amiable. This may be mistaken for an attachment or interpersonal relationship. Actually, there is no warmth, and the relationship can stand no separation or disappointments or demands; it shifts to the nearest new object as soon as the recipient is out of sight.

These are children who, in our terminology, have not learned dependency behavior. We are not concerned in this paper with cases such as these, but rather with those children who have built up a set of expectations with regard to how dependency needs are to be met and then suddenly and radically have to change them. What I am proposing is that overdependent children who become so as a result of disturbance during the first critical period will differ from overdependent children who become so as a result of a disturbance during the second critical period. The first group of children is more likely to be affected with regard to ego-aspects of personality whereas the second group is more likely to be affected with regard to superego-aspects of personality.

To make clear the reasoning behind this distinction we need to understand the different nature of the frustration involved during the two critical periods. In discussing the process of identification, Mowrer (1950) differentiates between two types of frustration. He says:

It is true that in both developmental and defensive identification the subject is "frustrated," but the different nature of the frustration in the two instances is noteworthy. In the one case it arises from a sense of helplessness and loneliness: the parent or parent-person is *absent,* and the infant wishes he were *present.* In the other case, the frustration arises from interference and punishment: the parent or parent-person is *present,* and the infant wishes he were *absent.* But the latter wish brings the average child into intolerable conflict: while he hates the parent for his disciplinary actions, he also loves the parent and experiences acute anxiety at the prospect of his really being separated, physically or emotionally, from him (or her).

Developmental identification, we may suppose, is a milder and simpler experience than is defensive identification, which has a violent, crisis-like nature. The one is powered mainly by biologically given drives ("fear of loss of love," in the analytic sense) and the other by socially inflicted discomforts ("castration fear" or, less dramatically, simply fear of punishment). The first presumably involves relatively little conflict; but in the latter case, conflict and attendant anxiety are outstanding.

The first type of frustration we see as occurring during the first critical period and, as a result, affecting the developmental or ego-aspects of identification. The second type of frustration occurs during the second critical period and as a result affects the defensive or super-ego aspects of identification.

Overdependent children produced during the first critical period will be children who have experienced helplessness; who have not been able to control the socializing agent at the time when recognition of the importance of that agent for one's own well-being was dawning. Therefore we can expect such children to be low in ego-strength, with resulting low level of aspiration and low frustration tolerance. Also, such children, while they cling to the socializing agent will tend to see that agent as a punishing figure rather than a helpful one. These things may not be true of over-dependent children produced during the second critical period. These children are more likely to be affected in the area of conscience. They will tend to resolve the anxiety generated by the frustration by overdoing the job of building a punishing voice inside. They will be rigid in their ideas of right and wrong, overconforming in behavior, unduly disturbed by the wrongdoings of other children. They will prefer well-defined structured situations to those which allow for more freedom of choice.

This is a sketchy picture of possible developments during critical periods in socialization. A necessary task for the future is spelling out in detail the relationship between dependency needs and other aspects of personality development during these critical periods.

SUMMARY

This paper examines some theoretical questions with regard to the origin of overdependency. According to the proposed theory, there may be two critical periods in the socialization process for the beginnings of over-dependency. One of these may be toward the end of the child's first year of life; the other when his parents begin to increase their demands upon the child. Disturbances of a serious nature during either of these periods may result in overdependency. It is suggested that the timing of the disturbance with regard to dependency needs may influence ego and super-ego development in particular ways.

5

Learning Theory and the Acquisition of Values*

Winfred F. Hill

Freud had sufficient creative genius and boldness to make the great leap from the empirical world of observables to the conceptual domain of theory without benefit of a strictly formal logic or the currently revered methods of statistical inference. His postulations of psychological processes like unconscious motivation, anxiety, repression, projection, identification, and the like have stimulated an almost unbelievably large number of experimental and clinical studies in psychology during the last three decades. Some of these investigations have aimed to discover the adequacy or inadequacy of Freud's psychoanalytic conceptions. The conclusions reached by research have been mixed, some supporting and some failing to support what appear to be reasonable deductions from psychoanalytic theory. Other psychologists have directed their energies toward coordinating the clinically inferred principles of psychoanalytic theory with the experimentally inferred postulates, corollaries, and theorems of contemporary behavior theory. The goal of these recent efforts is to achieve more rigorous hypothetical constructions that will combine improved scientific procedures with the intuitively apparent fruitfulness of the psychoanalytic model. Dr. Hill has set himself the task of coordinating such psychoanalytic dynamisms as identification, introjection, and internalization with the reinforcement principles of modern learning theory and showing how they are related to the acquisition of values.

The processes by which a child acquires the values of his culture and his various overlapping subcultures is, as a recent review of the subject points

* From Winfred F. Hill, "Learning Theory and the Acquisition of Values," *Psychological Review*, 1960, Vol. 67, pp. 317-331. (With permission of the author and the American Psychological Association.)

out (Dukes, 1955), still rather obscure. This obscurity is certainly not due to lack of interest in the topic. Psychologists, psychiatrists, anthropologists, sociologists, pediatricians, and educators have all given attention to the question of how children come to share the attitudes, ideals, and ethical standards of those around them. Nor is this interest undeserved, for few topics are of greater practical importance.

Perhaps this very convergence of interest from many directions is partly responsible for the difficulties involved in studying the topic. This area of research has become a battleground for conflicting terminologies, with one term often having a multiplicity of half-distinct meanings, and with what appears to be the same meaning often bearing different labels. Although many terms contribute to this confusion, three are of particular interest here: *identification, introjection,* and *internalization.* All involve some relation between an individual, hereinafter designated the subject (S), and another person or personalized entity, the model or M, such that S's behavior is in some way patterned after M's. However, these terms may refer either to a state of affairs or to the process which brought it about (Lazowick, 1955); the M may be a person, a group, or an idea (Glaser, 1958); and the relation may involve specific responses, broad meanings, or emotional reactions.

Some of the confusion as to the meaning of the term identification may be seen in the following uses. Lazowick (1955) distinguishes three main uses of the term identification in the literature: pseudoidentity, imitation, and personality change. He suggests that the term should be used only with regard to broad meanings, with imitation being the corresponding term for specific acts. Freud (1950) contrasts a boy's identification with his father, which forms the basis of his ego ideal, and his identification with his mother as an abandoned object cathexis. Davis and Havighurst (1947) maintain that a child will identify with his parents only if he loves them, but Anna Freud (1946) emphasizes identification with the aggressor. Lynn (1959) contrasts sex-role identification, which is "reserved to refer to the actual incorporation of the role of a given sex, and to the unconscious reactions characteristic of that role" (p. 127), with sex-role preference and sex-role adoption. He regards figure drawing as a measure of identification and choice of dolls for play as a measure of preference. Sears, Maccoby, and Levin (1957), however, use children's choices of dolls as a measure of identification. Sanford (1955), discouraged by such confusions of meaning, considers the possibility of abandoning the term identification altogether, but decides to retain it to describe a defense mechanism involving extreme adoption of M's behavior by S, a mechanism which is not important in normal personality development. Finally, this collection of meanings, diverse as it is, still omits those cases where identification is used as a synonym for loyalty or for empathy.

There is similar confusion concerning the meaning of introjection and internalization. Both carry the implication of values being incorporated into the personality. Hence, particularly with introjection, there is the suggestion of some relation with orality (Freud, 1950). However, Freud in the same discussion also uses introjection synonymously with identification. Parsons (1955), on the other hand, treats identification and internalization as synonyms.

The many discussions of these three terms in the literature seem to indicate that there are several processes involved but no generally accepted conventions for labeling them. A number of writers, including several already cited, have expressed discouragement at this state of affairs, but the usual result of such discouragement seems to be a redefinition of terms, which may clarify the particular exposition but which only serves further to confuse the field as a whole. Whereas Lynn (1959) believes that a term as widespread as identification must have potential usefulness, the present writer believes that clarity would be served by abolishing not only identification but also introjection and internalization from the technical vocabulary of personality development.

What, then, should be substituted? The topics to which the above terms have been applied certainly deserve discussion, and if the redefinition of the old terms is unsatisfactory, the introduction of new terms would be even worse. An answer may be found, however, in a sort of reductionism. Since the processes involved are learning processes, the existing vocabulary of learning is the obvious candidate for the job of describing them. It is quite possible, of course, that the existing vocabulary of learning theory will be inadequate for the complexities of value acquisition. However, if its use is carried as far as possible, the successes of this application should clarify our thinking about personality development, while any gaps which result should point to possible extensions of learning theory.

This approach involves treating human learning in a sociocultural environment in the same terms, at least for a first approximation, as animal learning in the environment of laboratory apparatus. For this purpose, the social rewards and punishments applied to humans may be treated as equivalent to the food pellets and electric shocks used with rats. Similarly, social roles are the equivalents of mazes which must be learned in order to obtain the rewards and avoid the punishments. Human beings of course constitute a far more variable environment than laboratory hardware, and one on which S can exercise greater influence. However, since most of the theory in this area is concerned with the adaptation of S to a relatively constant human environment (whether it be called culture, social system, or the personalities of the parents), this should not prove a serious stumbling block. There is ample precedent for such an approach in the writings of Dollard and Miller (1950), Mowrer (1950), Whiting and Child (1953), and others.

In addition, this approach treats values as nothing more than inferences from overt behavior. In principle this assumption should cause no difficulty. Few behavioral scientists would regard values (in the empirical, not the transcendental sense) as fundamentally different from such behavioristic constructs as Hull's (1943) habit strength or Tolman's (1949) equivalence beliefs. In practice, however, some theorists might take issue with this view on at least two bases.

For one thing, the measurement of values (including attitudes, ideals, and ethical standards) is commonly by verbal methods (see the review by Dukes, 1955). This leads to the suspicion that any measurement of values by nonverbal means must be inadequate, that only verbal measures can get at the significance of an act for an individual. However, verbal responses are part of the total behavior of the human organism and may be studied like other responses. The processes of unconscious motivation, semiconscious hypocrisy, and deliberate concealment all indicate that it would be unwise to treat verbal and nonverbal measures of values as equivalent. Rather than treat either verbal or nonverbal behavior as the true indicator of values and the other as a side issue, it seems more useful to study both and to ascertain empirically to what extent they lead to the same generalizations about a given S.

Another possible objection involves the distinction between specific acts and broad meanings, as in Lazowick's (1955) contrasting definitions of imitation and identification, noted above. This distinction between specific acts and broad meanings may refer either to the presence of mediating responses (see Osgood, 1953) or to the generality of the stimuli and responses involved. Neither of these distinctions, however, is dichotomous. Hull (1952) has indicated how a mediator, the fractional antedating goal response, may function in animal behavior, and Russell and Storms (1955) have demonstrated mediational processes in rote learning. Thus the mediation mechanism is by no means restricted to the "higher mental processes" of humans. As for the generality of the behavior and of the stimuli which guide it, this presumably represents a continuum from the most specific to the most inclusive categories. If, for example, washing the hands before meals is an example of imitation and cleanliness an example of identification, where would wearing clean clothes be classified? So, although the distinction between specific acts and broad meanings is a legitimate one, there are no sharp breaks on the continuum and there is no reason to assume that basically different laws are involved.

In view of the above considerations, an attempt to study the acquisition of values as a branch of learning theory appears justified.

KINDS OF REINFORCEMENT

The concept of reinforcement is basic to learning theory. While theorists are by no means unanimously agreed on the value of reinforcement terminology, there is little question that an empirical law of effect holds, that the consequences of an act influence its subsequent occurrence. A classification of kinds of reinforcers will be used here as the basis for analyzing the learning of values.

Primary Reinforcement. For the present purpose, three kinds of reinforcement may be distinguished: *"primary," secondary,* and *vicarious.* Placing "primary" in quotes indicates that it refers to the effects not only of innate physiological reinforcers but also of those social reinforcers which play a primary role in human motivation. Presumably the positively reinforcing effects of attention and praise and the negatively reinforcing effects of criticism, ridicule, and rejection are at least partly learned, but the nature of the learning process is obscure, and at the present level of analysis it seems preferable to treat praise for a human as comparable to food for a rat. The distinction between "primary" and secondary reinforcement is thus one of convenience between that which we take as given and that for which we can find a specific learned basis. Though arbitrary, this distinction is perhaps no more so than the decision as to whether food in the mouth should be considered a primary or a secondary reinforcer.

One particular kind of learning by "primary" reinforcement is the acquisition of a generalized tendency to imitate others. Miller and Dollard (1941) have indicated how a generalized tendency to imitate the behavior of others may be learned in the same way as any other class of responses. Although their demonstrations of imitation involved S's patterning his behavior after a leader who was present, Church (1957) has shown that rats can also learn to respond appropriately to the same cues to which the leader rat is responding. In spite of some negative animal evidence (Solomon & Coles, 1954), there is little doubt that humans can learn to pattern their behavior after that of other people, not only when the M is present, but also in M's absence by utilizing the appropriate environmental cues. As the child is repeatedly rewarded for imitative behavior in a variety of otherwise different situations, and as his capacity for abstraction increases, it seems plausible that a generalized imitative tendency would develop. It would be desirable, however, if the widespread anecdotal support for this deduction could be bolstered by experimental data.

The same process presumably applies to verbal instructions. The child is typically reinforced (though with some striking exceptions) for doing what others tell him to do. Hence (common parental impressions to the contrary notwithstanding), a generalized tendency toward conformity to verbal instructions may be expected to develop. With increasing intellectual development, this tendency should come to include conformity to fictional examples or to abstract ethical exhortations.

Secondary Reinforcement. Although no basic distinction is made here between primary and secondary reinforcement, there is one case frequently discussed in the literature where the acquisition of reinforcing properties by certain stimuli may be analyzed in detail. These stimuli are those which are connected with care of the child by adults, i.e., the non-essential aspects of nurturance. These include patterns of speech, facial expressions, gestures, and the like. Since these occur with those nurturant behaviors which are primary reinforcers, such as feeding and cuddling, they may become secondary reinforcers. By stimulus generalization, these behaviors should also be rewarding to the child (although less so) when produced by himself. As the child grows older and the parents expect him to take greater care of his own needs, he is more and more forced to provide not only his own primary reinforcers, but his own secondary reinforcers as well. Hence he may be expected to show some of the same mannerisms as his parents showed when caring for him.

This kind of learning appears to be one of those processes which Freud (1950) includes under the heading of identification or introjection, that in which abandoned object cathexes become incorporated into the ego. However, in the view presented here, the coincidence of abandonment and incorporation into the ego refers only to performance, not to learning. The secondary reinforcing value of the parental mannerisms is built up during the period of nurturance, but becomes evident in the child's behavior as nurturance begins to be withdrawn. This learning process has been discussed by Mowrer (1950, Ch. 24) in connection with the learning of language, and by Lindemann (1944) as a reaction to the death of a loved one. Although this process appears better adapted to the learning of rather trivial mannerisms, it is capable at least in principle of being adapted to more general and significant values as well.

Vicarious Reinforcement. Vicarious reinforcement does not have the same dignified status in learning theory as do primary and secondary reinforcement, but some such process appears necessary in order to explain some important human learning. Vicarious reinforcement involves the generalization of reinforcing effects from others to oneself, hence learning from the reinforcers which others receive. A given act is reinforced for S as a result of the act being performed by M, followed by reinforcement to M. For example, if S observes M trying to solve a problem by certain techniques and succeeding, S is more likely to use the same techniques when faced by a similar problem than if M had failed to solve the problem. Although most of the evidence for such learning is anecdotal, Lewis and Duncan (1958) have provided some evidence of it in a human gambling situation, and Darby and Riopelle (1959) have demonstrated it in discrimination learning by monkeys.

Although vicarious reinforcement involves selective imitation, it differs from the selectivity of imitation, described by Miller and Dollard (1941), in which S imitates some Ms and not others because of differential reinforcement received by S for imitating the two Ms. Vicarious reinforcement does not involve any reinforcers delivered directly to S; the discrimination of Ms to be imitated or not is made entirely on the basis of S's observation of M's experience. This distinction is emphasized by Campbell (in press). In Hullian terms, vicarious reinforcement involves the acquisition of K by observation.

This type of learning need not be restricted to the effect of particular reinforcers administered to M under specific conditions. Stimulus generalization should occur not only from M's behavior to S's but also from one act of M's to another. As a result, if M is frequently reinforced, S should find it rewarding to resemble M in general, including imitation of some of M's behaviors which S has never seen rewarded. Thus a beginning salesman (S) might treat a customer with extreme politeness because he had observed another salesman (M) making a large sale while using such behavior, and he might also smoke a cigar because he had observed his highly successful salesmanager (M) doing so. In the former case M's behavior (politeness) and M's reinforcement (a large sale) were paired, whereas in the latter case the reinforcement (business success) was a perennial experience of M, but not paired with the particular behavior (smoking cigars) in question. Both, however, are examples of vicarious reinforcement.

Vicarious reinforcement corresponds to identification as defined by Masserman (1946) and to that aspect of identification referred to by Kagan (1958) as "the motivation to command or experience desired goal states of a model" (p. 298). Freud's (1946) identification with the aggressor also fits under this heading if successful aggression is assumed to be reinforcing to the aggressor. Sanford's (1955) concept of identification also involves the adoption as M of someone perceived by S as successful.

Conflicting Sources of Reinforcement. Traditionally the terms identification, introjection, and internalization might be applied to any or all of the learning processes described above or to their end product, similarity between S and some M. Since for the most part these processes involve learning by imitation, require some kind of reinforcement, and result in similarity between S and M, it may be asked why detailed analysis of the rather subtle differences among them is called for.

The answer is apparent when the possibility of conflict is considered. Conditions for a given S may be such that one of these processes tends to produce one kind of behavior while another tends to produce quite different or even opposite behavior. Such a conflictful situation might be expected in a child reared by a nurturant mother, whose mannerisms would become secondarily reinforcing, and a domineering father, who would be perceived as successful in mastering the environment. Freud (1950) recognized the frequent occurrence of just such a conflict, but did not consider it necessary to use different words for the two learning processes. Another common conflict is between the tendency to imitate Ms whom S is directly reinforced for imitating (e.g., well behaved children) and the tendency to imitate Ms whom S perceives as successful (e.g., tough kids). Such conflict is inevitable to a certain extent in children, since they are not permitted to imitate their (presumably more successful) elders in all respects, but it is particularly prominent in members of low-status social categories (e.g., Negroes) who are often conspicuously not reinforced for imitating high-status Ms. In the broadest sense, any situation where there is discrepancy among what S is told to do, what he is rewarded for doing, and what he sees others doing is a potential conflict situation, and one in which the use of any single inclusive term such as "identification" obscures the relevant variables.

The occurrence of conflict among the various reinforcement processes makes possible a finer analysis of the acquisition of values than could be made otherwise. If there is perfect agreement among what S is told to do, what those who nurture him do, what those around him conspicuously master the environment by doing, and what he himself is directly rewarded for doing, there is little basis for judging how much each of these factors contributed to S's adoption of the values of those around him. By observing situations in which they conflict, greater knowledge of the efficacy of each kind of reinforcement may be obtained. Research in conflict situations might answer such theoretically and practically important questions as: "Does dominance or nurturance on M's part do more to make M effective in modifying S's values?"; "Do words and examples completely lose their efficacy if the appropriate behaviors, when elicited, are not reinforced?"; and "To what extent is behavior influenced by Ms presented verbally (e.g., in literature)?"

There is of course no special merit to the classificatory scheme presented here. Except for the concept of vicarious reinforcement, the writer has avoided attaching distinctive labels to the learning processes described. The purpose of this discussion was to show how the terminology of learning theory can be applied to processes of value acquisition which have been described by personality theorists. This not only serves as a step toward the integration of these two areas of study, but also suggests the probable usefulness of employing such independent variables as number, percentage, magnitude and delay of reinforcement, distribution of practice, and discriminability of stimuli in the study of value acquisition. As both learning theory and personality theory develop further, it is to be expected that any schema developed now will be at least partially replaced by newer concepts. Rather than developing in further detail the ideas suggested above, the remainder of this discussion will therefore concentrate on the application of this kind of thinking to a narrower area, the development of conscience.

CONSCIENCE

Negative values, or conscience, have received much more attention than positive values. Educators seeking to improve children's characters, psychoanalysts concerned with the tyranny of the superego, anthropologists trying to distinguish between shame and guilt cultures, and experimental psychologists noting the persistence of avoidance responses have shared this emphasis on values of the "Thou shalt not" variety. Because of this widespread interest in conscience, it is a particularly appropriate topic with which to illustrate the possibilities of the learning theory approach to the study of values. Sears, Maccoby, and Levin (1957), in their challenging book *Patterns of Child Rearing,* devote a chapter to the development of conscience in preschool children. Their treatment of the topic will serve as a starting point for the present analysis.

Criteria for Conscience. Sears, Maccoby, and Levin give three criteria for recognizing the operation of conscience in young children: *resistance to temptation, self instructions* to obey the rules, and *evidence of guilt* when transgression occurs. These three criteria are treated jointly as defining conscience, and no attempt is made to analyze their separate developments. Although the authors mention that the aspects of conscience do not necessarily all appear at once, they regard conscience as representing an internalization of control which is fundamentally different from external control, whether by force, fear of punishment, or hope of material reward. This treatment of conscience as essentially a single variable seems premature in our present state of knowledge; certainly the learning theory approach to personality advocated here would involve separate analyses of these diverse response patterns.

The first criterion, *resistance to temptation,* may be viewed simply as avoidance learning. Although this kind of learning is still a focus of theoretical controversy, much experimental data are available concerning it (Solomon & Brush, 1956). Sidman's (1953) studies of avoidance behavior without a warning signal and Dinsmoor's (1954) analysis of punishment show how feedback from an individual's own acts can become a cue for avoidance, and how persistent such avoidance may be. Although children can presumably learn to respond to more abstract characteristics of cues than can animals, there is no reason to regard a child's learning to avoid certain behaviors as fundamentally different from a rat's learning to do so. The fact that the child avoids the forbidden acts even in the absence of the parents is presumably due to the parents' having in the past discovered and punished (in the broadest sense of that word) transgressions committed in their absence.

This relating of conscience to avoidance learning suggests that independent variables known to be effective in animal avoidance learning would be among the most appropriate ones for study in connection with the development of conscience in children. Within certain limits, the greater the intensity of the punishments (Brush, 1957; Miller, 1951) and the shorter the delay between transgression and punishment, (Mowrer & Ullman, 1945; Solomon & Brush, 1956) the greater should be the resulting inhibition. Though the data are somewhat ambiguous, greater certainty of punishment might be expected to produce inhibition which would be more complete in the short run but also less persistent once punishment was permanently withdrawn (Grant, Schipper, & Ross, 1952; Jenkins & Stanley, 1950; Reynolds, 1958). This prediction suggests that even this one criterion of conscience may not be unitary, that different laws may apply depending on whether one asks how completely the child obeys the prohibitions or how long he continues to obey them after leaving the parental home. If partial reinforcement should turn out to be a crucial variable in the human situation, these two criteria might even be inversely related. The prediction also suggests that the question, "Is inconsistent discipline bad?" is far too simple; one must at least ask, "Bad for what?"

It must also be kept in mind that punishment is not restricted to physical chastisement or even to noxious stimuli in general, including scolding and ridicule. Withdrawal of positive reinforcers may be very effective as a punishment, a fact which complicates the analysis. As this is a much discussed topic in personality theory, it will be considered below.

Sears, Maccoby, and Levin's second criterion of conscience, *self-instruction*, obviously makes the human case different from the animal case, but it does not introduce any new motivational principle. One of the advantages of membership in the human species is the possibility of using verbal symbolization in dealing with one's problems. It is natural that a person learning an avoidance, like a person learning any other difficult response pattern, should give himself verbal instructions, especially since verbal coaching by others is so important in the learning of social prohibitions. Moreover, such self-instruction is an imitative act which might be learned according to any of the reinforcement paradigms discussed above. Presumably the learning of prohibitions proceeds differently in verbal and nonverbal organisms, but observations of the relation between moral statements and moral behavior (Hurlock, 1956, pp. 406, 411-412) argue against the assumption that there is a high correlation between verbal and other criteria of conscience, except as both are influenced by the values represented in the social environment.

The third criterion of conscience, *guilt* at violations of the prohibitions, is itself complex, with many verbal, autonomic, and gross behavioral aspects. However, the striking paradox about guilt, which has seemed to some students to set it apart from the ordinary laws of learning, is that it often involves the seeking of punishment. The person who has transgressed, rather than trying to avoid punishment, or even waiting passively for it to come, actively seeks out the authorities, confesses, and receives his punishment with apparent relief. He may also, or instead, go to great lengths to make restitution. Were it not for these phenomena of punishment-seeking and self-sacrificing restitution, it would be easy to dismiss guilt as merely the kind of fear associated with anticipation of certain sorts of punishment. As it is, the existence of guilt serves as an argument for regarding conscience as something more than the sum of all those avoidances which have moral significance in one's culture.

However, the attempt to distinguish between guilt-controlled and other behaviors has not been very successful. Though the distinction between guilt cultures and shame cultures has had a considerable vogue in anthropology (e.g., Benedict, 1946; Havighurst & Neugarten, 1955; Mead, 1950), the inadequacies of the distinction have been pointed out by Ausubel (1955) and by Singer (1953). Moreover, the relation between conformity to a standard and guilt when the standard has been violated is open to question. Shaw (1948) suggests that confession may even be so satisfying to some people that it constitutes a reinforcement for sinning. So, although the phenomena of guilt may raise difficulties for learning theory, these difficulties probably cannot be solved by using guilt to define a distinctive kind of learning.

The above considerations should suffice to indicate that conscience cannot be assumed a priori to be unitary. The extent to which short-run conformity, long-run conformity, self-instructions to conform, certain kinds of distress at having failed to conform, and voluntary confession of non-conformity are intercorrelated is a matter to be empirically determined. Moreover, even if high positive intercorrelations are found, it is possible that they may reflect correlations in the environment rather than any fundamental unity of process. If environmental pressures toward conformity vary markedly, artificially high correlations among the criteria of conscience are to be expected. However, even when this artifact is removed, an analysis of separate learning processes for different behaviors may still lead to the prediction of high correlations among the behaviors. Such an analysis is presented below.

Learning of Conscience. Sears, Maccoby, and Levin found that the development of conscience, as defined jointly by their three criteria, was greater in those children whose parents used love-oriented forms of discipline (praise, isolation, and withdrawal of love than in those whose parents used "materialistic" forms of discipline (material rewards, deprivation of privileges, and physical punishment). A similar finding, though not highly reliable statistically, is reported by Whiting and Child (1953, Ch. 11) in a cross-cultural study of guilt as measured by attitudes toward illness. This is consistent with the widely held view that the acquisition of parental values occurs most fully in an atmosphere of love (e.g., Ausubel, 1955; Davis & Havighurst, 1947). It is possible, however, that this finding may be due, not to love-oriented discipline as such, but to other characteristics of discipline which are correlated with it. The effect of this kind of discipline may be to accentuate the learning of several different responses, all of which contribute to the overall diagnosis of high conscience.

The various kinds of punishments commonly applied to children probably differ markedly in the temporal relations and the reinforcement contingencies involved. Physical punishment is likely to occur all at once and be over quickly, while punishment by deprivation of objects or privileges is likely to be either for a fixed period of time or for as long as the disciplinarian finds convenient. Discipline by withdrawal of love, on the other hand, probably much more often lasts until the child makes some symbolic renunciation of his wrongdoing, as by apologizing, making restitution, or promising not to do it again. The child is deprived of his parents' love (or, the parents would claim, of the outward manifestations of it!) for as much or as little time as is necessary to get him to make such a symbolic renunciation. When he has made it, he is restored to his parents' favor. If the normal relation between the parents and child is one of warmth, such discipline strongly motivates the child to make the renunciation quickly. On repeated occasions of transgression, punishment by withdrawal of love, and symbolic renunciation, the child may be expected not only to learn the renunciation response as an escape from parental disfavor but eventually to use it as an avoidance rather than merely an escape response. Thus if the wrongdoing is not immediately discovered, the child may anticipate his parents' impending disfavor by confessing in advance and making the symbolic renunciation.

The result of this hypothesized sequence of events is that the child makes a verbal response which is in effect an instruction to himself not to repeat his wrongdoing. The next time temptation comes, he is more likely to make this verbal response before transgressing. Although this does not guarantee that he will not trangress, it is likely to reduce the probability. If he succumbs to temptation, he is more likely to confess before being caught and thereby avoid the temporary loss of his parents' love. Thus if the above reasoning is correct, all three criteria of conscience should be present to a greater degree in the child who has been disciplined in this fashion than in other children. According to the present hypothesis, however, this will be due to the fact that punishment continues until the child makes a symbolic renunciation, rather than to the fact that the punishment involves withdrawal of love. If physical chastisement or loss of privileges are used in the same way, the same outcome is predicted.

A possible weakness of this hypothesis is that children might learn a discrimination between the symbolic and the actual avoidances, so that they would develop a pattern of violating parental standards, immediately confessing and apologizing, and then transgressing again at the next hint of temptation. If forgiveness is offered freely and uncritically enough, such a pattern presumably does develop. In this case the correlation among the criteria of conscience would be expected to drop, actual avoidance of wrongdoing no longer being associated with the other criteria. (For this reason, Sears, Maccoby, and Levin might have found smaller relations if they had studied older children.) However, if the parents' discrimination keeps up with the child's so that the child cannot count on removing all the parents' disfavor with a perfunctory apology, the efficacy of this kind of discipline should be at least partially maintained.

If this explanation of greater conscience in children disciplined by withdrawal of love is correct, why was greater conscience also found with the other kinds of love-oriented control? Since these were all found to be inter-correlated, and since their relations to the degree of conscience were uniformly low, interpretations either of separate techniques or of love orientation as a general trait are necessarily somewhat dubious. As an example of the difficulties involved, it may be noted that reasoning with the child is counted as a love-oriented technique solely on the grounds of its correlation with the other such techniques. Nevertheless, it shows a higher relation to conscience than do two of the three clearly love-oriented techniques. In view of such complexities, it seems legitimate to suggest that the crucial factor in those techniques associated with conscience may not be love orientation as such, but something else correlated with it.

To test this hypothesis, it would be necessary to have further detailed information of the sort that Sears, Maccoby, and Levin used, so that disciplinary methods could be classified according to the time relations discussed above. It is predicted that the parents' tendency to make termination of punishment contingent on symbolic renunciation would be correlated with love-oriented discipline. However, if each were varied with the other held constant, conscience should be more closely related to response contingency than to love orientation.

Along with this overall analysis of conscience, more detailed analyses could be made of the various components of conscience. According to the present view, intercorrelations among these criteria would be moderate for the entire sample and low when method of discipline was held constant.

The learning sequence discussed above is only one of several possible explanations of the Sears, Maccoby, and Levin finding. By suggesting that the crucial causal factor is not the distinction between materialistic orientation and love orientation, but another distinction correlated with it, the present hypothesis gains an advantage in objectivity and in practical applicability. Whether it also has the advantage of correctness must be empirically determined. The chief purpose of the present example is to point to the availability of ·such reductionist hypotheses in the study of values and to argue that they deserve priority in the schedule of scientific investigation.

Permanence of Conscience. It would be particularly desirable to have a follow-up study to compare evidences of conscience in kindergarten with those of the same people later in life, when they were no longer primarily under the direct influence of their parents. Such a follow-up would help to clarify the relation between short-run and long-run conformity discussed above. Is the child who thoroughly obeys all his parents' prohibitions also the one who sticks to these standards when his parents are no longer around and his new associates have different standards? Anecdotal evidence can be cited on both sides, though the bulk is probably in the affirmative. To the extent that current and later conformity are independent, what variables influence one more than the other?

Predictions from learning theory on this topic are by no means unambiguous. Nevertheless, two lines of reasoning may be suggested concerning the type of discipline likely to result in the most persistent avoidances. (Persistence here refers, not to absolute level of avoidance, but to relative lack of decrement in the strength of avoidance with time.)

The first line of reasoning is from the differences in the slopes of *generalization gradients* for different kinds of learning (Dollard & Miller, 1950). In most cases the contrast in slope is between approach (or excitatory) and avoidance (or inhibitory) tendencies. It appears, however, that the basic distinction is between response tendencies activated by innate and by learned (generally fear) drives (Miller & Murray, 1952). When stimulus conditions change, the resultant removal of cues for fear produces a greater weakening of response tendencies based on fear than of response tendencies based on other drives. Hence, the generalization gradient of responses and inhibitions based on fear is steeper than that of other responses and inhibitions. This implies that discipline based on fear should lose its efficacy more quickly than discipline based on rewards as distance from the disciplinarian or any other change in conditions increases. Since this difference in slope is found on continua both of distance (Miller, 1944) and of similarity (Miller & Kraeling, 1952; Murray & Miller, 1952), it seems reasonable to predict that it also applies to that complex continuum along which an individual makes the transition away from parental apron strings. It would follow from this analysis that of two inhibitions learned in childhood, equal in age and original strength, one learned from the threat of losing rewards would be more effective later in life than one learned from the fear-provoking threat of punishment.

In this analysis, the advantages of discipline by manipulation (including withdrawal) of reward would apply to any kind of reward, material or social, not merely to parental love. However, the desire to continue receiving love from the parents may persist after the child has outgrown the need for other parental rewards, such as gifts and privileges. Discipline by withdrawal of love, in an atmosphere of warmth, might therefore be even more effective than other forms of discipline by denial of reward in producing persistent avoidances.

The other line of reasoning, involving the *partial reinforcement effect,* argues for the persistence of conscience learned by the process outlined above, in which a symbolic renunciation of wrongdoing terminates punishment. Although the greater resistance to extinction of responses which have received less than 100 per cent reinforcement has been demonstrated primarily with positive reinforcement, it applies to negative as well (Humphreys, 1939-a, 1940; Grant, Schipper, & Ross, 1952). Partial reinforcement is of course present with all kinds of discipline, since punishment depends on the parents' moods and on the social situation, as well as on the child's being caught. However, the above analysis of the kind of punishment which terminates when the child makes a symbolic renunciation of wrongdoing suggests that such discipline may involve an additional source of partial reinforcement. As was indicated above, the child may learn that he can avoid punishment by confessing and apologizing. When this happens, the avoidance starts to extinguish. However, the discerning parent then learns not to accept the apology, and the child is punished anyway. The child must then make a more vigorous and convincing symbolic renunciation than before in order to terminate the punishment. In addition, the discrimination he has made between the symbolic renunciation and the actual avoidance is broken down; punishment can only be prevented by actual avoidance of wrongdoing. If, however, after a period of obedience he once more transgresses and then confesses, he is likely again not to be punished. This starts the cycle of extinction and reconditioning of the avoidance response going again, thus continuing to provide a reinforcement schedule in which only part of the child's transgressions are punished.

To predict that such partial reinforcement will retard extinction is admittedly problematic, both because of the complexity of the avoidance paradigm and because the unpunished transgressions are assumed to occur in blocks rather than randomly. Nevertheless, the hypothesis deserves consideration, not only as a prediction from learning principles to personality, but also as a case where the needs of personality theory might guide research in learning.

Although these two lines of reasoning agree in predicting maximally persistent conformity to parental prohibitions by children reared in an atmosphere of parental warmth and disciplined by withdrawal of love, they differ in their other predictions. To test these various hypotheses separately would require both short-run and long-run analyses of the effects of a variety of parental discipline patterns. The following hypotheses might be tested: (a) that discipline by deprivations (whether of things, privileges, or love) has more persistent effects than discipline by noxious stimulation (whether physical or social); (b) that where the child is taught to confess and apologize for his transgressions, avoidance behavior will go through cycles of extinction and reconditioning; and (c) that punishing only part of a child's transgressions results in more persistent obedience than does punishing all of them.

SUMMARY AND CONCLUSIONS

It is suggested that the terms identification, introjection, and internalization be replaced by detailed analyses in learning-theory terms of the acquisition of values. A reinforcement framework for such analyses is outlined, and examples are presented dealing with the concept of conscience and the factors influencing its development. It is argued that this would simplify terminology, encourage more precise study, and further the integration of learning and personality theories.

This analysis, like all attempts to integrate the harder-headed and the softer-hearted portions of behavioral science, is open to attack from both sides. On the one hand it may be objected that the present treatment is too cavalier with the interpersonal and intrapsychic complexities of personality development, that the internalization of values and the identification of one person with another cannot be treated as though they were nothing but the simple learning of a rat in a maze. The answer to this objection is that no "nothing but-ism" is intended; it is an empirical matter both to determine how far the principles of learning (not necessarily simple) can go in explaining personality development and to decide how much the additional principles suggested by some writers actually contribute to our understanding of the phenomena in question. The attempt to catch too much complexity at a single stroke may retard rather than advance our understanding.

On the other hand it may be objected that the interpretations given here are untestable, that the variables involve such diverse and subtle behaviors over such long periods of time as to defy adequate measurement. Admittedly the questionnaire, interview, and brief-observation techniques used in this area leave much to be desired. However, as long as applied behavioral scientists are called upon to deal with questions of personality development, poor data to guide their decisions are better than none. Study of learning of values by humans, guided by the principles of learning based on both animal and human studies, has the potential to make vital contributions to many theoretical and applied areas of knowledge. It is hoped that the present discussion may contribute something to that goal.

Part II

PHYSICAL FACTORS IN PSYCHOLOGICAL DEVELOPMENT

HUMAN behavior and personality are largely dependent upon the physical structure characterizing the human species. Many behaviors are species-wide; and when such universality is observed, it may be presumed with some degree of confidence that the behavior has in part a genetic basis. It is, perhaps, not an exaggeration to assert that when *all* aspects of human behavior are considered (often basic similarities are taken for granted and thus overlooked) more similarities than dissimilarities are to be found within the human group or within any other species. However, even when individuals are "similar" in behavior, differences will exist. Many such differences among individuals of any age are at least partially a reflection of inter-individual differences in total constitutional structure. And *within* an individual changes with increasing age in underlying constitution are at least partially responsible for changes in behavior and personality as the child matures through adolescence into adulthood, and advances on into later maturity and old age.

The biological system which constitutes the human organism is extremely complex. Four features, by no means separate in their action, may be mentioned in this brief foreword to illustrate the relationship between physical factors and behavior. First is the developing nervous system, changes in which represent the direct cause of new behaviors, not only *in utero* but also in early infancy and childhood. Its less direct, but no less important, role in intellectual growth will in many ways affect the course of later development during the maturing years to adulthood and into the decline of old age by influencing the ease with which behavior can be modified. New patterns of behavior emerge as the growing child becomes increasingly capable mentally; and as ability declines there may be loss or some modification of certain behaviors as they become impossible or more difficult of performance. The older person may become more rigid in his habits when compared with the young person partly because of changes in the structure of his aging nervous system. And important changes in sensory functions may limit the range of stimuli to which a person (perhaps of advanced age) is sensitive and alter his efficiency on the job and his responsiveness in social situations.

Although not unrelated to growth of the nervous system, a second phase of physical development to be noted includes the changes in motor capacity, strength, and general physical resiliency which run a fairly typical course of expansion during the years of childhood and adolescence and of constriction during the middle years and old age. Such changes will determine the degree of participation in all sorts of activities that are possible as age increases and will indirectly affect the roles of self-sufficiency and responsibility that a person is able to achieve in youth and maintain into his old age. As one views the total psychology of human growth and change the pervasive influence of growth up to physical prime and the later decline in physical strength, speed, and resiliency are apparent.

Third to be mentioned are the differences among people and the changes with age in endocrine constitution, factors which will have many striking and subtle effects and will determine or influence personality, temperament, and energy level. Normal changes in endocrine functioning with increasing age will give rise to new or shifting patterns of behavior. The advent of pubescence, to choose one example, and the resulting changes in biochemical constitution give impetus to the sex drive and are accompanied by a reorientation of interests in which the opposite sex plays a dominant role. And with decline in gonadal function in adult years, subtle changes in behavior occur as the motivational structure alters.

Fourth and finally, differences and changes in gross physical structure—height, weight, general physical appearance—will be found to play significant roles in determining the reactions of others to the individual or the individual's own reactions to himself. Psychologically important features may include sheer size (which plays an important role in a child's changing relations to adults) and the degree to which size conforms to or deviates from the cultural ideal for the particular sex; physical attractiveness in the form of bodily contours and build and facial characteristics; physical symptoms of aging such as graying hair or baldness, increased girth, changes in skin texture and pigmentation, springiness of step. Such physical characteristics, largely determined by heredity in the form they take and the age at which changes occur, are partial determiners of an individual's concept of himself and of his stimulus value to others, attitudes of extreme importance psychologically and socially.

It is especially noteworthy in considering the physical bases for behavior that the human organism, to a far greater degree than lower mammals, possesses a nervous system which permits extensive modification of its behavior and behavior potential by the experiences it has with its environment. The result is that human behavior and the developmental trends of growth and change that characterize the life span of individuals are the result of the interaction of genetic and environmental factors. This interaction is so complex that although it is a relatively straightforward matter to demonstrate that constitutional factors and environmental factors are important in psychological development, it has not been possible to demonstrate with any precision the *relative* importance of one as opposed to the other, nor has it been possible to demonstrate the precise way in which nature and nurture interact. To many students of behavior, especially to those interested in the applications of psychology, deficiencies in knowledge at this point are not too handicapping so long as the principle is recognized that the interactions of both genetic and environmental factors are involved in the determination of almost any type of human behavior.

Every individual's supply of genes, the bearers of hereditary factors, is given him once for all and inalterably at conception. For this reason, those interested in promoting human welfare, and in particular in fostering optimal personality development, tend to give greater emphasis to environmental factors, since the manipulation of the physical and social environment represents the most easily available means for reaching these ends. This should not imply that such workers fail to recognize the role of genetic factors in behavior and the importance of a sound physique. Surely all of them readily admit the desirability of appropriate study of the body, and of attempts to improve health and correct physical defects and physiological malfunctioning, through proper nutrition, provision of sensory aids, surgery, endocrine replacement or supplementation and general medical treatment.

The five papers grouped in this part have been selected to illustrate the role of physical factors in psychological development. The first is a modern statement of the nature-nurture "problem," emphasizing the continuous interactive effects of environmental and genetic variables, and also calling attention to some of the more promising techniques for determining how these influences operate. The next paper illustrates the basic importance of heredity by describing the great similarity of identical twins in senescence with respect to certain physical and psychological traits. Such twins, though possessing identical heredity, have not had exactly the same environmentally determined experiences. The third paper deals with "motor primacy," and relates certain aspects of behavioral development to the fact that neuro-motor mechanisms develop in advance of capacity to respond to the stimulation of sense organs. The fourth paper demonstrates the complex interaction of biological and cultural factors, as these are evident not only in adolescence but also later in young adulthood. The final paper in the part examines certain changes in perception during the aging process.

6

Heredity, Environment, and the Question "How?"*

Anne Anastasi

Fifteen years ago the question of the relative contributions of heredity and environment to psychological processes came to be regarded in many quarters as an unproductive query, perhaps suitable for a high school debating society but essentially sterile for the scientist. The unresolved issues were admittedly still very much alive but conceptualization had reached an apparent impasse. Then theorists and experimentalists like Beach, Dobzhansky, Hebb, and Scott came forward with new interpretations of the continuous reciprocal and interactive effects of the environmental and the genetic variables. From this fresh perspective the original question was reinterpreted in ways that stimulated a now rapidly developing area in psychology, the genetics of behavior. In this paper, Dr. Anastasi reviews the major events in this revitalized conception of the heredity-environment interaction. She also presents a detailed picture of the most promising "techniques for exploring the modus operandi of hereditary and environmental factors."

Two or three decades ago, the so-called heredity-environment question was the center of lively controversy. Today, on the other hand, many psychologists look upon it as a dead issue. It is now generally conceded that both hereditary and environmental factors enter into all behavior. The reacting organism is a product of its genes and its past environment, while present environment provides the immediate stimulus for current behavior. To be sure, it can be argued that, although a given trait may result from the combined influence of hereditary and environmental factors, a specific difference in this trait between individuals or between groups may be traceable to either hereditary or environmental factors alone. The design of

* From Anne Anastasi, "Heredity, Environment, and the Question 'How?,'" *Psychological Review*, 1958, Vol. 65, pp. 197-208. (With permission of the author and the American Psychological Association.)

most traditional investigations undertaken to identify such factors, however, has been such as to yield inconclusive answers. The same set of data has frequently led to opposite conclusions in the hands of psychologists with different orientations.

Nor have efforts to determine the proportional contribution of hereditary and environmental factors to observe individual differences in given traits met with any greater success. Apart from difficulties in controlling conditions, such investigations have usually been based upon the implicit assumption that hereditary and environmental factors combine in an additive fashion. Both geneticists and psychologists have repeatedly demonstrated, however, that a more tenable hypothesis is that of interaction (Haldane, 1938; Loevinger, 1943; Schwesinger, 1933; Woodworth, 1941). In other words, the nature and extent of the influence of each type of factor depend upon the contribution of the other. Thus the proportional contribution of heredity to the variance of a given trait, rather than being a constant, will vary under different environmental conditions. Similarly, under different hereditary conditions, the relative contribution of environment will differ. Studies designed to estimate the proportional contribution of heredity and environment, however, have rarely included measures of such interaction. The only possible conclusion from such research would thus seem to be that both heredity and environment contribute to all behavior traits and that the extent of their respective contributions cannot be specified for any trait. Small wonder that some psychologists regard the heredity-environment question as unworthy of further consideration!

But is this really all we can find out about the operation of heredity and environment in the etiology of behavior? Perhaps we have simply been asking the wrong questions. The traditional questions about heredity and environment may be intrinsically unanswerable. Psychologists began by asking *which* type of factor, hereditary or environmental, is responsible for individual differences in a given trait. Later, they tried to discover *how much* of the variance was attributable to heredity and how much to environment. It is the primary contention of this paper that a more fruitful approach is to be found in the question *"How?"* There is still much to be learned about the specific *modus operandi* of hereditary and environmental factors in the development of behavioral differences. And there are several current lines of research which offer promising techniques for answering the question "How?"

VARIETY OF INTERACTION MECHANISMS

Hereditary Factors. If we examine some of the specific ways in which hereditary factors may influence behavior, we cannot fail but be impressed by their wide diversity. At one extreme, we find such conditions as phenyl-pyruvic amentia and amaurotic idiocy. In these cases, certain essential physical prerequisites for normal intellectual development are lacking as a result of hereditary metabolic disorders. In our present state of knowledge, there is no environmental factor which can completely counteract this hereditary deficit. The individual will be mentally defective, regardless of the type of environmental conditions under which he is reared.

A somewhat different situation is illustrated by hereditary deafness, which may lead to intellectual retardation through interference with normal social interaction, language development, and schooling. In such a case, however, the hereditary handicap can be offset by appropriate adaptations of training procedures. It has been said, in fact, that the degree of intellectual backwardness of the deaf is an index of the state of development of special instructional facilities. As the latter improve, the intellectual retardation associated with deafness is correspondingly reduced.

A third example is provided by inherited susceptibility to certain physical diseases, with consequent protracted ill health. If environmental conditions are such that illness does in fact develop, a number of different behavioral effects may follow. Intellectually, the individual may be handicapped by his inability to attend school regularly. On the other hand, depending upon age of onset, home conditions, parental status, and similar factors, poor health may have the effect of concentrating the individual's energies upon intellectual pursuits. The curtailment of participation in athletics and social functions may serve to strengthen interest in reading and other sedentary activities. Concomitant circumstances would also determine the influence of such illness upon personality development. And it is well known that the latter effects could run the gamut from a deepening of human sympathy to psychiatric breakdown.

Finally, heredity may influence behavior through the mechanism of social stereotypes. A wide variety of inherited physical characteristics have served as the visible cues for identifying such stereotypes. These cues thus lead to behavioral restrictions or opportunities and—at a more subtle level—to social attitudes and expectancies. The individual's own self concept tends gradually to reflect such expectancies. All of these influences eventually leave their mark upon his abilities and inabilities, his emotional reactions, goals, ambitions, and outlook on life.

The geneticist Dobzhansky (1950, p. 147) illustrates this type of mechanism by means of a dramatic hypothetical situation. He points out that, if there were a culture in which the carriers of blood group AB were considered aristocrats and those of blood group O laborers, then the blood-group genes would become important hereditary determiners of behavior. Obviously the association between blood group and behavior would be specific to that culture. But such specificity is an essential property of the causal mechanism under consideration.

More realistic examples are not hard to find. The most familiar instances occur in connection with constitutional types, sex, and race. Sex and skin pigmentation obviously depend upon heredity. General body build is strongly influenced by hereditary components, although also susceptible to environmental modification. That all these physical characteristics may exert a pronounced effect upon behavior within a given culture is well known. It is equally apparent, of course, that in different cultures the behavioral correlates of such hereditary physical traits may be quite unlike. A specific physical cue may be completely unrelated to individual differences in psychological traits in one culture, while closely correlated with them in another. Or it may be associated with totally dissimilar behavior characteristics in two different cultures.

It might be objected that some of the illustrations which have been cited do not properly exemplify the operation of hereditary mechanisms in behavior development, since hereditary factors enter only indirectly into the behavior in question. Closer examination, however, shows this distinction to be untenable. First it may be noted that the influence of heredity upon behavior is always indirect. No psychological trait is ever inherited as such. All we can ever say directly from behavioral observations is that a given trait shows evidence of being influenced by certain "inheritable unknowns." This merely defines a problem for genetic research; it does not provide a causal explanation. Unlike the blood groups, which are close to the level of primary gene products, psychological traits are related to genes by highly indirect and devious routes. Even the mental deficiency associated with phenylketonuria is several steps removed from the chemically defective genes that represent its hereditary basis. Moreover, hereditary influences cannot be dichotomized into the more direct and the less direct. Rather do they represent a whole "continuum of indirectness," along which are found all degrees of remoteness of causal links. The examples already cited illustrate a few of the points on this continuum.

It should be noted that as we proceed along the continuum of indirectness, the range of variation of possible outcomes of hereditary factors expands rapidly. At each step in the causal chain, there is fresh opportunity for interaction with other hereditary factors as well as with environmental factors. And since each interaction in turn determines the direction of subsequent interactions, there is an ever-widening network of possible outcomes. If we visualize a simple sequential grid with only two alternatives at each point, it is obvious that there are two possible outcomes in the one-stage situation, four outcomes at the second stage, eight at the third, and so on in geometric progression. The actual situation is undoubtedly much more complex, since there will usually be more than two alternatives at any one point.

In the case of the blood groups, the relation to specific genes is so close that no other concomitant hereditary or environmental conditions can alter the outcome. If the organism survives at all, it will have the blood group determined by its genes. Among psychological traits, on the other hand, some variation in outcome is always possible as a result of concurrent circumstances. Even in cases of phenylketonuria, intellectual development will exhibit some relationship with the type of care and training available to the individual. That behavioral outcomes show progressive diversification as we proceed along the continuum of indirectness is brought out by the other examples which were cited. Chronic illness *can* lead to scholarly renown or to intellectual immaturity; a mesomorphic physique *can* be a contributing factor in juvenile delinquency or in the attainment of a college presidency! Published data on Sheldon somatotypes provide some support for both of the latter outcomes.

Parenthetically, it may be noted that geneticists have sometimes used the term "norm of reaction" to designate the range of variation of possible outcomes of gene properties (cf. Dobzhansky, 1950b, p. 161). Thus heredity sets the "norm" or limits within which environmental differences determine the eventual outcome. In the case of some traits, such as blood groups or eye color, this norm is much narrower than in the case of other traits. Owing to the rather different psychological connotations of both the words "norm" and "reaction," however, it seems less confusing to speak of the "range of variation" in this context.

A large portion of the continuum of hereditary influences which we have described coincides with the domain of somatopsychological relations, as defined by Barker et al. (1953). Under this heading, Barker includes "variations in physique that affect the psychological situation of a person by influencing the effectiveness of his body as a tool for actions or by serving as a stimulus to himself or others." Relatively direct neurological influences on behavior, which have been the traditional concern of physiological psychology, are excluded from this definition, Barker being primarily concerned with what he calls the "social psychology of physique." Of the examples cited in the present paper, deafness, severe illness, and the physical characteristics associated with social stereotypes would meet the specifications of somatopsychological factors.

The somatic factors to which Barker refers, however, are not limited to those of hereditary origin. Bodily conditions attributable to environmental causes operate in the same sorts of somatopsychological relations as those traceable to heredity. In fact, heredity-environment distinctions play a minor part in Barker's approach.

Environmental Factors: Organic. Turning now to an analysis of the role of environmental factors in behavior, we find the same etiological mechanisms which were observed in the case of hereditary factors. First, however, we must differentiate between two classes of environmental influences: (*a*) those producing organic effects which may in turn influence behavior and (*b*) those serving as direct stimuli for psychological reactions. The former may be illustrated by food intake or by exposure to bacterial infection; the latter, by tribal initiation ceremonies or by a course in algebra. There are no completely satisfactory names by which to designate these two classes of influences. In an earlier paper by Anastasi and Foley (1948), the terms "structural" and "functional" were employed. However, "organic" and "behavioral" have the advantage of greater familiarity in this context and may be less open to misinterpretation. Accordingly, these terms will be used in the present paper.

Like hereditary factors, environmental influences of an organic nature can also be ordered along a continuum of indirectness with regard to their relation to behavior. This continuum closely parallels that of hereditary factors. One end is typified by such conditions as mental deficiency resulting from cerebral birth injury or from prenatal nutritional inadequacies. A more indirect etiological mechanism is illustrated by severe motor disorder—as in certain cases of cerebral palsy—*without* accompanying injury to higher neurological centers. In such instances, intellectual retardation may occur as an indirect result of the motor handicap, through the curtailment of educational and social activities. Obviously this causal mechanism corresponds closely to that of hereditary deafness cited earlier in the paper.

Finally, we may consider an environmental parallel to the previously discussed social stereotypes which were mediated by hereditary physical cues. Let us suppose that a young woman with mousy brown hair becomes transformed into a dazzling golden blonde through environmental techniques currently available in our culture. It is highly probable that this metamorphosis will alter, not only the reactions of her associates toward her, but also her own self concept and subsequent behavior. The effects could range all the way from a rise in social poise to a drop in clerical accuracy!

Among the examples of environmentally determined organic influences which have been described, all but the first two fit Barker's definition of somatopsychological factors. With the exception of birth injuries and nutritional deficiencies, all fall within the social psychology of physique. Nevertheless, the individual factors exhibit wide diversity in their specific *modus operandi*—a diversity which has important practical as well as theoretical implications.

Environmental Factors: Behavioral. The second major class of environmental factors—the behavioral as contrasted to the organic—are by definition direct influences. The immediate effect of such environmental factors is always a behavioral change. To be sure, some of the initial behavioral effects may themselves indirectly affect the individual's later behavior. But this relationship can perhaps be best conceptualized in terms of breadth and permanence of effects. Thus it could be said that we are now dealing, not with a continuum of indirectness, as in the case of hereditary and organic-environmental factors, but rather with a continuum of breadth.

Social class membership may serve as an illustration of a relatively broad, pervasive, and enduring environmental factor. Its influence upon behavior development may operate through many channels. Thus social level may determine the range and nature of intellectual stimulation provided by home and community through books, music, art, play activities, and the like. Even more far-reaching may be the effects upon interests and motivation, as illustrated by the desire to perform abstract intellectual tasks, to surpass others in competitive situations, to succeed in school, or to gain social approval. Emotional and social traits may likewise be influenced by the nature of interpersonal relations characterizing homes at different socio-economic levels. Somewhat more restricted in scope than social class, although still exerting a relatively broad influence, is amount of formal schooling which the individual is able to obtain.

A factor which may be wide or narrow in its effects, depending upon concomitant circumstances, is language handicap. Thus the bilingualism of an adult who moves to a foreign country with inadequate mastery of the new language represents a relatively limited handicap which can be readily overcome in most cases. At most, the difficulty is one of communication. On the other hand, some kinds of bilingualism in childhood may exert a retarding influence upon intellectual development and may under certain conditions affect personality development adversely (Anastasi, 1958; Arsenian, 1945; Darcy, 1953). A common pattern in the homes of immigrants is that the child speaks one language at home and another in school, so that his knowledge of each language is limited to certain types of situations. Inadequate facility with the language of the school interferes with the acquisition of basic concepts, intellectual skills, and information. The frustration engendered by scholastic difficulties may in turn lead to discouragement and general dislike of school. Such reactions can be found, for example, among a number of Puerto Rican children in New York City schools (Anastasi and Cordova, 1953). In the case of certain groups, moreover, the child's foreign language background may be perceived by himself and his associates as a symbol of minority group status and may thereby augment any emotional maladjustment arising from such status (Spoerl, 1943).

A highly restricted environmental influence is to be found in the opportunity to acquire specific items of information occurring in a particular intelligence test. The fact that such opportunities may vary with culture, social class, or individual experiential background is at the basis of the test user's concern with the problem of coaching and with "culture-free" or "culture-fair" tests (cf. Anastasi, 1954; 1958). If the advantage or disadvantage which such experiential differences confer upon certain individuals is strictly confined to performance on the given test, it will obviously reduce the validity of the test and should be eliminated.

In this connection, however, it is essential to know the breadth of the environmental influence in question. A fallacy inherent in many attempts to develop culture-fair tests is that the breadth of cultural differentials is not taken into account. Failure to consider breadth of effect likewise characterizes certain discussions of coaching. If, in coaching a student for a college admission test, we can improve his knowledge of verbal concepts and his reading comprehension, he will be better equipped to succeed in college courses. His performance level will thus be raised, not only on the test, but also on the criterion which the test is intended to predict. To try to devise a test which is not susceptible to such coaching would merely reduce the effectiveness of the test. Similarly, efforts to rule out cultural differentials from test items so as to make them equally "fair" to subjects in different social classes or in different cultures may merely limit the usefulness of the test, since the same cultural differentials may operate within the broader area of behavior which the test is designed to sample.

METHODOLOGICAL APPROACHES

The examples considered so far should suffice to highlight the wide variety of ways in which hereditary and environmental factors may interact in the course of behavior development. There is clearly a need for identifying explicitly the etiological mechanism whereby any given hereditary or environmental condition ultimately leads to a behavioral characteristic—in other words, the "how" of heredity and environment. Accordingly, we may now take a quick look at some promising methodological approaches to the question "how."

Within the past decade, an increasing number of studies have been designed to trace the connection between specific factors in the hereditary backgrounds or in the reactional biographies of individuals and their observed behavioral characteristics. There has been a definite shift away from the predominantly descriptive and correlational approach of the earlier decades toward more deliberate attempts to verify explanatory hypotheses. Similarly, the cataloguing of group differences in psychological traits has been giving way gradually to research on *changes* in group characteristics following altered conditions.

Among recent methodological developments, we have chosen seven as being particularly relevant to the analysis of etiological mechanisms. The first represents an extension of selective breeding investigations to permit the identification of specific hereditary conditions underlying the observed behavioral differences. When early selective breeding investigations such as those of Tryon (1940) on rats indicated that "maze learning ability" was inherited, we were still a long way from knowing what was actually being transmitted by the genes. It was obviously not "maze learning ability" as such. Twenty—or even ten—years ago, some psychologists would have suggested that it was probably general intelligence. And a few might even have drawn a parallel with the inheritance of human intelligence.

But today investigators have been asking: Just what makes one group of rats learn mazes more quickly than the other? Is it differences in motivation, emotionality, speed of running, general activity level? If so, are these behavioral characteristics in turn dependent upon group differences in glandular development, body weight, brain size, biochemical factors, or some other organic conditions? A number of recent and ongoing investigations indicate that attempts are being made to trace, at least part of the way, the steps whereby certain chemical properties of the genes may ultimately lead to specified behavior characteristics.

An example of such a study is provided by Searle's (1949) follow-up of Tryon's research. Working with the strains of maze-bright and maze-dull rats developed by Tryon, Searle demonstrated that the two strains differed in a number of emotional and motivational factors, rather than in ability. Thus the strain differences were traced one step further, although many links still remain to be found between maze learning and genes. A promising methodological development within the same general area is to be found in the recent research of Hirsch and Tryon (1956). Utilizing a specially devised technique for measuring individual differences in behavior among lower organisms, these investigators launched a series of studies on selective breeding for behavioral characteristics in the fruit fly, Drosophila. Such research can capitalize on the mass of available genetic knowledge regarding the morphology of Drosophila, as well as on other advantages of using such an organism in genetic studies.

Further evidence of current interest in the specific hereditary factors which influence behavior is to be found in an extensive research program in progress at the Jackson Memorial Laboratory, under the direction of Scott and Fuller (1951). In general, the project is concerned with the behavioral characteristics of various breeds and cross-breeds of dogs. Analyses of some of the data gathered to date again suggest that "differences in performance are produced by differences in emotional, motivational, and peripheral processes, and that genetically caused differences in central processes may be either slight or non-existent" (Scott and Charles, 1953, p. 225). In other parts of the same project, breed differences in physiological characteristics, which may in turn be related to behavioral differences, have been established.

A second line of attack is the exploration of possible relationships between behavioral characteristics and physiological variables which may in turn be traceable to hereditary factors. Research on EEG, autonomic balance, metabolic processes, and biochemical factors illustrates this approach. A lucid demonstration of the process of tracing a psychological condition to genetic factors is provided by the identification and subsequent investigation of phenylpyruvic amentia. In this case, the causal chain from defective gene, through metabolic disorder and consequent cerebral malfunctioning, to feeblemindedness and other overt symptoms can be described step by step (cf. Snyder, 1949; Snyder and David, 1957, pp. 389–391). Also relevant are the recent researches on neurological and biochemical correlates of schizophrenia (Brackbill, 1956). Owing to inadequate methodological controls, however, most of the findings of the latter studies must be regarded as tentative (Horwitt, 1956).

Prenatal environmental factors provide a third avenue of fruitful investigation. Especially noteworthy is the recent work of Pasamanick and his associates (1956), which demonstrated a tie-up between socioeconomic level, complications of pregnancy and parturition, and psychological disorders of the offspring. In a series of studies on large samples of whites and Negroes in Baltimore, these investigators showed that various prenatal and paranatal disorders are significantly related to the occurrence of mental defect and psychiatric disorders in the child. An important source of such irregularities in the process of childbearing and birth is to be found in deficiencies of maternal diet and in other conditions associated with low socioeconomic status. An analysis of the data did in fact reveal a much higher frequency of all such medical complications in lower than in higher socioeconomic levels, and a higher frequency among Negroes than among whites.

Direct evidence of the influence of prenatal nutritional factors upon subsequent intellectual development is to be found in a recent, well controlled experiment by Harrell et al. (1955). The subjects were pregnant women in low-income groups, whose normal diets were generally quite deficient. A dietary supplement was administered to some of these women during pregnancy and lactation, while an equated control group received placebos. When tested at the ages of three and four years, the offspring of the experimental group obtained a significantly higher mean IQ than did the offspring of the controls.

Mention should also be made of animal experiments on the effects of such factors as prenatal radiation and neonatal asphyxia upon cerebral anomalies as well as upon subsequent behavior development. These experimental studies merge imperceptibly into the fourth approach to be considered, namely, the investigation of the influence of early experience upon the eventual behavioral characteristics of animals. Research in this area has been accumulating at a rapid rate. In 1954, Beach and Jaynes surveyed this literature for the *Psychological Bulletin,* listing over 130 references. Several new studies have appeared since that date.[1] The variety of factors covered ranges from the type and quantity of available food to

[1] Forgus, 1954; King and Gurney, 1954; Luchens and Forgus, 1955; Melzack, 1954; Thompson and Melzack, 1956.

the extent of contact with human culture. A large number of experiments have been concerned with various forms of sensory deprivation and with diminished opportunities for motor exercise. Effects have been observed in many kinds of animals and in almost all aspects of behavior, including perceptual responses, motor activity, learning, emotionality, and social reactions.

In their review, Beach and Jaynes pointed out that research in this area has been stimulated by at least four distinct theoretical interests. Some studies were motivated by the traditional concern with the relative contribution of maturation and learning to behavior development. Others were designed in an effort to test certain psychoanalytic theories regarding infantile experiences, as illustrated by studies which limited the feeding responses of young animals. A third relevant influence is to be found in the work of the European biologist Lorenz (1935) on early social stimulation of birds, and in particular on the special type of learning for which the term "imprinting" has been coined. A relatively large number of recent studies have centered around Hebb's (1949) theory regarding the importance of early perceptual experiences upon subsequent performance in learning situations. All this research represents a rapidly growing and promising attack on the *modus operandi* of specific environmental factors.

The human counterpart of these animal studies may be found in the comparative investigation of child-rearing practices in different cultures and sub-cultures. This represents the fifth approach in our list. An outstanding example of such a study is that by Whiting and Child (1953). Utilizing data on 75 primitive societies from the Cross-Cultural Files of the Yale Institute of Human Relations, these investigators set out to test a number of hypotheses regarding the relationships between child-rearing practices and personality development. This analysis was followed up by field observations in five cultures, the results of which have not yet been reported (cf. Whiting et al., 1954).

Within our own culture, similar surveys have been concerned with the diverse psychological environments provided by different social classes (Davis and Havighurst, 1946). Of particular interest are the studies by Williams and Scott (1953) on the association between socioeconomic level, permissiveness, and motor development among Negro children, and the exploratory research by Milner (1951) on the relationship between reading readiness in first-grade children and patterns of parent-child interaction. Milner found that upon school entrance the lower-class child seems to lack chiefly two advantages enjoyed by the middle-class child. The first is described as "a warm positive family atmosphere or adult-relationship pattern which is more and more being recognized as a motivational prerequisite of any kind of adult-controlled learning." The lower-class children in Milner's study perceived adults as predominantly hostile. The second advantage is an extensive opportunity to interact verbally with adults in the family. The latter point is illustrated by parental attitudes toward mealtime conversation, lower-class parents tending to inhibit and discourage such conversation, while middle-class parents encourage it.

Most traditional studies on child-rearing practices have been designed in terms of a psychoanalytic orientation. There is need for more data pertaining to other types of hypotheses. Findings such as those of Milner on opportunities for verbalization and the resulting effects upon reading readiness represent a step in this direction. Another possible source of future data is the application of the intensive observational techniques of psychological ecology developed by Barker and Wright (1955) to widely diverse socioeconomic groups.

A sixth major approach involves research on the previously cited somatopsychological relationships (Barker, Wright, Myerson, and Gonick, 1953). To date, little direct information is available on the precise operation of this class of factors in psychological development. The multiplicity of ways in which physical traits—whether hereditary or environmental in origin—may influence behavior thus offers a relatively unexplored field for future study.

The seventh and final approach to be considered represents an adaption of traditional twin studies. From the standpoint of the question "How?" there is need for closer coordination between the usual data on twin resemblance and observations of the family interactions of twins. Available data already suggest, for example, that closeness of contact and extent of environmental similarity are greater in the case of monozygotic than in the case of dizygotic twins (cf. Anastasi, 1958). Information on the social reactions of twins toward each other and the specialization of roles is likewise of interest. Especially useful would be longitudinal studies of twins, beginning in early infancy and following the subjects through school age. The operation of differential environmental pressures, the development of specialized roles, and other environmental influences could thus be more clearly identified and correlated with intellectual and personality changes in the growing twins.

Parenthetically, I should like to add a remark about the traditional applications of the twin method, in which persons in different degrees of hereditary and environmental relationships to each other are simply compared for behavioral similarity. In these studies, attention has been focused principally upon the amount of resemblance of monozygotic as contrasted to dizygotic twins. Yet such a comparison is particularly difficult to interpret because of the many subtle differences in the environmental situations of the two types of twins. A more fruitful comparison would seem to be that between dizygotic twins and siblings, for whom the hereditary similarity is known to be the same. In Kallmann's (1953) monumental research on psychiatric disorders among twins, for example, one of the most convincing bits of evidence for the operation of hereditary factors in schizophrenia is the fact that the degrees of concordance for dizygotic twins and for siblings were practically identical. In contrast, it will be recalled that in intelligence test scores dizygotic twins resemble each other much more closely than do siblings—a finding which reveals the influence of environmental factors in intellectual development.

SUMMARY

The heredity-environment problem is still very much alive. Its viability is assured by the gradual replacement of the questions, "Which one?" and "How much?" by the more basic and appropriate question, "How?" Hereditary influences—as well as environmental factors of an organic nature —vary along a "continuum of indirectness." The more indirect their connection with behavior, the wider will be the range of variation of possible outcomes. One extreme of the continuum of indirectness may be illustrated by brain damage leading to mental deficiency; the other extreme, by physical characteristics associated with social stereotypes. Examples of factors falling at intermediate points include deafness, physical diseases, and motor disorders. Those environmental factors which act directly upon behavior can be ordered along a continuum of breadth or permanence of effect, as exemplified by social class membership, amount of formal schooling, language handicap, and familiarity with specific test items.

Several current lines of research offer promising techniques for exploring the *modus operandi* of hereditary and environmental factors. Outstanding among them are investigations of: (*a*) hereditary conditions which underlie behavioral differences between selectively bred groups of animals; (*b*) relations between physiological variables and individual differences in behavior, especially in the case of pathological deviations; (*c*) role of prenatal physiological factors in behavior development; (*d*) influence of early experience upon eventual behavioral characteristics; (*e*) cultural differences in child-rearing practices in relation to intellectual and emotional development; (*f*) mechanisms of somatopsychological relationships; and (*g*) psychological development of twins from infancy to maturity, together with observations of their social environment. Such approaches are extremely varied with regard to subjects employed, nature of psychological functions studied, and specific experimental procedures followed. But it is just such heterogeneity of methodology that is demanded by the wide diversity of ways in which hereditary and environmental factors interact in behavior development.

7

Twin Studies on Senescence[*]

Franz J. Kallmann and Gerhard Sander

Since identical twins have identical heredity, they have often been utilized in studies of the effect of nature upon psychological characteristics. In general, identical twins have been found to be highly similar in mental traits (much more so than fraternal twins or siblings), and when reared apart the degree of difference found, while not great, varies roughly with the degree of contrast between their life histories. In the present study senescent twins—monozygotic and dizygotic or one-egg and two-egg pairs respectively—have been studied, and it is found that the identical twins are more similar than fraternal twins in their physical and mental traits even after 60 years or more of life. Dr. Kallmann interprets the findings as indicating the basic role of heredity and constitution in determining the variable ability to maintain physical and mental health and capacity until and through senescence.

Of the many basic secrets of human life processes the vicissitudes of senility continue to be one of the most perplexing biological challenges. It is also certain that the scores of social, economic, and psychiatric problems associated with old age have been multiplied by the progressive increase in man's average life span. One may remember that by 1980 probably one-half of our population will consist of persons over 45 years of age.

Since not only the times of onset and completion, but also the localization and severity, of senile manifestations appear to vary considerably from man to man, an intricate interaction of genetic and environmental influences may be assumed to be at work. The apparent complexity of this interplay requires investigation under experiment-like, but mankind-specific conditions. The method of choice for such an inquiry is the study

[*] Adapted and abridged from F. J. Kallmann and G. Sander, "Twin Studies on Senescence," *The American Journal of Psychiatry*, 1949, Vol. 106, pp. 29-36. (With permission of the senior author and the publisher, The American Psychiatric Association.)

of an unselected and statistically representative sample of twin pairs and their sibships (twin family method).

THE POPULATION STUDIED

In the organization of our survey it was decided to adopt survival up to the age of 60 and residence in the state of New York or some closely adjacent areas as the main criteria for selecting twin index cases. In order to assure a maximum degree of universality and completeness, our study has been arranged in such a manner that it includes institutionalized twin residents over 60 years of age as well as those aged twins who live outside of institutions and receive no old-age assistance. All of them are being seen at regular intervals so that they can be observed until the end of their lives. Their co-operation has been beyond expectation, largely in response to the very active support rendered not only by a great number of health and welfare agencies, hospitals and homes for the aged, but also by news services, local radio stations, and the general public.

With the aid of this co-operative organization it was possible during the first 3 years of the survey, that is, until January, 1948, to collect a total of 1,602 senescent twin index cases. Most of them are still alive, including 431 pairs of whom both partners survived. The oldest living twin has reached an age of 102 years, while the oldest pair is at present 95 years old. The sex distribution of our index cases shows a ratio of 697 males to 905 females for the entire sample, and a ratio of 464:584 for those twins who resided outside of institutions in the state of New York. This distribution is fully in accordance with statistical expectation, since the corresponding sex ratio for the total New York State population over 65 years of age is 478:570. The ratio of one-egg pairs in our sample is 237:548, which means that the proportion of one-egg pairs is about 30 per cent. There is nothing in various comparisons we have made to indicate that the collected sample of senescent twin index cases is not truly representative from a statistical standpoint.

PHYSICAL CHARACTERISTICS

The permanence in the physical likenesses of monozygotic pairs is often so striking that twin partners may be practically as indistinguishable in various stages of senescence as they had been in childhood or in their earlier years of maturity (Figure 1). The similarities usually include the degree of general enfeeblement or its absence, the graying and thinning of the hair, the configuration of baldness and senile wrinkle formation, and the type and extent of eye, ear, and teeth deficiencies (gerontoxon, senile cataract). Significant differences in these physical symptoms of aging are the exception in monozygotic pairs, while they are the rule and generally more pronounced in dizygotic pairs.

The tendency of one-egg twins to remain physically alike while advancing toward the end stage of senium is frequently expressed against the potential effect of modifying influences arising from entirely different environments. The differences in the life histories of the E twins (Figure

FIGURE 1. Life-long Indistinguishability of One-egg Twins as Illustrated by Pictures of the N Twins at Ages 4, 25, 60, and 85

2) were those between a married country doctor who had a large family and for over 50 years practiced medicine in the state of New York and a Western rancher who never married but was successful in breeding stock. Nevertheless, when the twin brothers met after many decades of separation, they were found to have resisted the development of complete baldness with approximately the same residual amount of hair.

That genetically determined likenesses of physique may withstand both age and environmental diversity seems illustrated equally well by the F twins (not shown), who, at the age of 95, are currently the oldest surviving pair in our survey. Their disparities of the past are collectively reflected in the rather interesting fact that one twin speaks English fluently and the other not at all, although both have been in this country for over 60 years. By visual means, however, it is still very difficult to tell them apart. In another senescent one-egg pair it was impossible to procure a photograph taken at an advanced age, but it is notable that these twin sisters developed very similar senile psychoses despite significant differences in their social and marital histories. In addition, the clinical developments paral-

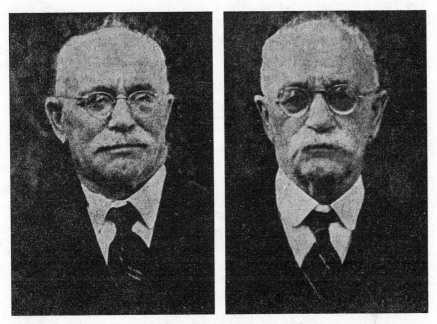

FIGURE 2. The *E* Twins at Age 73

leled each other to such an extent that both became totally blind and deaf in the same month, that they sustained massive cerebral hemorrhages on the same day, and their deaths were only five days apart shortly before their eighty-sixth birthdays.

MENTAL CHARACTERISTICS

With respect to mental changes associated with senescence, the emphasis of our study has been on the procurement of psychometric evidence for the presence or absence of genetically controlled variations in the human tendency, or resistance to the tendency, to deteriorate intellectually in relation to chronologically advancing age. The testing procedure was synthesized from various standard intelligence tests used for adults;

namely, the Wechsler-Bellevue Test, the Cornell-Coxe Performance Ability Scale, the Directions Test of Bronson Price, and the Terman and Merrill Revision of the Stanford-Binet Test.

Our test series includes only same-sexed and noninstitutionalized twin partners who were able and willing to co-operate to the extent of submitting to repeated and rather tedious mental examinations. In the first test round, as recorded in Table 1, these requirements were met by 77 index pairs. Most of them (51 pairs) were female, and over one-half (46 pairs) were monozygotic. The ages of the female pairs ranged from 60 to 87 years, while the educational backgrounds varied from the level of public school education in rural districts to those of professional groups.

Because of the obviously still insufficient number of male test pairs, the present comparison by means of Fisher's analysis of variance was limited to female pairs. In the continuation of this work, every effort will be made to equalize the test groups for the two sexes, although there has been no indication that psychometric variations in aging male twins might follow a different pattern.

In the tabulation of the female test results, the mean scores are given as well as the intrapair differences. With respect to the mean scores it is interesting to note that all of them are within the limits of normal expectation and practically alike for the two twin groups. There is no reason to believe, therefore, that with regard to intelligence or general vitality or any other aspect of biological development, a twin derived from only one-half of a fertilized ovum might tend to be inferior either to a two-egg twin or to the average single-born person.

Geriatrically it is of more obvious importance that 4 of the 6 test methods used (vocabulary, Kohs' blocks, digit span, and digit symbol substitution) render mean intrapair differences between the 2 members of index pairs, which are definitely smaller for monozygotic than for dizygotic pairs. The differences observed are statistically significant at the 1% level of confidence, which means that they would occur by chance only in one out of 100 comparable samples.

The inference to be drawn from these test results is that certain intellectual abilities depend on genetically produced potentialities, which in their measurable effects remain variable from man to man until senescence. Eventually, our total scale of psychometric comparisons will make it possible to analyze variations in the tendency to senile deterioration in relation to both constitutional and environmental influences.

LONGEVITY

One of the most essential biological aspects of senescence is that of longevity. On account of the observational long-range objectives of our study, the present analysis of intrapair differences in the life span of index pairs is based only on the histories of 58 pairs, of whom both members have already died of natural causes in the age group over 60. If it is correct to hypothesize that the capacity for longevity may primarily depend upon heredity, a comparison of the life span of monozygotic and dizygotic index pairs cannot yield more than minimum differences at this point. The obvious expectation would be that our dizygotic groups with still incomplete histories include the largest proportion of index pairs in whom only one member has been capable of surviving.

TABLE 1. Comparative Psychometric Findings in Female Twin Index Pairs

	Mean Test Scores		Intrapair Score Differences			
			Monozygotic Pairs		Dizygotic Pairs	
Type of Test	Mono-zygotic	Dizy-gotic	Mean	Standard Error	Mean	Standard Error
	Test Cases					
Vocabulary	29.5	27.0	2.0	0.33	4.5	1.03
Kohs' blocks	15.0	15.4	1.6	0.99	6.5	1.85
Memory for digits	9.9	9.8	1.2	0.14	2.0	0.45
Digit symbol substitution	33.5	30.5	4.4	0.84	9.5	2.15
Similarities	10.2	8.9	2.5	0.49	3.8	0.82
Motor coordination	68.3	68.4	12.4	1.02	14.5	2.64

In view of this reservation it is certainly impressive that the present discrepancy in the life spans of the two members of same-sexed pairs is about twice as large for dizygotic pairs as it is for monozygotic pairs. The total mean difference amounts to 36.9 months in the monozygotic group, to 78.3 months in the same-sexed dizygotic group, and to 126.6 months for all dizygotic pairs of opposite sex. Incidentally, the histories of the monozygotic group include one pair whose 2 members died the same day of similar natural causes at the age of 86, in addition to 2 pairs whose partners died only 5 and 25 days apart at the ages of 85 and 69 respectively, while there is no pair in the dizygotic group with a difference of less than 3 months.

The difference between monozygotic and same-sexed dizygotic pairs is approximately the same for the two sexes and is statistically significant at the 5% level of confidence. Unquestionably, if the differential trend continues at the present rate or possibly increases with the progress of the study, it would conclusively confirm the essentiality of genetic factors with respect to longevity.

DISCUSSION

The selection of the particular features presented in this paper has been necessary not only because of the abundance of accumulated material, but also because in 92 per cent of the index pairs the life history has not yet been completed by one or both members. All the available data serve to show, however, that the genetically determined likenesses of monozygotic twin partners have a tendency to persist throughout life, and in many instances are able to remain expressed during senescence to a remarkable degree. The similarities extend to physique and personality development, as well as to important aspects of the social, occupational, and reproductive histories, to the onset and type of senile psychopathology, and to length of life in general. With regard to certain basic elements which apparently control the variability of these phenomena, the extent of correspondence observed in one-egg pairs is apt to exceed by far that of two-egg pairs.

On the basis of our twin observations it is no longer questionable that *heredity and constitution play a basic role in determining the variable ability to maintain a state of physical and mental health until and through the period of senescence.*

Psychologically it is certain that satisfactory adjustment to aging can be attained only if the biological facts of life are clearly understood, and their acceptance is woven into a plain design of living. In a human world, old age is a comparative classification of vital efficiency and as relative in its definitions as is the faculty of being alive or the quality of being human.

8

Motor Primacy and Behavioral Development[*]

Weston A. Bousfield

It is apparent that many response tendencies are built into the organism on a genetic basis. Some behavior patterns appear spontaneously

[*] From Weston A. Bousfield, "The Assumption of Motor Primacy and Its Significance for Behavioral Development," *Journal of Genetic Psychology,* 1953, Vol. 83, pp. 79-88. (With permission of the author and The Journal Press.)

when the motor neurones and musculature reach a threshold state of maturity. Developmental psychologists conceptualize these emerging responses as being due to the maturing of "innate releasing mechanisms." Such motor patterns appear to be almost entirely independent of differential environmental conditions. For example, the human smile makes its appearance in the congenitally blind infant who has never seen this response in others. Infants bound to the swaddling board for the first six or seven months of life suffer no retardation in the acquisition of motor skills related to walking. The disappearance of the grasping reflex and the initiation of voluntary grasping seem wholly unrelated to opportunities for practicing this form of prehensile behavior. These motor responses, as well as many others, point toward the existence of inner mechanisms that initiate and release early patterns of motor response. Dr. Bousfield offers us an interesting proto-theory to account for the observed developmental trends in motor behavior during the early months of life.

This paper undertakes to consider what is here termed *the assumption of motor primacy*. It may be stated briefly as follows: *The neuro-motor mechanism develops in advance of capacity to respond to stimulation of sense organs.* The basis of this formulation is in Coghill's (1929) monograph on the development of amblystoma. Our interpretation of evidence, however, goes beyond Coghill. We shall attempt to indicate the usefulness of the assumption and its correlates in explaining certain characteristics of behavioral development, and to demonstrate the application of this approach to relevant theories.

EVIDENCE OF MOTOR PRIMACY

Coghill (1929) undertook to connect his observations on behavioral development with the results of a careful study of the growth of the embryonic nervous system. During the non-motile stage of amblystoma muscular reactions can be elicited only by direct stimulation. At this time both motor and sensory cells develop contact with their respective organs, but the lack of commissural connections prevents responses to sensory influx. The connecting cells are initially unipolar and extend axons to the motor cells on one side only. Later the central neurons become bipolar and establish contact with sensory axons on the opposite side of the cord. Such closing of reflex gaps progresses generally in a cephalocaudal direction. Axons are initially *naked protoplasmic threads*, and their lack of myelinization is associated with considerable diffusion of response. This description provides an explanation for the early flexure and coil stages in which a light touch to the anterior skin elicits first a movement of the head away from the side stimulated and later a cephalocaudal progression of bending down the entire side of the embryo. It would thus appear that during the early development of amblystoma the number of stimuli capable of eliciting motor responses is limited, and that reactions are apparently general in character. We need not be committed, however, to the generality of Coghill's total-pattern theory. As long as there are grounds for supposing the closure of simple reflex gaps, relatively specific response patterns are possible though they may be components of mass action. The studies undertaken in the past 20 years appear to confirm the developmental priority of the motor system. Hooker (1950), in a recent summary of evidence, reports general agreement on several facts of development. Included in these are the conclusions that the capacity to transmit nervous impulses develops in motor nerves prior to the sensory, and that the last components of the reflex arc to become functional are the sensory and very likely the intercalated elements. Hooker further indicates the probability that proprioceptive reflexes appear earlier than the exteroceptive.

We have implied that responses other than those elicited by direct stimulation of muscles depend on activation of sense organs. There is evidence, however, for supposing such an interpretation to be too narrow. Weiss (1941) demonstrated the occurrence of uncoordinated motor activity in the transplanted limb of a salamander larva when it received innervation from a deplanted section of spinal cord. There were no afferent fibers and the motor activity must have been due to spontaneous firing of cells in the fragment of spinal cord. Hebb (1949) and Weiss (1950) cite evidence from a variety of sources indicating the occurrence of spontaneous firing, and such autonomous activity is apparently an established property of aggregates of neural cells. This suggests that a basis is provided for neurally instigated motor responses that may occur without afferent influx.

Evidence significant for the assumption of motor primacy appears in the order of structural development of the human brain. The motor areas appear to develop in advance of other centers. Bolton and Moyes (1912) undertook a study of cellular differentiation of the cortex of a fetus 18 weeks of age. They found that the pyramidal cells in the frontoparietal region showed the most advanced development. This part of the cortex is the beginning one of the major motor pathways extending to the spinal cord. McGraw (1946) has reviewed this and other studies which similarly indicate relative precocity in the development of motor areas.

If our interpretation of evidence is valid, we may suppose that motor primacy is involved in the following correlated mechanisms: (a) Idiomuscular response consequent on direct stimulation of muscles. (b) Diffuse motor response consequent on sensory stimulation capable of inducing diffusion of excitation in motor tracts. (c) Spontaneous motor response consequent on the firing of cells in the central axis. (d) Isolated reflex response consequent on localized stimulation and mediated by a neural arc. (e) Concatenated response pattern consequent on the orderly coordination of two or more neuromotor units.

Except for the priority of idio-muscular response it is not intended that this enumeration should represent a strict temporal sequence. The treatment so far presents a general outline of the evidence indicating the developmental primacy of the neuro-motor mechanism. We shall now consider the usefulness of the foregoing assumptions in accounting for observed facts relating to behavioral development. An attempt will also be made to indicate certain of the variables having a bearing on the interpretation of experimental findings.

INTERPRETATION OF ASPECTS OF DEVELOPMENT

Spontaneous Behavior. Various investigators of behavioral development during the fetal period have noted the occurrence of behavior in the absence of imposed stimulation. Carmichael (1934) reported spontaneous movement as the first observable response in his study of the development of fetal guinea pigs. This movement comprised a lateral flexion of the neck accompanied by movement of the forelimbs. In a further study, Bridgman and Carmichael (1935) indicated the occurrence of spontaneous behavior 10 to 14 hours after responses elicited by stimulation. Hooker (1943) recorded the occurrence of spontaneous movements in the human fetus at the age of 9½ weeks. Responses to tactual stimulation were possible, however, at the earlier age of 8½ weeks. Windle (1950) concluded that the time of occurrence of spontaneous activity of the mammalian embryo within the uterus is unknown. However, he inferred that such activity probably occurs appreciably later than movements elicited by stimulation.

Available evidence thus indicates the early occurrence of motor activity in the absence of identifiable stimulation; generally the term spontaneous is used to describe such behavior. That such responses appear to be somewhat spasmodic in character is not surprising since the kinesthetic mechanisms permitting coordinated activity are relatively slow to develop. The study of Weiss (1941), to which reference has already been made, reports the occurrence of motor activity as a consequence of the firing of motor cells. We may venture the supposition that this type of neural activity accounts for behavior which should be labelled spontaneous. The time of occurrence of spontaneous behavior would depend on an optimum development of the cells of either motor or correlator neurons. What constitutes such optimum development cannot at the present time be specified. We do, however, have an important suggestion relating to the rate of growth of segmental neural systems, and Barron

(1950) has assembled evidence bearing on this problem. He points out that the growth of the limb parallels the growth of cells in the basal plate of associated regions in the central axis. There is an apparent tendency for limbs to appear relatively earlier in some animals than in others. The relative timing of development in axial and appendicular systems has a bearing on the appearance of local reflexes. If our analysis is valid we would suppose that with precocious limb development we should expect a relatively early appearance in the limbs of both reflex and spontaneous responses. The precise estimation of timing of the occurrence of spontaneous response may well depend on use of adequate instruments to detect action potentials in various muscles under conditions which exclude the possibility of sensory stimulation.

Motor Diffusion. The term motor diffusion is here employed to denote the essential variability, generality, and relative lack of gradient of response occurring in early development. For example, Minkowski (1922) observed that a tactual stimulus applied to the skin of the 135 mm. human fetus induced various reactions in different parts of the body. He observed that every section of the skin could serve as a reflexogenous zone, and that there was a tendency for the reactions to spread over the entire organism. The studies undertaken since Minkowski generally indicate the presence of diffuse and variable responses in the early stages of development. The issue of controversy appears to relate primarily to the relative proportion of the total responses that should be labelled isolated, discrete, or genuinely reflex in character. It is not surprising that motor diffusion appears also as a consequence of direct cortical stimulation. Fulton (1943) summarized evidence showing that isolated motor responses are difficult to obtain in the infant macaque. He believes this to be a consequence of the relatively undifferentiated character of the Betz cells and the lack of myelinization of the pyramidal tracts. The same phenomena appear also from work with human infants.

The assumptions necessary for an explanation of motor diffusion may be indicated in general terms. Motor primacy indicates a relatively rapid development in motor pathways. Myelinization of neurons comprising these pathways proceeds as an aspect of their structural development. Whether or not we can regard the myelin sheath as an insulating agent preventing the overflow of impulses, it appears that lack of myelinization is associated with lack of specificity of response. We also assume that afferent pathways from sense organs are relatively slow in establishing functional central connections. If this analysis is valid, it would follow that during the early stages of development, a limited number of stimuli, especially when they are intense, would be effective in eliciting diffuse motor responses. It should be noted further that evidence of motor diffusion would also be expected in spontaneous responses.

Dominance of Intrinsic Neural Activity. Gibbs and Gibbs (1941), in their survey of evidence on developmental changes in EEG, indicate the occurrence in newborn infants of large slow waves of one-half to two cycles per second. Waves of this type, according to Hebb (1949), are also characteristic of sleep or coma in older subjects, and are probably a result of hypersynchrony in the firing of cortical cells. Hebb suggests that the behavioral consequences of this hypersynchrony include a raised threshold for sensory stimulation, and a lack of the maintained and directed activity which generally is labelled voluntary or purposeful. Stimulation of receptors not only breaks up hypersynchrony, but is also necessary for the coordination and control of behavior. At birth intrinsic organization of cortical activity is dominant, and such organization is opposed to the organization consequent on sensory events. The assumption of motor primacy receives support from Hebb's interpretation, but at the same time suggests implications going somewhat beyond his analysis. The early deficiency in central connections with sense organs should contribute both to the heightening of sensory thresholds and to the maintenance of hypersynchrony. It may further be assumed that hypersynchrony is likely to result in the instigation of impulses over motor pathways, and that this type of intrinsic neural activity may sometimes be responsible for spontaneous responses.

Early Learning. Our discussion of early learning will center on evidence from human fetal and neonatal subjects. It appears that even at birth there is still a lag in the capacity to respond to stimulation, and that observable responses reflect the consequences of diffusion. It would follow that the response specificity required for the conditioning of specific reflexes would be more difficult to obtain at this time than at a later period. On the other hand, since diffuse responses are elicited with comparative ease during the fetal period, the conditioning of such responses should be possible at a relatively early age. The requirements for such conditioning would involve the use of: (a) an unconditioned stimulus capable of eliciting diffuse responses; (b) a conditioned stimulus which would not elicit diffuse responses. It would be unnecessary that the response to the conditioned stimulus be recordable. As long as conditioning could be established, the requirements for learning would be fulfilled.

Our survey of the literature yields evidence consistent with these deductions. As Wenger's (1943) extensive study has shown, the conditioning of specific reflex responses, e.g., lid closure to tactual vibration, in the neonate is difficult. Furthermore, the learning, in so far as it is indicated, is unstable. It appears he was able to establish the conditioning of some responses, but not in all his subjects. Among the difficulties he reported were those involved in the choice of both unconditioned and conditioned stimuli. Many stimuli elicited no observable responses, and the responses he was able to obtain tended to be diffuse and variable. Wenger's findings appear to be in accord with the conclusions reached by Pratt (1946) in his survey of studies of neonate learning.

Evidence relating to the conditioning of general activity, while limited, appears to be considerably more positive. In the present frame of reference, the general activity characteristic of the fetus and neonate is regarded as involving diffuse motor responses. Spelt (1948) reported success in an experiment designed to condition such responses in the fetus during the last two months of gestation. Employing a procedure suggested by Ray's (1932) early work, he used for his unconditioned stimulus a loud noise capable of eliciting fetal movements. This was combined with a vibrotactile conditioned stimulus. Three pairs of tambours attached to the mother's abdomen recorded the presence or absence of fetal movements in the general areas of the head, arms, and legs. The protocols also included signals given by the mother of felt movements. It was not expected that the records would furnish data on the comparative motility of the separate parts of the fetus. In addition to establishing conditioned responses, Spelt also reported success in demonstrating experimental extinction, spontaneous recovery, and retention over an interval of three weeks.

Marquis (1941) was able to establish the temporal conditioning of general activity in neonates. A group of infants was fed on a 3-hour schedule for the first eight days, and then shifted to a 4-hour schedule. Stabilimeters were used to obtain records of activity. The results showed adaptation to the 3-hour schedule, and an upset when a change was made to the 4-hour schedule. Furthermore, the activity cycles of the 3-hour group differed markedly from those of controls fed on a 4-hour schedule, and from those of a group placed on a self-schedule determined by their crying.

If our interpretation is valid, evidence of early learning tends to confirm the assumption of motor primacy and the correlated factor of diffusion. Such learning is limited on the one hand by the lag in responsiveness to stimulation, and on the other by the lack of response specificity.

Mention may appropriately be made here of the relevance of our assumptions to Hebb's (1949) concept of the cell assembly and his account of early learning. Primary learning, according to Hebb, involves the establishment of environmental control over groups of cells in the cortex and diencephalon through the building up of cell assemblies. These assemblies are necessary for the establishment of perceptual elements which must precede the emergence of complex perceptions. The formation of an assembly depends on the repetition of particular stimulation and on some degree of constancy of central action following such stimulation. Hebb calls attention to the slowness of this process even for simple perceptions. In relating Hebb's postulates to those of this paper, it may be said that the development of cell assemblies is retarded both by the limited nature of early sensory impact, and by diffusion which works against specificity of response in cortical association areas.

Theories of Development. Two general theories, essentially opposite in their implications, have emerged from the studies of early behavioral development. This opposition is between the *total-pattern* and the *isolated-reflex* points of view. Coghill (1929) was a total-pattern exponent. Development of behavior, he believed, involves the expansion of a general pattern which emerges as a perfectly integrated unit. Partial systems develop within the total pattern and acquire more or less specificity. Against this Gestaltic conception, and after extensive researches, Windle (1950) continues to subscribe to the point of view that early movements elicited by stimulation are reflex in nature and depend on functional reflex arcs. His point of view indicates that with progressive development of central reflex mechanisms, more complex and integrated patterns make their appearance. The so-called mass-activity observed by many investigators who have removed fetuses from the uterus is, he assumes, a consequence of asphyxia. During such a state, a diffuse discharge of most of the motor units may be induced by stimulation or may occur spontaneously.

Since, as already indicated, the appearance of specific reflex responses is related to the timing of the emergence of appendicular systems, it might seem attractive to suppose that the applicability of the total-pattern and isolated-reflex explanations would depend on the type of organism being considered. Several difficulties, however, are apparent in such an approach. Even in mammalian fetuses where appendicular development is relatively precocious, there is no general agreement on the validity of either the isolated-reflex or total-pattern explanations. Further, it is apparent that since such explanations have generated confusion, we should re-examine the problem in order to determine useful and experimentally verifiable assumptions. Nearly 20 years ago Carmichael (1934) stated that the formulation of general theories of development such as those denoted by the terms individuation and integration is premature. His observation is still valid.

SUMMARY AND CONCLUSIONS

It is obvious that the incidence of various forms of behavior must depend on the physiological mechanisms available to the organism, and the study of behavioral development should be guided by relevant premises derived from developmental physiology. Present evidence supports the assumption of the developmental priority of the neuro-motor system, and a corresponding lag in the capacity to respond to stimulation. The consideration of this assumption has led to the supposition of correlated mechanisms for the eliciting of muscular responses. This approach has been shown to be useful in accounting for various aspects of behavioral development, and at the same time furnishes a basis for the evaluation of relevant theories.

The literature shows considerable difference of opinion with respect to the facts of behavioral development and a consequent lack of agreement in theory. We would propose that the resolution of this problem depends in large measure on adequate definitions of the behavioral phenomena available for observation, and that such definitions should derive from tenable assumptions relating to the development of physiological mechanisms for response. Our analysis has led to the postulation of motor primacy and the definitions of five correlated mechanisms of motor reaction. If these assumptions are valid, there should be no essential disagreement on the facts they denote, and facts are necessary for both the generation and the testing of theory. As a general orientation for further study, we would suggest the following:

1. *Idio-muscular* response. More information is needed on the time when muscles are capable of responding to direct stimulation, the nature of such responses, and the types of effective stimuli.

2. *Diffuse motor response.* Motor diffusion denotes the occurrence of non-specific responses as a result of the spread of excitation over neural pathways. There is a need for more effective measures of this phenomenon and the conditions on which it depends. The latter would appear to include the physiological variables of the level of maturity of motor pathways, and the condition of the organism. Research is needed on the nature and locus of receptor stimulation capable of eliciting this type of response, and on the occurrence of diffusion as an aspect of spontaneous behavior. It would also be worthwhile to identify sequences in the spread of excitation.

3. *Spontaneous response.* Such responses would appear to depend on the firing of neural cell aggregates in either lower or higher centers. Further research might well be undertaken to determine the occurrence of such responses following the elimination of afferent influx of impulses from receptors.

4. *Isolated reflex response.* By definition the reflex is a constant type of response following the application of a specific stimulus. Such an element of behavior is assumed to depend on a neural arc connecting specific receptors with specific motor or glandular organs. The identification of isolated reflex responses is complicated, however, by the consequences of diffusion occurring in the central axis and presumably also in peripheral nerves. To be labelled as a specific reflex response, however, the behavior should be mediated by a functioning neural arc. Consideration should be given to the consequences of development occurring within its components.

5. *Concatenated response pattern*. As is the case with other types of response, it is apparent that the problem of identification is complicated by the occurrence of diffusion. There is no sharp transition between generalized and indeterminate responses on the one hand, and an orderly coordination of multiple responses on the other. It would seem necessary, however, to specify the components of the pattern being studied, and further to indicate their temporal relationships.

9

Physical Maturing Among Boys as Related to Behavior in Adolescence and Adult Years[*]

Mary C. Jones and Nancy Bayley

The preceding paper indicated relationships between neurophysiological growth and changes in motor behavior. The present paper is of broader scope, indicating that age of physical maturing and resulting differences in physical size and strength play important roles in personal and social adjustment as well as in behavior generally, and that these differences in behavior persist to some degree into the adult years. Such relationships can come about in various ways. Better physique and greater strength may rather directly determine competence in certain activities. More mature appearance, even sheer size, may result in treatment by adults which is different from that accorded the immature-appearing child of the same age. Expectation of more mature behavior may stimulate more mature efforts and accelerate psychological growth. Immature appearance and physical inferiority, on the other hand, may result in childish treatment by adults and feelings of inferiority in peer relationships. The present paper clearly indicates the extreme complexity of the relationships between physical change and status on one hand and psychological development and behavior on the other.

* Adapted and abridged mainly from M. C. Jones and N. Bayley, "Physical Maturing Among Boys as Related to Behavior," *Journal of Educational Psychology*, 1950, Vol. 41, pp. 129-148. (With permission of the senior author and the copyright holder, Abrahams Magazine Service, Inc.)

The problems of adjustment which are usually attributed to the adolescent period center around the youth's need to develop heterosexual interests, to select a vocation, and, in general, to acquire the status of adulthood in the eyes of his peers and of his elders. The impetus for the attainment of independent and mature status is undoubtedly related to the adolescent's physical changes, but the process of growing up is so complex and so interwoven with cultural factors that we have not yet been able to demonstrate more than a rather general relationship between physical and psychological phases of development.

It is well known that children mature at different rates, and reach the period of pubescence at different chronological ages. Although the psychological accompaniments of these differences in maturing can be examined in terms of mass statistics, this approach to the problem is often disappointing because of its tendency to obscure the intricacies of the growth pattern and the dynamics involved in the process of integration. Case reports of individual children have been somewhat more successful in their attempts to disclose the processes involved in the attainment of maturity, but the accumulation of individual life histories is a slow way in which to arrive at useful generalities.

The present report deals with two groups of boys who fall at opposite ends of a normal sample distributed on the basis of one developmental characteristic (skeletal age). In an attempt to find differentiating behavior characteristics, statistical comparisons of the two groups have been made and illustrative case material has been assembled for individuals falling at each extreme. The method, while providing no touchstone, does enable us to consider group differences without losing sight of the individual behavior patterns of members of the group.

A follow-up study was undertaken when the boys described in the main section of this report had reached age 33, in an effort to determine the long-term effects of rate of maturing upon personality.[1]

PHYSICAL CHARACTERISTICS OF THE EARLY-
AND LATE-MATURING GROUPS

The selection of contrasting extreme groups for the present study was on the basis of physical maturity assessments by the Todd standards for hand and knee. The groups included sixteen boys who were most consistently accelerated and sixteen who were most consistently retarded during the four-and-a-half years for which we had cumulative skeletal X-rays, beginning at an average age of fourteen years. The total distribution from

[1] These findings were reported in a later paper by Mary Cover Jones, "The later careers of boys who were early- or late-maturing," *Child Development*, 1957, 28, 113-128. Adaptation of this paper in the section of the present paper dealing with "Adult Differences" (pp. 133-136 in the present volume) is by permission of Dr. Jones and of the publisher of *Child Development*.

which these extremes were truncated consisted of 90 cases, a normal classroom sample of boys in an urban public school system.

On the average, the physically accelerated and the physically retarded boys, though of the same age, are separated by about two years in skeletal age (the criterion variable). Although some overlapping exists in the height of individual children at each age, the means of the groups are widely different. Even as early as eleven years all of the late-maturing are shorter than the mean for the early-maturing. At the mean age of fourteen years the distributions show an extreme separation; in the later years of adolescence the differences tend to decrease, and the predicted mature heights of the early- and late-maturing are very similar.

There is also an obvious divergence (with no overlap) when the two groups are compared in terms of physical maturity ratings. This is seen when Greulich's five-point standards of maturity[2] are applied to photographs taken at fourteen years of age. The characteristic rating at this age is 3. The mean of 16 early-maturing boys was 4.5 (close to the maximum), with no rating below 4. The mean of the 16 late-maturers was 2.0, with only two ratings of 3.

The boys who matured late were relatively very small from thirteen to fifteen years. In agreement with Bayley's study of body build in relation to skeletal maturing, they were characteristically slender built and long legged at all ages. Furthermore, their strength tests show them to have been relatively weak at the ages when they were lagging in size, and their scores in the Espenschade tests of athletic ability were in most instances below average. The early-maturing boys, on the other hand, were usually large, broad-built and strong, and tended to show good athletic skill throughout the period of our records. Their superiority in strength and physical skills was greatest at ages thirteen to fifteen, when their early growth spurt accentuated their differences in size as compared with the slower-growing average and late-maturing boys.

SOCIAL BEHAVIOR IN BOYS' GROUPS

The psychological records examined in connection with the present study include both observational measures and reputation scores. We shall present first the ratings made independently by three staff members when the boys were in small groups (usually six) in a same-sex, "free play" situation. These will be referred to as ICW (Institute of Child Welfare) ratings. The observations and ratings were concerned, in general, with social behavior and personal attributes which are important in social relationships.

The ratings have been converted into standard scores in which 50 represents the mean of the total group, with an SD of 10 points. The direction

[2] Based on ratings of pubic hair and external genitals.

and the degree of a child's deviation from the mean of his group are thus expressed in such a way that comparisons can readily be made between accelerated and retarded subgroups.

Figures 1 and 2 present cumulative standard score curves, from ages twelve to seventeen, for several traits involving personal appearance and emotional patterns. (Contrasts between the two groups at age sixteen with respect to various traits are presented later in Table 1.) As shown in Figure 1, the early-maturing are consistently rated as superior in physical attractiveness, with average scores which reach their highest value at age fifteen. In general, the group is about one SD above the mean total sample of boys. The late-maturing fall somewhat below the group mean, increasingly so from age twelve to age fifteen or sixteen. These differences in attractiveness of physique are complexly influenced by factors of size and of body build. Early maturing is not only associated with a more rapid growth in height, but also with mesomorphy. The boys in this group tend to be "well-built," muscular, and athletic. By contrast, the more slender, poorly-muscled build of the late-maturers was rated as relatively "unattractive" by the adult observers.

Early-maturers are found to be on the average more "masculine," the late-maturers more "childish" in their build, and, as might be expected, the early-maturers also were rated as giving somewhat greater attention to the amenities of personal grooming. This is expressed in cleanliness, attention to hair and nails, and neatness of clothing.

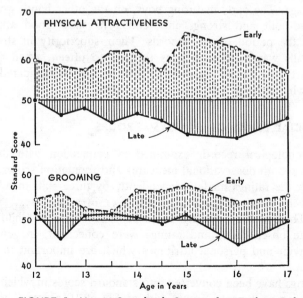

FIGURE 1. Mean Standard Scores for Early- and Late-maturing Groups, in Physical Appearance

The difference between the two groups in physical attractiveness is most marked at ages fifteen and sixteen. When ratings based on a composite of physique, grooming, and attractiveness of facial appearance were compared, so marked was the separation of the early- and late-maturing that all but one of the former fall above the average of the latter; only two cases among the late-maturing are rated above the central tendency of our total group of boys.

Another group of traits which may have developmental significance is that related to expressiveness. In these characteristics the early-maturing are close to the group average, but the late-maturing are consistently above the average. Similar differences were found for other traits involving expressiveness; comparisons were made for behavior defined, at contrasting extremes, as talkative-silent; active-stationary; busy-idle; peppy-indifferent; and laughing-sober. In each of these the early-maturing boys were distributed similarly to the total sample of boys; however, the late-maturing were consistently on the "expressive" side of the scale.

At least two factors are probably involved in determining this deviate position of the late-maturing. The first is a persistence of a childish activity pattern. A busy scurrying about, the noisy interchange of shouts and comments, is more characteristic of preadolescence than of later years; the adolescent often looks down upon such behavior as undignified, and adopts instead the role of a lounger, observing with tolerant superiority the childish antics of those younger than himself. A second factor is a reaction formation to inferiority. The "active small boy" may be expressing through his activity not merely a survival of an immature culture pattern, but may also use this, as the only technique he knows, to hold the attention of others and to compensate for a physically less favored status.

In this connection, it is instructive to consider the evidence concerning attention-seeking behavior. The late-maturing boys tend to vary around the average in the trait "matter-of-factness" and on the trait "unaffectedness." Their expressiveness is judged to have a more affected quality at ages sixteen and seventeen than in the years immediately preceding. Although the differences are small, this would be consistent with an interpretation emphasizing a "natural" or "childish" expressiveness in the earlier years of adolescence, and a more compensatory attention-seeking expressiveness in the later years. In contrast, the early-maturing are at these ages judged to be relatively nonattention-seeking: unaffected and matter-of-fact.

Also pertinent are the ratings for inhibition and relaxation in social situations (Figure 2). The late-maturing are relatively uninhibited, but they are also judged to be relatively tense. At age sixteen, the early-maturing are on the average approximately one SD above the group mean, in the direction of "relaxation," and the late-maturing are a similar distance below the mean, in the direction of "tenseness." The early-maturing are con-

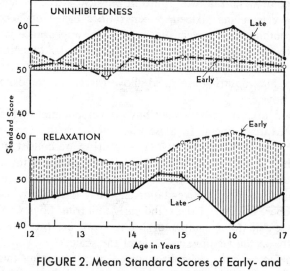

FIGURE 2. Mean Standard Scores of Early- and
Late-maturing Groups, in Emotional Patterning

sistently well-adjusted in this trait, while the late-maturing are in most
semesters on the less well-adjusted side of the scale.

Table 1 presents the significance of the differences between the early-
and late-maturing at age sixteen, based on t ratios. For all but two traits
on this list, differences are significant at the five per cent level or better.
In these two traits (animation and "uninhibitedness") significant differences are obtained when results are considered for all nine semesters in
which ratings have been recorded, from ages twelve to seventeen, and
analyzed in terms of the binomial test for consistency.[3] In attractiveness
of physique, grooming, and relaxation (higher for the late-maturing) differences are in the same direction in each of nine semesters, with a significance level of .002. Differences of the same consistency were obtained
for a number of other traits not included in Figures 1 and 2; these results
show that the late-maturing are significantly more busy, more active, more
"peppy," and more talkative. Differences at the 2 per cent level (in the
same direction for eight of the nine semesters) were found for eagerness,
social initiative, and sociability, in favor of the late-maturing. Differences
at the 7 per cent level (in the same direction for seven of the nine semesters) occurred in several additional traits, indicating a possibly greater
tendency for the early-maturing to be good-natured, and for the late-maturing to be attention-seeking and to enjoy games.

[3] Based on the probability that the difference in a series of paired measures will
occur in the same direction in a specified proportion of the instances. Since the same
subjects are involved, consistent differences are interpreted as independent of errors
in measurement, but they are not necessarily independent of initial sampling errors.

TABLE 1. Mean Standard Scores for Early- and Late-maturing Boys

	Early	Late	Level of Significance of Difference
Attractiveness of physique	60.6	45.0	.01
Grooming	54.6	49.8	.05
Animation	49.6	61.2	
Eagerness	47.9	59.3	.05
Uninhibitedness	52.5	60.2	
Matter-of-factness	60.5	43.6	.02
Unaffectedness	60.7	46.2	.05
Relaxation	61.1	40.6	.01

It may be noted that the two maturational groups show similar rather than different records in a number of traits of social importance. Thus, they present no marked nor consistent differences in observed popularity, leadership, prestige, poise, assurance, cheerfulness, or social effect on the group.[4]

In view of the relation of maturing to physical abilities, and of the high valuation placed upon athletic performance in the adolescent culture, it is perhaps surprising that differences in maturing are not reflected in such traits as popularity, leadership, or prestige. Case reports have made it clear that late-maturing is sometimes a primary source of social and personal maladjustment. On the average, however, the late-maturing boy succeeds in maintaining a fairly adequate status among his age-mates; very likely he is helped in this by his activity and other compensations, and it is also probable that some of the early-maturing are handicapped at times by the fact that they have outgrown their age group.

CLUBHOUSE RECORDS

Ratings and observations made in mixed group situations provide additional material for comparison of these two extreme groups of boys. These records were made in a variety of social situations, primarily in a clubhouse maintained by the Adolescent Study near the school playground. In this situation it was possible to observe and rate a youngster's "interest in the opposite sex," based on approved behavior, participation in dancing and other mixed social situations, and talking about the other sex. As might be expected, marked differences were observed in this trait: in each of six

[4] As previously noted, the measures reported up to this point are based on behavior among small groups of boys. Somewhat greater prestige differences are apparent, especially in the later years, when measures refer to behavior in mixed groups, or to reputation scores based on votes from both boys and girls (considered in a later section).

series of records, beginning at age thirteen-and-a-half, the early-maturing obtained average scores above the group mean, and the late-maturing were consistently below the group mean. In this as well as in attention-seeking and other expressive behavior, a tendency could be noted for the late-maturers to show their widest deviation from the early-maturers during the period when they were most different in physical respects; in senior high school the apparent differences diminished, but as will be seen in the subsequent discussion of reputation records, the development of a more mature pattern, in the late-maturers, does not necessarily imply a prompt change in their status in the peer culture.

The narrative records obtained in the clubhouse situation provide evidence of the numerous specific ways in which maturity differences are expressed. At a Saturday graduation party three of the early-maturers came to the party conspicuously late, a mark of sophistication not shown by any of the late-maturers. Three others had Saturday jobs, had been working all day and were eager to talk to adults about their work. Among the observer's comments about the early-maturers were such notations as "he dances well"; "seems to think of himself as an adult"; "acts a bit condescending"; "reserved, little energy output"; "ran, sat in the corner and flirted with Myra"; "cheek-to-cheek dancing"; "gay and assured, tried to cut in."

In contrast, these phrases described some of the boys who were of the same age but were late-maturing: "the first time I've ever seen him with a girl"; "he held his head tensely while dancing"; "didn't dance at all"; "acted extremely silly"; "Ronnie admitted he had been to only three dances before"; "Claude showed a beaming countenance at all times"; "began to wiggle and giggle."

REPUTATION WITH CLASSMATES

Another source of evidence concerning adolescent behavior and status is from the Reputation Test. Data are available from a series of tests in which classmates were asked to write down the name of anyone in the class conforming to certain descriptions. For example, "Here is someone who finds it hard to sit still in class," or at the other extreme, "Here is someone who can work quietly without moving around in his seat." Scores were obtained by determining the percentage of times a person was mentioned on a given trait description, and these measures were then transformed into standard scores in which 50 represented the "indifference point" (indicating no mentions at either extreme of the trait). Reputation scores are less differentiating than ratings; they tend to identify outstanding individuals, but may fail to distribute the middle range of cases who receive few or no mentions from their classmates. As a result differences between early- and late-maturing in average reputation scores are less marked than in average ratings by adults. However, a number of traits show differences which occur in the same direction on six testings, and are significant by the binomial test.

The late-maturing are consistently more "attention-getting," more "restless," more "assured in class," more "talkative," less "grown-up," and less likely to have older friends. On five out of six tests they are more "bossy," and less "good-looking."

Less consistency is found for traits which have been established as especially important for adolescent prestige. On judgments of "popular," "leader," "friendly," "daring," "active in games," and "humor about self," the late-maturing stand relatively well until the middle period of junior high school, and then tend to drop to lower status.

At the earlier ages the more active and energetic of those in the late-maturing group were not unsuccessful in winning social recognition. But the early-maturing were much more likely to get and maintain the kind of prestige accorded to athletes and officeholders. Two of the sixteen early-maturing boys became student body presidents, one was president of the boys' club (a position next in importance to that of student body president), several were elected to committee chairmanships, and four attained outstanding reputations as athletes. The sixteen late-maturing boys produced only one somewhat "important" officeholder (a class vice-president), and one athlete.

ADULT DIFFERENCES[5]

As noted in the introductory section of the present paper a follow-up was undertaken when the boys described in the foregoing pages had reached an average of 33 years of age. Eleven of the early-maturers and nine of the late-maturers were available for study at this age. Although some cases were lost from the original sample, the data of the follow-up group as reconstituted showed no substantial alteration in the adolescent differentials of the early- and late-maturing. What, now, are the differences between these groups at 33 years of age? The major findings are presented in Table 2.

The early-maturing average only half an inch taller, at 5 feet 10 inches; and 7 pounds heavier, at 172 pounds. These differences are not significant. In body build, the prediction is that the early-maturing would be more mesomorphic. The tendency is in this direction, but the differences are not significant. The chief thing to note is the wide range of physiques within each group (both in adolescence and in adulthood) and the marked consistency over the years. A slight change is apparent in the direction of

[5] See Footnote 1, p. 126, for reference to source of this section on adult differences.

TABLE 2. Summary of Statistical Findings for the Follow-up Comparisons

Physical Measures: Means

	Early		Late	
	Age 14	Age 33	Age 14	Age 33
Height	5 ft. 8 in.	5 ft. 10 in.	5 ft.	5 ft. 9½ in.
Weight	126.9 lb.	172 lb.	93.2 lb.	165 lb.
Endormorphy[a]	2.6	3.1	3.1	3.3
Mesomorphy[a]	4.5	4.6	3.9	4.3
Ectomorphy[a]	3.4	3.4	3.7	3.7

Psychological Scales

	Early	Late	Signif. of Difference[b]	r^c	Signif. Level
California Psychological Inventory					
Good Impression	25.6	15.7	.006	.50	<.01
Flexibility	9.7	13.8	.05	−.23	
Socialization[d]	13.9	20.3	.07	−.40	<.01
Impulsivity	17.1	23.4	.13	−.31	<.05
Dominance	31.7	27.4	.17	.26	
Responsibility	32.9	30.0	.19	.35	<.05
Edwards Personal Preference Schedule					
Dominance	19.4	12.6	.04	.40	<.01
Succorance	7.1	12.4	.05	−.48	<.01

[a] Rating on 7-point scale; 7 is high.
[b] Significance level, Wilcoxon Rank Test.
[c] Pearson product-moment correlation with skeletal age/chronological age, at 15 years.
[d] A low score indicates "socialization."

greater mesomorphy in eight of the nine late-maturing and they now present a somewhat more developed and sturdy appearance.

Some differences would be expected in constitutional indices of masculinity. Among the late-maturing, the majority of the original study and of those included in the follow-up were rated as having a deficiency in masculine development, at age 17. At age 33, however, Sheldon ratings of gynandromorphy in the two groups showed considerable overlap and only a small and nonsignificant difference in favor of the early-maturing.

Personality differences in adult life have been examined with reference to a number of criteria. Two sources of data to be considered here are Gough's California Psychological Inventory and the Edwards Personal Preference Schedule. The first of these attempts to appraise aspects of character and temperament which are significant for social living and interpersonal behavior and which are related to personal maturity and creative achievement. Eighteen scales are available which describe individuals in terms of social responsibility, tolerance, flexibility, academic motivation, self-control and the like.

Most of the above scales did not show significant differences between the groups. One outstanding exception is the scale entitled "good impression," (interest in, and capacity for, creating a "good impression" on others). Differences here favored the early-maturing with a significance at the .006 level. Some of the interpretative phrases associated with high scores on this scale include: "is turned to for advice and reassurance; fatherly; is concerned with making a good impression; is persistent in working toward his goal." High scorers on this "Gi" scale are also designated as responsible, cooperative, enterprising, sociable and warm.

In our groups the early-maturing tend in addition to obtain higher scores on the C. P. I. scales for socialization, dominance, self-control, and responsibility. Although none of these shows differences at a significance level better than .07, it is true that the early-maturing have high average scores and present a consistently favorable personality picture with regard to these important social variables.

The phrases and adjectives associated with high scores on these five scales (good impression, socialization, dominance, self-control, and responsibility) remind us strikingly of the social behavior and personal traits attributed, by their peers and by adults, to the early-maturing boys in adolescence. For the total group of 43 boys thus far included in the follow-up, a correlation of .50 (significant at the .01 level) was found between the "good impression" score on the C. P. I., and their level of skeletal maturity 18 years earlier. The corresponding Pearson r for the socialization score at age 33, and skeletal maturity at age 15, was .40, significant at the .01 level. For these correlations, skeletal quotients were computed (skeletal age over chronological age), to make allowance for slight differences in the age at which the skeletal X-rays were obtained.

One other scale yields an interesting difference, significant at the .05 level. This is the scale for what has been termed "flexibility." Those who score high on this scale are described by Gough as tending to be rebellious, touchy, impulsive, self-indulgent, assertive, and also insightful. Low scorers are described as deliberate, methodical, industrious, rigid, mannerly, overly-controlling of impulses, compliant. In these terms, the late-maturers tend to be more "flexible" than the early-maturers.

We might hazard the guess that some of the little boy behavior—the impulsiveness, playfulness and also the "touchiness" repeatedly noted in late-maturing adolescents—is mirrored in the description of high scorers on this scale. We might speculate further that in the course of having to adapt to difficult status problems, the late-maturers have gained some insights and are indeed more flexible, while the early-maturing, capitalizing on their ability to make a good impression, may have clung to their earlier success pattern to the extent of becoming somewhat rigid or over-controlled.

On the Edwards Personal Preference Schedule, two of the scales are discriminating for our groups at the 4 and 5 per cent levels respectively. The early-maturing group scores high on the *dominance* scale: "to be a leader, persuade, argue for a point of view," while the late-maturing score high in *succorance:* "to seek encouragement, to be helped by others, to have a fuss made over one when hurt." For the total group of 40 who took the Edwards test at around age 33, skeletal maturing at age 17 correlated .40 with dominance, and —.48 with succorance (both significant at the .01 level).

To those of us who have known these young men for over 20 years, some of the most interesting questions remain to be answered. What have been their successes and failures in achieving occupational and personal goals? All are married, and in each group the present number of children averages 2.3. Socio-economic ratings, based on homes and neighborhoods, show no differences for the two groups. There are no significant differences in average educational level, although a slightly higher proportion of the later-maturing have college degrees and the only college teacher is in this group.

There is some indication that more of the early-maturing have attained vocational goals which are satisfying and status-conferring. Among this group five are in professional careers; four are executives; one is a skilled mechanic and one in a clerical position. Of the executives, three are in positions of somewhat impressive status.

Among the late-maturing, four are in professions, two are still university students, two are salesmen, and one is a carpenter. None has attained an important managerial position and several, by their own account and the nature of their work, seem somewhat precariously unsettled.

CONCLUSIONS

A general picture emerges from the various ratings and characterizations of these two contrasting groups of boys. Those who are physically accelerated are usually accepted and treated by adults and other children as more mature. They appear to have relatively little need to strive for status. From their ranks come the outstanding student body leaders in senior high school. In contrast, the physically retarded boys exhibit many forms of relatively immature behavior: this may be in part because others tend to treat them as the little boys they appear to be. Furthermore, a fair proportion of these boys give evidence of needing to counteract their physical disadvantage in some way—usually by greater activity and striving for attention, although in some cases by withdrawal.

It is doubtful if any single event in the maturing process for boys can be compared in psychological importance to the menarche in girls. Skeletal age, as a measure of maturing, is relatively satisfactory with regard to reliability and stability. It is applicable at all ages from birth to adulthood, and is therefore well adapted to longitudinal studies of the same individuals throughout their period of growth. But skeletal age is revealed only by X-ray. Individual differences in this variable are hidden, and hence have received no cultural value-assessments. Feelings of perplexity or inferiority may arise, in relation to early or late skeletal maturing, only in so far as skeletal age is related to other physical features (such as size, strength, primary or secondary sexual characteristics) or to psychological changes in adolescence.[6]

It is not surprising that those who are retarded in skeletal development should often be directly aware of other aspects of physical retardation, and it is not surprising that this should lead to anxiety. We have seen, however, that there are many complicating factors, which make it difficult to predict the course which any individual adjustment will take. Some of our late-maturing boys enjoyed a degree of personal security, and status in other areas, which helped to balance their temporary physical inadequacies. Some of the early-maturing boys with fine physiques, nevertheless had disturbing accompaniments of rapid growth (such as severe acne), which tended to offset other advantages.

Our findings give clear evidence of the effect of physical maturing upon behavior. Perhaps of greater importance, however, is the repeated demonstration of the multiplicity of factors, psychological and cultural as well as physical, which contribute to the formation of basic personality patterns.

When available members of these groups were followed up at about age 33, it appeared that the adolescent handicaps and advantages associated with late- or early-maturing carry over into adulthood to some extent, and perhaps to a greater extent in psychological than in physical characteristics.

---

[6] Although skeletal age is highly correlated with other (more external) aspects of physical maturing, we must expect some regression toward the mean in such factors as growth of pubic hair, or other sexual characteristics, among boys selected at the extremes in skeletal maturing.

10

Changes in Perception of Verticality During the Adult Years[*]

Peter E. Comalli, Jr., Seymour Wapner,

and Heinz Werner

At one point or more during childhood many individuals heard their parents remark that "Grandfather (or Grandmother) is becoming childish." And true enough to youthful eyes, it probably did appear at the time that he (or she) was becoming shorter, thinner, and generally smaller in every way. It was also probably noticed that Grandfather sometimes failed to finish a story or that occasionally he became childishly jealous or unduly secretive. Despite such apparent regressions toward less mature behavior, one usually sensed, even as a child, that Grandfather or Grandmother could be turned to for a kind of detached and enduring wisdom that was not always available from one's parents. The following report by Drs. Comalli, Wapner, and Werner is related to the question of which psychological functions are lost in old age and which ones are retained relatively intact, if not necessarily distilled into something distinctly superior by the passage of time. These investigators suggest that oldsters do develop a more egocentric orientation, at least in their perceptions, which is more similar to that of childhood than to that held in adulthood; however, old people do not display any indications of reverting to the stimulus boundedness so characteristic of children's perceptions. Although this is only a tiny beginning toward answering the larger question of what is lost and what is retained in the psychological functions of the aged, it is sufficient to negate the generalization that old people simply regress to earlier patterns of behavior.

Recently we published a monograph (Wapner and Werner, 1957) devoted to the problem of perceptual development, or more specifically to the

* Adapted and abridged from Peter E. Comalli, Jr., Seymour Wapner, and Heinz Werner, "Perception of Verticality in Middle and Old Age," *Journal of Psychology,* 1959, Vol. 47, pp. 259-266. (With permission of the authors and The Journal Press.)

changes in spatial organization that occur during the course of growth. The study was undertaken within sensory-tonic theory which deals with perception in terms of "object organism" relationships and general developmental theory that specifies the ontogenetic changes in this relationship in terms of differentiation.

A number of experimental situations were employed in that study of perceptual development, one of which, pertinent to the present paper, concerns the perception of verticality. With subjects ranging in age from 6 to 20 years, two significant developmental trends in the perception of verticality were found. One concerns the effect of body tilt: within the lower age levels, a luminescent rod in a darkroom is perceived as vertical when tilted to the side at which the body is tilted, in contrast to higher age levels where it is perceived as vertical when tilted opposite the side of body tilt. The second effect is that of "starting position," i.e., the rotation of the apparent vertical to the side at which the rod is placed at the beginning of a trial; this effect is greatest for the lowest age levels and decreases with increase in age. The results were interpreted as being consonant with the general developmental principle that with increase in age there is increasing differentiation of self and object. Specifically, it was assumed that this lack of differentiation at the early age levels is manifested in two ways: (a) by "egocentricity," i.e., determination of the object world through the self (body) as referent, as evidenced by the effect of body tilt; and (b) by "stimulus boundedness," i.e., inordinate impact of initially presented stimuli, as evidenced by the effect of starting position.

The present study again is concerned with developmental changes in spatial organization, as reflected in perception of verticality, but deals with such changes that occur beyond the 20 year age level and in particular in old age; its further purpose is to compare these changes with those obtaining at younger age levels so that a total picture will be gained of the development of spatial organization between 6 to 80 years of age.

PROCEDURE

The Task. The task for S was to adjust, in a dark room, a luminescent rod so that it appeared vertical. The rod, 30 in. long and 1 in. wide, was rotated in the fronto-parallel plane and pivoted at its center; its angular displacement from the perpendicular was measured in half degrees. The task of adjusting the rod to apparent verticality was carried out under 12 conditions, viz., 3 conditions of body position (30° left tilt; erect; 30° right tilt) in combination with four conditions of starting position of the rod (30° left; 10° left; 10° right; 30° right). A different random order of presentation of trials was used for each S.

S sat in a chair which was pivoted below the seat permitting left and right tilts. The chair was provided with head rest, sides, and back, to make certain that the body was held firmly in place. While *S* was blindfolded, the chair and rod were set into positions required for the particular trial. *S,* after opening his eyes, instructed *E* to move the rod till it appeared vertical to *S*. *E* followed *S*'s instructions by moving the rod first in 2° steps, and finally in smaller steps. After adjustment of the rod to a physical position in which it appeared vertical, *S* was again blindfolded until the beginning of the next trial.

Measures Employed. The position in which the rod looked vertical to *S* (position of apparent vertical) was measured in degrees of deviation from the objective vertical (plumb line). Arbitrarily, an angular position clockwise of objective vertical, as viewed by *S,* is designated "+" (right tilt); and an angular position counterclockwise of objective vertical as "—" (left tilt).

SUBJECTS

A total of 75 men between the ages 20 and 80 were tested, 10 at each semidecade from 20 to 50 and 15 between 65 and 80. The *S*s between the ages of 20 and 50 were drawn from the Clark University Evening College and the local community; those between 65 and 80 years were drawn from a community old-age club.

RESULTS

Effect of Body Tilt. If one combines the data of the present study with those obtained previously for younger ages, a very interesting result becomes apparent. Figure 1 plots the mean positions of apparent vertical under the three body positions for the various age levels. Considering the effect of

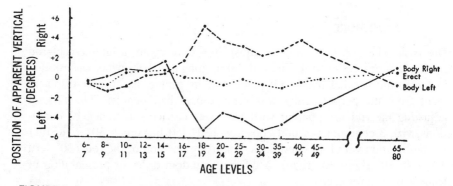

FIGURE 1. Developmental Changes in Effect of Body Tilt on Perception of Verticality Between 6 and 80 Years of Age.

body tilt for ages 20–50 there is confirmation of a finding that has been substantiated in many studies, viz., with body tilted left the apparent vertical is rotated to the right, and with the body right the apparent vertical is rotated to the left. In contrast, for both young boys, 6–15, and older men, 65–80, the apparent vertical is located at the same side as body tilt. The shift in the present study in the tilt relation of body and rod in old age, 65–80, as compared to ages 20–50 is statistically significant. Thus, at age levels 6–15, the apparent vertical is located to the same side as body tilt. Beyond the age of 15 the apparent vertical is located *opposite* body tilt. This relationship begins to reverse itself at about 45 years of age so that for the 65–80 age group the same relationship found at the early age level obtains. The interaction between age and body tilt is significant beyond the .01 level of confidence.

Starting Position. As mentioned above, by starting position effect is meant the influence of the position of the rod at the start of a trial on the final position in which it is seen as vertical. The developmental results for starting position from the present study, ages 20–80, are combined with a previous study covering ages 6–19 in Figure 2. The mean position of apparent vertical under the four starting positions of the rod is shown for the various age levels. The graph shows the effect demonstrated in many other studies with adults, viz., the physical position of apparent vertical is rotated relatively to the left under left starting position and relatively to the right under right starting position. The curves clearly indicate a significant decrease in the starting position effect between 6 and 19 years of age. Though there are fluctuations in the curves, no consistent developmental change is apparent

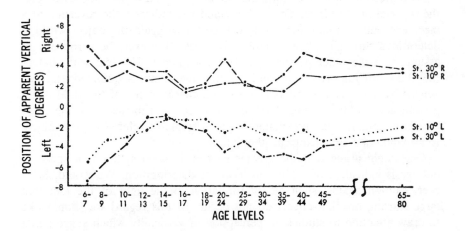

FIGURE 2. Developmental Changes in Effect of Starting Position on Perception of Verticality Between 6 and 80 Years of Age.

after age 19. The interaction of age and starting position is not significant for the adult years, 20–80.

SUMMARY AND DISCUSSION

The present investigation, together with the previous study concerned with early age levels, contributes to our knowledge concerning changes in spatial organization that occur through life. Striking differences in effect of body tilt depending on age level were found: for young boys 6–15 the apparent vertical is located to the *same* side as body tilt; between 16 and 50, however, the opposite effect occurs, viz., apparent vertical is located to the *opposite* side of body tilt; finally in older men, 65–80, the apparent vertical is again located to the *same* side of body tilt. The developmental changes in effect of starting position were found to occur only within the younger age range, viz., starting position effect is greatest at the lowest age level and decreases markedly until the 19-year level; following this there are no consistent developmental changes throughout the age levels studied.

Both of these effects occurring during the period of growth through adolescence were interpreted by us as an expression of the orthogenetic principle which states that the development proceeds from a state of globality, and lack of differentiation—in this case between self (own body) and object—to a state of increased differentiation. We interpret our results in accordance with this principle by assuming that at early stages of development lack of differentiation of self and object manifests itself in two ways: (*a*) by egocentricity—i.e., the formation of a frame of reference whereby the stimuli are interpreted in terms of body position; and (*b*) by stimulus boundedness—which refers to the inordinate impact of object stimuli.

As to our findings concerning the old age groups it is here suggested that the reversal in the tilt relation of body and rod indicates the reverting to a more egocentric organization of space, i.e., once again the object world is determined through self as referent. It would, however, be erroneous to assume that the older person operates in a manner identical with that of the child. An important difference is that the stimulus boundedness, evidenced by the large starting position effect, characteristic of the child is not present in the older person. That means, in contrast to the child, the older person maintains a relatively stable spatial frame of references not subject to the whim of every change in stimulation.

One might argue that the greater egocentric determination of space in old age is indicative of senility in terms of deterioration. We would, however, caution against such an interpretation in the light of the fact that large starting position effects do not occur. In this regard we should like to draw attention to studies on perception of verticality which suggest that stimulus boundedness, as indicated by large starting position effects, are associated with brain damage (Teuber and Liebert, 1958). Therefore, we would argue that the absence of increased starting position effects in old age coupled with egocentric position of the apparent vertical would define changes in spatial organization occurring in old age as part of normal ontogenetic development. It remains for future studies to determine whether a distinction can be made between normal and pathological perceptual changes in old age, one evidenced by the absence and the other by the presence of large starting position effects.

Part III

PROCESSES OF LEARNING AND PSYCHOLOGICAL ADJUSTMENT

THE LEARNING process has piqued man's curiosity since the earliest days of recorded history. Aristotle, the famous Greek philosopher who wrote on biological topics, proposed a number of rather simple principles to explain the manner in which learning takes place. Some later philosophers have considered the learning process as central to the problem of understanding man's cultural superiority over lower animals.

Near the close of the nineteenth and the beginning of the twentieth century the pioneer investigations of Ebbinghaus, Pavlov, and Thorndike brought the learning problem into the psychological laboratory. Since that time a large mass of data has been collected which is relevant to the conditions under which man learns new responses and discards old ones that are no longer useful to him.

How does man acquire the many symbolic concepts that do so much to facilitate his control over environmental circumstances—both those that are obstacles to and those that provide opportunities for the satisfaction of his needs? How does he use these concepts to solve problems on a "reasoning" basis? How can he "transfer" previous responses to a new problem in such a way that satisfactory adjustment takes place almost immediately? Why do some human individuals persistently strive for higher and higher levels of achievement? These are only a few of the questions for which philosophers and psychologists have sought—and continue to seek—acceptable answers.

The following papers are merely representative samples of the numerous investigations psychologists have conducted in the area of human learning. Bayley's report throws new light on what happens to learning aptitudes during the first four decades of life. This research is especially important because of its longitudinal design. The paper by Korchin and Basowitz is concerned with the effects of aging on different kinds of learning and adjustment capacities in the later years of life. These findings have direct implications for educational programs in which older adults are enrolled. The paper by Welford reports his insightful views of what changes in the psychoneurological functions occur during the life span and how these changes affect the learning and adjustment abilities of individuals during different periods of the ontogenetic span.

Although the search by contemporary psychologists for the major dimensions and dynamics of learning is still in progress, several important advances have been made to date. For example, the paper by Stevenson and Zigler shows that very young children learn to respond to the ever variable environment in a manner that tends to maximize the probability that they will be positively reinforced or rewarded. Egon Brunswik wrote convincingly on the significance of this manner of "reading" the environment for the goal strivings of human beings. Spiker, Gerjuoy, and Shepard document the function of language skills in the solution of a problem. Just how language serves as a mediating process in learning to solve problems is as yet conceptually vague; however, more and more developmental psychologists are turning their research efforts toward the field of verbal learning, apparently with the conviction that here lies the solution to the riddle of generalization and transfer so obviously important in human behavior.

At this point the reader's attention should be called to the several theories of learning that have been developed to explain what is now known about the learning process.[1] These various theories will have to be scientifically evaluated over the years on the basis of their rigor, range, and fruitfulness in interrelating and "ordering" the available factual information. Although some of the current theories of learning are "promising," no one of them is completely acceptable to a majority of contemporary psychologists.

---

[1] For a review of modern learning theories, see Ernest R. Hilgard and Gordon H. Bower, *Theories of Learning* (3rd ed.) (New York: Appleton-Century-Crofts, 1966).

11

Problem Solving and Verbal Mediation[*]

Charles C. Spiker, Irma R. Gerjuoy, and Winifred O. Shepard

One of the most baffling conceptual problems confronting modern psychology is the construction of a theoretical model to guide our groping efforts in the direction of understanding the role of verbal responses in learning, discrimination, generalization and transfer, and problem solving. It seems intuitively axiomatic that verbalized symbols sustain the higher mental processes that we call thinking. On the basis of introspection, individuals report "talking to themselves," asking themselves questions, weighing alternative answers, and making decisions. Watson, the pioneer American behaviorist, proposed that thinking is nothing more than subvocal speech. Subsequent research and theory have failed to support this extreme position, but it would be difficult to deny that verbalization very frequently accompanies learning and that it appears to be a useful guide in discrimination, generalization, and problem solving. In the present report, Dr. Spiker and his collaborators show that children who possess a verbal concept of middle-sizedness are able to use this language skill (or some associated function) in solving problems that involve the generalization or transfer of this concept to transposed situations. Research findings of this very basic type will probably have to accumulate for a long time to come, before a fruitful model of language functions in the higher mental processes can be constructed, but this study and a few others similar in design mark a beginning.

There has been a recent increasing interest in the relationship between the degree to which verbal names for stimuli are available to S and his subsequent discrimination performance with these stimuli. Several experi-

* From Charles C. Spiker, Irma R. Gerjuoy, and Winifred O. Shepard, "Children's Concept of Middle-sizedness and Performance on the Intermediate Size Problem," *Journal of Comparative and Physiological Psychology*, 1956, Vol. 49, pp. 416-419. (With permission of the authors and the American Psychological Association.)

ments with adults (Joan Cantor, 1955; Gagné and Baker, 1950; Goss, 1953; Rossman and Goss, 1951) and with children (Cantor, 1955; Gerjuoy, 1953; Shepard, 1954) have shown facilitation of discrimination learning following the learning of distinctive verbal responses to the discriminal stimuli. These experiments have involved nonrelational stimuli and verbal responses. The theoretical notions that have been utilized are "stimulus predifferentiation" as proposed by Gagné and Baker (1950) and "acquired distinctiveness of cues" as elaborated by Dollard and Miller (1950).

The present experiment attempts to determine the effect of the possession of a relational concept, middle-sizedness, upon the rate of learning to select the intermediate sized of three stimuli. Two groups of Ss were selected in terms of their performance on a test designed to determine whether or not the concept was understood. One-half of those Ss who understood and one-half of those who did not understand the concept were given a discrimination problem requiring a relational solution—that is to say, a problem in which the absolute size of the intermediate stimulus varied from trial to trial. The other halves of each of these groups were given a similar problem in which the intermediate stimulus was of the same size from trial to trial. Assuming that the possession of the relational concept facilitates relational learning, it is expected that the difference between the concept and no-concept groups will be greater on the relational than on the nonrelational problem. Statistically stated, the hypothesis is that there will be a significant interaction between level of understanding the concept and the type of criterion task.

METHOD

Subjects. The Ss were children from the preschool laboratories of the Iowa Child Welfare Research Station. They ranged in age from 40 to 67 months. The majority had had previous experience in experiments requiring discrimination learning with two-stimulus problems. So far as could be determined, none had served in experiments requiring the selection of the middle-sized of three stimuli. The majority of Ss were therefore familiar with similar experimental procedures at the time the experiment was begun, and in addition, the Es spent several hours in the preschool groups becoming acquainted with the Ss prior to the experiment.

Preliminary Test. From one to two weeks prior to the main experiment, 84 Ss were given a pretest during which E attempted to elicit from them the verbal response, "middle-sized" or "medium-sized." A total of six cards was constructed for this purpose, each having three stimulus elements which were homogeneous in form but different in area in the ratio 1:2:4. Each of three different forms (triangles, trapezoids, and circles) was represented twice in the series of six cards. These cards included two (one with triangles and one with trapezoids) with elements having areas of 8, 4, and 2 sq. in.: two (circles and trapezoids), of 4, 2, and 1 sq. in.; and two (circles and triangles), of 2, 1, and ½ sq. in.

The E first presented to S each of the six cards, saying each time, "This is the big one (pointing to the largest element), this is the little one (pointing to the smallest element), and this is the ——————?" If S verbalized "middle-sized," "medium-sized," or "medium one," to each of the six cards, the pretest was discontinued. If S failed to verbalize one of these names to each card, the test was continued by instructing S to put a finger on the "middle-sized" one. When all six cards had been presented in this way, the pretest was discontinued regardless of S's performance.[1]

On the basis of their performance on the pretest, two groups of 30 Ss each were selected. In one group, the "concept" group, were placed those Ss who responded consistently with one of the conventional terms for middle-sizedness. Those Ss were put in the "no-concept" group who did not use the conventional terms at all, who were not able to point consistently to the middle-sized stimulus upon instruction, and who did not select consistently the large or small stimulus upon being instructed to select the middle-sized stimulus.[2]

Stimuli for the Main Experiment. The stimuli were squares cut from black construction paper and pasted on white cardboard. The areas of the squares were ¼, ½, 1, 2, 4, 8, and 16 sq. in. The squares were arranged on the backgrounds in five groups of three in such a way that the ratio of the areas, from the smallest to the largest, was always 1:2:4. The three squares in each of the five resulting sets (size-series) were placed in the six possible spatial orders, generating a total of 30 cards differing from each other in the absolute sizes of the squares and/or in the spatial positions of the large, small, and middle-sized squares.

These stimulus materials were so arranged that two tasks were formed. Each S given Task A (the nonrelational task) was presented with just one

[1] Additional work suggests that it is advisable to use a third phase of the test for those Ss who respond consistently in the first phase with a name other than conventional terms for middle-sizedness, e.g., "mama one," "the kind of large one," etc. In the third phase, E instructs S to point to the "mama one," "the kind of large one," etc. Some such Ss are able to select consistently the middle-sized stimulus, and subsequently tend to learn the discrimination problems in much the same way as Ss who use the conventional names.

[2] This latter criterion was adopted after discovering that Ss who, in the second phase of the pretest, tended to respond consistently to the large or to the small stimuli subsequently learned the discrimination problem in much the same way as Ss who used the concept middle-sized correctly. Presumably, such Ss have had sufficient experience with the relational concepts "larger than" and "smaller than" that they are able to learn rather quickly to respond to the one that is not the larger and not the smaller of three stimuli.

of the five size-series so that the correct (middle-sized) stimulus was of the same absolute size from trial to trial. The six cards in a given size-series were presented to S five times each, providing a total of 30 trials. Each S given Task B (the relational task) was given all five size-series, the 30 cards being presented in a random order, providing a total of 30 trials. Thus, Task A required the Ss to select the middle-sized stimulus on each trial, and this stimulus was always of the same absolute size from trial to trial. Task B required the Ss to select the middle-sized stimulus on each trial, but the correct stimulus varied in absolute size from trial to trial. Or, again, while each S given Task A was required to select, on each of 30 trials, a stimulus of a given size when it was presented with a larger and a smaller one, each S given Task B was in effect presented with five such problems and allowed only six trials on each.

Experimental Design. The experiment was designed as a 2 x 2 factorial, with Tasks A and B constituting one factor, the two levels of understanding the concept "middle-sized" representing the second. Fifteen Ss from each concept level were assigned at random to each of the two tasks, thus yielding four groups. One group, C-A, consisted of Ss who knew the concept and were given Task A; a second group, C-B, who knew the concept and were given Task B; a third, NC-A, not knowing the concept given Task A; and a fourth, NC-B, not knowing the concept and given Task B. Each fifth of the Ss in Groups C-A and NC-A was assigned just one of the five stimulus size-series. This procedure was adopted in order to control for the possibility that the five size-series differed in difficulty due to differential discriminability of the stimuli.

Procedure. The S was brought into the experimental room and given the preliminary test. Following the test, he was shown the contents of a bag of dime-store toys and told that he would later play a game in which he would have a chance to win one of the toys. A few days later, he returned to the experimental room and was seated at a small table across from E. The S was instructed that he was going to play a game in which he would be able to win some money and that when he had won enough money, he would be able to buy one of the toys. The stimulus cards were then presented one at a time. The S was instructed on each trial to put a finger on one of the squares. If the square selected by S was the middle-sized one, E gave S a toy coin. If the selected square was either the large or the small one, S was not given a coin and E pointed to the middle-sized one, informing S that it was the correct one. The term "middle-sized" was never used in E's instructions to S. The E recorded on prepared record sheets each of S's choices, in terms of both the spatial position of the choice and the relative size of the stimulus selected. The order of presenting the stimulus complexes was the same for all Ss receiving Task A, and for all Ss receiving Task B.

TABLE 1. Means and Standard Deviations of Number of Correct Responses in 30 Trials

| Learning Task | Concept of Middle-sizedness | | | |
| | Concept | | No-Concept | |
	Mean	SD	Mean	SD
Nonrelational (A)	24.60	7.72	22.60	7.65
Relational (B)	21.40	8.81	10.20	2.47

RESULTS

The number of correct responses in 30 trials was determined for each S. The means and standard deviations for the four groups are presented in Table 1. An analysis of variance was performed and the results are shown in Table 2. Task B was significantly more difficult than Task A ($p < .001$), and the "concept" groups performed significantly better than the "no-concept" groups ($p < .001$). The interaction between concept levels and tasks is significant at the .025 level, indicating that the difference between the concept levels was significantly greater for Task B than for Task A.

As may be noted in Table 1, the standard deviation of Group NC-B is less than those for the other groups. This difference proves significant at less than the .01 level. Thus, it seems desirable to supplement the analysis of variance with nonparametric tests to determine whether or not the differences exposed by the analysis of variance may be attributed entirely to differences in variabilities. A criterion of 10 correct responses in the last 12 trials was arbitrarily chosen to define learning. Table 3 presents the number of Ss who met and the number who did not meet this criterion within each group. The χ^2 obtained for the 2×4 table was 26.9, ($p < .001$, $df = 3$.). When Group NC-B is eliminated from the table, the resulting χ^2 is 0.96 ($p > .50$, $df = 2$). When Group NC-B is compared with the other three groups combined, the χ^2 corrected for continuity is 22.9 ($p < .001$, $df = 1$).

The Mann-Whitney U test (1947) was applied to compare Group NC-B with C-B and with NC-A, using the number of correct responses in 30

TABLE 2. Summary of Analysis of Variance of Number of Correct Responses in 30 Trials

Source	df	Mean Square	F	p
Tasks (T)	1	653.4	12.91	.001
Concepts (C)	1	912.6	18.04	.001
T x C	1	317.6	6.28	.025
Within cells	56	50.6		
Total	59			

TABLE 3. Number of Ss in Each Group Meeting or Not Meeting Criterion of Ten Correct of Last Twelve Choices

Group	Learners	Nonlearners	Total
C-A	12	3	15
NC-A	12	3	15
C-B	10	5	15
NC-B	0	15	15

trials as the response measure. The obtained U in each case was significant at less than the .01 level. Groups C-A and NC-B, on the other hand, were compared by the more sensitive t test. The resulting t value was .34 $(p > .70)$.

The analyses indicate that Group NC-B performed at a significantly lower level than did the other three groups, whereas the hypothesis is tenable that the latter performed at about the same level.

DISCUSSION

The results of the experiment support the expectation that Ss who understand the verbal concept of middle-sizedness perform significantly better on the relational task than Ss who do not understand the concept, and that understanding the concept did not appreciably affect performance on a task that could be solved on a nonrelational basis. The question arises as to the plausibility of accounting for the difference between Groups C-B and NC-B in terms other than the possession of the concept. In any experiment in which the major variable is varied by subject selection rather than by experimental manipulation, an unequivocal answer to such a question cannot be given. In the present case, it is possible to eliminate one obvious possibility—chronological age. Although the concept groups averaged approximately 5½ months older than the no-concept groups, $(p < .01)$, the correlation between chronological age and number of correct responses in 30 trials is .08 for the nonrelational task and —.05 for the relational task.

It seems worth while to point out the relationship between the present experiment and the ones conducted by Kuenne (1946) and by Alberts and Ehrenfreund (1951). These investigators were concerned with the study of transposition behavior of children in the two-stimulus size problem as a function of mental age and chronological age, on the assumption that these variables reflected concept ability. Task B in this experiment may be conceived as a three-stimulus transposition problem, in which transposition occurs or does not occur from one trial to the next. The concept levels are substituted for the MA or CA levels used by the earlier investigators. Thus, the results obtained support the contention of Kuenne

(1946) that if *S* has appropriate concepts available (e.g., possession of the concept of middle-sizedness), transposition will be more likely to occur.

SUMMARY

The experiment was designed to test the hypothesis that the learning of a discrimination problem involving selection of the intermediate sized of three stimuli, where the absolute size of the stimuli vary from trial to trial, is facilitated by *S*'s possession of the verbal concept middle-sized. Sixty children were classified into two equal-size groups in terms of their levels of understanding of the concept middle-sizedness. One-half of each of these two groups was rewarded for selecting the middle-sized of three stimuli, where the absolute size of the stimuli varied from trial to trial. The other half of each of these groups was rewarded for selecting the middle-sized of three stimuli, where the absolute size of the stimuli remained constant from trial to trial. The results indicated that an understanding of the concept of middle-sizedness facilitated learning of the relational task more than it did the learning of the nonrelational task. These results were considered in relation to the findings of Kuenne (1946) and Alberts and Ehrenfreund (1951).

12

Probability Learning in Children[*]

Harold W. Stevenson and Edward F. Zigler

When an individual is faced with alternative but equally plausible ways of acting, none of which is successful every time in enabling him to reach the desired goal, he tends with the passage of time to try and retry all of the "reasonable" courses of responding. When the alternatives are clearly limited, the individual tries a particular one of them in approximate proportion to the percentage of times it has been previously successful in gaining positive reinforcement. For example, the professional gambler very seldom "draws to an inside straight,"

[*] From Harold W. Stevenson and Edward F. Zigler, "Probability Learning in Children," *Journal of Experimental Psychology*, 1958, Vol. 56, pp. 185-192. (With permission of the authors and the American Psychological Association.)

because prior experience (and formal knowledge of probabilities) indicates that this response is infrequently successful. However upon highly infrequent occasions the skillful gambler will risk this draw because it sometimes works. This sampling of stimulus and response universes that are seemingly appropriate to the solution of a given problem has been loosely conceptualized in Guthrie's contiguity theory of learning and given more rigorous attention in the recent statistical model detailed by Estes. In the following empirical study, Dr. Stevenson and Dr. Zigler show that children with mental ages of approximately six years (both normals and chronologically older feebleminded subjects) learn to respond to selectively reinforced alternatives in about the same ways as do adults. These investigators have further shown that it is possible not only to predict but also to manipulate the probabilities of different responses by special pre-experimental experiences that transfer to a later experimental situation.

There has been a great deal of interest during recent years in the investigation of probability learning in human Ss. In a large number of studies (Anderson and Grant, 1957; Estes, 1954; Estes and Straughn, 1954; Humphreys, 1939; Grant, Hake and Hornseth, 1951; Jarvik, 1951; Neimark, 1956) it was been found that Ss tend to match the stimulus probabilities with their guesses. At the same time, it has been found that under certain conditions Ss tend to maximize their frequency of choosing the more frequently reinforced stimulus. Among these are the presentation of a gambling task or a game of skill rather than a problem-solving task (Goodnow, 1955; Goodnow and Postman, 1955), an increased number of training trials (Detambel, 1955; Gardner, 1957), the presence of a distracting stimulus (Straughn, 1956; Wyckoff and Sidowski, 1955), and the lack of information concerning the appropriateness of some responses (Brand, Sakoda and Woods, 1957; Detambel, 1955; Neimark, 1956).

These studies have been done primarily with college students as Ss. It would be of interest to determine whether behavior similar to that of these Ss might be found with other populations of Ss, and to explore other conditions which might influence the tendency of Ss to choose the more frequently reinforcing stimulus. The present study, therefore, is concerned with testing normal and institutionalized feebleminded children in a situation similar to that which has been presented to adult Ss, and with determining whether the behavior of normal children in a probability learning task can be influenced by pretraining experience with different probabilities of reinforcement. Three experiments are presented and the hypotheses tested in each are discussed in later sections.

EXPERIMENT I

The purpose of this experiment is to determine whether the responses of normal children in a probability learning task are similar to those of adult Ss. A three-choice, contingent procedure was used in which the response to only one stimulus was reinforced. In this situation, adult Ss have been found (Neimark, 1956) to show a rapid increase in frequency of choice of the reinforced stimulus and to reach an asymptotic level of response slightly above that corresponding to the frequency of reinforcement.

Method. *Subjects.* The Ss consisted of 45 children attending nursery schools in Austin, Texas. The Ss were selected at random from among children of the appropriate CA enrolled in the schools. The average CA was 5.5 yr.

Apparatus. The apparatus consisted of a yellow vertical panel 22 inches long and 16 inches high on which was centered a row of three identical black knobs. The knobs, 1¾ inches in diameter, projected 1 in. from the panel and were 2 inches apart. A red signal light was mounted on the midline, 2 inches from the top of the panel, and a hole through which marbles were delivered was centered 7 inches from the bottom of the panel. The marbles fell from the hole into a small enclosed box. The box had a clear plastic top and front which enabled S to see the marbles but not to handle them.

A mechanism behind the panel provided for the dispensing of the marbles and for the measurement of latency of response. The switch by which E turned on the signal light also turned on an electric timer. When S pushed one of the knobs, the light was automatically turned off and the timer stopped. In addition, the knob dislodged a marble which fell down a chute into the box.

Procedure. The S was seated in front of the apparatus and was told that he was to play a game. The E demonstrated the apparatus and said, "When the light comes on, you push one of the knobs. If you push the correct knob a marble comes out here like this. Now every time the light comes on you push the knob that you think will get you the marble. Remember, just push one knob each time the light comes on." The S was told that he was to get as many marbles as he could and when the game was over he could choose two toys from a selection of toys including balloons, plastic figures, etc., which E showed him. The E took a position behind the apparatus and did not interact further with S during the experiment. A second E seated in a distant part of the room behind S recorded the responses and their latencies.

Three conditions which differed in the percentage of reinforcement of correct response were used. For each S, one of the three knobs (either L,

M, or R) was designated at the correct knob. The particular knob that was correct yielded reinforcement; choices of the other two knobs were never reinforced. In the three conditions the correct knob yielded 100 per cent, 66 per cent, and 33 per cent reinforcement, respectively. In the 66 per cent and 33 per cent conditions the trials on which a choice of the correct knob was reinforced were determined by a prearranged random schedule. The schedule was utilized in such a fashion that it insured S would receive the desired percentage of reinforcement of correct responses. Fifteen Ss were assigned at random to each of the three conditions. The Ss were given 80 trials and at the completion of the experiment S was allowed to select his prizes.

Results. The three groups differed consistently throughout the 80 trials in the incidence of correct response, as may be seen in Figure 1. An analysis of variance revealed that the differences among the groups were significant at beyond the .01 level $(F=7.39)$.

The general tendency seen in Figure 1 is for the frequency of correct response to increase for a short period and then to level off. The 33 per cent group did not show a significant improvement in performance between the first 20 and last 20 trials $(t=1.66, P>.05)$. The change in perform-ance from the first 20 to the last 20 trials was significant for both the 66

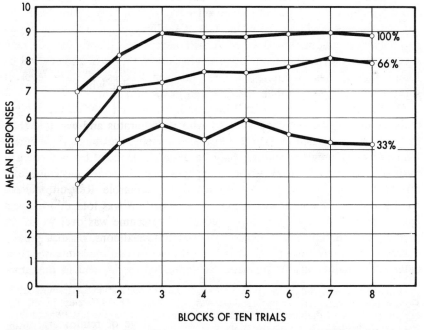

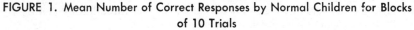

FIGURE 1. Mean Number of Correct Responses by Normal Children for Blocks of 10 Trials

per cent (t=4.00, P<.01) and the 100 per cent group (t=2.97, P<.01).[1]

The values of the asymptotic level of response, as estimated from performance on the last 20 trials, were .97, .79, and .53 for the 100 per cent, 66 per cent, and 33 per cent groups, respectively. The values are quite similar to those obtained by Neimark (1956), who tested adult Ss under similar conditions with 100 per cent and 66 per cent reinforcement. The asymptotic levels of response obtained by Neimark for the last 20 of 100 training trials were .99 for the 100 per cent group and .83 for the 66 per cent group.

There was a tendency for the average latencies of response in the 100 per cent and 66 per cent groups to decrease during the course of the 80 trials in the manner expected in learning problems of different difficulty. The changes for the 33 per cent group were more erratic and appeared to represent a different process from that of the other two groups. An analysis of variance of the latency scores of the three groups during acquisition is not significant (F<1).

EXPERIMENT II

Goodnow (1955), in an analysis of the determinants of choice behavior, has suggested that one of the conditions influencing whether or not S will maximize his guesses of the more frequently reinforced stimulus is the level of success S will accept in the task. Goodnow suggests that maximizing behavior will be found when S will accept less than 100 per cent success as a good final outcome, while other distributions of choices will be found when S has an interest in 100 per cent success or in a level of success which is greater than that allowed in the situation.

On the basis of this analysis, it may be hypothesized that different types of behavior will be obtained with Ss who differ in the degree of success that they have learned to expect. Normal Ss, such as those of Experiment I and of most previous studies, may be assumed to have learned, on the basis of their everyday experience, to expect a high degree of success. Maximizing behavior would not be predicted for these Ss. Institutionalized feebleminded children, however, may be assumed to have learned to expect and to settle for lower degrees of success. These Ss, therefore, would be predicted to maximize their choices of the reinforced stimulus to a greater degree than would normal Ss. It is the purpose of this experiment (a) to determine whether institutionalized feebleminded Ss do tend to maximize

---

[1] Forty extinction trials were given to these Ss immediately after the training trials. During the extinction trials no response was reinforced. The difference in the frequency of choice of the stimulus correct during training between the last 10 acquisition trials and the last 10 extinction trials was significant for the 66 per cent group (t=2.38, P<.05) and in the 100 per cent group (t=2.51, P<.05), but not for the 33 per cent group (t=1.46, P>.05).

their choices in such a manner, and (*b*) to determine whether their choices of the reinforced stimulus differ significantly from those found for the normal *S*s in Experiment I.

Method. *Subjects.* The *S*s consisted of 30 feebleminded children chosen at random from among individuals of appropriate MA and CA residing at the Austin State School. The individuals were all of the familial type of mental deficiency and no individuals with gross motor or sensory disturbances were used. The *S*s were selected so that their average MA would be comparable to that of the normal *S*s in Experiment I. Previous testing with the Stanford-Binet of more than 80 *S*s from the population from which *S*s in Experiment I were selected revealed an average IQ of 119. On the basis of this it was assumed that the *S*s in Experiment I had an average MA of approximately 6.5 yr. The average MA of the feebleminded *S*s was 6.1 yr. and their average CA was 12.8 yr.

Apparatus and procedure. The same apparatus and procedure employed in Experiment I were used. Ten feebleminded *S*s were tested in each of the three conditions.

Results. The frequencies of correct response made by the three groups of *S*s are presented in Figure 2. An analysis of variance of these data indicated

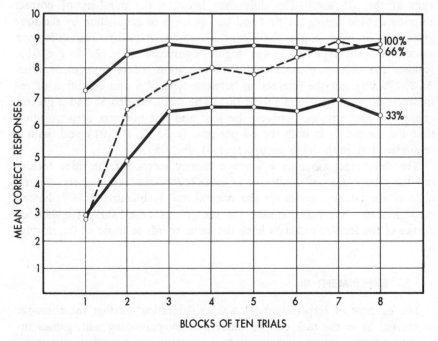

FIGURE 2. Mean Number of Correct Responses by Feebleminded Children
for Blocks of 10 Trials

that the three groups did not differ significantly in frequency of correct response $(F=2.91, P>.05)$. This is in marked contrast with the results for the normal Ss, where a highly significant difference among groups was found.

All three groups showed significant increases in frequency of correct response between the first 20 and last 20 trials. The difference is significant at less than the .05 level for the 100 per cent $(t=2.77)$ and 33 per cent groups $(t=2.48)$, and at less than the .01 level for the 66 per cent group $(t=6.69)$.

The normal and feebleminded Ss in the 100 per cent groups would not be expected to differ in frequency of correct response during the acquisition trials, for complete success is possible in these groups. The prediction is supported; the averages of 67.5 correct responses for the feebleminded Ss and 70.1 for the normal Ss do not differ significantly $(t=.33)$.

The feebleminded Ss, according to the hypothesis presented earlier would be predicted to show a higher frequency of correct response than normal Ss in the 33 per cent and 66 per cent conditions. Two measures were used to test this prediction, the total number of correct responses and the change in performance between the first and last quarters of the acquisition series. An analysis of variance of total number of correct responses for the four groups resulted in an F of 2.41, which is not significant at the .05 level. The difference between the numbers of correct responses made during the first and last quarters of acquisition by the four groups of Ss were highly significant $(F=5.35, P<.01)$. The difference associated with type of S was highly significant $(F=12.74, P<.01)$. Neither the difference associated with conditions of reinforcement $(F=3.22, P>.05)$ nor the interaction between type of S and condition of reinforcement was significant $(F<1.00)$. The feebleminded Ss had a greater change in performance between the first and last quarters of acquisition than the normal Ss in both the 66 per cent $(t=3.52, P<.01)$ and, with a one-tailed test, in the 33% group $(t=1.81, P<.05)$.

The differences among the average latency scores for the three feebleminded groups are not significant $(F=1.82, P>.05)$. An analysis of variance of the latency scores for the normal and feebleminded Ss indicated no significant differences among the six groups $(F<1.00)$. The latency curves of the feebleminded Ss have the same trends as those of the normal Ss.

EXPERIMENT III

The purpose of Experiment III was to determine whether the behavior of normal Ss in the task can be influenced by pertaining with games involving different frequencies of reinforcement. It is assumed, in the manner outlined in Experiment II, that there will be less of a tendency for maximizing behavior to occur with Ss who have learned to expect high degrees of success than with those who have learned to expect lower degrees of success. It is predicted, therefore, that Ss with pretraining on other tasks with high frequencies of reinforcement will show a significantly lower frequency of choice of the reinforcing stimulus than will Ss who have pretraining with lower frequencies of reinforcement.

Method. *Subjects.* The Ss consisted of 30 preschool children attending the same nursery schools as Ss in Experiment I. The Ss were selected at random from among the children who had not performed in Experiment I. The mean CA was 5.9 yr.

Apparatus. Four tasks were used—the learning task used in Experiment I and II and three experimental games. The apparatus for the learning task was modified so that a small open box from which S could remove the marbles replaced the enclosed box. A marble board, with 50 holes into which S could place the marbles, was also used.

The games were the Card Game, the Picture Game, and the Nursery School Game. The *Card Game* apparatus consisted of two sets of cards. The cards were constructed of 2 x 3-in. cardboard on which were mounted small rectangles of black or red paper. One set contained 12 red cards and the other contained 8 black and 4 red cards. The *Picture Game* apparatus consisted of (*a*) 12 cards similar to those in the Card Game, each bearing a rectangle of a different color; (*b*) a panel containing a 7-in. square milkglass screen; (*c*) a slide projector; and (*d*) 12 slides depicting different animals. The *Nursery School Game* apparatus consisted of (*a*) two green panels 17 in. square, each containing six hooks; and (*b*) 12 pictures of young children mounted in plastic covers with a wire loop at the top of each picture.

Two additional marble boards were also used; one containing 36 holes, and one containing 12 holes.

Procedure. The Ss were presented with the three games followed by the learning problem. The Ss were divided at random into two groups of 15 Ss each. Group 1 received 100 per cent reinforcement and Group 2 received 33 per cent reinforcement during the games. All Ss received 66 per cent reinforcement during the learning problem. The games were dissimilar to each other and to the learning task. Since the games did not involve learning, the different percentages of reinforcement could be given regardless of the specific responses Ss made.

The S was seated at a small table and was told, "We're going to play several different kinds of games today and you can win some nice prizes." The E displayed prizes of the same types used in Experiments I and II, and proceeded with the instructions for the first game. During these instructions S was told that he would receive marbles for correct responses and was shown a marble board which he was to fill. The marble boards for the two groups differed; the 36-hole marble board was given to Ss in Group 1 and the 12-hole marble board to Ss in Group 2. The number of holes in the marble board corresponded to the number of times that S would be reinforced during the period in which S played the three games. The S was further told that when he filled the marble board he would be given another marble board which he could fill and could exchange for his choice of prizes. The use of different marble boards during this period was introduced to insure that the two groups of Ss, although receiving different numbers of reinforcements, would have attained the same degree of accomplishment towards their goal. The S was then allowed to proceed with the three games. The order in which the three games were played was randomized among Ss.

The instructions and procedures for the three games are described below:

In the *Card Game,* one of the decks of cards was placed in front of S. He was instructed to draw one card at a time from the top of the deck. He was told that every time he drew a red card he would be given a marble for his marble board. The S was allowed to draw 12 cards. The decks were prearranged so that for Group 1 the top 12 cards were red, and for Group 2 the top 12 cards contained 4 red cards and 8 black cards randomly mixed.

In the *Picture Game,* S was shown the apparatus and was told that as pictures appeared on the screen he was to select the card that went with the picture. There was no principle by which S could select an appropriate card, and reinforcement was given arbitrarily, depending upon the group in which S was placed. For Group 1, all of S's responses were reinforced by E's telling S that he was correct and giving S a marble. For Group 2, 33 per cent of S's responses were reinforced. The four responses reinforced were determined by a prearranged random sequence.

In the *Nursery School Game,* S was told that the panels represented nursery schools and that half of the children in the pictures went to one nursery school and half to the other. The S was instructed to place each child in the nursery school which S thought the child attended. There was no principle by which the pictures could be separated and again reinforcement was given arbitrarily, depending upon the Group in which S was placed. All of S's responses in Group 1 were reinforced and 33 per cent of S's responses in Group 2. The responses reinforced in Group 2 again followed a prearranged random sequence.

After completing the games S was asked to give the filled marble board to E and was given the marble board containing 50 holes. The S was told that when this marble board was filled he could select his prizes. The E then introduced the learning task. The instructions for this task were identical to those described in Experiments I and II, except that S was told to remove the marbles from the box after each reinforced trial and to place them in the marble board. The procedure did not differ for Groups 1 and 2; all Ss were tested under the 66 per cent reinforcement schedule described in the previous experiments. The Ss were given 80 trials and were then given their prizes.

Results. The results of the study are presented in Figure 3. Following the initial 10 trials the groups differed consistently. The Ss receiving 100 per cent reinforcement on the games preceding the learning problem (Group 1) chose the correct knob less frequently than Ss who had received 33 per cent reinforcement (Group 2). The correct knob was chosen an average of 44.7 times in Group 1 and 56.6 times in Group 2. The difference is significant at beyond the .025 level with a one-tailed test ($t=2.11$).

DISCUSSION

In this study it was assumed that children learn to expect certain frequencies of reinforcement on the basis of their everyday experience, and that children living in a normal, responsive environment develop a higher expectancy of reinforcement than do children living in an institution. It was also assumed that the expectancies that children develop may be modified by manipulating the frequency of reinforcement that the

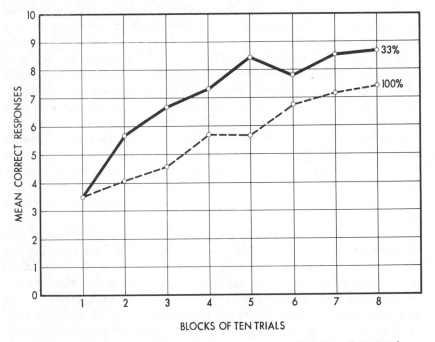

FIGURE 3. Mean Number of Correct Responses in Blocks of 10 Trials

child receives in an experimental setting. It was hypothesized that different types of behavior would be obtained with Ss who differ in the degree of success that they have learned to expect, and it was predicted that Ss with low expectancies would show a greater frequency of choice of the reinforcing stimulus than would Ss with higher expectancies. This would result from the attempt by Ss with higher expectancies to seek, through variable behavior, a means by which they could obtain a frequency of reinforcement corresponding to the frequency which they expect.

The total number of correct responses made by three groups of normal children receiving different percentages of reinforcement differed significantly, but the number of correct responses made by three groups of feebleminded children tested under the same procedure as the normal Ss did not. The two types of Ss differed significantly in rate of learning under both 66 per cent and 33 per cent reinforcement, but did not differ significantly under 100 per cent reinforcement. In learning a response which yielded 66 per cent reinforcement, normals Ss receiving 100 per cent reinforcement on pretraining games showed significantly poorer learning than did Ss receiving 33 per cent reinforcement on the pretraining games.

In Experiment I it was found that the mean response levels of normal children were similar to those for groups of adult Ss given 66 per cent and 100 per cent reinforcement in a similar situation (Neimark, 1956). The results are also similar to those of Messick and Solley (1957), who found that children tend to approach an asymptotic level of response in a probability learning situation.

In the 33 per cent and 66 per cent groups of Experiment I, a tendency was found for Ss to follow one of two modes of response; they either adopted the correct response relatively quickly or persisted in variable behavior throughout all of the trials. Individual differences in responses on a two-choice task have also been reported by Anderson and Grant (1957). It is of interest that even Ss who persisted in responding in a variable fashion were able to tell E at the end of the experiment which knob had yielded reinforcement. The fact that Ss knew the correct response but did not make it supports the view that Ss with a high expectancy are unwilling to accept a solution which yields low frequencies of reinforcement.

There are several alternative interpretations of the differences in behavior of the normal and feebleminded children which differ from the one previously presented. One that seems quite reasonable is that institutionalized children may have less experience in playing games than normal children, hence are less likely to know the nature of such games. If this were the case, their behavior might be similar to that of adult Ss who, when tested in an obscure task, tend to depart from the probability matching behavior found in less obscure matching tasks (Wyckoff and Sidowski,

1955). A second alternative interpretation is that feebleminded children may tend to choose the reinforced stimulus more frequently than do normal Ss because they are more rigid and tend to perseverate more than do normal Ss. This interpretation does not, however, appear to be tenable in light of the results of several recent studies in discrimination learning which show that normal and feebleminded Ss of the same MA do not differ in rigidity of response or in learning speed (Plenderlith, 1956; Stevenson and Zigler, 1957).

The results of Experiment III also provide support for the hypothesis that behavior in probability learning tasks is dependent upon Ss' expectations concerning level of reinforcement. The fact that pretraining with different frequencies of reinforcement affects behavior in a probability learning task is in accord with the results of experiments with adult Ss where the probability of reinforcement is shifted during the course of training. In these studies (Estes and Straughn, 1954; Goodnow and Pettigrew, 1955; Parducci, 1957), differences in behavior have been found as a function of the shift in probabilities of reinforcement.

The form of the curves for the two groups in Experiment III tends to differ from that of the group in Experiment I which also received 66 per cent reinforcement. The differences in the curves may be related to the differences in procedures used in the two experiments. In Experiment III, Ss were given a more defined goal than were Ss in Experiment I. The use of a more defined goal may lead to a greater tendency for Ss to maximize their choices of the reinforcing stimulus.

SUMMARY

Three experiments are reported which investigate the performance of children in a probability learning task. In Experiments I and II, normal and feebleminded children were tested on a problem where the correct response resulted in either 100 per cent, 66 per cent, or 33 per cent reinforcement. In Experiment III normal children were given pretraining on three nonlearning games with 100 per cent or 33 per cent reinforcement, and were then trained on the discrimination problem with 66 per cent reinforcement of the correct response. Predictions were made from an hypothesis relating performance to Ss expected frequency of reinforcement. Feebleminded Ss performed at a higher level in the 33 per cent and 66 per cent conditions than normal Ss and at a comparable level in the 100 per cent condition. The Ss in Experiment III receiving 100 per cent reinforcement during pretraining made significantly fewer correct responses in the learning problem than did Ss receiving 33 per cent reinforcement during pretraining.

13

Growth of Abilities into Adulthood*

Nancy Bayley

There has been much controversy regarding the nature of intellectual growth during the adult years, with cross-sectional and longitudinal studies showing different, and sometimes opposite, age trends. This problem, and at least one of the contributing factors to the inconsistency of the data, is discussed in a subsequent report in this volume (see Paper #21). The data presented in the following report are those most recently available from one of the major longitudinal studies being conducted in this country. It is of great interest that while verbal scores are continuing to increase until 36 years of age, some of the performance scores suggest the beginning of decrements. Will it turn out, when all of the data from Dr. Bayley's investigation have been collected during the next three to four decades, that the longitudinal and cross-sectional data will be in greater agreement than has seemed likely thus far? The reader's attention is also called to the changes taking place in women's intelligence scores between 16 and 36 years of age. Are these erratic variations the possible consequences of low levels of cultural stimulation and demand?

"What kinds of intellectual abilities show growth into adulthood? How are these related to concept learning? What are the implications for the teaching of concepts to adults?" The material reported here is most relevant to answering the first of these questions. Out of this material may come some suggestions which will be partial answers to the other two questions.

The findings from the Berkeley Growth Study may yield some partial answers to these questions because it is a less highly selected sample than Terman's gifted subjects, for example, and because the subjects have now been tested at 5 ages on the Wechsler scales, which contain both verbal and performance (nonverbal) subscales.

* Adapted and abridged from Nancy Bayley, "Learning in Adulthood: The Role of Intelligence." Chapter 8, pp. 117-138, in H. J. Klausmeier and C. W. Harris (Eds.), *Analysis of Concept Learning*, 1966, New York. (With permission of the author and the publisher, Academic Press.)

SUBJECTS AND TESTS

Although the subjects of the Berkeley Growth Study (Bayley, 1955; Jones & Bayley, 1941) are not a completely representative sample, they were selected at the time of their birth in 1928-1930 to represent a broad range of full-term healthy babies born in Berkeley, California, hospitals. Their fathers' education ranged from third grade to the M.D. and Ph.D. degrees, with a mean of 13.7 years of schooling (*SD*, 3.6 years). Attrition has changed the general nature of the sample very little over the 36-year period. It has not been possible to compare the general level of mental ability of these subjects with a random population, because of the unknown practice effects of the repeated testing these people have experienced in their 36 years. For the few who have not missed a single scheduled test, the number of tests taken is 42. The 30-year period starting with the Stanford-Binet at 6 years includes a total of 16 test ages.

As for the subjects' own achieved education, the distribution is wide, though it is weighted with a high proportion of cases with more than 16 years' education (there are 5 M.D.'s among the men tested so far at 36 years and potentially another M.D. and a Ph.D. will be tested). There is, at the other extreme, however, one case who remained in an ungraded class, achieving a barely third-grade level, and there are three others who did not complete high school. The mean education for the total sample of 58 longitudinally followed cases is 15.5 years. By sex the means are for 28 males 15.61, for 30 females 15.41; the *SD*'s are 4.10 and 1.54, respectively.

Most relevant for our present consideration will be an investigation of the scores earned by 52 of these cases tested on the Wechsler scales at some or all of five test ages: 16, 18, 21, 26, and 36 years. At the first four of these ages the test used was Form I of the Wechsler-Bellevue Intelligence Scale; at the 36-year test the Wechsler Adult Intelligence Scale (WAIS) was used. All of the tests were given by the same examiner (Bayley) except for 18 of the 26-year tests, which were given by Dorothy H. Eichorn.

AGE TRENDS IN TOTAL SCORES

Figure 1 represents the age curves of the means for the verbal and performance scale scores. The three upper lines show the age curves of scores for the males and females separately, and for a core sample, sexes combined, who were tested at all five ages. The means for the males and females are not composed of completely constant samples, as all tested cases were included in each of the appropriate age groups. It is clear from the curve of the constant sample, however, that the age trends in scores are not a function of variations in the composition of the sample. For comparative purposes the WAIS age norms are also represented for a similar range of ages (the lower curve).

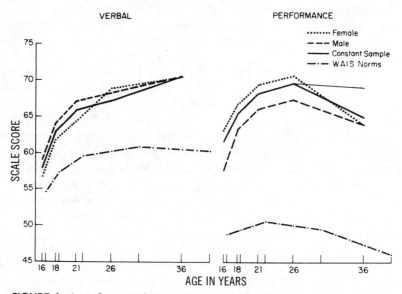

FIGURE 1. Age Curves of Mean Scores on the Wechsler Scales of Intelligence, for the Berkeley Growth Study. The Wechsler-Bellevue Test of Adult Intelligence (1939) was given at years 16, 18, 21, and 26; the Wechsler Adult Intelligence Scale (1955) at 36 years. The constant sample is composed of 25 cases of both sexes who were tested at all five ages. The 36-year point on the curve for the constant sample on the performance scale is shown both for the 36-year WAIS scores (heavy line) and for an estimated corrected score (light line). The number of cases at a given age varies for the female sample from 17 to 24, for the male sample from 16 to 22.

Another point necessary to consider here is the degree of equivalence between the Wechsler-Bellevue (W-B) and WAIS scale scores. It was not possible for us to give both forms of the test to our subjects at the same age, and differences between scores over a 10-year interval may be a function of either age changes or nonequivalence in scales, or both. In such published studies (Dann, 1957; Goolishian & Ramsey, 1956; Neuringer, 1963) as we have been able to find on the comparison of the scales at or near these ages, there appears to be no difference in difficulty levels of the verbal scale. On the performance scale, however, repeat tests on the same subjects gave scores averaging 3-5 points lower on the WAIS. We might assume, therefore, that an adjustment upward of 4 points on the performance scale of the WAIS will render the scores on the two forms of the scale approximately equivalent. The curve with such an adjustment at 36 years for the constant sample is indicated on the chart.

If we assume equivalence in difficulty at all five ages on the verbal scale, then we may say that the Berkeley Growth Study subjects clearly show an increase in scores with age over the entire span, though the rate of increase is decelerating. In comparison with the WAIS norms the Berkeley Growth Study increases are greater through 26 years. After this age our sample shows a slight continued increase through 36 years, whereas in the normative curve there is a mild decline in scores after 30. Although the males appear to score higher on the verbal scale at 16 through 21 years, there are no sex differences at the later ages, 26 and 36 years.

The performance scale presents a different picture. There are clear increments for the total sample and for both sexes from 16 to 26 years, with the females consistently scoring higher. The curves for males and females make no adjustment for performance score differences on the WAIS. If we were to add 4 points at 36 years to each of these curves, then the males would show no mean change in score between 26 and 36 years, while the females drop an average of 2½ points (about .3 of an *SD*). That is, unlike the Wechsler cross-sectional data, our longitudinal sample shows a tendency for stability in the performance scores with very little falling off in scores after 26 years. Such decline as there is occurs primarily in the females.

In summary, then, the Wechsler scores on our longitudinal sample either increase with age through 36 years on the verbal scale or remain stable with very little loss of level on the performance scale.

AGE TRENDS IN INDIVIDUAL TESTS

The nature of the age changes in the Wechsler scale mental functions may be investigated more closely by looking at the age trends in the scale scores of the separate tests. These are shown in Figure 2. Let us again assume that the two forms of the scale are approximately equivalent. The most consistent and marked increases in score over the 20-year interval are found for both sexes in three highly verbal tests: information, comprehension, and vocabulary. However, another verbal test, similarities, shows a leveling off after 26 years. This test has been changed only very slightly in the WAIS revision, and there may not be enough top in the scale to permit further increments. Alternatively, this kind of ability may have reached its own limits around 26 years.

Both the digit span and arithmetic tests level off after 26 years, with no increase in score at 36. Digit span is the one test which is entirely identical in the two forms of the scale. Although the scale scores for this test are different for the W-B and the WAIS, it has been possible to use raw scores to compare age changes in span. The curves for the raw scores are essentially the same as for the scale scores. Digit span is a test of capacity to retain discrete items in a short span of immediate recall. Immediate recall may be thought of as a basic tool in intellective functions, the capacity to hold in mind several abstract ideas in the associative processes of reasoning. If this is so, then a short span of immediate attention or recall could

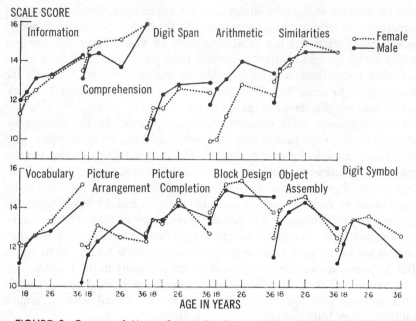

FIGURE 2. Curves of Mean Scores by Sex and Age for the 11 Wechsler Subtests, Berkeley Growth Study.

be a limiting factor in permitting processes of analysis and synthesis in thinking and the consolidation of knowledge in some organized and utilizable form. According to the tables of intercorrelation in the WAIS Manual, digit span correlated most highly with information, vocabulary, and arithmetic. These tests are presented orally, and call for just such a capacity.

Among the verbal subscales, digit span and arithmetic share similar growth curves, except for the fact that the females consistently do less well in arithmetic. This latter finding has been reported in many other studies. Within either sex, however, there is no further growth, but even, perhaps, a slight decline, after 26 years.

In general, it would appear that in the verbal portion of the Wechsler scales the more verbally constituted a test, the more likely it is that these subjects, and intellectually comparable persons, will continue to grow in the capacities tapped in the tests.

The performance subscales again present a somewhat different picture. However, the 36-year portion of these curves must be interpreted with caution. It is in the relative difficulty of these subscales that the WAIS is most different from the Wechsler-Bellevue. All five of the performance tests show a drop in score between 26 and 36 years. If, however, by using Neuringer's (1963) comparison of the scales on twice-tested 18 year olds, we make a rough adjustment in order to bring the relative difficulty of the scales into line, the drops for most tests are reduced. Actually, the men's performance on block design would appear to improve at 36 years, whereas picture arrangement, object assembly, and digit symbol would remain stable. Scores on picture completion, however, would drop even further. Using these adjustments, we would be able to conclude that in three of the performance tests the scores level off after 26 years, while in one (block design) scores continue to improve and in one (picture completion) there is a considerable loss.

What is most evident in the performance scale, however, is that at 36 years in four of the five tests the females do relatively poorly. This is in contrast to the earlier ages. For 16 through 26 years the females tended to surpass the males on these tests. The drop for females at 36 years (after scale adjustments not shown here) is most precipitous in picture completion, object assembly, and block design, and least in digit symbol.

To summarize the age trends on the performance scales, we find that, for this total longitudinal sample, growth continues through all five scales through 26 years, but then levels off, with the females showing a drop in scores after 26 years in several of the tests.

If we ask the relevance of these trends for the learning of concepts, we can at this point only reason by analogy to studies of learning and concept formation, which do not seem to have been compared on the basis of level of intelligence. One relevant recent study by Wiersma and Klausmeier (1965) may be cited. They found that of 48 females ranging in age from 20 to 51, the group of women 35 years and older took significantly longer than the younger ones to form the concepts in a task designed to measure speed of learning a concept. This task, which involved classifying cards according to indicated rules, may require types of concepts similar to those in several of the Wechsler scale tasks: namely, arithmetic, similarities, picture arrangement, block design, and object assembly. It is interesting to note that four of the five tests are scored partially for speed of response and that the Berkeley Growth Study women tended to lose ground in three of these five tests, while the men either improved or remained stable in all five.

These findings are by no means conclusive, but they are in line with other studies which show loss of speed in learning with advancing age. A possible age-related sex difference in this form of learning might be well worth exploring.

CONSISTENCY IN MENTAL ABILITIES

So far we have been concerned with general growth trends in increment or decrement in intelligence over the 20-year age span between 16 and 36 years. We may also ask how consistent over time are the scores earned in the several kinds of function as measured in the 11 tests of which the scale is composed.

The correlations between test ages are represented for the six verbal scales in Figure 3. In this chart the tests are arranged approximately in the order of least to most change in the content of the WAIS Scale from its counterpart in the Wechsler-Bellevue. That is, digit span is placed first because that test was left unchanged, while vocabulary is last because the WAIS uses an entirely new set of words. Within each scale the test-retest correlations are arranged according to the time interval between tests and to a generally ascending order of age at the later test. Thus, for digit span the first comparison is between 16 and 18 years, then 18 and 21, 16 and 21, 21 and 26, 18 and 26, 16 and 26, 26 and 36, 21 and 36, 18 and 36, and 16 and 36, the last of these being the full 20-year span. The solid dots represent correlations between the two different forms of the scale; the open dots represent correlations between retests on the Wechsler-Bellevue.

The general size of a correlation (indicated by the height above the zero base line) is in part a measure (in particular for the shorter retest intervals) of the reliability of the test. Consistency over time, or stability in a given function, should be indicated by the extent to which the level of correlation is maintained. That is, if a test is unreliable the rs will be low and often variable. If there are differing individual patterns in rate of growth, for example in vocabulary, we should expect the correlations to become progressively lower as the retest intervals become longer.

It appears, then, that digit span is relatively less reliable than information

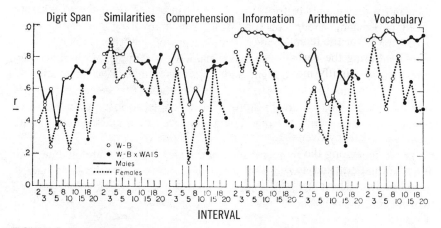

FIGURE 3. Berkeley Growth Study Test-retest Correlations for Wechsler Verbal Scale Scores. The subtests are presented in the order of least to most change in content from the Wechsler-Bellevue to the WAIS. The test-retest intervals are for years 16-18, 18-21, 16-21, 21-26, 18-26, 16-26, 26-36, 21-36, 18-36, and 16-36.

and vocabulary. It is also, for the males, surprisingly stable over the long intervals, though the shorter interval retest correlations tend to be low between 18 and 26 years. Both reliability and consistency are greater in the males in all six tests. This sex difference is conspicuous for vocabulary and information. The change in form of the test at 36 years does not appear to make any difference in these correlations.

Males are remarkably consistent in vocabulary scores: the r between 16 and 36 years is .95. In contrast, for the same interval the r for the females is only .49. Information has a closely similar pattern of sex differences in correlation.

Several of the lowest rs are at the intermediate ages and retest intervals, in particular for the women. This may very well be a period when there are large shifts in the women's motivations and attitudes toward intellectual and educational goals.

The same presentation of correlations is shown in Figure 4 for the performance tests. Digit symbol (which was changed only by extending its length) appears to be most reliable and stable, with block design second. In general the performance test correlations are lower than in the verbal tests. Block design is the one test in this group that is both more reliable and more consistent for the males. The females show no constancy of scores over the long intervals in block design. Their performance on picture arrangement is erratic. We might say that the males tend to be erratic in the 5–10-year intervals on object assembly and picture completion.

The consistency correlations for the combined scales, as is to be expected, are much more stable than the separate tests. They are also more stable for the males than for the females. The 20-year rs (16 to 36 years) for the males for verbal, performance, and full scale IQs are .94, .88, and .97, whereas for the females, given in the same order, they are .57, .67, and .69. Comparing the verbal and performance scales within a sex, the males appear to be slightly more stable in their verbal scale scores (r of .94 for verbal versus .88 for performance); the females may be relatively more stable in performance (r of .67 for performance versus .57 for verbal).

To summarize these patterns of consistency in test performance, we see greater consistency over this young adult age span in both short- and long-range scores among the males, and for the males most clearly in vocabulary and information, and to a lesser extent in similarities, digit symbol, and block design. These tend also to be the tests (notably vocabulary and information) which show continuing increments in capacity (for both sexes) through 36 years.

IMPLICATIONS FOR LEARNING

It appears from the foregoing analysis of scores for these Berkeley Growth Study subjects that their intellectual potential for continued learn-

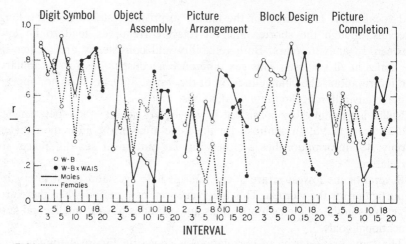

FIGURE 4. Berkeley Growth Study Test-retest Correlations for Wechsler Performance Scale Scores.

ing is unimpaired through 36 years. In the attainment of information and word knowledge their intelligence is continuing to increase. If we relate these results to the findings from other longitudinally studied adult subjects, such as those of Owens (1953), Bayley and Oden (1955), H. E. Jones (1959), and others, we may hypothesize that this increase in general verbal capacity may well be maintained through 50 years or longer. There is, however, very little research reported on the relation of intelligence level to learning in adults of various ages.

The extent of our knowledge about learning in adults has been discussed thoroughly by Jones and by Jerome in their chapters in Birren's *Handbook of Aging and the Individual* (1959). There is a surprisingly small amount of established knowledge in this field. I shall summarize it here only briefly.

There is evidence that in older persons loss in speed of mental processes is often compensated for by a greater fund of information and greater skill in its utilization. There is, on the other hand, probably increasing resistance with age toward expending the effort necessary to break old patterns of thought in order to learn new techniques and new ways of organizing knowledge. The extent to which these resistances are overcome may be matters of motivation and opportunity, rather than of intelligence. Jerome (1959), after reviewing studies of learning which predominantly show decline in learning ability after 35 years, says, "The data currently available do not provide an adequate basis for deciding whether or not the motivation-speed-indigence-ill-health syndrome can be accepted as a sufficient explanation of the observed age differences in learning performance" (p. 698). Clearly there is an area here for more carefully controlled studies of learning in adults as it relates to both age and intelligence.

14

Age Differences in Verbal Learning[*]

Sheldon J. Korchin and Harold Basowitz

"You can't teach an old dog new tricks," at least not *as easily* as you can a younger dog during the prime learning days of his early maturity. The foregoing appears to be a valid generalization about the adaptive plasticity of all organisms. In the first two editions of the present book we included a paper by Dr. Ruch on the relation of age to learning ability. The following report by Drs. Korchin and Basowitz describes a replication of the earlier research by Dr. Ruch. The findings of the two studies are in agreement that there is a substantial decrement in learning performance during old age; however, the organismic and personality variables that determine this decrement still remain obscure. Even though the findings reported in the present study are not in complete agreement with those reported earlier by Dr. Ruch, there does appear to be a consensus that the older learner performs best when he can draw heavily on past experience. Whether or not this results largely from physical limitations or from psychological predispositions remains in scientific debate.

The specific conditions which determine the relative ease or difficulty of learning for the older person, the importance of different types of material, learning situations, and the like, have been a concern of systematic and experimental work within the psychology of learning only in relatively recent years. Of considerable interest is a study by F. L. Ruch (1934). In his experiments Ruch had three age groups learn a pursuit rotor task, first in direct vision, then in mirror vision, and three lists of paired-associate materials. These tasks were presumed to differ not only in difficulty and novelty but also in the degree to which prior experience might enter to facilitate or disrupt present learning. Ruch concluded that older persons have least "deficit" in learning materials which are compatible with habitual behavior and greatest where the new learning contradicts earlier habits.

* Adapted and abridged from S. J. Korchin and H. Basowitz, "Age Differences in Verbal Learning," *Journal of Abnormal and Social Psychology*, 1957, Vol. 54, pp. 64-69. (With permission of the authors and the American Psychological Association.)

The present paper will consider the comparison of two groups, distinct in age, in their performance on Ruch's three verbal learning procedures. The purpose is twofold: (*a*) To repeat Ruch's study and to retest his hypothesis; and (*b*) To see whether further understanding can be gained about age-related changes in cognitive functioning generally.

METHOD

Two distinct age groups were used in the main study. The *young* group included resident physicians and graduate nurses. The *old* group consisted of residents of an institution for the aged. The *S*s were included in the older sample only if they were in good general health, were free from organic brain pathology, and had acceptable corrected vision.

Since the total young group was distinctly superior to the old in education and intellectual level, it was felt that a more direct and exact test of the differences in learning could be made using groups equated for general intelligence. Since vocabulary correlates well with general intelligence as measured by omnibus batteries and itself shows relatively little change with age, the Vocabulary test of the Wechsler-Bellevue Scale was used. The groups employed were two matched groups of 16 *S*s each. The young group had a mean unweighted vocabulary score of 26.8 with a standard deviation of 4.6; the old group 28.6 and 4.8, respectively. The young group consisted of 5 men and 11 women, with a mean age of 26.8; the old group of 8 men and 8 women, with a mean age of 78.1 years.

Each *S* was individually administered a modified version of the learning tasks described by Ruch. As in his experiment, *S*s had to learn three separate lists: 1. *Word Associates,* consisting of familiar, logically related word pairs such as Man–Boy; 2. *Nonsense Equations,* e.g., E × Z = G; 3. *False Equations,* e.g., 3 × 5 = 6. In the present study the task was changed somewhat from Ruch's original procedure. After preliminary tests, the length of list was reduced from 10 to 8 items and the number of trials from 15 to 6 in order to make the task easier and the session less fatiguing, particularly for the older *S*s.

Each list consisted of 8 units selected from the 10 used originally. Before each list was given *S* was first shown a sample pair and the task explained. After an initial presentation of the series, *S* was given 6 trials in which he was to anticipate the right-hand member of the pair when the left was first shown alone. The items were projected by a 35 mm strip film projector in a semidarkened room, each frame remaining in view for 4 seconds. The left-hand member of the first pair appeared alone for 4 seconds, both parts for 4 seconds, then the left-hand member of the second pair, and so on. Eight seconds were allowed between trials and about 2 minutes between lists. To prevent serial learning, the order of items was changed on each trial.

The instructions used were substantially the same as Ruch's. The S was encouraged to guess if uncertain. In presenting the lists of Nonsense and False Equations the items were divided at the equal sign, e.g., first $3 \times 5 =$ was shown, then $3 \times 5 = 6$.

RESULTS

In Table 1 are presented the mean scores for each of the three tests. Since there were 8 items and 6 trials, the highest possible score for an individual is 48. Young Ss clearly perform better on each task. The difference between the groups is significant in each case at the $p < .001$ level. Moreover, it is equally clear that for each group the Word-Associate learning was decidedly easier than either the learning of the Nonsense or False Equations, although, surprisingly, there is virtually no difference between the latter two.

Following Ruch's analysis for determining variation in the amounts of deficit among the three types of material, we can compare the difference between old and young on each of the tests. For the Word-Associates this difference in score is 13.81, for the Nonsense Equations 17.57, and for the False Equations it is 17.62 (Table 1). These values do not differ significantly from each other.

TABLE 1. Mean Learning Scores for Young and Old Groups

Group	N	Mean Age	Word Associates (WA)	Nonsense Equations (NE)	False Equations (FE)	$\dfrac{WA - NE}{WA}$	$\dfrac{WA - FE}{WA}$
Young	16	26.8	44.19	25.00	24.81	43.59	44.21
Old	16	78.1	30.38	7.43	7.19	74.86	74.96
$\text{Diff}_{M_y - M_o}$			13.81	17.57	17.62		

However, the difference between the groups in the learning of the three types of material can be viewed in another way. If we consider the proportional change between the tests it does appear that the older group has relatively poorer learning on both the Nonsense and False Equations when these are compared with the Word Associates. Subtracting the Word-Associate score and the Nonsense Equation score and taking this difference as a fraction of the Word-Associate score, the mean ratio $\dfrac{WA - NE}{WA}$ is 43.59 for the young Ss and for the old 74.86. The difference between these values is significant at the $p < .001$ level. Similarly, the ratio of Word-Associate score minus False Equation divided by Word Associate $\dfrac{WA - FE}{WA}$ is 44.21 for the young group and 74.96 for the old (Table 1), significant at the p<.001 level. From this analysis we may fairly conclude not only that the older Ss learn less in each of the three tasks but that they are proportionately more deficient in the learning of materials in which the facilitative effects of prior experience are minimized. However, we have not found evidence that interference materials are more difficult than nonsense materials.

The trial-by-trial learning curves for the two groups on each of the tests show the difference in performance already discussed to be visible throughout learning (Figure 1). The curves for the Nonsense Equations and False Equations are virtually identical within each group and each of these is distinct from Word-Associates levels.

Not only do the old and young groups differ in the amount of material learned, but they differ as well in the type of error made during the learning process. In Table 2 the total number of errors made by each of the groups on each of the three tasks is broken down into various types. In both the Word Associates and the Nonsense Equations there are three distinct types of error possible: S may not respond at all to the stimulus item (*No response*); he may give an associate which appears nowhere in the series (*Random response*); or he may respond with an item which although incorrect for the present stimulus item is appropriate elsewhere in the list (*Correct elsewhere*). For the False Equations list S can also give a response which represents a correct multiplication, or, conceivably, he can add or subtract the two numbers in the stimulus equation. Although the completion of the multiplication is of particular theoretical interest since it may represent the intrusion of the competing, albeit actually correct, response, addition or subtraction may also reflect habitual response to the implied

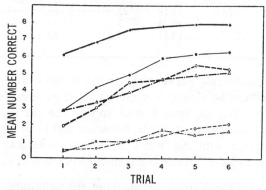

FIGURE 1. Learning Curves for the Old and Young Groups for Each of the Three Tests. The curves for the young are heavily drawn, for the old lightly drawn. The three tests are distinguished: Word Associates . . . Nonsense Equations . . . False Equations.

structure of an arithmetical problem. Scoring these errors does, of course, involve interpretation since such response might as well be a *Random response* or, in a particular case, *Correct elsewhere*.

There is considerable difference in the pattern of errors between the two groups (Table 2). On all three tasks the typical behavior of the older person is not to respond, distinctly less often to give a response that is *Correct elsewhere*. Compared to the old group, young *S*s have proportionally more of their errors of the latter type. The young are also more prone to give *Random responses* and in the case of the False Equations to multiply, add, or subtract the items, although there are few of these errors in either group.

Closer inspection of the trial-by-trial changes in the pattern of error gives further evidence of the difference between old and young learners. On all tasks on each successive trial the young group has relatively fewer of its errors in the *No response* class and an increasing proportion of *Correct elsewhere* errors. On the Nonsense Equations task, for example, of the total errors made by the young *S*s on the first trial 57% are *No response* and 30% *Correct elsewhere,* which changes gradually to 30% *No response* and 66% *Correct elsewhere* by the sixth trial. However, the old group preserves roughly the same proportions on each trial. Thus, for the same task, these *S*s start with 95% *No response* and 3% *Correct elsewhere* and by the last trial still have 92% and 8% of their errors in each of these classes. Although there is somewhat more tendency for the *No response* proportion to go down on the Word Associate and False Equation tasks, the pattern is basically the same. Thus, it is clear that simply not responding to a stimulus item is characteristic of the learning behavior of the older *S*s throughout; it is less common in the younger *S* at any point and declines greatly as learning proceeds.

DISCUSSION

There is no doubt that older persons in this as in Ruch's original study are less well able to master each of the learning tasks. As such, this finding is in agreement with a considerable body of material which shows a generally decreased ability to learn with advancing age. However, unlike Ruch, we have found virtually no difference between scores on the nonsense and interference materials and no evidence of a greater degree of deficit in the latter than in the former. However, it may be that the differences, though seemingly small, between Ruch's and the present procedure are sufficient to account for the obtained differences in results.

What we have found is that, compared to the level of attainment on Word-Associate learning, the older persons show proportionately poorer learning on *both* the new and the interference materials. In this sense, we can speak of greater deficit on both of these materials, although there is no

TABLE 2. Percentages of Various Types of Errors Made in Word Associate (WA), Nonsense Equation (NE), and False Equation (FE) Tests

Group	N	Mean Age	Test	Total No. of Errors	No Response	Random Response	Correct Elsewhere	Multiplication*	Addition*	Subtraction*
Young	16	26.8	WA	61	62	7	31			
			NE	368	45	7	48			
			FE	370	30	9	45	2	8	6
Old	16	78.1	WA	273	83	1	16			
			NE	649	92	1	7			
			FE	653	75	3	18	1	1	2

* These types of errors are possible only on the False Equation task.

difference between them. While it may be that older persons are uniquely prone to disturbed performance when required to reorganize existing habits, as has been suggested by a number of papers, the evidence of the present experiment suggests that the older individual will perform less well in any situation in which he must deal with material which is in any way novel. When the task at hand cannot be integrated with earlier experience, either because there is no precedent or existing precedent is inadequate or contradictory, learning suffers.

Older and younger *S*s differ also in their behavior during learning. The younger, as we have noted, are more likely to make some response to the stimulus item, to offer hypotheses, whether correct or incorrect, and as learning proceeds to have an increasing proportion of their errors responses which, although correct elsewhere in the list, are inappropriately given to the particular stimulus. The older *S* will either respond correctly or not at all, and this behavior is consistent from trial to trial.

We believe that three factors jointly determine this behavior of the older *S*s, although from available evidence we cannot judge their relative contributions.

1. The older person is more cautious. Despite the injunction to guess, it may be that older persons require greater certainty before they are willing to report. Although *S* knows that the item is equally incorrect whether he gives no response or a wrong response, he apparently prefers the error of omission to that of commission. This tendency to inhibit response in the uncertain situation may reflect a more profound personality defense of the aged through which the recognition of inadequacy is avoided.

2. The older person requires more time for the integration of a response. A condition of the experiment which may account for some of the differences may be the rapid pacing of the items. As the experiment was conducted *S* had to read the stimulus item, select, and report a response item within 4 seconds. Considerable work has shown that older persons require more time both for simple perceptual discrimination and in more complex decision-making. Moreover, requiring performance within arbitrarily short times can result in a significant reduction in the adequacy of that performance. Such findings would suggest that the processes of perceiving-judging-recalling-responding require more time for the older person than is available and that, perhaps, if the pacing were slower his behavior might differ less than that of younger individuals.

3. For the older person learning may principally involve the association of *discrete* stimulus-response combinations, and unlike for the younger person, may not include a prior stage in which the response items are first learned as belonging *somewhere* in the series, before they are attached to particular stimuli. That the pattern of errors is generally the same on all three learning tasks and that there are no important changes in pattern from trial to trial further suggest that the acquisition of separate and distinct

units may be a general characteristic of learning in the aged. Implicit in this view is the assumption that there are in general two patterns of learning: one in which there is first a more general learning from which particular associations are increasingly differentiated, and a second in which only the specific stimulus-response associations are formed. We might speculate that the second pattern, seen here in the behavior of aged persons, is generally characteristic of more constricted or rigid cognitive organization and might be found as well in the behavior of anxious or brain-damaged individuals.

From the first of these three views one assumes that the older learner may have available, but is unwilling to report, incorrect hypotheses. According to the second, the formulation of such hypotheses cannot be completed and reported within the time available. But on the last assumption neither caution nor time blocks response; rather there are fewer incorrect hypotheses available.

All of these factors, however, may be conceived as parts of the total aging process. In the aged there is a decreased ability to comprehend, organize, and integrate new experience both in perception and in memory. Integration is likely to be incomplete, often rigid or confused, and the integrative process requires greater time. Performance is most adequate where the individual can draw most heavily from past experience, most disturbed when novel behavior is involved. As a consequence the aged person seeks the security of the familiar, risks fewer failures by making fewer attempts, and so defends against the recognition of inadequacy.

15

Some Observations on Age and Skill*

A. T. Welford

There is a great temptation to be sentimental about the talents of older people. It is easy to persuade oneself that they retain all of the finer

* From AGEING AND HUMAN SKILL by A. T. Welford, published by Oxford University Press under the auspices of the Nuffield Foundation. 1958, London, pp. 283-289. (With permission of the author and the Oxford University Press.)

qualities of earlier years, while at the same time they are acquiring new psychological assets, especially those commonly ascribed to the vintage years of maturity. The facts simply do not support such an idealistic interpretation. As Dr. Welford reminds us, the number of active brain cells tends to diminish from young adulthood onwards. It seems foolish to believe that there are no degenerative changes in the central nervous system paralleling those that aging produces in other physical structures, changes which are clearly reflected in such attributes as weakened muscle tone and reduced skin elasticity. Although the older person may effectively compensate in many instances for deteriorating structures of the central nervous system, it seems probable, in Dr. Welford's opinion, that peak demands on the older individual's functional resources will reveal the following kinds of deficiencies: diminished channel capacity, lowering of the "signal-to-noise" ratio in neural transmission, and lessened capacity for short-term memory storage. Offsetting these inevitable losses in mental efficiency are the often-forgotten personal-social resources, special talents, and time-honored virtues of the aged—for example, an inclination to be concerned about the welfare of the poor, the oppressed, the deranged, and the other unfortunates who are always among us.

From a strictly empirical point of view the main results from the work we have conducted which occur again and again are, firstly, the obvious slowing of performance that goes with age, a slowing manifested not only in sensori-motor tasks but in perception, problem-solving and other situations in which it is the mental rather than the motor component which is stressed. Secondly, there is the increasing variability between one individual and another as we go up the age scale, which means that more often than not we find a substantial number of old people performing at a level at least equal to that of the average of a group of younger subjects. These two tendencies have frequently been demonstrated in the past and are indeed obvious to common observation. What has not been so noticeable in previous studies is a third point, namely, that the changes of performance with age very commonly become disproportionately greater as the difficulty of the task rises, so that relatively small age differences with easy tasks may be profound with similar tasks making rather more severe demands.

None of these tendencies is, however, regular enough from one situation to another for us to be able to regard it as implying any universal rule or law. Speed of performance does not always decline in the years from the twenties onwards and the actual form of the slowing when it occurs may belong to one of several different patterns. The increasing variability appears to be of more than one kind; sometimes, for example, the rise may be in absolute terms only, the relative variability remaining constant with age;

whereas in other tasks, older people may show both relatively as well as absolutely greater individual differences than do younger. The disproportionate effect of increased difficulty is by no means universal, and instances have been given in which the opposite has been observed. It is clear, therefore, that we must go beyond the readily observable facts to more fundamental principles of the operation of human sensory, central and motor mechanisms. This the work reported here has attempted to do by looking in detail at the nature and causes of changing performance among older people.

The studies have revealed clearly that the changes with age lie essentially in the central control and guidance of actions. In some cases they may represent the indirect effects of impairment to the peripheral organs of sense and motor action. For example, if we cannot see clearly we can compensate to some extent by looking for a longer time at what we have to observe, or if our hand becomes unsteady we can largely offset the resulting difficulty of making accurately graded movements by altering the manner in which we support and steady it. There is no doubt, however, that some, and probably the most important, age trends in performance are due directly to effects associated with age in the central mechanisms themselves. These may be thought of as due to changes in the central nervous system which are analogous to those more obvious changes in tissues we can see. They are organic in nature and are to be thought of as dispassionately as we think of the signs of maturing years in face and hands. Their effect upon behaviour is due to the fact that they occur in the tissue by which behaviour is mediated.

These effects would seem to be of two main types. The first is the lowering of the 'capacity' of the organism's 'information channel', due either to a reduction in the strength of the signals from one part of the mechanism to the next, or to an increase in the amount of random nervous activity (i.e., 'noise'), or to both. The reduction of 'signal-to-noise' ratio implied by these changes results in a need for stronger signals or for the integration of data over a longer time before it can become a sufficient basis for action. This applies not only to signals coming from the sense organs to the brain, but to the many stages of signalling within the brain itself. Because many mechanisms of this kind are involved, the form of slowing varies from one task to another according to which mechanism in the chain is setting the limit to the subject's performance—in other words, according to the demands of the task he is doing.

The second major effect of central change with age lies in a little-understood process seemingly common to short-term memory and conceptualization. We have described it as the holding in mind of a quantity of data so that it can be used simultaneously. It is conceived that data are somehow held in a form of short-term storage while other data are being gathered. Obviously, unless data can be so held, the amount of information that can be simultaneously applied to any problem is very small indeed. It would appear that in old people the amount than can be stored tends to diminish, and that what is stored is more liable than it is in younger people to interference and disruption from other activity going on at the same time. Such a decline in short-term retention would be capable of accounting for a very wide range of observed age changes in learning and problem-solving, although it must be recognized that the evidence at present available does not rule out other explanations.

Diminished channel capacity, lowering of 'signal-to-noise' ratio and lessened short-term storage would all on average tend to produce limitations of performance measurable by simple over-all achievement scores. It is important to recognize, however, that these limitations are not likely to exert their effects upon all parts or aspects or stages of a task equally. They will only become serious at certain points at which 'peak' demands occur leading to 'overloading'. Thus the pacing of performance by an external agency is likely to lead to occasional overloading of the subject's capacity to handle information, and complex problem-solving tasks may at certain points on the way to a solution make excessive demands for short-term retention, so that the capacity for this will limit the complexity of problem that can be tackled successfully. Intermittent overloads of these kinds may well be the cause of some of the momentary 'lapses' of attention to which both young and old are to some extent prone, and which are often said to increase with age.

A possible explanation of the limitation of both channel capacity and short-term retention is contained in the fact that the number of active brain cells tends to diminish from young adulthood onwards. Such a diminution would almost certainly lead to a lessening of signal strength in the brain: the fact that random activity would be averaged over a smaller number of cells would tend to increase the relative 'noise' level, and the reduced number of cells would mean less capacity for the establishment of the reverberant circuits which probably underlie short-term retention. The same kind of explanation might well account for other observed changes with age, for example, the finding by Botwinick and Shock (1952) that a mental task showed less fatigue effect among older people than it did among younger; if we can conceive of fatigue as in any sense an aftermath of overactivity of the brain, it is clear that reduction of signal strength would, in certain circumstances at least, reduce liability to fatigue effects.

This kind of explanation would not, however, explain the fact noted in many experiments that older people have a remarkable ability to compensate for any changes which may tend to impair their performance and show an automatic and unconscious ordering of their activity to make the best use of what capacities they have. This process of what we may call *unconscious optimization* is probably a feature of much if not most normal human performance. The fact that it is striking in later middle and old age indicates that whatever difficulties may be experienced at these times of life, the ability to organize behaviour 'strategically' has not been lost. It must be emphasized that such over-all planning should not be taken as in any sense supporting the view that there is 'a little man up aloft in control', but simply that behaviour is organized in a hierarchical manner, with different controlling processes operating on different time scales.

It is clear that each one of the areas of research surveyed here requires a great deal of further work. The results already obtained constitute little more than an extensive exploration and a beginning of the definition of essential problems. What has been achieved would seem to be the demonstration that certain age changes which might *prima facie* be due to either organic causes or to experience are likely to have been caused predominantly by the former. The time would now seem opportune for a more thorough-going study of the effects of experience, especially long experience, upon performance in later middle and old age. We do not know, for example, the relationship between demands early in life and the subsequent changes of performance level with age, although we know that moderate demands in childhood and adolescence appear to bring out an individual's potentialities better than demands which are either too high or too low, and we also know that age changes are less among individuals who show high achievement as young adults.

Research aimed at studying the results of long experience would seem inevitably to involve longitudinal studies following individuals over a considerable period of years and imply the need for the highly stable investigating groups that these longitudinal studies require. They would also seem to need considerable flexibility of thought in designing ways of studying performance. It would be necessary to solve the problem of how to study those performances in which older people excel and of how to discover in just what ways this excellence is attained. There is little doubt that the more thorough 'coding' in perception and in action that experience makes possible is potentially a means of offsetting the limitations we referred to earlier, and may often far more than compensate for them. Such 'coding' and the experience that lies behind it, is, however, highly individual, and it would seem necessary, therefore, to face the task of assessing uniquely individual abilities and their changes with age. It is difficult to do this in an acceptably scientific manner, but the task would seem not to be impossible. We might, for example, consider the progress over a number of years of those things which a man can do best, and compare these 'best' performances with other aspects of his ability. Again, a potentially useful line of approach is to measure really well-established skills such as those attained by industrial operatives at their work, because these are probably the most highly practised activities that we have available for study, apart from simple actions such as eating and walking.

Viewing our research findings from a strictly practical standpoint, we see that they provide no dramatic suggestions for the elimination or reversal of age changes. What they do indicate, however, is that in many tasks subjects, young and old alike, are working well within their capacities and that changes of capacity, even in old age, are unimportant. Perhaps more significant is the indication that where age changes do impinge upon performance some relatively trivial factor may often be limiting what can be done, so that comparatively small changes in the task could bring it within the capacities of older people. It follows that a promising line for future research in industry lies in attempting to change the layout of work or of machine tools in order to make them more suitable for operation by older people. It would seem likely that relatively minor modifications could profoundly affect the chances of success by older people at certain jobs: the modifications would benefit both young and old, but especially the latter. Attempts to 'fit the job to the man' in such ways would seem a far better approach to the problem of employment for older people than attempting to move men to other jobs. Older people who at the present time change their jobs seem seldom to take up work at a level appropriate to their past attainments, and in consequence a move in middle or old age usually leads to the wasting of skills which have been established and brought to a high level over a period of many years. Where changes of work must be made, we may expect that the acquisition of new skill would be easier if arrangements could be made for it to be acquired gradually over a substantial period of time—if, in other words, a man could always look "one jump ahead' and prepare for his new work in advance. The same might well be true of preparation for retirement.

An industrial medical officer once said to the writer that data were needed which would enable a doctor to prescribe work for older people much the same way as he now prescribes drugs or treatment. We are not yet in a position to make suggestions either for work or for leisure which attain this degree of definiteness. It is, however, fair to say that a foundation has been laid upon which such an "ergopoeia', analogous to the pharmacopoeia, can eventually be based, and the way has been shown round some of the extremely difficult problems besetting the studies of ageing in industry which must precede such specification.

In conclusion, it must be remarked with all humility that anyone who has a sympathetic interest in his fellow men and seeks to understand them cannot but recognize that everything which has been done so far towards the scientific study of ageing leaves aside some of the most characteristic and important qualities of older people, qualities which are elusive in nature and must be broadly classed as attitudinal. Many so-called attitudes and interests have been the subject of investigations which have shown changes in the patterns of what men and women consider desirable or important as they grow older, but over and above these are many qualities of attitude which have up to the present escaped systematic study. Some of these seem rather clearly based on organic or other fundamental factors; for example, the gnawing suspiciousness that seems to derive from deafness or loss of memory, the disagreeability and laziness which often result from failing energy, or, on the other hand, the gentle enjoyment of people that comes from the inability to pursue the energetic pastimes of former years, or the helpfulness to others that many old people show when increased leisure in retirement gives them opportunity for its practical expression.

Other attitudinal qualities do not seem to have any such clear and obvious organic foundations. For example, the bitterness resulting from failure to achieve ambitions, or the fearless simplicity that derives from having reconciled oneself to the fact that some of what one set out to do has been done and the rest can be forgotten. Perhaps we may say of these that old age is a *revealing* time when the best and the worst in us stand out in sharp relief.

Whatever the cause of these attitudes they are of profound practical and social importance and the understanding of them must surely form a part of the programme of future research in the field of ageing. How to proceed to study them in a significant way we do not yet know, and for the present all we can do is to remember what the pioneers of psychology realized, but has since often been forgotten, namely, that preconceived theory is a tool and a servant that must never be allowed to usurp a position of control. We shall do less than justice to our subject if we try to force these aspects of the behaviour of older people into the strait jacket of present psychological theories. For the present we must observe as accurately and objectively as we can, searching forward step by step, content never to be quite sure where we shall eventually arrive.

Part IV

THE ONTOGENESIS OF
MOTIVATIONAL PATTERNS

THE PAST two and a half decades of American psychology have witnessed a tremendous upsurge of interest in motivational concepts as explanatory variables in human behavior and in finding out more about motivation itself through research. This development has its roots in the progress of the science itself, but it probably received added impetus from the fact that substantial numbers of psychologists served as "clinical psychologists" in military service during World War II. In addition, the development during the past decade of a number of devices for measuring motivation stimulated and paved the way for new research undertakings.

The broad range of completed studies dealing with motivation, including psychological needs, illustrates the fruitfulness of the motivational concept. Motives instigate and give direction to behavior, and often serve to relate in meaningful fashion what seem superficially to be very diverse and inconsistent forms of behavior, thus providing a certain unity to behavior both as it occurs at any one moment and over long time-spans. Such concepts as the "inner-directed" and "other-directed" person illustrate this. In the "inner-directed" individual, a fairly consistent, integrated life plan may be revealed underlying many superficially diverse activities. The "other-directed" person, on the other hand, may respond quite differently in one setting as compared to another, depending on the nature of the external social pressures he happens to encounter, yet his "inconsistencies" may be seen to be external expressions of the same underlying tendency: to conform in thought or action with whatever is going on around him.

The several papers assembled in this part will serve to illustrate something of the origins of motives, and how they are expressed in adolescence and during the course of a life span in the things people like to do, in their interests, and in their changing goals. The first paper, by Professor Harry F. Harlow, and his associates, of the University of Wisconsin, is of special interest in its demonstration that a "need" to explore and manipulate is evident at very early ages—and may be considered one of the genetically determined drives. The second paper, by Professor McClelland and his associates, deals with the origins of the achievement motive, a motive highly valued in American society. The influence of interaction with parents, and the reward-punishment patterns characterizing the early home situation, are clearly evident in this investigation. The next paper is a classic by Professors Stone and Barker which contrasts sexually mature girls with sexually immature girls of the same age. The influence of endocrine changes in pubescence upon a broad array of interests is evident, but the differences are sufficiently small so that they suggest that such developments do not produce sudden changes but require substantial periods of time to influence behavior.

The next paper, by Professor E. K. Strong, shows changes in interests from the twenties through the fifties. If it is recognized that "interests" represent behaviors which have need-gratification value, their relevance to an understanding of motivational changes during the adult years is evident. Indeed, a systematic inventorying of interests represents one approach to the measurement of motives.

16

Manipulatory Motivation in Monkeys*

Harry F. Harlow, N. C. Blazek, G. E. McClearn

It is customary in contemporary psychology, almost without exception, to postulate the existence of some drive, need, goal-attraction, or other motivational state to instigate and sustain a behavior sequence in organisms. Freud assumed instinctual forces that may propel the human organism in deflected, or sublimated, form throughout life. Modern behaviorists hold that a few primary drives (like hunger, thirst, sex, and avoidance of noxious stimuli) may become elaborated through learning into many specific drive states. Field theorists, in their conceptions, use drives and the attractions of valenced goals to account for behavioral movement. Adopting the principle of parsi-

* From Harry F. Harlow, N. C. Blazek, and G. E. McClearn, "Manipulatory Motivation in the Infant Rhesus Monkey," *Journal of Comparative and Physiological Psychology*, 1956, Vol. 49, pp. 444-448. (With permission of the senior author and the American Psychological Association.)

mony, or Ockham's razor, most theorists prefer the postulation of as few "givens" in motivation as possible, and then proceed to account for the complexity of motivating states in the mature organism by processes of learning and acculturation. For example, it is proposed that the infant learns to need the presence of his mother because she is typically present when the primary need for food is being satisfied. This form of theorizing makes it important that we recognize the structure and function of all primary, or genetically transmitted, drives and needs. Otherwise we will feel obliged to claim a learning basis for motivating states that in fact are already provided by genetic-developmental processes. In the following report, Dr. Harlow and his collaborators report the findings of several experiments that show the operation of manipulation motives very early in the life of the infant rhesus monkey. It seems reasonable to assume that similar needs to explore and manipulate are also present in the human organism as genetically "givens."

The series of experiments included in the following paper deal with the manipulatory behavior of infant rhesus monkeys and comprise a portion of an extensive study utilizing six monkeys born and raised at the Wisconsin Laboratory. Although the primary concern of the investigation was the development of techniques and apparatus suitable for the maintenance and testing of the infant monkey, the obtained results provide information on manipulatory motives and on developmental aspects of learning based both on food and manipulatory incentives.

Previous experiments at the Wisconsin Laboratory demonstrated that the operation of manipulation motivation in adult monkeys was effective in maintaining persistently high levels of response and in facilitating the learning of mechanical puzzles and discrimination problems. These data have been summarized by Harlow (1953). Studies using adult animals, however, cannot determine the influence, if any, of homeostatic drives and associated incentives on the development of manipulation motives, or the influence of maturation on responsiveness to the various manipulatory incentives. Solution of these questions requires utilizing infant animals, tracing the development of their motivational and learning performances, and comparing their behaviors with those of their mature relatives.

EXPERIMENT 1. SINGLE-DEVICE PUZZLE TESTS

Method. *Subjects.* Six infant rhesus monkeys were used as Ss in this experiment. The sex of each animal, time of maternal separation, time of initial introduction of semisolid and of solid food, and age on the initial test day of the four described researches are presented in Table 1. Before and during the period in which this experiment was run, the monkeys were bottle- or cup-fed a milk formula, but supplementary solid foods were gradually introduced into their diets at the ages designated in Table 1. At no time during the testing periods was there food in the cages. The infants were housed within the same room, in individual wire-mesh cages 15 inches by 18 inches by 24 inches and were raised under condition similar to those described by van Wagenen (1950).

Apparatus. The apparatus used in the presentation of the stimuli consisted of a set of three gray panels 15 inches by 18 inches, so designed that any one panel could temporarily replace a cage end. Mounted on each of the panels was an array of nine identical devices arranged in rows and columns of three and mounted not less than 2 inches apart horizontally and 3 inches apart vertically. The three types of devices so utilized were small screen-door hook-and-eye units, cotter pins with small rings dangling from them, and small brass hasps.

The Gray Audograph recording unit was used by E to record observed behavior during the test period, and a stop watch was utilized to time the test interval.

Procedure. All Ss were given a single 5-minute test session with each of the three test panels on each day of testing, and the order of presentation of the boards was varied from day to day in a counterbalanced manner. Whenever possible, testing was conducted seven days a week, but there were numerous occasions when this was impractical. Monkeys 1 to 4 were tested for a total of 30 days, and the remaining two Ss were tested for 15 days.

At the beginning of each test S was restrained by E while the cage end was removed and the appropriate test panel fastened in place. When the panel was arranged with all devices in closed position, E released the animal, started timing, and began recording observations of S's behavior.

TABLE 1

							Discrimi-
		Maternal	Semi-		Single-	String-	Two-	nated
Animal		Sepa-	Solid	Solid	Device	Pulling	Device	Pin-
Number	Sex	ration	Food	Food	Puzzle	Test	Puzzle	Pulling
			Age at Introduction of Indicated Measure					
---	---	---	---	---	---	---	---	---
1	F	30	31	79	36	47	106	109
2	F	26	26	63	29	41	100	103
3	M	1	16	50	26	37	96	99
4	M	1	24	48	16	27	86	89
5	M	1	24	89	24	18		52
6	F	2	25	83	23	17		51

Items recorded included contacts with specific unopened devices, device opening, and contacts with opened devices. "Contacts" were defined as mouth or hand touchings and openings, such as removal of pins from the board, pulling down the loose flap of the hasp from the fixed portion, and lifting and disengaging the hook from the eye. "Successful responses" were defined as hook or hasp openings and pin removals.

A measure of the percentage of successful responses was obtained by dividing the total number of successful contacts by all contacts with devices, excluding contacts with devices subsequent to their opening. Thus, an increase in the percentage correct could result from either an increase in the number of successes or a decrease in the number of contacts preceding successes.

Results. The mean number of daily responses on successive five-day blocks for Ss 1 to 4 on each of the three devices is presented in Figure 1. A t test of the differences between means for days 1 to 5 and 26 to 30 reveals significant increase in the number of daily contacts with the hook and the hasp$(p<.02)$, and fails to indicate a significant difference between means for the pin responses $(p>.1)$. These data suggest that the response level on the single-device puzzle first increases and then remains relatively constant for a considerable period of time.

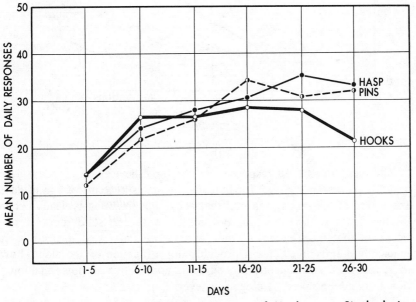

FIGURE 1. Mean Number of Daily Responses of Monkeys on Single-device Puzzle Tests

Figure 2 shows the percentage of successful responses on successive five-day blocks for both the four-S group, which was tested for 30 days, and the complete six-S group tested for the first 15 days on each of the three devices. The results of t tests indicate significant increases for the four-S group between initial and terminal blocks on the pin ($p<.01$) and hasp ($p<.01$) devices, but fail to show a significant increase for the hook device ($p>.1$). In the case of the pins, however, the result is not unequivocal inasmuch as a test for heterogeneity of variance indicated an F value significant at the .05 level.

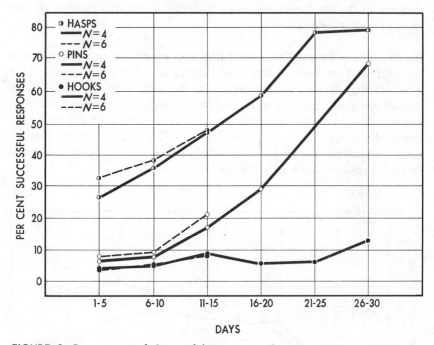

FIGURE 2. Percentage of Successful Responses for Pins, Hooks, and Hasps

The mean number of responses for the three devices on test days 1, 3, and 5 is plotted in Figure 3 for individual animals in terms of age in days. Inspection of the graph indicated that active manipulation typically occurs on the first test day and precedes contact with any solid food. It may be noted that monkey no. 4, the youngest animal tested, proved to be unusually nonreactive. This is probably not a function of age alone, however, for this S subsequently proved to be nonreactive on other manipulation tests administered at older age levels.

EXPERIMENT 2. STRING-PULLING MANIPULATION TEST

Method. *Subjects.* The same six infant monkeys again served as *S*s.

Apparatus. The apparatus consisted of a 15-in. by 18-in. Masonite panel with six holes 9/16 in. in diameter, spaced 2¼ in. apart and 8½ in. from the bottom of the panel. Six different types of string were led through these holes and attached to microswitches behind the panel by means of

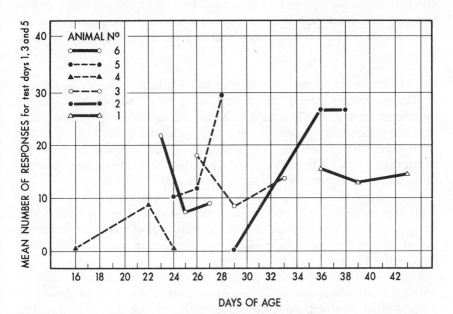

FIGURE 3. Mean Number of Responses on All Devices (Test Days 1, 3, and 5). Age in days is given on the abscissa.

Nuway snaps, making possible ready attachment and detachment of any string to or from any switch. Each switch, when activated, closed a circuit, which activated a Veeder-Root Counter. The nature and characteristics of the strings, which extended 6 in. below the holes in the panel, were as follows:

1. *Twine*—a heavy, stiff, white cord, 3/16 inches in diameter with a fairly coarse texture.
2. *Thong*—a length of brown leather shoe thong, 3/16 inches thick.
3. *Chain*—plumbers chain, a series of small, silver-colored balls 3/16 inches in diameter in fixed series on a wire.
4. *Ribbon*—pink, satin ribbon ¼ inches wide.
5. *Link*—small, brass, linked plumbers chain 3/16 inches wide.
6. *Shoelaces*—gaudy shoestring, 5/16 inches wide, with a red, yellow, and green plaid pattern.

A stop watch was used to time response latencies and test periods.

Procedure. The pattern of presentation of the strings was determined for every six-day period, independently for each animal, by means of permuted latin squares, and the Ss were tested for three successive six-day periods.

For a given test session, the appropriate pattern of strings was arranged, all counters were set to zero, and while S was restrained, the panel was attached, replacing one end of the cage. Timing was begun when S was released, and initial response latency was recorded to the nearest second. After 5 minutes the counters were read and the apparatus removed from the cage.

Results. The mean number of responses to all strings by the six Ss showed significant increase during the 18 test days. Total number of responses ranged from about 400 to over 1,200, and the individual differences were significant ($F < .05$). A similar range and significance were indicated for string preference. The strings arranged from highest to lowest in the order twine, thong, chain, ribbon, link, and shoestring. No evidence was obtained for significant differences among the six positions.

The average latency ranged from 38 seconds on day 1 to approximately 4 seconds on days 9, 12, and 16. In spite of wide day-to-day fluctuations the general trend was downward, and the Wilcoxon nonparametric test for paired replications indicates a significant decrease in mean latency from days 1 to 5 to days 13 to 18 ($p < .05$).

Figure 4 shows the number of daily responses on the first five days of testing for individual animals according to days of age. Five of the six Ss demonstrated clear-cut string-pulling behavior on the first test day. The sharp increase in level of initial response for animals more than 35 days old suggests that age may be a factor in determining the number of string-pulling responses an infant monkey will make.

EXPERIMENT 3. TWO-DEVICE PUZZLE TESTS

Method. *Subjects.* Monkeys 1, 2, 3, and 4 served as Ss.

Apparatus. The apparatus used for the presentation of manipulanda in this experiment was similar to that used in Experiment 1. Four puzzle-units were mounted on the gray test panel and the units arranged in rows and columns of two with a separation of approximately 5 inches. Each unit was composed of the hook and hasp devices combined in such a manner that the hook had to be released before the hasp could be opened.

Procedure. Each S was given a 5-minute experimental session once a day for ten days. Testing was conducted five days a week.

At the beginning of each session E restrained the animal while replacing one cage end with the test panel. When the panel was in place with all devices closed, E released S and started stop-watch timing and Audograph recording of S's contacts with the puzzles and S's behavior between contacts. The items recorded included contacts with specific components and units, openings, and contacts with opened devices. As in the previous experiment hook-opening required the disengaging of the hook from the

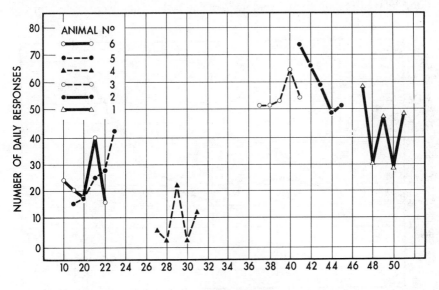

FIGURE 4. Number of Daily Responses on Test Days 1 to 5 on String-pulling Test. Age in days is given on the abscissa.

eye by an upward motion. Hasp-opening required a lateral motion to move the loose flap away from the fixed portion.

Percentage of correct responses was measured by dividing the hook or the hasp openings by the number of contacts with both devices up to and including the successful contact.

Results. The mean number of daily responses on successive two-day blocks for four Ss remained almost constant at 35, and no difference between blocks was significant. Thus, the group maintained a steady level of response, showing no sign of satiation during the ten days of testing.

Figure 5 shows the percentage of correct responses on both the hook and hasp components of the puzzle for successive two-day blocks, and the curves indicate trends toward improved performance. The differences between the initial and final test blocks as measured by t tests for correlated measures were not, however, statistically significant.

EXPERIMENT 4. DISCRIMINATED PIN-PULLING TESTS

Method. *Subjects.* The six rhesus infants utilized in the preceding studies served as Ss in the present experiment. In addition to the manipulation studies reported in this paper these monkeys had by this time received various other tests. Monkeys 1, 2, 3, and 4 had been given object discrimination, delayed response, and patterned-string tests. They were tested on the

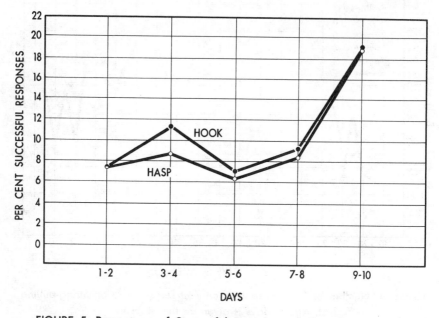

FIGURE 5. Percentage of Successful Responses on Two-device Puzzle
(4 animals)

two-device puzzles and the present experiment concurrently. Monkeys 5 and 6 had no previous experience on object discrimination, delayed response, or patterned-string tests and were never tested on the two-device puzzle.

Apparatus. The pins were presented to the Ss on a gray wooden panel which could be fitted over the end of the cage. The stimulus objects consisted of the ring-bearing halves of ordinary house keys. The objects were arranged on the panel so as to form two vertical columns and five horizontal rows. One member of each row was painted white and the other black. On each of the four panels, all of either the black or white key halves were removable and hence correct, while the keys of the other color were fixed and incorrect. The objects were separated from one another by a distance of 2¼ inches in the horizontal direction and 1½ inches in the vertical direction. Inversion of each of the boards made possible a second stimulus configuration. Thus, the four panels provided eight test configurations, four with white objects correct and four with black objects correct.

The Gray Audograph was used by *E* in recording behavioral observations during the test periods, and a stop watch was used for timing.

Procedure. All animals were given a 5-minute test session each day. The four oldest *S*s were tested for a total of 10 days, and the two younger

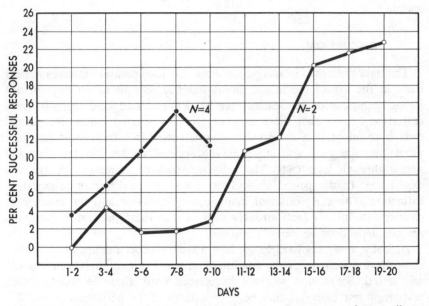

FIGURE 6. Percentage of Successful Responses on Discriminated Pin-pulling Tests. Test days are given on abscissa.

*S*s for 20 days. Each of the four older *S*s was tested on two panels (four stimulus configurations); white was correct on two configurations, black on the other two. The order in which the panels were presented was determined individually for each animal. Each configuration appeared once in each four-day test period. The two youngest animals were tested on one panel only (white correct), which was inverted to present the second configuration every other day.

At the beginning of each test session *E* restrained *S* while removing the cage end and putting the test panel in place. He then released *S* and started timing and recording. A system of symbols was used to indicate the animal's behavior in relationship to the pins.

Results. Figure 6 shows the percentage of successful responses by two-day blocks for both the two- and four-*S* groups. This measure was calculated in terms of "correct responses," defined as removals of mobile pins, divided by "incorrect responses," which involved either contacts with immobile pins or contacts with mobile pins which did not result in their removal.

A *t* test of differences between correlated means shows differences ($.05 > p > .02$) between mean per cent successful responses on days 1 to 2 and days 9 to 10 for the four-*S* group and between days 1 to 5 and 16 to 20 for the two-*S* group. Thus, in both groups there is evidence of learning.

DISCUSSION

The data presented in this paper show that manipulation motives appear early in the life of the infant rhesus monkey. By 20 to 30 days of age strong manipulation tendencies may be demonstrated, and there is every reason to believe that these motives probably existed before the formal tests were initiated in the present experiments. More frequently than not, puzzle manipulation and string-pulling appear on the first test day and persist through later tests. The behavior tends to increase with age and experience. In the period studied there was no evidence of satiation or extinction. The early onset of manipulatory behavior and the absence of clear-cut satiation effects strongly suggest that these motivated behaviors are not dependent on derived motives.

Actually, it is very hard to see how a second-order manipulation motive could have arisen under the conditions in which the animals were housed and tested. Solid food was not introduced until after the puzzle-device and string-test behavior had been demonstrated (experiments 1 and 2). Although semisolid food was spoon-fed the monkeys during this developmental period, it was given routinely at feeding time, never as a reward for searching behavior, and its ingestion involved little or no manual activity by the monkey. Conceivably, the manipulation motives might have been derived from conditioning to, and generalization from, the suckling activities, but this seems highly unlikely. Thus, the present data strongly indicate that manipulation behavior is self-sustaining and that it is not elicited by conditioning to any identifiable internal drive state, such as hunger, or some learned incentive, such as food.

SUMMARY

The manipulatory behavior of six infant rhesus monkeys was investigated during a series of four problems measuring motivation and learning based on manipulation motives. Testing was initiated when the *S*s were between 16 and 36 days of age and before the introduction of solid food.

Manipulation was found generally to increase in amount and efficiency with age and with practice. The results suggest that manipulatory behavior is self-sustaining and is not dependent upon, nor derived from, internal drives such as hunger or thirst, or their incentive systems.

17

Origins of Achievement Motivation[*]

David C. McClelland, John W. Atkinson, Russell A. Clark, and Edgar L. Lowell

The present paper is an excerpt from a book by Dr. David McClelland and his associates, a book which presents a fascinating array of research findings bearing on the origin and correlates of the achievement motive. Dr. McClelland's use of projective test procedures represented one of the early efforts to measure motives and has helped open up this important area of psychology to careful study. The present paper describes one phase of his research dealing with development of achievement motives in the context of the family during the years of early childhood. The types of training in independence that a child receives and the nature of the social and physical rewards which are bestowed upon him for his achievements at an early age prove to be related to the presence of achievement striving later. It should be noted that the research reported here represents some of the first research on this topic. As might be expected some of the conceptions proved to be overly simple. To appreciate the development of concepts and research designs the reader may wish to review the entire book from which this excerpt is taken and to contrast it with later work reported by Atkinson et al. (1958). He may also wish to examine a more recent volume which studies the character of achieving societies (McClelland, 1961).

* Adapted and abridged from pp. 288-306 of David C. McClelland, John W. Atkinson, Russell A. Clark, and Edgar L. Lowell, *The Achievement Motive*, Appleton-Century-Crofts, 1953. (With permission of the senior author and the publisher.)

Our hypothesis is that differences in achievement motivation are learned from the different experiences that children have. Since our earlier studies of sons' perceptions of the child-rearing practices to which they were exposed suggested a focus, we begin with the hypothesis that achievement motivation is a function of the stress placed on independence training. Actually, the hypothesis is also supported by our theoretical analysis of how the achievement motive is acquired out of the way in which the child is handled as he faces a variety of learning situations, common to all children in all cultures at all times. That is, nearly all children have to learn to walk and talk and all have to master some other skills such as reading, hunting, sewing, cooking, and the like. Cultures and parents as representatives of the culture will vary in the amount of pressure they place on their children for *early* mastery of such skills. The more they insist on early mastery, the more the child thinks in achievement terms, the greater the affect from meeting or failing to meet achievement standards, and so on. In short, the more the child is forced to master things, the greater his *n* Achievement, the more independent he becomes of his parents, and the more rejectant they are likely to appear to him.

PROCEDURE AND SUBJECTS

By far the most direct and conclusive test of our hypothesis that *n* Achievement is associated with stress on independence training has been made by Winterbottom (1953). She obtained *n* Achievement scores from stories told by 29 normal boys, 8-10 years old, in response to verbal cues under both Relaxed and Achievement-oriented conditions. Since her findings were substantially the same for scores obtained under the two conditions, and since we have some justification for believing scores obtained under Achievement orientation are the best measure of individual differences, we will report here only the results obtained with scores obtained under Achievement orientation. The verbal cues used in this condition were as follows:
1. A father and son talking about something important
2. Brothers and sisters playing. One is a little ahead
3. A young man alone at night
4. A boy with his head resting on his hands

The average *n* Achievement score for stories (each told in 4-5 minutes) in response to these cues was 5.69, SD=5.05.

The mother's attitude toward independence training was obtained from a questionnaire given the mother in an interview, the nature of which is best indicated by the "core" section dealing with training demands reproduced in part below.

Beside each statement there are two blanks. In the first one put a check mark if it is one of the things you want in your child by the time he is ten years old. In the second one put the approximate age by which you think your child should have learned this behavior. The sample below illustrates how to do this:

✔   10   To obey traffic signals and street lights when he is out alone

This mother has checked this as one of the things she wants in her child and she expects him to learn this by the age of 10 . . . Lots of books have been written on how a mother should treat her child but it's surprising how little information we have on what the people on the firing-line—the mothers—actually do. We would like you to answer these questions by telling us what you find works best with your child.

_____ _____ To stand up for his own rights with other children
_____ _____ To know his way around his part of the city so that he can play where he wants without getting lost
_____ _____ To go outside to play when he wants to be noisy or boisterous
_____ _____ To be willing to try new things on his own without depending on his mother for help
_____ _____ To be active and energetic in climbing, jumping and sports
_____ _____ To show pride in his ability to do things well
_____ _____ To take part in his parents' interests and conversations
_____ _____ To try hard things for himself without asking for help
_____ _____ To be able to eat alone without help in cutting and handling food
_____ _____ To be able to lead other children and assert himself in children's groups
_____ _____ To make his own friends among children his own age
_____ _____ To hang up his own clothes and look after his own possessions
_____ _____ To do well in school on his own
_____ _____ To be able to undress and go to bed by himself
_____ _____ To have interests and hobbies of his own. To be able to entertain himself
_____ _____ To earn his own spending money
_____ _____ To do some regular tasks around the house
_____ _____ To be able to stay at home during the day alone
_____ _____ To make decisions like choosing his clothes or deciding how to spend his money by himself
_____ _____ To do well in competition with other children
_____ _____ To try hard to come out on top in games and sports.

These items came from some interview scales developed by Whiting and Sears at Harvard University, and each one was rephrased as a restriction in another part of the questionnaire. For example, the first item in the above list became the following restriction to be filled out in the same way if the mother wanted it before age 10.

_____ _____ Not to fight with children to get his own way.

In many instances the restrictions indicated not only an absence of opportunity for independent action by the child but also positive restrictive action by the parent. The questionnaire covered a number of other matters, but these are the ones most relevant to our hypothesis.

RESULTS

Winterbottom's main results are summarized in Figure 1 and Table 1 which show that while the total number of demands made by mothers of sons with high and low *n* Achievement (above and below the median score) does not differ, the mothers of sons with high *n* Achievement ex-

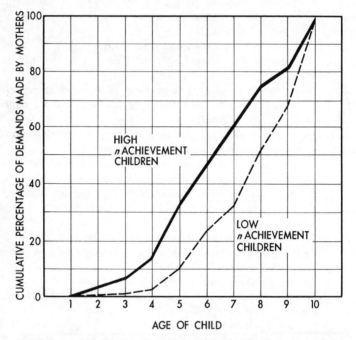

FIGURE 1. Cumulative Curves Showing the Proportion of Total
Demands Made Up to Each Age Level as Reported by Mothers
of Children Scoring High and Low on *n* Achievement
(Achievement orientation)

pect their children to have met independence demands much earlier in life. Thus, as the cumulative percentage curve in Figure 1 shows, by age 7 the mothers of sons with high *n* Achievement expect that over 60 per cent of the demands checked will have been learned, whereas the mothers of sons with low *n* Achievement expect that only about 33 per cent of their demands will have been learned. If the distribution of ages at which demands are to be learned is broken at age 8, the results shown in Table 1 are obtained. The sons with high *n* Achievement have mothers who say they require almost twice as many skills to be mastered below the age of 8 as are required by the mothers of sons with low *n* Achievement.

The "restrictions" data are also interesting although less conclusive.

In general, they parallel the "demands" results but with a minor and perhaps significant difference. The mothers of children with low n Achievement tend to check more restrictions over all ages (p∼.06, with a nonparametric test of association), while there is no difference in the total number of demands checked by the two groups of mothers. This greater restrictiveness shows up in Table 1 if one compares the ratio of demands to restrictions below the age of 8. Thus the mothers of "lows" make al-

TABLE 1. Average Number of Demands and Restrictions Required Below and Above Age 8 by Mothers of Children with High and Low n Achievement (Achievement orientation)

	Mothers' Demands		Mothers' Restrictions	
	Age 7 and Below	Age 8 and Above	Age 7 and Below	Age 8 and Above
Sons with High n Achievement (N=14)				
Mean	11.71	7.43	8.79	4.50
SD	4.68	4.62	3.56	3.42
Sons with Low n Achievement (N=15)				
Mean	6.07	12.13	5.80	9.60
SD	4.05	3.94	3.92	5.02
Difference between means	5.64	--4.70	2.99	−5.10
σ diff.	1.69	1.66	1.44	1.64
t	3.34	2.83	2.10	3.11
p	<.01	<.01	<.05	<.01

most as many restrictions (mean=5.80) as they do demands (mean =6.07), and the difference between them is not significant. But the mothers of "highs" make more demands (mean=11.71) than they do restrictions (mean=8.79) before the age of 8 at a nearly significant level (p<.08). Another part of the same picture is illustrated by the way the mothers of the "highs" tend to cease making restrictions at age 8 while the mothers of the "lows" increase their restrictions. It might be argued that this is just because the mothers of the "highs" always tend to put the pressure on earlier. After all, they also drop off in the *demands* they make from age 8 on. But this is an artifact, because there are a limited number of items on the scale. Thus for the mothers of the "highs" there are only 8.29 demands left on the average for them to check to be learned at 8 or above, and they check 7.43 on the average, or nearly 90 per cent of these. The mothers of the "lows" check around 85 per cent of the demands left for them. With the restrictions it is different. Here from age 8 on the mothers of the "lows" check about 67 per cent of the restrictions left to them while the mothers of the "highs" are checking only 40 per cent of the restrictions left to them.

What this adds up to may be simply summarized. The mothers of sons with low *n* Achievement tend to demand less in the way of independent achievement at an early age, and they tend to be more restrictive than the other mothers. It is worth noting in this connection that the one item among the restrictions which differentiated the mothers of the "highs" and "lows" most significantly dealt with not playing "with children his parents don't know or disapprove." Significantly more of the mothers checking this item had sons with scores below the median on *n* Achievement.

The mothers of sons with high *n* Achievement, on the other hand, represent an "individualistic" family pattern in that they stress early independent achievement. They also make more restrictions initially, though as Winterbottom (1953) showed in another type of analysis, the restrictions tend to come *after* the demands. What is more, the restrictions fall off more markedly after age 8, presumably after the child has mastered the necessary skills. The picture here is of a parent who urges her child to master a skill early (e.g., "to know his way around the city"), restricts him until he does (e.g., "not to play away from home"), and then lets him alone. In short, she has faith in her son's ability to master something and do it on his own, whereas the mother of a son with low *n* Achievement tends not to have that faith and to continue restricting her child to playing around the house.

It is especially revealing in this connection to look at the "demand" items on which the mothers of the "highs" and "lows" differed and did not differ. The greatest differences appeared on the following items which were demanded significantly more often before age 8 by the mothers of the "highs" than by the mothers of the "lows":

1. To know his way around the city
2. To try new things for himself
3. To do well in competition
4. To make his own friends

The mothers did not differ on such items as these:

1. To eat well alone
2. To look after his own possessions
3. To go to bed by himself
4. To do tasks around the house

The difference between these two types of items is clear-cut. In the latter, the child is urged to do something on his own *so that the parent won't have to do it*. If the child doesn't eat alone, then the mother has to feed him. In the former, the demand seems to relate more directly to the welfare of the child, *as an end in himself*, rather than as a means to the end of freeing the parent from some "caretaking" jobs, with respect to the child. If the child doesn't know his way around the city, his mother doesn't have to do it for him. The mother of the son with high n Achievement is interested in her son's developing away from her, in urging him to master things on his own, whereas the mother of the son with low n Achievement is willing to let such things slide and let him remain somewhat more dependent on her. Our initial hypothesis seems amply justified: *Achievement motivation in boys is associated with stress on independence training by their mothers.*

Before leaving this topic entirely, it is perhaps worth recording some very tentative additional findings which tend to show that the reverse is true of girls. Lowell obtained n Achievement scores in the usual way on Mormon boys and girls of high school age in a Southwest rural community. As part of another study, the mothers of a number of these children were interviewed on their socialization practices with respect to a younger child in the same family. Out of these interviews a rating on "severity of interference with a child's dependent responses" was made. In the case of the six families on whose older sons he had n Achievement scores, the correlation between n Achievement and severity of independence training was positive, as expected ($tau = +.41$, $p < .15$), but for the six families on whose older daughters he had n Achievement scores, the relationship was reversed ($tau = -.41$, $p < .15$). This is only a straw in the wind, but it is suggestive because the relationship for boys is "normal" even for so small a sample and because it is logical to assume that interference with dependency in girls, since it is more expected of women, may indicate a rejection by the mother either of the daughter or the female role. Such rejection would hardly be conducive to developing high n Achievement in the daughters, which is apparently associated with social acceptability (and possibly dependence) in women rather than with independent mastery.

A portion of our theory of motivation argues that a motive results from the pairing of certain cues with an affect-producing situation. Fortunately again, Winterbottom (1953) obtained data which bear directly on this problem. The questionnaire the mothers filled out contained the following item which came directly after they had answered the "demands" section:

When your child is learning how to do things like these, which of the following are you most likely to do when he does what you want? Mark your first three choices (1, 2, 3) in the space beside the ones you choose.

_____ Tell him what a good boy he is. Praise him for doing well

_____ Do nothing at all to make it seem special

_____ Show him that you expected it of him

_____ Kiss or hug him to show how pleased you are

_____ Give him a special treat or privilege

_____ Show him how he could have done even better

The theory makes at least one specific prediction as to how the mothers of sons with high *n* Achievement should check these alternatives. It is this: Primary physical affection (kissing and hugging) for fulfilling an achievement demand should produce the most certain and probably the largest affective change in young children associated with achievement situations. Therefore it should result in higher *n* Achievement in those children who experience it.

Fortunately, the mothers broke about even in whether they checked this item at all or not. The results may be summarized very simply as shown in Table 2. The hypothesis is confirmed: Mothers who use physical rewards

TABLE 2. Contrast with Respect to Achievement Need Between Sons of Mothers Reporting Physical Rewards and Sons of Mothers Not so Reporting

	Mothers Reporting Physical Rewards		*Mothers Not Reporting Physical Rewards*
Sons' Mean *n*			
Achievement score	7.60		3.64
SD	4.51		4.79
Difference		3.96	
ó diff.		1.80	
t		2.20	
p		< .05	

for fulfillment of achievement demands have sons whose average *n* Achievement score is twice that of the sons of mothers who use more attenuated means of affective arousal. Unfortunately, not enough mothers admitted using physical punishment for nonfulfillment of demands to check any hypothesis in this area. Also it was not possible to check the possibility that giving a "special treat" might also in some cases involve primary sensory affect and hence lead to higher *n* Achievement.

Needless to say, this evidence does not conclusively prove that affective arousal *produced* the higher achievement motivation. It may simply reflect the fact that the mothers who used it felt more strongly about achievement and put greater pressure of all kinds on their sons. But this hypothesis seems a little less reasonable than the first, because it seems more likely that the preferred mode of handling a child—e.g., through verbal, objective, or physical rewards—is a personality or ideological characteristic of the mother rather than a direct result of the intensity of the mother's own achievement drive. Further research will have to settle this question, but as of the moment, the data appear to support the "affective arousal" hypothesis as to the origin of motives.

18

The Attitudes and Interests of
Pre-Menarcheal and Post-Menarcheal Girls*

Calvin P. Stone and Roger G. Barker

The emerging interest in the opposite sex and in related social activities at adolescence would seem likely to be initiated by, or at least to receive some impetus from, the various biological changes which constitute sexual maturation. The present paper reports a study of this matter in which girls of the same age and socio-economic status but differing in pubescent status were asked to express their interests and attitudes on a comprehensive paper-and-pencil "test." The sexually mature girls in contrast to their immature age mates showed greater heterosexual interest, interest in self-adornment and in daydreaming, disinterest in physical exertion. Though endocrine changes thus seem to affect behavior, there was a marked similarity in the interests and attitudes of the two groups, suggesting that the total impact of sexual maturation is to be noted not so much in its immediate effects as in long-term effects observable over a period of years.

In some species of animals characteristic patterns of behavior appear *de novo* when puberal changes in the primary and secondary sexual characters and accessory organs of sex are most in evidence; in others, notably the primates, a limited amount of sexual play is said to appear before the puberal stage of development has been reached. In either case, however, observations permit us to assume that sexual drive is greatly augmented near the time of somatic puberty and in most, if not all, instances continues to wax in strength for some time thereafter by virtue of factors of maturation and sexual experience. Man, it is popularly believed, affords no excep-

* Adapted and abridged from C. P. Stone and R. G. Barker, "The Attitudes and Interests of Pre-Menarcheal and Post Menarcheal Girls," *Journal of Genetic Psychology*, 1939, Vol. 54, pp. 27-71. (With permission of Dr. Barker and the publisher, The Journal Press.)

tion to these basic generalizations; however, just as closely related species differ from each other with respect to specific details, so also man, with his complicated cultural heritage and social environment, may differ greatly even from the higher anthropoids which most nearly resemble him in structural and physiological organization.

Although this popular belief is one of long standing, scientists, so far, have made little progress in identifying new patterns of behavior in man that manifest themselves at puberty or new urges that are markedly augmented at this time. Moreover, little has been accomplished in developing methods of investigation that are likely to prove fruitful for the investigation of these or closely related problems. Investigators are still exploring for promising leads. It is with this type of exploratory research that the present study is to be identified. Our study has as its chief objective an inquiry as to whether pre-menarcheal girls differ significantly from post menarcheal girls of the same chronological ages and social status in their responses to questions concerning their attitudes and interests.

THE SUBJECTS AND PROCEDURE

The Contrasting Groups. The subjects were 1,000 girls of two large junior high schools of Berkeley, California. All of the girls of these two schools were subjected to the same routine of testing and physical measurements. Information, supplemented by records from the schools, was secured as to the race of each of the pupils. Those whose records were included in the study were American-born children of middle and north European stock, and with but few exceptions they have lived in California all their lives.

A woman assistant ascertained from each individual whether or not the menarche has been reached and, if so, the age at the time of the first mensis. This inquiry was made at the time the assistant was making the physical measurement, and was directed to the student in a matter of fact way in terms which were commonly used in the physical education and hygiene courses given in these schools. Especial care was taken to help the student fix the date, and we are of the opinion that this information on menarcheal age is not subject to the errors sometimes arising when the children are asked to make all of the necessary computations involved in fixing the date of the menarche.

The mean ages of the pre-menarcheal and post menarcheal subjects in five age groups are shown in Table 1. These means were computed from the original data giving the age to the nearest month. At all ages the post menarcheal girls are slightly the older, but the amounts of the differences, from 5 to 15 days, would appear to be quite insignificant for the functions involved in this study.

The socio-economic class frequencies in pre-menarcheal and post menarcheal subgroups closely approximate those expected upon the basis of the distribution in the total group. The computed chi square indicates that the obtained deviations from the expected frequencies would arise by chance in from 80 to 90 cases in 100. In view of this fact we may proceed in our study with the assumption that little or no difference exists between the pre-menarcheal and post menarcheal groups with respect to socio-economic status, and that this factor need not be taken into account in our further comparisons of these groups. It is important, however, to keep in mind the fact that our total group is not representative of the socio-economic distribution of the general population. Over 95 per cent fall into occupational categories that are above the level of the semi- and unskilled

TABLE 1. Number of Subjects and the Mean Ages in Months of Post Menarcheal and Pre-menarcheal Girls in the Five Age Categories Used in Item Analysis

	Age Category				
	1	*2*	*3*	*4*	*5*
Mean Age					
Post menarcheal	147.3	154.2	160.2	166.0	174.8
Pre-menarcheal	146.9	154.0	160.0	165.6	174.8
Number of Subjects					
Post menarcheal	36	54	90	94	243
Pre-menarcheal	137	87	63	49	40

classes, and all are from urban families. Because of this fact one must refrain from any generalizations concerning the relationship between menarcheal status and socio-economic status in general.

The Test and Testing Procedure. In assembling the items for the questionnaire used in this study we were guided materially by two considerations:

a. Preliminary work with the Pressey (1933) and the Sullivan (1934) tests had revealed a considerable group of items which differentiated pre-menarcheal and post menarcheal subjects of the same chronological ages fairly satisfactorily (Stone and Barker, 1937). These items concerned play interests, vocational interests, reading interests, fears, worries, and ideas of right and wrong. Pressey and Sullivan had found that chronological age groups could be differentiated on the basis of responses to these same items. Using the items suggested by our first study as a point of departure, we added items in those regions of interest which appeared most promising. These items were secured by searching through all of the questionnaire-type personality tests we could locate (in 1934) which had proven suitable for the ages we were to use.

b. In addition to following suggestions gained from the preliminary experiment we assembled items bearing upon certain hypothetical pre-menarcheal-post menarcheal differences which appeared promising; e.g., heterosexual interests, family adjustment, interest in adornment, play activities, vocational choice, etc. These groupings of items will be considered later in discussing the results. To secure such items other tests were scrutinized, school counsellors were interviewed, and groups of girls in a neighboring high school were asked by their counsellors for suggestions.

The children were examined in groups. An experienced test administrator (woman) conducted the test program with the aid of such assistants as she required from our testing personnel and from the staff of the school. The children were informed that there was no time limit for the test; they were instructed to work until all items had been checked. On the whole the pupils appeared to co-operate in the desired manner. A few individuals were amused by certain items, and also a few were unwilling to check all of the items because they regarded their own interests and attitudes as highly personal and not subject to interrogation by anyone. How many silently rebelled but checked the items anyway we have no way of telling.

Plan of Analysis. The frequency of occurrence of each response to each item was determined for each subgroup separately and converted into a percentage of the total of such possible responses. The standard errors of the differences in the percentages of pre-menarcheal and post menarcheal girls making each response at each age were then computed for each of the five age groups separately and the probabilities that the differences in the per cents were true differences were determined. For certain purposes it was obviously desirable to reduce the five values to a single value. This we have done by a method proposed by Pearson (1932).

In the case of certain items, both pre-menarcheal and post menarcheal groups favored a response so overwhelmingly that the percentage differences were unreliable. The data for these responses were dropped from further consideration. Our criteria for dropping responses were as follows: (a) in dealing with a single age group, an item was discarded if more than 90 per cent or less than 10 per cent of either the pubescent or the non-pubescent group checked the response in question; (b) in dealing with the combined age groups a response was discarded when in more than two of the nine subgroups 90 per cent or more, or 10 per cent or less of the subjects endorsed the response.

EVIDENCES THAT DIFFERENCES EXIST

Evidence that certain items of the questionnaire differentiated the pre-menarcheal and the post menarcheal groups was the first result obtained from the analysis of the data. Our next step was to inquire whether the differences obtained might be merely chance differences or whether they were true differences such as would arise only if the two groups of individuals really differed with respect to the functions covered by the questionnaire. Three lines of evidence bearing upon this question will be considered.

The first evidence concerns the form of the distribution of the critical ratios of the differences in the proportions of the post menarcheal and pre-menarcheal groups making each response to each item. If the differences were due to randomly operating factors the distribution of critical ratios should approximate the normal frequency curve. The crucial question is as follows: are the obtained differences greater than those which would be expected if the pubescent and nonpubescent groups did not differ in the frequency of their preferences for particular responses? Inspection of the percentage distributions of critical ratio frequencies for the five age groups combined indicated that the larger critical ratios occurred with greater frequency and the smaller critical ratios with lesser frequency than would be expected if only random differences were operating. The probability that these divergencies from the theoretical expectation might be due to chance has been tested in two ways with the following results: (a) according to the computed chi square such differences might arise by chance in less than one in a million times in the case of both the right- and the left-column responses; (b) the obtained standard deviations of critical ratio distributions of both the right- and the left-column responses are greater than expected by an amount approximately eight times their standard errors.

The second type of data which bear upon the main problem concerns the consistency with which different groups of pubescent and nonpubescent girls can be differentiated on the basis of their responses to the same questionnaire items. Data of this sort are available in the form of the items of the Pressey and Sullivan tests which were included in the present questionnaire. These items were included upon the basis of the extent to which they differentiated between 175 post menarcheal and 175 pre-menarcheal girls in the schools of San Jose and Redwood City in the year 1934 (Stone and Barker, 1937). The question may be raised as to whether these items differentiate the pre-menarcheal and post menarcheal girls of the present study as they did in the previous study. Appropriate statistical treatment indicated clearly that the responses did differentiate in the same general way on the two occasions although some responses were reversed. We have not attempted to measure the exact extent of this relation inasmuch as the form of the question was changed in certain instances and the form of the answer in others.

The third sort of evidence as to the reality of the differences in the way pre-menarcheal and post menarcheal girls respond to the questionnaire items is the consistency with which responses of approximately the same meaning differentiate between the pre-menarcheal and post menarcheal girls. The data indicated that there is a fair degree of consistency in the responses of our groups to items having similar or identical connotations.

This tendency is to be expected, of course, if the children are seriously considering each item and answering it according to the way it appeals to them.

NATURE OF THE DIFFERENTIATING ITEMS

While making up this questionnaire we had to use tentative hypotheses concerning regions or zones of interests and attitudes wherein pre-men-archeal-postmenarcheal differences were likely to exist. With these in mind, items were formulated or were selected from the available test or question-naire sources to tap these zones of interests and attitudes. For a considera-tion of the meanings of the differentiating responses, these items have been re-assembled and placed under the categorical headings used while making up the test. Sample items illustrating the several categories are presented in Table 2.

Naturally, any analysis based upon meaningful groupings of items is highly subjective because of a necessary degree of judgment one must exercise in deciding what items should be included in a given group and how the possible responses to the items should be interpreted. In the analysis which follows, we have tried, as far as possible, to avoid serious errors by taking only items whose responses seemed classifiable without equivocation. It is true, of course, that none of the items is indicative for a single region of interest exclusively; it is a matter of classifying the items into categories indicative of the dominant interest expressed by the re-sponse. Naturally it is to be regretted that some zones of interest have so few items that trends of differentiation can be indicated only in a very tentative way.

1. A number of items were grouped under the heading "heterosexual interests and attitudes" and the responses to these items were rated as to their significance with respect to heterosexual interests. Thus for Item 6, Subtest I, "go to dances," the response "not wrong" was rated as indicating more heterosexual interest than "wrong." For Item 12, Subtest I, "indulge in petting or necking," the response "not wrong" was rated as indicative of stronger heterosexual interest than "wrong."

Of the responses for which the percentage frequencies were adequate to meet our criterion there were 21 that were rated as indicating greater heterosexual interest. Nineteen of these were favored by a greater propor-tion of the post menarcheal than of the pre-menarcheal groups. Of the 20 responses indicating less heterosexual interest, 18 were favored by a greater proportion of the pre-menarcheal girls. These results suggest rather strongly that post menarcheal girls favor responses indicative of the stronger hetero-sexual interest.

2. A second group of items, totaling 42 in number, related to "family adjustments." For 35 of these items the percentage frequencies were ade-

quate for further consideration. Eighteen of the responses denoting adjustments were chosen in greater proportion by the pre-menarcheal girls; 17 were chosen in greater proportion by the post menarcheal girls. This result was somewhat surprising and ran counter to our *a priori* judgment concerning this zone of attitudes and interests. Certainly the above data give no support to the hypothesis that post menarcheal girls give more evidence of open revolt from parental discipline and home restrictions than pre-menarcheal girls.

3. Twenty-five items could be grouped under "adornment and display of person" and the responses to these items could be rated as indicating greater or less interest in adornment and bodily display. Twenty-four of the

TABLE 2. Sample Items Illustrating Various Types of Interests and Attitudes. In some cases the items have been paraphrased for presentation here.

1. *Heterosexual Interests and Attitudes*
   Do you find it easy to make friends with boys?
   Would you like to have more boy friends?
   Would you rather go to a party with a girl friend or with a boy friend?
   Would you rather go roller skating or to a dancing party?
2. *Family Adjustments*
   Does your mother understand you well enough that you feel like talking over your problems with her?
   Do your folks let you decide how to wear your hair?
   Do you think your parents are too strict with you?
   Do you wish you had more freedom?
3. *Interest in Bodily Adornment and Display*
   Do you like or dislike the use of cosmetics (rouge, powder, lipstick)?
   Would you like or dislike to design fine gowns?
   Would you rather make silk underwear or have stories read to you?
   Would you like or dislike to be a model or mannikin in a fashion show?
4. *Interest in Activities of Varying Degrees of Strenuousness*
   Do you like or dislike just loafing and being lazy?
   Do you like or dislike playing in the gym on the bars, rings, etc.?
   Would you like or dislike being on an athletic team?
   Would you like or dislike to climb cliffs?
5. *Worries, Fears* (each item is listed separately)
   Are you afraid or not afraid of: collisions, smothering, poison, fire, going down a dark street, guns, robbers, dogs?
   Do you worry or not about: being punished, feebleness, going insane, dying, dieting?
6. *Interest in Imaginative or Secretive Activities*
   Have you quite a few secrets you do not wish adults to know of?
   Have you secret ambitions and desires that you seldom talk about?
   Do you imagine lots of things that you never tell anyone?
   Do you sometimes pretend that you know things, so that people won't think you are very young and innocent?

above responses denoting greater interest had percentage frequencies that met our criterion. Of these, 18 were favored by a greater proportion of the post menarcheal girls than of the pre-menarcheal girls. The data indicating less interest are exactly the converse of the foregoing. In this zone of interest, our working hypothesis that post menarcheal girls would have a stronger interest in adornment and display of person has received relatively strong support.

4. Twenty-five items concerned games and activities of varying degrees of strenuousness. Again we have reported only those responses for which the percentage frequencies are adequate. Of the 22 responses indicating greater interest in the more strenuous activities, 19 are favored by a greater proportion of the pre-menarcheal than of the post menarcheal group. Of the 21 responses indicating less interest in strenuous activities, 19 were favored by a greater proportion of the post menarcheal than of the pre-menarcheal group. These results strongly support the view that with the onset of puberty there is a change in interest with respect to the expenditure of energy in strenuous exercises.

5. All items concerning fears, worries, and anxieties may be combined. Of the 50 responses which give an indication of relatively more fear, worry, or anxiety 30 are preferred by a greater proportion of the pre-menarcheal girls. Of the 61 responses indicating relatively less fear, worry, or anxiety 39 are favored by a greater proportion of the post menarcheal girls. Here we find a very slight tendency for the pre-menarcheal girls to indicate more fears than the post menarcheal girls.

6. Five items, four of which are listed in Table 1, refer to imaginative or secretive activities. In all five instances a greater proportion of the post menarcheal girls indicate that they engage in or are interested in imaginative daydreaming activities. It is regrettable that more items of this type were not used in the test battery.

INTEREST MATURITY

The items of the Pressey and Sullivan tests which were included in the present questionnaire were standardized by their authors in terms of the increasing or decreasing proportion of children who made each response with increasing chronological age. A mature response is one which uniformly increases in frequency with the increasing chronological age of children, and vice versa.

There was a very clear tendency in our findings for the responses preferred by the chronologically mature, according to the Pressey and Sullivan ratings, to be preferred also by post menarcheal individuals. This point is striking in view of the fact that the post menarcheal and the pre-menarcheal subjects compared are of comparable chronological ages. These data confirm those reported by us previously (Stone and Barker, 1937) in indicating that the interests of post menarcheal girls are more similar to the interests of relatively older girls than are the interests of pre-menarcheal girls of the same chronological age.

DISCUSSION

Regrettably, the methods employed in this study are not instructive as to what causal factors brought about the differences in responses by our pre-menarcheal and post menarcheal groups. It is generally known that certain physical changes associated with the menarche are to be accounted for in terms of specific tissue responsiveness to hormones of the anterior lobe of the pituitary and to hormones from the gonads. Perhaps certain behavioral changes as manifested in interests and attitudes also can be accredited to hormones from one or both of these glands. In this connection, however, one must not overlook or underestimate the importance of extrinsic factors, particularly those of an ideational type which undoubtedly would play a more potent role in man than in lower animals lacking man's cultural background. It is not unlikely that self-evident changes in adolescent physique (accelerated growth, enlargement of the accessory sexual organs, hirsuteness, etc.) and the onset of the menses give rise in the adolescent to new interests, new aspirations, and new conceptions of freedom and restrictions imposed by society on persons who have passed that milestone in development which historically has separated the child from the young adult. Finally, there may be differences in the social stimulation directed by adults to post menarcheal and pre-menarcheal girls. If so, these social pressures could account for new types of interests, attitudes, or other mental residuals that show up in adolescent responses to items of a questionnaire.

The aim of the present study did not include an investigation of the practical significance of differences in attitudes and interests of groups of pre-menarcheal and post menarcheal girls. In this connection, however, it is appropriate to recall that there was always a great amount of overlapping of the responses of the pre-menarcheal and the post menarcheal groups to individual items. Certainly interests and attitudes as tapped by our questionnaire differentiate the post menarcheal and pre-menarcheal groups much less strikingly than do anthropometric measures during these adolescent years.

19

Change of Interests with Age[*]

E. K. Strong, Jr.

Professor E. K. Strong, Jr., has personally done more research, and has stimulated more, on interest-patterns, especially as they relate to vocational activity, than perhaps any other investigator. An extensive summary of research on interests, including much material on changes during the adult years, is to be found in his volume *Vocational Interests of Men and Women* (1943). In the present paper, adapted from an earlier book by Professor Strong, he traces changes in specific interests and in interest patterns during the several decades of life from the twenties through the fifties. The changing orientations and motivations as age increases are clearly evident. Taken in conjunction with two other papers in this volume, by Bayley on intellectual change and by Korchin and Basowitz on the effects of age on learning (both in Part III), the finding in this study that with increased age there is less liking for new activities, especially those that interfere with established habits, assumes great importance. Adults who wish to understand children and adolescents should be particularly aware that their own orientations and values have changed with increased age, and they must make special efforts if they are to keep sensitive to the interests and problems of younger people.

The study here presented is restricted to the interests of adult men, and particularly to the question of how those interests change with age. The work was prepared not only to throw light upon the problems of later maturity but also to determine how changes in interest due to age may affect that phase of vocational guidance which is based upon the interests of young people. If interests change from year to year, they are not trustworthy guides to the choice of a career. If they do not change greatly, then they may be safely so employed. It is possible to conceive that interests may change rapidly up to a certain age and from then on change rela-

* Adapted and abridged from CHANGE OF INTERESTS WITH AGE by Edward K. Strong, Jr. with permission of the publishers, Stanford University Press. Copyright 1931 by the Board of Trustees of the Leland Stanford Junior University, renewed 1959 by Edward K. Strong, Jr. Also with permission of the author.

tively little. If this is so, then guidance based on interests would be possible during the later period of life but not in the earlier period. Wise vocational guidance in terms of interests depends upon the answers to the vital questions: How much do interests change? and, At what age do changes take place?

THE DATA UPON WHICH THIS INVESTIGATION IS BASED

Vocational Interest Test. With the author's Vocational Interest Blank, the attempt is made to discover the interests of a man by getting his reactions to a large sampling of everyday experiences. The blank has been used to determine whether or not a man's interests are in agreement with the average interests of men engaged in various occupations. There are 420 items on the blank, to each of which the individual reacts by indicating whether he likes (L), is indifferent to (I), or dislikes it (D). The 420 items comprise 100 occupations (e.g., actor, advertiser, architect), 54 amusements (golf, fishing, hunting), 39 school subjects (algebra, agriculture, arithmetic), 82 activities (repairing a clock, making a radio set, adjusting a carburetor), 63 peculiarities of people (progressive people, conservative people, energetic people), 42 miscellaneous items, and 40 estimates of present abilities and characteristics ("usually start activities of my group," "usually drive myself steadily," "win friends easily").

Men Included in This Study. The test just described was administered to 2,340 men between the ages of 20 and 60 years. In Table 1 are set forth the eight occupations to which the 2,340 men here studied belong and their distribution within the four age groups of 20 to 29 years, 30 to 39 years, 40 to 49 years, and 50 to 59 years. Throughout this report these four decades will be respectively referred to as the 25, 35, 45, and 55 age groups. The actual average ages of the four groups are 25.9, 34.8, 43.9 and 53.6 years, respectively. The 2,340 men are not as evenly distributed within the 32 subgroups as we should have liked. All available blanks were used except in the case of engineers, where only 100 were included in each of the three upper-age groups. The two groups of engineers and medical men have 76 or more at each age level. The groups of ministers have 50 or more. These three groups are well balanced. The groups of lawyers and Y.M.C.A. secretaries are poorly represented at age 55, with only 34 and 17, respectively; the group of writers is particularly poorly represented by 11 at 25 years, and the group of life insurance salesmen and school men includes only 29 men at age 25 and 34 men at age 55.

Since there are these marked differences in the total representation of each of the eight occupational groups at the four age levels, and also more particularly because there are very great differences in the interests characteristic of these occupational groups, it is necessary to equalize as far as possible the representation of each. Instead of basing our calculations upon the actual populations given in Table 1, the data for each of the 32 subgroups have been reduced to percentages and all calculations have been based upon these percentages; in a sense this procedure has the effect of increasing the population in each subgroup to 100. In no other way can the groups be equally represented. But when the reliabilities of calculations are determined, they are based upon the actual populations rather than upon percentages.

TABLE 1. Distribution of 2,340 Men Whose Interests Are Considered in This Research, According to Age and Occupation

Occupation	Age 20-29	Age 30-39	Age 40-49	Age 50-59	Total
Engineers	84	100	100	100	384
Lawyers	90	71	62	34	257
Insurance men	29	106	95	30	260
Ministers	52	63	51	50	216
Physicians	104	129	102	76	411
School men	34	107	71	33	245
Writers	11	41	59	56	167
Y.M.C.A. Secretary	200	142	41	17	400
Total	604	759	581	396	2,340

Certain errors are, however, inevitable in such a procedure, since it is impossible to obtain comparable samplings for the four age groups. In the first place the older age groups are different from the younger groups in the fact that they have survived to such ages. Not all of the younger men will live to be 35, 45, or 55 years of age. The younger age groups contain also some men who for one cause or another will not continue in their present occupations. In addition, each age group is composed of men born and reared under somewhat different social and environmental conditions. These must have had some effect upon the development of interests. Thus, for example, 55-year-old men had no opportunity in youth to drive an auto. Also the various occupations have changed in their demands and activities with the years. The young engineer, minister, or physician does not work along exactly the same lines as his father did upon entering the profession. When he is 55 years old he will probably find intrinsically different conditions from those confronting his father now. In addition to all such factors affecting the sampling of our four age groups there is one that peculiarly affects the 25 age group. A long period of preparation is essential for the occupations considered here; consequently very few men become established in their life-work before 30. They may have started before that date, but their names do not appear in membership lists much before that age. As a consequence, it is extremely difficult to locate men objectively assigned to the occupation who are under thirty years of age. In order to obtain data for the 25-year group, it has been necessary to include records of college graduates and graduate students. Although such records have been very carefully selected so as to include only those who have consistently shown by their actions that they will enter the occupation in question, the 25-year group because of this factor would seemingly be a poorer selection than the other three age groups. From internal evidence, it appears, however, that the 25-year group is nearly as good a sampling as are the other three groups.

GENERAL CONCLUSIONS

Certain of the more striking age trends have been illustrated in the three charts here included.[1] The major conclusions of the study, including the trends charted, are as follows:

Amount of Change in Interest. 1. There is no particular difference in the number of items used in this study that are liked or disliked at ages 25, 35, 45, and 55. (At age 25, 35 per cent of the items are liked and 30 per cent disliked, at age 55 the percentages are, respectively, 34 and 31, showing a decrease of one per cent in liking and an increase of the same amount in disliking.) According to this, older men are no more catholic in their interests than younger men; they have as many likes and dislikes as younger men but their likes and dislikes are not identical with those of younger men.

2. The average item increases or decreases in liking 7.5 per cent between ages 25 and 55. Men between 20 and 60 are in surprising agreement regarding the peculiarities of other people and their own characteristics, since there is less change from 25 to 55 regarding such items than the average of 7.5 per cent. They are least in agreement about their own activities and amusements, where changes greater than the average are found.

3. Change in interest does not take place uniformly from 25 to 55. In round numbers, 50 per cent of the total change occurs between 25 and 35, 20 per cent between 35 and 45, and 30 per cent between 45 and 55. There is little or no change from 55 to 65.

4. Changes in interests from decade to decade are not great. Differences between 35- and 45-year-old men (also 45 and 55) are less than the differences in interests between mechanical and electrical engineers (which correlate .92); and the differences between 25 and 35 (also those between 35 and 55) are about equal to the differences in interest between mechanical and civil engineers (which correlate .84). The differences between 25- and 55-year-old men are equal to the differences between purchasing agents and office men, or between vacuum-cleaner salesmen and the dis-

[1] Prepared by the editors of the present volume from data in the appendix of the original publication.

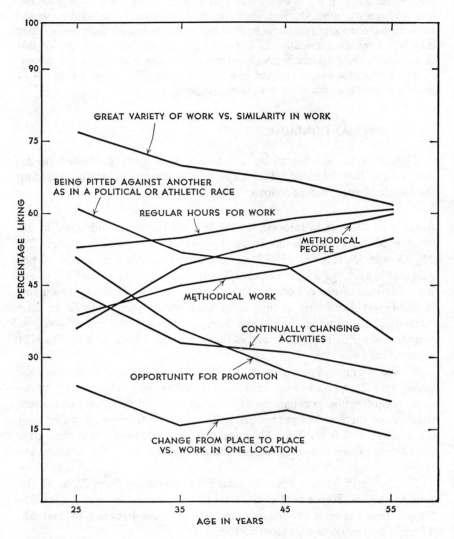

FIGURE 1. Showing Age Trends in Liking for Conditions Involving Little or No Change and Lack of Interference with Established Habits

trict managers who employ them. These differences between 25 and 55 are about one-half that found between architects and civil engineers, or about one-third that between life insurance men and mechanical engineers. Just as it has been found that individual differences in intellectual traits are much greater than sex or age or racial differences, so here, differences as represented by occupational interests are much greater than differences due to age.

Characteristics of Changes in Interest. 5. Items suggesting physical skill and daring, as "walking along the edge of a precipice" or "being an aviator," show the greatest change of all. Older men do not like such activities as do young men.

6. The next greatest change is registered by items suggesting change or interference with established habits or customs. (See Figure 1.) Thorndike reports evidence supporting his conclusion and summarizes it by saying that "adults are proverbially less ready to adopt new ways, even to try new ways, than adolescents." From the practical point of view of employing older men, we do not know whether Thorndike's finding of very slight diminution in ability to learn from 25 to 55 is more or less significant than our finding of pronounced increase in disinclination to change. Further research is greatly needed at this point.

7. With few exceptions, liking for occupations decreases with age. This applies not only to occupations one is not engaged in but also in many cases to one's own occupation. Decrease in liking occupations is probably another illustration of disliking change, for to enter any other occupation would necessitate decided changes in behavior.

Three orders of preference for occupations were obtained from three rather different groups of men. The three orders agree surprisingly (correlations between .91 and .98). Preference for occupations is little influenced by age but is somewhat influenced by the occupation of the rater. Estimated income of the occupation correlates only about .65 with preference, indicating that there are potent factors besides income influencing choice.

8. Linguistic activities of an oral or written nature decline in interest, but those involving reading increase in liking with age.

9. Many amusements are liked by large percentages at all ages. But there is a distinct tendency for all of them to decline except those that may be characterized as cultural. These increase in liking. Older men also prefer, more than younger men do, those amusements pursued largely alone in contrast to ones involving others. There is no question that older men are less interested in people associated with them whether in business or in amusement. How much of the changes reported here are due to genuine changes in men with age and how much are a reflection of changes in social life is a question; undoubtedly not all of it is due to the latter. Figures 2 and 3 depict certain changes in interest in amusements and in social activities.

Old people are likely to be lonely, as most of their lifelong friends are dead. Preparation for the enjoyment of old age should seemingly include the development of interest in activities that may be pursued largely alone. This our data clearly indicate. How far in addition older people can be trained in earlier life to enjoy activities with others, so that in later life they will participate in them, is a question. For a generation or two the

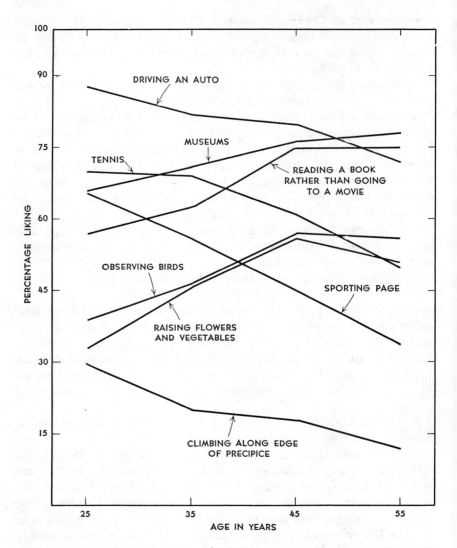

FIGURE 2. Showing Age Trends in Interest in Certain Amusements

experiment should be tried in order that the limits of enjoyment in old age from such sources may be ascertained.

10. Liking for people exhibiting desirable traits increases with age, as does disliking for people exhibiting undesirable traits. The difference in reaction to these two types of items is the greatest we have found. Evidently men are more unanimous in their likes and dislikes toward kinds of people than toward any other group of items.

11. Although there is a great variety of reactions to items describing

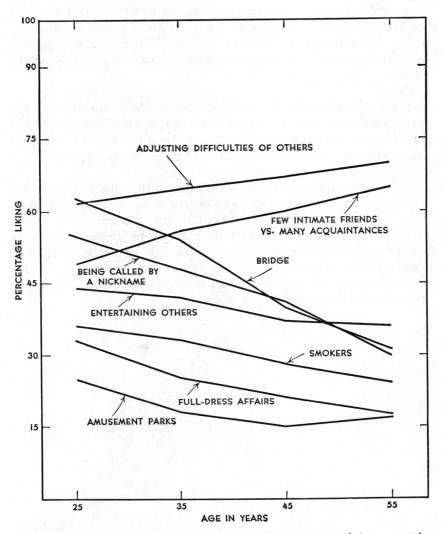

FIGURE 3. Showing Changes, Essentially "Decline," in Social Interest with Increased Age

working conditions, there seems to be no possibility of summarizing them in terms of the interests of men at different ages. This may be due to the fact that our data are based upon the likes of eight rather different occupational groups, comprising engineers, lawyers, ministers, writers, life insurance salesmen, school men, Y.M.C.A. secretaries, and medical men.

12. Older men are somewhat surer of their estimates of themselves than are younger men.

13. In general, the things we like most at 25 years of age are liked

better and better with increasing age, and the things we like least at 25 are liked less and less. This clearly holds true for our reactions to people and amusements and for our own estimates of ourselves. The reverse, however, is the case respecting occupations, school subjects, and general activities.

Changes Characteristic of All Eight Occupational Groups. 14. The changes indicated above might be due to averaging eight conflicting sets of data from as many distinct occupations. They are not. In practically every case, the change typical of all eight groups is also typical of each of the eight.

15. Although there are changes common to all eight groups, nevertheless the eight groups do not become more or less similar to the average of all eight as they advance in age. The differences between these groups (average inter-correlation is .008) far outweigh the differences between age groups or the changes common to all eight occupations. There is nothing here to suggest that the interests so characteristic of each occupational group wax or wane, or that the eight groups cannot be equally well differentiated at all four age levels.

Part V

PSYCHOLOGICAL GROWTH UNDER DIFFERENT SOCIAL-CULTURAL CONDITIONS

PARTS III AND IV contain illustrations of the fact that *what* man learns is dependent on environmental demand and stimulation. The papers in the present part were selected to document, in part, the effects of different social-cultural conditions on human behavior and styles of living. The first paper by Sears, Maccoby, and Levin was taken from a major research report on the significant variables in child rearing in middle class American homes. The book from which this paper was excerpted describes the most ambitious effort in the history of developmental psychology to identify the antecedent-consequent relationships existing between parental practices and the developing behavior patterns of children. It is hoped that the present paper will whet the reader's curiosity and interest sufficiently to lead him to study the complete volume, one that promises to become a classic in developmental psychology.

The paper by Simmons focuses on a very different developmental problem whose solution shows wide variations across cultures and subcultures. What are the attitudes of young and middle-aged persons toward the extremely aged, those who are sometimes with a dash of poetic license described as our "senior citizens." The primitive Eskimos and American Indians abandoned their weak and dependent elders to perish from cold and hunger when they could no longer keep pace with the demands of nomadic living. We favor the institutional solution of special homes for our elders—"living tombs" they are called by some cynical journalists. Simmons compares the roles of the aged in primitive and civilized societies and concludes, "Modern civilization has added more years to life, but it has left less life in the twilight years."

That there is cultural change, when a sufficient time perspective is permitted, is dramatically illustrated in the report by deCharms and Moeller. The values reflected in pupils' readers in 1800 as contrasted with those of 1950 remind us of just how substantially the American style of living has altered in a few generations. Has the tempo of cultural drift quickened, perhaps, since the coming of the electronic and space era? If so, it becomes exceedingly difficult to predict what values may prevail in the year A.D. 2100. The report by Jones examines the differences in attitudes and interests of ninth-grade pupils reared some two decades apart. The report by Kuhlen shows that cultural changes must be taken into account whenever we attempt to ascribe changes in behavior over time to developmental variables.

20

The Child-rearing Process*

Robert R. Sears, Eleanor E. Maccoby, and Harry Levin

How do the relatively unique ways of thinking, feeling, and acting that characterize different families and groups get transmitted to their offspring? Often this is done directly and formally, as in educational programs, but to a very substantial degree such transmission occurs through the informal interactions between parents and their children which occur in the course of child rearing. This paper analyzes and illustrates the process of child rearing, how the child activated by inborn drives learns, through a complex pattern of responding to a whole array of specific influences arranged by his parents or others, to become a particular "person." The present analysis of this process by Professors Sears, Maccoby, and Levin is incorporated in an unusually insightful paper.

Child rearing is not a technical term with precise significance. It refers generally to *all the interactions between parents and their children*. These interactions include the parents' expressions of attitudes, values, interests, and beliefs as well as their caretaking and training behavior. Sociologically

* Adapted from pp. 457-466, "The Child-Rearing Process" from PATTERNS OF CHILD REARING by Robert R. Sears, Eleanor E. Maccoby and Harry Levin. Copyright © 1957 by Harper & Row, Publishers, Incorporated. Reprinted by permission of the publishers.

speaking, these interactions are one separable class of events that prepare the child, intentionally or not, for continuing his life. If a society survives beyond one generation, it quite evidently has cared for some of its offspring, and has provided opportunity for them to develop the values and skills needed for living. Some of this learning comes from parent-child interaction, and much does not. Relatives, neighbors, and peers play an important role, too, as do teachers or others specifically charged with the training function. Once he is beyond infancy, a youngster's personality is always a product of more social experiences than just those offered by his parents.

Not all parent-child interactions are intended, by the parents, to train the child. Some are simply for caretaking, such as feeding and cleaning and protecting. Others are expressions of love or annoyance, of concern or pride—reactions that have no significant purposes for the child's future nor even for his control at the moment; but they are nonetheless elicited by the child and impinge on him when they occur. Child rearing includes all such interactions, for they all affect his behavior, and, whether by intention or not, change his potentialities for future action.

To understand the implications of these defining statements about child rearing, one must examine the apparent mechanisms by which parents and children influence one another. There are two ways. One is with respect to action and the other to learning. Action is what a person is doing on any given occasion; a theory of action attempts to define the conditions under which specified kinds of action do or do not occur. Anything a parent does to or with a child that has as its aim *control,* i.e., the changing or maintaining of a particular form of behavior, is an influence on action.

Learning, on the other hand, is the changing of a persons' potentialities for acting in the future; a theory of learning attempts to define the conditions under which a second presentation of a given situation will produce a different reaction from that elicited by the first presentation of the situation. Learning is the process involved in personality development. Parental behavior that is intended to *train* the child, to change his customary way of acting, is an influence via learning.

This distinction between action and learning is not always clear either to a mother or to a child. In one way this is just as well, but in another it leads to confusion. Actually, every interaction between two people has an effect both on their present actions and on their potentialities for future actions. An affectionate hug or a testy reprimand not only influences what the child is doing at the moment, but adds a small change into his expectations of what will happen on future similar occasions. This expectancy, in turn, increases or decreases the probability that he will act the same way in the future. Likewise, a mother's discipline—which she may view strictly as a method of training for the future—has

some immediate impact on the child and leads to a change in his behavior at the moment.

However, when a child has developed adequate language skills, it is
possible for a mother to make clear what her intentions are, whether to
control for the moment or to modify permanently. This verbal understanding helps a child discriminate somewhat the difference between his
"now" behavior and his "next." Better discrimination of his mother's
intent leads to more efficient learning.

The most convenient way to view behavior is not simply as action, but
as reaction. Every motion is a function of some immediately preceding
state of affairs. Some of these antecedent conditions are internal to the
person, such as thirstiness or a desire for affection. These include the
various organic drives as well as a good many wishes, ideas, desires, or
knowledge that can only be inferred to exist—sometimes from what the
person says, sometimes from other things he does, and sometimes simply
from a knowledge of what experiences he has had in the past. (It is safe
enough to infer, for example, that an adolescent who has gone four hours
without food, in the afternoon, has internal instigation to eat!)

Still other antecedents of behavior can be observed directly by an out-
sider—a smile or a request or a spank or a warning look. Not all those that
affect a child are equally noticeable to a disinterested stranger, of course.
When two people live closely together, they become sensitive to each
other's expressions, to postures, manners of movement, and expressions
of tension or mood. Even a husband may not note all the little signs of a
mother's impending actions that a child does. Or at least not the same ones.

One can distinguish two functions of the conditions which precede
action: to *direct* behavior and to *impel* it. Some conditions have more importance for the former purpose and others for the latter, while some do
both equally (e.g., a slap). By *directing* is meant giving a signal as to what
to do next. A child must move around in his world, and manipulate it to
a certain extent, if he is to stay alive and get satisfaction from living. He
must reach for the food in front of him, accept or refuse the glass of water
for drinking, comply with his mother's "no!" or suffer uncomfortable
consequences. In the life of a young child, a mother provides a great many
directive signals. Her words and her gestures, even the faint and intangible
expressions of mood in her gait or her posture, help him to find his way
around in his world and interact with it in the most effective fashion.

But there must also be some *impulsion* to action. Even a chocolate pie
has little directive effect on a child already full-fed: it does not make him
reach for it. The strongest impulsions in the beginning come from bodily
needs—the so-called primary drives. These are native and universal, and
some of them are referable to reasonably well understood physiological
processes. They initiate action with varying degrees of specificity. In the
newborn infant, for example, hunger and thirst may produce no more

than a general thrashing about and crying. In an older child they set off quite specific actions of asking for food or water, or of turning on a tap, or opening the bread box. The primary drives include hunger, thirst, sex tensions, fatigue, need for activity, waste elimination, optimum temperature maintenance, pain, and probably a number of metabolic ones. Also, the internal states of affairs reflected by the emotions of rage and fear probably belong in the same category. The impelling quality of primary drive states is a constitutional characteristic of the organism. The directed behavior with which the organism satisfies its needs is (in man) almost entirely learned. Furthermore, through learning, the child comes to want and need certain conditions, such as the presence of the mother. Learning is a crucial process underlying not only the child's actions in pursuing a goal but his choice of goals themselves. A brief consideration of the learning process, that is, of the principles by which life experiences change the child's potentialities for action, appears to be in order.

For purposes of description, it is convenient to break up the continuous flow of a person's behavior into segments called *action sequences*. These are somewhat arbitrary units that have the following qualities in common. Each starts with some impelling state of affairs, such as the state of being hungry (the hunger drive), and ends with a consummatory (goal) response (e.g., eating) that reduces the drive. Between the beginning and the end, there is a series of instrumental acts which puts the person in such contact with his environment that he can make the goal response; for instance, a child runs to his mother and asks for a sandwich. Actions that lead to gratification (whether conscious or not) are learned, and may be expected to occur more quickly, more skillfully and more customarily on future occasions when the child finds himself in a same or similar situation.

It is not only the acts immediately preceding gratification that are learned, however. For most activities, especially those that involve social interaction, there are intermediate (or concurrent) events that must be produced in order that the goal may be achieved. For example, a two-year-old child who is hungry needs co-operative action by his mother in order to perform his own goal response of eating. He may cry, or gesture, or ask in words for help. Whatever instrumental techniques he uses, the necessary event must be the same—his mother's giving him food. And he must learn to perform the necessary acts to produce her response. As time goes on, the child develops a "want" for any object, person, or social situation that happened to be associated with the original satisfying experience, and he will learn to perform whatever actions are necessary to produce the desired state of affairs.

It is important to keep in mind that this learning process is, in at least one respect, a highly *mechanical* one. The child learns to want *whatever events regularly occur* in the satisfying context. He does not discriminate between those that are physically efficacious and those that are simply inadvertent accompaniments. For example, the mother must nearly always be present when a child is fed; she orients herself toward him physically, looks at him, often smiles and talks while she is giving food. To the observer trying to decide which of the mother's acts are relevant to the child's food-seeking behavior, the mere handing out of food may seem all that is essential. But the orientations and other actions of the mother nearly always occur, too, and hence the child learns to want them as much as the giving of food. To him, they are part of the whole pattern accompanying the satisfaction of his hunger, and he learns to want the entire pattern. A new item has been added to the list of things the world can do for that child to make him happy—it can be labeled as "mother looking at me and smiling and talking."

When one considers the myriad situations in which children are rewarded throughout childhood, the variety of actions their mothers perform in the process of child rearing, it does not seem surprising that there are so many sub-goal systems of this sort. Or that there should be a unique set of them for each child. Every mother has her own temperament, her own attitudes, her own methods of rewarding and punishing. It is these ways of behaving that her child learns to want. If she is warm and loquacious, he will treasure demonstrativeness; if she is reserved, he will seek her normal reserved expressions toward him. It should be evident now why the term child rearing includes *all* the interactions between parents and their children, not just the ones which directly satisfy primary drives, or those that are consciously *intended* to have a training effect.

The problem of punishment must be raised in connection with both these kinds of learning. Punishment, in its broadest sense, is the inflicting of pain or anxiety. Such an act may be intentional on a mother's part, or it may not. From the standpoint of its effect on the child, any maternal act that hurts or shames or frightens the child is punishment. This is the technical, not the ordinary, use of the word.

The effects of punishment are relevant to both ongoing action and learning. Punishment motivates a child to do something which will reduce the pain created by the punishment; for example, something which will get him away from the source of pain. In the beginning, when there are only reflexes available, infants cry and thrash about. Gradually they learn to move away from external sources of discomfort, mainly sharp things and hot things. But when the source of pain is a punishing parent, the problem cannot be solved merely by avoidance, for the child is dependent upon the parent's presence for the gratification of many of his needs.

There are many kinds of behavior the child can learn in response to punishment that emanates from his mother. Those responses will be selected and retained which serve best to reduce the discomfort. What kind of behavior by him will placate the mother will depend to some extent on her personality characteristics. Sheer flight may work—if the mother has lost her temper or is irritably nagging. Passivity may help, or a counter-attack may do the trick. If the mother's punishing actions are accompanied by some indication of what behavior she *does* desire from the child, then he can follow this clue. And then his reaction to the punishment likely will be effective in reducing the pain.

Once a child develops a repertory of responses to threatening or punishing situations, he will use those that are appropriate to any specific instance. This does not mean that what he does will actually work. Many of the reactions to punishment that are learned in early childhood are quite ineffectual in later years. Bursting into tears may be useful at four, but it is less likely to be so at ten or twelve. Passivity toward a mother may be established because she stops punishing under those circumstances, but passivity in a threatened adult is often quite the least useful form of response. But usefulness or "sensibleness" is not the only determiner of behavior; both actions and desires are the products of previous learning experiences, and which ones are activated at any given moment depends on what situation is present.

Whether a particular action is effective for achieving its aim depends on what may be called the *response qualities* of the environment, that is, what reaction the environment can make to the actions the person imposes on it. A child may learn, as a great joke, to pummel his father's knee when his father is reading the newspaper. He learns to do this because his father always responds affectionately, rewardingly. If the child does the same thing to a newspaper reader on a train, he may get the same friendly response or he may get a swat on his behind. It depends on the response qualities of the man who, in this instance, is the relevant "environment" of the child. The effectiveness of a given action is only as great as is the similarity of the response qualities of the environment in which the behavior was originally learned. Since it is always possible for aspects of the new situation (man on train reading a newspaper) to resemble those of many previous ones, without there being any similarity in the environment's response qualities (the man is *not* tolerant and affectionate to this child at this moment), much human social behavior inevitably is maladaptive and "senseless."

We have said little about the intentional training that is a part of child rearing. From a mother's standpoint, there is much to teach a child, or to help him learn. There are all the motor activities that will enable him to manipulate his environment and to get around in it. There are eating habits, toileting, independence, responsibility, speaking and understanding of speech must be developed. He must learn what are desirable things to have, what to avoid. He must develop proper control of his aggressive impulses and his sex drive. He must learn what is good and what is bad. He must learn the names and functions of things, and the proper techniques of behaving toward other people. And much of this learning is not simply the adding of new responses to the collection he already has: it requires the replacing of undesired actions or attitudes or desires with ones the mother conceives as more appropriate.

Teaching is a delicate and complex process. It requires the selection of appropriate kinds of behavior for the child to perform, the providing of sufficient opportunity for him to practice them, the introducing of adequate motivation to induce him to do the practicing, and the insuring that he enjoys the rewards of his labors so that he will be inclined to repeat them. This is all there is to teaching—in theory. In practice, there is a serious stumbling block. A child often knows what he wants to do, knows how to do it in some degree, and insists on doing it. If his existing action patterns do not coincide with those his tutors would like to teach him, the teacher must undertake an additional task—eliminating his old actions. This is what makes the theoretically simple process so difficult. No child is ever a *tabula rasa;* he always has a repertory of actions that need replacing. Many of them he likes and does not want to change. Any one can teach a person whose desire to learn comes from being dissatisfied with what he already knows. But the socialization of children is not so easy. Many an action a mother wants to introduce comes in conflict with actions the child already has. She must find a way of eliminating the old before she can establish the new.

There is one infallible way to stop a child from doing what he is doing: start him doing something else. Like all panaceas, however, this one has a joker in it. *How* do you start him doing something else? Actions occur because the child wants something, and certain situations have impinged on him—situations to which he has learned to react with a specific kind of behavior. To change these actions, new wants or new situations must be introduced.

Much of the maternal control and teaching in child rearing is accomplished by manipulating the child's wants. Mothers quickly learn that a youngster can be induced to do all manner of things if these are a part of some pleasurable sequence of activities. If she joins him in cleaning up the toys, he works like a Trojan with her just to have her company and to gain the sense of being useful in an adult fashion. He can relish the wash-up job if she shows him how much fun it is to slop and squeeze the fluffy soapsuds. He will attend seriously to his table manners if she calls this "the grown-up way." To the extent that a mother can introduce new actions into already existing motivational systems, or can construct new goals and values by associating them with such desirable achievements as being *mature* or *big* or *strong* or *beautiful,* to that extent is child rearing made easy, and the inculcation of new actions made a pleasure for both teacher and learner.

But not *always,* with *every* child, can a mother think up an effective way of doing this. She has trouble during temper tantrums, some frights, some stubborn spells. When children have strong emotional reactions, they are not easy to control. But the real problem is not with the unmodifiability of the child, but with the fact that mothers are not always themselves calm or rational or profound. They get angry, frightened, tired, and neither their wit nor their wisdom can ever be perfect. The upshot of it is that they are not infrequently driven into interaction with children on a basis that has little to do with teaching. But teaching or not, the continuing interaction has a lasting effect on the child, in the sense that it affects his potentialities for future action as well as his present behavior.

Obviously not all, or perhaps even very much, of a mother's interaction with her child is of an intentional teaching variety. But the need to ensure the child's development, to socialize him, is always present and creeps into expression whenever the mother observes a kind of action, on the child's part, that she wishes to see modified.

It is these various changeworthy actions that cause the trouble. Some of them relate to eating habits or table manners, some to speech and language. Some involve cleanliness or neatness or orderliness or noise or play habits or interests. A large proportion, however, have to do with the child's relation to other people. After all, the word *socialization* does have a social reference. It means, in large part, the development of socially appropriate behavior, the proper (i.e., adult) kinds of interactions with others.

Child rearing is a continuous process. Every moment of a child's life that he spends in contact with his parents has some effect on both his present behavior and his potentialities for future action. Happily, the importance of many of these moments is small, but those that provide repetitions of common and consistent experiences add up, over the years, to the production of consistent ways of behaving toward the kinds of people he knows.

So much for the mechanics of interpersonal influence. Left at this, the process would seem to dictate a unique personality for each child. Every mother behaves differently, and hence even without constitutional variation every child should be different. Strictly speaking, this appears to be the case. Although the process by which learning occurs is the same for everyone, the specific environmental conditions that determine just what wants and actions will be learned are unique to each human being.

The researcher's task is not as impossible as this conclusion may suggest, however. He does not have to study every living human being, for his interest is in those aspects of personality that are common to many. There are quite a few dimensions of this kind. Our interest has been largely in those that describe mothers' child-rearing activities. These represent a part of mothers' personalities, just as our measures of eating problems, enuresis, aggressiveness, and other aspects of children's behavior are indicators of children's personalities.

21

The Significance of Cultural Change in Longitudinal and Cross-sectional Studies of Aging*

Raymond G. Kuhlen

The search for those developmental processes that will veridically describe the dimensions of growing up, and subsequent aging, is beset by many conceptual and technical difficulties. Throughout his professional career the late Raymond G. Kuhlen recurrently reminded his scientific colleagues that one cannot afford to overlook cultural change as a potential source of influence on observations made at different times in man's history. Differential cultural effects in a rapidly evolving society are inextricably confounded with developmental processes. Indeed, it is easy to interpret what are really cultural effects as being the concomitants of socially and culturally invariant age changes. In the following report Dr. Kuhlen reviewed the conceptual complexities of this problem, using measured intelligence as an example. He concluded from his analysis that both longitudinal and cross-sectional research designs are vulnerable to biased cultural intrusions. Although the present discussion centers on changes in intelligence, similar effects have been demonstrated (as noted by Dr. Kuhlen) in attitudes, religious beliefs, femininity, and even physical size.

A number of hypotheses may account for observed adult age trends in various psychological traits and may serve to explain or reconcile the contrasting trends in mental abilities revealed by cross-sectional and longitudinal studies of aging. In a paper published some twenty years ago the writer emphasized the role of cultural change in *cross-sectional* studies and concluded by stressing the merit of the longitudinal study as a means of

*Adapted from Raymond G. Kuhlen, "Age and Intelligence: The Significance of Cultural Change in Longitudinal vs. Cross-Sectional Findings," *Vita humana,* 1963, Vol. 6, pp. 113-124. (With permission of the author and the publisher, S. Karger, Basel/New York.)

minimizing the impact of that variable. In contrast, the present paper argues that cultural change contaminates *both* types of studies, but with opposing effects, such as to promote exactly the contradictions that have been found.

In the comments to follow, this argument is pursued, first, by examining the nature of the data to be "reconciled"; second, by noting the character of some of the cultural changes that have been evident during the last 40 or 50 years; third, by suggesting ways in which such changes may have differential impact upon different age groups as they are studied in cross-sectional and longitudinal procedures; and, finally, by suggesting ways in which research designs and procedures of data analysis might provide a better perspective in this matter.

THE NATURE OF THE DATA ON "INTELLIGENCE"

Putting aside for present purpose any detailed consideration of what is meant by "intelligence," the term may be defined in its barest operational sense: intelligence is what intelligence tests measure. Granting that this definition is a crude one, it is important to recognize that the basic data to be "reconciled" come from culturally based tests. It is well known that performance on such tests is influenced by cultural variables, by experience variables, and by personality and motivational variables; and that to a considerable degree such tests are broadly based *achievement* tests. This consideration is of first importance in evaluating longitudinal and cross-sectional data.

A second major consideration is that the trends suggested by current longitudinal studies are not yet determined with precision. We cannot be sure what it is we are contrasting when we compare the findings from longitudinal to the findings from cross-sectional data. Existing longitudinal studies of mental abilities suffer from one or more of the following deficiencies:

1. Abilities have usually been measured at only two, often widely separated, ages. In view of the fact that most functions studied are curvilinearly related to adult age, it is apparent that two points, which can establish only a straight line, are insufficient. Thus, Owens (1953) demonstrated that 50-year-olds did better than they themselves did at age 19; but previous studies indicate that performance on the Army Alpha test does not reach a peak until age 20.

2. The tests employed in some studies are relatively homogeneous and, instead of yielding measures of "general" ability, may provide trends for some single function similar to vocabulary ability. This criticism may be made of the Bayley and Oden (1955) follow-up of Terman's gifted group, though it is to the credit of this study that the data were obtained at a number of age-points in the adult life span.

3. A third criticism applicable to certain longitudinal studies is that they are, in a sense, make-shift studies, capitalizing on existing initial data. Useful as such analyses may be for exploratory purposes, it is extremely likely that influences which operate at one age and not at the other may result in differences which are mistakenly attributed to age. Tests administered to *groups* during freshman week in college, for example, are seldom administered under conditions of high motivation. When these same subjects are retested individually and under vastly different conditions of motivation at a later time, important questions can be raised as to the meaning of the obtained differences.

4. The carefully designed longitudinal studies now in progress have not been pursued long enough to yield definitive data. Probably the most important studies are those underway at the University of California (Berkeley), which have revealed continued gains in intellectual ability up to around 30 years of age, as thus far reported. It is not yet known whether performance begins to decline as these groups move beyond age 30.

In evaluating the findings from current "two-point" longitudinal studies, it may be worth recalling an earlier semi-longitudinal investigation which is rarely referred to in current papers, but which provided longitudinal data at *several pairs of points* during the adult years. In 1934 Catharine Cox Miles published a brief paper reporting data from the Stanford Later Maturity Studies. She had retested, after two years, different age samples of the basic study group. Scores did not continue to rise, but paralleled rather closely the decrements apparent in the cross-sectional data. McCulloch (1957) used a very similar semi-longitudinal procedure in the study of age trends in 937 retarded adults. His summary curve, covering the age range of 16 to 60, showed a high point at 30, with decline thereafter. These studies suggest that longitudinal data may also reveal a downward turn after a peak in relatively young adulthood, just as do the cross-sectional studies.

It is noteworthy that the trend apparent in the Miles study, although true for the total sample of 190 Ss, was not evident in a subgroup of 135 Ss who had voluntarily returned to be retested because of their interest in the study. In fact gains, instead of losses, were evident for this group, except for the oldest members. Mean losses throughout the age range resulted for the total sample when those additional 55 subjects were included who agreed to be retested only after vigorous recruiting efforts. This is a rather important point since it suggests that those volunteering for longitudinal studies may be different Ss over time from those not volunteering.

In contrast to the relatively tenuous longitudinal data now available, the cross-sectional data inspire more confidence in the curves they demarcate. The four principal cross-sectional studies are the 1933 Jones and Conrad investigation of a rural Vermont population with the Army Alpha test; the Stanford Later Maturity Studies (Miles and Miles, 1932) involving a sample in California tested with a brief form of the Otis; the standardization data of the Wechsler-Bellevue Scale (Wechsler, 1939); and the recent data of the Revised Wechsler Adult Intelligence Scale (Wechsler, 1958). In three of these studies performance reached a peak at age 20 and declined shortly thereafter. The 1955 Wechsler data, based on a stratified sample of the population, identified peak performance at around age 25, with linear decline evident shortly thereafter. Although there is a possible effect of cultural change in comparisons of the Wechsler data of the mid-1930's and the mid-1950's all four cross-sectional studies are consistent in showing an early adult peak performance, followed by regular decline.

Thus it may be argued that at the present time fairly adequate cross-sectional data are being compared with extremely tenuous longitudinal data; and the attempts to "reconcile" the findings or to draw firm conclusions may be somewhat premature.

CULTURAL CHANGE AND ITS IMPACT

There is now more "cognitive stimulation" in our culture than there was in earlier times. Older people when they were young not only received less stimulation through formal societal efforts (public schooling), but they were exposed to less informal stimulation through the media of mass communication. As is well known, length of schooling is highly correlated with measured intelligence; thus, "decline" in test performance evidenced in cross-sectional studies may be partially explained by the lower educational level of older individuals. It would seem clear that if intellectual stimulation is most important in younger years, older individuals, those who grew up at a time when verbal stimulation was relatively meager, would be handicapped.

If we consider the broad problem of cultural change as related to studies of aging, rather than considering only studies of intelligence, further complications are encountered. Different aspects of the culture do not change to the same degree or in the same direction over the same period of time. An interesting illustration comes from a study published recently (de-Charms and Moeller, 1962).[1] As revealed in an analysis of children's readers, there is a marked curvilinear relationship over time in the pressure put upon children for achievement. The evidence suggests an increase in achievement pressure from 1800 to 1890, a steady decrease thereafter through the 1940's, and other evidence indicates a recent increase again in the last few years.

If such a curvilinear relationship between cultural trends and time characterizes the life spans of adults now living (instead of encompassing a century and a half, as in the foregoing illustration), then cultural change

[1] Paper #23 in this volume.

will have a differential impact upon different age groups in cross-sectional studies. However, cultural change will also produce age "gains" or "losses" throughout the age span studied in the longitudinal studies, depending upon the historical time setting in which the longitudinal measures are taken.

To take another example, some data suggest a turn away from religion during the first three decades of the twentieth century and a shift in the opposite direction during the last two decades. Thus if studies of age changes in religion had been conducted in 1930, one might well have expected, in a cross-sectional study, that older people would be *more* "religious" than those younger. At the same time, 1930, a longitudinal study might well have shown that, with age, people became *less* religious. The reverse might be expected in studies carried out in 1960—in which during the first half of the adult life span, a cross-sectional study might well show younger people more religious than middle-aged, whereas a longitudinal study might show that, as persons moved from early to middle adulthood, they became more religious.

It becomes evident from the foregoing that a longitudinal study will, under the cultural circumstances of the last several decades, result generally in data showing that older individuals are "better" in the respect being measured than they were when first tested at a younger age; whereas a cross-sectional study will put the older individual at a disadvantage compared to the younger person when they are both being tested at the same time.

That cross-sectional studies are influenced by cultural change has, of course, long been recognized. It is not so widely recognized that the longitudinal study may yield data spuriously favorable to the older individual when marked cultural change is occurring in a positive direction. Indeed, developmental psychologists appear to have become so enamoured of the longitudinal study that many view it as the design of choice for almost any problem. Yet a careful comparison of the advantages and disadvantages of the cross-sectional and longitudinal methods for research on aging will show the two methods to be fairly well balanced. For some purposes the longitudinal study is the only method of obtaining the desired data; for other purposes the cross-sectional study is the method of choice.

Two studies demonstrate the point that what appeared to be age trends in longitudinal data were instead artifacts of cultural change: Nelson (1954) tested college students with an array of attitude scales and retested them fourteen years later. Marked trends in the direction of increased liberalism were noted. However, at the second testing a new sample of college students was obtained. The scores of this new group were about the same as those of the *re*test scores of the first sample. In another study by Bender (1958), Dartmouth College students were retested after a fifteen-year period with the Allport-Vernon Scale of Values. A marked trend in the direction of greater religious interest was noted. But again, test results from a new group of Dartmouth students tested at the time the first group was *re*tested suggested that the change in the first group was likely due to cultural change, not to age *per se*.

There seems little question that the tremendous changes in cognitive stimulation over recent decades can affect performance on intelligence tests just as dramatically as indicated in these attitude studies. Indeed, Tilton (1949) showed substantial gains in intellectual performance of World War II soldiers over World War I soldiers.

It might well be asked why cultural changes should affect different age groups differentially. Why are not people of all ages influenced to the same extent by the changing world in which they live? Several reasons suggest themselves. First, at least in the American culture, there are massive efforts to transmit the culture to the young through formal education. Thus the young get the quick advantage of new advances in knowledge. (A dramatic illustration is the fact that engineers can become rapidly outdated because of the rapid cultural change designated as "technical advance.") In addition to a very probable decline in learning ability with age, with handicaps especially evident when faced with new and different learning tasks, older people, as compared with younger, tend not to experience so directly the impact of cultural change. This is true (*a*) because of reduced need or motivation to learn (reflecting the decreased demand of the culture that they learn), (*b*) because of pressure of the work-a-day world, which denies the adult opportunities to interact with his broader environment, and (*c*) because of the tendency of older persons to insulate themselves psychologically from new features of their environment. One notes, in this last connection, that as people become older they tend to live in an increasingly restricted social matrix. This circumstance probably results partly from losses in energy, and possibly from psychological trends such as increasing habits of conservatism, caution, and avoidance tendencies—habits or practices which serve to reduce the anxiety generated by age-related losses. Despite these reasons, however, some of the cultural change reaches the older individual, with the result that compared to himself when younger, he is at a "higher" level.

DESIRABLE CORRECTIVES

While the arguments advanced above may explain why cross-sectional data may yield one type of age trend whereas longitudinal data may yield another, the basic question remains: What is the pattern of intellectual development and decline during the adult life span? As pointed out earlier, an answer to this question must necessarily await better data. If it should turn out that longitudinal data tend to show a peak at about age 30, the findings will be reasonably consistent with the cross-sectional data now available, and no reconciliation between the two types of studies will be necessary. If, however, longitudinal data should show that the peak is not reached until age 40, will this finding be due to practice effect, or to cultural change? Or do people actually continue to mature in the abilities measured by the tests? These questions cannot be answered in the absence of the data; yet when the data are in, they are likely to be subject to varied interpretations. Accordingly various porcedures should be explored for checking on the effect of cultural change and other influences.

One approach is the systematic replication of studies across time and across cultures. Data presently available from both types of "replication," though admittedly sparse, tend to emphasize the influence of culture. Probably the major replication study across time is to be found in the Wechsler data of the 1930s and the 1950s, both sets of data based on substantial samples. In one case the peak of intellectual ability is shown at age 20; in the other, at age 25. Has the peak of the growth curve of intelligence shifted in approximately one generation? Or is there reflected here the greater verbal character of the culture, the increased levels of education (the larger proportions of the population in high school; the widespread training programs available to young people in industry, in adult education programs, as well as in college)? Perhaps in the United States the important changes in cognitive stimulation have occurred in the last two or three decades, with the onset of commercial radio in the early 1920s to the saturation of the American public with television in the 1960s. Hereafter such cultural changes may be less dramatic. Replication studies across time may thus provide intelligence test data of considerable relevance.

A second approach to the problem is to examine trends on individual test items, items which are judged to be especially reflective of cultural change. While there are important advantages in generalizing across groups of items, as subtests conventionally do, a detailed inspection of single *item* trends would yield useful insights.

Third, an analysis of the cultural, dietary, "life style," and other characteristics of subgroups of subjects showing differential age trends might prove to be instructive. Although test-retest correlations are high, even over thirty-year intervals, they are not so high as to preclude quite different trends for different individuals, especially when longitudinal studies suggest larger variance in distribution of scores at older ages. There may be some advantage at this stage of our research in relatively exploratory types of studies, in this respect. It is becoming increasingly evident that we need a better conceptualization of the aging process than is presently available. Age itself is not a significant theoretical variable, but is mainly an index of time—time in which other things of psychological importance happen. An empirical approach to the identification of age-related variables which may prove to be the important independent variables should not be neglected.

A fourth suggestion concerns the general design of studies. Cross-sectional and longitudinal studies are generally considered to represent different basic designs. The importance of cultural change in the outcomes of both types of studies, however, makes obvious the necessity of combining the two approaches. Given the substantial amount of time and money required for a longitudinal study, it would be wise if the investigators added the small amounts necessary to obtain cross-sectional data at the same time, as a check on the influence of cultural change. In this connection, it may also be noted that the design of many current studies does not provide for control over practice effects. The recent study by L. R. Jarvik, Kallmann, and Falk (1962) and some observations of William A. Owens (1962), as yet unpublished, suggest that practice effect on test-retest may be an exceedingly important influence even over ten-year intervals.

Finally, it may be that we need some new conception and definition of intelligence. Many psychologists still take a somewhat biological view of intelligence, and interpret cultural influences upon test performance primarily as a source of error. Perhaps studies of the central nervous system will eventually provide "answers" regarding the nature of intelligence. Be that as it may, current intelligence tests are fundamentally based in the culture; and the growth curves of intelligence obtained by means of the tests are to a considerable degree a function of the particular measuring instruments used. For these reasons we shall probably never know the inherent nature of the intellectual growth curve through the use of such tests. Catharine Miles (1934) and Demming and Pressey (1957), among others, have pointed out that tests standardized on middle-aged adults rather than on children and adolescents would yield quite different "growth" curves.

New conceptions of intelligence may be emerging which place greater emphasis upon perception, thought processes, and reasoning; and which accord a greater role to experience and thus to cultural influences. For example, the distinction between "fluid" and "crystallized" intelligence, recently given elaboration by R. B. Cattell (1963), leads to specific predictions regarding adult age trends. Cultural and personality variables are assigned an important role in the determination of crystallized ability.

22

Role of the Aged in Primitive and Civilized Society[*]

Leo W. Simmons

The study of contrasting primitive cultures will often illustrate in strik-ing fashion the effects of culture upon personality development. And a contrast of these simple societies with infinitely more complex civilized societies may bring into sharp focus important features of the latter which otherwise might be unnoticed, or at least unappreciated as to their significance. The present paper by Dr. Simmons contrasts civilized society with primitive cultures with respect to the role and adjustment of their older members, and concludes that the role of the old in modern society is more hazardous.[1]

When we select a generous sampling of primitive peoples throughout the whole world—under different physical conditions and within different cul-tural milieus—and examine their attitudes toward aging and their adjust-ments to old age, we are bound to be impressed at first with the great variety of problems than can stem from senescence and the many con-trasting solutions that have been tried out and seem to work reasonably well in their cultural context. Later on, however, when we gain wider familiarity with the subject, we find that certain underlying uniformities appear in the many problems that arise and in the different adaptations that are made to them. It is these uniformities that interest us most, and some of them will be noted at the beginning.

What are some of the common underlying factors in the problem? In general, among primitive peoples, greater uniformity can be found in the interests which old people cherish than in the adjustments which are made

* Adapted and abridged from L. W. Simmons. "Attitudes toward Aging and the Aged: Primitive Societies," *Journal of Gerontology*, 1946, Vol. 1, pp. 72-95. (With permission of the author and the publisher.)

[1] A more detailed account of the attitudes toward the old in primitive cultures is to be found in Dr. Simmons' book, *The Role of the Aged in Primitive Society* (New Haven: Yale University Press, 1945).

to old age. It appears that, when minor differences are allowed for, the basic interests of the aged can be summed up roughly as fivefold:

1. To live as long as possible, at least until life's satisfactions no longer compensate for its privations, or until the advantage of death seems to outweigh the burdens of life.

2. To get more rest, release from the necessity of wearisome exertion at humdrum tasks and protection from too great exposure to physical hazards—opportunities, in other words, to safeguard and preserve the waning energies of physical existence.

3. To remain active participants in personal and group affairs in either operational or supervisory roles—any participation, in fact, being preferable to complete idleness and indifference.

4. To safeguard or even strengthen any prerogatives acquired in a long life, i.e., skills, possessions, rights, authority, prestige, etc.

5. Finally to withdraw from life, when necessity requires it, as honorably as possible, without too much suffering, and with maximal prospects for an attractive hereafter.

These, with minor variations, seem to be about what old people want in primitive societies—and perhaps elsewhere—and they may be summed up in the word security, if it is used with broad connotations.

There is, also, some uniformity in the adjustments that are made to old age. Everywhere the human cycle begins with the dependency of the young on those who are older, and usually ends with the dependency of the very old on those who are younger. The extent of dependency at either end varies with different societies, but where the chief difference lies is with respect to the aged. In this respect man is set apart from all other animals. For while animals, too, have a period of dependency of the young, provided for by the instinct to protect them on the part of those who are older, among lower animals, there is no period of dependency of the aged, and no instinct which impels others of their group to protect them. As soon as lower animals get to the point where they no longer can take care of themselves adequately, they perish.

Thus the problem of aging among human beings is basically a social and cultural one, involving conscious attitudes and feelings of responsibility or obligations on the part of members of the group, or the group as a whole, towards those who have become dependent through age. Accompanying this, there are also conscious efforts on the part of the aged to maintain their positions in the group and to insure support. A satisfactory old age for anyone, perhaps anywhere, depends chiefly upon the amount of persuasion that may be exerted upon the young and strong to serve and to pay homage to the needs and interests of the old and feeble. In primitive societies, aged individuals have received or achieved the greatest fulfillment of their interests through personal adjustments to such major institutions as the domestic organization, the economic system, government, magic and religion, and what may be called the learned or skilled professions. Basically, then, we may anticipate that security and survival in senescence are not a boon of nature, nor a gift of the gods; they depend upon the contributions which old people can make or the rights which they can command in the particular groups of which they are members.

Although there is more uniformity in the interests of old people in different primitive societies than in the adjustments which are made to senescence, there is, nevertheless, some degree of order discernible, varying with the stage of cultural development and physical and social factors. It may be of interest to note the contrasts which exist between primitive societies and our own civilization with respect to the treatment accorded the old and attitudes toward old age.

Some of these contrasts are quite obvious. One is immediately struck with the fact that primitive peoples generally have far less exact knowledge than moderns concerning the biological and medical aspects of aging, and so they indulge their fancy much more freely concerning the nature and significance of senescence. They have thus quite reasonably and seriously conceived many mythical, and to us fantastic, accounts of a golden age of perpetual youth, of the unnatural origin of old age and death, of exceptional persons able to escape both of these misfortunes, and of perennial endeavors to find lost or secret remedies for rejuvenation and longevity. In fine, the culturally conditioned meaning and interpretation of old age among primitive men and women is bound to be at variance with modern thought on the matter.

Another contrast that attracts attention is the fact that the average life time in primitive society is short, that most people die in youth or middle age, and that relatively few ever reach old age, whereas among advanced peoples a long life is a reasonable expectation of the average person. Thus old age, a rarity with them, is a commonplace with us. Indeed, a modest old age may provide a mark of distinction in itself, while in modern society only a centenarian achieves fame by survival. Nevertheless, a small proportion of primitives live to be as old as any civilized men or women, and they often receive considerable distinction. Therefore, although primitive man's chance for long life cannot compare with ours, senescence is for that very reason more impressive.

This greater distinction of very old people in primitive societies rests not only on the fact that there are relatively fewer of them; those who do manage to survive the rigors of primitive life seem generally to remain much more vigorous and active than old people in modern society. Under hard primitive conditions, weaklings are weeded out all along the line. Moreover, when they become totally helpless and dependent in old age they are soon eliminated in one way or another. In protected civilized society, however, even weaklings are preserved. The keeping alive of enormous numbers of very old and decrepit people is something relatively recent in the history of man. It is not surprising therefore that old age among us tends to be regarded as an unenviable state. And it would be even more so if we learned how to keep old people alive twice as long as we do now! There would be many more old people, and much feebler ones, all in competition with each other and with younger persons for the goods of life.

A further comment should be made concerning the larger proportion of old people who remain active, productive, and even essential in primitive as compared with modern societies. The fact seems to be that many primitive peoples have succeeded amazingly in providing means for utilizing the services of their few old people as long as they are able to move hand or foot in special kinds of labor, minding children, telling stories, executing feats of magic, performing rituals, supplying useful information, and making important decisions. These are all found to be worthy occupations of the primitive aged. Thus the opportunities for an old man or woman to be regarded as a treasured asset to the group are much greater than in modern societies. This is not to say that there are fewer useful functions in civilization that the aged can fill measurably well—indeed the reverse is true—but among us competition with the young is generally much stronger. Indeed, primitive cultures are frequently so well adapted to the capacities of old people that old age can become a more enviable period than the youthful years. The average old man or woman tends to be retired as relatively useless earlier and more definitely in modern civilization than in many primitive societies.

This leads to a further important contrast. The experience of aging in primitive societies seems to be more smoothly tapered and the onset of senescence less abrupt and freer of traumatic transitional phases than in modern civilization. No haunting calendar, no chronological deadline makes each birthday a well-marked milestone on the road to death. This keen awareness of chronological age is a modern experience of aging which has little place in primitive life. The primitive man has his superstitions, to be sure, but the calendar bugaboo is not one of them.

We have seen that another significant contrast lies in the prevailing attitudes towards death, the beliefs associated with dying, and the social significance placed on the manner and the means of death. With us it is axiomatic that the very aged are nearing death's door, and their unpleasant preoccupation with thoughts of death are almost taken for granted. But primitive oldsters are not so convinced that age must bring death, and when a patriarch does die, other explanations may be found to account for the catastrophe. It may well be that we, for all the benefits of civilization, are less well prepared to confront death than are primitive men.

One other contrast which is very apparent and of great importance is that generally in primitive societies the cultural context—economic, social, religious, and domestic—seems to be better geared to the capacities of the aged in primitive society than in advanced civilization, so that they may often continue to function effectively far into senescence. In modern societies, indeed, the basic institutional alignments seem to work largely to the disadvantage of old people. Among primitives expedient adjustments tend to be made by the aged themselves as they grow older, whereas in modern civilization protection for the aged is either insured by planned and legislated programs or by anxious preparations made during youth and middle age, through savings and otherwise.

Thus the question arises whether some serious losses have not come to old people with the advances of civilization. The price of a secure old age must be paid out of the prime of life, and then, in old age, the beneficiaries become functionless hangers-on, who have had their day in the field and are now relegated to the side lines—out of contact with the game of life—with too much time on their hands, and too little to do with it. Like unwanted children, in the way of others, they often come to feel out of tune with time and place. No matter how justly deserving one may be, a safe seat on the side is a poor substitute for an active place in the field. It is the passiveness of old age among us that makes it so unhappy. Modern civilization has added more years to life, but it has left less life in the twilight years.

23

Values Expressed in American Children's Readers: 1800-1950*

Richard deCharms and Gerald H. Moeller

The preceding papers in this chapter have emphasized the contrasts in cultural pressures and aims from group to group at a given time. Similar differences may be expected at different times within the same culture. The most striking characteristic of the modern world is change—change in goals, values, and processes of child rearing,

* Adapted and abridged from Richard deCharms and Gerald H. Moeller, "Values Expressed in American Children's Readers: 1800-1950," *Journal of Abnormal and Social Psychology*, 1962, Vol. 64, pp. 136-142. (With permission of the senior author and the American Psychological Association.)

as well as in technology. While this fact in itself is obvious, such changes are difficult to measure and to express in psychologically meaningful terms. The present paper is an interesting application of a method commonly used in psychological research—the analysis of projective test data—to an examination of the changes in particular values that have occurred during the course of a century and a half in the United States, changes which have borne directly on children at different periods in our history. What emerges is a dramatic illustration of the fact that cultural changes of a potentially most significant sort may occur.

Students of cultural change within the United States seem to have reached some agreement as to a trend observable within the last century. This trend, which deals with some of the basic values of our culture, may be seen as a change from what Weber (1930) called "the Protestant ethic" to what has been called the "social ethic" (Whyte, 1956). Specifically, the dominant value of individual salvation through hard work, thrift, and competition is seen as being replaced by "a belief in the group as the source of creativity; a belief in 'belongingness' as the ultimate need of the individual; and a belief in the application of science to achieve the belongingness" (Whyte, 1956, p. 7). In Riesman's (Riesman, Glazer, & Denney, 1950) terminology the basic trend is from inner-direction to other-direction.

Actually this process is circular in the sense that the cultural change is probably accompanied by a change in values which starts a new cycle. The psychologist likes to conceive of the basic variables in human behavior as being internally determined and thus breaks this circle and concentrates on motives as basic.

The aim of the present paper is to investigate psychological variables which it seems logical to predict will be associated with the cultural changes observed in the United States over the last century and a half.

Assuming that achievement motivation is a basic component of the inner-directed character type, and that affiliation motivation is a basic component of the other-directed character type, in the context of Riesman's cultural change thesis, one would predict a decline in over-all achievement motivation and an increase in affiliation motivation in the last century of United States history. Strauss and Houghton (1960) have found evidence giving some support to these hypotheses in the period since 1924 in a study of 4-H club journals. A meaningful relationship should also be found between achievement orientation and economic and technological change according to McClelland (1955).

A further aspect of Riesman's thesis is that the stage of inner-direction is preceded by a stage of tradition-direction. During this stage strict moral codes demand behavioral conformity of the individual. The change from a tradition-directed society to an inner-directed society involves a secularization in the sense that the individual must prove himself worthy as in Weber's (1930) Protestant ethic, rather than be told what to do by categorical imperatives. One might thus predict more reliance on moral teaching early in the history of the United States.

McClelland (1958) has developed a method of assessing achievement motivation in a culture by content analysis of literary products of the culture. Using this tool he found striking confirmation for his hypothesis that achievement motivation preceded the economic and technological development of Athenian civilization in classical Greece, a culture also discussed by Riesman.

McClelland's measure of motivation was developed originally to assess the motives of individuals (McClelland, Atkinson, Clark, & Lowell, 1953). The extension of it to apply to cultures raises questions as to what is being measured. It is obvious that a measure which has been shown to be related to individual motives would be expected to reflect the motives of the writer of any document chosen from a culture. In order to use such a measure as an indication of cultural orientation one does not have to assume that the motive score of an individual author is a measure of the cultural orientation alone. One must, however, assume that a portion of the score is a measure of the cultural orientation. The problem of reducing idiosyncratic components in the measure of cultural orientation becomes one of (a) sampling randomly many authors (b) under as similar conditions as possible (i.e., writing similar material) and (c) choosing materials which should place few restrictions on the author's fantasy.

All of the above advantages can be obtained by careful sampling of stories written for children's readers. In addition, the stories are actually written to be used in transmitting cultural values, and information on how widely they have been used gives at once some indication of cultural acceptance of the values contained in the book and of the extent of its influence. An example of the use of children's readers to assess values in many cultures has been presented by McClelland (1961).

The schema presented above predicts a relationship between cultural achievement orientation and behavior of the members of the culture which would lead to technological advance. Just as one might predict that an individual with high achievement motivation might strive for some unique accomplishment, one might also predict that a culture with strong achievement orientation would produce many inventions. A measure of the inventiveness of the culture at various periods in history might be obtained from the number of patents issued per population, and one could predict a relationship between this and a measure of cultural achievement orientation.

HYPOTHESES

The present study is an attempt to plot the incidence of achievement and affiliation imagery and moral teaching in a sample of children's readers from 1800 to the present. In addition, achievement imagery is to be related to data on the number of patents issued per population. The study was undertaken to test several hypotheses: (I) The incidence of achievement imagery in a sample of children's readers selected over the period 1800-1950 will decrease over the time period, (II) The incidence of affiliation imagery in the same sample of readers will increase over the time period, (III) The incidence of moral teaching in the sample will decrease over the time period, and (IV) The incidence of achievement imagery will be positively related to the number of patents issued, corrected for changes in population.

The hypotheses assume, with Riesman, that the nineteenth century in the United States was dominated by the inner-directed character type, and that the United States has recently been in transition from an inner-directed phase to an other-directed phase.

METHOD

A bibliography of reading textbooks with copyright dates ranging from 1800 to 1952 was compiled. An attempt was made to procure at least four books from each 20-year period beginning in 1800. Readers were excluded which were not in wide use during the period or which were used by religious affiliated schools. In the more recent periods from which more than four books were available, the choice of books was made randomly. In the periods in which fewer than four books were available the sample from each book was enlarged in so far as possible. Generally, the sample from each book was obtained by scoring every third page. In order to equate for number of pages available the score was the number of pages containing imagery per 75 pages sampled. A raw score was thus computed for every 75 pages sampled (i.e., 25 pages scored). The readers chosen for the study were, generally speaking, at a fourth grade level.

The pages selected from each book were scored independently by two scorers as to whether the page contained (a) achievement imagery, (b) affiliation imagery, or (c) a category called moral teaching. Achievement and affiliation imagery were scored according to the procedure outlined in Atkinson (1958). The subcategories usually scored in this procedure were not scored. The category Moral Teaching was developed and defined as explicit or implicit statements of judgment between right and wrong from the point of view of the author. The following (McGuffey, 1857) is an example of items which were scored for moral teaching:

The little boy took care of his faithful dog as long as he lived and never forgot that we must do good to others, if we wish them to do the same to us (p. 42).

Scorer reliabilities, based on presence of imagery only, were consistently high (Achievement Imagery=94 per cent, Affiliation Imagery=96 per cent, Moral Teaching=97 per cent).

The number of patents issued by the United States Patent Office and the United States Census figures were taken from governmental documents (United States Department of Commerce, 1960) and a patent index was computed by dividing the number of patents granted in a 20-year period by the population reported in the midyear of that period and multiplying by one million. This results in an index of patents issued per one million population during the period.

There are two methodological flaws in the procedure which it was felt might have had an effect on the results. In the first place, the technique of blind scoring was not employed. The scoring was done directly from the book; thus the scorer probably knew the date of the book. Second, since each score was based on 75 pages of text, some books were more heavily weighted than others and the individual values of their authors might have unduly influenced the results.

In order to correct these methodological flaws it was decided to repeat the study with a drastically smaller sample. A sample of 6 pages was chosen at random from each book, and the pages were typed and coded for blind scoring. Plots of the results of the two studies are almost identical and statistical significance was reached in most instances in the second study, although, as anticipated, the probability levels were not as great as in the first. This comparison of the two replications gives greater confidence in the results of the first study. The data presented here come from the first study.

RESULTS AND DISCUSSION[1]

Figures 1 and 2 present the mean imagery scores for achievement, affiliation, and moral teaching in each of the 20-year periods. Hypothesis I predicted a consistent decrease in achievement imagery. The data (see Figure 1) show a sharp decline since 1890, but a steady increase from 1800 to the peak at about 1890. Hypothesis II predicted a consistent increase in affiliation imagery from 1800 to the present. The data in Figure 2 show no consistent increase but do show a general trend with an unexpected drop in 1950 to the 1890 level. Hypothesis III predicts a decrease

[1] The results reported were submitted to statistical tests in both samples. Details are reported in the original article.

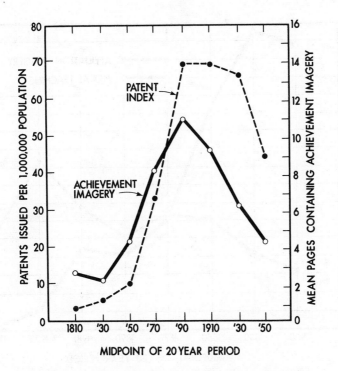

FIGURE 1. Mean Number of Pages (out of 25) Containing Achievement Imagery and the Patent Index

in moral teaching from 1800 to the present. The data show a striking confirmation. Hypothesis IV predicts a relationship between the amount of achievement imagery during a specific period and the index of patents issued per population. Figure 1 shows this relationship in graphic form. A striking relationship is apparent.

The data on achievement imagery do not confirm the original hypothesis which was obviously too simple. There are clear indications in both samples that achievement imagery increases to a peak around the turn of the present century and has steadily declined since then. This relationship is supported by the strikingly similar data from the patent index. The number of patents granted was used in preference to the number of applications for patents for two reasons: no record was kept of patents applied for until 1840 (this would have cut 39 years from the patent/population measure) and the very fact that a patent is issued is indicative of the "uniqueness" of the patent. Unique accomplishment is one of the criteria for scoring achievement imagery (Atkinson, 1958).

The data from both samples tend to confirm the hypothesis of increasing

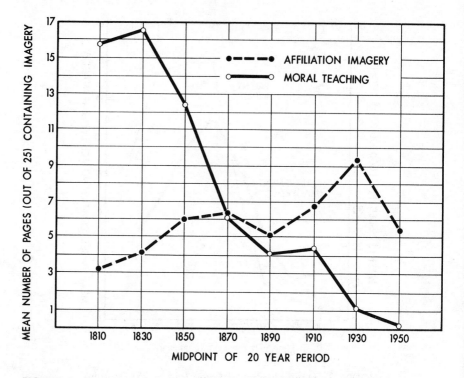

FIGURE 2. Mean Number of Pages (out of 25) Containing Affiliation Imagery
and Moral Teaching Imagery

affiliation imagery, although the results were not statistically significant in
the second sample. Certain aspects of the difference in type of affiliation
imagery through time are noteworthy. Much of the early and middle nineteenth century readers' affiliation imagery, though widely scattered, was
quite unsophisticated. In contrast, affiliation imagery in the period from
1920 was considerably more subtle. It was more difficult to score affiliation imagery in the earliest books in the study and it was in this period
that interrater reliability was lowest. The difficulty lay in differentiating
true affective affiliation imagery from a culturally sanctioned form of address. Thus "dear son," "dear father," and "my dear" were not scored
unless affect was also demonstrated since this was often mere conventionally approved formalism.

It is possible that this scoring difficulty could account for the results
found. This, in combination with the fact that the results were not significant in the second sample, suggests caution in interpretation of these
results.

The decline in the religious-moral emphasis in textbooks has long been noted by various researchers. Hart (1933), in analyzing selected popular magazines of the period from 1900 to 1930, found evidence of a general decline in the status of religion and religious sanctions. These findings are in general accord with the results of the present study. In the case of the school readers it may be argued that the diminishing frequency of moral references is a result of the secularization of the schools during the nineteenth century.

It should be noted that the first schools in the colonies were church-sponsored and, in many instances, the minister of the church also served as teacher to the children. The shift from church-sponsored to the public-sponsored and supported schools began about the time of the American Revolution and continued through most of the nineteenth century. However, since all the books in the present study were prepared for public schools, the decrease in moral teaching imagery indicates the cultural trend toward secularization which affected the management of the schools and was reflected in the books written for the schools even after they had become nominally secular.

The antecedent conditions of changes in values such as demonstrated here are very complex. As noted earlier theorists such as Riesman et al. (1950) stress the importance of psychological factors (character type) which lead to the examination of child rearing practices. Economic historians stress political and economic factors.

The findings of the present study fit very well the conceptual paradigm of Rostow (1960) who developed a general model of the stages of economic growth which distinguishes (a) precondition for take-off, (b) the take-off, (c) the drive to maturity, and (d) the age of high mass consumption.

In the United States, Rostow (1960) found that the traditional or agricultural society lasted until about 1840. The take-off occurred from 1843 to 1860. This appears to be the take-off period for achievement orientation also (see Figure 1). During the next period from 1860 to 1900, called by Rostow the drive to maturity, "some ten to twenty per cent of the national income was steadily invested, permitting industrial output regularly to outstrip the increase in population" (p. 9). The United States, according to Rostow's data and reasoning, reached technological maturity around 1900. This date is extremely close to the high points of achievement imagery and patent measures.

Rostow's (1960) preconditions for take-off are technological developments which might set the stage for increased social mobility, a factor mentioned by Riesman et al. (1950) as affecting child rearing practices. Rostow feels that during this period the idea that economic progress is possible and necessary for such ends as national dignity becomes prevalent in the culture and men come forward who are willing to mobilize savings, take risks, and engage in entrepreneurial activity.

The latter aspects have a distinctly psychological flavor. Men who take risks and engage in entrepreneurial activity are those who have high achievement motivation (McClelland, 1958). Recently economists have noted the importance of motivation and personality structure in economic growth. Thus Hagen (1958) discusses the role of the need for achievement, for autonomy, for aggression, for dominance, for affiliation, and for dependence in the beginning of economic growth. These motivational variables interact with economic and political variables to produce cultural changes.

As noted in the introduction, evidence for the importance of psychological factors such as motives and values in cultural change and economic growth has been presented by McClelland (1955, 1958, 1961). There are, moreover, studies which have made a start in uncovering the relationship between child rearing practices and achievement and affiliation motivation. Briefly, achievement motivation appears to be associated with early parental stress on independence training and mastery, coupled with a warm acceptance of the child (Winterbottom, 1958). Affiliation motivation is related to maternal acceptance and to parental stress on interpersonal involvement of the child (Gall, 1960).

These findings appear to be in accord with Riesman's analysis of the child rearing practices which lead to the inner- and other-directed character types. The parent rearing a child in the period of transition to inner-direction must equip him with a "gyroscope" which will fit him to remain on course in a society where it is impossible to foretell, due to increasing social mobility, what role he will be called upon to play. He must be equipped to be self-reliant and independent. These are the aspects which Riesman sees in nineteenth century child rearing. The antecedents of achievement motivation seem clear.

On the other hand, with increasing urbanization and population density which result from technological advance, the child is no longer pushed to be independent, but learns the importance of other individuals in the environment. He must be taught to win approval.

In summary we propose that motivation, or cultural orientation, be conceived of as an intervening variable standing between antecedent environmental factors associated with economic and political changes and consequent behavior resulting in cultural changes such as technological growth. Such an analysis should give increased explanatory power, since it is probable that motivation is a function of factors other than economic changes. For instance, cultural values affect child rearing practices and hence motives (McClelland, Rindlisbacher, & deCharms, 1955). Thus two cultures undergoing similar economic or political change may react quite differently due to the intervening variables of values, child rearing practices, and motives.

SUMMARY

Content analysis of children's readers from schools in the United States demonstrated a rise in achievement imagery from 1800 to about 1900 and then a steady decline. The achievement imagery curve was related to an index of the number of patents issued. A steady decline over the period 1800-1950 was found in the amount of moral teaching in readers. There was tentative indication of an increase in affiliation imagery.

The over-all picture presented by the data corresponds very well with certain cultural trends pointed out by students of cultural change. The data illustrate an interesting technique for obtaining objective data to investigate cultural historical hypotheses.

24

Changes in the Attitudes and Interests of Adolescents Over Two Decades[*]

Mary Cover Jones

The preceding paper analyzed important changes in our American culture but gave no evidence as to the degree to which such changes were reflected in the attitudes and values of the individuals reared in the succeeding generations. The present paper reverses the pattern; it focuses upon the differences between two groups of adolescents reared almost a generation apart, in the 1930's and in the 1950's, in the same neighborhoods. Although one can only guess what particular cultural changes produced the differences, the facts here reported suggest that the adolescent of the 1950's was in many respects an improvement over the 1935 model, at least in the community studied.

Are teenagers today more serious or more frivolous, more conforming or more rebelling, more sophisticated or more naive, than teenagers of a

* Adapted and abridged from Mary Cover Jones, "A Comparison of the Attitudes and Interests of Ninth Grade Students over Two Decades," *Journal of Educational Psychology*, 1960, Vol. 51, pp. 175-186. (With permission of the author and the American Psychological Association.)

generation ago? This is not a question which can have a general answer, since trends (if they occur) will not necessarily be in the same direction in different regions or in different social classes. However, where relevant data are available for known samples it seems desirable to report them and consider their implications in relation to other research in this field. What adolescents think, do, want is of interest from many different theoretical and practical points of view.

COMPARISON OF SAMPLES

In a state growing as rapidly as California, the population composition of some neighborhoods has changed so greatly that temporal trends would

TABLE 1. Socioeconomic Classification: Parents' Occupation
(Edwards 6-point Scale) (Expressed in percentages)

	1935	1953
1. Professional	07	17
2. Managerial	18	29
3. Semiprofessional	38	25
4. Skilled	29	25
5. Semiskilled	06	04
6. Unskilled	02	00
Median	3.12[a]	2.59[a]
SD	1.04[a]	1.12[a]

[a] These values are scale values on the Edwards Scale where a low score indicates higher socioeconomic status.

be difficult to disentangle from differences in social groups. Fortunately for our purpose, the neighborhoods involved in this study have to a fairly high degree maintained the stability which was noted at the time this junior high school was chosen for the longitudinal study.

Table 1 compares the distribution of parents' occupations (Edwards, 1933) in 1935 and 1953. An increase has occurred in professional and managerial occupations, and the total for white collar occupations has increased from 59 to 65%. Similarly, a slight upward shift has occurred in the neighborhood classifications; here the principal change has resulted from the opening of a neighborhood of new homes, and the diminished proportion remaining in an older neighborhood.

To some extent these changes reflect the general upward mobility in living standards, income and education which has occurred over this 18-year period. An additional contributing factor was a change in the elementary school sources of this junior high school population, a change in the direction of a more homogeneous middle class group, slightly above the former average.

If these changes had resulted in a very marked alteration of the social structure of the junior high school district, we would expect to find significant changes in the intelligence distribution. This has not occurred as is shown in Table 2.

As a further control on the comparability of the two populations in socioeconomic status, a subsample was selected of 40 cases for each sex

TABLE 2. Intelligence Test (IQ) Classification
(Expressed in percentages)

	1935[a]	1953[b]
130-139	02	01
120-129	06	12
110-119	27	30
100-109	38	30
90-99	21	18
80-89	05	07
70-79	01	02
Mean	105.49	105.18
SD	10.75	12.28

[a] Terman Group Test, Form A and B.
[b] Kuhlmann-Anderson.
Note: Although different tests were used, they have been shown to yield about the same mean and SD.

and each period under study (1935 and 1953), carefully matched on the basis of parents' occupation. The responses for the subsamples on a 139 item comparison were in general agreement with those of the larger sample. Because of the advantages of dealing with a larger sample, it was decided to use the total ninth grade population as the basis of this report.

SUBJECTS AND PROCEDURES

Results are discussed below for an inventory consisting of some 250 items pertaining to activities, interests, and attitudes. Levels of significance have been computed for the sexes separately in a comparison of earlier with later records. Sex differences within each temporal sample have been analyzed, as well as age trends over the seven-year period in the earlier, longitudinal sample.

Members of the Oakland Growth study, 72 boys and 70 girls, are represented in the 1935 testing, when they were in the ninth grade. For this group an interest record was administered yearly for seven years, an activity schedule yearly from the 9th through the 12th grade, and an opinion ballot in the 8th, 9th, and 11th grades.

For the 1953 comparison, all ninth-grade students in the same junior high school were tested. The boys numbered 95 and the girls 78. The additional test program in 1959 included 134 boys and 123 girls. Nonwhite students, now numbering about 20, were eliminated to maintain comparability with the earlier samples.

The test used in 1953 and in 1959 included a representative selection of items from three inventories used in the longitudinal study. It was administered in one class period of 50 min. Students were asked to check items organized on separate pages under such headings as Where I Went Last Week, and What I Read Last Week. They were asked to indicate whether they liked, disliked, or were indifferent to a number of items listed under titles such as Things to Own, or Things to Be: Occupations. Headings such as Things You Talk About were answered on a 5-point scale from Never to Very often. Attitudes were sampled under the heading My Opinion, which instructed the Ss to report whether they approved, disapproved, or sometimes approved the behavior or ideas listed.

The categories of items as presented were administrative rather than functional. Items belonging to a given functional classification (such as interest in sex-social activities) occurred under different phrasing in each of the nine parts of the test. Thus, preoccupation with mixed group activities and interest in the opposite sex might presumably be tapped by the subject's desire to own new party clothes, to go to a good dance hall, to want to stay out late, or to talk about dates. Similarly, a student might indicate that he or she went to a dance or read a love story last week, and approved of "permanents."

RESULTS

One fact is outstanding in our results. In the more recent tests, boys and girls in the ninth grade marked items in such a way as to indicate greater maturity and greater social sophistication. This is demonstrated in their responses to items which show an age trend in adolescence for the earlier study group. Some of these items, representing "juvenile" interests or immature behavior, are, in the longitudinal sample, rejected increasingly as boys and girls grow older. At the same time, other items which represent greater maturity of interests and attitudes become more frequently selected. For example, members of the adolescent study group, as they grew older, no longer wanted to "own a stamp collection," to read Boy's Life, to go to a "secret clubhouse" or to be "a detective." On the other hand, as they grew older, they more often checked such items as this week "I went to a dance"; I approve of "thinking about how I look"; I talk about "having dates."

On such age-relative items, we now find that ninth graders in the '50's are more comparable to the eleventh- or twelfth-grade students of 20 years earlier than to those of their own age.

Interest, activity, and attitude items which illustrate this tendency to check the more mature response have been grouped under subheadings such as social-sex interests, sense of responsibility, tolerance, and anti-aggression attitudes. For each of these categories, one item which illustrates the findings has been selected for discussion.

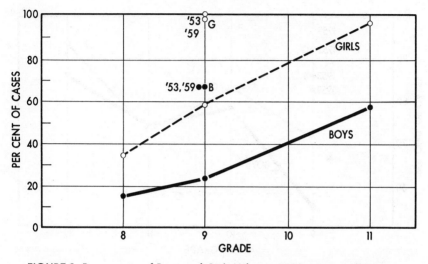

FIGURE 1. Percentage of Boys and Girls Who, in 1938, 1953, and 1959, Approve of Using Lipstick

In the area of social-sex or heterosexual preoccupation, Figure 1 shows the response for the item *I approve of the use of lipstick*. For boys and girls respectively, the solid and broken lines indicate age trends in the longitudinal sample, in the 1930's. The responses of ninth graders in 1953 and 1959 are also indicated; black circles represent the percentages for boys, open circles the percentages for girls. Lipstick symbolizes as well as any one specific item could, the sensitization in early adolescence toward a new sex role and toward being grown up. While its use is confined to girls, opinions about its use are not, as the figure indicates. The lag shown in the data for boys (as compared with girls) may indicate either less interest or active antagonism toward signs of maturing from members of the less mature sex who are being pressured into the heterosexual phase ahead of schedule.

The data show that by the 1950's (1953 and 1959), for both boys and girls, the percentage approving of the use of lipstick was higher in the 9th grade than in the 11th grade sample 20 years earlier. It is well known that there are social class and regional differences in attitudes toward the use of lipstick and other aspects of adolescent grooming. But here we find also a temporal difference in samples living in the same neighborhood and comparable in social status.

Other items in the category of social-sex interest for the most part revealed significant differences of a similar sort between 1935 and 1953 and between 1935 and 1959.

When we described the junior high school culture of our group in the

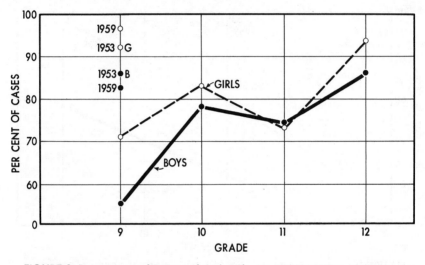

FIGURE 2. Percentage of Boys and Girls Who, in 1938, 1953, and 1959, Report That "This Week I Studied"

1930's, we interpreted their concern with social activities as in conflict with achievement motives of an academic nature. This preoccupation often seemed inconsistent with an interest in homework, in assuming responsibilities or in showing concern for any but their own narrow peer group activities. Does a similar situation hold today? Is an increased social interest accompanied by a decreased commitment in other areas?

Quite the contrary. These 14-year-olds in 1953 and 1959 can be described from their answers as more studious, more broadly interested in the contemporary scene, more tolerant in their social attitudes, more inclined to value controlled behavior and to disapprove of aggression or irresponsible behavior in others. Comparative results for the item *This week I studied* are shown in Figure 2. A significantly higher percentage of boys and of girls in the 1950's reported studying. The actual percentages in the ninth grade were virtually the same as those of high school seniors in the 1930's. Other items indicating a greater sense of personal and social responsibility, as marked in the more recent sample, are shown in

Table 3. There were more frequent reports of talking about their studies and talking about other school activities. They liked to go to school assemblies. Such responses indicate a more school-centered orientation in the '50's than in the '30's.

TABLE 3. Responsible Behavior

	Boys % Positive Response			Girls % Positive Response		
	1935	1953	1959	1935	1953	1959
Activities						
I studied	67	86	85	54	92	94
I took care of children	8	20	25	30	47	53
I earned some money	57	69*	69*	22	58	49
I read						
something about science	17	35	40	4	12*	17
The Bible	16	20*	21*	12	35	32
something about religion	8	19*	18*	11	28	30
I went to Sunday School	41	43*	40*	35	69	62
I went to Church	46	47*	56*	55	82	78
Conversations						
I talk about						
what you are going to be	58	77	69*	74	89	89
money and things you need	60	78	75	53	84	86
church and things about						
religion	21	46	45	33	72	71
studies, classwork	63	83	80	82	93	91
school activities	49	59*	64*	58	89	82
things about the govern-						
ment, politics	38	67	48*	14	51	30
Attitudes						
I approve of worrying						
about the future	12	27	31	5	17	32

* Comparisons with 1935 are starred for chi squares *not* significant at the .05 level or better.

A greater proportion said they earned money, took care of their clothes and their rooms, talked about what they were going to be when they grew up, and thought it appropriate to worry about the future (Table 3). This, in prosperous times as contrasted with depression years and (for the 1953 sample) before Sputnik!

The differences shown in Table 3 may be in part differences in the *Zeitgeist*, and in part a matter of situational changes. Thus, an increase in the number of young children, and the development of baby-sitting, may be largely responsible for the increase (especially among girls) in "taking care of children" and "earning money." The increased interest reported by both sexes in such items as "reading about science" and "talking about political matters" may define a generally higher level of intellectual-cultural maturity in the more recent junior high school samples. The markedly significant increases especially among girls in religious interests may reflect an additional factor; the percentages reached in the '50's are higher than any we obtained even in the 12th grade in the '30's (Figure 3).

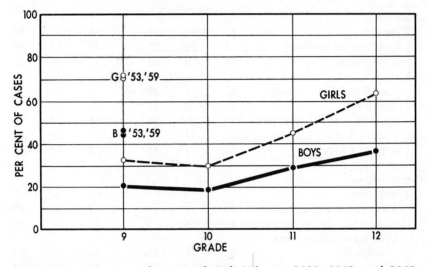

FIGURE 3. Percentage of Boys and Girls Who, in 1938, 1953, and 1959, Report "Talking About Religion"

Table 3 presents data for a number of items illustrating different aspects of tolerance. As shown in Figure 4, *I approve of foreigners* elicits a much more affirmative response in the '50's, from both boys and girls.

One group of items (approval of betting, gambling, etc.) suggests a more relaxed attitude which might be thought to be incompatible with the greater expressed interest in the church and its influences (as shown in the preceding table). However, this acquiescence does not extend to what might be classified as inconsiderate or aggressive behavior. The ninth graders of the '50's manifest more disapproval of antisocial behavior such as *"getting even"* or "doing what I want when I want to" (Figure 5).

Some of the responses discussed above suggest a greater socialization and also a more conforming attitude. The latter characteristic is frequently attributed to our present generation of young people. But not all items which connote acquiescence are approved by the recent samples as compared with the '30's. More adolescents countenance "disagreeing with my parents" and "saying exactly what I think." "Always doing what is expected" is indicated as much less acceptable.

More in line with the findings of the present study is an early report by Pressey (1946) on attitude changes between 1923 and 1943. Pressey was encouraged by "the general freeing of young people over the past 20 years . . . from a great variety of borderland social taboos, inhibitions and restrictions. . . ." A second trend which he applauded was "the growth of activities."

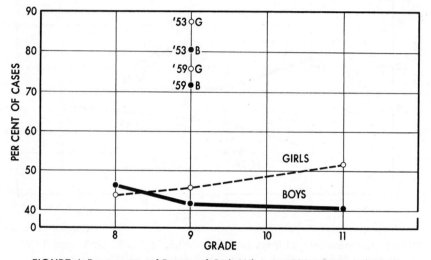

FIGURE 4. Percentage of Boys and Girls Who, in 1938, 1953, and 1959, Report That They Approve of Foreigners

SEX DIFFERENCES AND SEX ROLE PATTERNS

Check lists of children's interests, such as those employed in this study, have been used by a number of investigators to examine the development of sex role concepts and sex differences. For most of the items in the area of social-sex development the indication of mature interest is more marked in girls than in boys. More girls than boys report "going to a dance." More girls than boys report that they talk about dates and opposite-sex friends.

Earlier physiological maturing of girls (as compared with boys) would be expected to produce now, as formerly, an earlier maturing in social-sex development. However, it may be that the temporal trend in the direction of a generally earlier expression of heterosexual interest for both sexes, contributes to some blurring of sex role patterns as revealed in certain aspects of the data for the 1950's.

For example, this may account for the fact that in the 1950's boys' responses are more like those of girls on some items. More girls than boys checked that they manicured their nails, but between 1935 and 1959 the increase in percentage checking this item was significant only for boys.

Although greater social maturity in both boys and girls may be one factor which accounts for increased similarity of the sexes on some items, there is one area of interest in which results run counter to this observa-

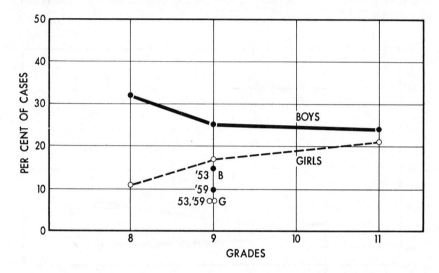

FIGURE 5. Percentage of Boys and Girls Who, in 1938, 1953, and 1959, Indicate Disapproval of the Antisocial Behavior of "Getting Even"

tion. The girls seem to have made a striking shift from passive to active interest in sports and athletic activities. In the earlier sample the percentage checking the positive response diminished from the 6th to the 12th grade. There was also a large sex difference in the 1935 sample, with boys showing more favorable attitudes.

Figure 6 gives the results for a representative item, showing the trend in percentage wishing *to own a baseball and bat*. Data are given for the 6th through the 12th grades in the '30's and also for the 9th grade in 1953 and 1959. Differences are significant for girls but not for boys. This finding suggests that the female role perception is expanding in the direction of greater activity and increased masculinity.

The question has been raised as to what the effect on the masculine role will be, if girls' interests are expanded to include traditionally masculine activities. We might conjecture that, for this sample at least, boys may be staking out a new claim in the borderland of social respectability involving betting and gambling (data not presented here). On the other hand, the increased heterosexual orientation of ninth-grade boys suggests that they may not be averse to sharing interests in some areas with girls.

In relation to psychological sex-role development the data are not definitive. There is some blending of sex-role patterns but only as it is expressed concomitantly with earlier social maturing. There is some expansion of feminine interests into the male domain, but this is principally seen in sports activities. In the area of vocational preferences, girls' interests seem

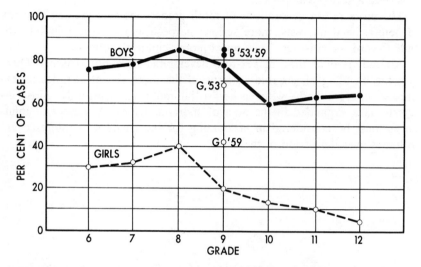

FIGURE 6. Percentage of Boys and Girls Who, in 1938, 1953, and 1959, Report Owning a Baseball and Bat

to be oriented toward supplementing the family income rather than toward a career. There is some constriction of the boys' vocational choices but this may be because we are comparing good times with the earlier depression era.

Members of the early growth study are now adults, some with adolescent offspring of their own. In interviews they often express their opinions about today's young people in contrast to their own remembered youth. They do not need to be told that adolescents now are more mature socially than in their day, though they may exaggerate the differences.

So, in a sense, the present attitudes of our original sample, and their contemporaries, now parents and citizens, are among the environmental factors affecting changes in the directions which we have seen. Parental influences, evidence of earlier maturing, altered school programs, historical events, all give direction to the secular trends in interests and attitudes recorded in this study.

SUMMARY

This report compares the activities, interests and attitudes of three ninth-grade classes in the same school but separated in time by 18 and 24 years (1935, 1953, 1959). The samples are closely similar in age and IQ distributions, and fairly comparable in a number of social measures. The earlier group provided age-trend data through tests given at regular intervals over a seven-year period.

The more recent generations of ninth graders indicate greater maturity of heterosexual interests, more serious purpose and a more tolerant attitude toward social issues. They reject more "childish" activities.

Alterations over time in sex-role development are not striking. There is some blending of sex-role patterns in the more recent samples as expressed concomitantly with earlier social maturing. Currently, girls' interests have expanded in the area of sports activities. A variety of influences must be considered in accounting for the changes in interests and attitudes over the period of the study.

Part VI

PATTERNS OF INTELLECTUAL GROWTH

INTELLIGENCE IS defined in various ways as the capacity of the organism to learn or to modify its behavior, as its capacity to think or to solve problems, or its capacity to deal with novel situations. Human intelligence is intimately related to the solution of problems involving the comprehension and use of symbols. Symbols include words, diagrams, numbers, equations, or formulas representing ideas and relationships of varying degrees of complexity. Intellectual skills play an important role in human adjustment, and changes in such competencies with increasing age are of extreme importance not only in their own right but also through the influence they exert on other facets of personality growth and change.

Much of the controversy in psychology regarding the relative importance of nature and nurture has been focused on intellectual growth. To what extent is intellectual ability determined by heredity? To what extent by environment? The paper by Burt involving identical-twin subjects indicates the extreme similarity in intelligence of twins of identical heredity and thus suggests that heredity plays the crucial role in determining variations in human intelligence. No matter how much one may be swayed toward an hereditary emphasis by Burt's argument, however, it seems important that all of us note that environmental influences of the kind that stimulate educational effort must still play an essential role in acquiring the grasp of symbols and the knowledge of processes which are required for an individual to make full use of the "raw" intelligence that he possesses. More subtle environmental influence in the home, family, and general social life will also be partially responsible for his level of aspiration and drive and for the quality of his adjustment, good or poor, which in turn are important factors in making the most of his ability. Indeed, the article by Kagan, Sontag, Baker, and Nelson describes how certain social conditions covary with steady increments and decrements in *measured* intelligence. The young child who is high in curiosity and competitive in his orientation toward life has a good chance both of succeeding in our culture and of making higher scores on tests of intelligence.

Though useful indicators of ability, "intelligence tests" are not perfect, and performance on such tests can be influenced by extraneous factors. Intellectual efficiency at one age may differ markedly from the efficiency of the *same* individual, beset perhaps by entirely different pressures, at another age. Thus the practical user of intelligence test scores will wish to pay particular attention to normal variations in indexes of intelligence with repetitions of the same or different tests. Some evidence on this point is included in the paper by Honzik, Macfarlane, and Allen.

Finally, among the papers here assembled is a discussion by Drs. Getzels and Jackson of their research into the characteristics of the creative individual, a topic high in current interest. Important discrepancies appeared between "intelligence" as measured by conventional tests and capacity for generating novel ideas and reacting in an unusual way to the environment. The "bright" person does not necessarily turn out to be the creative person. Such findings are particularly important when it is noted that conventional tests are utilized in screening students admitted to college, and that the individual who is conventional and who conforms to ordinary classroom expectations—e.g., the "academically promising" person—is likely to be the student who is considered creative by teachers. Especially needed today are better means of identifying the individual with truly creative potential, as well as knowledge of how to foster the development of creativity both in such individuals and in those with somewhat less creative ability. Drs. Getzels and Jackson's research represents an important step in this direction.

25

The Inheritance of Mental Ability*

Cyril Burt

How much of human intelligence, and which of its aspects, are potentially open to environmental influence? Certainly a man deprived of all contact with the logical-linguistic tools of civilized society would be regarded as intellectually dull if confronted with the problems of contemporary man. On the other hand, there are many instances of

* From Cyril Burt, "The Inheritance of Mental Ability," *American Psychologist*, 1958, Vol. 13, pp. 1-15. (With permission of the author and the American Psychological Association.)

This paper is based on the Walter Van Dyke Bingham Memorial Lecture given at University College, London, on May 21, 1957.

children born into good families and reared under what appear to be ideal conditions of tender loving care and verbal stimulation who remain forever retarded in the acquisition of intellectual skills. What proportion of the variations in human intellect can be reasonably attributed to variations in environmental stimulation and nurturance? Dr. Cyril Burt, emeritus professor of psychology of University College in London, England, offers little hope to the social reformer who may wish to improve man's eventual understanding and skill by a sustained program of environmental enrichment. Dr. Burt's estimates of environmental influence on intellectual development are very conservative, accounting for only about 8 to 12 per cent of observed variations in human intelligence. The reader will be impressed with the cogency of Dr. Burt's reasoning as well as the plausibility of his suppositions about the two different types of genes affecting mental development.

May I first say how deeply I feel the honour of being invited by the American Psychological Association, through its special committee, to deliver this lecture, and how grateful we are to Dr. and Mrs. Walter V. Bingham for their generosity in establishing such a lectureship. The problem which the founders had in mind happens to be one of special interest to us here in Britain; and it was with particular pleasure that we learnt that Mrs. Bingham and the committee had agreed that, on this occasion, the lecture should be given in this country and at this college. British psychologists, many of whom are gathered in this hall, are thus enabled to express their sincere and heartfelt admiration of the work carried out by Bingham himself, not only during two world wars, but also in time of peace, and not only in his own country, but also during his many visits over here. The valuable contributions that he made by his books, his numerous articles, and most of all perhaps by his tactful and untiring activities behind the scenes, I have already attempted to review elsewhere. Here therefore may I content myself with endorsing on behalf of British psychologists the well deserved tribute paid by Professor Egon Pearson on behalf of British statisticians.

In his own autobiographical chapter Bingham has himself observed that one of his "chief functions in life seems to have been to act as an emissary for psychology to the heathen"; and it was during one of these apostolic missions that, when he came to London a year or two before the first world war, he so kindly sought me out to discuss the paper I had just published while at Oxford on the measurement and inheritability of mental capacity (Burt, 1909). It was my first effort at research, and the first paper published in this country on mental tests. I still treasure the letter I received from Ward of Cambridge, who was in those days the acknowledged leader of psychology in this country and editor of our new and only journal of psychology. While accepting my paper, he added that I was myself an outstanding example of wasted capacity, in that I had "spent so much time and industry on a transient problem like mental testing, which held so little promise for the future." "Evidently," said Bingham, "Oxford must begin by converting Cambridge." And it was the encouragement I then received from him that emboldened me to persevere. As it turned out, Bingham's precognition of the future of mental testing was far more accurate than Ward's; and soon afterwards McDougall at Oxford, and Myers, then a young lecturer at Cambridge, succeeded in transforming British psychology from a branch of philosophy into a branch of science. In so doing both insisted that in the future "psychology must devote itself to the study of the individual and not merely to the study of mind in general."[1]

THE PROBLEM OF INDIVIDUAL DIFFERENCES

In Britain as in America, the earliest applications of the new techniques of mental testing were concerned chiefly with the lower end of the intellectual scale. They were readily accepted as practical aids to the doctor in diagnosing the mentally deficient, and to the teacher in discriminating the temporarily retarded from the irremediably dull. It was Bingham's firm belief that: "in the long run it would be even more profitable to discover and aid the bright and the supernormal than to ascertain and provide for the dull and defective."

In this country the traditional method of dealing with the problem was by means of what was popularly known as "the scholarship system." British teachers and parents were apt in those days to think of scholarships rather as a means for rewarding hard work than as a device for detecting and assisting impecunious talent. But considerable misgiving was felt over the erratic local distribution not only of scholarship winners but also of defectives. It was indeed widely affirmed that these variations in the numbers were "largely the result of the injustice of the ordinary methods of examination." Accordingly, in 1913 the London County Council took the unprecedented step of appointing an official psychologist. His chief duties were to act as referee for what were sometimes known as "problem children"—particularly in disputed cases of feeblemindedness and of scholarship ability.

In the surveys that I carried out in this capacity I found that, in the poorer districts of the East End, there were three times as many certified defectives, eight times as many backward pupils, but only one-tenth the number of scholarship winners as were reported in the well-to-do areas of

[1] The change that thus took place can be seen by comparing the treatment of individual psychology in the writings of Ward (e.g., *Psychological Principles*, pp. 433ff.) and in those of Myers (*Experimental Psychology*, 1911, Chap. VI & VII) and McDougall (*Psychology: The Study of Behaviour*, 1912, Chap. VI-VIII).

London. Who or what was to blame: the teachers, the homes, the traditional examination in arithmetic and English? Or the fact that the varying modicum of ability bestowed on each child was irretrievably fixed at birth? Environment or heredity, those seemed to be the alternative explanations; and each had its own enthusiastic advocates. As a rule the social reformers gave one answer and the psychologists the opposite.

During the nineteenth century the main champions of social reform were the philosophical radicals: Bentham, James and John Mill, and their various followers. Their motto was the maxim of Helvétius: l'éducation peut tout; or, as James Mill put it, "if education cannot do everything, there is hardly anything it cannot do." In psychology, their one basic law was the law of association; and the wide differences between one individual and another they attributed solely to the cumulative effects of association, through the operation of "habit, custom, training, and environmental opportunity or deprivation."

By the beginning of the twentieth century, however, most British psychologists had abandoned this simple creed. Impressed by the novel doctrines of the evolutionary school, they began to follow Darwin, Spencer, Huxley, and Galton in holding that the laws of heredity and individual variation applied to men as well as to animals, to mind as well as to body. "It is not so much," said Karl Pearson, "that the slums create the dullards, but rather that the duller stocks gravitate automatically to the slums." It followed that the only cure would be to start breeding citizens as we bred race horses, prize rabbits, or pedigree pups. Huxley's celebrated essay on the "Natural Inequality of Man" won over the few who still wavered. Most teachers were already converted by firsthand experience under the new scheme of universal education.

However, during the last few decades psychologists have been gradually discovering that the problem is far more complicated than either side had originally assumed. And, largely as a result, there has been yet another swing of the polemical pendulum. In part this is due to a reluctance to support what G. K. Chesterton once described as "the modernized dogma of predestination—a dogma calculated to paralyse all progress towards a welfare state"; in part it has been due to a fuller appreciation of the possibilities of experience and learning, which in turn has involved a reversion to something like a rejuvenated belief in the fundamental law of association.

To the British psychologist the experimental work on "conditioning" seemed to offer a more precise interpretation, on a more adequate basis, of the traditional doctrine of association as preached by Hartley and Mill; and the behaviourist school was widely welcomed as substituting a more profitable line of practical research for inconclusive speculations about heredity and innate endowment. As a result, we find contemporary educationists reminding each other of Bagley's (1912) well known dictum that, "except for a few cases of pathological deficiency, the factor of heredity plays a very small part in human life, as compared with the factor of environment"; while several of their psychological colleagues quote with approval the pronouncements of Watson: "there are inheritable differences in structure, but we no longer believe in inherited capacities." "Give me," he adds, "a dozen healthy infants, and my own world to bring them up in, and I'll guarantee to train any one of them to become any type of specialist I might select—doctor, lawyer, artist, merchant-chief, and even beggar-man or thief" (Watson, 1931, p. 104).

A glance through the current literature will show that, for the most part, the hypotheses which our younger psychologists desire to challenge are the two propositions which, at the beginning of the century, were accepted almost without question as justifying the organization of our system of education: first, the hypothesis of general ability, i.e., the view that "up to adolescence the chief differences distinguishing individual pupils are differences in 'general intelligence' "—a view which led the Chief Inspector of Schools to declare that, "with a few exceptions, each pupil may be taught in the same class for every subject, or, if mentally defective, sent to a special school on the ground that he is defective all round"; secondly, the hypothesis of mental inheritance, i.e., the view that the wide differences in the degree of general ability exhibited by various pupils were due mainly to genetic endowment.

The Hypothesis of General Ability. Of these two hypotheses the first was firmly rejected by the report of the "Norwood Committee"—a report which strongly influenced the reorganization of our national education as envisaged in the Education Act of 1944. The committee maintained that children differed far more in quality of ability than in amount; and recommended a tripartite classification of "secondary" schools, based on the doctrine that pupils fall into three main types: a literary or abstract type, to be educated at "grammar schools"; a mechanical or technical type, to be educated at "technical schools"; and a concrete or practical type to be educated at "modern schools." This conception was supported by several leading psychologists who argued that "the statistical analyses of Thurstone disclose no evidence for Spearman's factor of general ability, but only a number of 'primary abilities,' each more or less specialized" (Burt, 1943-6 and refs.).

The scheme has not worked out in actual practice so successfully as was hoped; and the proposal itself at once stimulated a large number of new inquiries. Those who still defend the tripartite theory seem to overlook the vast and varied character of the evidence that has since become available on the issue thus raised. As a rule they content themselves with citing one particular line of reasoning—usually the statistical. If, however, we take a wider view, we shall find that there are three or four independent chains of converging arguments, none perhaps irrefragable by itself, but all of them tending to rehabilitate the older view. The evidence on which these inferences rest is drawn from many different fields: introspection, observation, biology and neurology, as well as statistical research.

In point of fact, the distinction between "general ability" and "special abilities" was due, not (as is so widely supposed) to Spearman, but rather to Francis Galton, from whom Spearman, as he expressly states in his earlier papers, originally borrowed it. Spearman, however, went on to deny the existence of "special abilities" which Galton had supported, on the ground that they were "just relics or revivals of the obsolete theory of faculties" (Spearman, 1927). It is this aspect of the Spearman doctrine that the modern educationist repudiates, and with it he is a little too ready to discard "general intelligence" as well.

However, even Galton had been partly anticipated by previous writers who, in a vague and inchoate fashion, had inculcated a somewhat similar doctrine on the basis of speculative arguments, partly introspective, partly biological. Introspection, so the faculty school had claimed, revealed a sharp distinction between intellectual or cognitive qualities on the one hand and emotional or orectic qualities on the other. Spencer and his followers accepted this distinction, and supplemented it with biological arguments, which in those days were almost equally conjectural. During the evolution of the animal kingdom, and again during the development of each individual, the fundamental capacity which Spencer termed intelligence

. . . becomes [so he tells us] progressively differentiated into a hierarchy of more specialized cognitive capacities—sensory, perceptual, associative, and ratiocinative, much as the trunk of a growing tree ramifies into boughs and twigs (Spencer, 1870, Part iv).

Later writers were not so sure that the term cognition really furnished the best differentia: for them the real distinction was between directive or adaptive processes on the one hand and valuative or dynamic processes on the other; "intelligence," said Sully, "steers like a rudder; emotion and interest supply the steam." A similar reinterpretation has more recently been proposed by Piaget in his book on *The Psychology of Intelligence* (1950, pp. 4ff.).

Far more convincing to my mind is the neurological evidence. The alternative doctrine of distinct and independent abilities drew much of its support from early experiments on cerebral localization. These, it was claimed, ". . . appear to indicate that distinct functions—motor, sensory, perceptual, associative, linguistic, and the like—can be assigned to distinct and definite centres or areas within the brain." And this conclusion was apparently corroborated by the maps of cell structure subsequently produced by histologists like Campbell, Brodmann, and von Economo. Their inferences, however, have been severely criticized by more recent workers, like Bok, Lorente de Nò, and, at University College, by D. A. Sholl (1956). Few of the older map makers (he says) realized "the enormous amount of variability that exists between individual human brains." In their studies of comparable cortical areas from different specimens of *Ateles* Lashley and Clark (1946) have shown that the differences between different individuals are at least as large as the differences upon which the distinction of "architectonic areas" was based. Hence it now seems clear that the charts that used to figure in popular textbooks "greatly exaggerated the amount and the definiteness of the alleged localization, both as regards structure and as regards function."

After all, as Sherrington so frequently pointed out, in any one individual each anatomical tissue—skin, bone, hair, or muscle—tends to be of the same general character all over the body: minor local variations are often discernible; but in the same individual the variations are much slighter than those between one individual and another; and we should naturally expect the same to hold good of nerve tissue. Bolton's studies of the cerebral cortex, both in normal and defective persons, suggest that the quality of the nervous tissue in any given individual tends to be predominantly the same throughout: in low-grade defectives, for example, the nerve cells tend to be "visibly deficient in number, in branching, and in regularity of arrangement in every part of the cortex." The clinical work of Hughlings Jackson, the experimental researches of Sherrington, and the microscopical studies of the infant brain carried out more recently by Conel and de Crinis, seem in many ways to provide increasing confirmation for Spencer's theory of a "hierarchy of neural functions," developing stage by stage out of a simpler basic activity into higher and more specialized forms. Even if we cannot wholly accept Lashley's doctrine of the "mass action" of the brain, nevertheless the actual facts that he has reported are far more in keeping with a theory of general ability (and minor special abilities) than with a theory of major "special abilities" and no general factor. And Sholl himself concludes that "intelligence," like retentivity, is a "general attribute of all cortical tissue" (1957, p. 111).

Each of the foregoing arguments—from introspection, from biology, and from neurology—is admittedly inconclusive. The most we could so far claim is that, when taken in combination, the evidence from each of these separate fields sets up a fairly strong a priori probability in favour of Galton's twofold theory of general abilities plus special. It is at this point, therefore, that the psychologist is tempted to invoke the aid of statistical analysis. In my view, the function of statistics, at any rate in psychological research, is simply to provide a more rigorous method of testing alternative hypotheses. How then do the various hypotheses that confront us stand up to this ordeal?

Each of the three main suggestions leads to distinctive corollaries which are open to statistical verification. First of all, if, as Thorndike held, there was no such thing as a general factor, but only a set of independent abilities, then the cross-correlation between the tests or assessments for those abilities should be zero, or at least nonsignificant. They are not: they are always both significant and positive. Secondly, if, as Spearman maintained, there were no such thing as special abilities but only a single general factor, the intercorrelations for every test should diminish proportionately in the same descending order (except, of course, for nonsignificant deviations due to sampling and the like): in technical language, the table of intercorrelations should constitute a matrix of rank one. It does not.

The third hypothesis assumes the presence of both general and special abilities. In the early article to which I have already referred,[2] I endeavoured to apply to the correlations between mental tests the procedure which Karl Pearson had already elaborated for use with measurements of bodily characteristics. In this way I sought to compare each of my various tables of observed coefficients with the best fitting set of theoretical values deduced from the hypothesis of a single "general ability" only; this hypothetical ability was redefined as the "highest common factor" entering into all the processes measured in any given table.[3] The fit was moderately good, but by no means perfect. The differences between the observed and the theoretical values were accordingly tested for statistical significance; and the result was to disclose small but significant clusters of residual correlations, common to certain limited groups of tests only, thus plainly indicating the presence of certain supplementary abilities. This seemed definitely to clinch the double hypothesis put forward by Galton. Precisely the same conclusion was reached in many later analyses carried out both by myself and by other workers with larger numbers of pupils and a greater variety of tests (Burt, 1914-1931; 1917 and refs.).

[2] Those to whom this earlier (1909) paper is inaccessible will find the essential figures from one of the tables reproduced in books by Freeman (1926) and Thorndike (1914); Garnett (1921) reprints not only the observed values, but, beneath them, the theoretical values, the discrepancies, and the probable errors, as I myself had done. It should be noted that the procedure subsequently developed by Spearman (1927) was rather different. He preferred to secure independent assessments for intelligence, based on teachers' ratings, examination results, or, in later inquiries, the results of one or two accredited tests, and use them as "reference values." In other words, he used an *external* criterion; whereas I have used an *internal* criterion or "factor" derived from the intercorrelations themselves. My reasons were that both examination results and teachers' assessments were commonly influenced by the child's capacity to learn, i.e., by his memory, rather than by his sheer intelligence, and thus often reflected what the child had actually acquired rather than his innate capacity.

[3] The simplified formula used for this purpose in most of these earlier researches (Burt, 1917, p. 53) was the same as that subsequently adopted by Thurstone under the name of the centroid formula (1935, p. 94, Equation 13). When in addition "special abilities" were studied as well as "general ability," they were regarded as "group factors" obtainable by an arithmetical rotation of the "bipolar" factor matrix. I may add that we encountered a certain amount of evidence indicating that several of these special abilities were also largely dependent on heredity, but space does not permit me to deal with them here.

The factorization of correlations between persons and between successive occasions (with the same persons and tests) revealed, or at least very plainly confirmed, the constant presence of a random factor, which appeared to be due, not merely to sampling as ordinarily understood, but to something essentially characteristic of the working of the mind or brain. A somewhat similar conclusion has been independently reached by neurologists like Beurle, Cragg and Temperley, and Uttley and Sholl. Thus the type of "neuronal connectivity" suggested by the histological study of dendritic fibres strongly suggests "the semi-random arrangement of a machine working largely in accordance with the principles of probability" (Sholl, 1956 and refs.).[4] This partly agrees with, though it is by no means identical with, the doctrine of "equipotentiality" put forward by Lashley; and thus further supports the value of factorial procedures as a means of investigating variations in mental ability.

However, what is far more important from the practical standpoint of educational guidance is this: in nearly every factorial study of cognitive ability, the general factor commonly accounts for quite 50% of the variance (rather more in the case of the young child, rather less with older age groups) while each of the minor factors accounts for only 10% or less. With increasing age, the "group factors," which represent special abilities, contribute increasing amounts to the total variance; and this fact lends further support to the view that, as a result of maturation, cognitive ability progressively differentiates and tends to become more and more specialized (Burt, 1954 and refs.).

Be that as it may, whatever be our views on the various biological or neurological issues, we may, I think, safely say this: for purposes of prediction—forecasting what this or that individual child is likely to do in school or in after-life—the general factor is by far the most important, though admittedly not our only, guide. For all practical purposes, almost every psychologist—even former opponents of the concept of general intelligence, like Thorndike, Brown, Thomson, and Thurstone—seems in

---

[4] This is not the same as the "sampling theory" of Thomson, which maintains that the apparent emergence of "factors" is "a result of the laws of chance and not of any psychological laws": like all simplified theories, it seems to amplify just one aspect of mental process, at the expense of denying all the rest. What is needed is a model which will combine the "integrative action" of the nervous system with its "stochastic action." As I have suggested elsewhere (*Psychometrika*, 1909, p. 160), the mathematical model which most effectively does this is a classificatory model derived from Pearson's method of principal axes. The mechanical model would resemble, not the homeostat of Ashby or the mechanical tortoise of Grey Walter, but rather a classification machine like that proposed by Uttley and Sholl. Similarly a stochastical induction machine would seem to reproduce the results of human learning far better than the model adopted by Hull and his followers. It is therefore tempting to suggest that what has been called the A/S ratio—i.e., the proportionate amount of "association cortex" with which either a species or an organism is endowed at birth—would form an index primarily of the amount of its intelligence and only incidentally of its capacity to learn.

the end to have come round to much the same conclusion, even though, for theoretical purposes, each tends to reword it in a modified terminology of his own. And thus today, save for one or two occasional attacks, current psychological criticism is not so much concerned with the problem of "general intelligence," but is directed rather against the second of our two initial propositions: the assumption, namely, that individual differences in intelligence are hereditary or innate.

The Genetic Components. Here three distinct questions seem to be involved: (a) what evidence is there for the *fact* of inheritance, (b) what precisely is the *mode* in which intelligence is inherited, and (c) what is the *relative importance* of the genetic factor as compared with the environmental?

The Fact. In controversies about the facts of mental heredity most critics have tended to assume that the two causal agencies commonly discussed —heredity and environment—are not merely antithetical but mutually exclusive. The environmentalists apparently suppose that, once they have shown that intelligence tests are affected by environment, it follows that all differences in intelligence are due to nothing but environment. Similarly the thorough-going hereditarian is apt to talk as though he believed that differences in intelligence were due to nothing but genetic constitution. This is the old familiar fallacy which I am tempted to label "nothing-buttery." In point of fact, with a few rare exceptions, like eye colour or serological differences in the blood, every observable characteristic that geneticists have studied has proved to be the product of the joint action of both heredity and environment. There are, in short, no such things as hereditary characters: there are only hereditary tendencies.

Now, where two contributory factors, such as heredity and environment, are likely to be involved, the obvious procedure will be to keep first one and then the other as constant as possible, and observe the results in either case.

1. *Uniform environment.* As psychological consultant to the London County Council, I had free access to orphanages and other residential institutions, and to the private files of case records giving the history of the various inmates. My co-workers and I were thus able to study large numbers of children who had been transferred thither during the earliest weeks of infancy, and had been brought up in an environment that was much the same for all. To our surprise we found that individual differences in intelligence, so far from being diminished, varied over an unusually wide range. In the majority of cases, they appeared to be correlated with differences in the intelligence of one or both of the parents. Some of the most striking instances were those of illegitimate children of high ability: often the father (so the case records showed) had been a casual acquaintance, of a social and intellectual status well above that of the mother, and had

taken no further interest in the child. In such cases it is out of the question to attribute the high intelligence of the child to the special cultural opportunities furnished by the home environment, since his only home has been the institution.[5]

2. *Uniform heredity.* To secure cases in which the children's genetic endowment is the same, we may turn to assessments obtained from monozygotic or "identical" twins. The mother is not infrequently unable or unwilling to bring up two children at the same time, and one twin is consequently sent to a relative or to a foster home. Owing to the strong popular prejudice against separating twins, she not unnaturally tries, as a rule, to keep these arrangements secret. But patient and tactful inquiries show that cases of twins brought up in different environments almost from birth are in fact much commoner than is usually believed. We have now collected over 30 such cases (Burt, 1943-c; 1955). I reproduce the more important correlations for the twins in Table 1 and have added for comparison corresponding coefficients obtained from other pairs, both related and unrelated. As regards intelligence the outstanding feature is the high correlation between the final assessments for the monozygotic twins, even when reared apart: it is almost as high as the correlation between two successive testings for the same individuals. On the other hand, with school attainments the correlations are much lower for twins reared separately than for twins reared together in the same home.

Several of our critics—Heim and Maddox, for example—have cited the account of analogous cases (described by Newman and others) as proving that intelligence is dependent on environment. Thus, to take an oft-quoted pair, "Helen," who had been trained as a teacher, scored with the Stanford-Binet tests an I.Q. of 116; whereas her twin sister, "Gladys," brought up for much of her childhood in an isolated district of the Canadian Rockies, scored only 92. But, says Newman, her score

... was higher than we might expect considering her scant education; and ... it seems certain that the great deficiency in education had inhibited the development of the rather high grade of mental ability with which she was *endowed by heredity* (Newman, 1942, pp. 136-144).

Thus Newman's interpretation in no way conflicts with ours.

It is sometimes alleged (Maddox, 1957) that, since twins are born at the same time, the intrauterine environment must have been the same for

[5] Details are given in the various *Annual Reports of the Psychologist to the London County Council* (Burt, 1914-1931) and are summarized in Burt (1943-c). In the recent symposium on *Quantitative Inheritance* (Reeve and Waddington [Eds.], 1952), Woolf, quoting a later paper of mine, regrets that I have "based such far reaching conclusions on the study by Barbara Burks . . . covering only 214 foster children" (Burks, 1928). But the principal basis for my own conclusion was a series of investigations in residential schools under the LCC covering in the course of years over 600 cases. I cited Burks' inquiry merely to show how an independent investigator in a different country had arrived at much the same figures as my own.

TABLE 1. Correlations Between Mental and Scholastic Assessments

	Identical Twins Reared Together	Identical Twins Reared Apart	Nonidentical Twins Reared Together	Siblings Reared Together	Siblings Reared Apart	Unrelated Children Reared Together
Mental						
"Intelligence"						
Group Test	.944	.771	.542	.515	.441	.281
Individual Test	.921	.843	.526	.491	.463	.252
Final Assessment	.925	.876	.551	.538	.517	.269
Scholastic						
General Attainments	.898	.681	.831	.814	.526	.535
Reading and Spelling	.944	.647	.915	.853	.490	.548
Arithmetic	.862	.723	.748	.769	.563	.476

279

both before birth, even if later on their environments differ widely, and that quite conceivably it is the former that is crucial. As it happens, however, this rather gratuitous assumption reverses the actual facts. Embryological and obstetric records show that, particularly with twins developed from split ova, the position of each in the uterus, and the subsequent development, is liable to differ widely (Burt and Howard, 1956, pp. 123ff. and refs.).

I think, therefore, that it may be safely said that, apart from the influence of some preconceived theory, few psychologists nowadays would be inclined to contest the mere fact of mental inheritance: the most that can be plausibly alleged is that its influence is comparatively slight and distinctly elusive.

The Mode of Inheritance. The majority of those who still question the importance of mental inheritance, and many of those who support it, seem by preference to adopt entirely antiquated notions of the way in which inheritable characteristics are transmitted. If, as I have maintained, mental capacities are dependent on the physical characteristics of the brain (or, to speak a little more precisely, on the structural and biochemical qualities of the nervous system), then we should expect those capacities to be inherited in accordance with the same principles that govern the inheritance of physical characteristics; and these principles (except for obscure and apparently exceptional instances of extranuclear heredity) are essentially those commonly associated with the name of Mendel. Many British psychologists, however, feel a strong and not unreasonable prejudice against applying "atomistic theories like Mendel's" to explain the facts of mental life, and consequently, so far as they admit the possibility of mental inheritance at all, still cling to the old Darwinian principle of blended inheritance. On this view heredity means "the tendency of like to beget like" (the definition quoted by one of them from the *Oxford English Dictionary*). As a result, they commonly assume that the arguments for inheritance must consist in demonstrating resemblances between the parent and his children by means of correlations. When the two parents differ, then the child is still expected to consist in an intermediate blend of both.

The approach of the modern geneticist is the reverse of all this. As he views it, the real problem is rather to explain why in so many instances "like begets unlike." Both for the environmentalist and for the believer in blended inheritance, one of the most puzzling phenomena is the appearance, not merely of extremely dull children in the families of the well-to-do professional classes, but also of extremely bright children in families where both the cultural and the economic conditions of the parents would, one might imagine, condemn every child to hopeless failure. With the Mendelian hypothesis these anomalies are just what we should anticipate. However, the few critics who are familiar with the Mendelian explanation appear, as a rule, to suppose that it can apply only to discontinuous variations; and point out that intelligence, like stature, exhibits not discontinuous but continuous or graded variation. Hence, so they contend (sometimes citing the experiments of De Vries on "pure lines"), the apparent differences in intelligence between one individual and another must be due almost entirely to differences in environmental conditions.

Mendel himself was the first to indicate how his theory could be extended to account for this particular difficulty. When supplementing his experiments on the hybridization of peas by hybridizing beans, and (as before) crossing white flowered plants with purple, he found, that, whereas with peas the two types always sorted out with no hint of any intermediate color, with beans the offspring displayed "a whole range of hues from white to deep purple." This, he suggested, might be explained by postulating that with beans the color was determined, not by a single pair of alternative factors, but by a *number* of such pairs, each positive factor, when present, contributing a small additional amount of color. And if, as before, the recombinations are the effects of chance unions, then the resulting frequencies would obviously approximate to those of the normal curve.

However, in our early surveys of London children (Burt, 1914-1931; 1917), we found that, when complete age groups were tested, the distribution of intelligence departed significantly from that of a perfect normal curve: there was a swollen tail at the lower end, due to an excess of mental defectives, and a smaller enlargement at the upper end. This and other considerations led me to put forward the tenative hypothesis that innate variations in intelligence are due partly to unifactor and partly to multifactor inheritance: i.e., they result from Mendelian factors of two main kinds (no doubt overlapping), viz., (a) major genes responsible for comparatively *large* deviations, usually of an abnormal type, and (b) multiple genes whose effects are *small, similar,* and *cumulative.*

Karl Pearson (1904) endeavoured to test the Mendelian theory in its multifactorial form by comparing its implications with actual figures obtained for height, arm length, and similar physical measurements, collected by himself and Alice Lee, from over 2,000 students and their relatives. The expected correlations which he deduced for various degrees of kinship were in every case far smaller than the observed coefficients. He therefore emphatically rejected the hypothesis of Mendelian inheritance, and fell back on the older theory of blending. However, in deriving his formulae and his expected values, Pearson relied on an oversimplified model. Contrary to what we now know to be the case, he assumed that the effect of assortative mating—the tendency of like to marry like—could be ignored as negligible, and that dominance would in every case be perfect. Ronald Fisher has since undertaken the rather formidable task of deducing more appropriate formulae, which allow for these and other complicating factors (Fisher, 1918). And with these refinements the calculated correlations fit Pearson's own figures as well as could be wished.

My colleagues and I have applied Fisher's methods (suitably modified) to assessments for intelligence (Burt and Howard, 1956). The data were secured in the course of surveys of the entire school population in a representative London borough, and covered nearly 1,000 pairs of siblings, together with ratings for parents, and (so far as they were accessible) grandparents, uncles and aunts, and first cousins. The final assessments for the children were obtained by submitting the marks from the group tests to the judgment of the teachers who knew the children best: where the teacher disagreed with the verdict of the marks, the child was interviewed personally, and subjected to further tests, often on several successive occasions. The assessments for the adult members of the family were naturally far less accurate. Nevertheless, in almost every case the correlations computed from the actual data agreed with the theoretical values deduced from the multifactorial hypothesis far better than with the values deduced from any other hypothesis hitherto put forward. The only appreciable discrepancy occurred in the case of first cousins. Here, as for stature, the observed correlation for intelligence is larger than the theoretical; but the difference is not statistically significant, and could readily be explained if (as has been suggested above) variations in intelligence are affected by a few major genes as well as by numerous minor genes. I may add that on sorting out figures for cousins of maternal, paternal, and mixed kinship there is also some slight evidence suggestive of sex linkage.

The Relative Influence of Heredity and Environment. In practical work, however, the question most frequently raised is, not whether differences in intelligence are inherited, nor even how they are inherited, but rather what is the relative influence of heredity as compared with environment. To an omnibus inquiry like this there can be no single answer. We can only try to determine, for this or that type of environment, for this or that population, and for this or that type of assessment, how far the observable results appear to be influenced by each of the two main groups of factors.

As Fisher's analysis has shown, formulae analogous to those used to deduce the expected correlations from the theoretical variances can also be devised for deducing the amount of the constituent variances from the observed correlations. I have ventured to amplify Fisher's methods (mainly on the lines of later work by Mather and Sewall Wright) so as to allow for unreliability and for the systematic effects of environment, i.e., of environmental influences which are correlated with those of heredity, as well as for random effects. The genetic contribution may be regarded as comprising two distinguishable portions: that due to the "fixable" component (or, as Fisher expresses it, to the "essential genotypes") and that due to the "nonfixable" (i.e., deviations due to dominance and similar influences). The data analysed consist of (a) the marks obtained from intelligence tests of the ordinary type taken just as they stand and (b) adjusted assessments obtained by the supplementary methods already described (Burt and Howard, 1956).

From Table 2 it will be seen that, with the crude test results, taken just as they stand, nearly 23% of the total variance appears due to non-genetic influences, i.e., to environment or to unreliability, and about 77% to genetic factors; with the adjusted assessments only about 12% (or slightly more) is apparently due to nongenetic influences and 88% to genetic factors. This of course means that the common practice of re-lying on tests alone—usually a group test applied once only—is by no

TABLE 2. Analysis of Variance for Assessments of Intelligence

Source	Unadjusted Test Scores	Adjusted Assessments
Genetic component:		
fixable	40.51	47.92
nonfixable	16.65	21.73
Assortative mating	19.90	17.91
Environment:		
systematic	10.60	1.43
random	5.91	5.77
Unreliability	6.43	5.24
Total	100.00	100.00

means a satisfactory method of assessing a child's innate ability. Better assessments are obtained by submitting the test scores to the teachers for criticism or correction, and where necessary adjusting them by the methods described above. But such intensive inquiries would be too costly for routine use except in borderline cases.

Environment appears to influence the test results chiefly in three ways: (a) the cultural amenities of the home and the educational opportunities provided by the school can undoubtedly affect a child's performance in intelligence tests of the ordinary type, since so often they demand an ac-quired facility with abstract and verbal modes of expression; (b) quite apart from what the child may learn, the constant presence of an intel-lectual background may stimulate (or seem to stimulate) his latent powers by inculcating a keener motivation, a stronger interest in intellectual things, and a habit of accurate, speedy, and diligent work; (c) in a few rare cases illness or malnutrition during the prenatal or early postnatal stages may, almost from the very start, permanently impair the develop-ment of the child's central nervous system. The adjusted assessments may do much towards eliminating the irrelevant effects of the first two condi-tions; but it is doubtful whether they can adequately allow for the last.

LIMITATIONS INVOLVED IN THESE CONCLUSIONS

As in almost all scientific investigations, the hypothetical model which has formed the basis of our inquiry involves of necessity certain minor simplifications. In particular we have assumed, for purposes of calculation, a sharp distinction between the "major genes" of unifactor inheritance and the "polygenes" of multifactor inheritance, and have treated the latter as contributing equal and additive doses to the sum total of each child's innate intelligence. We have then supposed that the effects of the former would on the whole be excluded if the few obviously pathological cases (mostly found in special schools or institutions) were omitted from our final calculations. However, these assumptions have led several critics to accuse us of

. . . disrupting the individual personality into atomic bits and discrete pieces which have subsequently to be joined together like a mosaic. . . . Personality [it is argued] is not a mosaic but a seamless whole, and hence the entire Mendelian hypothesis with its particulate genes, each producing a unit-character or adding another unit to the same character, is quite inapplicable to the facts of conscious behavior, and therefore to the study of mental capacity.

Objections of this kind could of course be used just as well to prove that a neuronic theory of the central nervous system is incompatible with the facts of conscious behaviour or of individual variations in ability, since nerve cells or "neural bonds" are equally "particulate." Nevertheless, even those neurologists who prefer to start from a "field theory" do not wholly reject the neuronic hypothesis (cf. Sholl, 1956). In both cases the difficulties raised owe their force chiefly to the fact that there is a vast series of elusive processes intervening between theory and observable results which the critic is exceedingly apt to forget. Moreover, criticisms like those just cited plainly rest on an obsolete version of the Mendelian doctrine. No geneticist today, I imagine, accepts the hypothesis of the autonomous corpuscular gene; and the genotypic endowment of the individual can only affect the phenotypic resultant through the mediation of innumerable obscure biochemical steps.

In our original papers Howard and I tried carefully to guard against recurrent objections of this type. As we pointed out, the phrase "multiple factors" may be used to cover either (a) relatively numerous loci each with only two allelomorphs or (b) a single locus (or relatively few loci) each with numerous allelomorphs, or possibly (c) some combination of the two. Hypothesis b by itself would hardly seem to fit the facts. We are inclined to think that factors of all the various types may be operative in varying degrees, and that the attempt to classify factors or genes should not be too severely pressed.

We further assumed that in all probability the influence of such factors on the individual's observable intelligence was mainly the indirect result of their influence on the development of his central nervous system, and was presumably effected by modifying growth rates. And we expressly stated that the ultimate influence of any one "gene" upon intelligence might be but one of its multifarious consequences, and possibly a comparatively remote consequence at that. Some genes may have a larger share in the final result; others a smaller; and the rough classification of genes into "major" genes and "minor" was adopted primarily with a view to simplifying our general discussion.[6] We ourselves find the "theory of chromosomal hierarchy," advanced by Goldschmidt (1955), especially attractive as a basis for the ultimate hierarchical differentiation of mental ability.

However, this is not the place to enlarge on these speculative interpretations. We fully admit that the simplifications involved in our hypothetical model mean that the figures finally deduced can be no more than approximations. But we maintain that the error of approximation, however large, will nevertheless be smaller than the amount of "unreliability" inevitably involved in all such measurements.

In any case we must repeat that the conclusions reached are at best only valid in reference to the particular conditions under which they were obtained. They would not necessarily hold good (a) of other mental traits, (b) of different methods of assessment, (c) of a population of a different genetic composition, or (d) of a population at a different cultural level: much less would they hold good if there were any subsequent change (e) in the present distribution of environmental and genetic characteristics, or (f) in the influences affecting their mutual interaction.[7]

THE INHERITANCE OF OTHER MENTAL QUALITIES

The mental trait in which we have been chiefly interested is the general factor of "intelligence." This, we readily concede, is but one psychological ingredient in ordinary everyday behavior. Our critics are accustomed to reproach us for apparently ignoring the rest. There are several obvious reasons why we have dealt less fully with other determinants. The first and the most conclusive is that comparatively little evidence is as yet available in regard to the genetic composition of other mental factors. We

[6] If Mather's view that "the major genes occur only in euchromatin, while heterochromatin contains only polygenes" (Darlington and Mather, 1949, p. 151 and refs.) is eventually confirmed, there would be more adequate grounds for retaining a sharp distinction between the two modes of inheritance. However, this view is not universally accepted. For an alternative interpretation of the experimental results on which Mather largely relies, see the papers by Reeve and Robertson quoted in our article (Burt and Howard, 1956, p. 116). These writers incline more to what in the text I have called hypothesis *b*. But, as Howard and I contended, their alternative interpretation would affect only the method, not the results, of our statistical deductions.

[7] A more detailed reply to the criticisms urged by Woolf, Heim and Maddox will appear in the forthcoming issue of the *Brit. J. statist. Psychol.*, Burt, 1954, Part i.

have, however, in the course of our surveys, met with an appreciable number of cases which strongly suggest the inheritability of certain specific abilities and disabilities, or rather of certain ill-defined tendencies that presumably underlie such disabilities—particularly in our studies of memory, of visual, auditory, and kinaesthetic imagery, and of verbal, numerical, artistic, and musical aptitudes (Burt, 1914-1931). We have encountered other cases which suggest the inheritability of general emotional instability, of temperamental qualities like introversion and extraversion, and of certain quasi-instinctive tendencies like sex and bad temper (or "pugnacity," as McDougall would have termed it). But emotional tendencies are always much more liable to be influenced and altered by postnatal experiences, and in any case undergo considerable changes during the developmental stages, so that all attempts at assessment are apt to be precarious. The most convincing evidence is afforded by the family histories of children brought up in orphanages or residential institutions (Burt, 1943-a, especially p. 14 and refs.). In all these instances the evidence, such as it is, appears to indicate that each of the characteristics mentioned, cognitive and temperamental alike, are influenced both by unifactor and by multifactor modes of inheritance—the latter tending on the whole to predominate, but in varying degrees. This after all is what is commonly found in investigations on physical characteristics. Characteristics depending mainly (though not entirely) on the development of the long bones —such as arm length, leg length, stature, and perhaps the longer dimensions of the face and head—yield correlations of much the same magnitude as those obtained for general intelligence. Others, like cephalic index, breadth at hips, and particularly facial characteristics, seem to be rather more subject to the influence of single (or relatively few) genes, which often appear to exhibit almost perfect dominance. Variations in the cartilaginous features, and particularly those depending on flesh and fat, are far more readily affected by environmental influences (for data, see Tanner, 1953, and refs.).

But secondly there is a practical reason for concentrating attention first of all, and chiefly, on the inheritability of general intelligence. General intelligence, as we have seen, accounts for four times as much of the variance as any other identifiable factor. Galton's pronouncement is thus fully borne out by our own results:

. . general ability appears far more important than special gifts; and, where the allowance granted by nature is inadequate, the keenest will and the stoutest industry must strive in vain.

Moreover, the child's innate endowment of intelligence sets an upper limit to the best he can possibly attain. No one would expect a mongolian imbecile, with the most skilful coaching in the world, to achieve the scholastic knowledge of an average child. In the same way, no one should expect a child who is innately dull to gain a scholarship to a grammar school, or one whose inborn ability is merely average to win first class honors at Oxford or Cambridge. No doubt, in any individual case the ascertainment of this upper limit can never be a matter of absolute certainty: an I.Q. derived from tests alone falls far short of a trustworthy indication. Hence education authorities, like life insurance companies, have to follow Butler's maxim, and take probability for their guide. They cannot, however, afford to risk a lavish expenditure on cases where there are fairly heavy odds against success.

Nevertheless, it must be owned that, in Britain at any rate, the existing

TABLE 3. Estimates for Grammar School Entries

	General Population[a]	Proportions over +0.85 SD	Expected Entries	Actual Entries
Middle Class	20%	.40	.08 (40%)	55%
Manual Class	80%	.15	.12 (60%)	45%
Total	100%		.20 (100%)	100%

[a] The *Census of Great Britain* (1951) gives an estimate of 81.7 for males over 15, occupied or retired, falling into the classes of "Skilled," "Mixed," and "Unskilled" workers: these I have pooled in a single broad group.

administrative machinery is far less efficient than it might be. In an inquiry made just before the introduction of the Education Act of 1944 we found that "approximately 40 per cent of those whose innate abilities are of university standard are failing to reach the university" (Burt, 1943-c). The new arrangements proposed by the act, and the postwar changes in the economic circumstances of the various social classes, have appreciably altered the entries to "grammar schools"; but it is too early to say how far they have affected the composition of the universities. For grammar schools the entries vary considerably from one area to another and even from year to year. The general aim is apparently to provide a grammar school education for the brightest 20% of each age group; this corresponds to a borderline of about 113 I.Q. On this basis the round figures in Table 3 represent estimates deduced from the information so far available.

A more intensive survey of two contrasted areas ("industrial" and "prosperous") has just been published by J. E. Floud and her colleagues. Briefly their conclusion is that, in both areas, gross material handicaps have been greatly lessened, though not entirely eliminated. Nevertheless, in their view, the "problem of social wastage" is by no means overcome. The fact that, even today, a large proportion of the children from the working classes fail to reach the higher levels of scholastic instruction

Floud herself attributes to the way in which the "educational ladder" is still widely regarded as a "middle class prerogative," to be anxiously watched and jealously preserved (Floud, Halsey and Martin, 1956).

I myself should be inclined to look rather to a difference in the aims and aspirations which are traditional in the different classes. The consequences seemed clearly revealed by the differences in the aftercareers of LCC scholarship winners from the lower and the middle classes respectively whom my colleagues and I have been able to follow up (cf. Burt, 1914-1931; 1943-c, and refs.).[8] The figures show that the abler children from the working classes, even when they have obtained free places or scholarships at secondary schools of the "grammar" type, frequently fail to stay the course: by the time they are sixteen the attractions of high wages and of cheap entertainment during leisure hours prove stronger than their desire for further knowledge and skill, and easily overcome their original resolve to face a long prospect of hard sedentary work in *statu pupillari*. As a headmaster of a secondary school which receives both types of boy has put it:

The working class parent wants his boy to be "selected" chiefly to prove that "his child is as good as anybody else's"; having done so, he will withdraw him at the earliest possible opportunity: I do not press them, for the presence of those whose chief interest in life is television, Hollywood films, football pools, "the dogs," and "the girls" has not improved the tone of my school. And too often these "ignobler attitudes and crude ambitions" are shared by, and encouraged by, both parents and friends.

On the other hand, if I may quote the report of an experienced university teacher:

That section of the middle class which seeks, by paying fees that it can ill afford, to assist its children to climb, *via* a "public school" or an independent "grammar school," to a University education and a good honours degree in the humaner subjects, is animated by a traditional morale which is comparatively rare in children and parents from the other classes: those who nowadays come

[8] Additional evidence is furnished by the recent report of the Central Advisory Council for Education (England) on *Early Leaving*. In 1953, at the age of entry to the grammar school (11 plus), 66% of the top intelligence group were the children of manual workers; at the end of the grammar school period the proportion had fallen to 47%. Of those who drop out, some are "premature leavers," i.e., they leave voluntarily, as soon as they are legally able to do so; others fail to reach the top form and so leave at 16: of these many even fail to secure a school leaving certificate. In such cases, the award of a special place in the grammar school would seem itself to have been a wasted effort. Nevertheless, in the long run there may be certain compensating advantages to the community as a whole: even the early leavers may have gained something from the higher education to which they have been for a while subjected, and it would surely be a misfortune were all the brightest youngsters to forsake the social class into which they were born. Their continued presence there must help, not only to elevate its tone, but also (a point too often overlooked) to prevent its genetic constitution from being wholly depleted of its better elements.

here on grants, at no cost to themselves or their parents, are, on the whole, most irregular attendants, and the least satisfactory students.

Or, to quote a still more recent pronouncement of the High Master of St. Paul's:[9]

The parents are themselves imbued with four traditional ideals which they hand on to their posterity: self-discipline, a community spirit, the Christian religion, and a readiness to accept social responsibility even at the sacrifice of material enjoyments—a genuine *noblesse oblige.*

Underlying all these differences in outlook I myself am tempted to suspect an innate and transmissible difference in temperamental stability and in character, or in the neurophysiological basis on which such temperamental and moral differences tend to be built up. Tradition may explain much: it can hardly account for all. However, it would be idle to pursue such speculations here in the absence of more adequate data.[10]

NEED FOR FURTHER RESEARCH

To my mind the most pressing need at the moment is for more extensive research. Hitherto the most active investigators have been research-students, with little or no experience of the ways of children or the conditions of the classroom. For the requisite facilities, and for any supplementary information they may want, they have to rely on the goodwill of the busy teacher. And one important factor is still more often overlooked: the motivation of the children themselves. This takes two obvious forms. There is first what may be called direct or short distance motivation. As actual trial has repeatedly shown, neither pupils nor students are likely to exert their full powers in a test conducted merely in the interests of someone else's research; but when the examinees' entrance to grammar school or university depends on their performances, the average score may rise 5 to 10 I.Q. points higher. Secondly, there are the effects of indirect or long distance

[9] A. N. Gilkes, *Independence in Education,* 1957.

[10] Since my lecture was written and delivered, some further information has become available in the data published by the Association of Universities of the British Commonwealth (*Report of an Inquiry into Applications for Admissions to Universities,* 1957). It appears that at Oxford and Cambridge only 12% of the men and 7% of the women had fathers in manual occupations; at other universities the proportions were somewhat higher, namely, 31% and 19%, respectively. Among the general population 72% of the population would fall into the manual category. The report points out that to a large extent the decline must occur during the school period, and the real reason, it is suggested, is more often lack of zeal than lack of the requisite ability. "Differing environmental influences and aspirations seem mainly responsible for the fall from 66% at the point of entry to the non-fee-paying grammar school and 36% at the point of university entry. . . . Discrimination against those of humble social origin can be virtually ruled out."

Most education authorities nowadays tend to use what are misleadingly termed "intelligence tests" as tests of suitability for a grammar school. (Such tests, as I have

motivation: the influence of parental attitudes, of teachers' exhortations, and (most of all perhaps with British lads) of the social pressure that arises from the opinions and the comments of their school fellows, and from the tone and atmosphere of the school or class to which the pupil belongs. It is therefore hardly surprising if the results obtained in mere academic researches are at times disappointing, and evince a comparatively low. reliability.

I myself had the good fortune to be appointed a member of the school inspectorate, and so not only acquired a firsthand knowledge of the schools, teachers, and pupils, but enjoyed full authority to interrupt the timetable, examine private records, and requisition whatever information might be wanted. Here therefore I must again record my indebtedness both to the London County Council for facilitating these inquiries and financing their publication, and to the teachers, social workers, and school medical officers, who rendered such wholehearted cooperation in all our investigations. It is to be hoped that other education authorities will in the near future perceive the practical value of systematically organized inquiries of this kind, conducted on an official basis by those who know the schools from inside.

The basic researches must be carried out on children rather than on students or adults. With adults, it is much harder to achieve accurate assessments; innate tendencies are already obscured and overlaid; and detailed family histories difficult to obtain. In allocating adults to appropriate occupations, whether in civil life or in the fighting services, innate capacities are of little consequence, and accordingly tend to be ignored. As a result the severest critics of researches on heredity are generally those whose experience of mental testing has been gained in the adult field. This was manifest during the symposium recently arranged by the Psychological Section of the British Association. Several contributors, for instance, echoed remarks like those of H. E. Jones that "potential investigators should now be advised that the nature-nurture controversy has been shown to be an unproductive field of research" (Carmichael, 1946); and similar conclusions have more recently been voiced by writers like Maddox (1957), Renshaw (1957), and others, who deplore what they call "the resurrection of the nature-nurture controversy" as "wholly anachronistic."

But whether or not this is now the prevailing view among psychologists, it is not the opinion of leading geneticists. Goldschmidt, Snyder, Calvin

---

argued elsewhere, should rather be termed "tests of scholastic aptitude.") The original intention was that the "intelligence test" should, so far as possible, assess innate ability. Bright children with special verbal or literary abilities and interests were then to be allocated to grammar schools; and those with practical or mechanical abilities and interests, to technical schools. But for the majority the age of 11 plus is too early to make a satisfactory distinction. Hence the brightest still seem likely to be sent to secondary schools of the grammar type rather than to a technical school, even if more suited to the latter.

Hall, and Calvin Stone all deplore the neglect of genetic inquiries by psychologists of the present day. Goldschmidt in particular has criticized "the extreme belief of contemporary psychologists in the power of environment"—a belief which he ascribes to the "doctrine of universal conditioning, which has, until lately, dominated the behaviourist school" (Dunn, 1921). In this country eminent authorities like R. A. Fisher (1919; 1950) and Fraser Roberts (1940) have not only urged the importance of genetic studies for psychology, but have made noteworthy contributions of their own.

Mere statistical inquiries, however, can never suffice. In this country one of the most obvious needs is a series of intensive studies of able boys and girls similar to those already carried out on the backward, the defective, the neurotic, and the delinquent. The brilliant investigation of 1,000 gifted children, started by Terman and his colleagues over 30 years ago, and so assiduously followed up, furnishes an admirable model (Stone, 1947; Tanner, 1953). But nothing like conclusive answers can be given to the questions here raised until far more extensive research has been undertaken on the fundamental problems of psychogenetics. An adequate understanding of the basic processes can be secured only if we start with carefully planned experiments on lowlier creatures, where pure strains can be obtained, breeding controlled, and successive generations more speedily raised. When we know more about the genetics of intelligence in animals, we may be able to construct with greater confidence a more exact hypothesis regarding the transmission of intelligence in man.

SOCIAL IMPLICATIONS

After all, the practical importance of the issues involved is so profound and so far-reaching that it would be fatal to dismiss the problem as "unproductive" or "anachronistic" without attempting to settle it one way or the other. No democratic state can afford to pass it by. If in the end the views of the early pioneers should turn out to have been approximately correct—if "innate intelligence varies between limits at least as wide as I.Q.'s of 50 and 150," and if too "the average intelligence of the general population at maturity is little if at all above that of an average child of thirteen or thirteen-and-a-half"—then the bearing of genetic variation on the national and social questions of the present day would be all too obvious.

In our laudable eagerness to improve the lot of our own generation, we have been tempted to close our eyes to the effects of present policy on the generations to come. The over-all efficiency of the citizens who make up a nation or a state must in the last resort depend on what has been called its "chromosomal pool." Improved environmental amenities can of themselves ensure no lasting results; but the changes in a nation's genetic constitution are likely to prove irreversible. Throughout almost the entire Western world, and to a less extent in other areas as well, the last half-century or so has witnessed radical modifications in the conditions that previously governed marriage and fertility. Increased mobility, enhanced freedom, new means of production, new methods of government, the progressive reduction of the traditional barriers separating different peoples and different social groups, and, in our own country, the recent extensions of the educational ladder, all these transformations are visibly disturbing the stability alike of classes and of races. Almost inevitably they must alter the genetic constitution of what have hitherto been the dominant nations and the dominant stocks within those nations.

From history and from past experience we know full well how changes in the balance between inbreeding and outbreeding[11] can affect the later destinies of populations, remoulding them sometimes for good, sometimes for ill. Geneticists have repeatedly drawn attention to the processes at work, and indicated the need for studying the possible effects of contemporary trends (cf., e.g., Darlington and Mather, 1950, pp. 49ff. and Fisher, 1950, pp. 170ff.). Yet current sociological textbooks seem almost wholly to ignore them. Surely it is high time that the social psychologist should now take up the question and plan a systematic series of investigations on the intricate but highly important issues involved. May I therefore conclude by endorsing, in the strongest possible terms, the verdict of Stone (Dunn [Ed.], 1921), quoted by Bingham in the last letter he wrote to me:

It is a matter of shame and regret that only an amateurish beginning has been made by psychologists in applying modern genetic methods to fundamental study in the nature-nurture area.

And may we hope that in the near future Bingham's "deepest wish" may be fulfilled, and that "a small band of enthusiasts will come forward to explore afresh this urgent and many-sided field of research."

---

[11] British readers will find it instructive to compare current copies of such works as *Who's Who* with those of (say) 60 years ago, and note the changes in the pedigrees of the British clergy (who in the nineteenth century were probably the most inbred profession in the country) and in the ancestry of members of the British cabinet and Civil Service during that period. The recent work of Ginsberg, Glass, and Moss has shown very plainly how the extension of the educational ladder is altering the composition of the different social groups, though none of the writers has considered the possible genetic consequences. The most illuminating discussion is still that contained in the concluding chapters of Fisher's book on *The Genetical Theory of Natural Selection* (1930), especially Chap. X, "Reproduction in Relation to Social Class."

26

The Stability of Mental Test Performance
Between Two and Eighteen Years[*]

M. P. Honzik, Jean W. MacFarlane and L. Allen

This paper is unusual among the papers presented in this volume. It presents the results of repeated testing of the same individuals over the greater part of their lives prior to adulthood, and examines the patterns of intellectual growth of individuals. This paper and the paper by Bayley in Part III are representative of the type of "longitudinal" research done at the Institute of Child Welfare at the University of California (Berkeley). Such research permits an analysis of the factors related to the growth patterns of individuals that is impossible in the typical "cross-section" study. The results of this investigation are notable in showing the great variability in intelligence test performance that can characterize individuals, in suggesting the role of total life circumstance in determining test performance at a particular time, and in demonstrating the degree of accuracy with which adult "intelligence" can be predicted from test performance at various ages from two upwards. The findings of this investigation warrant careful consideration by those who use intelligence tests for practical purposes.

The contribution of the present study lies first in the fact that repeated individual tests were given at specified ages over a 16-year period to more than 150 children; and, second, in the fact that this group of children was selected so as to be a representative sample of the children born in an urban community during the late 1920's. Furthermore, since the Guidance Study has as its primary purpose the study of personality development and associated factors, it has been possible to note the relation of fluctuations or stability in rate of mental growth to physical ills, unusual environmental

* Adapted and abridged from M. P. Honzik, J. W. Macfarlane and L. Allen, "The Stability of Mental Test Performance between Two and Eighteen Years," *Journal of Experimental Education*, 1948, Vol. 17, pp. 309-324. (With permission of the authors and the publisher.)

strains or supports, and to evidences of tension or serenity within the individual child.

THE SAMPLE

The names of every third child born in Berkeley, California, between January 1, 1928, and June 30, 1929 were included in the Berkeley survey. A total of 252 children from the Berkeley Survey Group were asked to come to the Institute for their first mental test at the age of 21 months. At this age level, the group of 252 children was divided into two matched sub-samples of 126 children on the basis of socio-economic factors (parents' national derivation, income, father's occupation, socio-economic rating, neighborhood, and mother's age and education). One of these subsamples (of the Berkeley Survey) has been called the "Guidance Group" because of the program of intensive interviews had with the parents and children; the second group, which has had physical examinations and mental tests but fewer and less intensive interviews and these at a much later age of the child, has been called the "Control Group." The children in both groups were given mental tests at the age of 21 months. At ages 2 and 2½ years, only the children in the Guidance Group were tested. Thereafter, the testing program was the same for the two groups.

Every effort was made to test the children as nearly as possible on or near their birthdays. Actually, from 72 to 95 per cent of the children were tested within one month of their birthdays at the various ages up to and including 8 years.[1]

THE TESTING PROGRAM

During the preschool years, 21 months to 5 years, inclusive, each child was tested at successive age levels on the same test, either the California Preschool Schedule I or California Preschool Schedule II. At ages 6 and 7 the 1916 Revision of the Stanford-Binet was used, and thereafter the 1937 Revision. Beginning at age 9, a program of test alternation was begun which was designed to show the effects of a change in the form of the test on mental test constancy. All the children in both groups were tested on either Form L or Form M of the Stanford Revision at age 9 years. But at ages 12 and 14 years, only two-thirds of the groups were given mental

---

[1] As was to be expected in a longitudinal study, a number of children were unable to come in for one or more of the mental tests. The most frequent cause of a missed test was the family being "out of town." However, a number of families lost interest or became unco-operative as their children grew older; one child was killed in an automobile accident. At 18 years 153 of the 252 children were tested on the Wechsler-Bellevue. The reasons that the remaining 99 did not come in for a test are as follows: 50 "out of town," 33 unco-operative, 1 died, 9 "missed" the 18-year test due to changes in staff, illness, or transportation difficulties and 6 cases were closed.

tests; the remaining third of the groups was tested at ages 13 and 15 years. In presenting group results, the scores for ages 12 and 13 years have been considered together, as have scores for ages 14 and 15 years. The Wechsler-Bellevue Scale was administered at age 18. The I.Q.'s obtained on the Stanford tests and the Wechsler-Bellevue were converted into sigma or standard scores so that they would be in comparable form to the mental test sigma scores obtained between 21 months and 5 years.

Although these children were selected as a representative sample of urban children, their scores are considerably above the test norms. The average I.Q. on the Stanford-Binet at ages 6 and 7 years and on the Stanford Revision, Form L at 8 years varied from 118.3 to 118.7. During the age period 9 to 13 years, the average I.Q. was approximately 120. The highest average I.Q. of 123 was obtained for the test period 14 and 15 years; and the lowest I.Q. average (118.2) was earned on the Wechsler-Bellevue at 18 years. The percentage distributions of I.Q.'s are relatively normal at all ages at which the Stanford-Binet or Form L or M of the Stanford Revision were administered. But at 18 years, the distribution of I.Q.'s on the Wechsler-Bellevue suggests that this test lacks "top" or at least does not differentiate between the children earning the highest scores at the earlier ages. Bayley (1949) has another explanation for the decreased variability at maturity. She suggests that variability is greatest during the age periods when the children are acquiring the functions being tested and that variability becomes restricted with the approach to maturity of the particular processes being measured.

GROUP TRENDS IN MENTAL TEST STABILITY

Pearsonian coefficients of correlation between test scores earned at specified ages between 21 months and 18 years are shown in Table 1. These correlation coefficients are based on the scores of the children in the combined Guidance and Control Groups for all but two age levels (2 and 2½ years) when only the children in the Guidance Group were tested.

Correlations for adjacent ages indicate a fair degree of mental test constancy when the interval between tests is at a minimum. The range of correlations for adjacent ages varies from r equals .71 (between ages 21 months x 2 years; 2 x 2½ years; 3 x 3½ years; and 5 x 6 years) to r equals .92 for the ages 12 x 14 years on the Stanford Revision, Form L. However, the correlations decrease markedly with the interval between tests but tend to increase with the age of the children when tested.

The correlation between tests given at 2 and at 5 years (r equals +.32) suggests a prediction which is not much better than chance, but the magnitude of the test-retest correlation increases markedly with age. The writers are concerned that the correlations with the Wechsler-Bellevue (at the 18-year-old level) are not higher. Restricted variability, regardless of its

TABLE 1. Correlations Between Test Scores Obtained at Different Ages

Test	Age	N	California Preschool Schedule I or II				Stanford-Binet 1916		1937 Stanford Revision Form L					W-B
			2	3	4	5	6	7	8	9	10	12 / 13	14	18
California Pre-school Schedule I or II	1¾	234	.71	.52	.38	.39	.27	.29	.27	.26	.22	.19	.07	.07
	2	113		.69	.46	.32	.47	.46	.43	.45	.37	.36	.21	.31
	2½	114		.73	.57	.46	.37	.38	.37		.36		.26	.24
	3	229			.58	.57	.57	.55	.49	.53	.36	.51	.35	.35
	3½	215			.76	.71	.64	.60	.50	.59	.59	.48	.49	.42
	4	211				.72	.62	.59	.61	.59	.66	.62	.54	.42
	5	212					.71	.59	.70	.68	.75	.74	.61	.56
Stanford-Binet I or II	6-7	214						.73	.77	.80	.71	.71	.67	.61
	7	208						.82	.83	.82	.77	.85	.73	.71
1937 Stanford Revision Form L	8	199								.91	.88	.90	.85	.70
	9	90										.87	.87	.76
	10	107											.85	.70
	12	92											.92	.76
	14	120												.78
		51												.73

cause, is probably a contributing factor. Another factor may be the differences in the types of test items included in the Stanford and Wechsler-Bellevue tests.

EFFECT OF CHANGE OF FORM OF TEST ON MENTAL TEST CONSTANCY

The correlation between the 8- and 9-year tests for children tested on the same form of the Stanford (Form L) is .91; but the correlation is even higher for the remainder of the group who were tested on Form L at 8 years and Form M at 9 years (r equals .93). Comparison of the effect of change of form on the test-retest correlations is made for six age periods. In all of these comparisons, the difference between the test-retest coefficients, when the same or different forms of the Stanford test were used, was negligible. Average correlation when the same form of the Stanford-Binet Test was used was .87; when different forms were used the average correlation was .88.

CHANGES IN SCORES OVER CERTAIN AGE PERIODS

The correlation coefficients in Table 1 indicate the group trends with respect to the constancy of mental test performance. It is also of interest to know the extent of the changes in sigma scores or I.Q. which are occurring in individual children. Furthermore, the question arises as to whether the correlation between mental test scores is largely determined by a relatively small proportion of the cases or by the group as a whole. We have, therefore, prepared distributions of the range of sigma score changes for the entire 16-year period of testing. We find that the scores of three children have increased between 4 and 4½ sigma (roughly between 70 and 79 I. Q. points, assuming an approximate standard deviation of 17.5 I.Q. points); and the scores of two children have decreased a similiar amount. The sigma score curves for four of these five children are depicted in Figure 1D and Figure 1E. The most interesting aspect of these tremendous changes in scores is the fact that the changes are not made abruptly but consistently over a long period of time. However, the greatest changes do occur on the preschool tests. We have, therefore, prepared distributions showing the range of changes in sigma scores and I.Q.'s between 6 and 18 years. No child's sigma score changes as much as 4 sigma during the school years. But the scores of one child (case 764, Figure 1D) changes 3 sigma; and those of four others between 2.5 and 2.9 sigma.

Since educators and clinical workers use I.Q.'s rather than standard scores, we have prepared a distribution of the range of changes in I.Q. during the 12-year period 6 to 18 years for the two groups, Guidance and Control. These tabulations are shown in the following table.

Changes in I.Q. of 30 or more points of I.Q. are shown by 9 per cent of the children in the Guidance Group and 10 per cent in the Control Group. The I.Q.'s of over half of the children showed a variation of 15 or more points of I.Q. at some time during the school years, and a third of the group varied as much as 20 points of I.Q.

Although it is extremely important to point out the possibility of marked changes in scores in individual cases, it is equally important to emphasize that the scores of many children change only slightly with respect to the group from one age period to the next. And it is only when the changes are

I.Q. Changes Between 6 and 18 Years	Guidance N Equals 114 %	Control N Equals 108 %	Total N Equals 222 %
50 or more I.Q. pts.	1	—	.5
30 or more I.Q. pts.	9	10	9
20 or more I.Q. pts.	32	42	37
15 or more I.Q. pts.	58	60	59
10 or more I.Q. pts.	87	83	85
9 or less I.Q. pts.	13	17	15

consistently in one direction, or the other, over a period of years, that the range of variation becomes as great as 3 or 4 sigma (or over 50 I.Q. points).

STABILITY AND INSTABILITY IN THE MENTAL TEST SCORES OF INDIVIDUAL CHILDREN

Mental test sigma score curves have been drawn for all of the children in the Guidance Study. In this sample of 252 children, we have found individuals whose mental test scores have remained relatively stable at either a high, average, or low level over the entire period of testing (21 months to 18 years). Other children have shown highly inconsistent scores in their mental test performance. Examples of varying degrees of constancy of mental test performance are shown in Figure 1.

Consistently Low Scores (Figure 1A) Case 504, a girl, had a mother who attended college two years and a father who graduated from college. The child was defective at birth, which showed up not only in tests (her I.Q.'s varied from 67 to 53, sigma scores from −3 to −4½) but in her whole developmental history. Clinical diagnosis was microcephaly, probably secondary to prenatal injury early in M.'s pregnancy.

Consistently Average Test Scores (Figure 1B) Case 976, showing consistently average and fairly stable test scores, is a girl of immigrant parents whose mother had schooling until 16 and whose father had schooling until age

12. The father provided a very substantial income and status to his family with his prestige-giving business success. Her mother, lonely in a new country, overprotected her daughter, especially in her early years. The mother slept in her daughter's room until she was 9. This girl's two highest scores (I.Q. 137) occurred at age 9 (following tonsillectomy ending a long period of chronic infection) and at 14 (during a period of more freedom from home, and more social opportunity and success). Her lowest score after her preschool years occurred at 18 after the death of her father.

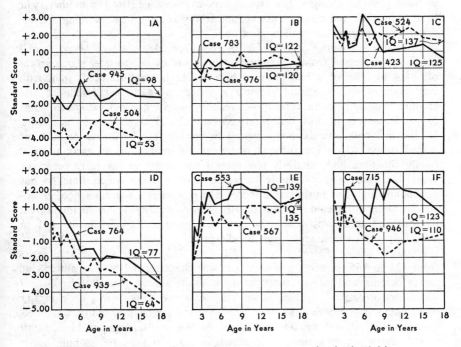

FIGURE 1. Stability of Mental Test Scores in Individual Children

Relatively Consistent High Scores (Figure 1C) Case 423 presents a high-scoring girl whose mother is a normal school graduate and whose father obtained a post-graduate university degree. Her highest test score was obtained at 6. Her scores continued high but sagged during late adolescence. She is attractive, artistically talented, and socially successful. She got very high grades in the elementary and junior high school years. Her lowest test scores are at ages 9 and 10, a period of fatigue and poor posture and a period during which she strained to excel, and at year 18 where her sigma score showed a drop. Her high school years were characterized by much less interest in intellectual success, which she regarded as unfeminine and interfering with getting good dates; and her motivation in all test situations was markedly below that of her early years. Scholastic mediocrity was consciously sought and obtained, serving not only her date objective, but her emancipatory revolt against parents who placed a very high value on grades and a very low value on her boy friends.

Steadily Decreasing Mental Test Scores (Figure 1D) Case 764 is an example of a gradual lowering of I.Q. from 133 to 77, and sigma scores from +1 to −3. She is an only child, born when her mother was 44, the father 37. The estimated I.Q. of the mother is 65 to 70. The father is a skilled mechanic. The parents went to school until age 14.

Obesity began in late preschool years and increased steadily until medical advice was finally followed at age 14 (height 5 ft. 2 in., weight 160 lbs. at 13). Weight was normal at 17. There were, however, no I.Q. variations in relation to these physical changes. She was always over-indulged by the mother, who lived to feed her and keep her young, and who was always complaining that her daughter never gave her enough affection.

Case with Increasing Scores (Figure 1E) Case 553 is a boy whose mental test scores increased from a preschool sigma score of −2 to later sigma scores of +2.4 in spite of a bad physical history. He is small-statured, thin, with very poor musculature, and presents a history of early ear infections and chronic bronchitis from infancy—headaches (early glasses), stomach pains (appendectomy); he has had three operations and three serious accidents. He has had only one six-month period in his life free of illness. In spite of a frail frame, which has suffered many serious indignities, an early strained family situation, and relatively low mental test scores in his early preschool years, his tested ability steadily increased until 9, from which time he has maintained high and fairly stable scores. His mother is a normal school graduate; his father completed high school. His greatest security lies in his intellectual interests and achievements, but he has made good social adjustments and an amazingly good adjustment to his handicaps.

Highly Variable Scores (Figure 1F) Case 715, a girl whose I.Q. varies from 121 to 165, presents a history that was characterized by intermittent but severe eczema and asthma throughout the entire testing period. Ages 3 to 7 constituted a particularly bad period; age 9, where there was a drop in I.Q. of 12 points, was a period not only of asthma and poor vision but of acute economic insecurity and family uneasiness. At age 10, during her highest test period, she was taking two cc. of adrenalin daily to keep her asthma under control.

Added to health strain, social strain became more acute for her at 12 when she entered junior high school and continued through high school. It was a period of overweight, disfiguring eczema, and marked mother-daughter strain. Not only did the girl belong to a racial minority group, but she was not at one with them because of her marked intellectual interest, unshared by others in her racial age group, at school or in the neighborhood. Her mother is a high school graduate; her father had three years in college.

At the time of the 18-year test she was very much below par as she was recovering from an acute period of asthma.

In selecting mental test curves to include in this study, the writers were impressed by the fact that the children whose scores showed the greatest fluctuations were children whose life experiences had also fluctuated between disturbing and satisfying periods. Two such cases are 715 and 946 in Figure 1F.

There is only one further generalization that seems justifiable on the basis of mental test curves of only 12 children, and that is the fact that the records of all eight children showing consistent trends have final mental test scores which are similar to their parents' ability, as judged by their education, and socio-economic rating. Of the four children whose scores either decreased markedly or were consistently below the average for the group, three children were from homes which were low in the socio-economic scale and had parents with less education than the average for this Berkeley sample. One common factor in the decreasing scores of cases 935 and 764 may be the stimulating effect of affectionate parents on their only children in the early years. These parents with less than average ability could not continue to offer intellectually stimulating environments as their children grew older, nor can the hereditary factors with which they were endowed be discounted. The microcephalic youngster with low scores was the child of parents with above average intelligence. This case should probably be considered the result of an intra-uterine disturbance unrelated to hereditary or post-natal environmental factors.

On the other hand, the four children with increasing or consistently high scores had parents with more than average education (seven of the eight parents were college graduates). Superior hereditary and environmental factors were unquestionably contributing to the mental test records of these children.

SUMMARY AND CONCLUSION

A group of 252 children, who comprise a representative sample of the children living in an urban community, were given mental tests at specified ages between 21 months and 18 years. These data have been analyzed to show the extent of the stability of mental test performance for this age period. The results may be summarized as follows:

1. Mental test constancy for the age period 21 months to 18 years is markedly dependent upon the age at testing and the interval between tests. That is, group prediction is good over short age periods, and mental test scores become increasingly predictive after the preschool years.

2. Distributions of the extent of the changes in I.Q. for the age period 6 to 18 years show that the I.Q.'s of almost 60 per cent of the group change 15 or more points; the I.Q.'s of a third of the group change 20 or more points; and the I.Q.'s of 9 per cent of the group change 30 or more points. The I.Q.'s of 15 per cent of the group change *less* than 10 points of I.Q. The group averages on the other hand, show a maximum shift in I.Q. over this age period of from 118 to 123.

3. Some individuals show consistent upward or downward trends in I.Q. over a long period resulting in changes of as much as 4½ sigma or 50 I.Q. points.

4. Inspection of the mental test curves of the individual children included in this paper indicates that changes in mental test scores tend to be in the direction of the family level, as judged by the parents' education and socio-economic status.

5. Children whose mental test scores showed the most marked fluctuations had life histories which showed unusual variations with respect to disturbing and stabilizing factors. However, there were other children whose scores remained constant despite highly disturbing experiences.

In conclusion, it should be re-emphasized that, whereas the results for the group suggest mental test stability between 6 and 18 years, the observed fluctuations in the scores of individual children indicate the need for the utmost caution in the predictive use of a single test score, or even two such scores. This finding seems of especial importance since many plans for individual children are made by schools, juvenile courts, and mental hygiene clinics on the basis of a single mental test score. Specifically, it should be noted that a prediction based on a 6-year test would be wrong to the extent of 20 I.Q. points for one out of three children by the age of 18 years, and to the extent of 15 I.Q. points for approximately six out of ten children.

27

Personality and IQ Change[*]

Jerome Kagan, Lester W. Sontag, Charles T. Baker, and Virginia L. Nelson

The IQ's obtained for the majority of children remain remarkably stable during the developmental years. However, research evidence collected during the last three decades clearly demonstrates that the IQ's of some children may vary substantially over long periods of time. These variations have been shown to be systematically related to grossly defined social and cultural conditions like nursery school attendance

* From Jerome Kagan, Lester W. Sontag, Charles T. Baker, and Virginia L. Nelson, "Personality and IQ Change," *Journal of Abnormal and Social Psychology*, 1958, Vol. 56, pp. 261-266. (With permission of the authors and the American Psychological Association.)

and institutional care. Under normal life circumstances a few children display a consistent downward trend in IQ, while in others there is a consistent rise as they grow older. What are the psychological concomitants of these trends in rate of psychological growth, trends that are too substantial and too consistent to be attributed to errors of measurement? In the following report from the Fels Research Institute at Yellow Springs, Ohio, Drs. Kagan, Sontag, Baker, and Nelson show that the children in whom IQ consistently increases are highly motivated toward achievement and competitive striving and are highly curious about nature. Although the details of these findings are intrinsically interesting, the reader may be equally interested in the instruments and analytical procedures employed by the present investigators in securing the evidence from which they make these inferences.

Research on mental development during the last twenty years has indicated that a child's IQ score does not necessarily remain constant with age (Bayley, 1940; 1949; Bradway, 1944; Sontag, Baker and Nelson, 1955). Several reports (Richards, 1951; Sontag, Baker and Nelson, 1955; Wellman and McCandless, 1946) suggest that changes in environmental conditions can depress or raise IQ level and it is sometimes implied that these changes may be explained by recourse to personality variables. The purpose of this paper is to demonstrate that changes in IQ during childhood are correlated with certain personality predispositions as inferred from projective test data. The personality variables under study include (a) need for achievement, (b) competitive strivings, (c) curiosity about nature, and (d) passivity.

Performance on an IQ test is assumed to be a function of at least two major variables; the variety of skills and abilities the person brings to the test situation and his motivation to perform well on the test (Bayley, 1940; Haggard, Davis and Havighurst, 1948). Since the IQ scores of some children change markedly during the school years, it seems plausible to assume that those children who show marked increases in IQ have a very strong motivation to acquire or develop the various intellectual skills tapped by an IQ test and to perform well in a testing situation. It is suggested that need for achievement, competitive strivings, and curiosity about nature motivate the acquisition and improvement of cognitive abilities and by so doing facilitate increases in tested IQ.

The social environment often awards praise and recognition for intellectual accomplishment, and school age children with a high need for achievement might seek to gratify this need through intellectual activity. Thus it was predicted that children showing marked increases in IQ would produce more achievement imagery on the TAT than those with minimal gains in IQ.

Secondly, the school environment emphasizes competitive intellectual activity, and children with strong competitive needs would be highly motivated to acquire the intellectual skills which result in successful competition with one's classmates. Thus it was predicted that children showing IQ gains would show more competitive strivings than children displaying minimal gains in IQ. In choosing an index of competitive strivings, besides the related measure of TAT achievement fantasy, it was decided to use aggressive content on the Rorschach. The bases for this choice rested on the assumptions that (a) incidence of aggressive imagery reflected degree of aggressive motivation and (b) competition was a socially accepted form of aggressive behavior. For in competition, as in aggression, the child desires to defeat another individual and assert his superiority over him. The population of children in this study is predominantly middle class and apt to place strong inhibitions on direct, overt expression of aggression. Therefore, there would be a tendency for the individual with high aggressive motivation to seek socially accepted channels for aggressive expression such as competitive activity with peers. Thus it was predicted that children showing IQ gain would report more Rorschach aggressive content than those with minimal gain because of their greater competitive predisposition.

A third motive that might facilitate a child's acquisition of knowledge and skills in dealing with the environment could be curiosity about nature. Interest in birth, death, sexual anatomy, and other processes of nature is a frequent phenomenon in young children. It is suggested that the more intense this curiosity the greater the motivation to acquire the habits which would gratify this motive. Since reading, questioning, and manipulating the environment are effective behavioral methods of gratifying one's curiosity, it might be expected that the highly curious child would be more likely to develop these skills and therefore apt to gain in IQ score. The TAT measure used to evaluate curiosity was presence of themes of interest in nature and its phenomena. For the Rorschach, it was hypothesized that concern with the body might reflect, in part, heightened interest in natural processes, and it was suggested that anatomy content might be more frequent for children who showed marked IQ gains than for those with minimal increases in IQ. It is recognized that many clinical psychologists regard anatomy content in adults as indicative of psychopathology. This study is concerned with the correlates of IQ gain rather than psychopathology, and it is not implied that children who show increases in IQ are completely free of conflict. Secondly, it was felt that the determinants of anatomy content for children might be different from those which produce this content in adults.

A final prediction dealt with the predisposition to behavioral passivity.

The children who show IQ gains have been characterized as having high need achievement, competitive strivings, and curiosity about the environment. This constellation of motives implies that when these children are confronted with a problem, they would have a tendency to attack and attempt to solve the problem rather than withdraw from the situation or seek help. On this basis, it was predicted that children who showed IQ gains would be less likely than those with minimal IQ increases to characterize their TAT heroes as passive in attitude or behavior.

The Fels Research Institute is uniquely equipped to test these ideas about IQ change since it has continuous longitudinal information on the development of a sample of normal children. These data include intelligence and projective tests, observations of the children, and reports on the parent-child interaction. In a recent study, Sontag, Baker, and Nelson (1958) related personality information on a sample of children with changes in IQ and found that those children who showed marked increases in IQ were rated as more competitive, more likely to display self-initiated behavior and less passive than those who showed decreases in IQ. The TAT and Rorschach protocols were not utilized in making these personality ratings, and the results from this study served as a major stimulus for the present investigation.

METHOD

A sample of 140 Fels subjects (Ss), 70 of each sex, were chosen for study because a fairly complete record of test information was available on them. From ages 2½ to 6, the Stanford-Binet intelligence test (1916 or 1937 revision) administered to most Ss twice yearly, on their birthdays and six months after their birthdays. From ages 6 to 12, most Ss received alternately Form L or Form M of the 1937 revision annually on or near each S's birthday. All of the tests were administered by one of the authors (VLN). The mean IQ of the Fels population is near 120, with standard deviation varying from 14 to 20 IQ points.

In order to obtain groups of Ss who showed the most change in IQ score from ages 6 to 10, a smoothed longitudinal plot of each S's IQ was prepared by averaging the mean of three consecutive test scores around each age. This procedure is explained in detail in other reports (Baker, Sontag and Nelson, 1955; Sontag, Baker and Nelson, 1955). This technique tends to eliminate erratic variations in IQ and hopefully furnishes a more valid measure of IQ changes. Then each S's smoothed IQ at age 6 was subtracted from his smoothed IQ at age 10, and this distribution of differences, positive if S gained in IQ and negative if S lost in IQ, was divided into quartiles. This report deals with the projective test information on those Ss in the two extreme groups; those who increased and those who decreased the most in IQ score. These will be called Group A, the IQ ascenders, and Group D, the IQ descenders, respectively. There was no significant difference between the mean IQ of the two extreme quartiles at age six, the means being 119 and 116 for Groups A and D respectively. The average amount of increase in IQ for Group A was larger (plus 17 points) than the corresponding decrease for the members of Group D (minus 5 points) and while 46 per cent of Group D lost five or more points, every child in Group A gained 10 or more points during the years 6 through 10. The mean IQ of the entire sample of 140 tends to increase slightly from ages 6 to 10, probably as a result of practice effects with the same test. Since every S in Group D showed a decrease in IQ, it might be inferred that the members of Group D did not benefit from practice and familiarity with the test, and it is probably more accurate to view Group D Ss in this light rather than as Ss who showed marked decreases in IQ score.

The projective tests used in the analysis were the Rorschach and selected TAT pictures. Two factors governed the choice of the TAT cards which were analyzed. Because the protocols were gathered over a period of years, there was not complete comparability for all Ss for the number of cards administered. Secondly, the specific hypotheses of the study dictated the cards chosen for analysis and Cards 1, 3 BM, 3 GF, 5, 6 BM, 12 F, 14, and 17 BM were selected for analysis. The age at which the TAT protocols were administered ranged from 8-9 to 14-6 with median at 11-6 and 80 per cent of the protocols obtained between the ages of 11 and 12. The age at which the Rorschachs were administered ranged from 6-5 to 13-6 with median at 10-5 and 63 per cent of the sample having had the test between ages 10 and 11. Since the Rorschach and TAT were administered by different examiners there was no comparability with respect to inquiry or probing. Thus, the analysis of both the Rorschach and TAT was restricted to the S's spontaneous verbalization to the stimulus before any questions or inquiry were conducted by the examiner. The protocols were scored for the following fantasy categories.

1. Need Achievement on the TAT. Achievement imagery on the TAT was scored according to the definition of McClelland et al. (1953); and themes involving a reference to competition with a standard of excellence were scored achievement imagery.

2. Rorschach Aggression. The definition of aggressive content on the Rorschach included (a) people, animals, or creatures engaged in physical or verbal aggression, e.g., fighting or quarreling, (b) explosive objects or explosions, e.g., volcanoes, bombs exploding, fireworks, and (c) objects or animal parts normally regarded as instruments of aggression, e.g., spears, rifles, clubs, guns, knives, horns, and claws.

3. Intellectual Curiosity about Nature. For the TAT, curiosity was defined in terms of themes in which someone is interested in the processes or phenomena of nature. Curiosity on the Rorschach was restricted to anatomy or X-ray responses of internal organs or boney parts, e.g., stomach, backbone, ribs.

4. Passivity. Because of the limited amount of thematic material in the spontaneous performance, themes of passivity were limited to stories in which the central figure was described as sleepy, tired, or resting.

TABLE 1. Distribution of Ss by Sex and Direction of IQ Change
Used in the Analysis of the TAT and Rorschach

Group	TAT Boys	TAT Girls	Rorschach Boys	Rorschach Girls
Group A	22	11	22	10
Group D	10	20	9	18
Both groups	32	31	31	28

The fantasy categories were independently scored by the senior author and an assistant without knowledge of the S's IQ scores. Reliability was very high because of the limited amount of content scored for each response and the objectivity of the definitions. Percentage of agreement for the three TAT categories was 95 per cent and for the two Rorschach categories 99 per cent.

RESULTS

Although there was a total of 70 Ss in the two extreme quartiles, not all of the Ss had Rorschach or TAT data for the age range under study. Table 1 shows the distribution of Ss, by sex and direction of IQ change, for the TAT and Rorschach analyses. Because there are approximately twice as many boys as there are girls in Group A, all comparisons were first made separately by sex and results were only combined if the direction of the result for both boys and girls in the same IQ group was in the predicted direction.

1. Need Achievement. All achievement themes, save one, occurred to Cards 1 and 17 BM. The typical achievement story to Card 1 concerned a boy who wanted to master the violin and/or become a famous violinist, while the typical achievement theme to 17 BM involved competitive activity with regard to rope climbing. Table 2 shows the percentage of Ss in each group reporting achievement imagery plots to Cards 1, 17 BM, and to both pictures.

For both Cards 1 and 17 BM, more male and female *S*s in Group A reported achievement imagery than the boys or girls of Group D. For Card 1, the difference between Group A and Group D girls is reliable at the .03 level; the difference for boys is in the predicted direction but not significant. For Card 17 BM, the difference between Group A and Group D boys is significant ($P=.03$) and in the predicted direction for girls. All P values are for one tail and were evaluated using the exact method sug-

TABLE 2. Percentage of Ss Reporting Achievement
Imagery to Cards 1 and 17 BM

TAT Card	Group A			Group D		
	Boys	Girls	Boys and Girls	Boys	Girls	Boys and Girls
Card 1	36.4	50.0	40.6	27.3	15.0	19.4
Card 17 BM	36.4	30.0	34.4	0.0	15.0	9.7
Cards 1 and 17 BM	22.7	10.0	18.8	0.0	0.0	0.0

gested by Fisher (1943). When the sexes were pooled, comparisons between Group A and D were significant not only for Cards 1 and 17 BM separately but also for the number of *S*s telling achievement imagery to both Cards 1 and 17 BM ($P<.10$, .03, and .01 respectively). Thus, the *S*s who showed increases in IQ were more prone to structure Cards 1 and 17 BM in terms of achievement oriented behavior than the *S*s in Group D.

2. Aggressive Content on Rorschach. There was no significant difference between Groups A and D or between boys and girls with respect to the mean number of responses per protocol, and the mean for the entire sample was 27 responses. There was no difference between Group A and Group D girls with respect to percentage of each group reporting one or more aggressive responses per protocol (30.0 per cent for Group A versus 33.0 per cent for Group D). However, the difference between Group A and D boys approached significance with 59.1 per cent of the former and 22.2 per cent of the latter reporting one or more aggressive images ($P=.07$). Thus, the prediction of a correlation between IQ increase and aggressive imagery held only for the boys. Because of the tentativeness of this result and the more speculative nature of the hypothesis relating competitive striving and aggressive content, an attempt was made to validate this finding by analyzing a later Rorschach protocol for the boys in Groups A and D. Not all of the boys had Rorschachs administered to them at a later age, and only 15 Ss in Group A and five in Group D were available for analysis. The median ages at the time of administration were 13-8 and 15-0 for Groups A and D respectively, and there was no significant difference in the lengths of the protocols of the two groups. The results were in the same direction for 86.7 per cent of Group A, and 20.0 per cent of Group D reported one or more aggressive images, and this difference is highly significant $(P=.01)$.

3. Intellectual Curiosity. The only TAT card eliciting curiosity plots was Card 14, and the typical theme described a person gazing at or interested

TABLE 3. Percentage of Ss Reporting Themes of Curiosity
to Card 14

Sex	Group A	Group D
Boys	40.0	18.2
Girls	30.0	5.0
Boys and girls	37.5	9.7

in the stars or the heavens. Table 3 shows the percentage of each group telling such themes to Card 14.

Both the boys and girls in Group A told more themes of interest in the stars or heavens than the males and females in Group D $(P=.14,$ $P=.10$, respectively) and combining of the sexes yielded a highly significant difference between Groups A and D $(P<.01)$.

4. Anatomy and X-ray Responses on the Rorschach. There was no difference between Group A and Group D girls reporting one or more anatomy responses (30.0 per cent versus 38.9 per cent for Groups A and D respectively). For the boys, 31.8 per cent of Group A and 0.0 per cent of Group D reported anatomy or X-ray imagery, a difference that approached significance $(P=.06)$. This finding was also validated on the same sample of 20 boys that was used to check the differences in aggressive content. The results were in the same direction with 60.0 per cent of Group A and 20.0 per cent of Group D reporting anatomy content $(P= .15)$.

5. Passivity. Card 3 BM accounted for most of the passivity themes and the groups were compared with respect to the incidence of stories to Card 3 BM in which the central figure was sleepy, tired, or resting. Table 4 shows the percentage of each group telling such themes. Both the boys and girls in Group D showed more passivity themes than the boys and girls in Group A. Although only the difference for the girls was significant (P=.06), when the sexes were pooled the difference was highly reliable (P<.03).

Cards 3 GF, 5, 6 BM, and 12 F did not furnish data relevant to the hypotheses under test and these results are not summarized.

DISCUSSION

In the main, the hypotheses about the differences between Groups A and D have been verified. Boy and girl ascenders produced more TAT

TABLE 4. Percentage of Ss Reporting Themes of Passivity
to Card 3 BM

Sex	Group A	Group D
Boys	9.1	27.3
Girls	10.0	45.0
Boys and girls	9.4	38.7

achievement imagery and curiosity about nature than Group D children and male ascenders displayed more aggressive content on the Rorschach than the boys in Group D. The higher incidence of aggressive imagery for the boys who gained in IQ was interpreted as reflecting stronger competitive motivation. Finally, the Ss in Group D were presumed to have a more passive orientation since they were more likely to perceive the ambiguous figure on Card 3 BM as sleeping or tired. The relation between Rorschach anatomy content and IQ gain was the most tentative finding.

The results are interpreted as indicating that high motivation to achieve, competitive strivings, and curiosity about nature may motivate the acquisition of intellectual skills and knowledge which, in turn, facilitates increases in tested IQ. If one accepts the generally assumed notion that boys are more competitive and achievement oriented than girls, the fact that there were twice as many boys in Group A as there were girls supports the present interpretation. A recent study using the Edwards Personal Preference Schedule found that high school boys obtained higher need achievement scores than high school girls (Klett, 1957).

These results are not interpreted as indicating that strong achievement, competitive, and curiosity motives are the only variables involved in producing gains in IQ. The Ss in this study are all average or above in IQ and there is not adequate sampling of children with lower IQ levels. One would not expect Ss with low IQ's or language handicaps to suddenly show an interest in reading despite achievement needs or intellectual curiosity. The child who spends increased time reading because of a heightened interest in natural processes must have already learned the basic reading skills so that this behavior is not a difficult or unlikely choice for him.

Similarly, needs for achievement and successful competition should only motivate attempts at improvement of intellectual abilities in a social milieu where praise, recognition, and superior status are awarded for such accomplishment. That is, achievement-oriented children from homes in which intellectual activity was praised would probably be more likely to master intellectual skills than achievement-oriented children from homes in which such accomplishment was not rewarded. In a cultural environment where athletic ability, fighting prowess, or success with the opposite sex was highly valued, one might expect the child to choose these behavioral channels to gratify his achievement and competitive needs. The parents in the Fels population are predominantly middle class and tend to place importance on intellectual accomplishment. A large majority of the parents have attended college, and since enrollment in the Fels program is voluntary it might be inferred that only parents who valued knowledge and scientific pursuits would be predisposed to become part of the research population. Thus, the children under study tend to come from homes which value intellectual ability.

Study of the educational attainment of the parents of the Ss in Groups A and D revealed no significant difference between the groups with respect to the percentage of families in which both parents attended college (57.1 per cent for Group A versus 42.9 per cent for Group D; $P > .30$). Although there is a slight difference favoring the educational level of Group A families, the difference was not dramatic. There may be important differences between Groups A and D with respect to the differential encouragement of intellectual achievement, but measurement of these differences would probably require variables more refined than educational level of the parents. However, even though parental emphasis on intellectual activity may increase the child's desire to improve his cognitive skills, the child's predisposition to adopt or rebel against parental values should selectively influence his motivation to strive for intellectual accomplishment. Thus, the type of relation between parent and child may be an important factor in this process.

Finally, there is the possibility that genetic and/or constitutional variables may play a role in facilitating marked IQ changes. There is considerable data indicating that genetic factors influence general IQ level but less evidence relevant to the role of these variables in producing childhood increases in IQ score. For most of the children in our population, IQ's tend to level off during the ages 6-10 and most of the marked changes in level occur during the preschool years. However, the exact relationship between genetic variables and IQ change has yet to be determined. The phenomenon of IQ increase during the school years is admittedly complex and it is not implied that the child's motives are the major factor. However, it is suggested that personality needs may influence this process.

Perhaps the most accurate generalization is that for middle-class children with average or above IQ levels, strong achievement, competitive, and curiosity needs may facilitate IQ gains by motivating the child to master intellectual skills.

A final implication of these findings is that they add indirect evidence for the usefulness of the Rorschach and TAT as research instruments. Validation of a predicted relationship between TAT achievement imagery and IQ gain increases one's confidence in the hypothesis that TAT plots can serve as an index of achievement-oriented tendencies. The results of the Rorschach analysis suggest that aggressive content may be an index of an individual's aggressive predispositions but not necessarily a measure of his tendency to express direct, physical aggression. Although Sontag, Baker, and Nelson (1958), using behavioral observations, rated the boys in Group A as more competitive than those in Group D, there was no difference between these groups with respect to intensity or incidence of direct verbal or physical aggression or destruction of property. We have assumed that competition is a socially approved form of aggressive behavior and the higher incidence of aggressive content for Group A boys was presumed to be a result of their more intense competitive strivings. Some clinicians who use projective tests are too prone to focus on predictive statements about direct, physical aggression when confronted with a protocol containing aggressive content. One is apt to overlook the fact that the individual may have alternative behavioral channels for expression of aggressive motives.

SUMMARY

For a group of 140 boys and girls in the Fels Research population on whom continuous Binet IQ data were available, a distribution of IQ change was obtained by subtracting each $S's$ smoothed IQ at age 6 from his smoothed IQ at age 10. This distribution of differences was divided into quartiles, and the Rorschach and TAT protocols of the upper, (maximum increase in IQ) and lower (maximum decrease in IQ) quartiles were analyzed and compared. The results showed that in comparing the Ss who showed IQ increases with those showing IQ decreases, the former had, on the TAT, significantly more (a) achievement imagery on Cards 1 and 17 BM and (b) themes of curiosity about nature on Card 14, and significantly fewer themes of passivity on Card 3 BM. For the boys only, more of the Ss who increased in IQ had anatomy responses and aggressive imagery on the Rorschach. The results were interpreted as indicating that high need achievement, competitive striving, and curiosity about nature are correlated with gains in IQ score because they may facilitate the acquisition of skills that are measured by the intelligence test.

28

An Intellectually Gifted Child*

Leta S. Hollingworth

One of the noteworthy accomplishments of Professor Leta S. Hollingworth (now deceased) was her contribution to our somewhat meager knowledge of the characteristics and potentialities of exceptionally brilliant children. Professor Hollingworth's work with intellectually gifted children did much to stimulate a new interest in the special educational problems of such children, and in the development of a new type of curriculum for them. Interest in the education of the gifted child has increased steadily during the last two decades. Special classes and merit scholarships for the intellectually gifted, these potentially great contributors to our culture, are now fairly common. The following report describes the family background, interests, and educational career of one of Professor Hollingworth's brilliant subjects. Children with IQ's above 180 on the Stanford-Binet Intelligence Scale are exceedingly rare—probably fewer than five in every 100,000 births! The precocious development of intellectual deviates like "Child D," in the following report, tends to support our confidence in the validity and usefulness of modern scales of mental growth.

Child D was brought to the attention of the writer as being a child of remarkable endowment. He was at that time 7 years, 4 months old and had a Mental Age of 13 years, 7 months, with an IQ of 184 (S-B).

D was descended from Russian Jews in the paternal branch and from English Jews in the maternal branch. D's father immigrated to America at an early age. He is a high school graduate and was a student of engineering but abandoned these studies in the third year to do newspaper work, and later entered the advertising business in a large city. His leisure is spent in writing, and he has published a number of books, including three novels and a philosophical drama dealing with religion. His first

* Adapted from Chapter 7 in Leta S. Hollingworth, *Children Above 180 IQ,* 1942, Yonkers, N.Y. World Book Co. (With permission of the estate of Dr. H. L. Hollingworth and Harcourt, Brace, & World, Inc., Publishers.)

book, a novel, was published when he was 21 years old. He was 28 when D was born.

D's mother went to school for only a few weeks and has been largely self-taught. Before marriage she was statistician and registrar in a large philanthropic organization. She has published stories, reviews, and poems, and a book on education. She has always taken part personally in the education of D. She was 26 years old when D was born. D is an only child.

PRESCHOOL HISTORY

D cut his first tooth at 4 months of age. He could say words at 8 months and talked in sentences at 11 months. In November, 1910 (8 months), he said "little boy" when his shadow appeared on the wall. D could stand, holding to chairs, at 9 months of age, and he walked alone at 11 to 12 months. At the age of 18 months, while sitting on his mother's lap as she sat before a typewriter, he learned to read by looking at the letters. At 2 years 6 months his vocabulary (incomplete) was 1690 words.

This child was not placed in school at the usual age because he did not fit into the school organization. At the time he should have entered kindergarten D could read fluently and could perform complicated arithmetical processes. His intellectual interests were far beyond those of even the highly selected children of a private kindergarten. Therefore, his parents kept him out of school and obtained the companionship of other children for him by sending him to a playground. It is very interesting to note how D made social contacts with the other children while pursuing his own interests. For instance, he published a playground newspaper called "The Weekly Post." He composed, edited, and typed this paper, issued at intervals, and it had a regular playground circulation.

DIVERSIONS AND INTERESTS

At the age of 7 years D's favorite amusements were skating, "Mechano," reading, playing ball, writing, tabulating, solitaire, chess, and numerical calculation in all its forms. As development has proceeded, he has continued most of these recreations, turning more and more, however, to games of intellectual skill. He likes other children and likes to be with them; he has established relations with them by editing newspapers for them, teaching them about nature, and the like. Play in the sense of mere purposeless sensorimotor activity has not been enjoyed by him.

From the age of about 4 years to about the age of 7, D was greatly interested in an imaginary land which he called "Borningtown." He spent many hours peopling Borningtown, laying out roads, drawing maps of its terrain, composing and recording its language (Bornish), and writing its history and literature. He composed a lengthy dictionary—scores of pages —of the Bornish language. The origin of the words "Borningtown" and "Bornish" is not known. It seems possible that D's imaginary land may have arisen out of the mystery of being born.

D had piano lessons for several years, and he displayed remarkable ability to deal with the mathematical aspects of music. He composed music before he had any instruction in playing musical instruments. He was able to compose music which he could not himself play.

From earliest childhood D felt a need for concepts and for words to express them that are not to be found in dictionaries. His occupation in this field he called "wordical work." Some examples are recorded by his mother in the following note dated December, 1916.

Was having his dinner and being nearly finished said he didn't care to eat any more, as he had a pain in his actum pelopthis. He explained that his actum pelopthis, actum quotatus, serbalopsis, and boobalicta are parts of the body where you sometimes have queer feelings; they don't serve any purpose. He said he also had a place called the boobalunksis, or source of headaches; that the hair usually springs out from around the herkadone; that the perpalensis is the place where socks end, and the bogalegus is the place where legs and tummy come together. He also named one other part, the cobaliscus or smerbalooble, whose function is not explained. The definitions are exactly as he gave them in each instance.

D invented many games. To illustrate this aspect of his mental capacity, there are his designs for three-handed and four-handed checkers. D held that these would be better games than two-handed checkers because they are more complicated. A description of the games invented by D, together with his mathematical calculations concerning the chances and probabilities in each, would fill many pages.

Throughout childhood he spent hours playing with numerical relation-ships. These calculations cover hundreds of pages. By the age of 12 years D had finished college entrance requirements in arithmetic, algebra, geometry, and trigonometry, all with high marks.

By the age of 10 years D's chief interests had come to center in science and it continued to center there. His classifications of moths, birds, and the like and his observations of their life cycles are "monumental."

Figures 1 and 2 illustrate his interest in physical science. They have been taken from his notebooks and state problems which occurred spon-taneously to him and for which he tried experimentally to find solutions. During a series of experiments "to determine the path of a tack," it is reported that "the house was full of tacks" which had been used in at-tempting solutions.

Determine the appearance of a finger, F, to two eyes, E_R and E_L,
focussed on a pole R at point P_S along lines E_RR and E_LR.

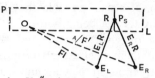

Thru R pass plane PL ∥ to the plane of the eyes. Draw a line from
E_L (which is nearer to F than E_R) to F, cutting PL in O. Draw E_RO; thru
F pass a plane ∥ to PL and crossing E_RO in A. Thru A pass F' ∥ F.

F' and F are the positions of F to E_R and E_L

                                                                                        D.

So it can be shown that 2 other eyes would see F in positions F
and F″.

∴ 4 eyes focused on R see F as F, F, F′, and F″.

                                                                                        D.

FIGURE 1. Copy of Work Done by D "For Fun,"
March 28, 1921, Aged 11 Years 1 Month

SCHOOL HISTORY

In the September following his ninth birthday D entered upon formal
instruction in the junior high school. In the autumn following his tenth
birthday he entered senior high school, from which he was graduated at
the age of 12 years, with a scholastic record which won for him two scholarships.

He was admitted to a large Eastern college at the age of 12 years 6
months (1922-1923), and made a superior record throughout the course. It
was very interesting to see that D continued to discover means of obtaining
social contacts in spite of the great difficulties due to his extreme youth
and his intellectual deviation. Thus it is not easy to plan how a 12-year-
old boy might successfully participate in college athletics when the median
age of college freshmen is over 18 years, but this problem was not too difficult for D. He presented himself to compete for the post of coxswain
on the freshman crew where, other things being equal, light weight is an
advantage.

He was graduated from college, with Phi Beta Kappa honors, in 1926,
at the age of 16 years 2 months. At that time he was ambitious for a career
in science.

D undertook graduate work, with distinction, in the field of chemistry.
He became an industrial chemist with an important position in the re-
search phases of the motion-picture industry. His death occurred in
September, 1938 (at age 28 years).

Discussion of the determination of the course of a freed tack, T, connected with other tacks by rubber bands.

A. Fig. 1.

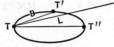

When connected to a tack T′ by band B.
Draw T T₁ or L.
T freed will travel along L, answer.

B. Fig. 2.

When connected to 2 tacks T′ and T″ by 2 bands B and B′.
Answer: Along L, the bisector of

T′ and TTT″.

C. Fig. 3.

The same as B, but only 1 band B.
Answer same as to B.

D. Fig. 4.

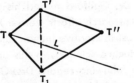

When connected to 3 tacks by any number of bands.
Draw T′ T₁, and treat as in B and C.

D.

FIGURE 2. The Path of a Tack—Work Done by D at Age 11 years

29

The Highly Intelligent and the Highly Creative Adolescent: A Summary of Some Research Findings[*]

J. W. Getzels and P. W. Jackson

Over thirty years ago Stoddard and Wellman in their *Child Psychology* noted that the creative aspects of human intelligence had been grossly neglected by psychological theorists and test-makers. This neglect continued until approximately 1950, when the distinguished psychometrician Dr. Guilford turned his attention to the measurement of creativity. His research efforts were instrumental in stimulating fairly widespread interest in creative human talent. Dr. Getzels has been one of the most productive scientists in this area of inquiry during the last ten years. In the following report, Drs. Getzels and Jackson show that high intelligence and high creativity do not necessarily go hand in hand. Their findings support the conclusion that the highly intelligent adolescent who is less creative is oriented toward obtaining the right or the customary answer while his highly creative but somewhat less intelligent contemporary is one who "diverges" from what is customary and "seems to enjoy the risk and the uncertainty of the unknown."

"Giftedness" in children has most often been defined as a score on an intelligence test, and typically the study of the so-called gifted child has actually been the study of children with high I.Q.'s. Implicit in this unidi-

* The research described here was supported by a grant from the U.S. Office of Education. A full report of the work is contained in J. W. Getzels and P. W. Jackson, *Creativity and Intelligence: Explorations with Gifted Students* (New York: John Wiley and Sons, 1962). The present article originally appeared in C. W. Taylor (Ed.), *The Third (1959) University of Utah Research Conference on the Identification of Creative Scientific Talent* (Salt Lake City: University of Utah Press, 1959). It also appeared in C. W. Taylor and F. Barron (Eds.) *Scientific Creativity: Its Recognition and Development* (New York: John Wiley and Sons, 1963). This paper is reproduced here by permission of the authors and the University of Utah Press.

mensional definition of giftedness, it seems to us, are several types of confusion, if not outright error.

First, there is the limitation of the I.Q. metric itself, which not only restricts our perspective of the more general phenomenon but places on the one concept a greater theoretical and predictive burden than it was intended to carry. For all practical purposes, the term "gifted child" has become synonymous with the expression "child with a high I.Q.," thus blinding us to other forms of potential excellence.

Second, we have frequently behaved as if the intelligence test alone represented an adequate sampling of *all* intellectual functions. For example, despite the recent work on cognition and creativity, the latter concept is still generally treated as if it applied only to performance in one or more of the arts. In effect, the term "creative child" has become synonymous with the expression, "child with artistic talents," thus limiting our attempts to identify and foster cognitive abilities related to creative functioning in areas other than the arts.

And finally, third, there has been a failure to attend sufficiently to the difference between the *definition* of giftedness as given by the I.Q. and the variations in the *value* placed upon giftedness as so defined. It is often taken for granted, for example, that the gifted child is equally valued by teachers and by parents, in the classroom and at home; that he is considered an equally good prospect by teachers and by parents to succeed as an adult; and that children themselves *want* to be gifted. It is demonstrable that none of these assumptions can be held without question. Empirical data indicate that the gifted child is *not* equally valued by teachers and by parents, in the classroom and at home; he is *not* held to be an equally good prospect to succeed as an adult; and children themselves do *not* necessarily want to be gifted, at least not in the traditional sense of the term.

Despite its longevity, there is nothing inevitable about the use of the I.Q. in defining giftedness. Indeed, it may be argued that in many ways this definition is only an historical happenstance—a consequence of the fact that early inquiries in this field had the classroom as their context and academic achievement as their major concern. If we moved the focus of inquiry from the classroom setting, we might identify qualities defining giftedness for other situations just as the I.Q. did for the classroom. Indeed, even without shifting our focus of inquiry, if we only modified the conventional criteria of achievement, we might change the qualities defining giftedness even in the classroom. For example, if we recognized that learning involves the production of novelty as well as the memorization of course content, then measures of creativity as well as the I.Q. might become appropriate in defining characteristics of giftedness.

The series of studies, of which the one we shall describe below is a part, is based on the foregoing considerations. Broadly speaking, these studies attempt to deal not only with intelligence as the quality defining giftedness but also with such other qualities as creativity, psychological health, and morality. Comparisons between groups of adolescents who are outstanding in these qualities serve as the basic analytic procedure of the research.

PROBLEM

The central task we set ourselves in the specific part of the research we shall present here was to differentiate two groups of adolescents—one representing individuals very high in measures of intelligence but *not* as high in measures of creativity, the other representing individuals very high in measures of creativity but *not* as high in measures of intelligence—and to compare the two groups with respect to the following questions:

1. What is the relative achievement—achievement as defined by learning in school—of the two groups?

2. Are the two groups equally preferred by teachers?

3. What is the relative need for achievement—as measured by McClelland's Index of Need: Achievement of the Thematic Apperception Test —of the two groups?

4. What are the personal qualities the two groups prefer for themselves?

5. What is the relation between the personal qualities preferred by the two groups for themselves and the personal qualities they believe teachers would like to see in children?

6. What is the relation between the personal qualities preferred by the two groups for themselves and the personal qualities they believe lead to "success" in adult life?

7. What is the nature of the fantasy productions of the two groups?

8. What are the career aspirations of the two groups?

IDENTIFYING THE EXPERIMENTAL GROUPS: SUBJECTS, INSTRUMENTS, PROCEDURES

The experimental groups were drawn from 449 adolescents of a Midwestern private secondary school on the basis of performance on the following instruments:

1. Standard I.Q. tests. Either a Binet, a Wechsler Intelligence Scale for Children, or a Henmon-Nelson score was available for each adolescent. The scores obtained from the WISC and the Henmon-Nelson were converted by regression equation to comparable Binet I.Q.'s.

2. Five creativity measures. These were taken or adapted from either Guilford or Cattell, or constructed especially for the study, as follows:

a. Word Association. The subject was asked to give as many definitions as possible to fairly common stimulus words, such as "bolt," "bark," "sack." His score depended upon the absolute number of definitions and the number of different categories into which these definitions could be put.

b. Uses for Things. The subject was required to give as many uses as he could for objects that customarily have a stereotyped function attached to them, such as "brick" or "paper-clip." His score depended upon both the number and the originality of the uses which he mentioned.

c. Hidden Shapes. The subject was required to find a given geometric form that was hidden in more complex geometric forms or patterns.

d. Fables. The subject was presented with four fables in which the last lines were missing. He was required to compose three different endings for each fable: a "moralistic," a "humorous," and a "sad" ending. His score depended upon the appropriateness and uniqueness of the endings.

e. Make-Up Problems. The subject was presented with four complex paragraphs each of which contained a number of numerical statements, for example, "the costs involved in building a house." He was required to make up as many mathematical problems as he could that might be solved with the information given. His score depended upon the number, appropriateness, and complexity of the problems.

On the basis of the I.Q. measure and a summated score on the five creativity instruments, the two experimental groups were formed as follows:

1. The High Creativity Group. These were subjects in the top 20% on the creativity measures when compared with like-sexed age peers, but *below* the top 20% in I.Q. ($N=26$).

2. The High Intelligence Group. These were subjects in the top 20% in I.Q. when compared with like-sexed age peers, but *below* the top 20% on the creativity measures ($N=28$).

With the experimental groups thus defined it is possible to approach each of the research questions in turn.[1]

Question 1: What is the relative school achievement of the two groups?

As the data in Table 1 indicate, the results were clear cut and striking. Despite the similarity in I.Q. between the high creatives and the school population, and the 23-point difference in mean I.Q. between the high creatives and the high I.Q.'s, the achievement scores of the two experimental groups were *equally superior* to the achievement scores of the school population as a whole.

---

[1] As might be expected, the creativity measures and I.Q. were not independent, the correlation between the two ranging from .12 to .39.

It was evident at this point that the cognitive functions assessed by our creativity battery accounted for a significant portion of the variance in school achievement. Moreover, since our creative students were not in the top of their class by I.Q. standards, their superiority in scholastic performance places them in the rather suspect category of so-called "over-achievers." This dubious classification often implies that the observed I.Q.-achievement discrepancy is a function of motivational (as opposed to cognitive) variables. It is assumed that the motivational elements pushing

TABLE 1. Means and Standard Deviations of Highly Creative and Highly Intelligent Groups on Experimental Variables

		Total Population* (N=449)	High I.Q. (N=28)	High Creative† (N=24)
I.Q.	X̄	132.00	150.00§	127.00
	s	15.07	6.64	10.58
School	X̄	49.91	55.00§	56.27§
achievement	s	7.36	5.95	7.90
Teacher-	X̄	10.23	11.20‡	10.54
preference ratings	s	3.64	1.56	1.95
Need for	X̄	49.81	49.00	50.04
achievement (T=scores)	s	9.49	7.97	8.39

* For purposes of comparison the scores of each experimental group were extracted from the total population before *t*-tests were computed.
† Two subjects omitted because of incomplete data.
‡ Significant at the .01 level.
§ Significant at the .001 level.

the student to outdo himself, as it were, are linked in varying degree to pathological conditions. We would raise the issue, at least for our present group, of whether it is motivational pathology or intellectual creativity that accounts for their superior scholastic achievement. Indeed, we wonder whether the current studies of cognitive functions other than those as-sessed by standard I.Q. tests do not underscore the need for re-examining the entire concept of "overachievement."

Question 2: Which of the two groups was preferred by teachers?

To answer this question we asked the teachers to rate all students in the school on the degree to which they enjoy having them in class. The ratings of the two groups were then compared with those of the entire school population.

The results, which are shown in Table 1, were again quite clear cut. The high-I.Q. group stands out as being more desirable than the average stu-dent; the high-creative group does not. It is apparent that an adolescent's desirability as a student is not a simple function of his academic standing. Even though their academic performance, as measured by achievement tests, is equal, the high-I.Q. student is preferred over the average student, whereas the high-creative student is not.

This finding leads one to suspect either that there are important variables, in addition to the purely cognitive ones, that distinguish the experimental groups, or that the discriminating cognitive functions are themselves differently preferable in the classroom. Actually, these alternatives should not be posed as either-or, since, as we shall demonstrate, evidence can be adduced which tends to support both points of view.

Question 3: What is the relative need for achievement of the two groups?

In effect, we wanted to know here whether the superior school achievement of the high creatives—by I.Q. standards, their so-called "overachievement"—could be accounted for by differences in motivation to achieve. To answer this question we administered six of the McClelland *n* Achievement stimulus-pictures. Each picture was shown on a screen for 20 seconds, and the subjects were given 4 minutes in which to write their responses. The results are presented in Table 1 and show no differences in Need for Achievement between the high creatives, the high I.Q.'s, and the total school population.

This failure to find differences does not, of course, mean that differences in motives do not exist. We could, and did, use other assessment procedures aimed at identifying motivational and attitudinal differences between the experimental groups. The next group of three questions deals with our efforts in this direction.

Question 4: What are the personal qualities that the two groups prefer for themselves?

Question 5: What is the relation between the personal qualities preferred by the two groups for themselves and the personal qualities they believe teachers prefer for them?

Question 6: What is the relation between the personal qualities preferred by the two groups for themselves and the personal qualities they believe lead to "success" in adult life?

Answers to these questions were obtained from data provided by an instrument called the Outstanding Traits Test. This instrument contains descriptions of thirteen children, each exemplifying some desirable personal quality or trait. For example, one child is described as having the highest I.Q. in the entire school, another as being the best athlete, another as having the best sense of humor, another as being the best looking, and another as being the most creative person in the school.

Our subjects ranked these thirteen children in three ways: (1) on the degree to which they would like to be like them; (2) on the degree to which they believed teachers would like them; (3) on the degree to which they believed people with these various qualities would succeed in adult life.

The entire population of the school almost without exception ranked "social skills" first as the quality in which they would like to be outstanding, and "athletics," "good looks," "high energy level," and "health" last. In view of this very high agreement, we reranked the responses, omitting the uniformly ranked qualities. The findings we are reporting here are on the reranked data.

The high I.Q.'s ranked the qualities in which they would like to be outstanding in the following order: (1) character, (2) emotional stability, (3) goal directedness, (4) creativity, (5) wide range of interests, (6) high

Table 2. Rank-order Correlations among Subsections of the
Outstanding Traits Test

	Subjects	
Components of Correlations	*I.Q.* *(N=28)*	*Creative* *(N=26)*
"Personal traits believed predictive of success" and "personal traits believed favored by teachers"	.62	.59
"Personal traits preferred for oneself" and "personal traits believed predictive of adult success"	.81	.10
"Personal traits preferred for oneself" and "personal traits believed favored by teachers"	.67	—.25

marks, (7) I.Q., (8) sense of humor. The high creativeness ranked the qualities in the following order: (1) emotional stability, (2) sense of humor, (3) character, (4.5) wide range of interests, (4.5) goals directedness, (6) creativity, (7) high marks, (8) I.Q. Most noteworthy here is the extraordinarily high ranking given by the creative group to "sense of humor," a ranking which not only distinguishes them from the high-I.Q. group (who ranked it last) but from all other groups we have studied.

Perhaps the most striking and suggestive of the differences between the two groups are observed in the relation of the qualities they want for themselves to the qualities they believe lead to adult success and the qualities they believe teachers favor.

For the high-I.Q. group, the rank-order correlation between the qualities they would like to have themselves and the qualities making for adult success was .81; for the high creativity group it was .10. For the high-I.Q. group, the correlation between the qualities they would like to have themselves and the qualities they believe teachers favor was .67; for the high-creativity group it was —.25. The data are presented in Table 2.

In effect, where the high-I.Q. adolescent wants the qualities he believes make for adult success and the qualities that are similar to those he believes his teachers like, the high-creative adolescent favors personal qualities having no relationship to those he believes make for adult success and are in some ways the reverse of those he believes his teachers favor.

These findings reflect directly on the answers to two earlier questions —the one on teacher ratings and the one on the relationship between creativity and school achievement. If the desirability of students in the classroom is related to the congruence or discrepancy between their values and their teacher's values, then in the light of the above data it is hardly

TABLE 3. Categorization of Fantasy Productions of Highly Creative and Highly Intelligent Groups

Content-Analysis Categories	High I.Q. (N=28)		High Creativity (N=24)		
	Frequency*	%	Frequency*	%	χ^2
Stimulus-free theme	11	39	18	75	5.31†‡
Unexpected ending	17	61	22	92	5.05‡
Presence of humor	7	25	17	71	9.16§
Presence of incongruity	10	36	17	71	5.06‡
Presence of violence	13	46	18	75	3.27
Playful attitude toward theme	9	32	21	89	14.04§

* Numbers in the frequency column represent the subjects whose fantasy productions fit the corresponding categories.
† Yates correction was applied in the computation of chi squares.
‡ Significant at the .05 level.
§ Significant at the .01 level.

surprising that our high-I.Q. students are favored by teachers more than are our creative students. Furthermore, if the motivational impetus represented by a concern with adult success and a desire to emulate the teacher is absent or weak among creative students, the observed relationship between creativity and school achievement becomes all the more significant.

Question 7: What is the nature of the fantasies of the two groups?

In addition to scoring the *n* Achievement protocols conventionally for the single achievement theme, we analyzed the *total content* of the stories. We first sorted "blind" 47 protocols written by matched creative and noncreative subjects. This blind sorting resulted in only 7 misplacements. Using the categories suggested by this sorting, we then systematically analyzed the protocols of the two experimental groups. The analysis showed striking differences in the fantasy productions of the high I.Q.'s and the high creatives. The creatives made significantly greater use of *stimulus-free themes, unexpected endings, humor, incongruities, and playfulness.* The data are presented in Table 3.

Here, for example, in response to the stimulus-picture perceived most often as a man sitting in an airplane reclining seat returning from a business trip or professional conference, are case-type stories given by a high-I.Q. subject and a high-creative subject.

The high-I.Q. subject: Mr. Smith is on his way home from a successful business trip. He is very happy and he is thinking about his wonderful family and how glad he will be to see them again. He can picture it, about an hour from now, his plane landing at the airport and Mrs. Smith and their three children all there welcoming him home again.

The high-creative subject: This man is flying back from Reno where he has just won a divorce from his wife. He couldn't stand to live with her anymore, he told the judge, because she wore so much cold cream on her face at night that her head would skid across the pillow and hit him in the head. He is now contemplating a new skid-proof face cream.

Or one more, this in response to the stimulus-picture most often perceived as a man working late (or very early) in an office:

The high-I.Q. subject: There's ambitious Bob, down at the office at 6:30 in the morning. Every morning it's the same. He's trying to show his boss how energetic he is. Now, thinks Bob, maybe the boss will give me a raise for all my extra work. The trouble is that Bob has been doing this for the last three years, and the boss still hasn't given him a raise. He'll come in at 9:00, not even noticing that Bob had been there so long, and poor Bob won't get his raise.

The high-creative subject: This man has just broken into this office of a new cereal company. He is a private-eye employed by a competitor firm to find out the formula that makes the cereal bend, sag, and sway. After a thorough search of the office he comes upon what he thinks is the current formula. He is now copying it. It turns out that it is the wrong formula and the competitor's factory blows up. Poetic justice!

Recall that these stories were written in group sessions, often more than a hundred adolescents in the same room, with the maximum writing time 4 minutes per story. "Skid-proof face cream!" "Cereal that will bend, sag, and sway!" It seems to us that it is this ability to restructure stereotyped objects with ease and rapidity—almost "naturally"—that is the characteristic mark of our high-creative as against our high-I.Q. subjects.

One other characteristic is well illustrated by a number of the stories. This is a certain mocking attitude on the part of the creatives toward what they call the "all-American boy"—a theme that is almost never mentioned by the high I.Q.'s. Here, for example, are two responses to the stimulus-picture most often perceived as a high school student doing his homework:

The high-I.Q. subject: John is a college student who posed for the picture while doing his homework. It is an average day with the usual amount of work to do. John took a short break from his studies to pose for the pictures, but he will get back to his work immediately after. He has been working for an hour already and he has an hour's more work to do. After he finishes he will read a book and then go to bed. This work which he is doing is not especially hard but it has to be done.

The high-creative subject: The boy's name is Jack Evans and he is a senior in school who gets C's and B's, hates soccer, does not revolt against convention, and has a girl friend named Lois, who is a typical sorority fake. He is studying when someone entered the room whom he likes. He has a dull life in terms of anything that is not average. His parents are pleased because they have a red-blooded American boy. Actually, he is horribly average. He will go to col-

TABLE 4. Quantity and Quality of Occupations Mentioned by the Experimental Groups on Direct and Indirect Sentence Completion Tests*

Test	Group	Number of Occupations Mentioned			Unusual Occupations	
		Total	$\overline{X}$	s	Number Mentioned	Number of Ss Mentioning
Direct	I.Q. (N=28)	51	1.82†	1.09	6	5‡
	Creative (N=26)	68	2.61†	1.41	24	16‡
Indirect	I.Q. (N=28)	100	3.57‡	1.81	12	10†
	Creative (N=26)	130	5.00‡	1.80	29	17†

* t was used to test differences between means in the fourth column; χ^2 was used to test differences between frequencies in the seventh column.
† Significant at .10 level.
‡ Significant at .01 level.

lege, take over his dad's business, marry a girl, and do absolutely nothing in the long run.

This "anti-red-blooded boy" theme is also quite consistent with the creatives' rejection of "success," which was mentioned earlier.

Question 8: What are the career aspirations of the two groups?

We have just begun the analysis of the data in this area. But this much is already clear—the two groups do indeed give different occupational choices and career aspirations. The data are presented in Table 4.

When the two groups were asked, on sentence-completion type questionnaires, to report the kinds of occupations they would like to have, the high creatives mentioned a significantly greater variety of occupations than did the high I.Q.'s. When the types of occupations mentioned are divided into conventional and unconventional career categories—for example, doctor, engineer, businessman, were classified as conventional; inventor, artist, spaceman, disc jockey, as unconventional—18% of the high I.Q.'s give unconventional career aspirations; 62% of the high creatives give such aspirations.

DISCUSSION

Several conceptual formulations may be adduced to account for the present data. In the context of this conference, however, we suggest that Guilford's factors of convergent and divergent thinking are highly relevant. Discussing the production of tests to assess these factors, Guilford (1957) states:

In tests of convergent thinking there is almost always one conclusion or answer that is regarded as unique, and thinking is to be channeled or controlled in the direction of that answer. . . . In divergent thinking, on the other hand, there is much searching about or going off in various directions. This is most easily seen when there is no unique conclusion. Divergent thinking . . . [is] characterized . . . as being less goal-bound. There is freedom to go off in different directions. . . . Rejecting the old solution and striking out in some new direction is necessary, and the resourceful organism will more probably succeed.

It seems to us that the essence of the performance of our creative adolescents lay in their ability to produce new forms, to risk conjoining elements that are customarily thought of as independent and dissimilar, to "go off in new directions." The creative adolescent seemed to possess the ability to free himself from the usual, to "diverge" from the customary. He seemed to enjoy the risk and uncertainty of the unknown. In contrast, the high-I.Q. adolescent seemed to posses to a high degree the ability and the need to focus on the usual, to be "channeled and controlled" in the direction of the right answer—the customary. He appeared to shy away from the risk and the uncertainty of the unknown and to seek out the safety and security of the known.

Furthermore, and most important, these differences do not seem to be restricted to the cognitive functioning of these two groups. The data with respect to both intellectually oriented and socially oriented behavior are of a piece, and the findings with regard to each of the eight questions can be put into the same conceptual formulation. The high I.Q.'s tend to converge upon stereotyped meanings, to perceive personal success by conventional standards, to move toward the model provided by teachers, to seek out careers that conform to what is expected of them. The high creatives tend to diverge from stereotyped meanings, to produce original fantasies, to perceive personal success by unconventional standards, to seek out careers that do not conform to what is expected of them.

Turning to the social implications of this research and, indeed, of the great bulk of research dealing with creativity, there seems to be little doubt as to which of these two personal orientations receives the greater welcome in the majority of our social institutions. Guilford (1957), who quite clearly perceived this social bias, states:

[Education] has emphasized abilities in the areas of convergent thinking and evaluation, often at the expense of development in the area of divergent thinking. We have attempted to teach students how to arrive at "correct" answers that our civilization has taught us are correct. This is convergent thinking. . . . Outside the arts we have generally discouraged the development of divergent-thinking abilities, unintentionally but effectively.

It is, we believe, unfortunate that in American education at all levels we fail to distinguish between our convergent and divergent talents—or, even worse, that we try to convert our divergent students into convergent students. Divergent fantasy is often called "rebellious" rather than *germinal;* unconventional career choice is often labeled "unrealistic" rather than *courageous.* It is hoped that present work in cognition will help modify some of the stereotypic attitudes regarding children's thinking.

Part VII

THE DEVELOPMENT OF LINGUISTIC SKILLS

FACILITY in the use of language is one of the richest gifts a person can have for interpreting and adjusting to the world around him. As Hayes's report shows, a chimpanzee, lacking sufficient verbal ability to acquire any substantial number of these language-conceptual tools, cannot approximate the higher mental processes of man. Thus, language-conceptual functioning accounts for a large part of those behavior patterns which are unique to *human* adjustment.

The reports included in the present part are representative of some of the more interesting investigations of language-conceptual growth in the psychology of human development. The theoretical paper by Brown helps to clarify some of the current controversies over the direction of language growth during childhood—whether from the concrete toward the abstract, or vice versa. The extremely bright child is, *on the average,* markedly precocious in acquiring the various language skills. However, it is also well known that many social factors may "mask" the individual's underlying language ability. The case study by Rigg is an interesting example of a child with high intellectual ability whose use of language was markedly depressed during the first years of life. The insightful analysis by McCarthy of sex differences in language development and disorders pinpoints many of the social-cultural variables related to the acquisition of language skills.

30

A Chimpanzee Learns to Talk*

Cathy Hayes

Man is the only animal that has developed a well-structured skill of oral communication. This uniquely human talent permits him to instruct, direct, persuade, and entertain other members of his species who have a common language background. Did man first acquire this skill by some biological-social accident, or is it a truly unique gift exclusively restricted to his species at least during this particular period in evolutionary history? Would it be possible to initiate and develop this skill among other higher-order species of animals by utilizing the principles and procedures of modern learning theory? While they were associated with the Yerkes Laboratory of Primate Biology in Orange Park, Florida, Drs. Catherine and Keith Hayes attempted to secure partial answers to such questions by rearing a chimpanzee in their own home, giving her all of the love and attention they would have bestowed on a human infant and child, together with as much tuition as she showed any capacity to profit from. A chimpanzee was regarded as a good choice of subject for this investigation because chimpanzees are generally agreed to be closest to man in the phylogenetic scale of evolutionary ascent. Their efforts to teach the female chimpanzee, Viki, to say simple words like "Mama," "Papa," and "cup" were finally rewarded after months of painstaking instruction that involved manual manipulation of her lips in combination with selective positive reinforcements. The reason for Viki's difficulties in acquiring the skills of oral communication provide grounds for a better understanding of the maturational components in human speech. Dr. Catherine Hayes's engaging comments on their successes and failures in Viki's education provide a charming as well as informative account of one aspect of the socialization process.

Our experiment had been born of scientific curiosity. We had wondered why apes do not learn to talk, since their vocal apparatus is similar to man's,

* From THE APE IN OUR HOUSE by Cathy Hayes. Copyright 1951 by Catherine Hayes. Reprinted by permission of Harper & Row, Publishers.

and since they are able to learn many tasks which are seemingly more difficult than speech. The art of language cannot require very much intelligence, we argued, considering that the human child of one year is already beginning to master it. Why should not an ape, raised in a completely human fashion, acquire human speech? One scientist has marveled that deaf, dumb, and blind children have been taught by "beings they could not see to use language they could not hear." Surely an educated chimpanzee should be able to do as well, we reasoned.

However, while many people have reasoned that apes *should* be able to speak, the literature reveals very few apes who have done so. It is reported that a chimpanzee named Peter who was performing on the stage at the beginning of this century was able to say "mama" on command. A decade later Dr. William Furness, after months of hard work, taught an orangutan to say "papa," and later "cup." These two cases only served to sharpen our curiosity. Why couldn't we teach an ape enough language to communicate its needs and feelings? Why should this not happen easily and spontaneously under the proper conditions?

Viki came into our lives with the usual vocal repertoire of a baby chimpanzee. Although she never cried like a human infant, Viki had two sounds to indicate degrees of distress. She had a shrill scream for the worst possible thing that could happen to her—losing her hold and falling. For any lesser terror she protruded her rubbery lips into a funnel shape and said, "Oo oo, oo oo," apprehensively.

At one week of age, she said, "Uh uh uh uh," to anyone who bent over her crib. Sometimes this greeting came like breathy panting; again it was as explosive as a scolding. At five weeks of age she gave her first "chimp bark" when someone tried to restrain her. It was a sharp "rhow!" not unlike the bark of a small dog. She thereafter used it to express surprise or anger. At fourteen weeks of age she began making chimpanzee "food barks." When she mildly anticipates approaching food, the barks are indistinguishable from her greeting sound, but if she is really interested, the food barks become a staccato stream of "e's" (as in wet), the lips drawn back over the teeth.

All these sounds are standard chimpanzee vocalizations. They are instinctive, appearing in all chimpanzees, and persisting into adulthood with little change. Proof that they are inborn lies in the fact that they appeared without coaching in Viki, who had been raised apart from the other apes. These sounds are called up automatically when the animal is emotionally aroused and are no more under control than the knee jerk reflex. In fact we have come to designate them as Viki's "reflex sounds." Since Viki was being constantly stimulated by the attentions of the experiment, and since her reflex sounds burst out in response to this excitement, she probably made more different sounds than the human infant until the age of three months. So far the baby has only cried, with perhaps a few "coo's" of satisfaction.

Moving Viki's lips to form an "m," as in "mama."

After two weeks, a touch with one finger was sufficient.

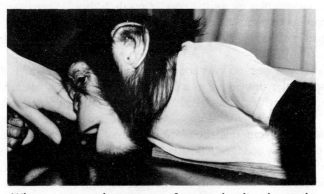

When we stopped putting our finger to her lip, she put her
lip to our finger.

Pictures by Dr. Keith J. Hayes

At about three months, however, a remarkable thing happens to the human baby. Without apparent provocation, it begins to make sounds with its lips: "m's," "p's," and "b's" combined with vowel sounds like "oo" and "ah." Then, obviously delighted, the baby begins to play with other syllables. The stream of chatter grows more varied and more frequent. Driven by an undeniable urge, the child chatters almost constantly. His babbling includes not only the syllables of his native language, but all other known languages as well.

The importance of babbling as a basis for human speech probably cannot be overestimated. To the onlooker, the babbling baby is obviously having fun, but at the same time he is learning to use his lips, tongue, and breathing in different combinations. He is gaining control of these until in time he will be able to produce whatever sound he pleases. He is developing *the motor skill of vocalization.*

When the human is about five months old, he begins repeating his simple syllables and may say something like "mama-mamam ma mah!" or "dada-dada da!" Hearing this, his parents are overjoyed and proudly celebrate "Baby's first word." In response to the attention it gets him, Baby may repeat the word many times, although he will not know what it means until months later. It is here that the deaf child, who has been babbling, becomes mute—when further learning depends on listening to himself and grown-ups.

The normal child learns many words by hearing people speak. By receiving praise for only certain sounds, he concentrates on his native tongue and abandons the incoherent hodgepodge of his early chatter. This then is how a child learns intelligible speech and the whole long hard struggle has its beginnings in the play behavior called babbling.

Apes do not babble—at least not much. As an infant, Viki lay in her crib perfectly silent. If we spoke to her, she made her greeting sound and various monosyllables as well: "poo," "pwah," "bra," "bee," and "wha," but as soon as we went away, she fell silent again. This was the first sad fact we had to face in trying to teach an ape to talk: They babble very very little.

Once she said "ee oo" without provocation, and repeated it several times, apparently enjoying the sound of her own baby voice. At other times she played with "ah ho" and "ba hoo" or simply gargled a bubble of saliva to form a continuous "k." We were delighted and immediately drew false hope from this. Soon Keith's first question every night was "What did Viki say today?" And I would recite the "ah goo's," "pee oo's," and "coo ee's." Some days I had choice stories to tell, about Viki challenging her echo in Mrs. Clarke's spacious living room, or how she addressed a gathering of visitors with a stream of "uuh uh's" so varied in volume and inflection that everyone insisted that Viki was "talking."

But suddenly at four months of age Viki's spontaneous chatter fell off sharply. She still made the chimp noises with which she had come equipped, but we heard less and less of her "babbling," which had never approached the human level in either quantity or variety. Now, at an age when the human child begins making every conceivable sound, Viki grew increasingly silent until in the evening, when Keith asked me what she had said during the day, I found myself replying, "Nothing at all."

There were a few encouraging little flare-ups, like the day she went Hawaiian with remarks like "ah ha wha he" and "ah wha he o." But these exceptions only made the next day's silence more discouraging. Finally the only unprovoked vocalization we heard was a baby-soft "goo ah" as we tucked her in at night. It was so wistful a sound and so small a remnant of her earlier promise that it broke our hearts to hear it.

At this point we realized that Viki would not learn to speak by herself. She would have to be taught by the same methods used when children for one reason or another do not learn to speak naturally. We would literally have to put words into her mouth by shaping her lips and tongue with our fingers to form the various syllables. In special schools throughout the country, speech-handicapped children are thus helped to a more satisfying life. The teacher manipulates the child's mouth parts, demonstrates exhalation of breath, and lo! the child says "ma," "pa," "ee," "oo" or whatever. There are other techniques, including one in which the child watches the teacher's mouth and his own in a mirror and imitates her movements. All methods are long and tedious, but great success often results.

Since Viki's vocalization had become so infrequent, we decided that before starting her training in specific sounds, we would do well to give her some practice in making any sound at all on command. And since it has been suggested that apes lack an "urge to speak," we supplied that urge in the form of food, the standard lure for which Viki had been working all her life. From now on Viki would be required to vocalize for her supper much as a dog is taught to "speak."

She was five months old the day I first held out a portion of milk and said, "Speak!" She looked at the milk, and then at me, and of course said nothing. I waited for fifteen minutes and then rose to leave. As I moved away, worried little "oo oo's" broke the silence and I quickly rewarded her for making the sound. The milk tasted good and Viki sputtered food barks which earned her a few more portions. Then as her appetite wore off, we spent more long moments gazing at the food and each other. I kept saying "Speak!" and Viki kept saying nothing, but each time I rose to leave, she cried, and thus she earned her supper.

Viki was not really speaking *on command*. We were tricking noises out of her by arousing her emotionally in a way which automatically calls up chimpanzee reflex vocalizations. We hoped that in time she would see the connection between making sounds and getting fed, and would then speak of her own free will in order to get fed more quickly. We became very ingenious at making her "speak." We got food barks by stirring the food vigorously, by letting her smell it, and by pretending to eat it ourselves. A sure way to draw her worried "oo oo's" was for me to start leaving the room, a cause for great anxiety since my presence was as vital to her as food at this time. Once Keith and I fed each other until Viki cried for fear that she would get nothing at all to eat. Thus for five discouraging weeks we struggled to make Viki "speak."

Suddenly one day when she was ten months old, she began making a very strange new sound. The first time we heard it we were surprised and vaguely displeased for it was an ugly sound, hoarse and strained. It was like someone whispering "ah" as loudly as possible and with great effort. When Viki said it her face contorted while her eyes assumed the tense preoccupied stare of a stutterer. Then from her lips burst this rasping, tortured "ahhhhh." She then confidently reached for the milk, so that we concluded she had at last gotten the idea of speaking for food. From then on, whenever we told her to speak, she replied with this straining "ahhh," and we came to call it her "asking sound."

Why was it so terribly hard for Viki to make this sound? As we pondered this question, and re-examined our notes on Viki's "speaking" for food, we realized an astonishing fact. Before our coaching *Viki had been completely unable to make any sound at all on purpose.* She made chimp noises, yes, but these were *beyond her control.* They were merely reflex expressions of her feelings. If she could have uttered even these voluntarily, she would have spoken up more quickly to get her food. As it was, she had to be disturbed before these burst out, and except for the chimp noises, Viki had been voiceless!

Why was Viki unable to vocalize when she wanted to, when her supper depended upon it? Perhaps because the ape, for all its humanlike vocal apparatus, lacks the neural organization necessary for voluntary speech; perhaps because she did not babble; perhaps some interdependent combination of the two was responsible for Viki's shortcoming. In any case until now she could not vocalize on purpose. She had lacked *the motor skill of vocalization.*

Now that Viki had this single voluntary utterance, the "asking sound," she used it in many "asking" situations besides meals. She asked to be gotten up in the morning, to be taken off the potty, to be given a towel out of reach, and apparently just for fun. She vocalized thus while doing other unrelated problems. One day while she sat on a chair and I sat on the floor, she said "ahhhh" for one toy after another as I held them up to her. Finally she was completely surrounded by toys. Then she seemed to realize that she had been taken advantage of. With a big saucy grin, she pushed the whole pile down upon me.

Now we were ready to give Viki some words. All we needed to do, we said blithely, was to hold her lips in the proper position, tell her to speak, and out would come human syllables. We hesitated for four more months hoping that her asking sound would become easier for her to make and for us to listen to, but since it did not change, we decided to get on with her first word. We chose "mama" because this is a very primitive sound. It is frequently the child's first word, and some variation of it is an almost universal designation of the female parent. Also it is easy to manipulate the mouth to form an "m", nothing more than pressing the lips together and then releasing them while the subject says "ahhh."

When Viki was fourteen months old Keith began this training at her morning meal. Holding her on his lap, he slipped his hand around her head so that his thumb was on her upper lip and his other fingers cradled her chin. In this position he could work her lips open and shut to form the m. Then with the portion of food in his other hand and Viki in her early morning hunger, he would tell her to speak. As she made her asking sound, he pressed her lips together and apart, and she said, "ma, ma."

She soon got the idea and began to inhibit her asking sound until Keith's fingers were on her lips. If he was too slow in getting ready, Viki often took his hand and put it in the helping position. Then looking up at him, she would strain her lips forward against the manipulating hand and say her "mama." If she was really hungry the word came out fiercely with a thrust of the head. One of our friends commented that this was the first time he had ever heard "mama" said like a cussword. As her hunger decreased at the end of each session, she leaned back on Keith's lap with her taut little tummy in the air and grinned lazily.

In a short time Keith became aware that her lips were moving under his fingers, forming the word by themselves. He stopped helping her then, although he did not yet remove his fingers. Instead he gradually moved them around to the side of her head until only the tip of his index finger was touching her upper lip. Finally even this was removed, and one morning, only two weeks after the mama training started, Viki said her first unaided "mama."

Having established language as her major shortcoming, we had proceeded in an attempt to overcome it by special methods. We had been working for the past month on a new technique with which we hoped to enlarge Viki's vocabulary. We would place her on the table before us, and then perform some simple act, such as clapping our hands or blowing a whistle, meanwhile saying, "Do this!" To get the reward (a jelly bean or a bit of marshmallow) Viki must repeat our actions. At first she merely stared at us blankly, and we had to put her hands through the motions. She picked up the idea quickly, however. At eighteen months of age she was able to "do this" in imitation of six different acts. She could blow the whistle, pat the end of the whistle as she blew it, clap her hands, pound on a can, draw a stick along a toy timpani, or put a wooden bead on a string, whichever task we demonstrated. Later we would introduce sounds and mouth movements into this "Imitation Series." Perhaps after enough sessions of "do this," Viki would be able to "say this" in imitation.

As Viki approached two years of age the Imitation Series paid off by giving her a second word. It had started as a play sound very like a human's Bronx cheer. It was a repulsive sound to us, but we were determined not to discourage any vocal play. Since the original purpose of the Imitation Series had been as an aid in speech training, we had added the cheer to her "do this" repertoire when she was twenty months old. Two months later we began insisting on softer and shorter "p's" with relaxed lips. Finally at twenty-three months, we called for just two "p's" in succession. The result was a whispered but perfectly audible "papa." She immediately used "mama" and "papa" interchangeably in asking for food or favors, since she had no idea what either word meant as yet.

Since the Imitation Series had already proved useful as a language aid by giving Viki her second word, we now added several more sounds and mouth movements to our list of "do this'es." These included a kissing sound, clicking the teeth, sticking out the tongue, "tsk," and "k," which she made by holding her hand over her nose and exhaling with the back of the tongue against the soft palate. We did not teach Viki how to make these sounds; she had previously made them in play as many chimpanzees do. In that respect they are similar to the human child's babbling. However, they are not voiced, but are produced by mouth movements and vibration alone. What we taught her was merely to repeat these sounds back to us when we produced them—which chimpanzees do not ordinarily do.

Since her language deficit involved understanding as well as speaking, we were also coaching her to touch her nose or ear on command, or to give us her hand or her foot when we asked her to. Sometimes she did this excellently; on other days she was completely confused.

At a party she had asked the guests for food and drink by saying "Mama" and "Papa." How were we to give her the idea that I alone was "Mama" and Keith was "Papa" if she must use these words for all needs and toward all people? A few days later I was talking to Henry Nissen about the possibility of using her play sounds to give her more words.

"She has a 'k' sound, which she can repeat after us, and a 'p' as in 'papa.' If we could teach her to string 'k' and 'p' together, we would get a primitive 'cup.' "

Viki had been listening to our conversation, and when she heard us join her two favorite play sounds, she immediately said, "k-p."

"She did it!" Henry exclaimed. "She just *said* cup." He sounded a little indignant as he always does when we underestimate the abilities of any chimpanzee.

Viki's third word immediately became her best. She practiced it by herself, and since her thirst is practically unquenchable, she said "cup" perhaps a hundred times a day. Even at three it is her most dependable word and it definitely means "I want a drink."

Through language, the individual at a very early age begins to acquire knowledge secondhand from teachers, books, and daily communication with other people, infinitely more knowledge than he could ever gain through personal experience. Language conveys not only information, but ideals, traditions, and abstract philosophy. It fosters that cumulative thing —invention. It enables the mechanic and the mathematician to make use of each other's skills. And this has been going on for thousands of years in man.

This aspect of our intellectual life is so characteristic of our species that we take it very much for granted, and seldom appreciate how mentally ineffective each of us would be if we had to function strictly as individuals. Much has been made of the human brain's ability to cope with any change in our environment. But no one man, isolated from birth could do this very well. It is man's collective brain, working over the centuries, which has made us increasingly versatile. It is man's unique ability to communicate knowledge which has led to that peculiarly human product, civilization.

Since apes do not acquire language to any significant extent—not even privileged apes like Viki, who are coached intensively on it, and who could profit a great deal by it—it seems unlikely that apes ever have or ever will develop a civilization.

31

How Shall a Thing Be Called?*

Roger Brown

Mental development as viewed by one group of theorists—for example, the early behaviorists—consists of the gradual acquisition and inte-

* From Roger Brown, "How Shall a Thing Be Called?" *Psychological Review*, 1958, Vol. 65, pp. 14-21. (With permission of the author and the American Psychological Association.)

gration of many relatively specific intellectual skills. The hypothesized trend is from the concrete and particular toward the abstract and general. Opposed to this conception are the theorists who insist that all development occurs by continuous differentiation of already integrated structures and functions. Organismic and Gestalt psychologists who typically adopt such a point of view conceive of mental growth as a gradual differentiation of pre-existing integrated wholes, moving from the general toward an increasing number of particulars. Vocabulary growth in young children proves not to be completely consistent with either of these opposing conceptions. Some concepts move toward the abstract and others toward the specific with increasing maturity. Dr. Brown offers an interesting explanation for these diverse trends in children's verbalizations. In his view adults in the child's linguistic environment verbally categorize objects in a maximally useful way for their purposes and some of these categorizations fall in the middle of the abstract-concrete continuum. Therefore children patterning their verbalizations after this adult model sometimes move toward the concrete and at other times toward the abstract depending on what is maximally useful for their own communication needs.

The most deliberate part of first-language teaching is the business of telling a child what each thing is called. We ordinarily speak of *the* name of thing as if there were just one, but in fact, of course, every referent has many names. The dime in my pocket is not only a *dime*. It is also *money*, a *metal object*, a *thing*, and, moving to sub-ordinates, it is a *1952 dime*, in fact a *particular 1952 dime* with a unique pattern of scratches, discolorations, and smooth places. When such an object is named for a very young child how is it called? It may be named *money* or *dime* but probably not *metal object, thing, 1952 dime,* or *particular 1952 dime*. The dog out on the lawn is not only a *dog* but is also a *boxer*, a *quadruped*, an *animate being;* it is the *landlord's dog*, named *Prince*. How will it be identified for a child? Sometimes it will be called a *dog*, sometimes *Prince*, less often a *boxer*, and almost never a *quadruped*, or *animate being*. Listening to many adults name things for many children, I find that their choices are quite uniform and that I can anticipate them from my own inclinations. How are these choices determined and what are their consequences for the cognitive development of the child?

Adults have notions about the kind of language appropriate for use with children. Especially strong and universal is the belief that children have trouble pronouncing long names and so should always be given the shortest possible names. A word is preferable to a phrase and, among words, a monosyllable is better than a polysyllable. This predicts the preference for *dog* and *Prince* over *boxer, quadruped,* and *animate being.* It predicts the choice of *dime* over *metal object* and *particular 1952 dime.*

Zipf (1935) has shown that the length of a word (in phonemes or syllables) is inversely related to its frequency in the printed language. Consequently the shorter names for any thing will usually also be the most frequently used names for that thing, and so it would seem that the choice of a name is usually predictable from either frequency or brevity. The monosyllables *dog* and *Prince* have much higher frequencies according to the Thorndike-Lorge list (1944) than do the polysyllables *boxer, quadruped,* and *animate being.*

It sometimes happens, however, that the frequency-brevity principle makes the wrong prediction. The thing called a *pineapple* is also *fruit.* *Fruit* is the shorter and more frequent term, but adults will name the thing *pineapple.* Similarly they will say *apple, banana, orange,* and even *pomegranate;* all of them longer and less frequent words than the perfectly appropriate *fruit.* Brevity seems not to be the powerful determinant we had imagined. The frequency principle can survive this kind of example, but only if it is separated from counts like the Thorndike-Lorge of overall frequency in the printed language. On the whole the word *fruit* appears more often than the word *pineapple* (and also is shorter), but we may confidently assume that, when pineapples are being named, the word *pineapple* is more frequent than the word *fruit.* This, of course, is a kind of frequency more directly relevant to our problem. Word counts of general usage are only very roughly applicable to the prediction of what will be said when something is named. What we need is referent-name counts. We don't have them, of course, but if we had them it is easy to see that they would improve our predictions. Bananas are called *banana,* apples *apple,* and oranges *orange* more often than any of them is called *fruit.* The broad frequency-brevity principle predicts that *money* and *dime* will be preferred to *metal object, 1952 dime,* and *particular 1952 dime,* but it does not predict the neglect of the common monosyllable *thing.* For this purpose we must again appeal to imagined referent-name counts, according to which dimes would surely be called *dime* or *money* more often than *thing.*

While the conscious preference for a short name can be overcome by frequency, the preference nevertheless affects the naming act. I have heard parents designate the appropriate objects *pineapple, television, vinegar,* and *policeman;* all these to children who cannot reproduce polysyllabic words. Presumably they use these names because that is what the referents are usually called, but the adult's sense of the absurdity of giving such words to a child is often evident. He may smile as he says it or remark, "That's too hard for you to say, isn't it?"

Some things are named in the same way by all adults for all children.

This is true of the apple and the orange. Other things have several common names, each of them used by a specifiable group of adults to specifiable children. The same dog is *dog* to most of the world and *Prince* in his own home and perhaps on his own block. The same man is a *man* to most children, *policeman* to some at some times, *Mr. Jones* to the neighborhood kids, and *papa* to his own. Referent-name counts from people in general will not predict these several usages. A still more particular name count must be imagined. The name given a thing by an adult for a child is determined by the frequency with which various names have been applied to such things in the experience of the particular adult. General referent-name counts taken from many people will predict much that the individual does, but, for a close prediction, counts specific to the individual would be needed.

The frequencies to which we are now appealing have not, of course, been recorded. We are explaining imagined preferences in names by imagined frequencies of names. It is conceivable, certainly, that some of these specific word counts might be made and a future naming performance independently predicted from a past frequency. Probably, however, such frequencies will never be known, and if we choose to explain particular naming performances by past frequencies we shall usually have to infer the frequency from the performance.

BEYOND THE FREQUENCY PRINCIPLE

A frequency explanation is not very satisfying even when the appeal is to known frequencies. The question will come to mind: "Why is one name more common than another?" Why is a dog called *dog* more often than *quadruped* and, by some people, called *Prince* more often than *dog?* Perhaps it just happened that way, like driving on the right side of the road in America and on the left in England. The convention is preserved but has no justification outside itself. As things have worked out, coins are usually named by species as *dime, nickel,* or *penny* while the people we know have individual names like *John, Mary,* and *Jim.* Could it just as easily be the other way around? Might we equally well give coins proper names and introduce people as types?

The referent for the word *dime* is a large class of coins. The name is equally appropriate to all members of this class. To name a coin *dime* is to establish its equivalence, for naming purposes, with all other coins of the same denomination. This equivalence for naming purposes corresponds to a more general equivalence for all purposes of economic exchange. In the grocery one dime is as good as another but quite different from any nickel or penny. For a child the name given an object anticipates the equivalences and differences that will need to be observed in most of his dealings with such an object. To make proper denotative use of the word *dime* he must be able to distinguish members of the referent category from everything else. When he learns that, he has solved more than a language problem. He has an essential bit of equipment for doing business. The most common names for coins could not move from the species level to the level of proper names without great alteration in our nonlinguistic culture. We should all be numismatists preparing our children to recognize a particular priceless 1910 dime.

Many things are reliably given the same name by the whole community. The spoon is seldom called anything but *spoon,* although it is also a piece of *silverware,* an *artifact,* and a *particular ill-washed restaurant spoon.* The community-wide preference for the word *spoon* corresponds to the community-wide practice of treating spoons as equivalent but different from knives and forks. There are no proper names for individual spoons because their individuality seldom signifies. It is the same way with pineapples, dimes, doors, and taxicabs. The most common name for each of these categorizes them as they need to be categorized for the community's nonlinguistic purposes. The most common name is at the level of usual utility.

People and pets have individual names as well as several kinds of generic name. The individual name is routinely coined by those who are disposed to treat the referent as unique, and is available afterwards to any others who will see the uniqueness. A man at home has his own name to go with the peculiar privileges and responsibilities binding him to wife and child. But the same man who is a one-of-a-kind *papa* to his own children is simply a *man* to children at large. He is, like the other members of this large category, someone with no time to play and little tolerance for noise. In some circumstances, this same man will be given the name of his occupation. He is a *policeman* equivalent to other policemen but different from *bus drivers* and *Good Humor men.* A policeman is someone to "behave in front of" and to go to when lost. To the kids in the neighborhood the man is *Mr. Jones,* unique in his way—a crank, bad tempered, likely to shout at you if you play out in front of his house. It is the same way with dogs as with people. He may be a unique *Prince* to his owners, who feed and house him, but he is just a *dog* to the rest of the world. A homeless dog reverts to namelessness, since there is none to single him out from his species. Dimes and nickels have much the same significance for an entire society, and their usual names are fixed at this level of significance. People and pets function uniquely for some and in various generic ways for others. They have a corresponding variety of designations, but each name is at the utility level for the group that uses it. Our naming practices for coins and people correspond to our nonlinguistic practices, and it is difficult to imagine changing the one without changing the other.

The names provided by parents for children anticipate the functional structure of the child's world.[1] This is not, of course, something parents are aware of doing. When we name a thing there does not seem to be any process of choice. Each thing has its name, just one, and that is what we give to a child. The one name is, of course, simply the usual name for us. Naming each thing in accordance with local frequencies, parents unwittingly transmit their own cognitive structures. It is a world in which *Prince* is unique among dogs and *papa* among men, *spoons* are all alike but different from *forks*. It may be a world of *bugs* (to be stepped on), of *flowers* (not to be picked), and *birds* (not to be stoned). It may be a world in which *Niggers,* like *spoons,* are all of a kind. A division of caste creates a vast categorical equivalence and a correspondingly generic name. *Mr. Jones* and *Mr. Smith* do not come out of racial anonymity until their uniqueness is appreciated.

Adults do not invariably provide a child with the name that is at the level of usual utility in the adult world. An effort is sometimes made to imagine the utilities of a child's life. Some parents will, at first, call every sort of coin *money.* This does not prepare a child to buy and sell, but then he may be too young for that. All coins are equivalent for the very young child in that they are objects not to be put into the mouth and not to be dropped down the register, and *money* anticipates that equivalence. A more differentiated terminology can wait upon the age of storegoing. Sometimes an adult is aware of a child's need for a distinction that is not coded in the English lexicon. A new chair comes into the house and is not going to be equivalent to the shabby chairs already there. A child is permitted to sit on the old chairs but will not be permitted on the new one. A distinctive name is created from the combinational resources of the language. *The new chair* or *the good chair* is not to be assimilated to *chairs* in general.

Eventually, of course, children learn many more names for each thing than the one that is most frequent and useful. Sometimes a name is supplied in order to bring forward an immediately important property of the referent. A child who starts bouncing the coffee pot needs to be told that it is glass. Sometimes a name is supplied to satisfy the child's curiosity as to the place of a referent in a hierarchy of categories. Chairs are *furniture*

---

[1] The equivalence of dimes and their distinctiveness as a class from nickels and pennies is strongly suggested by the appearance of individual coins as well as by their names. Variations in size, weight, and hue are far greater between classes than within a class. This, of course, is because coins are manufactured in accordance with a categorical scheme which is also represented in our names for coins. It is possible, then, that a child might structure coins in the culturally approved manner if he never heard them named at all. However, we cannot be sure that an untutored child would not put all shiny new coins into one class and all the dingy specimens into another. When the referents are not manufactured articles but are such things as dogs, people, flowers, and insects, it is clear that autochthonous factors in perception do not force any single scheme of categorization. The names applied must be the child's principal clue to the locally functioning scheme.

and so are tables; carrots are a *vegetable* but apples are not. Probably, however, both children and adults make some distinction among these various names. *The* name of a thing, the one that tells what it "really" is, is the name that constitutes the referent as it needs to be constituted for most purposes. The other names represent possible recategorizations useful for one or another purpose. We are even likely to feel that these recategorizations are acts of imagination, whereas the major categorization is a kind of passive recognition of the true character of the referent.

THE CHILD'S CONCRETE VOCABULARY

It is a commonplace saying that the mind of a child is relatively "concrete" and the mind of an adult "abstract." The words "concrete" and "abstract" are sometimes used in the sense of subordinate and superordinate. In this sense a relatively concrete mind would operate with subordinate categories and an abstract mind with superordinate categories. It is recorded in many studies of vocabulary acquisition (e.g., Internat. Kinder. Union, 1928; Smith, 1928) that children ordinarily use the words *milk* and *water* before the word *liquid;* the words *apple* and *orange* before *fruit; table* and *chair* before *furniture; mamma* and *daddy* before *parent* or *person;* etc. Very high-level superordinate terms like *article, action, quality,* and *relation,* though they are common in adult speech (Thorndike and Lorge, 1944), are very seldom heard from preschool children (Internat. Kinder. Union, 1928). Presumably this kind of vocabulary comparison is one of the sources of the notion that the child's mind is more concrete than the mind of the adult.[2] However, the vocabulary of a child is not a very direct index of his cognitive preferences. The child's vocabulary is more immediately determined by the naming practices of adults.

The occasion for a name is ordinarily some particular thing. In the naming it is categorized. The preference among possible names seems to go to the one that is most commonly applied to the referent in question. That name will ordinarily categorize the referent so as to observe the equivalences and differences that figure in its usual utilization. There are not many purposes for which all liquids are equivalent or all fruits, furniture, or parents; and so the names of these categories are less commonly used

---

[2] From the facts of vocabulary acquisition alone it is not possible to draw safe conclusions about cognitive development. Such conclusions rely on something like the following set of assumptions. A subject, whether animal or human, is ordinarily credited with a cognitive category when he extends some distinctive response to new instances of the category and withholds it from noninstances. Words, when used to denote new referents, are such a distinctive response. If children speak words they probably can make correct denotative use of them, and so the presence of the word in a child's vocabulary may be taken as evidence that he possesses the category to which the word makes reference. The instances of the category are presumed not to be differentiated by the child unless he uses words for such differentiations. If all

for denotation than are the names of categories subordinate to them. It is true that words like *article, action, quality* and *relation* are rather common in adult written English, but we can be sure that these frequencies in running discourse are not equaled in naming situations. Whatever the purposes for which all articles are equivalent, or all actions or qualities, they are not among the pressing needs of children.

It is not invariably true that vocabulary builds from concrete to abstract. *Fish* is likely to be learned before *perch* and *bass; house* before *bungalow* and *mansion; car* before *Chevrolet* and *Plymouth* (Smith 1926). The more concrete vocabulary waits for the child to reach an age where his purposes differentiate kinds of fish and makes of cars. There is much elaborately concrete vocabulary that is not introduced until one takes courses in biology, chemistry, and botany. No one has ever proved that vocabulary builds from the concrete to the abstract more often than it builds from the abstract to the concrete. The best generalization seems to be that each thing is first given its most common name. This name seems to categorize on the level of usual utility. That level sometimes falls on the most concrete categories in a hierarchy (proper names for significant people), and vocabulary then builds toward the more abstract categories (names for ethnic groups, personality types, social classes). Utility sometimes centers on a relatively abstract level of categorization (fish) and vocabulary then builds in both directions (perch and vertebrate). Probably utility never centers on the most abstract levels (thing, substance, etc.), and so probably there is no hierarchy within which vocabulary builds in an exclusively concrete direction.

In the literature describing first-language acquisition (McCarthy, 1946) there is much to indicate that children easily form large abstract categories. There are, to begin with, the numerous cases in which the child over-generalizes the use of a conventional word. The word *dog* may, at first, be applied to every kind of four-legged animal. It sometimes happens that every man who comes into the house is called *daddy*. When children invent their own words, these often have an enormous semantic range. Wilhelm Stern's (1920) son Gunther used *psee* for leaves, trees, and flowers. He used *bebau* for all animals. Lombroso (Werner, 1948) tells of a child who used *qua qua* for both duck and water and *afta* for drinking glass, the contents of a glass, and a pane of glass. Reports of this

of these assumptions are made it would seem to follow that the direction of vocabulary growth (from subordinate to superordinate or vice versa) reveals the direction of cognitive development. When the assumptions of such an argument are explicitly stated, it is clear that they are too many and too doubtful. Obviously words may be spoken but not understood; objects may be differentiated by nonlinguistic response even though they are not differentiated linguistically. However, it is not my purpose here to quarrel with these assumptions but rather to show that, even when they are accepted, the facts of vocabulary growth do not compel the conclusion that cognitive development is from the concrete to the abstract.

kind do not suggest that children are deficient in abstracting ability. It even looks as if they may favor large categories.

There are two extreme opinions about the direction of cognitive development. There are those who suppose that we begin by discriminating to the limits of our sensory acuity, seizing each thing in its uniqueness, noting every hair and flea of the particular dog. Cognitive development involves neglect of detail, abstracting from particulars so as to group similars into categories. By this view abstraction is a mature rather than a primitive process. The contrary opinion is that the primitive stage in cognition is one of a comparative lack of differentation. Probably certain distinctions are inescapable; the difference between a loud noise and near silence, between a bright contour and a dark ground, etc. These inevitable discriminations divide the perceived world into a small number of very large (abstract) categories. Cognitive development is increasing differentiation. The more distinctions we make, the more categories we have and the smaller (more concrete) these are. I think the latter view is favored in psychology today. While there is good empirical and theoretical support (Gibson and Gibson, 1955; Lashley and Wade, 1946; Lewin, 1935) for the view that development is differentiation, there is embarrassment for it in the fact that much vocabulary growth is from the concrete to the abstract. This embarrassment can be eliminated.

Suppose a very young child applies the word *dog* to every four-legged creature he sees. He may have abstracted a limited set of attributes and created a large category, but his abstraction will not show up in his vocabulary. Parents will not provide him with a conventional name for his category, e.g., *quadruped,* but instead will require him to narrow his use of *dog* to its proper range. Suppose a child calls all elderly ladies *aunt.* He will not be told that the usual name for his category is *elderly ladies* but, instead, will be taught to cut back *aunt* to accord with standard usage. In short, the sequence in which words are acquired is set by adults rather than children, and may ultimately be determined by the utility of the various categorizations. This will sometimes result in a movement of vocabulary toward higher abstraction and sometimes a movement toward greater concreteness. The cognitive development of the child may nevertheless always take the direction of increasing differentiation or concreteness.

The child who spontaneously hits on the category four-legged animals will be required to give it up in favor of dogs, cats, horses, cows, and the like. When the names of numerous subordinates have been mastered, he may be given the name *quadruped* for the superordinate. This abstraction is not the same as its primitive forerunner. The schoolboy who learns the word *quadruped* has abstracted from differentiated and named subordinates. The child he was [previously] abstracted through a failure to differentiate. Abstraction after differentiation may be the mature process, and abstraction from a failure to differentiate the primitive. Needless to say, the abstractions occurring on the two levels need not be coincident, as they are in our quadruped example.

SUMMARY

Though we often think of each thing as having a name—a single name —in fact, each thing has many equally correct names. When some thing is named for a child, adults show considerable regularity in their preference for one of the many possible names. This paper is addressed to the question: "What determines the name given to a child for a thing?" The first answer is that adults prefer the shorter to the longer expression. This gives way to the frequency principle. Adults give a thing the name it is most commonly given. We have now come full circle and are left with the question, "Why is one name for a thing more common than another?"

It seems likely that things are first named so as to categorize them in a maximally useful way. For most purposes Referent A is a spoon rather than a piece of silverware, and Referent B a dime rather than a metal object. The same referent may have its most useful categorization on one level (*Prince*) for one group (*the family*) and on another level (*dog*) for another group (*strangers*). The categorization that is most useful for very young children (*money*) may change as they grow older (*dime* and *nickel*).

With some hierarchies of vocabulary the more concrete terms are learned before the abstract; probably the most abstract terms are never learned first, but it often happens that a hierarchy develops in both directions from a middle level of abstraction. Psychologists who believe that mental development is from the abstract to the concrete, from a lack of differentiation to increased differentiation, have been embarrassed by the fact that vocabulary often builds in the opposite direction. This fact need not trouble them, since the sequence in which words are acquired is not determined by the cognitive preferences of children so much as by the naming practices of adults.

32

Sex Differences in Language Development*

Dorothea A. McCarthy

Although the findings of empirical research are not clear-cut, or even completely consistent in every instance, it appears to be a trustworthy generalization that boys and girls differ substantially in language development. Language disorders and difficulties like stuttering and reading retardation are much more common among boys than girls. What genetic-learning interactions produce these sex differences in the acquisition of language skills? In the following report, Dr. McCarthy presents some interesting and highly plausible hypotheses to account for the general acceleration of language functions among girls as contrasted with boys. These hypotheses are more than sheer speculation because they are derived from the available research evidence by a psychologist who has devoted her productive professional life almost exclusively to research and theory about language growth.

There has appeared in the literature considerable evidence indicating that American white boys are slightly later than girls in practically all aspects of language development which show developmental trends with age (Carmichael [Ed.], 1946, pp. 551-555). These differences seldom are statistically significant, but the careful observer cannot ignore the amazing consistency with which these small differences appear in one investigation after another, each being conducted by a different experimenter, employing different techniques, different subjects, and sampling different geographical populations.[1]

Sex differences in favor of girls are present as soon as children begin to talk; that is, at about the age of onset of true language as distinct from prelinguistic utterances. Irwin and Chen present curves showing the number of speech sounds from birth to 2½ years, which are practically

---

* From Dorothea A. McCarthy, "Some Possible Explanations of Sex Differences in Language Development and Disorders," *Journal of Psychology,* 1953, Vol. 35, pp. 155-160. (With permission of the author and The Journal Press.)

[1] A recent investigation by Anastasi and D'Angelo (*J. Genet. Psychol.,* 1952) reports a sex difference in favor of boys among five-year-old Negroes.

identical for the two sexes for the first year of life, but these curves begin to diverge in favor of the girls in the second year of life when true speech emerges.

Although the developmental differences between the sexes are small in magnitude, they seem to be of considerable importance for the later acquisition of the more complex and secondary language forms for the effect seems to be cumulative. All statistics on the incidence of language disorders, particularly on the incidence of stuttering and of reading disabilities, reveal that language disturbances occur much more frequently among boys than among girls in most American reports (Bennett, 1938; Loutitt, 1947; Yedinack, 1949). Series of case studies of language disorders show that rather than being evenly divided between the sexes, from 65 to 100 per cent of such disorders occur among boys. The roots of the sex differentiation in language development must be sought in early infancy, for the differences appear at an extremely early age and the vital importance of imitative babbling in the establishment of language patterns is well recognized. Stengel (1947) has stressed especially the importance of the so-called "echo-reaction" stage in which the baby babbles back to the mother approximations of the sounds made by her. This is pleasant and satisfying to the infant and is considered to facilitate identification with the adult who provides the language model. Wyatt (1949) also emphasizes the importance of the emotional quality of the early mother-child relations and the fact that the learning of the mother's speech is achieved through a process of unconscious identification. The mother is thus the child's first language teacher and as such is the first mediator of this vital cultural heritage.

The usual environmental situation in our culture is somewhat different for the boy infant than for the girl infant. Children of both sexes are usually cared for by, and have the constant companionship and speech model of, the mother. This experience in early language development is likely to be more satisfying for the girl than for the boy infant as she identifies more readily with the mother. The boy baby, on the other hand, needs to identify with, and to imitate, the father's speech, of which he is likely to hear a minimum in our culture. When he does hear the father's speech and tries to imitate it, the experience must be much less satisfying for him than for the girl who can produce a fairly satisfactory echo-reaction to the mother's voice. The tremendous difference in voice quality of the adult male whose voice has changed with the attainment of maturity, and the small high-pitched voice of the boy infant certainly must make the echo-reaction stage much less satisfying for the male infant. It may even be quite confusing and perhaps even fear-producing, since loud sounds often produce fear in the young child. It may be argued that girls also experience the father's voice, about as much as do boys, but they probably feel less need to imitate and to identify with him than do boys for they are already making good progress in echoing the speech of the mother, and are finding considerable security and satisfaction in so doing. It is conceivable therefore, if this interpretation is correct, that contacts with the father would be less disturbing and less confusing to girl than to boy infants.

The writer has elsewhere (1946-47, 1949) pointed out that language disorders in older children seem to be due to emotional insecurity based on attitudes of parental rejection. A second hypothesis which could account at least in part for the observed sex difference in language is that it may be due to differential parental attitudes towards the two sexes. Adoption agencies in the American culture usually have many more requests for girls than for boys for placement. If the same sex preference is present among true parents, that seems evident in instances in which prospective parents have their choice, it is reasonable to assume that girl babies are more often welcomed, and hence are given greater warmth, affection, and security from the very beginning, than are boys in our present day society.[2]

One of the reasons which may account for this preference is that boys are usually more active physically, and hence more difficult to control. Goodenough (1931) has shown that boys have more frequent and longer anger out-bursts than girls, that they are the objects of more disciplinary measures, and are usually handled more harshly than are girls. This would seem to indicate that they are more often frustrated by parental treatment, and must therefore experience a greater degree of emotional insecurity, which could lay the groundwork for later language disabilities as well as other behavior disorders.

If, as was pointed out above, the boy child finds less satisfaction in echoing the mother's speech, he will presumably repeat the activity less often than the girl, who, as pointed out above, finds such activity more pleasant. Thus, there may be a differential in amount of linguistic practice, and in the degree of satisfaction derived therefrom by the two sexes in our culture which may tend to make a cumulative difference in experience in favor of girls.

In our culture, the boy is encouraged in active games, and even at the nursery age, when he is acquiring language skill, he is sent outdoors to play more often than the girl. This separates him from further adult linguistic stimulation. Boys are also more likely to engage in play with blocks and wheel toys and objects low in conversational value. Girls on the other hand are encouraged in indoor play with dolls, household toys, and table-play which have been shown to be of high conversation value (Van Alstyne, 1932). Girls too are more likely to be permitted around the kitchen and other centers of household activity, and thus to have more constant adult attention. Girls are then more likely to be found within

[2] Studies of minority groups representing cultures which welcome boys should throw further light on this problem.

question-asking range of the mother and thus are more likely than their brothers to enjoy maternal contact and linguistic stimulation.

As the child finds satisfaction in echoing back the mother's utterances, the mother in turn finds it satisfying to engage in vocal play with the child. The girl child, however, being better able to identify with the mother, will probably be more responsive than the boy, so that the mother again may unconsciously give more linguistic practice to the girl than she does to the boy. Thus, it is conceivable, if these hypotheses are correct, that the ground-work is laid for greater conversation and companionship between mother and daughter than between mother and son. Such factors certainly seem worth considering in attempting to interpret the dynamics of the sex differences which are found. It becomes more understandable, in the light of such factors, why boys often interpret maternal behavior as rejecting and hence more of them feel insecure in their family relationship than is the case among girls.

There are of course some instances of language disorders among girls. One may ask in the light of the above interpretations, how the relatively rare occurrence of language disabilities among girls can be accounted for. In the writer's clinical experience girls with language disorders have always had severely disturbed relationships with the mother so that the identification with the mother through language probably never occurred or was seriously distorted. Usually the relationships with the father were either nonexistent or contacts were so infrequent or of such poor quality that they in no way compensated for the deprivation of maternal care, affection, and opportunity for identification.

Many language disorders are first noticed at the time of school entrance. Retardation and poor articulation which have been tolerated within the family circle become obvious. Unfavorable comparisons with other children contribute still further to the insecurity of already insecure children. At this time, adjustment must be made, not only to a new group of one's peers, often in a highly competitive situation, but also to another adult, usually another female, who becomes identified in the child's mind with the mother. When the mother-child relations in the preschool period have been of a wholesome quality, and a secure child enters the school situation, little difficulty arises. However, as has been outlined above, the average boy is more likely to enter school feeling somewhat insecure and rejected and to have a less healthy relationship with his mother than the average girl. His predispositions therefore toward the female teacher are more likely to be fraught with a greater degree of anxiety, which may interfere with effective learning; and hence he is somewhat more likely to have difficulty with reading and other verbal skills in the academic situation than the average girl. Being about six months less mature linguistically than the average girl with whom he now has to compete in oral language, he is slower in beginning reading. His performance with the primer is likely therefore to be frustrating to the teacher whose aim is often centered on teaching reading skills early, and her behavior toward the boy is therefore likely to be one of further rejection, contributing still more to his insecurity. The basic anxiety so accumulated interferes with effective learning and the stage is set for the problem or typical boy behavior which Wickman (1928) found so frustrating to teachers. If the child happens to encounter a teacher who is not well adjusted, who lacks insight into his behavior and into her own attitude, she will behave in what Anderson (1939) describes as a "dominative" rather than an "integrative" way, and the vicious circle of frustration and aggression in the school situation becomes well established, and another non-learner in verbal skills, a potential problem child, is added to the rolls. It should also be remembered that the physical limitations of the classroom are undoubtedly more frustrating to the naturally more active boy than they are to the girl who is accustomed to and accepts sedentary play.

It is always possible to postulate differences in native endowment to account for the sex differences observed. Yet, it does not seem as though this explanation should be resorted to until account has been taken of the various environmental factors which certainly are operative in present day American culture. These interpretations are offered as tentative explanations which may operate as indicated in the long run when averages for large numbers of cases are considered. They are advanced in an effort to harmonize evidence from genetic studies on the one hand, and from various clinical investigations on the other hand. They must not be construed as operating in every individual case, for the individual differences within each sex group are indeed great, and hence almost everyone can point to individual cases of boys who are accelerated and girls who are retarded for their ages in language. It seems to the writer, however, that such dynamisms as have been outlined·in this paper probably operate in the directions indicated with sufficient frequency to account for the small differences found in the averages for the two sexes at early ages in the genetic studies, and for the resultant cumulative effects observed in the clinical data at later ages.

33

Language Growth and Intellectual Status[*]

Melvin G. Rigg

The size of a child's vocabulary is one of the best single indicators of how "bright" he is, at least as intelligence is commonly measured. Mentally dull children are typically retarded in the acquisition of verbal concepts, while exceptionally bright children usually demonstrate their intellectual precocity by using abstract words at an early age. Professor Leta S. Hollingworth found that children above 180 IQ on the Stanford-Binet Intelligence Scale almost invariably demonstrated their intellectual superiority through accelerated vocabulary growth. Since the positive relationship between vocabulary growth and intellectual development is generally recognized by parents and teachers, adults frequently estimate a child's intellectual status from his spontaneous use of verbal concepts. That this may be a hazardous practice, leading to quite erroneous conclusions, is clearly demonstrated in the following report by Dr. Rigg. The child's spontaneous oral vocabulary is related to a number of psychological variables of which intelligence is only one.

Size of vocabulary has been regarded as the best single indication of intelligence. The failure of a child to develop normally in this respect would consequently appear to be a very bad sign. Occasionally, however, we find a child who breaks all the rules, and Carolyn is a case in point.

At the age of two Carolyn could say only thirteen words, as follows: bread; butter; bye; daddy; gak (milk); here; is; it; mother; there; wow-wow; Gaga (Arthur); Gak (Jack).

The writer has made little attempt to indicate how these words actually sounded. The child's pronunciation was extremely "dutchy," and the parents often despaired of being able to reduce it to exact phonetic symbols. The pronunciation did not improve greatly until she started to school

[*] Adapted and abridged from Melvin G. Rigg, "A Superior Child Who Would Not Talk," *Child Development*, 1938, Vol. 9, pp. 361-362. (With permission of the author and the Society for Research in Child Development.)

at the age of six, when, under the direction of an excellent primary teacher, rapid progress was made.

Whether this faulty pronunciation was connected with the abnormally slow vocabulary development is an interesting question. No other explanation suggests itself. Carolyn is the daughter of a college professor. The mother was before her marriage also a college professor. Carolyn has a brother two years older, and has always played with other children. The home in no way presents an environment which is unusual.

The full extent of Carolyn's early vocabulary deficiency can be appreciated only by a comparison with the accomplishments of other two-year-olds. After a search of the literature, the writer found a total of thirty-three cases of two-year-old children for whom vocabulary counts have been made. These vocabularies range from 5 to 1400 words. The mean is 520 and the mid score is 507. Among these thirty-three cases, Carolyn ranked next to the lowest.

These thirty-three counts represent attempts to list the actual words in each child's vocabulary. It is true that the different totals are not directly comparable, since each investigator formulated his own rules as to what should constitute a separate word. But this consideration can scarcely cover up a discrepancy between 13 and 520 words! It is also true that most of these children were very superior in intelligence, sons and daughters of college professors, and living in homes that were above average from the intellectual point of view. But since Carolyn belonged in this class herself, the point furnishes no excuse for her poor showing.

Smith, in attempting to estimate the total vocabularies of twenty-five two-year-olds by means of a vocabulary test, found a mean of 272 words. These children are presumably less brilliant than most of those for whom total counts have been made, although they were considered somewhat above average. But their vocabulary development was still far above that of Carolyn.

During her third year Carolyn made rapid progress, and at the age of three had a spoken vocabulary of 652 words. However, for nineteen published vocabulary counts of three-year-old children, the mean is 1230 and the mid score, 1139. The range is 48 to 2282. Smith, using a vocabulary test, estimated the average vocabulary of 20 three-year-olds to be 896 words. Drever reports four slum children as averaging 376 words. Carolyn was superior to these slum children, but was inferior to Smith's cases and far behind most of the cases for whom total vocabulary counts have been made.

Even at the age of three, however, Carolyn gave evidence of intellectual superiority. She was given the Stanford-Binet test (1916 form) and earned an I.Q. of 133, passing all of the three-year tests, four tests at year four, and two tests at year five.

At the age of four, Carolyn had a spoken vocabulary of 1019 words.

Twelve published vocabulary counts at this age have a mean of 2092 words, a mid score of 1818, and a range from 1019 to 4200, Carolyn's total being the lowest. Smith's 26 four-year-olds were estimated to have an average vocabulary of 1540 words. Their average I.Q. was 109. Drever reports five four-year-old slum children to average 451 words. Carolyn's vocabulary development was still relatively poor, especially in view of her intelligence rating.

No further vocabulary counts were made for Carolyn. She started to school at the age of six. The next spring, at the age of six years, ten months, she was again given the Stanford-Binet test (1916 form). She passed all the tests at year eight, four tests at year nine, two tests at year ten, and two at year twelve, making an I.Q. of 139. Her performance in vocabulary was at the norm for year eight. This fact indicates that her early vocabulary deficiency had by this time been made up. Some two months later she was retested by a clinician at the Ohio State University, and earned an I.Q. of 137. As a result of superior work in Grade One, she was given a double promotion to Grade Three. She adjusted herself to this change and has continued to earn very satisfactory marks.

At the age of eight years, ten months, Carolyn was again given the Stanford-Binet test (1937 revision). Her I.Q. was 147. This gain was of course to be expected, since the 1937 revision gives higher ratings to superior children. At this time she knew 20 words of the revised vocabulary, the norm for average adults! Her vocabulary development was indicated as definitely superior.

CONCLUSION

In the opinion of the writer, two important deductions can be made from this case. First, even an extreme deficiency of vocabulary development at two years of age does not necessarily indicate deficiency of intelligence. Second, it does not necessarily even indicate a relative vocabulary deficiency in later years.

Part VIII

GROWTH OF SOCIAL VALUES AND ATTITUDES

PSYCHOLOGISTS have adopted many different theoretical approaches to the problem of describing and predicting social values and attitudes. In Freud's theoretical system this problem is stated in terms of the dynamic principles of ego and super-ego development. In modern behaviorism the problem is formulated with the aid of a series of theoretical constructs like secondary needs and secondary reinforcement. Regardless of such theoretical differences there is unanimity of opinion among psychologists that social attitudes and values are of fundamental importance in understanding the complexities of human behavior and adjustment.

The studies included in this part are, by and large, empirical in design. They have definite implications for social planning and educational guidance. They also demonstrate the difficulties involved in obtaining clear-cut generalizations in those areas of human behavior where ethical and moral norms enter.

The first paper, by Harris and his associates, not only describes a scale for the measurement of responsibility in children, but presents some findings that run counter to many preconceptions held by parents as to how a sense of responsibility may be fostered. The assignment of home duties and chores, commonly practiced with the intention of promoting responsibility, proved to be unrelated to attitudes of responsibility. Instead the most responsible child seems to be the generally well-adjusted child. Responsibility, like other complex traits, is interwoven with other facets of personality, rather than being a simple, relatively unitary characteristic. In this respect, it is an array of attitudes similar to attitudes taken toward occupations (see the papers by Kulberg and Owens and by Rosenberg in Part XI) in reflecting a general behavioral predisposition (of the type labeled personality) which has complex and diffuse origins.

The paper by Radke-Yarrow and her associates reports data which have direct relevance to the early social differentiations of children. Many children resolve related adjustment problems by accepting the social attitudes and values of adults and older children. Thus both the "good" and the "bad" of the older generation's social values are transmitted *with little change* to the younger generation. Social reinforcement—reward and punishment—is doubtless an important factor in this process of transmission.

The next paper, by Adelson and O'Neil, shows the different processes involved in the social development of adolescents. This paper is especially interesting because of the conceptual and analytical procedures used by the investigators to make inferences about the dimensions of social maturing and acculturation.

The next paper is a classic study by Hartshorne and May of character organization and development. This paper illustrates the difficulties involved in transmitting *only the culturally desirable* social values and attitudes to young children. Ethical ideals are based on a variety of specific experiences. Without careful guidance these experiences may deviate markedly from the verbal models of ethical conduct provided by adults. Anderson and Dvorak's results show another difficulty which is typically encountered in the transmission of culturally desirable values and attitudes. Although indoctrinated by parents at an early age, young people "extract" their ethical ideals from their own experiences. These social values may not be completely in harmony with the attitudes of adults whose experiences were drawn from a different social period or who exhibit differences in personalities reflecting a variety of changes associated with age. Anderson and Dvorak's data tend to document this conflict in values between different generations. The paper by Schaie shows that at least one dimension of adult personality (rigidity-flexibility) is probably an important correlate of *functional* intelligence during the adult years, as well as an important influence on the next generation through the relative acceptance of changing trends in child-rearing practices.

34

Personality Characteristics of Responsible Children*

Dale B. Harris, A. M. Rose, Kenneth E. Clark, and Frances Valasek

Most parents naturally hope that their children will grow up to be responsible citizens—responsible for their own maintenance and welfare and willing to assume some responsibility for the well-being of their associates and for the improvement of general social conditions. Some years ago parents thought these ends might best be reached by "easing" the child into the responsibilities of the mature adult. Children were assigned home duties that were gradually increased in number and significance for the welfare of the family as the children grew older. In the days when the larger society was less complex and the family more nearly dominated the socialization process, this approach may have been reasonably successful. However, such practices are no longer sufficient. In the following report, Dr. Harris and his collaborators demonstrate something of the structural complexity of the concept of responsibility and also show that the responsible child is the generally well-adjusted child who has enjoyed parental trust and faith, shared in many activities at home, participated in making family decisions, and met on many occasions both the approval and the disapproval of his parents. Rearing a responsible and mentally healthy child cannot be accomplished merely through bench-mark practices like assigning home duties and chores. Rather it involves meaningful and rewarding interactions with parents who care and take the time and pains to influence their children in all the ways that will occur to alert, conscientious, and well-informed parents.

* From Dale B. Harris, A. M. Rose, Kenneth E. Clark, and Frances Valasek, "Personality Differences between Responsible and Less Responsible Children," *Journal of Genetic Psychology*, 1955, Vol. 87, pp. 103-109. (With permission of the senior author and The Journal Press.)

In other papers (Harris, Clark, Rose & Valasek, 1954) we have described two measures of responsible attitudes and behavior in children and adolescents and have shown that "responsibility," as these scales measure it, has little or no relation to home chores and duties. This lack of relationship was demonstrated by an item analysis of a home duties questionnaire supplied by highest and lowest scoring children on the two measures of responsibility. The relationship of responsibility to personality characteristics is of interest. Is responsibility associated with qualities from a mental hygiene point of view—lack of emotional tension, good family adjustment, favorable adjustment ratings made by teachers, or is responsibility associated with rigidity, anxiety, overweaning, need for recognition, com-

TABLE 1. Numbers of Children Included in This Analysis

	Boys	Girls	Totals
Low Responsibility	163	167	330
High Responsibility	137	133	270
Total	300	300	600

pulsive attention to details, characteristics which might not be so satisfactory from a mental hygiene viewpoint?

A number of other measures were available for the town and rural children in the sample. These measures (identified in Table 2) included a recreational activities inventory, a teacher's rating scale of 18 characteristics, a family adjustment inventory, an inventory composed of a variety of interest and attitude items which have been found to discriminate between delinquents and non-delinquents, and various socio-economic and home background information items.

Using two criterion measures, as described in another paper (Harris, et al., 1954-b), children high and low in responsibility were identified.

From the original sample of slightly under 3,000 children representing rural and small town environments in Minnesota, deviate quarters were segregated, amounting to about 1,500 children in all. These deviate quarters, high and low, were split at random to provide two criterion groups (one high and one low) for the validation of certain scales, and two additional cross-validation groups. The present study is based on the responses of children in these cross-validation samples. Table 1 gives the number of children in this set of sub-samples.

Significant differences between mean scores of these groups were found for many of the personality measures referred to above, indicating some association between those measures and "responsibility," as measured by our two scales. The *t* values are listed in Table 2, by instrument.

Table 2 does not, of course, show the mean scores of the responsible and of the less responsible groups. Rather uniformly, these subgroup means

TABLE 2. *t* Values Calculated for Differences Between Mean Scores of High and Low Responsibility Children, for a Number of Personality Measures

	Boys *t*	Girls *t*
General background data		
IQ (when available, Otis Group test)	8.04	9.00
Socio-Economic Index (Sewell, 1943)	3.58	5.54
Father's Education	2.04	2.42
Mother's Education	2.13	3.27
Play Activities—(Lehman and Witty Play Quiz)		
Total number of different activities	1.73	2.98
Solitary Activities	2.98	1.74
Competitive Activities	1.94	4.13
Activities requiring strenuous physical exertion	2.77	3.05
Anti-social play activities	0.50	1.57
Family Adjustment Scale (Brown, *et al.*, 1947)		
Common participation, parent and child	3.76	5.42
Approval-disapproval experienced by the child	7.37	7.33
Regularity in the home	7.95	9.25
Confidence shared, parent and child	5.70	7.20
Sharing in family decisions	5.48	4.30
Parents' trust and faith	6.49	5.98
Child's acceptance of the home standards	6.93	6.77
Parents' attitudes towards child's peer group activities	5.91	5.26
Interparent relations	9.46	9.86
Total score on Family Adjustment	9.46	9.82
Interest-attitude test items—selected from Pressey's Scale by Durea (1937, 1941)		
Number of delinquent items checked as "liked"	3.98	3.40
Number of delinquent "fears"	5.25	5.13
Number of delinquent "wrongs"	2.09	3.48
Number of delinquent items checked as "admired"	2.14	3.09
Total delinquent items marked	4.21	4.99
Number of non-delinquent items checked as "liked"	.34	1.28
Number of non-delinquent "fears"	1.67	3.66
Number of non-delinquent "wrongs"	1.41	1.09
Number of non-delinquent items checked as "admired"	2.97	2.45
Total non-delinquent items checked	1.35	1.15
Moral Judgment items (Bartlett & Harris, 1936)		
Socially approved attitudes held	2.81	2.65
Socially disapproved attitudes held	2.83	3.17
Ratio of approved to disapproved items	2.73	2.77
Psychoneurotic items (Bartlett & Harris, 1936)	8.53	7.28
Pupil profile form (Anderson, 1952)		
(a linear-type rating scale, composed of 20 items)	15.60	13.43

$$\begin{aligned} p\ .01 \quad & t = 2.61 \\ p\ .05 \quad & t = 1.98 \\ p\ .10 \quad & t = 1.65 \end{aligned}$$

"straddle" the general mean for a particular instrument. Invariably, the subgroup means depart from the general mean in the expected direction, i.e., the responsible children obtain a score "higher" or "more desirable" than the general mean, whereas the reverse is true for less responsible children. There are a few exceptions. While responsible and less responsible children are differentiated (.05 probability level) with respect to both fathers' and mothers' education, the mothers of both responsible and less responsible children exceed the general mean of mothers in amount of education. The same is true for fathers, where the subgroup means for fathers of high and low boys, and high and low girls, are at or exceed the general mean for fathers.

One or two additional "reversals" are worthy of mention. Although high and low responsibility children are differentiated on the play activities report, the direction of the differences is not always in keeping with quantity of activities. Responsible girls engage in significantly fewer total activities. Responsible children, both boys and girls, engage in fewer competitive activities in relation to total, and fewer activities requiring physical exertion in relation to total than do less responsible children. Responsible boys (but not girls) engage in fewer solitary activities than do the less responsible.

Items from the Pressey Interest Attitude Scales (1933), shown by Durea (1937, 1941) to differentiate between delinquent and non-delinquent children, were included in the measures given these children. Items picked more often by non-delinquents (marked as "non-delinquent" in Table 2) seldom reach the same levels of significance in differentiating between responsible and less responsible children as do items picked more often by delinquents (marked "delinquent" in Table 2). This fact also suggests the way in which "responsibility" may be related to adjustment, since negatively stated items, or items of less socially acceptable content, have been shown to be more powerful in discriminating degrees of adjustment than do positively stated items (Rundquist, 1935).

The family adjustment scale shows highly significant differences between responsible and less responsible children. The responsible child reports a home which is desirably oriented toward him and shows constructive attitudes in return. Certainly, responsibility as measured in this study is more associated with the quality of personal and emotional relationships between parent and child than it is with number of home chores (Harris, *et al.,* 1954-b).

It appears that responsibility as measured in this study, even though the measures were validated against carefully prepared definitions, phrased in terms of social behavior (Harris, *et al.,* 1954-a), is closely associated with general emotional and personal adjustment.

This raises the question as to the specific personality components of "responsibility," and to determine these it seemed desirable to use a technique like the Guttman scale analysis (1950) to determine the unidimensional components of the two measures of responsibility. The first step was for two persons independently to classify the items into what appeared to be meaningful categories relevant to personality. While the two persons set up different numbers of classes and gave them different names, there was a high degree of relationship in the item content they gave the assumed scales. The Guttman process was then applied to each of the assumed scales.

We find that the 42 original items of the "citizenship" measure of responsibility fell into seven categories and that five of these categories are scalable if terms are dropped. From this we can conclude that the Citizen-

TABLE 3. Scales Emerging from the Citizenship Measure of Responsibility

A. *Lack of group-centeredness* (Reproducibility=89%)
   No.
   5   We ought to let Europe get out of its own mess. (disagree=1 point)
   9   Every citizen should take the time to find out about current events even if it means giving up some spare time. (agree=1)
   20   A person who does not vote is not a good citizen. (agree=1)
   31   When a person does not tell all his income in order to get out of paying some of his taxes, it is just as bad as stealing money from the government. (agree=1)
   33   School teachers complain a lot about their pay, but they get as much as they deserve. (disagree=1)
   38   We ought to worry about our own country and let the rest of the world take care of itself. (disagree=1)
   43   Police cars should be specially marked so that you can always see them coming. (disagree=1)

B. *Conformity to social norms* (Reproducibility=87%)
   No.
   4   I would sneak into a movie if I could do it without being caught. (disagree=1)
   8   In school I am sometimes sent to the principal for being bad. (disagree=1)
   10   I have played hookey from school. (disagree=1)
   32   I have never been in trouble with the law or police. (agree=1)
   35   My parents often object to the kind of boys and girls I go around with. (disagree=1)

C. *Personal independence* (Reproducibility=89%)
   No.
   16   I usually work things out for myself rather than get someone to show me how. (agree=1)
   28   When I work on a committee, I like to run things. (agree=1)
   29   I find out what others think before I make up my mind. (disagree=1)
   34   In school my conduct gets me into trouble. (disagree=1)

TABLE 3. (continued)

D. *Possession of constructive interests* (Reproducibility=88%)
   No.
   2   I like to read about science. (agree=1)
   3   I would like to be an auto racer. (disagree=1)
   15   I sometimes do something dangerous just for the thrill of it. (disagree=1)
   19   When I get bored I like to stir up some excitement. (disagree=1)
E. *Strong and "non-authoritarian" personality* (Reproducibility=88%)
   No.
   1   I am afraid to see a doctor about sickness or injury. (disagree=1)
   11   Other children often make mean remarks about me behind my back. (disagree=1)
   12   It is hard for me to act natural in a group. (disagree=1)
   13   When someone does me a wrong, I want to pay him back if I can. (disagree=1)
   18   I feel that I have often been punished when I didn't deserve it. (disagree=1)
   21   I would like to wear clothes that cost a lot. (disagree=1)
   27   Everything is turning out just like the Bible says it will. (agree=1)
   30   Watching a fire gives me a special kind of thrill. (disagree=1)

ship measure contains at least five unidimensional scales. The assigned titles of these, the specific items making them up and their coefficient of reproducibility are presented in Table 3. The names of the scales are, of course, arbitrary, but we have found it meaningful to give the following names to these five dimensions of responsibility: lack of group-centeredness, conformity to social norms, personal independence, possession of constructive interests, strong and "non-authoritarian" personality. None of these scales was found to scale with any other into a larger scale. They rather represent distinct dimensions of personality describing the socially responsible child. Care should be exercised before generalizing from a child's position on one dimension to his position on another dimension.

In the same way the items in the "Teacher's Check List" were examined in terms of manifest content and four assumed scales were postulated. By applying the Guttman analysis, all four of these classes of items were found to scale, but three of the scales were found to form a single large scale. Thus two scales emerged from the Teacher's Check List; their names, item content, and coefficient of reproducibility are listed in Table 4. We conclude that the "Teacher's Check List" contains two dimensions, one representing the child's dependability in carrying out a task, and the other representing the extent to which the child's attitude to others and to cultural values conforms to the expectations of the larger society.

TABLE 4. Scale Emerging From the Teacher's Check List
Measure of Responsibility

A. *Dependableness* (Reproducibility=93%)

No.

20   Keeps appointments. (check=1)

21   Dawdles at his work. (no check=1)

22   Is very conscientious. (check=1)

23   Is usually late for appointments. (no check=1)

26   Always forgets to do assigned homework. (no check=1)

27   Can never be depended on to complete a job. (no check=1)

28   Must be continually prompted to finish a task. (no check=1)

29   Takes the initiative in assuming responsibility. (check=1)

30   Gets down to work without being prodded by others. (check=1)

33   Finishes assigned work whether checked up on or not. (check=1)

34   When assigned homework, does only part of the assignment. (no check=1)

36   Sees jobs to be done and does them without waiting to be asked. (check=1)

37   Feels a strong obligation to finish well whatever he undertakes. (check=1)

40   Carries through an undertaking about as well as others of his age. (check=1)

41   Takes his share of the burdens in planning as well as in executing plans. (check=1)

42   Quits work as soon as the "whistle blows," even in the middle of a job. (no check=1)

44   Works steadily and does not bother other people while teacher is out of room. (check=1)

46   People soon learn it is useless to assign him important tasks even if he is willing to accept them. (no check=1)

48   Likely to drop or neglect a difficult responsibility without bothering to notify anyone or find a substitute. (no check=1)

B. *Conformity to expectations of larger society* (Reproducibility=96%)

24   Takes good care of school property. (check=1)

31   Is careless about employer's and school's property. (no check=1)

32   Is quite responsible for his age. (check=1)

39   Lets others do the work he has agreed to do for his class or club. (no check=1)

35

Social Perceptions and Attitudes of Children*

Marian Radke-Yarrow, Helen G. Trager, and

Hadassah Davis

These investigators demonstrate that children acquire most of their social prejudices toward other racial and religious groups largely through interactions with their parents, other socially biased adults, and prejudiced peers. For example, young children who have never had direct social contact with Negroes express almost the same kinds of attitudes toward Negroes as children do who interact daily with various members of this group. The following highly abridged version of Drs. Radke-Yarrow, Trager, and Davis' report (retained from the first and second editions of this volume) also provides many other insights into the genesis of racial and religious intolerance during early childhood. As the world shrinks in functional size with faster and more convenient methods of transportation and communication, the understanding and control of bias and prejudice become increasingly important to our social welfare, and perhaps even to our sheer survival.

This research is an investigation of young children's perceptions and attitudes concerning racial and religious groups. Data were obtained on the nature of children's social concepts and their awareness of social values, conflicts and status differences—as these reactions are related to racial and religious groups. The findings are considered, also, in terms of theories of attitude development and influences of group membership upon the individual.

The subjects were 250 children of kindergarten, first, and second grades. The data were obtained in two sessions with each child. Interviews were carried out with the aid of a series of pictures (see examples of the Social Episodes Test in Figures 1 and 2) which permit the projections of content

* Adapted and abridged from Marian Radke-Yarrow, Helen G. Trager, and Hadassah Davis, "Social Perceptions and Attitudes of Children," *Genetic Psychology Monographs*, 1949, Vol. 40, pp. 327-447. (With permission of the senior author and The Journal Press.)

FIGURE 1. Religious Symbol Picture (Synagogue).
Example of pictures occurring in the Social Episodes Test

and attitudes regarding racial and religious groups, and which permit the examiner to probe particular aspects of attitudes. The pictures are of simple social situations involving children on a playground, in a school-room, and on a city street. The situations are sufficiently ambiguous to elicit a variety of interpretations. After initial interpretations by the child, racial and religious identifications are introduced by the examiner. Questions were asked by the tester beginning with general open-ended questions and progressing to probing, specific ones.

The Social Episodes Test is an effective technique for studying social perceptions and attitudes. The pictures bring responses of considerable variety and elaboration. They provide sufficiently interesting and ambiguous fields to permit the children, after the tester's introduction of group labels, to create story themes in which group factors can be ignored or can be incorporated with neutral, friendly or hostile interactions.

FIGURE 2. Barrier Picture (Race barrier).
Example of pictures occurring in the Social Episodes Test

SUMMARY OF FINDINGS

1. Cultural Content and Attitudes Relating to Racial and Religious Groups Are Learned Early in Childhood. Almost all the children studied show some differentiation of their social environment in group terms. At a minimum this differentiation involves an association of group labels with some fragment of personal experience ("Catholic is St. Anne's school") or with hearsay ("Colored is bad"). At the other extreme of differentiation, some children describe group characteristics and customs in detail; they describe status positions and group conflicts; they express their own feelings toward the groups and see social relations among different persons modified by such various considerations as:

"White don't like colored, but maybe they know the boy (and will let him play)."

"They (children in picture) are saying, 'I don't like these people. I hate them and they are too fresh.' I don't say that to hurt other people's feelings. I play with them."

The groups studied (Negro, white, Catholic, Protestant, Jewish) are not equally familiar to the children. While none of the subjects fails to recognize Negro and white differences, many are unable to supply content for one or more of the religious groups. "Catholic" is unknown to 19 per cent of the white children and 53 per cent of the Negro children; "Protestant" is unknown to 61 per cent of the white children and 87 per cent of the Negro children; and "Jewish" is unknown to 21 per cent of the white children and 59 per cent of the Negro children.

Group differentiations are made at various levels of understanding: (a) The group label is only a thing, something to do, an institution, but without clear reference to people (Catholic is "beads;" Jewish is "pickles;" Protestant is "sing songs"). (b) Group labels represent classifications of people along clearly or vaguely defined dimensions ("Jewish is people" or "Catholic, Jew, any kind of people, Protestants"). (c) Group labels stand for transitory conditions or behavior which make one a certain kind of person or give one a certain kind of experience ("When he gets dirty he turns into a colored boy"), ("You are Catholic when you go to Catholic school"). (d) Group labels represent classifications of people about whom evaluations are made ("They are saying the Catholic people are no good. Some people just hate Catholic people").

Varying shades of hostility and friendliness are expressed toward each of the groups. Group differences are recognized as signals for various kinds of "appropriate" social behavior. The group receiving the greatest amount of hostility and rejection is Negro. Responses toward Negro correspond to adult culture patterns: (a) segregation of white and Negro ("White and colored can't play together"); (b) racial hostility ("I don't like nigger kids"); and (c) stereotypes of Negro character ("tough," "dirty," "kill whites").

The white children ascribe aggression to both races. When it is aggression in the sense of exclusion and rejection, it is more frequently seen as expressed by whites; when it is physical aggression it is more frequently attributed to Negroes. The Negro children have learned the same culture patterns of rejection by the white group and hostility between the races. The effects of this awareness upon self-concepts are discussed below.

Regarding the religious groups, expressions of aggression are more frequent against Jewish than against Catholic and Protestant. The nature of the aggressions against each religious group again follows cultural prescriptions, and, more evidently than in the case of Negro and white, follows the peculiar patterns of the immediate neighborhoods (see 2 below).

Based on responses to questions, "Is this little boy glad he is —— (Negro, white, Catholic, Protestant, Jewish)?" and "Why?" the relative acceptance of each group compared with every other group was obtained. The results are, in general, in line with the status positions of these groups in American culture. The groups, in ascending order of acceptance, are Negro least accepted, Jewish next, and Catholic and Protestant next, about equal. (It is hazardous to interpret too literally the results on "Protestant," since it is an unfamiliar term to many children.) The order of acceptance is the same when responses of children who do not belong to the group in question and responses of children who are members of the group in question are considered separately.

2. The Social Learning Concerning Racial and Religious Groups Reflects the Particular Cultural Context in Which the Child Lives. Local neighborhood patterns and family group memberships are among the important subcultural differences which influence the responses. In a neighborhood in which tensions exist between Italian Catholics and Jews, the children show a heightened awareness of these groups. They tend to classify people with reference to these groups; thus, if told "These children are Jewish," a probable continuation by the child is "These others are Italian." They express competitive and hostile attitudes toward one or the other group. In another neighborhood, in which Protestant and Catholic religions are an issue, the children are more aware of Protestant than in any other neighborhood, and the in- and out-groups in their story themes are frequently Protestant and Catholic. "Jewish" is a more remote out-group, often classified as "not American." Similar, though less striking, local variations appear in the children from other neighborhoods. There is much less neighborhood variation in responses on Negro than on religious groups.

3. The Child Learns the Adults' Attitudes Toward Groups. Adult values and interpretations of the social world play a considerably more prominent role than do interpersonal experiences of the child with members of any one of the groups. The role of the adult as intermediary can be inferred from the children's references to parents' admonitions ("Sometimes other people's mothers don't like Protestants to play with Catholics"); to adult accounts of experience ("A colored man gave my father [taxi-driver] a dollar tip"); to religious teachings which "justify" attitudes ("They put God on the cross and that's why they [children in the picture] don't like them," "I learned about colored and white in Sunday School"); and to generalizations which are probably formulated by adults ("If you're kind you play with everybody").

Many of the statements which express the child's own reactions to a group are of the kind, "It is bad to play with ————" or "I don't like ————." They are rarely of the kind in which personal experience alone leads to a negative reaction, such as the hypothetical response, "I played with a Negro boy; he was mean to me, and therefore, I don't like

Negroes." There are numerous responses which show that prohibitions or expectations set up by adults either prevent personal experience which is available in the child's environment and by which the child could form his own opinions ("If she's white she's allowed to play in people's yards") or which predispose him to negatively affected perceptions of his experience ("Well, my mother said that sometimes colored people beat up white children").

4. The Extent of the Learning about Groups and the Degree of Crystallization of Attitudes Increase with the Age of the Child. Increases in social learning correlated with age are in the direction of greater *awareness* of group conflicts, patterns of exclusion, and forms of stereotyping and derogation; and in the direction of greater *acceptance* of prejudiced attitudes. There is no age trend (between kindergarten and second grade) in the accuracy of information about groups. There are as many misconceptions and distortions of facts among the older children as among the younger.

The following changes with age indicate increasing crystallization of attitudes. (a) Where picture interpretations are made in racial or religious terms rationalizations are given for the behavior projected. (b) The attitudes expressed by the child toward a given group tend to be the same each time that group appears. (c) A philosophy of behavior toward persons or groups is expressed. (d) The group label and its "meaning" become attached to people rather than to symbols or institutions or behavior. (e) The child shows personal involvement in responding to the pictures, sometimes through identifying himself with the child pictured, sometimes in showing emotional reactions to groups other than his own.

5. When Allowed to Discuss the Topic, Children Show Considerable Interest in Cultural Differences. Combined with This Interest Is an Awareness of the "Verboten" Nature of the Topic. In initial reactions to the interview topic there is, invariably, a reserve, an uneasiness, or an effort to avoid the mention of race and religion. This is most evident in reactions to Negro and white, especially by Negro children.

After a permissive situation has been established, the children's responses indicate their many ideas, curiosities, and also some preoccupations about racial and religious differences. It is apparent, too, the topics are discussed by the children among themselves.

6. Group Membership Is One Aspect of the Self-Concept of Children. Many of the children interviewed indicate a sense of own group membership. This is most frequent in regard to racial belonging. The child identifies himself with one race, usually with a preference for one or the other race implied or expressed.

Self-awareness of religious group belonging is less frequently apparent. Jewish children show greater awareness than either Catholic or Protestant children. Negro children very rarely identify themselves in religious terms. There is confusion, too, for some children who are uncertain as to whether they are Protestant or Catholic. Only a very few children who volunteer their religious group identify themselves incorrectly.

It should be noted that nonmembership in a group may be sensed by the child with as much import for his self-picture as membership in a group ("I'm glad I'm not Catholic," and a Negro girl referring to Negro child in picture, "She wishes she was white").

7. Group Membership Is Related to the Child's Needs for Acceptance. From the findings discussed above, certain effects of group membership upon the child's feelings of acceptance and rejection are inferred: (a) Group-belonging is seen by the children as one determinant of acceptance in play groups. The most marked influence in this regard is with racial membership. (b) Group-belonging is linked with conflicts which the child anticipates will occur in his social relations with his peers. (c) Some children find security in belonging to a group which they perceive as most desired ("I'm glad I am a white boy. Some colored people say, 'I wish I was a white boy and [the children] would like to play with me.'" "They wishes they was American like us."). (d) Concepts of groups which give an inherent "badness" or "goodness" to members of these groups contribute an abasing or enhancing quality to the child's self-image.

8. Negative Self-Feelings and Personal Conflict Concerning Group-Belonging Arise Frequently in Minority Children. Many children experience serious ego-threats as a result of group prejudices. Negro children reveal most vividly and most often the feelings of insecurity resulting from anticipated rejection or insult from the white children. The same phenomenon appears among the Jewish children. On occasion, Catholic and Protestant children show an anxious concern over an anti-Catholic or anti-Protestant remark which has been the topic of competitive discussion among their playmates. Experiences of social conflict by some of the minority group children have given rise to ambivalent feelings toward their own group,—expressions of self-hatred at an early age.

9. The Effect of Group Membership upon the Self-Concept Varies with the Role of the Particular Group in Society. This May Be to Increase or to Decrease the Importance of the Group Membership for the Individual. The frequency with which children identify themselves by group membership and the function of the identification varies with the group and neighborhood to which the children belong. The importance which identification assumes is appreciably greater (as evidenced by the kind and amount of content offered in the interview) for children belonging to minority groups or to groups involved in local community conflicts, than for children whose group is not greatly involved in cultural tensions. The role of group variables for the individual child cannot be predicted solely on the basis of cultural forces, but factors of intrafamily relations and personality modify attitudes, intensify or diminish cultural conflicts experienced by the child.

CONCLUSIONS

The findings of this study challenge a number of familiar assumptions and practices concerning children. It has been assumed that awareness of group differentiations, psychological needs arising out of group memberships and social prejudices do not develop until later childhood and the teen age. The data demonstrate the falsity and danger in this assumption. Some of the implications for the formal and informal education of children are clear. If the personal-social needs of children in our culture are to be met, their awareness, interests, fears and securities related to group factors must be dealt with. This cannot be postponed until adolescence, but must be begun in preschool and early school years.

Research on children's concepts of the world has explored with great thoroughness children's abilities to comprehend time, space, physical phenomena, etc. Research on methods of teaching these facts is extensive. But children's concepts of anthropology and sociology have not had the benefit of the same amount of research effort. For the most part, the concepts are allowed to "just grow" without the benefit of planned teaching and without regard to the gross and damaging misconceptions which develop. Surely these social concepts are not more difficult, and surely they are not less important in personal development than concepts in arithmetic, geography, physiology, etc.

To proceed as if group differences did not exist is to ignore the cultural context in which children live, for society does not ignore differences; family customs and values and names and languages all reflect group-derived variations. A rule of silence about differences not only fails to help the child to achieve a better understanding of group factors, but the silence may also be perceived by him as tacit agreement with societal prejudices.

There is much evidence to indicate that children's perceptions of groups develop out of adult values and the status quo; that is to say, that many of the children have opportunity for only the kind of learning about groups which involves stereotypes and rejection, especially of groups not present in the child's environment.

The training needed is of the kind which faces cultural diversities in the form and in the situations in which the child experiences them (as the child differs from his playmates, as he observes rituals, customs, characteristics for which he knows no explanation); and which provides him with information and attitudes and social techniques required for adjustment in a culturally diverse world.

36

Growth of Political Ideas in Adolescence[*]

Joseph Adelson and Robert P. O'Neil

In a search for the most productive strategies for pursuing their work, scientists often find it necessary to simulate natural proceedings, to set the stage for particularly desired events, or in other ways to dictate the limits cf some conceptually needed set of antecedent-consequent relationships. These manipulations constitute the operational components of the experimental method, an approach that has served man so well during the past four to five centuries. Only in the past three or four decades, however, have these research strategies been viewed as possible avenues to greater knowledge of sociocentric development during childhood and adolescence. Some of the novel theorizing and courageous experimentation by Kurt Lewin in the late 1930s pointed the way. More recently a widespread reappraisal and a broader acceptance of Piaget's contributions to developmental theory and methodology have accelerated the production of research studies that simulate social problems and conflicts through the use of verbally played games. The following report by Drs. Adelson and O'Neil is an excellent example of how effectively this approach can be utilized to reveal a generous measure of the cognitive processes that culminate in social-political maturity.

[*] Adapted and abridged from Joseph Adelson and Robert P. O'Neil, "Growth of Political Ideas in Adolescence: The Sense of Community," *Journal of Personality and Social Psychology,* 1966, Vol. 4, pp. 295-306. (With permission of the authors and the American Psychological Association.)

During adolescence the youngster gropes, stumbles, and leaps towards political understanding. Prior to these years the child's sense of the political order is erratic and incomplete—a curious array of sentiments and dogmas, personalized ideas, randomly remembered names and party labels, half-understood platitudes. By the time adolescence has come to an end, the child's mind, much of the time, moves easily within and among the categories of political discourse. The aim of our research was to achieve some grasp of how this transition is made.

Our early, informal conversations with adolescents suggested the importance of keeping our inquiry at some distance from current political issues; otherwise the underlying structure of the political is obscured by the clichés and catchphrases of partisan politics. To this end, we devised an interview schedule springing from the following premise: Imagine that a thousand men and women, dissatisfied with the way things are going in their country, decide to purchase and move to an island in the Pacific; once there, they must devise laws and modes of government.

Having established this premise, the interview schedule continued by offering questions on a number of hypothetical issues. For example, the subject was asked to choose among several forms of government and to argue the merits and difficulties of each. Proposed laws were suggested to him; he was asked to weigh their advantages and liabilities and answer arguments from opposing positions. The interview leaned heavily on dilemma items, wherein traditional issues in political theory are actualized in specific instances of political conflict, with the subject asked to choose and justify a solution. The content of our inquiry ranged widely to include, among others, the following topics: the scope and limits of political authority, the reciprocal obligations of citizens and state, utopian views of man and society, conceptions of law and justice, the nature of the political process.

This paper reports our findings on the development, in adolescence, of *the sense of community*. The term is deliberately comprehensive, for we mean to encompass not only government in its organized forms, but also the social and political collectivity more generally, as in "society" or "the people."

The very ubiquity of the concept determined our strategy in exploring it. We felt that the dimensions of community would emerge indirectly, in the course of inquiry focused elsewhere. Our pretesting had taught us that direct questions on such large and solemn issues, though at times very useful, tended to evoke simple incoherence from the cognitively unready, and schoolboy stock responses from the facile. We also learned that (whatever the ostensible topic) most of our questions informed us of the child's view of the social order, not only through what he is prepared to tell us, but also through what he does not know, knows falsely, cannot state, fumbles in stating, or takes for granted. Consequently we approached this topic through a survey of questions from several different areas of the schedule, chosen to illuminate different sides of the sense of community.

METHOD

Sample. The sample was comprised of 120 youngsters, equally divided by sex, with 30 subjects at each of 4 age-grade levels—fifth grade (average age, 10.9), seventh (12.6), ninth (14.7), and twelfth (17.7). The sample was further divided by intelligence: At each grade level, two thirds of the subjects were of average intelligence (95-110) and one third of superior intelligence (125 and over), as measured by the California Test of Mental Maturity. For each grade, school records were used to establish a pool of subjects meeting our criteria for age, sex, and IQ; within each of the subgroups so selected, names were chosen randomly until the desired sample size was achieved. Children more than 6 months older or younger than the average for their grade were excluded, as were two otherwise eligible subjects reported by their counselor to have a history of severe psychological disturbance.

This paper will report findings by age alone (to the next nearest age) and without regard to sex or intelligence. We were unable to discover sex differences nor—to our continuing surprise—differences associated with intelligence. The brighter children were certainly more fluent, and there is some reason to feel that they use a drier, more impersonal, more intellectualized approach in dealing with certain questions, but up to this time we have not found that they attain political concepts earlier than subjects of average intelligence.

The interviews were taken in Ann Arbor, Michigan. We were able to use schools representative of the community, in the sense that they do not draw students from socioeconomically extreme neighborhoods. The children of average IQ were preponderantly lower-middle and working class in background; those of high intelligence were largely from professional and managerial families. Academic families made up 13% of the sample, concentrated in the high IQ group; 5% of the "average" children and somewhat over one quarter of the "brights" had fathers with a professional connection to the University of Michigan. In these respects—socioeconomic status and parental education—the sample, which combined both IQ groups, was by no means representative of the American adolescent population at large. Yet our inability to find differences between the IQ groups, who derive from sharply different social milieux, makes us hesitate to assume that social status is closely associated with the growth of political ideas as we have measured them, or that the findings deviate markedly from what we would find in other middle-class suburbs.

Interview. The aims, scope, and form of the interview schedule have already been described. In developing the schedule we were most concerned to find a tone and level of discourse sufficiently simple to allow our youngest subjects to understand and respond to the problems posed, yet sufficiently advanced to keep our older interviewees challenged and engaged. Another aim was to strike a balance between the focused interview—to ease scoring—and a looser, more discursive approach—to allow a greater depth of inquiry and spontaneity of response. Our interviewers were permitted, once they had covered the basic questions of a topic, to explore it more thoroughly.

The interviews were conducted at the school. There were six interviewers, all with at least some graduate training in clinical psychology. The interviews were tape-recorded and transcribed verbatim. Those conducted with younger subjects were completed in about 1 hour, with older subjects in about 1½ hours.

Reliability. In order to appraise the lower limits of reliability, only the more difficult items were examined, those in which responses were complex or ambiguous. For five items of this type, intercoder reliabilities ranged from .79 to .84.

RESULTS

When we examine the interviews of 11-year-olds, we are immediately struck by the common, pervasive incapacity to speak from a coherent view of the political order. Looking more closely, we find that this failure has two clear sources: First, these children are, in Piaget's sense, egocentric, in that they cannot transcend a purely personal approach to matters which require a sociocentric perspective. Second, they treat political issues in a concrete fashion and cannot manage the requisite abstractness of attitude. These tendencies, singly and together, dominate the discourse of the interview, so much so that a few sample sentences can often distinguish 11-year-old protocols from those given by only slightly older children.

The following are some interview excerpts to illustrate the differences: These are chosen randomly from the interviews of 11- and 13-year-old boys of average intelligence. They have been asked: "What is the purpose of government?"

11A. To handle the state or whatever it is so it won't get out of hand, because if it gets out of hand you might have to . . . people might get mad or something.

11B. Well . . . buildings, they have to look over buildings that would be . . . um, that wouldn't be any use of the land if they had crops on it or something like that. And when they have highways the government would have to inspect it, certain details. I guess that's about all.

11C. So everything won't go wrong in the country. They want to have a government because they respect him and they think he's a good man.

Now the 13-year-olds:

13A. So the people have rights and freedom of speech. Also so the civilization will balance.

13B. To keep law and order and talk to the people to make new ideas.

13C. Well, I think it is to keep the country happy or keep it going properly. If you didn't have it, then it would just be chaos with stealing and things like this. It runs the country better and more efficiently.

These extracts are sufficiently representative to direct us to some of the major developmental patterns in adolescent thinking on politics.

Personalism. Under *personalism* we include two related tendencies: first, the child's disposition to treat institutions and social processes upon the model of persons and personal relationships; second, his inability to achieve a sociocentric orientation, that is, his failure to understand that political decisions have social as well as personal consequences, and that the political realm encompasses not merely the individual citizen, but the community as a whole.

1. "Government," "community," "society," are abstract ideas; they connote those invisible networks of obligation and purpose which link people to each other in organized social interaction. These concepts are beyond the effective reach of 11-year-olds; in failing to grasp them they fall back to persons and actions of persons, which are the nearest equivalent of the intangible agencies and ephemeral processes they are trying to imagine. Hence, Subject 11A seems to glimpse that an abstract answer is needed, tries to find it, then despairs and retreats to the personalized "people might get mad or something." A more extreme example is found in 11C's statement, which refers to government as a "he," apparently confusing it with "governor." Gross personalizations of "government" and similar terms are not uncommon at 11 and diminish markedly after that. We counted the number of times the personal pronouns "he" and "she" were used in three questions dealing with government. There were instances involving six subjects among the 11-year-olds (or 20% of the sample) and none among 13-year-olds. (The most striking example is the following sentence by an 11: "Well, I don't think she should forbid it, but if they, if he did, well most people would want to put up an argument about it.")

Although personalizations as bald as these diminish sharply after 11, more subtle or tacit ones continue well into adolescence (and in all likelihood, into adulthood)—the use of "they," for example, when "it" is appropriate. It is our impression that we see a revival of personalization among older subjects under two conditions: when the topic being discussed is too advanced or difficult for the youngster to follow or when it exposes an area of ignorance or uncertainty, and when the subject's beliefs and resentments are engaged to the point of passion or bitterness. In both these cases the emergence of affects (anxiety, anger) seems to produce a momentary cognitive regression, expressing itself in a loss of abstractness and a reversion to personalized modes of discourse.

2. The second side of personalism is the failure to attain a sociocentric perspective. The preadolescent subject does not usually appraise political events in the light of their collective consequences. Since he finds it hard to conceive the social order as a whole, he is frequently unable to understand those actions which aim to serve communal ends and so tends to interpret them parochially, as serving only the needs of individuals. We have an illustration of this in the data given in Table 1. Table 1 reports the

TABLE 1. Purpose of Vaccination

	Age			
	11	13	15	18
Social consequences (prevention of epidemics, etc.)	.23	.67	1.00	.90
Individual consequences (prevention of individual illness)	.70	.33	.00	.10

Note: $\chi^2 = 46.53$, $p < .001$. In this table and all that follow $N = 30$ for each age group. When proportions in a column do not total 1.00, certain responses are not included in the response categories shown. When proportions total more than 1.00, responses have been included in more than one category of the table. The p level refers to the total table except when asterisks indicat significance levels for a designated row.

answers to the following item: "Another law was suggested which required all children to be vaccinated against smallpox and polio. What would be the purpose of that law?"

A substantial majority—about three quarters—of the 11-year-olds see the law serving an individual end: personal protection from disease. By 13 there has been a decisive shift in emphasis, those children stressing the protection of the community. At 15 and after, an understanding of the wider purposes of vaccination has become nearly universal.

Parts and Wholes. Another reflection of the concreteness of younger adolescents can be found in their tendency to treat the total functioning of institutions in terms of specific, discrete activities. If we return to the interview excerpts, we find a good example in the answer given by Subject 11B on the purpose of government. He can do no more than mention some specific governmental functions, in this case, the inspecting of buildings and highways. This answer exemplifies a pattern we find frequently among our younger subjects, one which appears in many content areas. Adolescents only gradually perceive institutions (and their processes) as wholes; until they can imagine the institution abstractly, as a total idea, they are limited to the concrete and visible.

Table 2 is one of several which demonstrates this. The subjects were

TABLE 2. Purpose of Income Tax

	Age			
	11	13	15	18
General support of government	.23	.33	.47	1.00*
Specific services only	.23	.17	.23	.00
Do not know	.53	.50	.30	.00

Note: p level refers to row designated by asterisk.
* $\chi^2 = 9.54$, $p < .05$.

asked the purpose of the income tax. The responses were coded to distinguish those who answered in terms of general government support from those who mentioned only specific government services. (In most cases the services referred to are both local and visible—police, firefighting, etc.) We observe that the percentage of those referring to the government in a general sense rises slowly and steadily; all of the high school seniors do so.

Negatives and Positives. Before we leave this set of interview excerpts, we want to note one more important difference between the 11- and 13-year-olds. Two of the former emphasize the negative or coercive functions of government ("To handle the state . . . so it won't get out of hand"; "So everything won't go wrong . . ."). The 13-year-olds, on the other hand, stress the positive functions of the government—keeping the country happy or working properly. This difference is so important and extensive that we will treat it in depth in a later publication, but it should be discussed at least briefly here. Younger subjects adhere to a Hobbesian view of political man: The citizenry is seen as willful and potentially dangerous, and society, therefore, as rightfully, needfully coercive and authoritarian. Although this view of the political never quite loses its appeal for a certain proportion of individuals at all ages, it nevertheless diminishes both in frequency and centrality, to be replaced, in time, by more complex views of political arrangements, views which stress the administrative sides of government (keeping the machinery oiled and in repair) or which emphasize melioristic ends (enhancing the human condition).

The Future. The adolescent years see a considerable extension of time perspective. On the one hand, a sense of history emerges, as the youngster is able to link past and present and to understand the present as having been influenced or determined by the past. On the other, the child begins to imagine the future and, what may be more important, to ponder alternative futures. Thus the present is connected to the future not merely because the future unfolds from the present, but also because the future is *tractable;* its shape depends upon choices made in the present.

This idea of the future asserts itself with increasing effect as the child advances through adolescence. In making political judgments, the youngster can anticipate the consequences of a choice taken here and now for the long-range future of the community and can weigh the probable effects of alternative choices on the future. The community is now seen to be temporal, that is, as an organism which persists beyond the life of its current members; thus judgments in the present must take into account the needs of the young and of the unborn. Further, the adolescent becomes able to envision not only the communal future, but himself (and others) in possible statuses in that future as well.

The items which most clearly expose the changing meaning of the future are those dealing with education. When we reflect on it, this is not surprising: Education is the public enterprise which most directly links the generations to each other; it is the communal activity through which one generation orients another toward the future. Several questions of public policy toward education were asked; in the answers to each the needs of the communal future weigh more heavily with increasing age. One item runs: "Some people suggested a law which would require children to go to school until they were sixteen years old. What would be the purpose of such a law?" One type of answer to this question was coded "Continuity of community"; these responses stress the community's need to sustain and perpetuate itself by educating a new generation of citizens and leaders. Typical answers were "So children will grow up to be leaders," and "To educate people so they can carry on the government." Looking at this answer alone (analysis of the entire table would carry us beyond this topic), we find the following distribution by age (see Table 3).

TABLE 3. Purpose of Minimum Education Law

	Age			
	11	*13*	*15*	*18*
Continuity of community	.00	.27	.33	.43

Note: $\chi^2 = 11.95, p < .01$.

Another item later in the interview poses this problem: "The people who did not have children thought it was unfair they would have to pay taxes to support the school system. What do you think of that argument?" Again the same category, which stresses the community's continuity and its future needs, rises sharply with age as shown in Table 4.

TABLE 4. Should People Without Children Pay School Taxes?

	Age			
	11	13	15	18
Continuity of community	.10	.10	.47	.60

Note: $\chi^2 = 18.61, p < .001$.

Finally, we want to examine another education item in some detail, since it offers a more complex view of the sense of the future in adolescent political thought, allowing us to observe changes in the child's view of the personal future. The question was the last of a series on the minimum education law. After the subject was asked to discuss its purpose (see above), he was asked whether he supports it. Almost all of our subjects did. He was then asked: "Suppose you have a parent who says 'My son is going to go into my business anyway and he doesn't need much schooling for that.' Do you think his son should be required to go to school anyway? Why?"

Table 5 shows that as children advance into adolescence, they stress increasingly the communal function of education. Younger subjects respond

TABLE 5. Should Son Be Required to Attend School
Though Father Wants Him to Enter Business?

	Age			
	11	13	15	18
Yes, education needed to function in community	.00	.23	.43	.77***
Yes, education good in itself	.03	.23	.20	.27
Yes, education needed in business	.40	.47	.23	.13
Yes, prevents parental coercion	.57	.47	.43	.23

Note: p level refers to row designated by asterisks.
*** $\chi^2 = 25.54, p < .001$.

more to the father's arbitrariness or to the economic consequences of the father's position. They are less likely to grasp the more remote, more general effects of a curtailed education—that it hinders the attainment of citizenship. Representative answers by 11-year-olds were: "Well, maybe he wants some other desire and if he does maybe his father is forcing him";

and ". . . let's say he doesn't like the business and maybe he'd want to start something new." These children stress the practical and familial aspects of the issue.

Older subjects, those 15 and 18, all but ignored both the struggle with the father and the purely pragmatic advantages of remaining in school. They discoursed, sometimes eloquently, on the child's need to know about society as a whole, to function as a citizen, and to understand the perspectives of others.

Older subjects see education as the opportunity to become *cosmopolitan,* to transcend the insularities of job and kinship. For the older adolescent, leaving school early endangers the future in two ways. On the personal side, it threatens one's capacity to assume the perspective of the other and to attain an adequate breadth of outlook; thus, it imperils one's future place in the community. On the societal side, it endangers the integrity of the social order itself, by depriving the community of a cosmopolitan citizenry.

Claims of the Community. We have already seen that as adolescence advances the youngster is increasingly sensitive to the fact of community and its claims upon the citizen. What are the limits of these claims, the limits of political authority? To what point, and under what conditions can the state, acting in the common good, trespass upon the autonomy of the citizen? When do the community's demands violate the privacy and liberty of the individual? The clash of these principles—individual freedom versus the public welfare and safety—is one of the enduring themes of Western political theory.

A number of questions in the interview touched upon this topic tangentially, and some were designed to approach it directly. In these latter we asked the subject to adjudicate and comment upon a conflict between public and private interests, each of these supported by a general political principle—usually the individual's right to be free of compulsion, on the one hand, and the common good, on the other. We tried to find issues which would be tangled enough to engage the most complex modes of political reasoning. A major effort in this direction was made through a series of three connected questions on eminent domain. The series began with this question:

Here is another problem the Council faced. They decided to build a road to connect one side of the island to the other. For the most part they had no trouble buying the land on which to build the road, but one man refused to sell his land to the government. He was offered a fair price for his land but he refused, saying that he didn't want to move, that he was attached to his land, and that the Council could buy another piece of land and change the direction of the road. Many people thought he was selfish, but others thought he was in the right. What do you think?

Somewhat to our surprise, there are no strong developmental patterns visible, though we do see a moderate tendency (not significant statistically, however) for the younger subjects to side with the landowner (see Table 6).

TABLE 6. Which Party Is Right in Eminent-domain Conflict?

	Age			
	11	13	15	18
Individual should sell; community needs come first	.30	.20	.30	.40
Detour should be made; individual rights come first	.60	.47	.27	.37
Emphasis on social responsibility; individual should be appealed to, but not forced	.10	.17	.17	.07
Ambivalence; individual is right in some ways, wrong in others	.00	.13	.27	.17

The next question in the series sharpened the issue somewhat between the Council and the reluctant landowner:

The Council met and after long discussion voted that if the landowner would not agree to give up his land for the road, he should be forced to, because the rights of all the people on the island were more important than his. Do you think this was a fair decision?

The phrasing of the second question does not alter the objective facts of the conflict; yet Table 7 shows decisive shifts in position. It is hard to be

TABLE 7. Should Landowner Be Forced to Sell His Land?

	Age			
	11	13	15	18
Yes, rights of others come first	.40	.37	.63	.70
No, individual rights come first	.57	.50	.33	.07**
No, social responsibility should suffice	.03	.10	.00	.23

Note: p level refers to row designated by asterisks.
** $\chi^2 = 12.17$, $p < .01$.

sure why: perhaps because the second question states that the Council has considered the matter at length, perhaps because the Council's decision is justified by advancing the idea of "the people's rights." Whatever the reason, we now see a marked polarization of attitude. The younger subjects —those 11 and 13—continue to side with the landowner; those 15 and 18 almost completely abandon him, although about one quarter of the latter want to avoid coercion and suggest an appeal to his sense of social responsibility.

These findings seem to confirm the idea that older adolescents are more responsive to communal than to individual needs. Yet it would be incorrect to infer that these subjects favor the community willy-nilly. A close look at the interview protocols suggests that older adolescents choose differently because they reason differently.

Most younger children—those 13 and below—can offer no justification for their choices. Either they are content with a simple statement of preference, for example; "I think he was in the right"; or they do no more than paraphrase the question: "Well, there is really two sides to it. One is that he is attached and he shouldn't give it up, but again he should give it up for the country." These youngsters do not or cannot rationalize their decisions, neither through appeal to a determining principle, nor through a comparative analysis of each side's position. If there is an internal argument going on within the mind of the 11- or 13-year-old, he is unable to make it public; instead, he seems to choose by an intuitive ethical leap, averring that one or the other position is "fair," "in the right," or "selfish." He usually favors the landowner, because his side of the matter is concrete, personal, psychologically immediate, while the Council's position hinges on an idea of the public welfare which is too remote and abstract for these youngsters to absorb. Even those few children who try to reason from knowledge or experience more often than not flounder and end in confusion.

What we miss in these interviews are two styles of reasoning which begin to make their appearance in 15-year-olds: first, the capacity to reason consequentially, to trace out the long-range implications of various courses of action; second, a readiness to deduce specific choices from general principles. The following excerpt from a 15-year-old's interview illustrates both of these approaches:

Well, maybe he owned only a little land if he was a farmer and even if they did give him a fair price maybe all the land was already bought on the island that was good for farming or something and he couldn't get another start in life if he did buy it. Then maybe in a sense he was selfish because if they had to buy other land and change the direction of the road why of course then maybe they'd raise taxes on things so they could get more money cause it would cost more to change directions from what they already have planned. [Fair to force him off?] Yes, really, just because one person doesn't want to sell his land that don't mean that, well the other 999 or the rest of the people on the island should go without this road because of one.

In the first part of the statement, the subject utilizes a cost-effectiveness approach; he estimates the costs (economic, social, moral) of one decision against another. He begins by examining the effects on the landowner. Can he obtain equivalent land elsewhere? He then considers the long-range economic consequences for the community. Will the purchase of other land be more expensive and thus entail a tax increase? Though he does not go on to solve these implicit equations—he could hardly do so, since he does not have sufficient information—he does state the variables he deems necessary to solve them.

The second common strategy at this age, seen in the last part of the statement, is to imply or formulate a general principle, usually ethico-political in nature, which subsumes the instance. Most adolescents using this approach will for this item advert to the community's total welfare, but some of our older adolescents suggest some other governing principle—the sanctity of property rights or the individual's right to privacy and autonomy. In either instance, the style of reasoning is the same; a general principle is sought which contains the specific issue.

Once a principle is accepted, the youngster attempts to apply it consistently. If the principle is valid, it should fall with equal weight on all consequently, exceptions are resisted. And to the question of the land-owner's threatening violence: "They shouldn't let him have his own way because he would be an example. Other people would think that if they used his way, they could do what they wanted to." Even a child who bitterly opposes the Council's position on this issue agrees that once a policy has been established, exceptions should be resisted.

The Force of Principle. Once principles and ideals are firmly established, the child's approach to political discourse is decisively altered. When he ponders a political choice, he takes into account not only *personal* consequences (What will this mean, practically speaking, for the individuals involved?) and pragmatic *social* consequences (What effect will this have on the community at large?), but also its consequences in the realm of *value* (Does this law or decision enhance or endanger such ideals as liberty, justice, and so on?). There is of course no sharp distinction among these types of consequences; values are contained, however tacitly, in the most "practical" of decisions. Nevertheless, these ideals, once they develop, have a life, an autonomy, of their own. We reasoned that as the adolescent grew older, political principles and ideals would be increasingly significant, and indeed would loom large enough to overcome the appeal of personal and social utility in the narrow sense.

To test this belief we wanted an item which would pit a "good" against a "value." We devised a question proposing a law which, while achieving a personal and communal good, would at the same time violate a political ideal—in this case; the value of personal autonomy. The item ran "One [proposed law] was a suggestion that men over 45 be required to have a yearly medical checkup. What do you think of that suggestion?" The answer was to be probed if necessary: "Would you be in favor of that? Why (or why not)?" Table 8 shows the distribution of responses.

The findings are interesting on several counts, aside from offering testimony on the degree to which good health is viewed as a summum bonum. The 11-year-olds, here as elsewhere, interpret the issue along familial and

TABLE 8. Should Men over 45 Be Required to Have
a Yearly Medical Checkup?

	Age			
	11	13	15	18
Yes, otherwise they would not do it	.50	.07	.00	.03***
Yes, good for person and/or community	.50	.80	.70	.60
No, infringement on liberties	.00	.13	.27	.37**

Note: p level refers to rows designated by asterisks.
** $\chi^2 = 11.95$, $p < .01$.
*** $\chi^2 = 33.10$, $p < .001$.

authoritarian lines. The government is seen in loco parentis; its function is to make its citizens do the sensible things they would otherwise neglect to do. But our primary interest is in the steady growth of opposition to the proposal. The basis for opposition, though it is phrased variously, is that the government has no business exercising compulsion in this domain. These youngsters look past the utilitarian appeal of the law and sense its conflict with a value that the question itself does not state. These data, then, offer some support to our suggestion that older adolescents can more easily bring abstract principles to bear in the appraisal of political issues. Strictly speaking, the findings are not definitive, for we cannot infer that all of those supporting the law do so without respect to principle. Some of the older adolescents do, in fact, recognize the conflict implicit in the question, but argue that the public and personal benefits are so clear as to override the issue of personal liberties. But there are very few signs of this among the younger subjects. Even when pressed, as they were in a following question, they cannot grasp the meaning and significance of the conflict; they see only the tangible good.

DISCUSSION

These findings suggest that the adolescent's sense of community is determined not by a single factor, but by the interaction of several related developmental parameters. We should now be in a position to consider what some of these are.

1. *The decline of authoritarianism.* Younger subjects are more likely to approve of coercion in public affairs. Themselves subject to the authority of adults, they more readily accept the fact of hierarchy. They find it hard to imagine that authority may be irrational, presumptuous, or whimsical; thus they bend easily to the collective will.

2. With advancing age there is an increasing grasp of the *nature and needs of the community.* As the youngster begins to understand the structure

and functioning of the social order as a whole, he begins to understand too the specific social institutions within it and their relations to the whole. He comes to comprehend the autonomy of institutions, their need to remain viable, to sustain and enhance themselves. Thus the demands of the social order and its constituent institutions, as well as the needs of the public, become matters to be appraised in formulating political choices.

3. *The absorption of knowledge and consensus.* This paper has taken for granted, and hence neglected, the adolescent's increasing knowingness. The adolescent years see a vast growth in the acquisition of political information, in which we include not only knowledge in the ordinary substantive sense, but also the apprehension of consensus, a feeling for the common and prevailing ways of looking at political issues. The child acquires these from formal teaching, as well as through a heightened cathexis of the political, which in turn reflects the generally amplified interest in the adult world. Thus, quite apart from the growth of cognitive capacity, the older adolescent's views are more "mature" in that they reflect internalization of adult perspectives.

4. We must remember that it is not enough to be exposed to mature knowledge and opinion; their absorption in turn depends on the growth of *cognitive capacities.* Some of the younger subjects knew the fact of eminent domain, knew it to be accepted practice, yet, unable to grasp the principles involved, could not apply their knowledge effectively to the question. This paper has stressed the growth of those cognitive capacities which underlie the particular intellectual achievements of the period: the adolescent's increasing ability to weigh the relative consequences of actions, the attainment of deductive reasoning. The achievement of these capacities—the leap to "formal operations," in Piaget's term—allows him to escape that compulsion toward the immediate, the tangible, the narrowly pragmatic which so limits the political discourse of younger adolescents.

5. In turn the growth of cognitive capacity allows *the birth of ideology.* Ideology may not be quite the right word here, for it suggests a degree of coherence and articulation that few of our subjects, even the oldest and brightest, come close to achieving. Nevertheless there is an impressive difference between the younger and older adolescents in the orderliness and internal consistency of their political perspectives. What passes for ideology in the younger respondents is a raggle-taggle array of sentiments: "People ought to be nice to each other"; "There are a lot of wise guys around, so you have to have strict laws." In time these sentiments may mature (or harden) into ideologies or ideological dispositions, but they are still too erratic, too inconsistent. They are not yet principled or generalized and so tend to be self-contradictory, or loosely held and hence easily abandoned. When younger subjects are cross-questioned, however gently, they are ready to reverse themselves even on issues they seem to feel strongly about. When older subjects are challenged, however sharply, they refute, debate, and

counterchallenge. In some part their resistance to easy change reflects a greater degree of poise and their greater experience in colloquy and argument, but it also bespeaks the fact that their views are more firmly founded. The older adolescents, most conspicuously those at 18, aim for an inner concordance of political belief.

These, then, are the variables our study has suggested as directing the growth of political concepts. We must not lean too heavily on any one of them: The development of political thought is not simply or even largely a function of cognitive maturation or of increased knowledge or of the growth of ideology when these are taken alone. This paper has stressed the cognitive parameters because they seem to be so influential at the younger ages. The early adolescent's political thought is constrained by personalized, concrete, present-oriented modes of approach. Once these limits are transcended, the adolescent is open to influence by knowledge, by the absorption of consensus, and by the principles he adopts from others or develops on his own.

37

Age Differences in Rigidity-Flexibility and Intelligence over the Adult Life Span[*]

K. Warner Schaie

It is a familiar observation that older people are inclined to resist change, to define the new in terms of the old, to be cautious and conservative, and generally to be less open to new experience. These characteristics are associated in one type of psychological theorizing with the variable of rigidity which ranges over one end of the rigidity-flexibility continuum. In the accompanying report Dr. Schaie examines the hypothesis that knowledge of individuals' positions along the rigidity-flexibility continuum might enable one to predict their differential declines in scores on intelligence tests during the later decades of adult life. Briefly stated, the hypothesis holds that one might expect

* Adapted and abridged from K. Warner Schaie, "Rigidity-Flexibility and Intelligence: a Cross-Sectional Study of the Adult Life Span from 20 to 70 Years," *Psychological Monographs*, 1958, Vol. 72, No. 9, 26 pp. (With permission of the author and the American Psychological Association.)

that the more rigid the individual is during the peak years of his intellectual functioning, the greater would be the decrements in his measured intelligence (and inferred cognitive effectiveness) during the decades of middle and old age. Although the findings of Dr. Schaie's research are by no means a simple, straight-forward demonstration of the validity of this hypothesis, they do provide strong support for his hunch that measures of rigidity-flexibility are significantly related to scores on tests of intelligence over the entire span of adult life and that the patterning of these relationships may, indeed, be predictive of an individual's differential intellectual decline, beginning in the forties and extending into extremely old age. It should be borne in mind, of course, that these findings are from a cross-sectional study, as the author cautiously notes in the title of this report. Findings from longitudinal investigations (as illustrated in Paper #13 of this volume) are sorely needed to test the fruitfulness of the rigidity hypothesis in a more convincing manner.

If one considers some of the conventional age gradients for many traits and abilities, one finds a fairly rapid rate of change during the early maturational period and a gradual slowing down as the developmental peak is reached and passed. From then on the developmental process is characterized by a gradual decrease in the effectiveness and personal adjustment of most individuals. Enough individual variation is found at each age level, however, to demand the introduction of additional explanatory factors.

If socially effective and mature behavior is taken to be a function of the individual's ability to adjust without difficulty to changes in the pattern of cognitive and social stimuli which makes up his environment, one might then consider these individual differences to be an effect of a more or less complex interaction of initial potential ability and changing ability to utilize this potential for the acquisition of new behavior patterns. One might then go further to suggest that the individual who is most able to adjust to the stress imposed by changes in the patterns of environmental stimuli will tend to respond in a socially effective manner longer than his less flexible peer. Given reasonably constant environmental conditions it might be possible to measure a person's ability to adjust to change, once he reaches maturity, and to predict his personal gradient of decline in effective behavior.

The class of behavior which has been closely studied in the past and which approximates fairly well the psychological aspects of adjustment to change has usually been subsumed under the heading of "behavioral rigidity."

Behavioral rigidity may be defined as:

. . . a tendency to perseverate and resist conceptual change, to resist the acquisition of new patterns of behavior, and to refuse to relinquish old and established behavior patterns.

This definition may seem rather broad, but a set of behavioral consequences can readily be deduced which are amenable to observational test.

From such a definition one can deduce, for example, that a rigid person dislikes to change patterns of interpersonal relationships, has difficulty in changing from one activity to another, is less efficient in activities requiring alternation and continuous readjustment of motor activities, etc.

As the result of a series of factor analyses it was possible to show that this concept could best be described by a three-dimensional system: "motor-cognitive rigidity," "personality-perceptual rigidity," and "psychomotor speed."

The motor-cognitive rigidity factor seems to indicate the individual's ability to shift without difficulty from one activity to another; it is a measure of effective adjustment to shifts in familiar patterns and to continuously changing situational demands. The personality-perceptual rigidity factor seems to indicate the individual's ability to adjust readily to new surroundings and change in cognitive and environmental patterns; it seems to be a measure of ability to perceive and adjust to unfamiliar and new patterns and situations. The psychomotor speed factor finally indicates an individual's rate of emission of familiar cognitive responses. A high score on this factor would seem to imply superior functioning efficiency in coping with familiar situations requiring rapid response and quick thinking.

It is suggested that the level of functioning of an individual with respect to cognitive and perhaps other behavior traits may be predictable in terms of a more central factor which might be measured by a three-dimensional rigidity factor system and possibly well approximated by a composite score formed by a linear combination of the three factor scores.

Such a formulation might also be useful for the prediction of adult age changes in various types of socially important behavior classes, provided it can be shown that not only level of functioning but also maintenance of basal level of functioning over the adult age span can be meaningfully related to this central factor.

HYPOTHESES

An empirical description of the rate of change observed on the variables to be measured is of interest in any event, but it is timely now to state the hypotheses concerning the influence of behavioral rigidity upon mental abilities with age. Briefly they are as follows:

Hypothesis I states that:

Behavioral age changes are a function of the individual's lack of ability to adjust to change and can thus be predicted for an advanced age from a knowledge of his standing on the rigidity-flexibility dimension at the basal age.

If this hypothesis is correct, the correlations between the Test of Behavioral Rigidity (TBR) and Thurstone's Primary Mental Abilities Test (PMA) would be expected to increase systematically with age.

Hypothesis II states that:

Behavioral age changes occur concomitantly with decreasing adjustment to change and the level of function for individuals at any given age level is therefore predictable from knowledge of either dimension.

If this hypothesis were true one would expect to find significant but constant correlation throughout the adult age range, with possibly slightly decreasing values towards the upper end of the range.

Hypothesis III states that:

Behavioral age changes and changes in rigidity-flexibility show no significant relation whatsoever.

In this case insignificant correlation throughout the adult age range would be expected.

Hypothesis IV, finally, is the obverse of Hypothesis I. It states that:

Lack of ability of an individual to adjust to change may be a function of some other behavior variable and may be predictable for his old age from a knowledge of that variable at the basal age.

Again correlations between PMA and TBR would be expected to rise with age and the direction of the relation would be testable by means of the analysis of covariance.

THE ASSESSMENT OF BEHAVIORAL RIGIDITY

In earlier studies a battery of tests of rigidity, some of which were selected from the literature and others of which were newly constructed, had been factor analyzed. Since developmental studies were anticipated, the final test battery retained only those tests which appeared applicable to young adults as well as to mature and senescent populations. For practical reasons, the battery was further restricted to tests suitable for group administration, and an effort was made to retain those tests where social status and educational level were of minimal importance in influencing test results.

The factor analysis of these tests, using a modified version of the multiple-group method, resulted in the isolation of three factors termed motor-cognitive rigidity, personality-perceptual rigidity, and psychomotor speed. The original test battery was shortened by deleting the two tests which contributed the lowest factor loadings to their respective factor scores. The remaining four subtests yielded seven scores and require about 30 minutes for administration.

1. The Capitals Test. The S copies a paragraph first as it is printed on a sample card and then once more, substituting capitals for lower case letters and vice versa; e.g. Original: "The Duke DREW his sword." Second time: "tHE dUKE drew HIS SWORD." Two and one-half minutes are allowed for each part, and an estimate of rigidity is obtained by dividing the number of correctly written words in the test series by the number of correctly written words in the practice series. The number of words in the practice series is used as one of the psychomotor speed estimates.

2. The Opposites Test. This test contains three series of 40 stimulus words each. In the first series, the S is required to respond by giving the opposite of the words listed. In the second list, he responds with a synonym of the word listed. The last list finally presents a mixture of stimuli to which S must respond with either the synonym or the antonym. When the stimulus word is printed in capitals, the synonym is required; when small letters are used, the antonym is the required response. The number of correct responses on the first two series gives another psychomotor score. Two rigidity scores are yielded by this test. The first measures accurate cognitive shift and is based on the third series only. It is given by dividing the number of rigid (i.e. inappropriate) responses by the total number of responses given on this series. The second rigidity score measures the influence of rigidity in inhibiting rapid cognitive shift and is given by the formula Number of correct responses in the third series divided by one-half the number of correct responses in Series 1 and 2. Two minutes are allowed for each series.

3. Scale of Rigidity (R scale). This is a 22-item scale of general statements which Gough (1951) found to be empirically related to rigid behavior. These items are mixed among 44 masking items which in themselves can be scaled as a measure of social responsibility (Gough, McCloskey, & Meehle, 1952). The score is the number of flexible responses favorably endorsed by the S.

4. The Rigidity Index (P scale). This is a 9-item inquiry as to rigid modes of behavior. It contains questions like: "Do you feel strongly inclined to finish whatever you are doing in spite of being tired of doing it?" The score is also the number of flexible responses.

Once the factorial structure of the test battery was known to be essentially three dimensional, it was possible to write appropriate regression equations to permit an estimate of factor scores from knowledge of the test scores of subjects on the original variables having high loadings on the specified factors.

THE ASSESSMENT OF MENTAL ABILITIES

One of the common criticisms of tests of intelligence has been the lack of readily identifiable subtest meaning and the high subtest intercorrelations. Thurstone's Primary Mental Abilities Test, Intermediate Form (Thurstone and Thurstone, 1947), seemed the best instrument for the purposes of this study.

The battery consists of five subtests designed to cover the presumably independent factors listed below with the description furnished in the test manual (Thurstone and Thurstone, 1949).

1. Verbal-Meaning (V) is the ability to understand ideas expressed in words. It is used in any activities in which information is obtained by reading or listening to words.

2. Space (S) is the ability to think about objects in two or three dimensions. It is perhaps best described as the ability to imagine how an object or figure would look when it is rotated, to visualize objects in two or three dimensions, and to see the relations of an arrangement of objects in space.

3. Reasoning (R) is the ability to solve logical problems—to foresee and plan. It is probably the most important of the mental abilities. The person with good reasoning ability can solve problems, foresee consequences, analyze a situation on the basis of past experience, and make and carry out plans according to recognizable facts.

4. Number (N) is the ability to work with figures—to handle simple quantitative problems rapidly and accurately. It involves primarily speed and accuracy in handling numbers.

5. Word-Fluency (W) is the ability to write and talk easily. It differs from Verbal-Meaning because it is concerned with the speed and ease with which words can be used, rather than with the degree of understanding of verbal concepts.

SUBJECTS

Subjects for this study were obtained in the course of a cooperative research project from the membership of a prepaid medical plan. The total pool of potential subjects over 16 years of age available from this organization consisted of about 18,000 members. A stratified random sampling procedure picked the names of 2,818 potential subjects who were then contacted and asked to volunteer. In response to this request positive replies were obtained from 451 men and 459 women, a total of 910 subjects. Because of conflicting time schedules and other sources of attrition, such as incomplete test records, the final sample consists of 500 subjects ranging in age from 20 to 70 years. The sample was divided into ten 5-year intervals, each containing 25 men and 25 women.

As seems inevitable in studies employing volunteer Ss, there was a tendency for the better-educated levels of the pool of potential Ss to participate. In spite of this fact a great range of educational background was found. Mean number of years of schooling varied from 11.0 years for the 61–65-year-old group, which was lowest, to 14.1 years for the 26–30-year-old group. These differences are significant but would seem to reflect the increased educational opportunities available for the younger Ss, rather than differences in the population from which the Ss were obtained, since these changes run pretty close to the general census data. It should be noted, though, that the mean educational level for all subgroups is somewhat above that of the general population.

All Ss were rated as to their occupational level on a scale ranging from 0 to 9 using the major classifications of the United States Census Bureau, ranging from "unskilled labor" to "professional." Where the occupation "housewife" was given, the occupational rating of the husband was used. On this rating scale, the sample attained a mean rating of 6.0, which is higher than the population average but is probably quite close to the population distribution in a metropolitan area like Seattle. The mean occupational levels for different age groups vary from 5.2 to 6.4 points. These age differences show a systematic trend, achieving a peak in the 46–50-year period and showing some decline thereafter. The mean income level for the entire group was equivalent to a total annual family income of about $4,500. The distribution of marital status is homogeneous with respect to age, except for the youngest group (where there is a high incidence of people presumably before the stage of establishing families) and in the oldest groups (where evidence is found of family dissolution through the death of one of the partners). Eighty-five per cent of the total sample was married.

The sample is not quite as representative for the lowest and highest population segments, but in terms of the socioeconomic characteristics given is probably an adequate sample of the upper 75% of the American social structure. This is probably as good a population sample as can be constituted without the use of captive populations.

AGE CHANGES IN THE MEASURE OF RIGID BEHAVIOR

As was indicated in the section on the test material, the Test of Behavioral Rigidity used in this study yields seven different subtest scores, which, when combined according to appropriate weighting formulae, will yield three factor scores and a composite rigidity score which is a linear combination of these factor scores. Figure 1 gives the means for the factor scores for each of the subgroups, and indicates systematic age changes on all the rigidity dimensions. Analysis of variance tests show differences between age groups to be significant at the 1% level of confidence for every variable. It may thus be concluded on the basis of these data that people do become more rigid with increasing age on all the dimensions of rigidity measured.

To give a better view of the extent of change in these scores, the absolute decrement in T-scores from the mean score of the most flexible group has been plotted for all groups. These are shown in Figure 2. It appears that the most dramatic decline is found on the motor-cognitive rigidity dimension, while the least (though still highly significant) change occurs on the

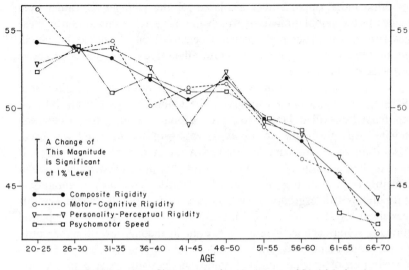

FIGURE 1. Age Changes in the Measures of Rigid Behavior.

personality-perceptual dimension. Significant decrements at the 1% level of confidence prevail for the motor-cognitive rigidity dimension beginning with the 26–30-year-old group. On the personality-perceptual rigidity dimension, however, the decrement is not significant until the 41–45-year-old group is reached. On the psychomotor speed dimension, significant decrement is noted at age 31–35; and finally, on the composite rigidity scores, significant decrement is noted beginning with the 36–40-year-old group.

From these data it would appear that loss of flexibility would become noticeable in the forties and fifties, and that by the fifties an average loss of approximately one population *SD* has occurred. In terms of the dimensions tested it appears then that, whether by maturational change or environmental effect, there is a progressive and significant decrement with age in the ability of the average adult to react to environmental change.

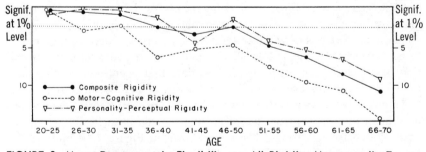

FIGURE 2. Mean Decrement in Flexibility on All Rigidity Measures (in *T*-score points from mean of most flexible subgroup).

Correlations were also computed, separately for each age group, among the factor scores and between the factor scores and the composite score. There did not seem to be any significant age trends in these intercorrelations.

AGE CHANGES IN MENTAL ABILITIES

All PMA raw scores were converted into T-scores to make them comparable to the rigidity scores, again using the mean and SD of the whole sample as the point of reference. Figure 3 shows the means for each of the five mental abilities which were measured as well as for the composite IQ scores. The ages given on these graphs are the midpoints of the subgroups.

Age changes on all five mental abilities, as well as on the composite IQ, are found to be significant at the 1% level of confidence. It will be noted, however, that the form of these gradients differs among the individual abilities. The peak level of performance is, with the exception of Reasoning, found at a later level than is suggested by comparable studies with other intelligence tests. On the composite IQ score, the peak level is reached by the 31–35-year-old group. The peak levels of performance for the individual abilities are: Verbal-Meaning, 31–35 years; Space, 26–30 years; Reasoning, 20–25 years; Number, 46–50 years; and Word-Fluency, 31–35 years.

These findings indicate a wide range in the age trends for specific mental abilities. Since all the peak levels appear in the period from 20 to 50 years,

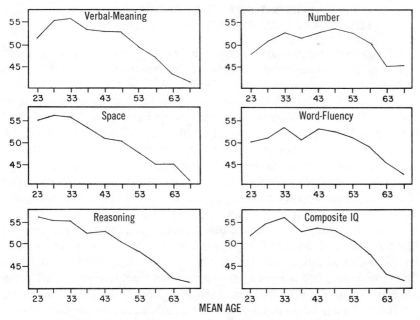

FIGURE 3. Age Changes in the Primary Mental Abilities.

this differential rise and decline of abilities might help to explain the tendency for global intelligence scores, when plotted against age, to show minimally significant decline for the period of the middle years and then, about age 50, to show steeper decrements. When results were examined in terms of the absolute decrement in T-score points from the mean peak levels for each of these abilities, it appeared that there is variability not only in age of peak performance, but also in the age level at which a significant decrement from the peak level is first noticed. Thus, for the composite IQ score, a significant decrement is first observed for the 36–40-year-old group. The ages for the individual mental abilities at which significant decrements are first seen are Verbal-Meaning, Space, Reasoning and Word-Fluency, 36–40 years; while for Number it does not occur until age 56–60.

More variation is shown in the rate of decrement. Decrements are assumed to become behaviorally noticeable if they have a magnitude of 5 points (½ SD) and marked if they exceed 10 points (1 SD), then these findings would indicate that such decline becomes noticeable at the following age levels: Verbal-Meaning, 51–55; Space and Reasoning, 46–50; Number and Word-Fluency, 61–65; and total IQ, 51–55. Decrement in the mental abilities according to the above criterion would be considered marked at the following ages: Total IQ, 61–65; Space and Reasoning, 56–60; Verbal-Meaning, 61–65; and Number and Word-Fluency probably in the seventies, if these age trends continue systematically.

THE RELATION BETWEEN CHANGES IN
BEHAVIORAL RIGIDITY AND MENTAL ABILITIES

After considering the age changes in both rigidity and mental ability measures, the next step in the analysis of the experimental evidence is concerned with changes in the relationship between the two sets of measures. Correlations were therefore computed between the composite rigidity score and the Primary Mental Abilities as well as between the individual Test of Behavioral Rigidity factor scores and the Primary Mental Abilities test.

Figure 4 indicates that there is a general tendency for these correlations to be significant and to be relatively constant over the adult age range, except for a slight drop in the older age groups. Correlations for samples of the magnitude here used are significant at the 5% level of confidence if they exceed .27 and at the 1% level of confidence if they exceed .35.

While the changes in the relation between rigidity and the Primary Mental Abilities scores are fairly consistent, they are by no means uniform for the different rigidity dimensions or the individual mental abilities. It should be noted that the personality-perceptual rigidity score shows lower correlation with the Primary Mental Abilities scores throughout, and at the top end of the age range seems to have no relation at all to the global intelligence score. This is in contrast to the motor-cognitive rigidity and the

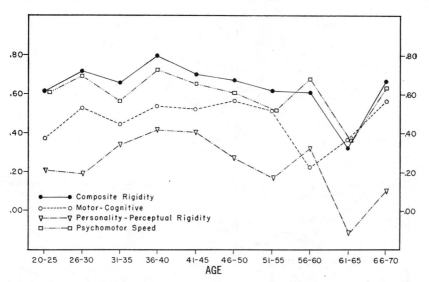

FIGURE 4. Correlation Between Test of Behavioral Rigidity Scores and Primary Mental Abilities Composite IQ.

psychomotor speed scores, which correlate significantly with the Primary Mental Abilities scores throughout.

Since the composite rigidity score appears to show, on the whole, the highest correlations with the individual PMA scores, its relationship with each of the individual mental abilities has been plotted in Figure 5. It will be noted that the correlations are again significant over the entire age range, except for Space, with some apparent decrease in the correlations with age. The slopes and levels of these age gradients, however, differ among the abilities, with little or no significant drop in the correlations with Reasoning and Word-Fluency, fairly marked drop for Verbal-Meaning and Number, and relatively low or insignificant correlation with Space.

On the basis of the preceding results it appears that Hypotheses I and IV are not tenable, while, with the possible exception of the relationship with Space, evidence favorable to Hypothesis II has been presented. A more formal statistical test of these hypotheses was made by means of analyses of variance and covariance. The results again favored Hypothesis II.

DISCUSSION

The results of the present study suggest that both rigidity-flexibility and measures of mental ability may be useful to predict level of functioning at any given age level. Although measures of three distinct rigidity dimensions were used, it appears that a linear combination of these factors had the best predictive power and that such a composite score discriminated best on other variables.

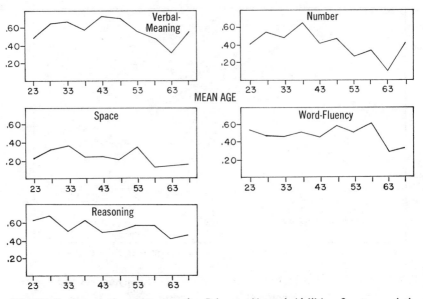

FIGURE 5. Correlation Between the Primary Mental Abilities Scores and the Composite Rigidity Scores.

The rigidity-flexibility dimension was found to be of almost equally discriminative power throughout the adult age range, even though restriction of the range of observed rigidity measures occurred at the upper age levels. This finding might be interpreted by the suggestion that the rigidity measures may give an indication of how well an individual is able to make use of his capacities. Thus an individual who scores high on the Test of Behavioral Rigidity probably makes effective use of his capacities, while one who scores low does not. No direct evidence on this point is given in this study, however, and one would probably have to define independent indices of optimal functioning to be correlated with our rigidity measures for further evidence.

It was noted that, among the rigidity factor scores, the ones showing highest relations with other measures were the motor-cognitive rigidity and the psychomotor speed scores. These scores presumably are indices of the difficulty in adjusting to change in familiar tasks and the ability to emit familiar responses and were expected to correlate best with the measures of cognitive behavior. The personality-perceptual rigidity score showed only low correlation with the cognitive material, but its inclusion in the composite score raised the predictive power of the latter.

This study presents additional evidence to show significant age decrements in important aspects of behavior. Considerable differences are also shown to exist among different measures as to their peak age of performance, the slope of the decrement gradient, and the variability of individuals at given age levels.

SUMMARY

1. An analysis was made of studies of developmental changes in adult behavior, and explanatory models using the concept of behavioral rigidity were considered.

2. Significant age differences were found on all measures of mental abilities and behavioral rigidity. There was considerable difference in the decrement shown on the different measures, in the ages of peak perform- ance for the different abilities, in the changes in variability, and in the rate of decline.

3. Correlations between the measures of rigidity and mental ability and an analysis of variance and covariance were used to test the principal hy- potheses. The correlations between the measures of rigidity and the mental abilities were found to be significantly high throughout the adult age span with a tendency to decrease toward the upper end of the age continuum. When the analysis of covariance was used to adjust the between-group differences on the mental abilities for the effect of rigidity, significant differences remained.

4. On the basis of this evidence the hypothesis which favors interaction between rigidity-flexibility and intelligence at every age level seems to be supported.

38

Studies in the Organization of Character*

Hugh Hartshorne and Mark A. May

The problems of character education are both tremendously important and tremendously complex. In considering character psychologically,

* Adapted and abridged from Hugh Hartshorne and Mark A. May, "A Summary of the Work of the Character Education Inquiry," *Religious Education,* 1930, Vol. 25, pp. 607-619, 754-762. (Published by permission of Dr. May and the publisher, The Re- ligious Education Association, New York City.)

investigators have not only the problem of identifying the behavior, which in practice may mean measuring it, but also the problem of evaluating this behavior against a standard of ethical conduct. Since the American culture (or any modern culture) is characterized by not one but many ethical standards, the problems which researchers encounter are multiplied, as indeed are the problems of parents and educators in promoting desirable "character" development in children. The widely known and important Character Education Inquiry, directed by Professors Hartshorne and May, is a series of studies (published in several volumes) which attempted to measure character by means of actual conduct tests and to examine the nature and organization of character as revealed by these tests. The present paper is adapted and abridged from a summary of this extensive research.

Although conducted in the 1920's, the Hartshorne and May investigation remains the classic study, and one which still has much to offer the serious student interested in psychological research dealing with ethical conduct. In view of the problems that beset the modern world, it is not surprising that this field has again become the object of extensive research investigation by psychologists.

The character education inquiry was launched at Teachers College, Columbia University, in September, 1924, at the request of, and under a grant from, the Institute of Social and Religious Research, and under the general supervision of Professor E. L. Thorndike.

At the outset, several approaches to the study of character were open, but the character testing approach was chosen, for several reasons. Not only is this relatively neglected approach basic to any fresh scientific research into the nature of character and its manner of growth, but studies of the relative value of current methods of moral and religious education and of experiments to discover improvements in technique depend, to a degree rarely appreciated, on the availability of ways of *measuring results*. Plans and programs which have no experimental basis, and which may be as likely to damage character as to improve it, are produced by the score. Hundreds of millions of dollars are probably spent annually by churches, Sunday schools and other organizations for children and youth, with almost no check on the product—a negligence of which no modern industry would be guilty. Through lack of tests for predicting effective living a vast amount of time and no one knows how much money are probably thrown away on expensive and intricate devices for moral and religious education.

Although the main form of the research was the development of tests for the measurement of progress in character education, it happened, as is often the case in scientific investigation, that the by-products of the investigation are of greater importance than the main results. This paper thus is concerned not only with the tests developed, but also with the nature of character traits and their concomitants.

THE TESTS DEVELOPED

Tests of Moral Knowledge. One of the most important intellectual abilities in character is that of being able to foresee the social consequences of acts. Accordingly, we devised a test that was intended to measure the child's ability to foresee the types of consequences that might follow from simple types of activity, such as starting across the street without looking both ways, getting into fights on the playground, giving away money that had been saved for another purpose, and similar commonplace activities well within the range of experience of school children.

In the first instance, the children were simply asked to write after each statement of an act all the things they could think of that might happen. They were asked to list both the good things and the bad. This gave a rough measure of what one might call the child's social imagination.

In a second test a situation is briefly described, and the child is asked to check the sentence that tells what is the best thing to do. For example, if you are very hungry at a party when only light refreshments are served, what is the right thing to do: (1) Eat little and say nothing? (2) Try to eat a lot without being noticed? (3) Leave the party and go to a restaurant? (4) Tell the hostess that her refreshments are too light?

It does not particularly matter, therefore, whether the child gives the answer which he thinks has the approval of the teacher and examiner, or guesses at what he is expected to say, or gives his own personal view. This point has been urged as a criticism against this type of testing, but we have regarded it as precisely that which we wish to measure.

Still another sample of the tests of intellectual factors is what we originally called a provocations test. Presumably there are conditions under which such conduct as lying, cheating, stealing, and the like, might be relatively desirable. What we wish to know is where the child draws the line. For example, under what conditions would the child justify stealing or lying? This is how we attempted to measure it: We told, in simple, one- or two-sentence stories, of things that children have done, describing briefly the circumstances. Then we asked for a vote on whether or not this act under these circumstances was right, wrong or excusable. For example, on the way to Sunday school Jack matched pennies with other boys in order to get money for the Sunday school collection. Was this right, wrong or excusable under the circumstances? We compiled a list of many similar situations and asked the children to vote on them. This gave information on the extent to which and the conditions under which a child will excuse types of action that fall below the ideal standard.

These tests, which we have called, for the want of a better name, moral knowledge tests, have satisfactory statistical reliability and validity. Their scientific quality is on a par with the best intelligence tests and school achievement tests.

Conduct Tests. In the field of actual conduct, we have developed tests covering four types of behavior—deception, co-operation, inhibition, and persistence. Before describing samples of these tests, a word should be inserted concerning the general theory of conduct testing. We have proceeded on the assumption that the only sense in which conduct can be measured is by taking samples of it. If they are representative and there are enough of them, his future conduct may be predicted from them.

In the study of honesty, or rather its opposite, deceit, we sampled the tendencies of children to cheat, steal and lie. Of the cheating type of conduct, we took fourteen samples of classroom situations, four of situations involving athletic contests, three of situations involving parties or parlor games, and two of school work done at home. We also took two samples of the lying tendency and two of stealing. The lying and stealing tests, however, were not widely used.

Examples of situations involving cheating in the classroom are such as copying answers from an answer sheet that was given out for the purpose of correcting papers at the close of the test, of adding answers in a speed test after time had been called, or violating the rules in the solution of a puzzle, or opening the eyes in doing a stunt that was to be accomplished with the eyes closed. The essential feature of these tests is that a child is placed in an ordinary classroom situation and given a task to perform which has in it an opportunity for cheating, but the situation is so arranged that if a child cheats or attempts to deceive the experimenter he unwittingly leaves a record of his conduct.

The next series of behavior tests is in an entirely different area. They represent types of behavior that are ordinarily described as helpfulness, co-operation, self-denial, self-sacrifice, charity and the like. We have used the term "service" to cover all of these. The plan for testing the service tendency is in general the same as that for testing the deception tendency and involves the setting up of a situation with an appeal and at the same time a resistance. Sample situations involving self-denial or self-sacrifice are these: inviting the child to come to school a half hour early in order to make pictures for hospital children; asking boys to give up their manual training project (in one case the building of a wooden automobile model) to make wooden toys for hospital children; presenting children in an orphan's home each with nineteen cents and asking them to vote how they would distribute it between self, bank and charity (a check-up was made to determine precisely what they did with this money).

Another type of conduct that we attempted to measure is persistence. Here, again, we had two series of tests, one for groups and the other for individuals. The plan was to set up a situation involving a task and note the length of time a child would stick at it. One task was that of solving magic squares; another, that of solving a very difficult mechanical puzzle; another, that of reading a story printed in a confusing manner.

To summarize now the conduct tests, we have taken twenty-three samples of situations involving deception or dishonesty, five samples of situations involving service, four samples of situations involving inhibition, and five samples of situations involving persistence. Add to this sampling of conduct some five hundred samples of imaginary situations in which the children are required to make some kind of an intellectual decision, and some 350 situations in which they are required to express a preference or desire, and you have then a fairly good picture of the scope of the tests of the Character Education Inquiry which have been brought to the point of actual use.

VALIDITY OF THE TESTS

We are now ready to raise the question as to the extent to which we have measured character. It is obvious that no one of these tests is an adequate measure of all there is to character. The question is whether or not any combination of them in any sense adequately measures character. This question can be answered only experimentally.

In order to find out the extent to which the tests measured character, it was necessary to secure data on the conduct, ideals, attitudes, social adjustments, reputation and environmental background of these children, quite apart from the scores derived from the tests themselves. We were fortunate in securing a large body of such data on a sufficient sample of the children who had been tested to enable us to determine the extent to which the character test scores correlate with these character factors.

Two main sources of information against which our tests were checked were: (1) The child's reputation among his teachers, classmates, and leaders; and (2) pen portraits of the character of one hundred children based on all available data, arranged, by sixty-three judges, according to the desirability of the character described.

Reputation. Reputation as a criterion of character has been used by numerous investigators and, on the whole, the results have been disappointing. Profiting by the mistakes of predecessors, we attempted to free our reputation data from the influence of prejudice and gossip so that the results would reflect as true a picture as possible of the facts on which the ratings were based. For example, instead of asking a teacher to give her general impression of the co-operativeness of a pupil, we asked her to check the one of five statements which seemed to her to describe best this behavior. One such group of five statements is as follows: (1) Works with others if asked to do so. (2) Works better alone; cannot get along with others. (3) Works well and gladly with others. (4) Indifferent as to whether or not he works with others. (5) Usually antagonistic or obstructive to joint effort. Similar statements were worked out for twenty-two types of conduct.

We also secured the opinions of pupils concerning the conduct of their classmates by the use of an instrument called the "Guess Who" test. The "Guess Who" test is a series of twenty-four descriptions of types of conduct characteristic of school children. Each child reads over each description and writes after it the names of his classmates who seem to him to be described by it. For example, one of the descriptions is: "Here is a crabber and knocker. Nothing is right. Always kicking and complaining." The children are asked to write down the names of their classmates who they think are described in these terms. This instrument turned out to have very high reliability and high validity.

In addition to these two devices, three others were used, so that the total reputation score of the child was a composite of the opinions of his teachers, classmates, and leaders. When this score was freed statistically from the effects of prejudice, it showed remarkable correspondence with the scores derived from the objective tests. When all of the conduct scores were combined into a single score, and all reputation scores combined into a single score, the correlation between the two, corrected for attenuation, is .94. These are exceedingly high values and are extremely significant.

But character is more than conduct and more than reputation. When we include in our character score not only conduct but also moral knowledge, social attitudes, the child's background and his reactions to it, all of which are parts of his character, the correlations run even higher. In fact, the raw correlation is .70, which, when corrected for attenuation, rises to .988. In other words, character so far as it is represented in reputation, is completely accounted for by performance on an extended series of tests which measure conduct, culture, social opinion and attitude.

Character Portraits. While these results seemed significant and even somewhat startling, we were not satisfied to let the matter rest here. We pushed the validation procedure a step further, in an attempt to check our character tests against a more unified and concrete criterion.

We took at least one step in the direction of concreteness by developing a scale of character as a whole. That is, we attempted to handle our specific data not in terms of their summation but in terms of their organization. Our technique consisted in the building of character sketches on the basis of our records. We selected one hundred children from one of our populations, on whom we had a rather complete set of data. The data on each child were written up in the form of a pen portrait or a description of his conduct, attitudes, reputation, intelligence and background, including what information we were able to secure regarding the second criterion, namely, the adequacy of the child's social functioning. These one hundred portraits were then ranked by sixty-three judges according to the degree of character exhibited by each. These rankings were surprisingly uniform and yielded a scale of character sketches with a reliability of .98.

The next step in the procedure was to find the correlation between each of the elements in the total composite and this general character scale. The results show that reputation stands in closest relation to total character as measured by this scale. Moral knowledge and social attitudes come next, conduct next, cultural background and personal factors, such as intelligence and age, come last. When all the conduct scores are added together, however, the correlation between conduct and character is about as high as between reputation and character, both being around .8.

Consistency. The consideration of this question led us to construct another type of criterion which resembles the one just described in being built on quantitative data. It differs, however, in one important respect. While both of the criteria described above rely on judgments and opinions, in this one all subjective factors are eliminated, and it is derived from the objective data themselves. The same one hundred cases used in the construction of the pen portrait criterion were also used for the building of this objective criterion, and scores on the moral knowledge tests, conduct tests, tests of emotional instability, home background, school marks, deportment and reputation were classed into twenty-three groups. This gave twenty-three character scores for each of the one hundred individuals. These scores were treated in two ways: first, they were summed up, as usual, in an average score; and, second, the variability of each individual's scores around his own mean was computed. Thus, for each individual, we have an average score and a variability score. The variability score was called his consistency score.

Our character score represents consistency multiplied by level. An individual who has a high average score but a low consistency score will have a relatively low index or score. But the individual who has a high average score and a high consistency score will receive the highest index or score. That is, the child who is consistently good will receive the highest score, whereas the child who is consistently bad will receive the lowest score.

A character score was thus computed for each of the one hundred children whom we have been discussing. This score, in a sense, represents our final effort as a criterion. It correlates .72 with reputation, which, it will be recalled, was our first criterion, and .81 with the criterion derived by having judges rank the pen portraits of character.

The conclusion reached as a result of our attempts to construct satisfactory character tests is that if a large number of samples of conduct, knowledge, attitude, intelligence, background, and social adjustment are taken, and if the general algebraic level for each individual is determined, and, at the same time, if the variability of each individual's scores around his own mean is computed, a combination of these two values will indeed yield an index or score of character.

THE SPECIFICITY OF MORAL CONDUCT

A great deal of moral education has been built on the assumption that character is a structure of virtues and vices. In our studies in actual conduct, we see that there is very little evidence of unified character traits. The evidence for the specificity of conduct is (1) the low intercorrelation between sample tests of the same type of behavior, (2) the normal distribution of honesty scores in a population of children, and (3) the tremendous differences in situations in the amount of dishonesty they elicit. If honesty were a trait which you either have or do not have, then we would expect the distribution of honesty scores to be bimodal; that is, at one end of the score we would have a piling up of saints and at the other end of the scale a piling up of sinners, with nothing much in between. The exact opposite of this is the truth. At the dishonesty end of the scale, there are very few. That is, we find very few children who cheated twenty-three times in twenty-three chances. At the honesty end of the scale we also find very few children who are honest twenty-three times in twenty-three chances. Most of them are sometimes honest and sometimes dishonest.

KNOWLEDGE AND CONDUCT

If you ask the same question regarding "rightness" or "wrongness" of conduct of fifty perfectly honest children, that is, children on whom we have no evidence of cheating, they will give you the same kinds of answers in about the same proportion as the cheaters. We made similar studies of four or five hundred questions, and the results were nearly always the same —no differences. Then we tried to determine the relationship between knowledge in general and conduct in a specific situation. Again the correlations were very low. So we finally pooled together all of our moral knowledge scores on each individual, on the one hand, and all the conduct scores, on the other, and correlated these in a very widespread and heterogeneous population, with a resulting coefficient of about .50. Thus we find no specific relations between moral knowledge and conduct, but only general relations.

FACTORS RELATED TO CHARACTER

Age. We can say with considerable certainty that within the limits of the present research there is practically no correlation between age and conduct, except, perhaps, in the case of the scores on the persistence tests. The results of our persistence tests do show that older children are inclined, on the whole, to be somewhat more persistent than younger children. This, however, may very well be accounted for by differences between older and younger children in the amount of interest in the tasks set by our tests. In the case of deception, we found that the older children were, in fact, a little more inclined to be deceptive than the younger children. This is rather significant in view of the amount of money and energy that has been spent on their moral education.

With moral knowledge, however, the case is quite different. Here we do find correlations with age, though of somewhat less magnitude than between moral knowledge and intelligence or school achievement. As children grow older, they become more appreciative of ideal standards, and their opinions and attitudes conform more closely to those of educated adults.

Sex. Our tests show no consistent sex differences in the matter of deception but rather wide and significant differences in service and self-control. In the tests of helpfulness, co-operation and charity, girls are slightly better than the boys. Their teachers, however, rate them very much better than the boys. In the tests of inhibition, the girls are markedly better than the boys and consistently so. In persistence, the differences are very slight and vary with the test situation. In moral knowledge, attitudes and opinions, the differences again are very slight but favor the girls.

Intelligence. Nearly all of the children with whom we have worked were tested with the Thorndike Group Intelligence Test. We estimate that if all honesty tests were combined on a large population of children, the correlation with intelligence would probably run as high as .60. In the case of service, inhibition and persistence, however, the correlations are somewhat lower. Evidently intelligence is more closely related to honesty than to any of these three types of behavior.

As would be expected, the correlations between intelligence and moral knowledge are almost as high as between one intelligence test and another. They are equally as high as between intelligence and school achievement. They run in fact from about .5 to about .9. This close relation between intellect and the abilities measured by these tests indicates what a strong part intelligence actually plays in the development of a child's social concepts and ability to make ethical discriminations.

Socio-economic Background. We find significant differences in honesty between children whose parents are engaged in the professional occupations and children whose parents are unskilled laborers. We take this to indicate that the general social and economic background of the child is an important factor in his honesty. It is also an important factor in his social attitudes and opinions, and also in his knowledge of right and wrong.

A careful study was made in one community of the homes of the fifty most honest and fifty most dishonest children. This revealed certain important differences between home conditions of these two groups of children. The homes from which the worst offenders came might be best characterized as exhibiting bad parental example, parental discord, bad discipline, unsocial attitudes toward children, impoverished community and changing economic or social situation. The homes from which the more honest children came revealed the opposite of these conditions.

Schooling. Turning now to school influences, we begin with the Sunday school. In the matter of honesty, co-operation, inhibition and persistence, we find a general tendency for children enrolled in Sunday schools to exhibit more desirable conduct than the children who are not enrolled in Sunday schools. But, on the other hand, we find (and this is especially true of honesty) that there is practically no correlation between frequency of attendance at Sunday school and conduct. Apparently it is only necessary to be enrolled. It is clear that we have here an excellent illustration of selection. It is the better trained children who are enrolled in the Sunday schools in the first place.

In our studies of the influence of the day school, we found that different types of school experiences are accompanied by differences in the conduct, knowledge, and attitudes of children. For example, children who attend private schools, particularly the more progressive schools, are markedly more honest in their school work than are children who attend conventional public schools. This question was investigated rather thoroughly with a long series of experiments. Aside from the fact that children who attend private schools are a selected group coming from the better homes and better environments, we find that progressive methods are more likely to foster situations in which honest behavior is the natural result than are more conventional methods. Schools, however, differ widely among themselves, and there are enormous differences between different classrooms, indicating an influence of the teacher, an influence of the morale of the group, or both. These phenomena have been investigated, and we find that the attitude of the teacher toward her pupils is a factor of considerable significance. Whenever this attitude is frankly co-operative and sympathetic, the children are likely to be more honest, more co-operative and to show higher degrees of self-control than in cases where the attitude of the teacher is unsympathetic, arbitrary, and dictatorial.

EDUCATIONAL IMPLICATIONS

Contradictory demands made upon the child by the varied situations in which he is responsible to adults not only prevent the organization of a consistent character but actually compel inconsistency as the price of peace and self-respect.

There is introduced, therefore, one conclusion. This relates to the building of a functioning ideal for society which may serve at once as a principle of unified or consistent response and as a principle of satisfactory social adjustment. Such a policy or principle must, therefore, be derived from the inherent nature of social life and growth as experienced by the child himself. It must not only be scientifically sound in the sense that it presents a workable theory of life; it must also emerge in the minds of the children through their own guided experiments in living.

It can hardly be expected that most children can be taught to be responsive to social ideals unsupported by group code and morale. When the individual is made the unit of educational effort, he is so abstracted from life situations as to become more and more of a prig in proportion as his teachers succeed with him, and more and more the victim of a disorganized and detached mind in proportion as they fail. The normal unit for character education is the group or small community, which provides through co-operative discussion and effort the moral support required for the adventurous discovery and effective use of ideals in the conduct of affairs.

39

Differences Between Three Generations in Standards of Conduct*

Alice Anderson and Beatrice Dvorak

This brief and interesting paper, apparently written in the student days of the investigators, reports one of the few efforts to study objectively the differences in attitudes and moral views characterizing adults of different age levels. It was found that adults of the grandparental generation made moral judgments more frequently on a "right or wrong" basis; their college-age grandchildren reached decisions more frequently on the basis of prudence or aesthetic standards. These findings suggest some of the psychological barriers that divide generations, though they do not indicate whether the differences are due to differences in the cultural backgrounds in which the three gen-

* Adapted and abridged from Alice Anderson and Beatrice Dvorak, "Differences Between College Students and Their Elders in Standards of Conduct," *Journal of Abnormal and Social Psychology,* 1928, Vol. 23, pp. 286-292. (With permission of Dr. Dvorak and the American Psychological Association.)

erations studied grew up or perhaps due to changes more immediately associated with advancing age as such. Some evidence, for example, suggests that the tendency to see things in terms of "black and white" may be connected with an increased sense of psychological insecurity among older persons.

PURPOSE AND PROCEDURE

The aim of the present study was to discover on which of four standards college students most frequently claim to base their conduct, and to determine whether the standard most frequently chosen differed for grandparents, parents and youth. In order to accomplish this end we devised a multiple-choice questionnaire of fifteen behavior situations, to each of which four choices of answer were given. One of these answers dealt with the situation according to the right and wrong standard, another according to the standard of prudence or intelligent judgment, a third according to the standard set by public opinion, or of doing what the crowd does, and a fourth according to the aesthetic standard. Sample items follow:

If you were at a party where everyone else was drinking which of the following things would you do: (1) refuse absolutely because you believed it wrong; (2) drink with the crowd; (3) refuse because the actions resulting from intoxication would be distasteful to you; (4) refuse because you believed it unwise or unhealthful to drink alcohol?

If you were in a "petting party" would you: (1) pet also for fear of being called a "poor sport"; (2) refuse to pet because you consider it wrong; (3) refuse to pet because it is "awfully poor taste"; (4) pet because everyone else did, and you see no logical reason why you shouldn't?

If friends of yours were contemplating a divorce on what ground would you try to dissuade them because: (1) divorce is contrary to your standards of right and wrong; (2) divorce would interfere with the welfare and happiness of their children; (3) the divorce would create an unbearable scandal; (4) divorce would cause them to lose caste socially?

The questionnaire is brief and inadequate in many respects, and some objections may be raised against the scoring key. Furthermore it may be charged that certain of the questions which are especially pertinent for students are irrelevant for their elders. Questions on creating, studying, and petting would probably not occur in a list of conduct questions made out for parents and grandparents. The merit of this questionnaire lies in the fact that it was made out by students for the use of students. But the results from its use on older age groups are quite consistent.

The questionnaire was given to several different groups including college students, parents, and grandparents. The college group comprised 30 men and 30 women, most of whom were of sophomore standing, and were co-students in a course in an elementary psychology laboratory. The groups of parents and grandparents were obtained at social gatherings of our parents' and grandparents' friends; 21 fathers, 27 mothers, 13 grandfathers and 21 grandmothers were thus obtained.

RESULTS

From the graphs in Figure 1 it is evident that both grandparents and parents claim to solve most of these 15 problems of conduct on the basis of the right and wrong standard; the other standards are preferred in the order of prudence or intelligent judgment, aesthetic appeal, and public opinion, or social approval. College youth prefers to make its decisions according to the standard of prudence or intelligent judgment, its second choice is the aesthetic standard, its third is the standard of right and wrong, and its fourth choice is that of public opinion.

Slight sex differences appear within each age group, the most striking of which is that college women prefer the aesthetic standard more than do college men, and they prefer the standard of prudence less than do college men. We surmise that the explanation of this difference lies in the fact that aesthetic appeal is still considered by the men a bit effeminate, and not quite so manly as the standard of prudence or intelligent judgment.

As shown in Table 1 the greatest differences appear between grandpar-

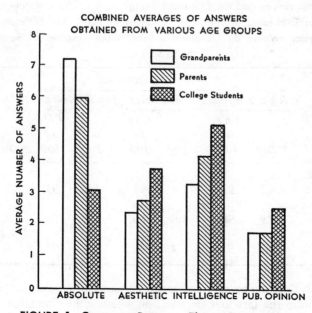

FIGURE 1. Contrasts Between Three Generations in Their Reliance on Various Types of Moral Standards

ents and college students; between these two age groups the difference is most significant on the right and wrong standard, and next most significant on the standard of prudence. Parents stand midway between students and grandparents on all of the standards; they differ most significantly from the student group on the standard of right and wrong, and they are most significantly different from the group of grandparents on the standard of prudence. These results tend to confirm the theory that the standard of right and wrong as a basis for conduct is rapidly dying and that the standard of prudence is being set up in its place. The standard of aesthetic morality is more preferred by college students than by parents or grandparents, and has already been accepted by college women almost to the same extent as has the standard of prudence.

We realize that the people who answered these questionnaires probably do not base their actions on the standards on which they claim to base them. They are doubtless far more swayed by public opinion and far less activated by cool reason or prudence than their answers would indicate. Although their answers are a product of rationalization, nevertheless it is likely that individuals can be appealed to by the standard on which they rationalize their conduct, whereas an appeal emphasizing the rightness or wrongness of an act might influence grandparents and parents, and appeal to college youth on the basis of prudence or aesthetics would probably be more effective.

TABLE 1. Differences and the Statistical Significance of the Differences Between Age Groups Expressed in Terms of "Chances in 100" That Differences in the Same Direction Would Be Obtained in an Infinite Number of Repetitions of the Experiment

	Standards							
	Right & Wrong		Aesthetics		Prudence		Public Opinion	
Groups Compared	Diff.	Ch's in 100	Diff.	Ch's in 100	Diff.	Ch's in 100	Diff.	Ch's in 100
Grandparents and youth	4.1	99+	1.4	92	1.9	95	.8	77
Parents and youth	2.9	98	1.0	86	1.0	83	.8	77
Grandparents and parents	1.2	93	.4	79	.9	97	0	50

This study does not reveal whether the standards of conduct have actually changed within the last four decades, or whether the standards of youth are always different from those of middle and old age. It may be that if the same students were to answer these questions twenty years hence, then answers would approximate those of the parents in this study.

To conclude:

1. College students differ from parents and grandparents in the standards on which they base their conduct, in that they prefer the standards of prudence and aesthetics to that of right and wrong.

2. The greatest differences in standards of conduct occur between age groups rather than between sex groups.

3. All groups tend to eschew the standard of public opinion.

4. Since they make prudence and aesthetics their chosen standards for rationalizing their conduct college students probably could be appealed to on the basis of those standards far more effectively than on the standard of right and wrong.

Part IX

CHANGING PATTERNS OF INTERPERSONAL RELATIONSHIPS

MAN'S relationships to man constitute one of the most baffling conceptual-theoretical problems in modern science. The overlapping disciplines of social psychology, sociology, and cultural anthropology are all focused on aspects of the diadic interaction in its various complex forms. The developmental psychologist is interested in the dimensions of interpersonal responses as they vary with the maturity of the participants. The basic patterns of social response are undoubtedly formed and selectively reinforced within the home. Other things being equal, children reared in socially suspicious and hostile homes tend to display these characteristics in their own social behavior. Fortunately other things are not always equal for such children.

In their report Horrocks and Buker present convincing evidence that the growing child gradually learns to maintain a more and more stable quality in his interpersonal relationships. The paper by Kuhlen and Houlihan illustrates the effects of a changing social climate on interpersonal relations between boys and girls. The findings of this study show an increasingly easier social relationship as we progress through the middle of the twentieth century.

A pattern of behavior that elicits approval and acceptance at one developmental level may become a social debit at a later age. The paper by McCandless, Castaneda, and Palermo shows some of the complex relationships between level of anxiety in children and social status within the group. These studies are, of course, only illustrative of the many variables that potentially influence interpersonal relationships.

Marriage brings with it a host of new demands for interpersonal compromises and the alternate satisfaction of the needs of first one and then the other partner. The report by Terman throws some much-needed light on factors that influence marital happiness and success. Terman's findings also show the wide range of differences in marital happiness in different families. It appears that a few marital partners are exceptionally well adjusted, a few abysmally unhappy, and the majority distributed at various points between these two extremes. The remaining paper in this part, that by Crawford, suggests some of the possible antecedents of marital happiness by an analysis of attitudinal differences between contrasting social subgroups within one culture. All of the papers in this part show that developmental status has a significant influence on the quantity and quality of interpersonal relationships.

40

Friendship Fluctuations During Childhood*

John E. Horrocks and Mae E. Buker

Man is a social animal with strong needs to relate himself significantly and meaningfully to others of his own kind. Social isolation, real or threatened, is a powerful motivating force for producing changes in human behavior. The initiation and maintenance of close friendships is one of the important ways that man guards himself against the loss of meaningful human contact so important to his feeling that living is a worthwhile experience. The maintenance of friendships neces- sarily involves mutual and reciprocal need satisfactions. To be a friend, a prerequisite of having a friend, the child must learn to delay and compromise some of his own egoistic needs in deference to the needs of another. This learning is based on many developing psycho- logical functions—perceptual awareness of another's needs, tolerance for frustrating circumstances, and acceptance of delayed gratification, to name only a few. It seems reasonable to expect that the growing child would acquire these socially important skills in the same gradual manner that he acquires his skill in reading or arithmetical computa- tion. In the following report, Dr. Horrocks and his collaborator show that the capacity for enduring friendships is gradually acquired during childhood and adolescence, as hypothesized. Just as some individuals never learn to read or engage in arithmetical reasoning, it seems prob- able that some persons never learn how to form and maintain a friend- ship. It also seems probable that the skills necessary for developing satisfying friendships are teachable.

* From John E. Horrocks and Mae E. Buker, "A Study of the Friendship Fluctua- tions of Preadolescents," *Journal of Genetic Psychology*, 1951, Vol. 78, pp. 131-144. (With permission of the senior author and The Journal Press.)

In a previous study Horrocks and Thompson (1946, 1947) investigated the degree of friendship fluctuation among 1874 adolescent boys and girls. It was the purpose of the present study to investigate the degree of fluctuation in pre-adolescent friendships and to compare the results with those obtained by Horrocks and Thompson in their earlier study. The development of acceptable social behavior has frequently been stressed as one of the more important aims of education. An inquiry into the stability of friendship among children in the various years of school, particularly as it changes or remains constant from year to year should serve as a further step toward an understanding of the development of social behavior. Many of the early studies of interpersonal relationships were concerned with the development of methods of observing the social behavior of the child. Recently the emphasis has shifted to the observation and measurement of the child's acceptance by his contemporaries and to interaction in social groups. Friendship is one form of acceptance and plays an important rôle in group interaction.

SUBJECTS

The 366 subjects originally selected for participation in this study were obtained from a suburban community near Columbus, Ohio, and consisted of all the children in one of that community's two elementary schools enrolled in grades one through five, and those in one session of the kindergarten. The children were in 14 different classrooms which ranged between 20 and 36 in population, with the exception of the kindergarten which had a population of 65. Ages ranged from 5 through 10 years and the sample consisted of 179 girls and 187 boys. The children came from families whose socio-economic status was considerably above that of the average American family. Intelligence quotients ranged from 75 to 128 with the median well above 100.

As is almost inevitable in a school situation, the sample of the testing periods varied somewhat due to absence, the admission of new students moving into the community, withdrawals, and classroom changes. About 90 per cent of the sample was common to all testing periods, or 327 out of 366 individuals. Table 1 presents the number of subjects, classified by chronological age, who were present at all testing periods. Of the total population of 366 enrolled in the grades represented in this study, 327 were actually present at both testing periods. After the collection of data the names of those absent at one or both of the testing periods were eliminated as *selectors* of best friends, although this did not affect their status as *selectees*.

PROCEDURE

All of the children selected for this study were given a slip of paper upon which the following request was mimeographed:

Please write below the names of your three best friends, or the children you like best in your classroom. List the one you like best first; second best, second; and third best, third.

Three numbered lines were provided for the subjects to write down the names of their three best friends. Each classroom in the study was self-contained, and so each classroom teacher explained verbally what the students were to do, emphasizing that the best friend's name was to be placed first and that friends outside the classroom were not to be named. With the kindergarten children it was necessary for the teacher to interview each child privately and also to record his response. In the first and second grades and in some of the other rooms, a list of the names of the children in the room was placed on the board. This served to help the children in spelling the names of their friends and called to mind the names of the children who were absent at the time the test was given.

Two weeks later the children were again asked to list their three best friends in order of preference. Slips of paper were supplied upon which the same directions used the first time were mimeographed. The following sentences were added:

Your best friends now may or may not be the same as your best friends two weeks ago. Write the names of the ones you like best now.

Special help was again given to the younger children.

TABLE 1. Number of Subjects Present at Both Testing Periods

Chronological Age	Boys	Girls	Boys and Girls
5	16	20	36
6	19	25	44
7	36	25	61
8	35	31	66
9	30	33	63
10	28	29	57
Total	164	163	327

Four weeks later another measure of friendship fluctuation was determined in the same manner as the first and was in turn followed by a retest after two weeks. Thus, two two-week testing periods, four weeks apart, were employed in this study, making a total time span of eight weeks. The study was made during March and April in order to have allowed the children to have been in the same classroom together since September.

The two-week interval was selected (a) because it was believed that it gave the children a short enough time so that they would have some opportunity to remember whom they had chosen in the first choosing situation, yet it was considered a long enough time to allow the presence or absence of characteristic trends in fluctuation to be shown through a comparison of the data on both tests: and (*b*) because it was desired for the purpose of the research that the results of the present study be comparable with the previous one made by Horrocks and Thompson.

A two-week testing period four weeks after the first two-week period was given to determine whether or not what is true of a given two-week period is also true of a later two-week period.

The method used in determining friendship fluctuation was the same as that devised by Horrocks and Thompson for their study. Their method of computing the friendship fluctuation indices was as follows: The three friends chosen by each subject during the second choice situation were compared with the three friends chosen two weeks previously.

If the friends chosen the second time duplicated in personage and rank order the friends chosen two weeks previously, the index of friendship fluctation was considered to be zero.

If the friends chosen the second time duplicated in personage but differed in rank order from the friends chosen two weeks previously, an index of friendship fluctuation was computed by assigning a numerical value of one to each rank that a friend of the second choice situation was separated from the rank initially assigned to him; e.g., if the original rankings were: like best, John; second best, Bill; third best, Carl; and the second rankings were: like best, Carl; second best, John; third best, Bill; the fluctuation index as computed by this procedure would be four; since Carl is removed two ranks, Bill one rank, and John one rank from the original rankings.

If the subject during the second choice situation chose among his three best friends boys or girls whom he had not previously chosen, the following numerical values were assigned to these new friends; two for a person not previously mentioned who became the subject's third-best friend during the second choice situation, three for a person not previously mentioned who became the subject's second-best friend, and four for a person not previously mentioned who became the subject's best friend. Table 2 may help to clarify the procedure employed to obtain this over-all index of friendship fluctuation.

TABLE 2. Subject, Female, Age 10

	First choice situation	Second choice situation
Best friend	Mary	Mary
Second-best friend	Patricia	Jane
Third-best friend	Jane	Doris
Friendship Fluctuation Index: 3		

RESULTS

The results of the first two-week testing period have been reported first. Unless otherwise designated, reference is to the results of this period.

The means and standard deviations of the distributions of friendship

TABLE 3. Sex Differences by Age in Indices of Friendship Fluctuation

Chronological Age	Girls		Boys		
	Mean	SD	Mean	SD	t
5	5.80	2.87	4.75	2.20	1.21
6	5.20	2.65	5.42	2.66	0.27
7	5.44	2.17	4.86	2.38	0.98
8	4.65	2.66	4.23	2.35	0.67
9	3.79	1.87	4.27	3.10	0.73
10	3.55	2.53	3.21	2.12	0.54

fluctuation for the various chronological age levels are presented in Table 3. These data are based on an analysis of 163 girls and 164 boys. In this table are also presented the results of statistical comparisons of the distributions of friendship fluctuation of boys and girls at the various age levels. Table 4 presents the means and standard deviations of the distributions of friendship fluctuation for the various grade levels.

The t's obtained in the statistical analyses presented in Table 3 and 4 indicate that the small differences in friendship fluctuation between the boys and girls at each of the chronological-age and grade levels can reasonably be attributed to random errors of sampling. From these statistical analyses one cannot reject with a reasonable degree of confidence the null hypothesis that there are no differences in friendship fluctuation between the boys and girls at the various age and grade levels.

The magnitude of the standard deviations for both sexes demonstrates that there are considerable individual differences in the stability of friendships at all of the chronological-age and grade levels studied.

As shown in Tables 5 and 6 there appears to be for both boys and girls a trend toward greater stability in friendship with increasing age or grade level, but with about the same amount of individual variation within each age and grade level.

The results of the statistical analyses comparing the fluctuation index of each chronological age group of girls with that of every other age group of girls are presented in Table 7. The obtained t's indicate that, comparatively, the mean fluctuation indices of the 9- and 10-year-old girls are significantly lower than the means of the 5-, 6-, and 7-year-old girls. The differences between the means of the other age groups of girls are not statistically significant at acceptable levels of confidence.

TABLE 4. Sex Differences by Grade in Indices of Friendship Fluctuation

| | Girls | | Boys | | |
Grade	Mean	SD	Mean	SD	t
Kindergarten	5.59	2.86	4.89	2.13	.86
1	5.04	2.63	5.25	2.47	.29
2	5.45	2.41	4.91	2.58	.84
3	4.57	2.53	3.89	2.27	1.05
4	4.08	2.13	4.31	3.08	.34
5	3.08	2.31	3.27	2.21	.28

TABLE 5. Boy-Girl Composite Indices of Friendship Fluctuation by Age

Chronological Age	N	Mean	SD
5	36	5.33	2.65
6	44	5.30	2.65
7	61	5.10	2.31
8	66	4.42	2.52
9	63	4.02	2.54
10	57	3.39	2.33

TABLE 6. Boy-Girl Composite Indices of Friendship Fluctuation by Grade

Grade	N	Mean	SD
Kindergarten	40	5.28	2.57
1	51	5.14	2.55
2	64	5.17	2.52
3	61	4.15	2.38
4	65	4.18	2.60
5	46	3.17	2.26

Statistical analyses, presented in Table 8, indicate that the mean fluctuation index of the 10-year-old boys is significantly lower than the means of the 5-, 6-, and 7-year-old boys. The differences between the means of the other age groups of boys are not statistically significant at acceptable levels of confidence.

TABLE 7. Results of Statistical Comparisons of the Distribution of Friendship Fluctuation Indices of the Six Chronological Age Groups of Girls

5	6	7	8	9	10	Chronological age
					—	10
				—	.41 (60)	9
			—	1.48 (62)	1.62 (58)	8
		—	1.22 (54)	3.00** (56)	2.91** (52)	7
	—	.34 (48)	.76 (54)	2.24* (56)	2.29* (52)	6
—	.71 (43)	.46 (43)	1.40 (49)	2.72** (51)	2.74** (47)	5
5	6	7	8	9	10	

Chronological age

* In the above table the upper numbers are the *t*'s for the various chronological age group comparisons. The numbers in the parentheses represent the numbers of degrees of freedom for the various *t* values. Those *t* values statistically significant at the 5 per cent level of confidence are indicated by a single asterisk; while those significant at the 1 per cent level of confidence are designated by two asterisks.

TABLE 8. Results of Statistical Comparisons of the Distribution of Friendship Fluctuation Indices of the Six Chronological Age Groups of Boys

5	6	7	8	9	10	Chronological age
					—	10
				—	1.51 (56)	9
			—	.06 (63)	1.79 (61)	8
		—	1.11 (69)	.84 (64)	2.89** (62)	7
	—	.75 (53)	1.59 (52)	1.35 (47)	2.95** (45)	6
—	.79 (33)	.16 (50)	.74 (49)	.59 (44)	3.85** (42)	5
5	6	7	8	9	10	

Chronological age

* In the above table the upper numbers are the *t*'s for the various chronological age group comparisons. The numbers in the parentheses represent the numbers of degrees of freedom for the various *t* values. Those *t* values statistically significant at the 1 per cent level of confidence are designated by two asterisks.

The statistical analysis of the combined data for boys and girls are presented in Table 9. The results indicate that the mean fluctuation indices of the 9- and 10-year-old elementary school children are significantly lower than the means of the 5-, 6-, and 7-year-olds. The mean of the 10-

TABLE 9. Results of Statistical Comparisons of the Distribution of Friendship Fluctuation Indices of the Six Chronological Age Groups of Girls and Boys Combined

						Chronological age
					—	10
				—	1.40 (118)	9
			—	.89 (127)	2.34* (121)	8
		—	1.58 (125)	2.45* (122)	3.98** (116)	7
	—	.40 (103)	1.73 (108)	2.51* (105)	3.75** (99)	6
—	.05 (78)	.43 (95)	1.65 (100)	2.38* (97)	3.53** (91)	5
5	6	7	8	9	10	

Chronological age

* In the above table the upper numbers are the t's for the various chronological age group comparisons. The numbers in the parentheses represent the numbers of degrees of freedom for the various t values. Those t values statistically significant at the 5 per cent level of confidence are indicated by a single asterisk; while those significant at the 1 per cent level of confidence are designated by two asterisks.

year-old group is also significantly lower than the mean of the 8-year-old group.

From the foregoing analysis it would appear that there is a trend toward greater stability with increasing chronological age, and that the onset of such stability tends to begin somewhat earlier with girls than it does with boys.

COMPARISON WITH THE PREVIOUS ADOLESCENT STUDY

Since the procedures and techniques used in the present study were identical with those used by Thompson and Horrocks (1947) in their study of friendship fluctuations among urban adolescents, it is possible, to some extent, to compare the friendship stability of urban youth at the various age levels included in these two studies. However, it should be noted that there are differences in the school samples included in these two studies. An attempt was made in the Thompson and Horrocks study to select schools enrolling pupils from average socio-economic status families, while in the present study the subjects are drawn from a single school system enrolling a large number of children from families of above average socio-economic status. While the populations of the communities utilized in both studies were approximately the same, the communities in the earlier studies were self-contained cities located some distance from the nearest large population center, while the community used in the present study was a suburb immediately adjoining a comparatively large metropolitan center, although it did possess an independent business and shopping district of its own. Under the circumstances the communities involved are not directly comparable, although they have many things in common; and this fact should be kept in mind in interpreting the comparative results cited.

The results of the statistical analysis comparing the fluctuation index of each chronological age group from year five to age 18 are presented in Table 10. In this table the data from the Thompson and Horrocks study have been combined with those of the present study. The obtained t's indicate that, comparatively, the mean fluctuation of the 9- through 18-year-old groups are significantly lower than the mean fluctuation indices of the 5-, 6-, and 7-year-olds. The mean fluctuation indices of the 12- through 18-year-old children are also significantly lower than the means of the 8-year-old group. In addition the means of the 16-, 17-, and 18-year-old groups are significantly lower than those of the 9- through 15-year-old group. The differences between the means of the other age groups are not statistically significant at acceptable levels of confidence.

This statistical comparison indicates that there is a significant trend toward greater stability in friendship with increasing chronological age from year five through year eighteen on the basis of the index used.

The means of the friendship fluctuation indices for the boy-girl composite population are also presented graphically in Figure 1. The combined data for these 1296 urban boys and girls show a consistent downward trend in friendship fluctuation from year 5 to 17.

RELATION BETWEEN FRIENDSHIP FLUCTUATION AND SOCIAL ACCEPTABILITY

Under the assumption that low social acceptance by one's age mates might serve to increase a child's fluctuation status, it was decided to compare the friendship fluctuation index with a social acceptance index.

In setting up a social acceptance index two criteria had to be met. First, since several groups were involved the social acceptance index had to be of such a nature that it would have uniform significance regardless of the size of the group. Second, the index would be most efficiently stated in numerical terms to facilitate the computation of a coefficient of correlation between the

TABLE 10. Results of Statistical Comparisons of the Distribution of Friendship Fluctuation Indices of the Fourteen Chronological Age Groups*

Chronological age				Chronological age				
	18	17	16	15	14	13	12	11
17	.79 (177)	—						
16	1.81 (196)	1.72 (309)	—					
15	3.31** (207)	4.12** (320)	2.46 (339)	—				
14	3.64*** (145)	4.59*** (258)	3.03** (277)	.71 (288)	—			
13	3.70** (215)	4.78** (328)	3.07** (347)	.52 (358)	.26 (296)	—		
12	3.09** (145)	3.63** (258)	2.07* (277)	.23 (288)	.90 (226)	.73 (296)	—	
11	3.32** (68)	3.56* (181)	2.48* (200)	.86 (211)	.35 (149)	.54 (219)	1.01 (149)	—
10	2.96** (88)	3.38** (201)	2.03* (220)	.03 (231)	.56 (169)	.38 (239)	.21 (169)	.75 (92)

TABLE 10. (continued)

Chronological age	5	6	7	8	9	10	11	12	13	14	15	16	17	18
9					—	1.40 (118)	.45 (98)	1.78 (175)	1.29 (245)	1.03 (175)	1.64 (237)	3.63** (226)	4.95** (207)	4.11** (94)
8				—	.89 (127)	2.34** (121)	1.23 (101)	2.85** (178)	2.41* (248)	2.08* (178)	2.74** (240)	4.81** (229)	6.16** (210)	4.84** (97)
7			—	1.58 (125)	2.45* (122)	3.98** (116)	2.54* (96)	4.71** (173)	4.36** (243)	3.92** (173)	4.65** (235)	6.65** (226)	8.00** (205)	6.19** (92)
6		—	.40 (103)	1.73 (108)	2.51* (105)	3.75** (99)	2.62* (79)	4.23** (156)	3.93** (226)	3.60** (156)	4.17** (218)	5.90** (207)	7.02** (188)	5.90** (75)
5	—	.05 (78)	.43 (95)	1.65 (100)	2.38* (97)	3.53** (91)	2.50* (71)	3.96** (148)	3.67** (218)	3.37** (148)	3.90** (210)	5.38** (199)	6.38** (180)	5.58** (67)

Chronological age

* Upper numbers are the t's for the age group comparisons. Numbers in parentheses are the degrees of freedom for the t values. One asterisk is a t value statistically significant at the 5 per cent level of confidence. Two asterisks are the t's significant at the 1 per cent level of confidence.

two indices. To meet these criteria the following scoring system was devised: first choice, 3 points; second choice, 2 points; third choice, 1 point. Thus, if a child in the first testing or choosing situation received one first-place choice, three second-place choices, and two third-place choices, he would have a score of 3 plus 6 plus 2, or a total of 11 as his social acceptability rat-

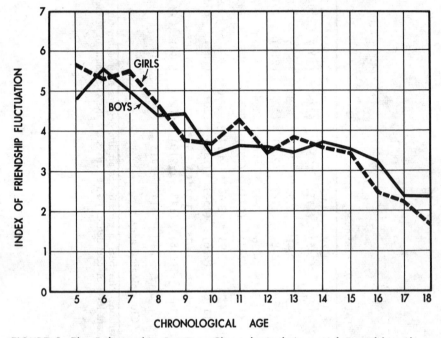

FIGURE 1. The Relationship Between Chronological Age and Friendship Fluctuation for an Urban Sample of 585 Boys and 647 Girls

ing. Table 11 shows the distribution of the friendship fluctuation index and the social acceptability index scores throughout the entire testing group.

A product-moment coefficient of .065 was obtained between friendship fluctuation index and the social acceptability index. Thus, there is practically no relationship between a person's friendship fluctuation and his acceptance by his group as determined by this study. The individual who is well accepted by his group and the one who is poorly accepted by his group will each tend to fluctuate in his friendships to about the same degree.

COMPARISON OF THE FIRST AND SECOND TESTING PERIODS

For purposes of comparison, the means and standard deviations for the various grade levels are presented in Tables 12 and 13. Corresponding tables for the first testing period are Tables 3 and 4.

From these tables it may be seen that the results obtained at the second testing period are not dissimilar to those secured at the first testing period. However, the *t*'s obtained in the statistical comparison of the distribution of friendship fluctuation of boys and girls at the various age levels at the

TABLE 11. A Scatter Diagram of the Friendship Fluctuation Index Scores and the Social Acceptability Index Scores at the First Testing Period

Friendship fluctuation index scores	*Social Acceptability Index Scores*																
	0-4	5-9	10-14	15-19	20-24	25-29	30-34	35-39	40-44	45-49	50-54	55-59	60-64	65-69	70-74	75-79	Total
9	18	7	2	4	2	1	1		1								36
8	2	2	0	2	0	1					1						8
7	14	12	1	4	4	1			2								38
6	10	6	6	2	2	4		2			1					1	34
5	11	15	7	3	1	0		2									39
4	18	9	4	10	6	1		3	1								52
3	6	6	4	5	1	4	1	1	1								29
2	17	18	13	9	2	2	1		1								63
1	0	0	0	0	0	0											0
0	14	7	3	2	0	1							1				28
Total	110	82	40	41	18	15	3	8	6	0	2	0	1	0	0	1	327

second testing period are on the whole higher than those obtained at the first testing period. There is a significant difference in friendship fluctuation between boys and girls at age 8, as is indicated in Table 12. However, in view of the lack of significant differences revealed in both testing periods one is led to conclude that there are probably no reliable differences in friendship fluctuation at the age levels included in this study. It is true, however, that both testing periods showed a tendency toward greater stability of friendship with increasing age.

DISCUSSION

The results of the present study apply, of course, only to the sample used in the study. Different results might well be obtained with other representative samples. The study does seem indicative, however, of the general trend in friendship development of the child as he progresses throughout the public schools from kindergarten through grade twelve. However, in view of the large individual variations it is apparent that here as in other phases of the child's development there are individual growth patterns.

From previous sociometric studies it is also true that results depend upon the nature of the question asked. In this study the question was

TABLE 12. Sex Differences by Age in Indices of Friendship Fluctuation at the Second Testing Period

Chronological Age	Girls		Boys		t
	Mean	SD	Mean	SD	
5	5.91	2.67	4.59	2.35	1.59
6	5.00	2.70	5.07	2.27	.10
7	3.85	2.29	4.79	2.77	1.47
8	4.70	2.30	3.47	2.28	2.16*
9	3.46	1.53	4.03	2.57	1.08
10	2.90	2.51	2.78	2.11	.19

* Significant at the 5 per cent level.

TABLE 13. Boy-Girl Composite Indices of Friendship Fluctuation by Age at the Second Testing Period

Chronological Age	N	Mean	SD
5	39	5.33	2.63
6	54	5.04	2.48
7	65	4.42	2.62
8	68	4.01	2.37
9	69	3.72	2.11
10	56	2.84	2.33

asked, "who is your best friend?" The person responding might well ask, best friend for what, and in the absence of any definition by the testor, make his own definition. In an unpublished study made at Ohio State University, the senior author found low correlations among persons nominated when best friends for various specific purposes were asked for. Further, each subject was compelled to confine his nominations to his grade group. It is possible that a number of the subjects would have preferred to nominate someone outside the grade group, and a somewhat different pattern of fluctuation might have ensued. Still, confining the selection to the immediate group did furnish a picture of the friendship situation *within* that particular group.

The method of computing the index might also be called into question particularly since there was no accurate quantitative way of indicating the values of given positions on the list of best friends. For the purpose of the index it was assumed that a second choice position was as far removed, in comparative selection strength, from a first choice position as a third choice position was removed from a second choice position. It may well have been that for many subjects first and second choice were equal and which person they listed in first as compared to second position was purely a chance matter.

Further research is needed in the direction of discovering the factors that determine friendship and friendship fluctuations, and a series of such studies are now underway at Ohio State University.

SUMMARY

The purpose of this study was to investigate the degree of friendship fluctuation among elementary school children and to compare the degree of fluctuations with that of urban adolescents as determined by Thompson and Horrocks (1946). All of the children from grade one through grade five in a suburban public school, and one of the two kindergarten groups coöperated in this study. The children ranged in age from 5 to 10 years of age. There were 163 girls and 164 boys in the group.

Friendship fluctuation was determined by pupil choices through the use of a sociometric test. The procedure and techniques used by Thompson and Horrocks were used in the present study. The subjects were asked to list their three best friends on two occasions, 14 days apart. Four weeks later another measure of friendship fluctuation was determined in the same manner. Analyses which included an index of friendship fluctuation were made of their responses.

The data showed a trend toward greater stability in friendship with increasing chronological age and a corresponding higher grade placement. These findings support the results of the previous adolescent study. The means of the friendship fluctuation indices for the various chronological age groups included in the two studies tended to form a continuous curve, showing a consistent downward trend in friendship fluctuation from year five to year eighteen.

Analysis revealed practically no relationship between a person's friendship fluctuation and his acceptance by his group.

The results of the first and second two-week testing periods were similar. Both showed a trend toward greater stability in friendship with increasing chronological age.

41

Anxiety in Children and Social Status[*]

Boyd R. McCandless, Alfred Castaneda, and David S. Palermo

How fares the anxious child in establishing satisfying social relationships with other children? It can be inferred, according to modern behavior theory, that he will have a stronger drive which might activate more habit tendencies to initiate and maintain social relations with others. On the other hand, a high drive can elevate many different response patterns above threshold, and the possibility arises that the anxious child may thereby appear to be capricious and unpredictable in his approach-withdrawal responses in social situations. Outweighing even these possibilities is the question of the social-stimulus value of the anxious child in a given cultural milieu. How is the "eager-beaver" viewed in the early childhood society of middle-class American life? In the following paper, Dr. McCandless and his collaborators, Drs. Castaneda and Palermo, show some of the interesting relationships between manifest anxiety and social status.

There have been several studies (Baron, 1951; Bonney, 1942 and 1947; Greenblatt, 1950; Grossman and Wrighter, 1948; Hardy, 1937; Kuhlen and Bretsch, 1947; Northway, 1944; Northway and Wigdor, 1947; Young, 1944) since 1937 dealing with the connection between adjustment and sociometric status in child populations. All have provided at least some support for the hypothesis of a moderate positive relationship between the two ("better adjusted" children are more popular), although Northway and Wigdor (1947) find some evidence of a curvilinear relationship. A recent review of sociometric validity (Mouton, Blake, and Fruchter, 1955-b) summarized a number of studies of adults that also lend support to this hypothesis.

* From Boyd R. McCandless, Alfred Castaneda, and David S. Palermo, "Anxiety in Children and Social Status," *Child Development*, 1956, Vol. 27, pp. 385-391. (With permission of the authors and the Society for Research in Child Development.)

In the child field, the hypothesis has been most recently (and perhaps most rigorously) supported by Thorpe's (1955) research with British school children. He studied 980 children in 34 classes, mean chronological age 12.8 years, using a scale that has been shown to possess some validity which he adopted from Eysenck. This test includes seven different "scales" which, grouped, are used to define "neuroticism." Thorpe obtained a pooled r of $-.152$, standard error .034, between "neuroticism" and sociometric status.

In the other child studies mentioned above, the adjustment measure has generally been a global inventory such as the California Test of Personality (Grossman and Wrighter, 1948) or the Mental Health Analysis, Elementary or Intermediate Series, Form A (Baron, 1951; Greenblatt, 1950). Rorschachs have also been used (Northway and Wigdor, 1947), as well as teachers' or observers' ratings, interviews, case histories (Bonney, 1942 and 1947; Hardy, 1937; Northway, 1944) and problem check lists (Kuhlen and Bretsch, 1947).

Previous studies by the present authors have reported the form, scoring, norms and reliabilities (Castaneda, Palermo and McCandless, 1956-a) for the children's form of the manifest anxiety scale (CMAS), as well as data concerning relationships of the scale with performance in complex learning situations (Castaneda, et al., 1956-b; Palermo, et al. 1956) and in the area of academic achievement (McCandless and Castaneda, 1956). The literature demonstrating predictive power for Taylor's (1953) adult form of the manifest anxiety scale is voluminous. The authors have also been interested for some time in sociometric techniques from the points of view both of their reliability and usefulness (McCandless, 1942 and 1955).

SOCIOMETRIC PROCEDURES AND RESULTS

Two teacher-administered sociometric techniques were administered, the rank method to nine classes, the rate method to six classes of public school fourth, fifth and sixth grade children. These were repeated, same methods for same classes, one week later to determine test-retest reliability. The population taking both tests numbered 369 children, 194 boys and 175 girls. The sociometric was a one-question "friend" instrument. This choice of a one-question, rank and rate sociometric was due to the authors' quest for a very simple instrument which could be administered by teachers from prepared instruction and data sheets.

The rank method was administered (by sexes rather than whole classes) in this fashion: a mimeographed list of all girls in a class was distributed to each girl, a list of all boys to each boy in a class. Children were instructed to enter a (1) after the name of their very best friend, a (2) after the name of their second best friend, and so on until every child but the one doing the ranking had a different number after his name, the largest number (n) being the number of boys or girls in a class, excepting the child doing the ranking.

The rate method was also given by sex. A sheet similar to the rank sheet was handed to each boy or girl, with the names of all the boys or girls in a class in a column down the left hand side of the page. A line to the

TABLE 1. Test-retest Reliabilities (One-week interval, product-moment) for Rate and Rank Methods of Assessing Sociometric Status, by Grade Groups and by Sex

	Class									
	1		*2*		*3*		*4*		*5*	
Grade & Sex	N	r	N	r	N	r	N	r	N	r
4B	8(r)	.93**	15(r)	.75**	9	.77*	10	.92**	15	.99**
4G	11(r)	.98**	10(r)	.70*	15	.90**	15	.92**	10	.97**
5B	10	.93**	17	.95**	11	.95**	16(r)	.96**	16(r)	.55*
5G	12	.80**	16	.96**	13	.96**	7(r)	.91**	16(r)	.96**
6B	11	.95**	18	.90**	13(r)	.94**	7(r)	.91**	18	.94**
6G	5	.91*	12	.98**	10(r)	.94**	11(r)	.82**	12	.96**

Note—An (r) preceding a coefficient indicates that it was obtained by the rate method.
* Significant at less than the .05 level.
** Significant at less than the .01 level.

right of each name included five equidistant check points, each subsumed by a number from (1) to (5) reading from left to right. The child was instructed to check a point for each name other than his own, a (1) if the child was a "best friend," a (3) if he didn't know the child very well or neither liked nor disliked him, and a (5) if the child "is not my friend," etc.

Table 1 gives reliability figures (product moment r's) by class, grade and sex for the two methods of sociometric assessment. The scores on which these correlations are based are the average rating or the average ranking received by a child. This score was the average of all ranks or ratings given by other children of his own sex to a given child. Consequently the lowest score represents the most popular child for a sex-class group. However, for clearness of presentation, signs of correlation coefficients in Table 2 have been changed so that a negative correlation means that there is a tendency for the more anxious children to be less popular, and vice versa.

There is no clearcut reliability difference between the rate and the rank methods; of the four reliabilities below .80, three were obtained by use of the rate method, two of these three being for fourth grade groups; and of the 12 reliabilities of .95 or more, only three were obtained by the rate method. Only four of the 30 reliabilities computed fail to reach significance at less than the .01 level. Two of these were obtained by the rank, two by the rate method, and all four were significant at less than the .05 level. Median test-retest reliability for the rate method (12 measures for six classes) was .92; and for the rank method (18 measures for nine classes) was .95. However, correlation range for the rate method (.55-.98) was greater than for the rank method (.77-.99).

TABLE 2. Pooled Product-moment Correlations by Grade and Sex Between CMAS Scores and Sociometric Status

Grade and Sex	N Classes	N Individuals	r
4B	5	58	−.28*
4G	5	62	−.23
5B	5	72	−.51**
5G	5	69	−.75**,†
6B	5	73	−.16
6G	5	53	.01

* Significant at less than the .05 level.
** Significant at less than the .01 level.
† This is an estimate based on five fifth grade classes, the correlation population of which proved to be nonhomogeneous at just below the .05 level (all other class populations were homogeneous). The correlations and N's for the five classes were: 1. $r = -.90$, $N = 14$; 2. $r = -.55$, $N = 17$; 3. $r = -.46$, $N = 15$; 4. $r = +.03$, $N = 7$; 5. $r = -.81$, $N = 16$.

At a more general level, this study indicates that a single question, teacher-administered-by-group sociometric, sexes separated, results in high reliabilities as judged by test-retest at a one-week interval. The reliabilities compare favorably with the studies reviewed by either Mouton, Blake and Fruchter (1955) or by Witryol and Thompson (1953).

ANXIETY SCALE PROCEDURES AND RESULTS

The hypothesis for this section of the study was that there would be a negative relationship between anxiety and social acceptability in fourth, fifth and sixth grade public school children (i.e., that more anxious children would be less popular). Subjects were 387 fourth, fifth and sixth graders from the public schools of a midwestern town of about 27,000 population. There were 203 boys and 184 girls. The population completely overlaps the sociometric population described above, differences in N being due to absences on retests for the sociometric. All relationships reported here are between a first administration of the CMAS and the sociometric assessment. Rank and rate methods of collecting sociometric data are combined in this portion of the study, since there were no significant differences in their relationship with CMAS scores between the two methods.

Table 2 shows correlations by grade and sex of the CMAS scores and sociometric status. The CMAS, as was also true of the sociometric assessments, was administered by classroom teachers. It was also repeated a week later to provide the reliability data reported in Castaneda, et al., (1956-a).

The over-all picture from Table 2 supports the hypothesis of a negative relationship between anxiety and social status (more anxious children are less popular) although there is clear variation by grades. The reasonably substantial N's, both of classes and individuals, the relative consistency by sexes in a grade and the frequency of significant correlations all argue against the notion of random variation as an explanation of this correlation pattern. Fourth graders, boys and girls, have low negative r's (for fourth grade boys r is significant at less than the .05 level, and r for fourth grade girls misses the .05 significance level by only .02). Correlations for both fifth grade boys and girls are significant at less than the .001 level, while sixth graders' r's hover close to zero. A social class differential cannot be argued, since the fourth, fifth and sixth graders are drawn by groups, each group coming from the same school. One can only suspect different social interaction patterns which are a function of unknown factors, possibly of grade and age (including physical maturity), teacher influence, or other, and look further for reasons for the variability.

As a check on within-class similarity (for which teachers might possibly be thought to be most responsible) an analysis of variance was run to test the relationship of within-groups variance (within a given class) to between groups variance (all grades and classes). Utilizing the 15 classes, including the one fifth grade class of girls (class 1, footnote, Table 2) that contributed most heavily to nonhomogeneity, the resulting F was 1.80, which is nonsignificant for 14 and 15 d.f. (F=2.43 is required for .05 level of significance). Eliminating this class, F equalled 3.60, which is significant for 13 and 14 d.f. at between the .01 and .02 levels. This analysis suggests very tentatively that there is a tendency for a given class, regardless of sex, to follow a given pattern of anxiety-social status relationship. The over-all nonhomogeneity of the correlations in Table 2 lends further support to this idea.

However, this over-all nonhomogeneity (the null hypothesis of no difference in the total correlation population is rejected at less than the .01 level) is due most heavily to the single class of fifth grade girls mentioned above. Dropping this single half-class enables us to retain the null hypothesis at between the .20 and .10 levels, and results in an average correlation between anxiety and social acceptance of —.32, significant at less than the .001 level. Average r's for boys and girls respectively (dropping the single deviant class of fifth grade girls) are —.33 and —.30, both significant at less than the .01 level.

SUMMARY AND CONCLUSIONS

High reliabilities, using the test-retest method at a one-week interval, were obtained for single-question friendship sociometrics administered by classroom teachers. The rank and rate methods were administered to fourth, fifth and sixth grade populations, the sexes separated, to obtain these reliabilities. There is a suggestion that the rank method is slightly more reliable, although differences in reliabilities between the two methods are slight.

Relationships between scores obtained by using the children's form of the manifest anxiety scale, and sociometric status, were predominantly negative (i.e., the more anxious youngsters were the less popular) for both boys and girls. These relationships were high for fifth graders, moderate for fourth graders and approximately zero for sixth graders. There is some indication that there may be characteristic "class climates" not dependent upon differences between the sexes. This, at a speculative level, may possibly be said to be related to the influence of the teacher on the class. An over-all lack of homogeneity of the correlation population supports the notion of "class climate," although when one half class of deviant fifth grade girls is dropped, the correlation population shows homogeneity. The resulting average correlation between anxiety and sociometric standing is then —.32, statistically significant. The authors believe, however, that looking at the correlations by grade and sex provides a more meaningful way of regarding the data than does concentration on the average r.

42

Social Heterosexual Development Among Urban Negroes and Whites[*]

Carlfred B. Broderick

The most noticeable social change accompanying puberty and the onset of adolescence is a growing interest in the opposite sex. The findings of Dr. Broderick's research document this well-known change in striking fashion, but more importantly they bring to light significant differences between American Negroes and whites in the many values and sentiments that lead the individual toward marriage. White girls and boys turned out to be clearly differentiated on their total heterosexual "scores," girls being more heterosexually oriented; Negro boys and girls were very similar to each other. The matrifocal family pattern of the lower-class Negro seems evident in these findings, especially in the Negro boy's increasingly less favorable attitude toward marriage as he moves into late adolescence.

Most research on the development of heterosexuality is concerned with either the earliest or the latest stages in the process. The focus is either on the problem of sex role learning and identification among young children or on the sexual and social dilemmas of later adolescence and early adulthood. The purpose of this paper is to compare patterns of social heterosexuality of Negroes and whites during the relatively uncharted middle period from ten through 17 years of age.

In the larger study from which these data were drawn, four major components of social heterosexual development have emerged. The first component of heterosexual orientation is a positive attitude toward the general subject of romantic interaction with the opposite sex. This diffuse approval is reflected, for example, in one's enjoyment of romantic movies or in one's

* Adapted and abridged from Carlfred B. Broderick, "Social Heterosexual Development Among Urban Negroes and Whites," *Journal of Marriage and the Family,* 1965, Vol. 27, pp. 200-203. (With permission of the author and the National Council on Family Relations.)

positive attitude toward marriage. The second component builds upon the first and involves an emotional attachment to some particular member of the opposite sex. Items on whether a boy has a girl friend or has been in love get at this factor. At the earlier ages, these items most often index emotional rather than social involvement, since the level of reciprocation is typically very low. At the later ages, they more often are associated with reciprocal social behavior as well as feelings. The third component might be negatively defined as the absence of social prejudice toward the opposite sex as a class of persons. This social openness is expressed primarily in sociometric items, although items on playing kissing games at parties also bear on it since this would necessarily involve mixed parties. The fourth and most advanced component of social heterosexuality during this age span involves actual social interaction on a romantic pair basis. This component of heterosexuality is tapped by questions on such interactions as serious kissing, dating, and going steady.

For the purpose of comparing the two racial groups, a simple index of social heterosexuality was developed from the nine questionnaire items used as examples above. These nine were chosen from a much larger number of items on a self-administered questionnaire to represent all of the four basic components of heterosexuality and to show evidence of construct validity; that is, each item differentiated between the sexes or among ages or communities in a meaningful way and related consistently to other variables. The exact wording and derivation of each item is given in Table 1.

Based on his responses to these items, each individual was assigned a social heterosexuality score. These scores ranged from zero to nine depending on how many of his responses were positive (heterosexual). A score of nine would indicate that the individual definitely wanted to get married someday, he liked the love scenes in movies, he had a girlfriend, he had been in love, he had named at least one member of the opposite sex among his five closest friends, he had played kissing games at parties, he had seriously kissed a girl on his own initiative, he had begun to date, and he had gone steady at least once. Someone with a score of zero, on the other hand, would have felt or experienced none of these things.

SAMPLE

The sample consisted of 1,262 young people. It included all the fifth through twelfth graders attending school within the district on the day the study was made. The area in which these young people live is part of the industrial complex of a middle-sized Pennsylvania city. Its economy is dominated by heavy industry and by a nearby military installation of some size.

Just over one quarter of the sample were Negroes. The primary ethnic origins of the white families were Eastern European. Although they lived

TABLE 1. Nine Items Contributing to the Social Heterosexuality Score

1. "Would you like to get married someday?" *Yes* response was scored as positive, *No* and *Don't Know* were scored as negative.
2. Under a cartoon showing a group of boys and girls watching a love scene (a couple embracing) on the screen of a movie theater, the questions: "How do the boys feel about what they are seeing?" and "How do the girls feel about what they are seeing?" The responses concerning one's own sex group were considered a measure of one's own attitude. They were coded as *positive* (they enjoy it; they wish they were doing that) or *other*, which included a range of negative, neutral, and conditional responses.
3. "Do you have a girl friend now?" (Or "Do you have a boy friend now?" for the girls.) *Yes* or *No.*
4. "Have you ever been in love?" *Yes* or *No.*
5. "Name your best friend" and "List any others you like almost as well." (Five spaces were provided in all.) This item was scored positively if one or more members of the opposite sex were listed among the friends.
6. "Sometimes people play kissing games at some of their parties. Have you ever played kissing games?" *Yes* or *No.*
7. "Kissing in kissing games is usually just for fun. At other times a kiss may mean something special. Have you ever seriously kissed a girl?" ("A boy," if the respondent was a girl.) *Yes* or *No.*
8. "Have you ever had a date?" *Yes* or *No.*
9. "How many times have you gone steady?" Once or more often were counted as positive responses.

in the same community, sent their children to the same schools, and derived their income from the same employers, there were several important differences between the circumstances of the Negro and white families in the sample.

Most fathers of both races were blue-collar workers, and although there were members of both races in each occupational category, Negroes were underrepresented among the foreman, skilled, and semi-skilled and overrepresented among the unskilled. The difference in occupational distribution of the two groups was significant at the .001 level.

In addition to these occupational differences, there were important differences in the family composition of Negroes and whites in the sample. Thirty-five percent of the Negro families had been broken by either death, divorce, or separation, whereas only 13 percent of the white families had been disrupted (the difference is significant at the .001 level). The sibling constellations of the two groups were also quite different. The proportion of only children among the white subjects was almost twice as great as among the Negro subjects (17 percent compared to nine percent). On the other hand, nearly twice as many Negro as white subjects reported having both brothers and sisters (60 percent compared to 36 percent). These figures indicated that the Negro subjects came from large families far more often than the white subjects.

Since there were these substantial socio-economic and familial in addition to racial differences between the two groups to be compared, it might be argued that any difference in the pattern of social heterosexual development of Negroes and whites might be explained solely on the basis of these uncontrolled background factors. Unfortunately, with the present sample it was not possible to control on these factors (occupation, family stability, and family size) because the numbers in some cells would have become too small. It was possible, however, to test for the independent influence of these factors within one race (the white race) by examining the relationship of each background variable to each of the nine items of the social heterosexuality score. Only one item, attitude toward marriage, was significantly related to these background factors. Children from white-collar homes and from stable families were significantly more positive in their attitudes toward marriage than were children from blue-collar or broken homes. This relationship probably helps to explain why Negroes had a substantially lower percentage of positive responses than whites on this item and on no other item. This cannot, however, account for the results reported below, since its effect is to reduce rather than to exaggerate the overall relationship between race and heterosexuality reported in this paper.

For purposes of comparison, each of the races was subdivided by age groupings (10-11, 12-13, 14-15, and 16–17-year-olds) and by sex. Table 2 indicates the manner in which the 1,262 subjects were distributed among

TABLE 2. Total Number in Each Analytical Cell*

| Age | White | | Negro | |
	Boys	Girls	Boys	Girls
10-11	79	77	25	37
12-13	143	104	49	47
14-15	166	154	52	50
16-17	100	98	46	35
Total	488	433	172	169

* All significance statements for the remainder of the paper are based on simple t-tests or Chi-square tests, whichever is appropriate. The .05 level of significance is accepted throughout.

the resulting 16 groups. Ten-year-olds were underrepresented since any below the fifth grade level were not included in the sample. Sixteen- and 17-year-olds were also underrepresented because of substantial school dropouts at these ages.

FINDINGS

The mean social heterosexuality scores for each of the 16 groups described above are presented graphically in Figure 1. It can be seen that among whites, girls were significantly more heterosexual in their social orientation than boys at every age. In fact, at every age the mean score for white girls is higher than the mean score for boys two years older than themselves. An analysis of the particular items which contribute to this overall sex difference (Table 3) shows that girls gave more heterosexual responses than boys on wanting to get married (significant at every age), claiming a boyfriend/girl friend (significant at every age), having been in love (significant at 10-11 and 12-13), and having kissed "when it meant something special" (significant at 12-13 and 14-15). Except for the kissing item, these items all involve romantic attitudes rather than social behavior; and it is worth noting that despite the striking sex differences on these items, there were no corresponding differences on involvement in kissing games, cross-sex friends, dating, or going steady.

This same sex differential was observed among Pennsylvania rural and suburban white youth involved in other phases of the larger project. As can be seen in Figure 1, however, urban Negro subjects did not conform

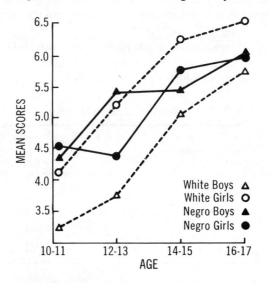

FIGURE 1. Mean Social Heterosexual Scores of Negroes and Whites by Sex and Age.

Differences between means are significant at or beyond the .05 level as follows: (*a*) between white boys and white girls at every age, (*b*) between Negro boys and Negro girls at ages 12-13, and (*c*) between Negro boys and white boys at ages 12-13.

TABLE 3. Percent of Positive Responses
to Each Item by Age, Sex, and Race

Item—Age	White		Negro	
	Boys	Girls	Boys	Girls
1. Marriage				
10-11	57	87[a]	71	76
12-13	63	89[ab]	60	74
14-15	61	90[a]	67	85
16-17	77[bc]	90[a]	58	84[a]
2. Romantic movie				
10-11	45	80[a]	68[b]	70
12-13	53	82[a]	75[b]	73
14-15	62	83[a]	83[b]	78
16-17	62	88[a]	62	79
3. Girlfriend/Boyfriend				
10-11	49	68[a]	65	64
12-13	49	66[a]	71[ab]	51
14-15	45	76[a]	58	72[c]
16-17	46	78[a]	62[b]	71
4. Love				
10-11	39	60[a]	46	57
12-13	47	62[a]	60	48
14-15	60[c]	72[b]	57	67
16-17	61	69	67	67
5. Cross-sex friend				
10-11	31	29	52	54[b]
12-13	30	38	48[b]	45
14-15	54[c]	59[c]	49	58
16-17	60	71	81[bc]	75
6. Kissing games				
10-11	49	53	68	62
12-13	61[c]	81[ac]	92[bc]	72
14-15	80[c]	83	87	84
16-17	83	78	85	86
7. Serious kiss				
10-11	22	21	38	39[b]
12-13	28	41[ac]	51[b]	48
14-15	50[c]	62[a]	62	65
16-17	72[c]	73	79[a]	59
8. Date				
10-11	20	18	16	20
12-13	30	29	49[abc]	21
14-15	69[c]	70[bc]	69[ac]	48[c]
16-17	89[c]	82[c]	93[c]	88[c]

TABLE 3. (continued)

Item—Age	White		Negro	
	Boys	Girls	Boys	Girls
9. Steady				
10-11	27	17	40	27
12-13	34	46[ac]	59[ab]	34
14-15	49[c]	57	58	44
16-17	59	66	63	51

[a] Significant differences between the sexes ($p < .05$).
[b] Significant differences between the races ($p < .05$).
[c] Significant differences from previous age ($p < .05$).

to the usual pattern. Negro boys did not trail Negro girls in their hetero-sexual orientation or involvement. In fact, the only significant difference between the sexes was at 12-13, when the boys' mean score exceeded the girls'. At that age, the Negro boys, significantly more often than the girls, reported having a girl friend/boyfriend, having begun to date, and having gone steady (Table 3). The latter two in particular involve heterosexual social interaction rather than romantic fantasy. The Negro boys also are significantly more heterosexually oriented than white boys at ages 12-13. (The difference approaches significance at ages 10-11 also.) The items differentiating them are the same those setting the Negro boys apart from the Negro girls at that age, with the addition of the romantic movie, cross-sex friends, and the two kissing items. These differences may reflect the fact that Negro boys tend to be sexually involved at an earlier age than white boys. The difference effectively disappears at ages 14-15, by which age it may be assumed that the white boy has caught up with his Negro counterpart.

One additional observation might be made about the item on attitude toward marriage. It was mentioned earlier that lower-class status and unstable home life tended to be associated with negative feelings about the desirability of getting married someday. Nevertheless, among white subjects of every class, attitude toward marriage tended to become more positive at each age. This pattern held not only in this community, but in all of the other communities studied in the larger project. It held for the Negro girls in the present sample. Among the Negro boys, however, the reverse held true. As can be seen in Table 3, at 10-11, 71 percent of these boys felt sure that they wanted to get married some day; at 12-13, the percentage had dropped to 60 percent; and, after a brief rally at 14-15 (back to 67 percent), it dropped finally to 58 percent at 16-17. This suggests a process of progressive disillusionment with marriage among teen-age Negro boys in this community. It seems probable that high levels of unemployment among Negro males help to make the acceptance of family responsibility unattractive. The prominence of matrifocal family patterns among lower-class Negro families might also contribute to the negative attitude toward marriage which these data reveal. If longitudinal research confirms the reality and universality of this progressive disillusionment, it may help to clarify the dynamics of marital instability among Negroes.

43

Change in Adolescent Heterosexual Interest Over Time*

Raymond G. Kuhlen and Nancy B. Houlihan

Interest in the opposite sex is obviously governed by social as well as by biological factors. As shown by comparative sociological and anthropological surveys, the mores and folkways governing the mingling of the sexes during adolescence vary greatly among contemporary cultures. The data of the present study by Drs. Kuhlen and Houlihan indicate that the social climate in the United States is changing in ways that encourage freer interactions between the sexes. In this study, adolescents were asked in 1942 and in 1963 to choose peers as companions for various activities. They chose peers of the opposite sex significantly more frequently in 1963 than in 1942, approximately a generation earlier. These findings clearly show that cultural factors are strongly influential in encouraging or discouraging these types of social interaction. It seems probable, as a number of world observers have commented, that all social lines of demarcation between the sexes are continuing to fade away with further passage into the twentieth century.

* Adapted from Raymond G. Kuhlen and Nancy Bryant Houlihan, "Adolescent Heterosexual Interest in 1942 and 1963," *Child Development,* 1965, Vol. 36, pp. 1049-1052. (With permission of the senior author and the Society for Research in Child Development.)

A number of writers and popular opinion have suggested that children today become interested in the opposite sex at an earlier age than they did a generation ago. Thus far evidence presented on this issue is somewhat less than direct, there being no comparisons between actual data obtained by identical procedures at different points in time in the same places. The present note reports a comparison of the frequency of cross-sex choices in grades 6 through 12 in the spring of 1963 compared to frequency of such choices in the same schools in the spring of 1942, as reflected in responses to the same questionnaire. In view of a seemingly greater current emphasis in the culture of the United States upon social interaction, and particularly interactions between sexes, it was predicted that a larger proportion of today's youngsters would make cross-sex choices than was true at the earlier testing.

SUBJECTS AND METHOD

In 1942, a sociometric questionnaire was administered to slightly more than 100 boys and 100 girls in each of grades 6, 9, and 12 in six central high school systems in central New York (Kuhlen & Lee, 1943). In the spring of 1963, in connection with another study, the same questionnaire was readministered in four of these six schools, but, because of population increases, the number of subjects was much larger. Also, at the latter testing, data were obtained for each of grades 6 through 12. The number of subjects at the time of testing is recorded in Table 1.

TABLE 1. Number of Subjects

	Grades						
	6	7	8	9	10	11	12
1942							
Boys	109	—	—	120	—	—	108
Girls	120	—	—	124	—	—	119
1963							
Boys	167	120	182	194	148	119	104
Girls	159	135	147	180	159	137	110

The questionnaire employed was a sociometric instrument in which each subject was asked to indicate a first and second choice of companions for nine activities: (1) occupying the next seat in the classroom, (2) attending the movies, (3) going for a walk, (4) going skating, (5) making things (as model boats, dresses, etc.), (6) playing outdoor games, (7) playing indoor games, (8) studying schoolwork, (9) reading for fun. The only restriction placed upon an individual's choice was that he must choose from his own grade. As earlier noted, the questionnaire used in 1963 (including instructions) was identical to the one used in 1942.

It was, of course, necessary to utilize the same procedure for analyzing the data as was employed in the 1942 study, and, accordingly, results are presented in terms of the proportion of children of each sex and grade level who made at least one choice involving a member of the opposite sex, or was chosen at least once by a member of the opposite sex.

RESULTS

The results for all seven grades obtained in 1963 and for grades 6, 9, and 12 obtained in 1942 are shown in Table 2. Since a directional predic-

TABLE 2. Percentages of Boys and Girls at Various School Grades in 1942 and 1963 Who Chose the Opposite Sex, Were Chosen by the Opposite Sex; and Were Chosen by No One as Companions

	Grades						
	6	7	8	9	10	11	12
Boys choosing girls							
1942	45.0	—	—	72.5	—	—	75.0
1963	48.8	68.9	69.2	79.9*	81.6	83.3	91.0**
Girls choosing boys							
1942	39.2	—	—	59.7	—	—	63.0
1963	52.8*	46.7	69.6	72.9*	68.3	72.7	82.7**
Boys chosen by girls							
1942	31.2	—	—	49.1	—	—	65.8
1963	46.7**	40.0	40.7	47.4	54.7	69.4	74.0
Girls chosen by boys							
1942	30.8	—	—	52.4	—	—	59.7
1963	39.6	46.7	51.7	52.2	59.1	43.7	61.8
Boys chosen by no one							
1942	5.5	—	—	5.0	—	—	1.9
1963	5.9	5.8	7.1	8.2	4.7	9.2	5.7
Girls chosen by no one							
1942	2.5	—	—	3.2	—	—	4.2
1963	2.5	2.2	2.7	3.8	3.7	4.3	5.4

* Difference between 1942 and 1963 percentages significant at the .05 level.
** Difference significant at the .01 level.

tion was made, the .01 and .05 levels of significance relating to reliabilities of differences were determined for one-tailed tests.

It will be noted that all of the six comparisons involving the *choosing* of the opposite sex are in the predicted direction and that five of those six differences are statistically significant. Thus, the hypothesis of greater heterosexual interest today (in 1963) compared to 21 years ago is supported. In contrast, only one of the six comparisons involving proportions *chosen by* the opposite sex is reliable. Apparently, about the same proportion of boys and girls have the qualities that attract choices of the opposite sex today as was true in the early 1940's, the greater interest in heterosexuality being evident in the *choosing* rather than in the being chosen. Although the more recent data contained a number of minor irregularities, the substantial drop in percentage of girls *chosen by* boys at the eleventh grade level is notable. Since no particular explanation presents itself, it is assumed tentatively that this decrease is due to sampling error.

Two minor findings may be mentioned. The first involves the number of social isolates, those chosen by no one. About the same proportion fell in this category at all grades in 1963 as in 1942, none of the differences being significant. The second finding (also in agreement with the results of the 1942 study) relates to the greater frequency of cross-sex choices by boys as compared to girls, a difference that is fairly consistent in direction, though only two of the five differences favoring boys are significant at the .05 level or beyond. Since girls generally appear to show earlier social and heterosexual interest than do boys, it seems reasonable to interpret the present finding as reflecting less reticence on the part of boys in expressing overtly an interest in particular girls, rather than as implying earlier and greater interest in the opposite sex on their part.

DISCUSSION

Although the present writers have no information as to whether the population of these communities has changed over the 21 years in ways that would result in more frequent cross-sex choices (Kanous, Daugherty, and Cohn [1962], suggest that there are more such choices in lower socioeconomic groups), the facts do seem to lend support to the view that adolescents show greater heterosexual interest now than a near generation ago. However, the data show a greater heterosexual interest throughout the age range and do not necessarily suggest an earlier *onset* of interest. Earlier studies (E. Campbell, 1939) suggest a V-shaped curve during the school years, with cross-sex choices being more frequent in the very early grades and in the high-school years. An *earlier* emergence of heterosexuality could be shown only by data that indicated that the age of greatest unisexual choice (i.e., the trough of the V) occurred at an earlier age now than a generation ago. The present study does not encompass a broad enough age range to answer this question. However, there is no evidence that this V-shaped curve has been "flattened" with passage of time.

44

Psychological Factors in Marital Happiness*

Lewis M. Terman

Two reasons may be noted why marital adjustment is worthy of the most serious scientific study. In the first place, happiness in marriage is the expectation of most young people and most of those who are married but who are unhappy in that relationship would probably like to look forward to greater happiness or to find ways to remedy their unhappiness. In the second place, the happiness or unhappiness of parents in their marriage will play a significant role in determining the kind of psychological environment in which their children are reared. Professor Lewis M. Terman conducted one of the most important large-scale investigations which have sought to assess the factors most closely associated with happiness and adjustment in marriage. In this paper, which is mainly the summary chapter of his book reporting the results of the research, are presented the essential findings and conclusions reached. The paper also includes some indication of changes that occur in marriage relationships and adjustment as age and the duration of the marriage increase. This paper is included as one of the "classics." More recent research (Winch, 1958; Ort, 1950) has focused upon the "meshing" of needs, personality, and expectations of individual couples as factors in mate selection and marital happiness.

An examination of recent contributions to the literature on marriage reveals a great diversity of opinion about the factors most responsible for marital success or failure. On practically every aspect of the problem the pronouncements by leading authors are highly contradictory. The explanation of this situation lies partly in the bias of authors, partly in their willingness to generalize from inadequate data, and partly in the use of faulty techniques in the collection of information.

A study was accordingly planned which would investigate for a larger number of subjects the relationship between happiness scores and a great

* Adapted and abridged mainly from the summary chapter (Chapter 16). (By permission from *Psychological Factors in Marital Happiness*, by L. M. Terman. Copyright, 1938. McGraw-Hill Book Co., Inc.)

variety of possible factors, including not only personality factors, but also background factors and factors having to do with sexual adjustments in the marriage. By the use of an improved technique for assuring anonymity of response, data were secured on these three sets of variables from 792 married couples who filled out the information schedules in the presence of a field assistant. The group studied represents a reasonably good sampling of the urban and semiurban married population of California at the middle and upper-middle cultural levels, though the sampling appears to be somewhat biased in the direction of superior marital happiness.

THE MEASURE OF HAPPINESS USED

The marital happiness score which was computed for each subject was based upon information regarding communality of interests, average amount of agreement or disagreement between spouses in 10 different fields, customary methods of settling disagreements, regret of marriage, choice of spouse if life were to be lived over, contemplation of separation or divorce, subjective estimates of happiness, direct admission of unhappiness, and a complaint score based upon domestic grievances checked in a long list presented. Graded weights were assigned the various possible responses to these items on the basis of intercorrelations, and the total happiness score of a given subject was the sum of the weights corresponding to his individual responses. The resulting numeral score is a serviceable index of the degree of satisfaction that a subject has found in his marriage even though it cannot be regarded as a precise quantitative measure of such satisfaction.

The happiness scores ranged from practically zero to a maximum of 87 points, with a mean of 68.40 for husbands and 69.25 for wives. The respective standard deviations of the distributions were 17.35 and 18.75. The distributions for husbands and wives agreed closely throughout and were markedly skewed in the direction of high happiness. The scores of husbands and wives correlated to the extent of approximately .60, showing that the happiness of one spouse is to a surprising degree independent of the happiness of the other. This finding is new and perhaps rather significant. Its newness is probably explained by the fact that no previous investigation based upon a large group of subjects had secured its data by methods which prevented collaboration between husband and wife in filling out the information schedules. It is significant in the suggestion it carries that the degree of satisfaction which one finds in a marriage depends partly upon one's own characteristic attitudes and temperament and so need not closely parallel the happiness of one's marital partner.

SOME TRENDS WITH AGE IN MARITAL LIFE

Two types of evidence are included here bearing on changes that occur in marriage relationships and adjustment as age and duration of marriages increase. The first relates to general happiness in marriage; the second to sex life.

Since our data show little correlation between happiness scores and present age of the subjects, they could not be expected to show a very high correlation between happiness scores and length of marriage. It is in fact only —.028 with husband's happiness and only —.048 with wife's. The mean length of marriage in our population is 11.4 years, the standard

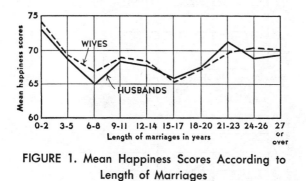

FIGURE 1. Mean Happiness Scores According to Length of Marriages

deviation of the distribution is 7.4 years, and the range is from less than 1 year to more than 27 years. With so wide a range any consistent relationship between happiness and length of marriage should be reflected in the correlation coefficients. The fact that these are practically zero means either that no appreciable relationship exists or that it is nonlinear.

Figure 1 shows trends with duration of marriage in mean happiness scores. An extreme low falls at the interval 6 to 8 years, after which there is a slight rise followed by a second low at 15 to 17 years. There is nothing to indicate a drop in happiness at a so-called "danger period" after 20 years; in fact, the period from 21 years onward rates only a little less happy than the first 2 years of the marriage. The low point at 6 to 8 years must be in part due to the waning of honeymoon happiness and in part to growing discord in certain marriages which will later be dissolved by divorce. But the tide of divorce does not flow unabated over the matrimonial shores. It is highest at around 10 years after marriage. After 20 years its force has been largely spent, and from this point onward the curves in Figure 1 are relatively flat. There is no evidence at the extreme end of the curves that the mellowness of old age is dissipating previously existing discord to an extent sufficient to cause a final rise in the average of happiness.

Doubtless many readers will be surprised that the relationship between happiness and length of marriage is as low as it is. Almost everyone seems to believe that most marriages are very happy for a time and that after a honeymoon period the happiness rapidly fades. To some degree this occurs.

It is probable, however, that in some marriages a period of early conflict and maladjustment is followed by increased understanding and content-

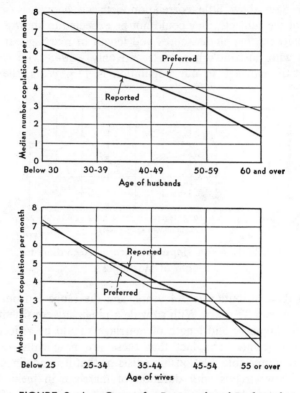

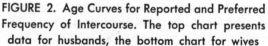

FIGURE 2. Age Curves for Reported and Preferred
Frequency of Intercourse. The top chart presents
data for husbands, the bottom chart for wives

ment and that changes in the two directions largely cancel each other. One must also allow for the possibility that even though the sum total of satisfaction with marriage may not change quantitatively during the years, it may change qualitatively in ways which are not brought to light by our happiness scale.

Information regarding changes in frequency of intercourse with increased age is contained in Figure 2. Data are presented for actual reported behavior as well as for preference. The upper chart in Figure 2 shows the curve of husband's preferred frequency to be above that of reported frequency at every age, the difference between the two ranging from one to two copulations per month. In the lower chart, however, it is seen that for wives the curves for reported and preferred frequency almost coincide throughout their course. This suggests that the frequency with which intercourse occurs in marriage is governed much more by the wife's than by the husband's preference.

It will be seen that the rate of decrease in reported frequency of intercourse is represented by almost a straight line. The phenomenon in question differs in this respect from the usual age curves for either physical or mental abilities. These almost invariably show a plateau, or near plateau, following a rapid rise to maximum and lasting for 5 to 15 years before decline begins. It is possible that in this case the plateau comes too early and lasts too short a time to be disclosed by our data; or it may be that frequency of intercourse in marriage is affected by motivational and other psychological factors which prevent it from reflecting accurately the waning of sexual drive.

The husband's curve of preferred frequency shows almost a straight-line drop through the 50 to 59 decade, after which the rate of decline appears to be less rapid. However, the N for decade 60 to 69 is very small and the mean not very reliable. In the case of wives the curve for preferred frequency shows a straight-line drop through decade 35 to 44, then almost a plateau through the decade 45 to 54, and a greatly accelerated decline thereafter. The decade 45 to 54 spans the menopause period in women, and the near plateau for the wives at this period confirms the observation frequently reported in the literature that sexual desire in women ordinarily shows little decrease at this time and in individual cases is even intensified.

PERSONALITY CORRELATES OF MARITAL HAPPINESS

The information schedule that was filled out by the subjects contained 233 personality test items dealing with interests, attitudes, likes and dislikes, habitual response patterns, and specific opinions as to what constitutes the ideal marriage. Of these, approximately 140 were found to show an appreciable degree of correlation with the happiness scores of either husbands or wives. The various possible responses to the valid items were then assigned score weights roughly in proportion to the extent to which they differentiated between subjects of high and low happiness scores. This made it possible to compute for each subject a "personality" score, which was merely the sum of the weights corresponding to the responses the subject had given. The personality score may be thought of as in some degree an index of the subject's temperamental predisposition to find happiness rather than unhappiness in the marital relationship. This index correlates approximately .46 with the marital happiness scores of each spouse. Evidently the attitudes and emotional response patterns tapped by the personality items are by no means negligible as determiners of marital happiness.

By noting and classifying the individual items that differentiate between subjects of high and low happiness, it has been possible to piece together descriptive composite pictures of the happy and unhappy temperaments. For example, it is especially characteristic of unhappy subjects to be touchy or grouchy; to lose their tempers easily; to fight to get their own way; to be critical of others; to be careless of others' feelings; to chafe under discipline or to rebel against orders; to show any dislike that they may happen to feel; to be easily affected by praise or blame; to lack self-confidence; to be dominating in their relations with the opposite sex; to be little interested in old people, children, teaching, charity, or uplift activities; to be unconventional in their attitudes toward religion, drinking, and sexual ethics; to be bothered by useless thoughts; to be often in a state of excitement; and to alternate between happiness and sadness without apparent cause.

The above characterizations hold for the unhappy of both sexes. In many respects, however, the differences between the happy and unhappy follow a different pattern for husbands and wives.

The qualities of personality that predispose a person to happiness or unhappiness in his relations with others are of course far from being the sole cause of success or failure in marriage. Their importance, however, is so obvious from our data that the problem calls for further investigation, preferably by a combination of the statistical and clinical approaches.

BACKGROUND CORRELATES OF HAPPINESS

Background factors which in these marriages were totally uncorrelated with happiness scores, or for which the correlation was so small as to have almost no practical significance, include family income, occupation, presence or absence of children, amount of religious training, birth order, number of opposite-sex siblings, adolescent popularity, and spouse differences in age and schooling. Nearly all of the factors in this list have been regarded by one writer or another as highly important, especially presence or absence of children in the home and differences between husband and wife in age and schooling.

It is doubtless true that the presence of children often prevents the breaking up of a marriage, but the evidence indicates that it has little effect on the general level of marital happiness. Childless women past middle age do show a slight tendency to be less happy than the average, but childless men of this age tend to have happiness scores above the average. If there are individual marriages that are made more happy by the presence of children, these appear to be offset by other marriages that are made less happy.

From the vantage point of our data it appears that much nonsense has been written about the risks entailed by marrying on inadequate income or by marrying out of one's age or educational class. The correlation of income with happiness scores is zero. The happiest wives in our group are those who are from 4 to 10 years older than their husbands; the happiest husbands are those who are 12 or more years older than their wives. Moreover, the spouses of these subjects rate as happy as the average for the entire population of subjects.

As for religious training, if this was ever a factor in marital happiness it appears no longer to exert such an influence.

We may designate as of slight importance the factors that show a barely significant relationship to the happiness of one or both of the spouses. This list includes age at marriage, absolute amount of schooling, rated adequacy of sex instruction, sources of sex information, age of learning the origin of babies, number of siblings, circumstances of first meeting between the spouses, length of premarital acquaintance, length of engagement, attractiveness of opposite-sex parent, resemblance of subject's spouse to subject's opposite-sex parent, amount of adolescent "petting," and wife's experience of sex shock or her age at first menstruation. No factor in this list is sufficiently related to marital happiness to warrant a prediction weight of more than one point[1] for either husbands or wives. There has been a vast amount of exaggeration about the risks to marital happiness of early marriage, brief premarital acquaintance, indequate sex instruction, adolescent "petting," and a history of sex shock on the part of the wife.

Expressed desire to be of the opposite sex tends to be associated with unhappiness in wives but not in husbands. A premarital attitude of disgust toward sex is unfavorable to happiness, and more so in men than in women. Frequent or severe punishment in childhood is reliably associated with unhappiness in both husbands and wives. The items mentioned in this paragraph carry a maximum prediction weight of two points for at least one of the spouses.

Next are five items carrying a maximum weight of three points for one spouse and two points for the other. They are: estimates on husbands and wives of their relative mental ability, parental attitudes toward the subject's early sex curiosity, amount of conflict with father, and amount of attachment to both father and mother.

As to relative mental ability, the most favorable situation is equality or near equality. Marked mental superiority of husband makes for happiness in the wife but for unhappiness in the husband; marked inferiority of husband makes the wife unhappy but does not greatly affect the husband.

Subjects whose parents rebuffed or punished them because of their early sex curiosity are definitely less happy than the average, this effect being somewhat more marked in husbands than in wives.

Strong attachment to either parent is markedly favorable to happiness,

[1] The "prediction weights," ranging from one to five points, were based on the reliability of the differences between characteristics of two extreme groups (high and low happiness) of husbands and wives taken separately.

especially in the case of husbands. Conflict with the father is unfavorable to happiness, especially in the case of wives.

We come now to the four most important of the background items: happiness of parents, childhood happiness, conflict with mother, and type of home discipline. All of these carry a maximum weight of four or five points.

Happiness of parents rates highest, with a maximum weight of five points for husbands and four for wives. This item is more predictive of success or failure in marriage than a composite of half a dozen items such as income, age at marriage, religious training, amount of adolescent "petting," or spouse difference in age or schooling.

Hardly less important is the rated happiness of respondent's childhood, with a maximum weight of four points for each spouse. Carrying the same weights is absence of conflict with mother. It appears that a record of conflict with mother constitutes a significantly greater threat to marital happiness than a record of conflict with father.

Childhood discipline that is firm, not harsh, is much more favorable to happiness than discipline that is lax, irregular, or excessively strict.

The 10 background circumstances most predictive of marital happiness are: (1) superior happiness of parents, (2) childhood happiness, (3) lack of conflict with mother, (4) home discipline that was firm, not harsh, (5) strong attachment to mother, (6) strong attachment to father, (7) lack of conflict with father, (8) parental frankness about matters of sex, (9) infrequency and mildness of childhood punishment, (10) premarital attitude toward sex that was free from disgust or aversion.

The subject who "passes" on all 10 of these items is a distinctly better-than-average marital risk. Any one of the 10 appears from the data of this study to be more important than virginity at marriage.

SEX FACTORS IN MARITAL HAPPINESS

Our study shows clearly that certain of the sex factors contribute materially to marital happiness or unhappiness. It shows no less clearly that others which have long been emphasized by sexologists as important are practically uncorrelated with happiness scores. The data in fact indicate that all of the sex factors combined are far from being the one major determinant of success in marriage.

Among the items yielding little or no correlation with happiness are both reported and preferred frequency of intercourse, estimated duration of intercourse, husband's ability to control ejaculation, methods of contraception used, distrust of contraceptives, fear of pregnancy, degree of pain experienced by wife at the first intercourse, wife's history of sex shock, rhythm in wife's sexual desire, ability of wife to experience multiple orgasms, and failure of the husband to be as dominant as the wife would like him to be in initiating or demanding intercourse.

The sex techniques that many writers regard as the primary key to happy marriage may be worth cultivating for their immediate sensual returns, but they exert no appreciable effect upon happiness scores. Their absence or imperfection is evidently not a major source of conflict or a major cause of separation, divorce, or regret of marriage. What is even more surprising, it appears that such techniques have no very marked effect on the wife's ability to experience the orgasm.

On the other hand, the wife's happiness score (though not her husband's) is reliably correlated with the amount of pleasure that she experienced at her first intercourse, and the husband's happiness is reliably correlated (negatively) with the wife's tendency to prudishness or excessive modesty.

Five of the sex items that correlate quite markedly with the happiness scores are: number of sexual complaints checked, rated degree of satisfaction from intercourse with spouse, frequency with which intercourse is refused, reaction of the spouse who is refused, and frequency of desire for extramarital intercourse. The correlations, however, probably do not mean that the factors in question are to any great extent actual determiners of happiness or unhappiness. It is more likely that they are primarily symptoms. The discontented spouse rationalizes his (or her) unhappiness by finding fault with the sexual partner and at the same time develops longings for extramarital relationships.

Among the sex factors investigated are two that not only correlate markedly with happiness scores but are in all probability genuine determiners of them: viz., the wife's orgasm adequacy and husband-wife difference in strength of sex drive.

Two measures were available on relative strength of sex drive. One of these was the ratio (computed for each subject) between actual and preferred number of copulations per month; the other was based on husband's and wife's ratings of their relative passionateness. The two measures agree in showing that equality or near equality in sex drive is an important factor in happiness. As the disparity in drive increases to the point where one spouse is in a more or less chronic state of sex hunger and the other in a state of satiety, the happiness scores of both drop off significantly.

First in importance among the sex factors is the wife's orgasm adequacy, which correlates about .30 both with her own and with her husband's happiness score. It is of special interest that orgasm inadequacy of the wife affects her husband's happiness almost as unfavorably as her own. Between wives of the "never" group and wives of the "always" group, there is a difference of 16.3 points in mean happiness, and a difference of 13.0 points in the mean happiness scores of their husbands. Nevertheless, one finds every grade of happiness both in the "never" group and the "always" group. Adequacy of the wife in this respect favors happiness but does not guarantee it, while on the other hand a considerable minority among the inadequates have happiness scores above the general average.

THE RELATIVE IMPORTANCE OF SEXUAL AND PSYCHOLOGICAL COMPATIBILITY

Our data do not confirm the view so often heard that the key to happiness in marriage is nearly always to be found in sexual compatibility. They indicate, instead, that the influence of the sexual factors is at most no greater than that of the combined personality and background factors, and that it is probably less. The problem is complicated by the fact that the testimony of husband and wife regarding their sexual compatibility is influenced by their psychological compatibility. Couples who are psychologically well mated are likely to show a surprising tolerance for the things that are not satisfactory in their sexual relationships. The psychologically ill-mated show no such tolerance but instead are prone to exaggeration in their reports on sexual maladjustments. The two sexual factors of genuine importance are wife's orgasm adequacy and relative strength of sex drive in the two spouses.

Part X

PSYCHOLOGICAL DEVELOPMENT AND ADJUSTMENT WITHIN THE SCHOOL ENVIRONMENT

NO ONE DENIES that the process of educating children is one of the most important activities of society. Much education, and almost all of certain types, goes on informally in the home, in the neighborhood, and in the larger community, especially within the partially or wholly informal groups of which the child, adolescent, or adult is a member. Society has, however, established formal institutions charged with the responsibility for educating the young and assigned a fundamental role in transmitting the culture to young people and in preparing them for happy, effective living in a complex and dizzily changing world.

The scope of the job to be accomplished requires the use of mass educational methods involving some standardization of curriculum and procedure. Yet a high degree of individualization is required by the nature of the learning process and by the vast range of differences among children in their purposes, personal and emotional traits, and background abilities and skills. It is the inability to provide the optimal degree of this individualization of instruction, as well as some insensitivity to the need for it on the part of many teachers and school administrators, that results in much academic frustration, especially in the case of children who do not fit the typical pattern.

But the school is more than a place where culture is transmitted and skills taught. Schooling represents a significant phase of the child's social life, and the school is a new world of varied human contacts demanding adjustments on the part of the child entering school for the first time, a world where friendships are made, where those who do not easily make friends feel their isolation more, where minority and economically less favored groups may feel especially keenly their lack of status and acceptance. The school is the hub of many group activities of children, and especially of adolescents. Through its social program, extracurricular program and school government, the school has innumerable opportunities to promote growth both in desirable personal qualities and in general competence for social living.

The papers in this part are chosen to emphasize not so much the academic impact of the schools on children as their personal-emotional impact and to suggest not so much how schools might do more to recognize the individuality of children as how children adjust and react to the school. The first paper in this part is on the behavior patterns of children in nursery school and the influence of various preschool curricula on children's psychological growth and adjustment. The paper by Schrupp and Gjerde shows how teachers' evaluations of pupils' behavior problems have changed since the classic Wickman investigation was made nearly 40 years earlier. Teachers have moved closer to the attitudes expressed by psychological and psychiatric specialists during this time. However, the report by Meyer and Thompson demonstrates that the teachers today still harbor unverbalized and unadmitted biases that may function to the detriment of the mental health of the boys. The study by Shaw and McCuen also demonstrates the differential response of boys and girls to the school environment, in this instance as it relates to the need to achieve, to accomplish something. These studies are representative of a vast number of psychological investigations of personal and social variables related to the direction of the school's program, the effectiveness of its curricula, formal and informal, and the competence and skills of its teaching personnel.

45

Comparative Social Adjustments of Elementary School Pupils with and Without Preschool Training[*]

Merl E. Bonney and Ertie Lou Nicholson

Three studies of the effect of nursery school or kindergarten experience upon later social adjustment in elementary school are summarized. The findings are inconsistent. A reliable difference was

* Adapted and abridged from Merl E. Bonney and Ertie Lou Nicholson, "Comparative Social Adjustments of Elementary School Pupils with and without Preschool Training," *Child Development*, 1958, Vol. 29, pp. 125-133. (With permission of the senior author and the Society for Research in Child Development.)

found in one study, i.e., the effect was shown to be good, but no difference was found in the other two. It is noteworthy that the beneficial effects were found in the case of a high-quality nursery school. What is important here is the demonstration that those activities— apparently ranging from the activities of a nursery school (as in this study) to psychotherapy (see the paper by Levitt in Part XIII)—which are presumed to have beneficial outcomes, are not necessarily effective. It is through such negative results as well as through positive findings that scientific knowledge and educational practice and applied psychology in general advances. While systematic research often confirms "common sense" (or common expectations and observation), often it does not. Such negative findings stimulate further search for the significant variables within the total complex labelled "nursery school," etc., which may make some programs effective, whereas others fail.

Educators, psychologists, and sociologists have generally agreed upon the importance of early childhood in the formation of personality and character. No doubt this emphasis is well placed. However, there is still much to be found out about the conditions or kinds of experiences which make for significant differences in subsequent development. It is the major purpose of this paper to present a report of some efforts to evaluate the extent to which nursery school and kindergarten experiences can be shown to make a difference in classroom social adjustments in subsequent elementary school grades. The primary question to be answered is: Can those children, as a group, who have had these preschool socializing experiences be shown to have measurable advantages in subsequent years in classroom social adjustments as compared with children in the same classes who have had no nursery school or kindergarten training?

This report consists of a review of three studies bearing on this question, together with a discussion of the findings.

FIRST STUDY

Methods and Subjects. The first study to be reported was conducted by Angell (1954) as a part of her graduate work at North Texas State College. Her subjects were 78 children in two kindergartens, two first grades, one second grade, and one third grade in two schools in Denton, Texas. These children were divided into 39 pairs with one pupil of each pair having attended a nursery school while the other member of each pair had not.

In order to help equate these pairings the two pupils put together within each class were similar in sex, fathers' occupational level, and number of siblings in the family. Classification of fathers' occupations was based on the Revised Scale for Rating Occupations as given in Warner, Meeker, and Eells (1949).

All of the children in the above listed grades responded to a one-criterion sociometric test involving several choices per pupil for preferred playmates. Total scores were calculated for each pupil on the basis of this measurement.

The teachers in four of the classes, including kindergarten through third grade, rated all the pupils included in their respective classes on the Winnetka Scale for Rating School Behavior and Attitudes. This scale has twelve subdivisions, but the ratings obtained on all of these are summarized into five major trait-categories as follows: Cooperation, Social Consciousness, Emotional Adjustment, Leadership, and Responsibility. The teachers did not know the purpose of this study when they made their ratings.

Findings. The difference between the mean sociometric scores of the nursery and non-nursery school pupils was found by *t* test to be significant at the .02 level of confidence.

In the four classes in which teacher ratings were obtained there were 23 of the 39 pairings described above. When the mean score of the Winnetka Scale in each of the five major categories for the 23 pupils who had attended nursery school was compared with that for the 23 non-nursery school pupils, only one of the differences was found to be statistically reliable, this at the 5 per cent level for the trait designated Social Consciousness.

Summary. These findings clearly show that the pupils who had attended nursery school had a reliable advantage over the non-nursery school pupils in receiving positive choices from their classmates, but they showed a reliable advantage in only one out of five traits from the standpoint of teacher ratings on the Winnetka Scale.

SECOND STUDY

Methods and Subjects. The second study was a master's thesis completed at North Texas State College by Nicholson (1957). Her subjects were 402 children in grades one through six in a public elementary school in a predominantly lower-middle class neighborhood in Dallas, Texas.

The first step in this study was to send a questionnaire to all the parents of all the pupils in this school asking them to supply information on whether or not their children had attended a nursery school or a kindergarten, or both. Of nearly 1000 questionnaires sent out, approximately 900 were returned. From these returns it was possible to select 14 classes (out of 32 classes available in the school) in which approximately 50 per cent of the pupils had had some type of preschool training. There were two classes on each of four grade levels and three classes on each of the other two grade levels.

Of the 402 pupils included in this study a little over 200 had had no formal preschool training. Of the nearly 200 who had had some type of preschool experience, approximate one-fourth had attended a nursery school, about one-half had attended a kindergarten, and the remaining one-fourth had attended both a nursery school and a kindergarten.

Classroom social adjustment was measured by sociometric testing and by teacher nominations.

In each of the 14 classes the pupils made four choices for others in their respective rooms with whom they would most like to eat lunch, and also four choices for the pupils they would select as candidates for the "Best Citizen of the Year" award—an annual custom in this school. These two criteria were used because they were both appropriate to all six grade levels in this school. Each child's total choice-status was based on his combined score from both of these criteria.

Teacher nominations were obtained by having each teacher list the upper one-fourth of pupils in her class who were regarded by her as making the most effective and satisfactory social adjustments within her classroom group; also, each teacher listed those whom she considered to be in the lowest fourth in reference to classroom social adjustments. All these listings were made before the teachers knew anything about the purposes of the investigation.

Findings. One of the major hypotheses which was tested in this study was whether the factor of preschool attendance or nonattendance was related to being in the upper or the lower halves of the sociometric distributions of the respective grade groupings. In order to have sufficient cases for statistical treatment the several classes on each grade level were combined, but all grade-level groupings were treated separately. The number of cases on the six grade levels ranged from 49 to 85 with a median of 67.

Using four-fold contingency tables each category was then compared with every other category. Because of the small number of cases in some cells an allowance for discontinuity was made by applying Yates' correction in computing the chi squares. When these data were assembled, it was found that none of the chi squares was statistically significant. These findings obviously do not support the hypothesis that there was a significant relationship between choice-status, as measured in this research, and preschool attendance or nonattendance.

A second hypothesis tested in this investigation was that the teachers' listings of pupils in the upper and lower fourths from the standpoint of classroom social adjustments, as described above, would show a reliable relationship to the fact of preschool attendance or nonattendance. This hypothesis was also tested by chi square, using Yates' correction. None of these relationships proved to be even close to statistical significance.

A third hypothesis bearing on the carry-over value of preschool training was tested by forming matched groups. On each grade level those pupils who had attended some type of preschool were matched with nonattending pupils in regard to the following factors: sex, age, fathers' occupational classification, and IQ's obtained from a group-administered intelligence test. On the basis of this matching the following number of pairs was obtained on each grade level from the first through the sixth: 23, 33, 34, 24, 20, 28. When the t test was applied to each of these experimental and control groupings, as they were related to sociometric choice-status on each grade level, none of the differences was found to be statistically significant. Only one of them even approached the .05 level of confidence.

Summary. It is clear that these findings provide no evidence that those pupils who had attended some type of preschool had, as a group, any advantage in personal-social behavior over those who had had no preschool training, either from the standpoint of acceptability by classroom peers or on the basis of teacher evaluations.

THIRD STUDY

Methods and Subjects. The third study was concerned with four sixth grade classes in the Denton, Texas, public schools. The pupils in each of these four sixth grades responded to a two-criteria sociometric test involving choices for preferred playmates and for desired associates in classroom group work. Also, each of the four teachers listed the names of those pupils whom she considered to be in the upper fourth of her class in "over-all good adjustment to the classroom social situation," and those she considered to be in the lowest fourth of her group on the same criterion.

Findings. In three of the four sixth grades approximately 35 per cent of the pupils had attended either nursery school or kindergarten. In these classes the average number of choices received on the two sociometric criteria combined was very nearly the same for the preschool and the non-preschool groups. The actual difference was less than one point in each of the three classes.

In the remaining sixth grade 80 per cent of the pupils had attended either nursery school or kindergarten, or both. In this class the preschool pupils received an average sociometric score which was nearly twice as large as that received by the non-preschool pupils. This is obviously a marked advantage but probably should not be used as a basis for generalization because of the very unbalanced proportions of the two groups being compared in this class.

If the analysis of teacher placements into upper and lower fourths, as described above, is confined to the three classes in which the number attending some type of preschool amounted to approximately 35 per cent of each class, the conclusion is reached that these placements were unrelated to the factor of preschool attendance or nonattendance. Both the upper and lower fourths in each class included preschool and non-preschool pupils in numbers which were very close to what would be expected from their proportional representation in their respective groups.

Considering all four of the sixth grades, an effort was made to see if those pupils who had attended *both* nursery school and kindergarten would show up better on the sociometric testing and the teacher placements than those who had not attended either type of preschool. In all four classes combined there were 20 pupils who met this condition. An inspection of their average choice-status in their respective classes and their listings on the teacher placements failed to show any advantage for these pupils except in the room mentioned above in which only 20 per cent of the children had had no preschool training.

An effort was made to isolate the influence of the factor of preschool vs. non-preschool attendance by comparing these two groups in each class on the basis of IQ's, fathers' occupational classification, and family size. The IQ's were obtained by administering the California Short-Form Test of Mental Maturity. The fathers' occupational classifications were based on the same scale used in the first study. Family size was based on the number of siblings within six years of the age of each pupil being studied.

In none of these three variables was the difference between the preschool and the non-preschool groupings large enough to warrant statistical treatment. All the average IQ differences were less than seven points, and in three of the four classes the differences were only two or three points. All the differences between average scores for fathers' occupational classifications were less than one point with the exception of the class in which only 20 per cent of the pupils had not gone to preschool. In this class those who had attended preschool possessed an obvious advantage in fathers' occupational level.

In regard to family size the means and medians for all the groups were very similar, the largest single difference being less than one-half of a point.

Summary. From the foregoing data it is clear that the over-all picture is one of no significant differences between the preschool and non-preschool pupils in social adjustments in the sixth grades studied.

DISCUSSION

Other studies which have been designed to evaluate preschool education, particularly the nursery school, have shown some definite advantages for this type of education, although these advantages have not always been very outstanding or consistent on various types of measurements. One question which would naturally be raised in a report of this kind is in regard to the *quality-level* of the preschool training which any particular group of pupils receives. The only basis available for dealing with this point in reference to the three studies which constitute the main body of this report is the proportion of subjects that attended a nursery school or a kindergarten sponsored by one of the two state colleges in Denton, the assumption being that these preschools are probably representative of the best kind of training available. In the first study conducted by Angell nearly all the pupils had had their training in a college-sponsored preschool, and it was this study which showed the most clear-cut advantage for the preschool pupils.

One experimental study by Thompson (1944) is especially pertinent to the matter of quality-level since his evidence showed that nursery school pupils whose teachers manifested toward them a large amount of warm friendly and helpful relationships made much more progress in various aspects of personal-social behavior than did a similar group of nursery school pupils whose teachers were considerate but who were somewhat detached and gave help only when it was specifically requested. These findings suggest that one of the essential characteristics of a preschool of high-quality level is a large amount of personal-social interaction not only between the pupils but also between the pupils and their teachers. Unfortunately, information is lacking on the extent to which this kind of relationship was present in the great majority of preschools that have been studied.

These results lead to the conclusion that if early socialization experiences are going to possess significant carry-over values into subsequent years they probably will need to be of a particularly high quality-level in reference to interpersonal rapport between the pupils and their adult supervisors and also in regard to adequate provision for meeting the varying needs of individuals.

It seems likely that many educators and child psychologists have had too much naive faith in the adjustment or curative values of group socialization, without sufficient attention being paid to whether or not the activities engaged in are actually helping those who need some assistance as opposed to simply perpetuating an established social hierarchy.

If this is a valid statement, then it follows that nursery school and kindergarten teachers should become more critical of their programs, particularly from the standpoint of planning more exercises, both in the school and with parents, which are designed to help those who show obvious signs of personal and social maladjustments.

46

Teachers' Attitudes Toward Behavior Problems of Children: Changes Over Time*

Manfred H. Schrupp and Clayton M. Gjerde

Teachers have important responsibilities for the mental health of school children and should provide the best possible environment for their psychological development. Accordingly, it is highly desirable that teachers be sensitive to any form of behavior in a child which suggests that he has a psychological problem, one which could result in poor future adjustment. This study is a replication of a widely cited study done in the 1920's. It suggests—and similar studies are in agreement—that teachers today have a much clearer understanding of the psychological significance of children's behavior than was true a generation ago, but that their judgments still differ from the judgment of "experts" in significant ways. In addition to a demonstration of this important trend, the reader's attention is directed toward the nature of the differences, since these differences probably are similar to (even though less pronounced than) those that are found between educated parents and specialists in understanding children's behavior problems.

Wickman's study of teachers' attitudes toward behavior problems of children, published in 1928, has been quoted ever since as evidence that teachers are unable to recognize as serious those problems so designated by clinicians. The very fact that his study has so frequently been quoted should have been influential in changing teachers' attitudes. Certainly teacher education programs have devoted increased time and effort to the development of a "mental hygiene viewpoint." It would therefore seem desirable to determine whether the attitudes of teachers of today correlate as poorly with those of mental hygienists as the professional literature im-

* Adapted and abridged from Manfred H. Schrupp and Clayton M. Gjerde, "Teacher Growth in Attitudes toward Behavior Problems of Children," *Journal of Educational Psychology*, 1953, Vol. 44, pp. 203-214. (With permission of the senior author and the copyright holder, Abrahams Magazine Service, Inc.)

plies. The major purpose of this study was to compare present-day teachers' attitudes with attitudes of earlier teachers and mental hygienists and with mental hygienists of today. To facilitate direct comparisons with Wickman's results, his procedures were repeated as closely as practicable.

WICKMAN'S PROCEDURE

In his study, Wickman had a group of five hundred eleven teachers and a group of thirty mental hygienists rate the seriousness of fifty behavior traits of children. He found that the ratings made by the teachers correlated about zero with the ratings made by the mental hygienists, and that there appeared to be wide discrepancies between the two groups with regard to the kinds of behavior problems which were considered serious. In interpreting his study, it should be noted that the ratings were made by the teachers and hygienists on the basis of distinctly different instructions. Wickman was careful to point this out in his report:

"The techniques employed for measuring the reactions of the mental hygienists to behavior disorders, therefore, differed in certain respects from the methods employed in measuring teachers' reactions. In the rating scales for teachers the adoption of three precautionary techniques for controlling the teachers' responses will be recalled . . . : (1) the directions to teachers for rating were phrased in such a way as to secure responses to the *present* problem, and the question of the significance of the present behavior disorder upon the *future* development of the child, though possibly unavoidably implied, was not definitely raised. The task set was to rate the degree of maladjustment represented by the immediate problem. (2) Care was also taken to establish in the teachers a mental set for responding to the "seriousness of" the amount of "difficulty produced by" the particular type of troublesome behavior. The assumption was that the degree to which teachers found a certain problem serious, difficult, or undesirable represented the amount of attention they directed to the problem and the effort exerted towards its modification. (3) Then, too, in order to elicit the first, unrationalized reactions, the teachers were instructed to rate as rapidly as possible, and a time limit was imposed for completing the ratings.

"The precautionary techniques utilized in measuring the teachers' attitudes were exactly reversed in eliciting the attitudes of the mental hygienists. (1) Instead of evaluating the *present* problem, the mental hygienists were directed to rate the significance of the problem in terms of its effect on the *future* life of the child. . . . (2) Though the terms "seriousness" and "difficulty" of a problem were retained in the directions for rating, the concept of the "importance" of the behavior problems was emphasized and replaced the concepts of "consequence" and "undesirableness." (3) Instead of issuing instructions for rating as rapidly as possible and imposing a time limit for completing the ratings, as in administering the scale to teachers, an attempt was made to elicit from the mental hygienists responses that were intellectually controlled and evaluated. The directions read, 'Try to make this a professional opinion that is as free as possible from your emotional reactions.' " (Wickman, 1928, pp. 119-121.)

The substance of this quotation has often been overlooked when the results of Wickman's research have been discussed. Mitchell (1942), in a study conducted in 1940 with teachers from the same school systems used by Wickman, employed a modification of the original Wickman scale, as well as a modification of the directions. Sixty-three mental hygienists also rated the traits, following the same directions used with the teachers. He reported a correlation of .70 between teachers and mental hygienists. He also reported a correlation of .21 between Wickman's teachers of 1927 and his mental hygienists of 1940, indicating a possible shift in the opinions of mental hygienists. Here, again, the higher relationship between teachers and mental hygienists could be due to the fact that these two groups followed the same directions in making their ratings.

PROCEDURES OF THE PRESENT STUDY

In the present study, Wickman's schedules were employed with the teachers and mental hygienists, without modification of any kind, either in the schedule of behavior traits itself or in the directions. It was therefore possible to make direct comparisons of present findings with those of twenty-four years ago. It should be remembered, however, that in this study, as in Wickman's, the results do not permit a direct comparison of teachers and clinicians as professional groups. Here, as in Wickman's study, the careful and considered judgment of the clinicians was used as the most nearly ideal criterion possible for evaluating the teachers' rapid, unrationalized reactions to the behavior problems.

The teachers' schedule and a personal data sheet were sent to 199 teachers, selected at random from regularly employed teachers in the secondary and elementary schools of San Diego, California. Of the 199 schedules distributed, 127 (63.8 per cent) were returned, and 119 (59.8 per cent) were usable. Of the 119 teachers responding, fifty-nine were from the elementary level, and sixty from the secondary level.

Thirty-seven mental hygienists completed the clinicians' schedule, and they were employed by public school guidance agencies or clinics, as were those in the Wickman study. The group was composed of one psychiatrist, twelve psychologists, twenty-four school social workers and visiting teachers. As will be shown later, the ratings by these clinicians correlated highly (.80 to .88) with clinicians in 1927 and in 1940, which suggests that these groups were quite comparable in their attitude toward behavior problems of children, insofar as the Wickman scale measured them.

As in the Wickman study, the respondents were asked to rate the behavior traits by marking on a line, scaled on the teacher's form from "Of no consequence" to "An extremely grave problem," and on the clinicians' form from "Of no importance at all" to "Of extremely great importance." The responses were quantified by the use of a scale ranging from 0 to 20, as described by Wickman, thus permitting the determination of mean scale scores on each trait for teachers and clinicians. It was possible then to compute product-moment correlations between the means of the ratings by the teacher group and the means of ratings by Wickman's clinicians, Mitchell's clinicians, and those involved in the present study. In addition, similar correlations were determined between the means of ratings made by groups of teachers in 1927, 1940, and 1951, and between the means of the ratings made by clinician groups in the same years. These correlations are presented in Table 1.

RESULTS

Using the ratings of the clinicians of 1927 as a criterion, there is evidence of definite increase in agreement between clinician and teacher attitudes, as the correlation of .43 is statistically significant at the one per cent level.

TABLE 1. Clinician and Teacher Intercorrelations on Attitudes Toward Behavior Problems of Children

	1951 Tchs.	1940 Tchs.	1927 Tchs.	1951 Clin.	1940 Clin.
1927 Clin.	.43**	.35*	−.04	.88**	.80**
1940 Clin.	.61**	.70**	.21	.88**	
1951 Clin.	.56**	.54**	.09		
1927 Tchs.	.76**	.78**			
1940 Tchs.	.81**				

* Significant at the five per cent level.
** Significant at the one per cent level.

Although the greatest change appears to be between 1927 and 1940, this cannot be assumed since Mitchell's 1940 group of teachers rated the behavior problems following the same directions employed in the case of the clinician group. For the same reason, the correlation between the 1940 clinicians' ratings and the 1940 teachers' ratings (.70) may not be directly comparable to those obtained in 1927 and 1951. However, the 1951 teachers' ratings correlated .61 with those of the 1940 clinicians, a considerable and significant gain over the .21 reported by Mitchell between the 1927 teachers' ratings and the 1940 clinicians' ratings.

If the ratings of the clinicians involved in the present study (hereafter referred to as "1951 clinicians") are used as a criterion, we again see a significant increase in the correlations between teachers' and clinicians' ratings. The 1927 teachers' ratings correlated only .09 with those of 1951 clinicians, while the ratings by 1951 teachers correlated .56 (significant at the one per cent level) with those of the 1951 clinician group. Here, too, the increase appears at first glance to be greater from 1927 to 1940 than from 1940 to 1951, but this may again be due to the fact that the 1940 teachers followed essentially the same directions in rating the traits as did the 1951 clinicians. This was not true in the case of the 1951 teachers.

Correlations between ratings by the three clinician groups (.88, .88, .80) are all significant at the one per cent level, and of higher order. For the teacher groups the same is true, with correlations ranging from .76 to .81. As mentioned earlier, this suggests that the teacher and clinician groups are distinct groups rather than being random samples from the same population. To determine if this was true for the 1951 teacher and clinician groups, each group was randomly divided into two subgroups of approximately equal size. Product-moment correlations were then computed between the mean scale scores of the subgroups. This correlation was .94 for the two teacher subgroups, and also .94 for the two clinician subgroups, again indicating that teachers and clinicians were distinct and fairly homogeneous groups.

In general, the correlations presented in Table 1 suggest that a definite increase in agreement between teachers and clinicians took place between 1927 and 1951, and that this increased agreement is probably due primarily to a change in the attitudes of teachers rather than of clinicians. Assuming (1) that the Wickman scale actually measures attitudes toward behavior problems of children, (2) that clinicians' ratings constitute a valid criterion, and (3) that the teachers studied are reasonably representative groups, it can be concluded that teachers' attitudes of this kind have improved significantly in the last twenty-four years.

Another method of indicating the relationships between two groups is by comparison of ranks. Examination of the rank orders indicates that some significant disagreements still exist between teachers and clinicians in their rating of seriousness of behavior traits. Among the fifty traits, there were sixteen for which the rank difference between ratings by 1951 teachers and clinicians was 15 or greater. These are listed in Table 2 in the order of their rank differences.

The evidence in Table 2 suggests that teachers, compared with clinicians, still tend to be more concerned with those behavior traits which appear to be transgressions against orderliness and, perhaps, morality, and less concerned with those traits which appear to be related to withdrawal. Again, it must be remembered that this difference may be due, in part at least, to the differences in directions given to the two groups. However,

TABLE 2. Traits on Which Greatest Disagreement Appears When
Rated by 1951 Teachers and Clinicians

Traits Rated More Serious by Teachers	Rank Difference	Traits Rated More Serious by Clinicians	Rank Difference
1. Impertinence, defiance	26.5	1. Shyness	31
2. Impudence, rudeness	26	2. Suspiciousness	27.5
3. Obscene notes, pictures, etc.	24	3. Dreaminess	25.5
4. Disobedience	24	4. Fearfulness	22
5. Disorderliness	24	5. Sensitiveness	20.5
6. Heterosexual activity	23	6. Overcritical of others	19
7. Masturbation	20	7. Imaginative lying	16
8. Untruthfulness	16	8. Nervousness	16

TABLE 3. Traits on Which Greatest Disagreement Appeared When
Rated by 1927 Teachers and Clinicians

Traits Rated More Serious by Teachers	Rank Difference	Traits Rated More Serious by Clinicians	Rank Difference
1. Masturbation	38	1. Unsocial, withdrawing	39.5
2. Destroying	35	2. Sensitiveness	38
3. Profanity	32	3. Shyness	36.5
4. Smoking	31	4. Overcritical of others	36
5. Impertinence, defiance	30.5	5. Suspiciousness	35
6. Disobedience	30	6. Fearfulness	31
7. Disorderliness	25.5	7. Resentfulness	25
8. Obscene notes, pictures, etc.	24.5	8. Sullenness, sulkiness	23
9. Heterosexual activity	24	9. Domineering, overbearing	21.5
10. Laziness	19	10. Dreaminess	21.5
11. Untruthfulness	18	11. Suggestible	20
12. Truancy	16	12. Unhappy, depressed	19.5
13. Impudence	15.5	13. Tattling	17
		14. Physical coward	16
		15. Easily discouraged	15.5

it seems likely that the differences reflect a real difference in attitude between the two groups, since Mitchell's data also support this conclusion in spite of the fact that his groups followed identical directions in making the ratings.

The difference between 1951 teachers and clinicians, as indicated in Table 2, does not appear as large as the difference between 1927 teachers and clinicians as shown in Table 3. It will be noted that, for the 1927 groups, there were twenty-eight traits in which there was a rank difference of 15 or more, as compared with sixteen for the 1951 groups. The magnitude of the difference between teachers' and clinicians' ratings also tend to be greater for the 1927 groups.

SUMMARY

This study was an attempt to re-examine certain conclusions, presented by Wickman in 1928 and still widely cited, as to the attitude of teachers towards the behavior problems of children. In an effort to closely approximate a replication of the Wickman study, the experimental design duplicated that used by Wickman.

The findings may be summarized as follows:

1. This comparison showed, insofar as the groups studied can be considered representative, that the attitudes of teachers of 1951 agreed much more closely with the "ideal criterion" than did teachers of 1927. This was evidenced primarily in three ways:

    (a) The correlation between the means of ratings of the 1951 teacher and clinician groups was .56, compared with —.04 in Wickman's study of 1928.

    (b) None of the traits listed among the ten most serious by one group was listed among the ten least serious by the other group. Wickman found five traits so rated.

    (c) As shown in Tables 2 and 3 the extent of disagreement between teachers and clinicians in 1951 was not as great as was true in 1927.

2. Disagreements between attitudes of teachers and the criterion attitude established by clinicians, though not as pronounced as in 1927, still exist, and these disagreements are of the same nature as those pointed out by Wickman. Those responsible for teacher education, both pre-service and in-service, evidently need to continue to emphasize what might be called "a mental-hygiene viewpoint."

3. In fairness to both professional groups, the data from this study, as well as Wickman's study, should be interpreted in the light of the experimental design. It is likely that teachers' attitudes will never approximate very closely the "ideal criterion attitudes" as established by clinicians, since good teachers will always need to be concerned about temporary, but disturbing, behavior in the classroom.

47

Teacher Interactions with Boys as Contrasted with Girls*

William J. Meyer and George G. Thompson

The quality of the interpersonal relationship between a teacher and her or his pupil is singularly important in determining the effects of formal education on a child's psychological growth and adjustment. It would be difficult for a normal boy or girl to remain completely indifferent to the teacher's demands, restrictions, and persuasive influence. The teacher, by the very symbol of her position of authority, possesses a tremendous power for bestowing or withholding reinforcement. Her judgment of what constitutes good or bad behavior, or proper and improper, determines what pupil behavior will elicit her approval or disapproval—even though she may have only a dim awareness of the basis of her evaluations. In the following report, Drs. Meyer and Thompson show that women teachers display significantly greater disapproval of what the boys do than of what the girls do in the classroom. This differential treatment is not only visible to a nonparticipating observer, but is also apparent to the boys and girls themselves. In this study it is inferred that the woman teacher's values do not permit her to condone the greater assertiveness and aggressiveness of the normally adjusted male pupil.

This study was designed to investigate the relative frequency of women teachers' approval and disapproval evaluations of sixth-grade male as contrasted with female pupils. The relevant data for this study were obtained by means of two independent techniques: thirty hours of direct observation of teacher-pupil interactions in each of three classrooms; and, the use of a modification of the "Guess Who?" technique to determine if the children

* From William J. Meyer and George G. Thompson, "Sex Differences in the Distribution of Teacher Approval and Disapproval among Sixth-grade Children," *Journal of Educational Psychology,* 1956, Vol. 47, pp. 385-397. (With permission of authors and the copyright holder, Abrahams Magazine Service, Inc.)

themselves were aware of any sex differences in their teachers' approval and disapproval evaluations.

There is considerable agreement among psychologists that the use of approval by the teacher results in better learning and probably in better overall adjustment (Hurlock, 1924; Ojemann and Wilkinson, 1939). Some studies (Olson and Wilkinson, 1938; Snyder, 1947) have shown that personal maladjustments in teachers have deleterious effects on the adjustment level of the children in their classes.

In a series of studies by Anderson et al. (1945, 1946b), using a sample of kindergarten-age children, the data indicate that teachers typically use statements of a dominative nature in their interactions with the children in their classes. Anderson further reports that the teachers in his study tended to levy most of their dominative and/or integrative overtures on only a few pupils to the relative neglect of the other children in the classroom. Further evidence of this nature is reported in a study by deGroat and Thompson (1949) using four sixth-grade classrooms. In addition to reporting inequities in teacher approval and disapproval they also found that teachers give more praise to the youngsters who are brighter, better adjusted and higher achievers. The more poorly adjusted and the duller children were observed by these investigators to receive more disapproval from their teachers.

The purpose of the present investigation is to shed more light on the ways in which teachers respond toward the pupils in their classrooms. Extensive research findings have been reported in the literature (Goodenough, 1931; Hayes, 1943; Radke, 1946; Sears, 1951; Tuddenham, 1952) which consistently show that boys are more aggressive and generally more "unmanageable" than girls. It is our hypothesis that this "masculine" behavior will result in male pupils receiving a larger number of dominative, or punitive, contacts than girls from their teacher, who is usually a woman from the middle socio-economic stratum of our society. That is, we feel that the behavior of boys in the typical classroom is of such a nature as to make it less acceptable to teachers who probably attempt to perpetuate certain middle-class standards of what "good" classroom behavior should be. We believe that girls usually display behavior more in conformity to the standards perceived as "good" by the average elementary school teacher and will therefore receive fewer disapproval contacts and more approval contacts from their teachers.

Assuming that the above hypotheses are supported by the data we would also predict that children of elementary school age will recognize, and take for granted, that boys receive more disapproval and blame from their teachers than girls.

EXPERIMENTAL PROCEDURE

In order to test the hypothesis that boys receive a larger number of dominative, or disapproval, evaluations from their teachers than do girls, teacher-pupil interaction within three sixth-grade classrooms were recorded for a total sample of thirty hours per classroom. These time samples of classroom behavior were spread over an entire school year. Among other things being studied, interactions between teachers and pupils were classified into two categories: (a) praise contacts (teacher initiated interactions with a child in which she verbally expressed approval of some behavior which the child had displayed), and (b) blame contacts (teacher initiated interactions with a child in which she verbally expressed disapproval for some bit of behavior which the child had displayed). Observer agreement for the praise classification ranged from eighty-four to one hundred per cent with a median of approximately ninety-two per cent. Observer agreement for the blame classification ranged from fifty-seven to one hundred per cent, with a median of approximately ninety-three per cent.

In an attempt to cast some light on children's perceptions of any sex differences in teacher disapproval, a modified "Guess Who?" approach was employed. The "Guess Who?" approach used in this study required each child to nominate fellow class members for a number of situations in which children are receiving approval or disapproval from their teacher for some behavior. (See deGroat and Thompson [1949] for a more complete description of these scales and information about their reliabilities.) The behavior descriptions were selected on the basis of their familiarity to children and contain a fairly representative sample of situations in which children typically receive either approval or disapproval from their teachers. Each child was required to list the names of four of his classmates whom he thought fitted each of the behavior descriptions most adequately.

RESULTS

Fisher's *t* test was used to determine the reliability of the obtained sex differences.[1] The difference between disapproval contacts received by boys and by girls from their teachers was statistically significant in each of the three classrooms. As predicted, the boys received the larger number of disapproval contacts. These differences may be interpreted according to our hypothesis as supporting the notion that teachers are responding with counter-aggression to the greater expression of aggression by boys. The re-

---

[1] This test assumes that the samples being compared are homogeneous with respect to their variance. Frequently this assumption had to be rejected in some of the group comparisons. In such cases a more conservative test of significance was used which makes some allowance in the error term for heterogeneity of variance. This technique is presented in detail in Cochran and Cox (1950).

sults obtained in analyzing the teachers' praise contacts with boys and girls are presented in Table 2. The only statistically significant differences obtained for this variable was in school B. However the boys received more praise than the girls in each of the classrooms. It may be that the teachers are attempting to reinforce any positive behavior that the boys may display.

TABLE 1. Sex Differences in Frequency of Teachers' Disapproval Contacts

	Classroom A		Classroom B		Classroom C	
	Boys	Girls	Boys	Girls	Boys	Girls
N	10	9	12	14	17	16
Mean	11.10	2.67	10.75	2.79	10.06	1.44
S.D.	7.62	2.18	9.27	2.42	14.42	1.59
t	3.20**		3.11**		2.37*	
F	12.22**		14.67**		130.36**	
t.01†	3.30		3.10		2.92	

* Significant at the five per cent level.
** Significant at the one per cent level.
† See footnote 1.

TABLE 2. Sex Differences in Frequency of Teachers' Approval Contacts

	Classroom A		Classroom B		Classroom C	
	Boys	Girls	Boys	Girls	Boys	Girls
N	10	9	12	14	17	16
Mean	9.90	9.67	10.50	5.50	3.71	2.69
S.D.	6.10	7.65	5.33	2.53	2.95	1.99
t	0.074		2.50*		1.15	
F	1.57		4.43**		2.19	
t.05†	—		2.19		—	

* Significant at the five per cent level.
** Significant at the one per cent level.
† See footnote 1.

Or this tendency to praise boys more than girls may reflect compensatory behavior for guilt feelings created in the teacher by her excessive agressiveness toward boys. Either interpretation, or any one of the several others that could be offered, is highly speculative.

The data presented above are based on the extensive observations of an objective observer who played no functional role in the classrooms. The data presented in the following section reflect the teachers' approval and disapproval contacts as viewed by their pupils.

"GUESS WHO?" DATA

Analysis of the "Guess Who?" data was performed along the same lines as the data obtained by direct observation. A comparison of the pupils' nominations of their peers on the disapproval items revealed statistically significant differences between boys and girls for two of the three schools.

TABLE 3. Sex Differences in Children's Nominations For Teacher Disapproval

	Classroom A		Classroom B		Classroom C	
	Boys	Girls	Boys	Girls	Boys	Girls
N	10	9	12	14	17	16
Mean	21.60	5.33	42.33	9.71	33.82	5.18
S.D.	13.33	5.68	43.06	8.13	55.87	8.26
t	3.39**		2.79**		2.03	
F	5.51**		28.07**		19.21**	
t.01†	3.26		3.10		—	

** Significant at the one per cent level.
† See footnote 1.

TABLE 4. Sex Differences in Children's Nominations for Teacher Approval

	Classroom A		Classroom B		Classroom C	
	Boys	Girls	Boys	Girls	Boys	Girls
N	10	9	12	14	17	16
Mean	11.00	34.33	23.58	31.42	23.71	21.60
S.D.	12.93	32.64	18.51	25.08	35.75	25.70
t	2.09		0.856		0.242	
F	6.376**		1.835		19.35**	
t.01†	—		—		—	

** Significant at the one per cent level.
† See footnote 1.

This can be interpreted as showing that the boys are viewed by the girls as well as by their male peers as being involved in more situations which evoke disapproval from their teachers.

Analysis of the children's responses to the items related to teacher approval produced no significant differences between boys and girls.

A final analysis of the "Guess Who?" data was performed in an attempt to determine how boys as contrasted with girls perceived the teacher's approval and disapproval biases. The choices made by the boys and by the girls for the approval and disapproval items were separately analyzed. It seemed unreasonable to use the t test in this situation because of the unequal numbers of boys and girls in the classroom. Therefore the groups were equated by converting the frequencies of nominations to percentages and working with percentage differences.

The results of the statistical analysis of boys' nominations on the disapproval items show that boys respond as if they usually received more blame from teachers than do girls. It would appear that boys are quite

TABLE 5. Choices Made by Boys and by Girls on Teacher Disapproval Items

	Classroom A				Classroom B				Classroom C			
	Boys Choosing		Girls Choosing		Boys Choosing		Girls Choosing		Boys Choosing		Girls Choosing	
	B	G	B	G	B	G	B	G	B	G	B	G
N	8	9	8	9	14	12	14	12	17	16	17	16
%	89.77	10.23	83.09	16.91	88.37	11.63	73.05	26.95	88.70	11.20	82.21	17.79
CR	5.60**		3.64**		6.10**		2.65**		7.03**		4.84**	

** Significant at the one per cent level.

TABLE 6. Choices Made by Boys and by Girls on Teacher Approval Items

	Classroom A				Classroom B				Classroom C			
	Boys Choosing		Girls Choosing		Boys Choosing		Girls Choosing		Boys Choosing		Girls Choosing	
	B	G	B	G	B	G	B	G	B	G	B	G
N	8	9	8	9	14	12	14	12	17	16	17	16
%	36.98	63.01	34.07	65.92	56.95	43.04	24.58	75.42	57.56	42.43	46.22	53.77
CR	1.11		1.38		0.72		3.01**		0.88		0.44	

** Significant at the one per cent level.

sensitive to the disapproval of their teachers. Table 5 shows that the girls also respond as if boys receive more teacher disapproval.

There is little consistency in the nominations made by the boys for the praise items. In schools B and C the boys react as though they typically receive more praise than girls, although this difference is not statistically significant. In contrast to the boys' responses, the girls feel that they receive more praise, particularly in school B where the difference is statistically significant. These results might be interpreted as meaning that children fail to recognize any definite dichotomy in the teacher's distribution of praise contacts.

DISCUSSION

The general findings of this study support the hypothesis that the male pupil receives reliably more blame from his teacher than the female pupil. Moreover, the boys recognize that they are the recipients of a higher incidence of teacher disapproval. We feel that these data lend indirect support to the notion that "masculine" behavior is not tolerated by the typical teacher who in turn attempts to inhibit such behavior by means of punishment.

Davis and Havighurst (1947) have discussed at length the divergence of cultural mores between lower-class children and their middle-class teachers. Their work may best be summarized in the assertion that the goals defined by the middle-class teacher do not receive reinforcement from the lower-class child's peer group or from his family. Teacher initiation of punishment for "misbehavior" only serves to reinforce an already existing dislike for school and further leads to peer group reinforcement. A similar (but by no means identical) interpretation appears relevant to the present discussion. Our society's definitions of acceptable male and female behavior are divergent particularly with respect to aggression. For example Radke (1946) in her monograph on the relationship of parental authority to child behavior reports that the fathers in her sample felt that aggressive, assertive behavior on the part of boys was less undesirable than the identical behavior in girls (and in many cases was deemed highly desirable). The mothers felt that aggression was unacceptable behavior in either sex but in general they were in agreement that aggressive behavior is more unacceptable in girls. In another study specifically related to the notion that aggressive behavior is more unacceptable in the female culture is a study by Sears et al. (1946). These writers predicted that in father-absent homes, wherein the child is brought up by the mother, boys would be less aggressive than in father-present homes in which the boy models his behavior after the father. The results of their study support the "sex-typing" hypothesis as presented above. Bach (1946) reports similar evidence in support of the "sex-typing" hypothesis.[2] Apparently the social mores of the typical female teacher, at least with respect to aggressive, assertive behavior, are in sharp contrast to the behavioral tendencies of the typical male youngsters. The behavioral tendencies of the female child are, however, in close agreement with those of her teachers. We feel that the above generalization accounts to a high degree for the data reported in this study. Our argument becomes somewhat stronger when the work of Wickman (1938) and a follow-up study by Mitchell (1942) are included in the discussion. These investigators found that teachers perceive aggressive

---

[2] Though there is insufficient evidence at this time the present writers feel that the factor of innate sex differences in aggressive tendencies should not be overlooked. See Beach (1948) for suggestive findings.

nonconforming behavior as more serious than withdrawal behavior. More recently Kaplan (1951-52) has reported that the aggressive child was deemed annoying to almost three-quarters of the teachers in his sample. The present investigation suggests that perhaps teachers react to the aggressive behavior of children with counter-aggression, a vicious circle for both pupil and teacher.

Consistent with the above interpretation is the larger amount of variation found among the male pupils as contrasted with the female pupils. In a culture such as ours in which the father is away from the home during most of the child's waking hours (and in some instances pays only cursory attention to the youngster when at home), it appears obvious that both the male and female child are more directly influenced by the mother. Many boys, however, will be influenced more by their fathers and peer culture than by the mother because of identification with the masculine role in our culture. Our belief is that these more "masculine" boys are the ones who receive the greater share of teacher disapproval. Such an interpretation appears consistent with the work of Sears (1946) and Bach (1946).

The foregoing discussion has certain implications for the student of child development and education. If our interpretation of the teacher and male-pupil relationship is accurate, then the fact that boys dislike school more than girls is understandable. The daily punishment received by the boy for behavior he really does not consider "bad" must certainly be anxiety producing. If the anxiety created in the school situation becomes sufficiently intense, it seems reasonable that tension reduction can be achieved by means of avoiding school. It is known that more boys leave school at an earlier age than girls (Tenenbaum, 1939-40).

Perhaps of even more importance is the effect of this teacher-disapproval generated anxiety on the general personality adjustment of male pupils. It is unfortunate that we do not have evidence on the changes in adjustment level of the children in our sample, but studies by Ojemann and Wilkinson (1939) and others indicate that consistent teacher dominance has deleterious effects on the adjustment of children. We can only speculate as to the nature of these adjustment problems but such behavioral manifestations as nervousness, withdrawal and lack of self-confidence are a few of the known symptoms.

We feel that the consistent trends in our findings imply that teachers' negative attitudes towards their male pupils arise from a lack of appreciation for the term "normal" male child. In our culture, aggressive outgoing behavior is as normal in the male as quiescent nonassertive behavior is in the female. The teacher who attempts to thwart this behavior by means of threats and punishment can only meet with frustration since the boy is confronted with a conflicting social code. A more reasonable plan to follow would seem to be one in which the excess energy and tensions of the male child could be discharged on some constructive activity. Planned physical education classes will do much to dissipate aggressive needs in a socially acceptable manner. Perhaps most important of all, however, is the knowledge that some degree of aggressive behavior is a normal part of development in both boys and girls and should be treated not as a personal threat to the teacher but as sign of "normal" social and personality development.

SUMMARY

The purpose of this study was to investigate sex differences in teacher distribution of approval and disapproval among three sixth-grade classrooms. Data relevant to the children's perceptions of their teachers' attitudes towards boys and girls were also collected. Using the discrepancies in attitude between males and females in our culture toward aggressive behavior as the basic underlying variable, the hypothesis was offered that boys, who are more aggressive and nonconforming than girls, would receive more disapproval contacts from their teachers than girls. Girls being quiescent and more conforming than boys would as a consequence receive more approval from their teachers than boys. We further hypothesized that both boys and girls will be aware of the differences in their teachers' attitudes towards them.

In order to test the foregoing hypothesis three sixth-grade teachers and their pupils were directly observed for a total of thirty hours per classroom. All teacher initiated contacts of an approval or disapproval nature were recorded. The measurement of the children's perceptions of teacher attitude was accomplished by means of a variation of the "Guess Who?" technique. The pupils were asked to list the names of four students who best fitted a series of statements of a teacher approval nature and of disapproval nature. Analysis was made of the number of children of each sex chosen for the approval items and for the disapproval items.

Statistical analysis of the data clearly supports our hypothesis with respect to male pupils. In all three schools the boys received reliably more disapproval from their teachers than the girls. We also found that both the boys and the girls nominated more boys for the disapproval items than girls. This difference was statistically reliable. With respect to the second hypothesis concerning girls, the data did not yield any clear-cut differences. If any trend was present it was in a direction opposite to that predicted. These results indicated that the teachers in our sample tended to have fewer contacts with the girls in their classrooms.

The results of this investigation were interpreted as being consistent with the notion of a sex difference in attitude towards aggressive behavior. The conclusion was drawn that teachers attempt to "socialize" the male child by means of dominative counter-aggressive behavior. The negative consequences of this situation for the child are discussed.

48

Age of Onset of Academic
Underachievement in Bright Children[*]

Merville C. Shaw and John T. McCuen

In order to understand the significance of nonintellectual factors in
school learning, many studies have been conducted in the past two
decades analyzing differences between school "underachievers" and
"overachievers," i.e., between those who do notably poorer or markedly better than would be expected on the basis of their measured
intelligence. When do overachievers begin to show this tendency to
use their ability to better advantage in school? The present study
shows that boys who are overachievers as seniors tend to have been
overachievers from the time they entered school. But girls who are
overachievers in the senior year are not differentiated from underachieving girls until they have reached junior high school. Just why
this is so was not gone into, but the investigation suggests that certain
significant factors may be motivating the girls in early adolescence. It
is a reasonable inference that the social and heterosexual orientation
of the girls during this period acts upon the need to achieve in school,
and in a way that it does not in the boys. In short, educational achievement reflects the performance of a total individual.

The purposes of the present study were to determine whether there is any
specific academic level at which academic underachievement can be said
to begin and to discover the subsequent pattern of achievement. The information resulting from the study has both practical and theoretical implications. On the practical side, the problems of prevention and reme-
diation of academic underachievement might conceivably be effected by
such results. It appears from previous research that underachievement
among high school sophomores is not a surface phenomenon which is

* Adapted and abridged from Merville C. Shaw and John T. McCuen, "The Onset of
Academic Underachievement in Bright Children," *Journal of Educational Psychology,*
1960, Vol. 51, pp. 103-108. (With permission of the senior author and the American
Psychological Association.)

easily modifiable, but rather is related to the basic personality matrix of the individual. If it is true that academic underachievement is related to basic personality structure, then such behavior is likely to occur during the early elementary school years. Specific information regarding the point at which underachievement actually begins has implications both for preventive and remedial measures that may be undertaken.

Such information also has implications from a theoretical point of view. The problem of the genesis of achievement motivation has been a topic of concern to McClelland and his associates. [See Paper #23 in the present volume.] Hypothesizing that the scores of college males on the McClelland Achievement Motivation Test would be effected by child rearing practices of their parents, they were able to isolate certain differences between subjects who received high scores and those who received low scores. Their criterion of achievement has not been validated as a predictor of academic achievement, however, and it would not be reasonable to conclude from their results that academic underachievement had its origins in parental child rearing practices. Should it be found that academic underachievement is present in the earliest school years, and is found with some consistency in the same individuals throughout their school careers, more credence could be placed in the general findings of McClelland et al. as they related to academic underachievement.

METHOD

The general plan of the study was to select Ss who were in the upper 25% of the school population with regard to ability and to classify them as achievers or underachievers on the basis of their cumulative grade-point averages in Grades 9, 10, and 11. The intelligence measure used was the Pinter General Ability Test: Verbal Series, which was administered to all Ss included in the study at the time they were in Grade 8. A student who achieved an intelligence test score which placed him in the upper 25% of the population (over 110) and who had earned a grade-point average below the mean of the class he was in, was classified as an underachiever. A student who earned a GPA above the average of his class, and whose IQ was over 110, was classified as an achiever. Those who fell exactly at the class average, which was 2.40 on a four point scale, were not included in the study. Only eleventh- and twelfth-graders were included.

A further criterion for the inclusion of an S in this study was that he must have attended school only in the school district served by the high schools in the study. All Ss, then, have had all of their formal education in a single school district. This criterion was established in order to reduce the variability in grades and educational philosophy which would be introduced by the inclusion of *S*s who had moved from one school district to another.

A single high school district with two large high schools whose combined enrollment was over six thousand was selected for use in the study. In addition to the factor of size and the presence of a fairly representative population from the socioeconomic point of view, it was also important to conduct the study in a school system where specific grades (A, B, C, etc.) were used at both the elementary and high school levels.

One hundred sixty-eight students met all of the criteria for inclusion in the study. This group was divided further into four subgroups of male Achievers, male Underachievers, female Achievers, and female Underachievers, for purposes of comparison. Much research has shown the necessity of treating males and females separately in studies of underachievement. In order to obtain groups whose mean intelligence scores were not significantly different it was necessary to eliminate 8 males and 18 females from the sample. All of those eliminated were from the Achiever groups. The final groups consisted of 36 male Achievers, 36 male Underachievers, 45 female Achievers, and 17 female Underachievers.

Following the final selection of *S*s, the academic record for each student from Grades 1 through 11 was obtained. In the case of elementary school grades it was necessary to convert from letter to number grades. This was done on a four point scale to keep elementary grades comparable to high school grades. Thus, an A became 4.0, a B became 3.0, etc. Each *S*'s grade-point average for each grade (not a cumulative grade-point average) was then computed. Mean grade-point averages for each group at each grade level were then computed.

RESULTS

The comparison of male Achievers and Underachievers indicates that a difference significant at the .01 level is found in the GPA of the two groups beginning at the third-grade level, and that this difference increases in significance at each grade level up to Grade 10, where it decreases somewhat. It remains significant at the .01 level, however. A difference in grade-point average in favor of the Achiever group actually exists at Grade 1 and becomes larger at Grade 2, but it is not significant at the .05 level of confidence in either of the first two grades.

Graphic presentation renders these results even more striking. Figure 1 indicates that while the general trend of grades in both groups tends to be the same, there is never any overlap. It also shows clearly the decline in mean difference between the two groups at the tenth- and eleventh-grade levels which is due primarily to a drop in the mean grade-point average of the Achievers, rather than a rise in the grades of the Underachievers.

Comparison of the female Achievers and Underachievers presents quite a different picture from that seen in the male groups. Through Grade 5 the Underachievers actually exceed the Achievers in GPA, although not at a significant level of confidence. At Grade 6 the Achievers obtain a higher mean GPA for the first time, and from that point until Grade 10 this difference increases every year, although it does not reach significance

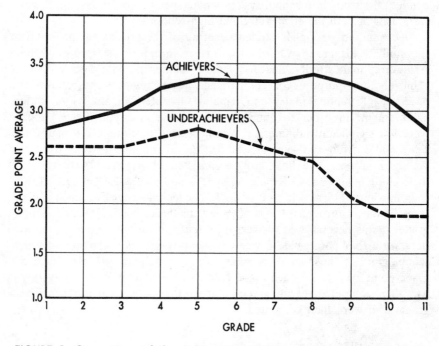

FIGURE 1. Comparison of the Achievement Patterns of Male Achievers and Underachievers from Grade 1 through 11

until Grade 9. From Grade 9 through 11 the difference is significant at the .01 level.

As in the case of the data on males, the data on females are most clearly understood through graphic presentation. Figure 2 contrasts these two groups. As was the case with the male groups, there is again a tendency for the mean grade-point averages of the two groups to diminish slightly in the last year of high school, and again this can be accounted for by a drop in the grade point average of the Achiever group, rather than an increase in the Underachiever group.

With regard to the male Underachievers it would appear reasonable to say that the predisposition to underachieve academically is present when the Underachiever enters school. It is also safe to say that, in comparison to the Achiever controls, the problem becomes steadily more serious until

Grade 10, at which time it becomes only slightly less serious, due primarily to a drop in grade-point average on the part of the Achiever group.

Comparison of the female groups does not present nearly so clear cut a picture. As has been found in other studies of underachievement, there is a great deal of difference between what we find to be true of males, and what

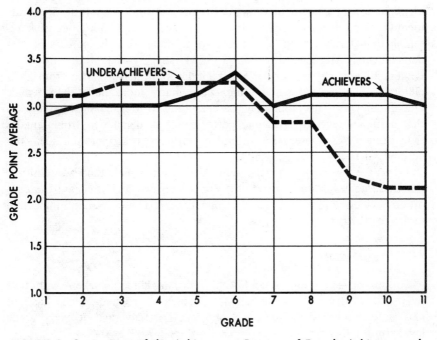

FIGURE 2. Comparison of the Achievement Patterns of Female Achievers and Underachievers from Grade 1 through 11

seems to be true in the case of females. The present study provides no clues which would explain why Underachieving females actually tend to do better than Achieving females in the first five grades, nor do we have any facts which would explain the precipitous drop they take, beginning in Grade 6. The fact that actual underachievement among the female group does not show itself until Grade 6 does not completely rule out the possibility of the presence of a predisposing factor at the time the female Underachiever enters school. The timing of the drop in GPA of female Underachievers is just about right for the start of puberty. We may hypothesize that females do not display their self-directing tendencies to the same extent that males do until they approach adolescence.

Another justifiable conclusion to be drawn is that underachievement is not a temporary phenomenon in the life of these Ss, but rather is chronic in nature. In comparison to the control group, the male Underachievers have been obtaining grades below their ability level since Grade 1. The female Underachievers have been performing below their ability level since Grade 9, and have tended to do so since Grade 6. This finding lends weight to the previously stated hypothesis that academic underachievement is not an easily modifiable surface phenomenon.

The most obvious implication of the study is the need for the early identification of Underachievers. At the present time, very little deliberate identification of such students is taking place. Much more intensive research than has yet been done needs to be done with the parents of Underachievers. McClelland et al. (1953) suggest that the parents of Underachievers do not demand a high level of performance from their children. The present study found very many more male than female Underachievers. This would suggest according to McClelland's hypothesis, that a higher level of academic performance is demanded from females than from males. Observation would not appear to support this idea, but certainly it needs intensive study.

What are the factors in the school situation which tend to reinforce the Underachievers predisposition to underachieve; and what are the conditions which might forestall its appearance? These too are important topics for further study.

SUMMARY

Groups of senior high-school Achievers and Underachievers with IQ's over 110, all from the same school system and grouped on the basis of sex, were compared on the basis of grade-point average at every grade level from 1 through 11.

Results for males indicated that the Underachievers tended to receive grades lower than the Achievers beginning in Grade 1, and that this difference became significant at the .01 level at Grade 3. From Grade 3 to Grade 10, the difference increased in significance every year. In Grades 10 and 11 the difference was reduced somewhat, but remained significant at the .01 level.

Results for females indicated that female Underachievers actually exceeded Achievers in grade-point average for the first five years of school, although not at a significant level of confidence. Beginning in Grade 6 Underachievers began a precipitous drop in grade-point average and remained below the Achiever group from Grade 6 through Grade 11. The difference became significant at Grade 9.

Part XI

VOCATIONAL ORIENTATION AND ADJUSTMENT

THE TYPE of occupation an individual enters and at which he spends his life has exceedingly important effects upon his way of life and the satisfaction he gets from it. Aspirations out of line with capabilities may lead to immediate or eventual conflict and unhappiness; work uncongenial to one's interests or personality may create boredom or discontent which carries over and influences adjustment in other aspects of living. To the end that occupational choice may be wise, educational institutions spend large funds and much effort in "guidance" activities planned to help young people make proper orientations. In American society, a man's achievement or loss of status tends to be linked with his economic or occupational success or failure. Failure to find a place in the economic world is a major factor in the adjustment problems of adolescence. Loss of personal status upon retirement in old age (either voluntary or forced) and continued feelings of uselessness as new employment is difficult to find represent important facets of the adjustment problem in old age.

The course of the work life from early preferences and aspirations to eventual retirement may be viewed from three different vantage points. There is, first of all, the worker's own view of things—*his* interest and aspirations, *his* satisfactions and dissatisfactions, the problems *he* encounters on the job. Second, the work life may be viewed from the point of view of the culture. Employers have certain biases regarding the employment of workers of different ages, with the result that certain age groups (especially the young and the old) may be penalized. Jobs may be more difficult to obtain at certain ages, unemployment more likely. In the third place, the work life may be viewed from the standpoint of the actual record, and evaluated in terms of productivity, per unit costs, merit ratings, income, accidents and illness rates. It is not implied that these are three completely independent variables. They are interrelated in important ways, and attention to points of disparity, as well as to points of similarity, will contribute to better understanding. It is noteworthy, for example, that the facts of the actual work record of the older worker seem to be at variance with common *views* of his productivity. Thus the need for broader "education" of employers is suggested.

Four papers have been assembled in the present part to illustrate the types of theorizing that are being done and the nature of current research on certain aspects of occupational orientation and career. The first paper describes in a series of generalizations the factors involved and the nature of the process of occupational choice and career development. This is followed by a paper reporting a study of the early antecedent conditions associated with later vocational interests. The third paper makes it clear that orientation toward a career is related to the major traits of an individual, not only in the type of occupation he prefers, but in respect to the satisfaction he expects to derive from it. The part concludes with a paper on the creative and the productive years of scientists and literary men.

49

Some Generalizations Regarding Vocational Development*

Donald E. Super, J. O. Crites, R. C. Hummel, H. P. Moser, P. L. Overstreet, and C. F. Warnath

The past two decades have witnessed a growing interest in the theory of vocational choice. In contrast to earlier conceptions which implied that a vocational "choice" was made essentially once and for all, at a particular point in life, newer views assert a long-term developmental process. In contrast to earlier descriptions of choice which emphasized an intellectualistic matching of aptitudes with job requirements, modern views include personality and motivation among the factors of prime importance. Among those who have contributed most to the development of the theory of vocational choice is Professor Donald E. Super. In this paper, which is adapted from a chapter in a monograph dealing with vocational development, Dr. Super and his collaborators have set down certain generalizations, or "postulates," which together constitute a tentative approach to theory and which embody the develop-

* Adapted and abridged from pp. 88-96 of Donald E. Super et al., *Vocational Development: A Framework for Research.* New York: Teachers College, Columbia University, 1957. (With permission of the senior author and the Bureau of Publications, Teachers College, Columbia University.)

mental, person-oriented conceptions that dominate much of today's research in this field.

An outline of a theory of vocational development is necessarily tentative and based upon inferences from research findings and experience. Although such a tentative theory leaves a number of questions unanswered, it provides a basis for the identification of relevant areas for study.

Some of the unanswered, or incompletely answered, questions are indicated in what follows. These particular questions have been selected because they concern specific aspects of vocational behavior. These questions point out areas in which investigation is needed, and serve to emphasize certain central assumptions upon which a framework for research may be built. Suggested answers to the questions, in the form of propositions or postulates, are discussed. In several instances attention is called to some appropriate research techniques and to possible lines of further research and inquiry. Most of the propositions need further exploration, although the first three are well established and need only verification and clarification of details. Many of the propositions are similar to, and have been derived from, those which Super had proposed earlier (1953). Until more comprehensive data are available on the psychological and sociological factors in vocational development, the nature of vocational development theory will necessarily be exploratory rather than systematic. It therefore seems advisable at this time to formulate working principles, instead of prematurely attempting to deduce testable hypotheses.

WHAT IS THE NATURE OF VOCATIONAL DEVELOPMENT?

The first three propositions describe the general nature of the vocational developmental process. They are essentially postulates, in need of further investigation so that they may be verified where already outlined and clarified where they are at present vague.

Proposition 1. *Vocational development is an ongoing, continuous, and generally irreversible process.* Vocational preferences and competencies, and the situations in which people live and work, change with time and experience, making choice and adjustment a continuous process. This process may be described as a series of life stages, in each of which the individual is expected to manifest certain specific types of behavior. The life stages are, respectively, those of growth, exploration, establishment, maintenance, and decline. It appears that the exploratory stage may be further subdivided into the fantasy, tentative, and realistic phases, and the establishment stage into the trial and stable phases. These stages seem to occur regularly in the course of normal vocational development within our culture.

Proposition 2. *Vocational development is an orderly, patterned process and thus predictable.* Every individual in a relatively homogeneous culture is expected to master much the same series of developmental tasks, if his development is to continue unimpeded. Physical development is basically determined by the process of growth; its course is similar for all individuals of the same sex, and changes occur at about the same stage of each individual's life. Developmental tasks set by cultural pressures are also largely the same for all individuals in a relatively homogeneous culture. Furthermore, the culture expects that vocational development will eventually result in vocational adjustment. The criterion of vocational adjustment is apparently basically the same for all individuals. It is the individual's long-term satisfaction with the efficiency of his vocational behavior. It is suggested that such satisfaction depends upon the meeting of socialized objectives, which include vocational success as viewed by the individual himself and to a lesser extent by other persons who are important to him.

Proposition 3. *Vocational development is a dynamic process of compromise or synthesis.* Interaction between the behavioral repertoire and the developmental tasks that must be mastered, between existing responses and new stimuli, is involved in vocational development. It also involves a relatively little understood process of compromise between, or synthesis of, personal and social factors, self-concept and reality, newly learned responses and existing patterns of reacting. Thus, vocational development may be described as a dynamic process involving the interaction and integration of many psychological and social factors. This fact of multiple causation must be recognized in order to account adequately for the phenomena of vocational development.

Patterns of behavior become differentiated and integrated into repertoires of habits and skills, which in childhood and adolescence are manifested in the classroom, in peer-group activities, in athletics, in community organizations, and in part-time work. Aspirations are formulated. Successes and failures are experienced. Increasingly realistic roles are played, tested, and modified as the self-concept develops and as integration of apparently unrelated aspects of the personality is achieved. The roles which are taken in childhood and adolescence are crucial to development, as are the changes which take place in these roles and their organization into a consistent concept of self. They foreshadow the roles the individual will seek to take as an adult wage-earner. The adolescent embarking upon his high school career is confronted with curricular and other choices of vocational significance. He must begin to work out a compromise between, or synthesis of, ideal-self and real-self, between the fantasy world and the world of work, between self and society (Super, 1951).

WHAT IS THE NATURE OF THE OCCUPATIONAL CHOICE-MAKING PROCESS?

Although information is available on numerous aspects of adolescent development and the patterns of behavior which emerge during this period, more comprehensive data are needed on what determines levels of vocational aspiration, identification with role models, the nature of the compromise or synthesizing process, and the implementation of the self-concept in making an occupational choice. Certain lines of inquiry in other areas of psychological investigation are suggestive, however, of new approaches to some recurrent problems in research on vocational behavior. Experimental studies of level of aspiration and its relationship to certain personality factors present suitable theoretical models and research designs which might be used in determining relationships between various levels of vocational aspiration (Lewin, *et al.*, 1944). Recent theoretical formulations of the nature of the identification process are applicable to a study of the relationship between identification with role models and occupational choice or occupational adjustment (Mowrer, 1950). Cronbach (1953) suggests novel uses of the techniques of self-sort and of correlation between persons, which are relevant to the study of identification as well as the investigation of vocational status and stereotypes. The method of the comparison of individuals under various conditions (Mowrer, 1953), especially on two or more occasions, not only has important implications for cross-sectional studies but is significant for the development of new methods of trend analysis for longitudinal investigations.

From consideration of the effects of role-taking upon the development of the self-concept, and the effects of both these factors upon vocational development, three propositions may be derived:

Proposition 4. *Self-concepts begin to form prior to adolescence, become clearer in adolescence, and are translated into occupational terms in adolescence.* It is assumed that basic development of the self-concept occurs in childhood; that adolescence provides a period of exploratory experiences in which the concept of self is elaborated and clarified; and that interests, values, and capacities are integrated and attain vocational meaning through the development of the self-concept and through testing it against reality.

Proposition 5. *Reality factors (the reality of personal characteristics and the reality of society) play an increasingly important part in occupational choice with increasing age, from early adolescence to adulthood.* As the individual matures, leaves school, and enters the world of work, he must deal with the developmental task of assuming vocational responsibilities which involve differing duties, values, and motivations. The neophyte worker must learn to cope with the new realities of competitive striving which are characteristic of the labor market and the work place. He experiences and is confronted with problems of continual status evaluation, and he must adjust to new modes of group membership (Miller and Form, 1951).

Proposition 6. *Identification with a parent or parent substitute is related to the development of adequate roles, their consistent and harmonious interrelationship, and their interpretation in terms of vocational plans and eventualities.* There is reason for believing that identification with a role model of the same sex is related to satisfactory work adjustments in a society which places considerable emphasis upon proper sex differentiation (Darley and Hagenah, 1955; Friend and Haggard, 1948; Tyler, 1951). Desiring to play a socially approved role which has an adequate occupational equivalent and becoming established in an occupation in which one can play a desired role are essential aspects of job satisfaction.

WHAT FACTORS AFFECT THE PATTERNING OF CAREERS?

Basic to an adequate explanation of vocational behavior is the postulate that development through the life stages derives from the interaction of various influences, as stated above in Proposition 3. Biological, psychological, economic, and sociological factors combine to affect the individual's career pattern. The importance of different types of influences probably varies in different life stages, because now one aspect of behavior, then another, is pre-eminent throughout the span of development. In each succeeding stage of life, the individual faces the necessity of coping with new and frequently more complex social demands while adequately performing some of the tasks of earlier stages of development.

Will an individual have a career pattern typical or atypical of his parental socioeconomic group? To what extent are entry, intermediate, and regular adult occupations determined by parental socioeconomic level? What part do intelligence, interests, status needs, and values play in the formation of the career pattern? How do the economic conditions of the labor market affect the patterning of an individual's career? These and other questions are pertinent for research on the nature of career patterns, since the occupational level attained and the sequence frequency, and duration of trial and stable jobs are affected by a complex of interrelated factors.

There is a lack of comprehensive data on the interaction of various sociological and psychological factors which conceivably affect patterns of vocational development. An analysis of studies reported by Davidson and Anderson (1937), Miller and Form (1951), Bell (1940), and Hollingshead (1949) suggests that research on career patterns should be genetic in design to allow the identification of psychological and sociological themes related to vocational development (Super, 1954). Both cross-sectional and longitudinal studies are essential to an investigation of the lines and rate of movement from entry to regular adult occupations, the factors associated with the direction and pace of the movement, and the possible causes of deviation from expected patterns of vocational development. The accurate forecast of future vocational development rests upon appraisal of the individual at selected points in time and examination of trends in individual and group career patterns over a period of time.

Numerous propositions can be formulated with respect to the dynamics of career patterns, and only some of the more important relationships among certain psychological, sociological, and economic factors are indicated in this discussion.

Proposition 7. *The direction and rate of the vertical movement of an individual from one occupational level to another is related to his intelligence, parental socioeconomic level, status needs, values, interests, skill in interpersonal relationships, and the supply and demand conditions in the economy.* To verify hypotheses derivable from this proposition, test scores, socioeconomic rankings, and quantified interview analyses can be related to measurements of direction and rate of vertical movement in the career pattern.

Proposition 8. *The occupational field which the individual enters is related to his interests and values, the identifications he makes with parental or substitute role models, the community resources he uses, the level and quality of his educational background, and the occupational structure, trends, and attitudes of his community.* One method for testing hypotheses based on this proposition is presented in the following section. It involves obtaining the necessary information about an individual and his circumstances while he is still in high school, determining the occupation which he subsequently enters, and identifying the factors which are significantly different from those of individuals in other occupations or occupational families.

HOW CAN SATISFACTORY CAREERS FOR AN INDIVIDUAL BE PREDICTED?

One of the basic elements in the theory of vocational development presented here is the concept of the occupational multipotentiality of the individual (Super, 1953).

Proposition 9. *Although each occupation requires a characteristic pattern of abilities, interests, and personality traits, the tolerances are wide* *enough to allow both some variety of individuals in each occupation and some diversity of occupations for each individual.* It has been well established not only that individuals differ in their abilities, interests, and personalities but also that workers in different occupations are distinguished by the possession of distinctive ability patterns (Paterson and Darley, 1936). What has not been generally recognized is that multipotentiality implies two rather different relationships. First, there is the relationship of the individual's abilities to success or satisfaction within an occupation or a group of occupations. The problem of prediction is one of determining in which occupation an individual will perform best or be happiest. The second relationship between individual characteristics and occupational ability patterns is one of belonging. It involves the question: What occupational group has abilities, interests, and personality traits most resembling those of a specific individual?

Proposition 10. *Work satisfactions depend upon the extent to which the individual can find adequate outlets in his job for his abilities, interests, values, and personality traits.* When the individual can find expression of his psychological characteristics in his work, he has the opportunity to develop feelings of self-realization, of belonginess, and of status. This is particularly true of men; it is less often true of women, for whom marriage often provides more complete self-fulfillment.

Proposition 11. *The degree of satisfaction the individual attains from his work is related to the degree to which he has been able to implement his self-concept in his work.* It is assumed that vocational development is in part the development of a self-concept and that the process of vocational adjustment is in part a process of implementing the self-concept, of finding a way of taking the role to which one aspires.

SUMMARY

A number of research questions have been considered and some of their implications for further research have been indicated. Propositions pertaining to various aspects of vocational development have been formulated in the hope of stimulating further research and providing a frame of reference for it.

50

Some Life History Antecedents of
Engineering Interests[*]

Gordon E. Kulberg and William A. Owens

The point of view described in the previous paper by Super implies
that the "roots" of careers are to be found in the early life histories
of individuals. Of current writers, perhaps Dr. Anne Roe (1957) has
most persuasively argued the importance of early home background
and a child's relationship to his parents as conditioners of the young
person's orientation to the world of work. While not designed specifically to test the validity of Dr. Roe's formulations, the research
reported in the present paper aimed at identification of the differences
in life history antecedents associated with different vocational orientations. Specifically, this brief paper reports significant differences between two groups of college engineering students, those whose scores
on the well-known Strong Vocational Interest Blank indicated orientation toward, for example, "sales engineering" while the other group
showed inclinations toward "pure research." The former group was
characterized more by a history of interest in people and social situations, the latter by interest in things and ideas.

The serial investigations of Roe (1951a, 1951b, 1953) imply that motivation plays a vital role in high-level scientific achievement. Terman's
monograph (1954) on gifted scientists and nonscientists contains an
affirmation and some specific evidence to the effect that *interest* measures
are among the better group discriminators. Each investigator has made
reference to data regarding the genesis of critical scientific or research
motivations.

Since interests *do* appear to be of vital importance in the context of
high-level achievement, and since relatively little is known regarding their

* Adapted and abridged from Gordon E. Kulberg and William A. Owens, "Some
Life History Antecedents of Engineering Interests," *Journal of Educational Psychology*,
1960, 51, pp. 26-31. (With permission of Dr. Owens and the American Psychological
Association.)

origins and development, the present study was designed to cast some light on their antecedents in one restricted area. Specifically, its purpose is to indicate some of the life history correlates of measured interest in the broad field of engineering and in two of its most dissimilar branches—research and sales.

METHOD

The problem thus formulated was attacked by correlating responses to a 100-item scored life history form with scores obtained on the Engineering scale of the Strong Vocational Interest Blank, and with two profile scales derived therefrom by Dunnette (1957). These latter, hypothesized to represent the poles in engineering interests, are for Sales Engineering and Pure Research.

Measuring Devices. The Strong Vocational Interest Blank is well known and requires no comment. Items of the life history questionnaires were in multiple choice form and of two types. Forty items involved alternatives, presumably on a continuum, from which only one could be chosen by an individual respondent. The other 60 items involved dichotomous response options, with a common stem, such that several options could be chosen by a given respondent. Thus, the total number of response options was 348.

Subjects. The subjects were mechanical engineering freshmen who entered Iowa State College, in that curriculum, during the fall of 1957, or who transferred into it prior to the middle of the quarter. Only 111 of a possible 148 were available for inclusion. It seems probable that poor attitude and inappropriate interests were prominent among the reasons for this attrition. If so, there may be some restriction in the range of interests reported here and, thus, some minimizing of the magnitude of interest vs. life history relationships.

Chronology. Subjects completed the life history during the regular sequence of freshmen testing and the Strong during a required engineering orientation course two months later.

Product-moment correlations, or their equivalent, were subsequently obtained between each item of the life history and score on each of the three scales of the Vocational Interest Blank. Dichotomous items which did not have at least 6% of the cases in the smaller response (or nonresponse) category were dropped from the computations but were nevertheless utilized to describe the groups.

Item Selection. Items from the life history were deemed related to engineering interests if they correlated at or above the 5% level ($r = 0.18$) with one of the three interest scales, or if they correlated 0.17 with one of these scales, had small variance and "made sense" in themselves and in relationship to other significant items. (Item variance was thus taken into account because of its effect on the magnitude of item-scale correlations.)

Since this study did not involve cross-validation in the conventional sense, it is axiomatic that some of the correlations reported are attributable to chance. Brozek and Tiede's formula (1952) was utilized to lend assurance that chance *alone* could not account for them. The fact that allegedly opposing interests (research vs. sales) are, in fact, frequently accompanied by quite *opposite* life history antecedents offers assurance of another sort, since the totality of such an outcome can hardly be attributed to chance.

RESULTS

As previously noted, high consensus, dichotomous options, elected by 94% or more of the subjects, were used only to characterize or describe the respondents. Thus, they may be typified as follows: (*a*) they were single, had siblings, were reared by both parents, had a hobby; (*b*) did *not* enjoy lectures in high school; (*c*) expected college to be more difficult, were not "life of the party" personalities; (*d*) were permitted to go out over week-ends; (*e*) worked during high school; (*f*) had early (indirect) sex information; (*g*) and did not feel that they would enter management.

In similar fashion, the parents of the respondents are typified as follows: (*a*) they owned or rented a home; (*b*) owned a car; (*c*) lived together; (*d*) either wanted their son to enter a profession or had no preferences; (*e*) and, they were engineers, managers, farmers, or skilled tradesmen, or were in private business; (*f*) they were *not* doctors, teachers, lawyers, salesmen or unskilled laborers.

Following identification of the items involving "thin splits" each of the remaining 252 response options were correlated with scores on each of the three interest scales. This yielded a total of 756 correlations ranging from .44 to —0.35. Eighteen of these were significant at the .01 level, and 64 were significant at the .05 level. Utilizing Brozek and Tiede's formula (1952), the probability of obtaining either result by chance is less than .0001.

The items themselves, the response options and their correlations with the given interest scale, or scales, appear in the tables which follow. Table 1 contains *all* the items correlated with the Engineering Interest scale, plus options common to one or both of the other two scales, as indicated. Table 2 contains all remaining items correlated with the Pure Research Interest scale, plus options common to the Sales Engineering scale; and Table 3 contains only the items correlated with the Sales Engineering Interest scale alone. An attempt has also been made to arrange the items

TABLE 1. Life History Items Correlated with Engineering Interest, and for Some Items with Pure Research and/or Sales Engineering Interests

Item	Correlation		
	Engineering	Pure Research	Sales Engineering
Elementary			
During my youth when teams were being chosen for games, I was usually picked:			
near the end	.19		
near the first	−.24		.27
I was usually the one doing the choosing		−.20	
High School			
When you were in school (grade or high) where did you and your friends *most* often get together?			
On the street corner	.22		−.29
At your house		−.19	
At a friend's home			.23
What grades did you make in science courses in high school?			
(Coded 1-4, D's to A's)	.28		
What were your main subjects in high school?			
Business or Commercial	.20		
Which were most difficult?			
Commercial courses, bookkeeping, typing	−.18		
Which were easiest?			
History, economics, civics	−.18		.25
Natural Science, Biology, Zoology			−.20
Which type of courses did you most enjoy?			
Discussion	−.31		
Natural Science, Biology, Zoology		.26	−.23
Which of the following offices did you hold at any time in high school?			
Chairman of an important student committee or club	−.24	.32	
Never held any		.20	−.18
When you were 15 years of age, how many living brothers and sisters did you have?			
(Coded 1 to 5, no brothers or sisters vs. 4 or more.)	−.27		.23
When did you first consider entering college?			
In junior high	.19		
Have always planned to come			.21
After (H.S.) graduation, but not in service			−.18

TABLE 1. (continued)

Item	Correlation		
	Engi-neering	Pure Research	Sales Engi-neering
Contemporary and future			
What are your present hobbies?			
Music	−.20		
Which one of the following has caused you the most difficulty in the past 6 months?			
Nothing special	−.21		
When some difficult problem is bothering you with whom do you usually talk it over?			
No one	.23		−.33
Father			.19
What sort of work do you like?			
With things	.32		−.35
With ideas	.21		−.21
What type job do you feel you will eventually take?			
Design	.29		−.24
Sales	−.28		
Research			−.26
What sort of work do you like?			
With people	−.33		.43
How do you feel about jobs requiring routine operations, calculations, etc.?			
Rather enjoy once I get hang of it	−.19		.27
Dislike them but would take one if well paid			−.17

chronologically, although in the case of the sales engineers it seemed necessary to utilize a general category for items which appeared to spread over the entire range, and to assign arbitrarily items which might have been allocated to either of several positions.

DISCUSSION

To summarize the tabular results presented, the possessor of typical engineering interests appears somewhat as follows: first, he has a history of painful and/or not completely necessary or successful personal-social contacts and of some adjustment problems. Second, he has a history of superior achievement in science courses and of more enjoyment of and more success in quantitative and utilitarian courses than in linguistic and social studies courses. Third, he has a history of long career planning, of liking to

TABLE 2. Life History Items Correlated Only with Pure Research Interest Plus
Options Common to Sales Engineering Interest

	Correlation	
Item	Pure Research	Sales Engineering
Preschool		
At what age was your father when you were born?		
(Coded 1-4, about 20 vs. about 35)	.24	
High School		
How much money did your family have while you were going to high school?		
About as much as my classmates	.24	
Do not know, or had not considered it	−.24	
To which of the following recreational activities have you devoted the most time in the past 5 years?		
Music, art, dramatics	−.24	
Who was the most influential in your decision to go to college?		
Another adult, teacher, minister	−.22	
Friends		.18
About how often have you changed your mind about your future vocational plans since entering high school?		
(Coded 1-4, have not changed vs. too many times to remember)	−.27	
Have still not decided	.24	
Contemporary		
Parental occupation:		
Manager or supervisor	−.17	.23
Private business	−.23	.21
Where do you belong in a list of 100 typical people in the kind of job you can do best?		
(Coded 1-4, lowest one-third vs. best 5%)	−.24	
How good do you think you are, or could be, as a supervisor?		
(Coded 1-4, in the lowest one-half vs. in the top 5%)	−.29	.34
Don't know	.20	

work with things and ideas as opposed to people, and of enjoying creative work and disliking routine.

This pattern of typical engineering interests seems intensified in the case of subjects having interests of research engineers. They appear somewhat unique in being more clearly from middle-class homes, being intellectually

TABLE 3. Life History Items Correlated Only with Sales
Engineering Interest

Item	Correlation Sales Engineering
High School	
How would you classify yourself as a student in high school?	
(Coded 1-5, poor to considerably above average)	.17
Which of the science courses did you take while in high school?	
Physics	.24
Which of the math courses did you take in high school?	
Advanced algebra, Trigonometry	.24
(at least part of a semester)	.21
What school projects or activities did you participate in while in high school other than athletics?	
Student council,	
Class offices	.25
How many elective offices did you hold while in high school?	
(Coded 1-5, none to 11 or more)	.21
What size school (high) did you attend?	
(Coded 1-5, rural area vs. over 25,000)	.21
During your last two years in high school, about how many hours a week did you spend on athletics?	
(Coded 1-5, none vs. 15 or more)	.23
As you grew up, how did you feel about high school?	
(Coded 1-5, cordially disliked vs. liked it very much)	.41
Where did most of your spending money come from during the years you were in high school?	
Partly allowance, partly earnings	.22
Contemporary and future	
How many very close friends do you have today?	
(Coded 1-5, none to 8+)	.26
How often do young people, outside of your immediate family, come to you for advice?	
(Coded 1-5, never to constantly)	.17
If single, how often do you date, on the average?	
(Coded 1-5, do not date vs. more than 2 a week)	.22
Do you consider yourself a relaxed person?	
Yes	.17
What type job do you feel you will eventually take?	
Sales	.44
Contemporary and future	
How close to Iowa State College is your home?	
(Coded 1-5, less than 20 miles to 200 or more)	.25
General	
About how large was the town in which you grew up?	

TABLE 3. (continued)

	Correlation
Item	*Sales Engineering*
(Coded 1-5, rural area to over 25,000)	.21
Was your mother employed and away from home, at least part time while you were growing up?	
(Coded 1-5, yes, she started before I was 6 years old vs. no)	.28
How much influence did your parents exert over your choice of friends?	
Objected to a few	.24
How often did you feel that you agreed with your parents concerning things in general?	
(Coded 1-5, we never disagreed vs. we hardly ever agreed)	.28

independent, having a considerable breadth of academic curiosity and success, and being somewhat lacking in self-confidence in general and in confidence in their supervisory ability in particular.

These first two patterns are virtually completely reversed in the instance of subjects having the interests of sales engineers. Indeed, the relationships of many identical life history items to scores on this scale are precisely the opposite of those noted earlier. Here the picture is one of success in dealing with people, of liking linguistic and nonscience courses, and of enjoying people more than things and ideas.

Among the limitations of this investigation are the following: First, the broad patterns of antecedents of engineering interests which have been traced here may not be peculiar to engineering. Further studies are needed to determine this; although the fact that such large differences exist between (research vs. sales) subgroups *within* the occupation suggests that measurable differences between occupations also exist. Second, the intercorrelations between the various life history items are not known. For example, it may be that possessors of a marked interest in engineering are not, typically, social leaders because, like many superior students, they are educationally accelerated and thus somewhat less mature than their fellows. Third, sweeping generalizations based upon so circumscribed a sample would be clearly unwarranted. Fourth, it should of course be recognized that this study involves only the correlation of one set of questionnaire results with another; the inherent weaknesses of the method are therefore multiplied. Fifth, in the absence of a conventional cross-validation, it may be assumed that the broad pattern of these results is correctly drawn, but it must also be recognized that some specific relationships are attributable to "chance."

SUMMARY AND CONCLUSION

Overall, the subjects of this investigation who exhibited a marked interest in engineering were young men with a history of academic superiority and of more satisfactory experiences with things and ideas than with people and social situations. This pattern was intensified in the case of research engineering interests and reversed in the case of sales engineering interests.

51

Personality and Career Choice*

Morris Rosenberg

During recent years psychologists and sociologists have been giving a great deal of attention to the hows and whys of vocational choices, and have emphasized the role of personal factors—psychological needs and personality—in vocational orientation. Roe (1957) has discussed the influence of early home factors; Super (1951) has viewed the process of choice as one of role-playing wherein a person gradually tests his self-concept against the realities of the tentatively "chosen" occupation; Tiedeman (1961) has examined the decision process as involved in effecting harmony between a person and his work. In this paper by Rosenberg we have clear evidence that tentative choices of career, and attitudes toward occupations generally, cannot be separated from the more general personal characteristics and values of the individual. In an important sense, consciously or unconsciously, one selects an occupation which he perceives as having the potential of satisfying his needs and which is compatible with his personality.

What influence do personality factors have upon occupational choice? Suggestive hypotheses are plentiful, but systematic data are scarce. One might hypothesize, for example, that a person who is psychologically in-

* Reprinted with permission of the publisher from *Occupations and Values* by Morris Rosenberg. Copyright 1957 by The Free Press, a corporation. Adapted mainly from Chapter 4, pp. 36-47. Also with permission of the author.

secure or anxious might seek a steady, secure job; that a compulsive per-
fectionist might seek to attach himself to an organization requiring a rigid
adherence to precise rules; that an "oral" personality might select a verbal
occupation (law, teaching); that the "anal" type might seek work providing possibilities for acquisition (business); that a detached personality
might select an occupation allowing him independence (art, medicine, exploration); that an extrovert might choose outgoing or exhibitionist occupations, such as acting or salesmanship; that an introvert might choose
"thoughtful" or self-sufficient occupations (science, poetry); that an
"authoritarian" personality might choose occupations involving a rigid
system of domination, such as the army; that a sado-masochist (in
Fromm's sense, 1941) might select an organization involving a rigid delineation of authority; that an "other-directed" personality (Riesman, *et al.,*
1950) might choose an occupation requiring sensitivity to the needs of
others; that an "inner-directed" type might select an occupation in terms
of a rigid sense of values; and so on.

Systematic tests of such hypotheses are rare. The problems of obtaining
adequate indices of such complex personality types, of controlling the influence of multitudinous non-personality factors, and of relating these personality characteristics in a specific way to occupational values and choices
are extremely complex. In the present study, we did not delve deeply into
the personality structures of our respondents, but we did utilize certain
items designed to give us a glimpse of some of their personality traits. Since
the study of this problem area is still in its bare beginnings, it appears
worthwhile to utilize the crude data available to consider whether certain
aspects of personality structure are in some way related to occupational
values and choices.

PROCEDURE

A representative sample of 2,758 college students were queried about
their occupational, educational, economic, political, religious, and social
values. In 1952 a new values study, placing special stress on students'
reactions to the prospect of impending military service but also including
data on occupational and other values, was conducted with 4,585 college
students selected on a representative basis from eleven universities throughout the country. In the second study, it proved possible to re-interview
944 students from Cornell University who had participated in the first
investigation, thus enabling us to examine trends and changes in the values,
attitudes, and behavior of these people.

A key area of interest in these studies was the problem of occupational
choices and occupational values; as a consequence, a large number of items
were included in both studies which were designed to shed light on the

determinants of occupational choices and on the special role which values played in directing the occupational decision. The present report is based upon the analysis of these data.

THE INFLUENCE OF SELF-CONFIDENCE

We may begin by looking at the common-sense notion of self-confidence. Everyone is familiar with the self-confident type of person. He is the kind of man who strikes us as very sure of himself; he is relatively unworried, is not hypersensitive, is usually in good spirits. On the other hand, there is another type of person—the opposite of the first—who is constantly worried, never appears able to relax, lacks a basic feeling of being worthwhile, constantly worries about doing things wrong. Most people we know, of course, fit somewhere between these two extreme types.

In an effort to determine whether our respondents could be ranged along this hypothetical continuum, we presented them with the following four questions:

(1) I usually don't have enough confidence in myself.   A D ?[1]

(2) I get upset if someone criticizes me, no matter who it is.   A D ?

(3) How would you say you feel most of the time—in good spirits or in low spirits?

   _____Very good spirits

   _____Fairly good spirits

   _____Neither good nor bad

   _____Fairly low spirits

   _____Very low spirits

(4) Are you the sort of person who lets things worry you or don't you let things worry you?

   _____Let things worry me very much

   _____Let things worry me quite a bit

   _____Let things worry me somewhat

   _____Don't let things worry me

If we tentatively assume that the person who gives the "positive" responses is the "self-confident" or "self-assured" type, and that the one who gives the "negative" responses is the "anxious" or "insecure" type, then the question arises: How will the individual's degree of self-confidence influence his orientation toward his career?

In the first place we find, as one would expect, that the self-confident people are more optimistic about their occupational futures. Students were asked what occupational values they hoped to satisfy in their work, and then were asked how many of these values they actually expected to satisfy. Eighty per cent of the most self-confident people expected to satisfy "most of them," compared with 55 per cent of the least self-assured.

[1] A stands for agree, D for disagree, and ? for undecided.

Similarly, the self-confident men are the most optimistic about their economic futures. When asked how much money they expected to earn ten years after college graduation 56 per cent of them expected to earn over $10,000 compared with 32 per cent of the least secure men. On the other hand, 25 per cent of the former, compared with 44 per cent of the latter, expected to be earning under $7,500.

These findings suggest that the anxious or insecure person tends to be relatively discouraged about his career before he starts. He is less likely to think that his work will really give him what he wants out of it and he is less likely to feel that he will make much money at his job.

While it is not immediately clear how self-confidence would influence occupational choice, one empirical finding affords a suggestive hint. At one point in our study, respondents were presented with a list of six characteristics and were asked to check the two characteristics most essential for success in the fields they had chosen. One of the qualities on this list was "organizing and administrative ability." Our data show that students expecting to enter the fields of hotel management, business, sales-promotion, farming, government work, and personnel work, are the most likely to feel that "organizing and administrative ability" are very essential for success in their work. We will call these six occupations the "organizing-administrative" fields.

The interesting finding which emerges is that 46 per cent of the most self-confident people chose one of the "organizing-administrative" occupations, but that this was true of only 20 per cent of the most anxious people (Table 1). In addition, as we would expect, the self-confident person is most likely to believe he possesses this ability (Table 2).

Why should this be so? Although we lack data to check our interpretation, our hypothesis would be that a person who chooses an occupation requiring organizing and administrative ability, such as hotel management, business sales-promotion, running a farm, is one who is willing to *assume responsibility* for his actions. He is willing to make decisions and face the consequences of his actions, is willing to "take charge" when things have to be done, is willing to assume control of things and people. If this is so, then it is understandable that a person who is basically self-confident would be quite willing to enter such occupations.

"SELF-OTHER" ATTITUDES

One aspect of personality which has received increasing attention in recent years is the concept of "self-other" attitudes—attitudes which influence the individual's characteristic way of relating to other people. There is reason to believe that the way an individual relates to others will be reflected in his selection of those values he hopes to satisfy in his work and in his occupational choice. This is not to say that personality "causes" values; rather, our argument is that the selection of certain occupational values is partly an *expression* of certain personality characteristics which are not themselves values. An illustration of the type of finding we would anticipate on the basis of this hypothesis would be the following: if an individual tends to have a strong need for affective ties to others, if he is

TABLE 1. Self-Confidence and Selection of "Organizing-Administrative" Occupations (Men)

| Occupational Choice | Self-Confidence | | | | |
	Low 1	2	3	4	High 5
Select "organizing-administrative" occupation	20%	26%	29%	34%	46%
Do not select "organizing-administrative" occupation	80	74	71	66	54
N	(91)	(332)	(445)	(203)	(70)

TABLE 2. Self-Confidence and Belief That One Possesses Organizing and Administrative Ability (Men)

| "Organizing and administrative ability" | Self-Confidence | | | | |
	Low 1	2	3	4	High 5
Believe they have it	40%	39%	55%	59%	68%
Do not believe they have it	60	61	45	41	32
N	(93)	(333)	(456)	(204)	(70)

strongly oriented toward obtaining warmth and affection, then he will particularly value the opportunity to *work with other people* in his occupational practice. In other words, his basic interpersonal attitude *will find expression* in the gratification he seeks from work.

As Horney (1945) has observed in her works, there are three basic ways in which an individual may relate himself to others: he may "move toward," "move against," or "move away from" people. To simplify our notation, we will use Horney's terms to characterize these types. Those who seek to "move toward people" are known as "the compliant type"; those who seek to "move against people" are called "the aggressive type"; and those who seek to "move away from people" are referred to as "the detached type."

Since adequate data were not available in our study to enable us to differentiate these types in a sophisticated fashion, it was necessary to use various indirect questions in an effort to classify respondents crudely in terms of "pure" types.

The detached personality type has been characterized as one who desires to maintain his emotional distance from others; he tends to be deeply concerned with his independence and the expression of his individuality. Fundamentally resistant to coercion or domination of any sort, he chiefly wants no interference from the world. In our study, we characterized people as detached if they said they were concerned with being "independent" (rather than "successful" or "well-liked"), said they were bothered at being given orders by others, considered it relatively unimportant for them to be well liked by different kinds of people, and said that, when in a group, they preferred to make decisions themselves rather than having others make the decisions.

The compliant type, on the other hand, is particularly concerned with approval, acceptance, warmth, support. He "likes everyone," is anxious to please them, is willing to be dominated but is reluctant to dominate others. We have classified people in this category if they said they were anxious to be "well-liked," were not bothered by being given orders but were bothered at giving them, and expressed a positive view of human nature.

The aggressive type, finally, is concerned with mastery, control, domination and conquest in the external world. This person is anxious to be top dog in a dog-eat-dog world; he respects only the powerful and successful. Respondents have been classified as belonging to this type if they were chiefly concerned with being "successful" (rather than independent or well-liked), if they said they did not mind giving orders to other people, and if they said that "if you don't watch yourself, people will take advantage of you."

THE SELF-OTHER TYPOLOGY AND OCCUPATIONAL VALUES

If our indices have successfully differentiated people in terms of self-other orientations, then we would expect the detached people to be more likely than others to stress "freedom from supervision" and "the chance to be creative and original" as occupational values. The detached type is, in the first place, characterized by a deep-seated resistance to coercion or domination of any sort. The fact that 66 per cent of the detached people ranked "leave me relatively free of supervision" high as an occupational value, compared with 36 per cent of the others, suggests that a person who is predisposed to emphasize independence in a variety of life situations will, when asked about his occupational values, stress the notion of freedom from control in this area as well.

Similarly, the fact that the detached person is so highly conscious of his unique individuality would help to account for his tendency to emphasize creativity and self-expression in his work (Table 3). It is this desire to be unique, different, and special which represents one of the strongest appeals of detachment, and it is understandable that this desire should tend to be reflected in occupational values.

When we turn to the *aggressive* personality type, a different occupational value constellation greets us—the "extrinsic-reward" values. The aggressive type is concerned with domination and mastery; it is well known that one very fertile area for the manifestation of such dominance in American

TABLE 3. Detached Type and Occupational Values

	Detached Type	All Others
"Leave me free of supervision"		
Ranked high	66%	36%
Ranked low	7	14
"Permit me to be creative and original"		
Ranked high	68%	46%
Ranked low	8	13
Either "freedom" or "creative"		
Ranked high	84%	63%
Ranked low	14	24
N	(146)	(982)

society is the occupational field. Two ways of pushing ahead in the world and thereby establishing one's superiority over others are to earn "a good deal of money" and to gain a high degree of "status and prestige." It is these values, it turns out, that the aggressive people are particularly apt to select. As Table 4 indicates, nearly three-fourths of the aggressive people ranked one of these values highly important, compared with less than two-fifths of the remainder of the respondents. The general desire for success and mastery appears to be expressed specifically in the occupational area in the form of a desire for prestige and possession.

Finally, the *compliant* type—the type who wants to be liked, accepted, welcomed, who wants to do things for others—tends to project his personality into the occupational realm by stressing "people-oriented" values. He tends to stress that an ideal job must enable him to "work with people rather than things" and must give him an "opportunity to be helpful to others" (Table 5). This individual, anxious to please and be helpful, seeks a work experience which will enable him to do so.

It would appear, then, that if we are able to isolate relatively "pure" personality types, we find that these personality characteristics tend to be expressed in the selection of occupational values. In what sense is it mean-

TABLE 4. Aggressive Type and Occupational Values

	Aggressive Type	All Others
"Earn a good deal of money"		
Ranked high	61%	31%
Ranked low	2	14
"Give me social status and prestige"		
Ranked high	44%	20%
Ranked low	9	22
Either "money" or "status"		
Ranked high	73%	39%
Ranked low	10	30
N	(186)	(942)

TABLE 5. Compliant Type and Occupational Values

	Compliant Type	All Others
"Opportunity to work with people"		
Ranked high	53%	33%
Ranked low	14	28
"Opportunity to be helpful to others"		
Ranked high	45%	31%
Ranked low	14	21
Either "people" or "helpful"		
Ranked high	74%	48%
Ranked low	22	38
N	(96)	(1032)

ingful, then, to speak of "values" and "personality" as separate concepts? Essentially, all we mean by the aspect of personality discussed here is some predisposition to behave in a certain fashion in a large number of situations. Values, too, are criteria which determine behavior, but which are socially defined as good or bad. Among the various things which the society encourages the individual to want (or not want), he will tend to select those which most closely agree with his underlying orientation. In this sense, occupational values would be a reflection of personality.

SELF-OTHER ORIENTATION AND OCCUPATIONAL CHOICE

Every occupation has some interpersonal quality about it—the chance to enjoy interaction with other people, or to dominate them, or to get away from them; and, as we will show later, the students are keenly aware of the importance of interpersonal factors in their careers. In principle, then, the individual's self-other orientation might well have some bearing on his occupational choice. However, it is actually rather difficult to pin down this influence, since the same occupation potentially can satisfy so many different values for different people. Thus, personality alone can rarely determine a *specific* choice, although it may represent a channeling factor determining one's broad *area* of choices.

In general, we would expect that if a student selects those values which are congenial to his "self-other orientation," he would also tend to choose an occupation in which, it is generally believed, these values can be satisfied.

Take, for example, the compliant personality type. This person, who wants to be well liked and to establish friendly relations with other people, tends to select "people-oriented" values. We would thus expect him to be more likely than others to select those occupations in which these values could be fulfilled. Students entering the fields of social work, medicine, teaching, social science, and personnel work were most likely to hold people-oriented values. It turns out that 43 per cent of the compliant people chose one of these occupations, compared with 24 per cent of the students classified as detached or aggressive.

Similarly, it was observed that people entering the fields of real estate or finance, hotel management, sales-promotion, law, advertising, and business (unspecified) tended to emphasize the extrinsic rewards of work. These are the values stressed by the aggressive personality type. Our data show that 32 per cent of those classified as aggressive chose one of these fields, compared with 20 per cent of the detached and compliant people.

The detached personality type, finally, would be expected to choose an occupation in which he felt the values of freedom from supervision and creativity and originality could be realized. Students selecting the fields of art, architecture, journalism-drama, and natural science tended to place the greatest stress on these values. It turns out that 30 per cent of those classified as detached selected one of these fields, compared with 14 per cent of the aggressive and compliant people (Table 6).

An additional item of evidence is available to suggest that the detached person tends to select an occupation which is consonant with his personality needs. We have noted that the detached person tends to value his independence and freedom and dislikes anything hinting at regimentation or coercion; consequently, when he chooses a type of "firm or outfit" in which he would like to work, we would expect him to select one which would grant him *independence* of action and to avoid the pressures of regularity and hierarchical discipline of a large-scale organization. It is interesting to note, therefore, that when the respondents were asked what type of "firm or outfit" they would like to enter, only 15 per cent of the detached people chose the category "private firm, organization, or factory," compared with 36 per cent of the other people in the study. Thus the selection of a certain type of organization appears to be associated with a desire to maintain an emotional distance between oneself and other people.

Although the crudeness of our indices prevents us from making any final judgments on the subject, the results appear sufficiently suggestive to in-

TABLE 6. Personality Typology and Choice of Occupational Area

Occupational choice:		
Social work, medicine, teaching, social science, and personnel	Compliant 43% (185)	Detached and Aggressive 24% (314)
Real estate, hotel, sales, law, advertising, & business (unspec.)	Aggressive 32% (188)	Detached and Compliant 20% (311)
Art, architecture, journalism- drama, and natural science	Detached 30% (126)	Compliant and Aggressive 14% (373)

dicate that the way a person characteristically relates to others will influence the type of career he selects. In principle, it does seem to make good sense to assume that an individual who "moves toward people," wants to be loving and helpful, will be guided toward a general area of occupations in which friendly, frequent contact with others is inherent in the structure of the occupation. Similarly, a person who needs to express control, mastery, or domination will move toward that general area of occupations in which this desire can find expression. Finally, an individual who wants to have as little as possible to do with others, wishes to maintain his emotional distance from people, would tend to avoid occupations in which others are likely to make demands upon him. In other words, if the individual relates to others in a characteristic way in a variety of life situations, it would not be surprising to find that this type of relationship influences his occupational values and occupational choice.

52

The Creative Years in Science and Literature[*]

Harvey C. Lehman

How productive are people of various adult ages? It is often assumed by industry that marked decrements occur in the older years in workers' ability to produce, and thus that per unit costs are higher when older workers are used. Practically no evidence is available on the actual productivity of the average older worker, but what is available suggests only slight decline which possibly may be compensated for by such factors as greater stability on the job. Regarding age and outstanding productivity and accomplishment—sufficiently important to become a matter of record, as publications and patents—a great deal of information has been assembled, much of it by Dr. H. C. Lehman, the author of this paper. After publishing the present paper in 1936, Dr. Lehman published many others dealing with such questions as age of recipients of large earned incomes, age of leadership, age of quality production vs. quantity production, age of greatest physical skill and the like. Not only are the facts here presented intrinsically interesting, but they have important implications regarding the education and utilization of potential contributors to science and the liberal arts. Too often, it might seem, graduate school studies encroach on the most productive years. And perhaps universities, industry, and society at large should give thought to personnel practices which drain off time and energy that might, perhaps, better go into further creative effort.

What are man's most creative years? At what ages are men likely to do their most outstanding work? In 1921 Professor Robert S. Woodworth, of Columbia University, published this statement in his book, *Psychology: A Study of Mental Life:* "Seldom does a very old person get outside the limits of his previous habits. Few great inventions, artistic or practical, have

* Adapted from H. C. Lehman, "The Creative Years in Science and Literature," *Scientific Monthly*, 1936, Vol. 43, pp. 151-162. (Reprinted from *Scientific Monthly* by permission of the author and the American Association for the Advancement of Science.)

emanated from really old persons, and comparatively few even from the middle-aged . . . The period from twenty years up to forty seems to be the most favorable for inventiveness." The present investigation represents an attempt actually to canvass various kinds of endeavor to determine whether scientists and other creative workers display more creative thinking at some chronological age levels than at others.

PROCEDURE

In general, the procedure followed in this investigation has been to study authoritative histories and source books which list various noteworthy contributions in various fields and to examine biographical sources to obtain information regarding the total production of individuals, the date of birth and death of the worker, as well as the date of the production, usually patent or publication. The following procedure followed in the case of chemistry illustrates the method:

In his book, *A Concise History of Chemistry,* Professor T. P. Hilditch (1911), of the University of Liverpool, presents the names of several hundred noted chemists and the dates on which these chemists made their outstanding contributions to the science of chemistry. Professor Hilditch's book was chosen for study because, in the first place, he is an able worker in the field of chemistry and, in the second place, because four of the writer's colleagues were unanimous in their judgment that the contributions listed by Hilditch form an essential part of the chemistry panorama.

Another reason may be noted: When he was selecting important contributions in the field of chemistry, Professor Hilditch was *not* studying age differences in creativity. He was probably therefore not even aware of age differences. This fact is of considerable importance in so far as the present study is concerned. Certainly, when studying the creativity of persons of different chronological ages, an investigator should divest himself of all bias for or against any particular age levels. And this impartial attitude is most likely to be attained when the compiler of a list of outstanding achievements is thinking *not* of age differences but solely of outstanding achievement.

If each age group is to be judged fairly, account must be taken of the fact that the number of individuals that are alive at each successive age level will decrease. Certainly, if more men are alive at the younger age levels than at the older age levels, the younger age groups might achieve more merely because of their greater numerical strength. Adequate allowance for the unequal numbers of individuals alive at the various age levels was therefore made. Each of the age curves in this paper presents the *average* number of contributions per chronological age level. Full and adequate allowance is thus made for the larger number of youthful research workers.

One final word with reference to the problem of technique. It obviously is not possible to study the entire life work of individuals who are still living and achieving. In the first place, it is almost impossible to judge the real significance of quite recent work. Moreover, we have no way of knowing what the living chemist will accomplish during his later years. The present study includes therefore data for deceased individuals only. For the deceased person the record is reasonably complete and future events will probably change the record only slightly.

Following this general plan age curves of productivity were constructed for the following areas of endeavor: chemistry, mathematics, physics, astronomy, invention, short-story writing, great poetry.

FINDINGS

To save space the findings for the various fields are charted in Figure 1 though in the discussion attention will be focussed on the findings for first one line of endeavor and then another. In the instance of chemistry, the question arises as to why the curve rises so much more quickly than it descends, and why it descends so quickly after reaching its maximum. One interpretation suggests that the older chemists may have become more discriminating during their later years and that the older men may therefore have disdained to publish findings which they regarded as of minor importance. If this explanation were a valid one the contributions of the older men should be superior in quality to the contributions of the young chemists. As a means of ascertaining the facts with reference to this matter, three of the writers' colleagues from the chemistry department of Ohio University were asked to select the 100 *most important or most significant* chemistry contributions that were listed in Hilditch's book. The peaks of the resultant curves appeared *at slightly younger ages* than the peak shown in Figure 1. Clearly, the alleged superior discriminative ability of the older men does not explain why maximum productivity occurs at such a relatively early age.

Another view was expressed that the young chemist who displays marked ability by the early publication of important research findings is likely, sooner or later, to be advanced to an administrative position. That is to say, the more gifted young chemist is often made head of his department or placed in some other administrative post which absorbs his time and energy and precludes further research. If the present study had been limited solely to the creative work of chemists, one might accept this hypothesis. However, similar age-curves were constructed for inventors, physicists, mathematicians, astronomers, poets, short-story writers and several other kinds of workers. It is true that the precise age level at which the several curves reached their peaks varied somewhat. The shapes of the curves also differed. Nevertheless, for most kinds of endeavor that the writer has thus far studied, the peak has been found to appear at a rela-

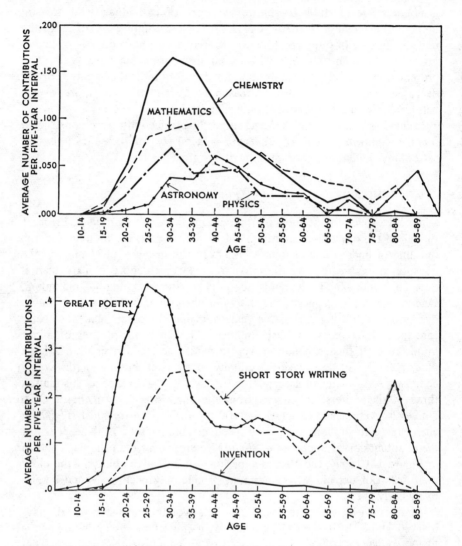

FIGURE 1. Age Trends in Productivity in Various Areas of Science and Literature

tively youthful age. Therefore, the theory that the early and marked decrement in the productivity of the chemists was due solely or even largely to the pressure of administrative and classroom duties is of very doubtful validity.

If the present study had been limited to the creativity of scientists only, one might have been led to the spurious belief that classroom and administrative duties are the sole reasons why the foregoing curves start descending at such relatively early ages. A glance at the curve for great inventions should suffice to dispel such a belief. The case of Thomas A. Edison is of special interest since he was very active as an inventor throughout his entire life. However, age 35 was Mr. Edison's most productive year. Moreover, during the four-year interval from ages 33 to 36 inclusive, Edison took out a total of 312 United States patents. This was more than a fourth (28 per cent) of all the United States patents that were taken out by Edison during an inventive career that lasted for more than 60 years. Figure 2 shows Edison's productivity at various ages and this single record fits well the general pattern set forth in Figure 1.

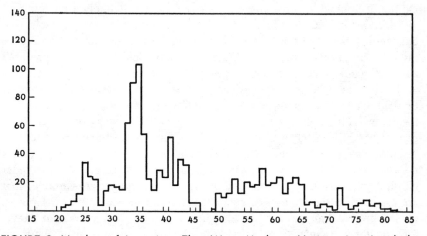

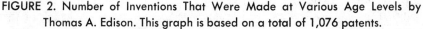

FIGURE 2. Number of Inventions That Were Made at Various Age Levels by Thomas A. Edison. This graph is based on a total of 1,076 patents.

DISCUSSION

It should not be assumed that Figure 1 sets forth, for every type of work, the relative creativity of men of different chronological ages. The writer does not mean to convey the impression that he has obtained typical creative-work curves. Indeed, he doubts very much that such a thing as a typical creative-work curve exists.[1]

To those who regard scientific information as the most precious asset

[1] Editorial note: In a later publication ("Man's Most Creative Years," *Scientific Monthly*, 1944, Vol. 59, pp. 384-393) Dr. Lehman concludes as follows: (1) Within any given field of endeavor, not one only, but numerous age-curves can be constructed which show the rise and fall of creative output at successive age levels. (2) The shape of any one of these various curves is in part a function of quality of performance. (3) As compared with an age-curve which sets forth quantity of performance at successive age levels, the peak of a curve which presents age data for performances of the highest quality is likely to be more narrow or pointed. (4) Within any given field of endeavor, quality of output and quantity of output are not necessarily correlated, output of the very highest merit tending to fall off at an

that the human race has accumulated, the above findings will perhaps bring a feeling of regret. Such persons may wonder if steps might not have been taken for increasing the scientific productivity of the older men. It is theoretically conceivable that an educational foundation, or some wealthy individual, might relieve the more capable research men of their routine and other time-consuming duties. If it be assumed that the older men have not lost their ability to do outstanding research work, the problem of actually motivating them (and certain other problems) would, of course, still remain unsolved.

Upon the basis of the foregoing data, what is one finally to conclude? Do the decrements in creativity at the older age levels imply a corresponding decrement in ability to create? Certainly not! It seems probable that outstanding potential ability must be present in the individual who makes original and noteworthy contributions in any field. However, potential ability alone does not guarantee accomplishment. Indeed, it is doubtful that genius is solely the fruit of any single trait. It is the belief of the writer that the fruits of genius are, on the contrary, a function of numerous integers, including both the personal traits of the individual worker, environmental conditions that are not too hostile, and the fortunate combination of both personal traits and external conditions. If the foregoing hypotheses be valid ones, the following conclusion seems inescapable. At the older chronological age levels, some one or more of the numerous variables that are essential to the fruition of genius tend either to wane or to disappear. At the present time we are not able to identify all the factors that enable a particular individual to exhibit genius. Therefore, in instances where the fruits of genius are lacking we are not able to state precisely which of the needed ingredients are wanting. As regards the decrement that has been set forth herein, it can be said only that the decrement is probably due not to any single causal factor but rather to a complex group of undetermined causal factors. Any statement much more specific than the foregoing would obviously be highly speculative and of doubtful validity.

---

earlier age level than does output of lesser merit. (5) Since quality of output and quantity of output are imperfectly correlated, no very accurate comparison of the ages of greatest creative efficiency in the several fields of science can be made unless the contributions are first equated upon the basis of their quality.

Part XII

STABILITY OF PSYCHOLOGICAL GROWTH OVER TIME .

How WELL can one predict the future station of an individual by knowledge of his present status? Research has shown that some types of prediction are highly accurate when measurements of the relevant variables are available. Some attributes do appear to be highly consistent over time when individuals are not exposed to rapidly changing environmental conditions. Other characteristics, however, are not so stable. The first paper in this part, by Anderson, provides a view of changing adjustment over the school years, showing interesting trends in the development of different types of behavior. This report demonstrates the difficulties involved in making long-term predictions of the more complex personality tendencies. Changes in the person and in the general environment may make it possible for some poorly adjusted children to achieve a good, or even superior, adult adjustment, while some who are well-adjusted as children may not fare so well as adults. Although the correlations between adjustment scores over time are generally positive, they are modest in magnitude. There is nothing in these findings to discourage those who are convinced that the child's misfortunes can be ameliorated by appropriate social reforms. Jones's report suggests that the human organism may sometimes appear inconsistent over time simply because we are viewing too restricted a sample of the important variables. It may be necessary to draw on concepts and data from the other life sciences to demonstrate the essential continuity and consistency of the human personality.

The paper by Kelly illustrates that some attributes of the human personality are far more stable than others over the early decades of adult life. Attitudes seem the most susceptible to change. This may be, however, only a phenotypical change, as Kelly notes. The person may be genotypically consistent as he reorients his style of living to changing conditions. A possible rubric for these reorientations is presented in the provocative paper by Frenkel-Brunswik. That report shows that what is carried forward may be highly consistent and stable even though the phenotypical details appear jumbled and chaotic. It seems probable that further progress in research related to the relative consistency of the human personality during the life span will have to await additional conceptual advances in personality theorizing and the psychometric refinements that these advances might guide and support.

53

The Long-Term Prediction of Children's Adjustment*

John E. Anderson

This extensive investigation provides important normative data regarding psychological development during the school years, and also indicates how difficult it is to predict outcomes in terms of later adjustment. Although many studies have demonstrated a basic continuity in development, in the sense of long-term persistence of adjustment patterns, the present research illustrates the dangers of overgeneralizing this trend. The differential findings for boys and girls revealed in this investigation suggest that the criteria for "good adjustment" and the factors involved may well vary for the sexes. Those students interested in the psychology of adolescence will be interested in the fact that the present data do not support the frequently made claim that adolescence is a period particularly marked by internal conflict and turmoil.

There are two major purposes for which the psychologist measures children. The first is assessment, which seeks to determine the present status of the child with regard to any aspect of behavior. To do this the psychologist obtains "norms," that is, statistical averages on measurements made upon adequate numbers of children sampled with reference to sex and socio-economic status at various age levels. Assessment is a very important

* Adapted and abridged from *A Survey of Children's Adjustment Over Time, A Report to the People of Nobles County*. Minneapolis, Institute of Child Welfare and Development, University of Minnesota, 1959. (With permission of Dr. Anderson and the Institute of Child Welfare and Development, University of Minnesota.) This study was supported in part by Research Grant M-690 from the National Institute of Mental Health, U. S. Public Health Service. The substance of the present paper has also appeared in Ira Iscoe and Harold W. Stevenson (eds.), *Personality Development in Children* (pp. 28-72), University of Texas Press, 1960.

function because it facilitates the diagnosis of difficulties and thus makes possible good treatment and assistance in surmounting difficulties.

But because the child has a future, a second purpose emerges, that of prediction. What will he be like some years hence if present tendencies continue? If we know how to predict, we can lay out an educational program that will use a person's capacities, as in the case of gifted children; or we can give protection and care, as in the case of retarded children. When persons are selected for expensive education, for jobs with long continuity, or for training for complex tasks, the problem of prediction over time emerges.

THE SUBJECTS OF THE STUDY

Over 2400 children in Nobles County, Minnesota, participated in the study. In general, the analysis of the population reveals a farming county, with the businesses typically associated with farming. The population is overwhelmingly native white; the average educational level of the population is very close to the national average; and the distribution of intelligence is normal.

In 1950, children from 9 to 17 years of age were tested. From the results we obtained information on changes with age and differences with sex for all the areas of adjustment measured. Between 1950 and 1954 the measures given in 1950 were analyzed and revised. In 1954, all children from 9 to 17 years of age were examined with the new tests developed from the 1950 tests. This also gives us a check on age relations and sex differences. A further check arises out of a comparison of the 1950 and 1954 tests, inventories, and ratings on the same children who, when in grades 4 to 8, took the 1950 tests and who, four years later when in grades 8 to 12, took the 1954 tests.

The 14- to 17-year-olds who were tested in 1950 were followed up in early adult life. A sample of 75 boys was followed up in 1954 and 1955 when they were from 19 to 22 years of age with adjustment measures. A sample of 75 girls were similarly followed up in 1956 when they were 20-23.

A second type of follow-up was also employed. The cohort[1] of children who in the 6th grade took the 1950 tests at the age of 11, were given the 1954 tests at the age of 15 in the 10th grade and were followed up at the age of 18 after graduation from high school to determine how well they were getting along. Some information was obtained about every child in this age cohort, whether he had continued in school or not.

---

[1] The word "cohort" is used to designate this group. It is a word used by the U. S. Census to designate all the persons born within a limited period of time who move forward together thereafter through life and experience.

THE MEASURES EMPLOYED

In the following paragraphs a brief general description of the tests and measures used for Predictors in 1950 and in 1954 is given, together with a short description of the manner in which the outcomes in adjustment were measured.

1950 Predictors. In 1950 the children filled out a number of personality inventories and tests. Fourteen tests and schedules took six hours of the child's time. There were scales measuring the child's attitudes toward his family, his sense of responsibility, his work and attitudes toward work based on his experience in home duties and chores, his interests and play activities, and his favorable attitudes toward experience. There was also a scale made up of items that in previous studies had been answered differently by delinquent and by nondelinquent children. The items had to do with personal-social attitudes, and with the child's fears and worries. From school records, we obtained the Intelligence Quotients of the children. In addition to information about the education and occupation of each parent, we also had several measures of socio-economic or cultural status. On the basis of a check against the current adjustment of the children, five scores were selected from the inventories given the children to be combined into a Pupil Index, which is used as a general score to predict future adjustment.

Because we wished to see how well ratings made by teachers would predict future adjustment of children, three rating forms were filled out by the teachers in 1950. These ratings concerned the child's responsibility, his personality traits, and his adjustment in the classroom or home room. Scores on these were combined to form the 1950 Teacher Index.

1954 Predictors. From the children in 1954 we had scores on two measures developed out of the 1950 instruments by selecting the best questions from 678 items. One of these measured adjustment, and the other measured both adjustment and maturity. We also had a shortened test of the favorable attitudes of the child to his experience, a short test of his likes, a new measure of his family relations, and a revised form of the scale that measured his sense of responsibility. From a combination of the scores on these instruments we developed a new Pupil Index of adjustment.

In 1954 we had information similar to that obtained in 1950 on intelligence, socio-economic status, and home background, in a somewhat more extended form. We also had a new set of teachers ratings of children based on a revision of the 1950 measure. The score on the personality ratings was used as a Teacher Index.

Outcomes. In designing measures of outcomes in terms of later adjustment, the type of information that can be secured about a person's relation to the demands of life must be considered. There is first the record made by the person in school, community, and on the job, which is the most obvious sign of his success. Such information may be regarded as the objective aspect of the person's life and can be obtained from various records. Next, there are the person's own feelings about himself and his view of his relation to others. Does he feel happy and satisfied with his life? Does he think he gets along well? Such information may be regarded as more subjective evidence of the person's life adjustment and is obtained from the person himself. Last, there are the impressions made by the person upon other people. How is he seen by others who know him? Some who know him very well are likely to balance his traits and feelings against his objective record. Finally, an interview with the person himself secures information about his accomplishments and feelings. The psychologically trained interviewer may thus balance the objective and the subjective aspects of the process of adjustment. In our follow-up studies we attempted to secure information about the person for each aspect of his life, such as work, recreation, education, and family life, from each of the sources, that is, from the records, the person's own statement about himself, the impressions others had of him, and the judgment of skilled psychological interviewers with psychological training. In spite of the fact that some emphasize the objective record, while others emphasize the subjective aspects of life, and in spite of the difficulty of defining adjustment, we feel that we obtained measures which, taken alone or combined, justify the use of the word adjustment in a general over-all sense.

In the 1954-56 Follow-up, several methods were used to measure outcomes. The young adults now out of school were interviewed by expert interviewers for information about their adjustment in various life areas (such as vocation, family, leisure, social, etc.) and were rated within each area. The young persons who were interviewed also rated themselves within each of the areas covered by the interview and also filled out a list of questions about their morale and adjustment. An estimate of the opinion in which they were held by other persons was obtained by talking to key people in the community who had known them in various ways. Thus information about adjustment was obtained from four sources: (1) evaluation by a professional, (2) self-evaluation, (3) evaluation by others, or their community reputation, and (4) the results of the Morale Inventory. The scores on these measures were combined into an Adjustment Index.

In the 1950-54-57 Follow-ups of the age cohort, we have five measures of outcome in terms of adjustment: (1) reports on community reputation, (2) ratings on adjustment by others who knew the person, (3) school grade, (4) school ratings, and (5) records of participation in school and community activities. A factor analysis led us to combine the first four measures into an Adjustment score and to use the Participation score as an independent measure.

CHANGES IN BEHAVIOR WITH AGE

Of the many age curves available, we have selected a few to illustrate principles of normal child development. In the figures which follow, all scores have been reduced to the same statistical base by the use of standard deviation units. This permits cross comparison of measures since all are drawn to the same scale. The figures have been drawn to show the relation of the characteristic measured to age, which is represented from left to right. The center line shows the average for all ages and for both sexes combined. Generally, the more desirable "better" behavior is that above the center line or average.

The change with age in work habits and in attitudes toward the family is shown in Figure 1. The dotted line which represents work habits moves steadily upward at about the same rate throughout childhood and adolescence and reveals the growing capacity of the child to meet the demands for work. The solid line shows the changes in attitudes toward the family. Note the rapid improvement in attitudes during the period of childhood and the smaller amount of change during adolescence or above the age of thirteen. Over the whole age range, however, significant progress is made. We can think of the older child, on the average, as a better worker and as more favorably inclined toward his family. In this figure there is no strong

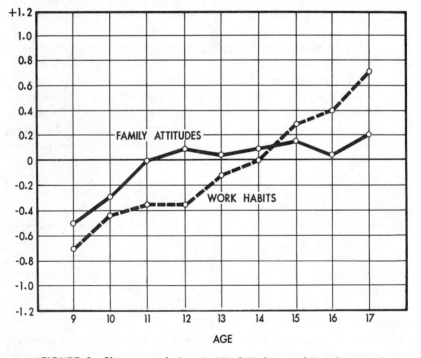

FIGURE 1. Changes with Age in Work Habits and Family Attitudes

evidence that adolescence is commonly a time of rebellion against parents, or of a deterioration in work habits.

In Figure 2 two types of age relations are shown, one of which increases, the other of which decreases with age. The solid line shows the change in the child's sense of responsibility. Note the marked improvement in the earlier years with the plateau from 11 to 13 years, which is followed by later improvement. This curve is based on the revised scale for responsibility given in 1954.

The dotted line shows how the range of children's interests and activities decreases with age. A similar result has been obtained by other investigators. It is usually interpreted as showing that as the person becomes older he becomes more deeply involved in a smaller number of activities than he was as a child. But an interesting relation to adjustment also appears in our data. If we study the children within any single age level, the better adjusted children seem to have more interests and activities. But if we study the relation of range of interest to adjustment over the entire age span, the opposite relation appears, namely, the better adjusted children move into deeper interests earlier. Good schools often make use of the principle revealed by this chart since they provide many activities and subjects for the earlier years with all children participating, while for older children they provide special opportunities for selected children.

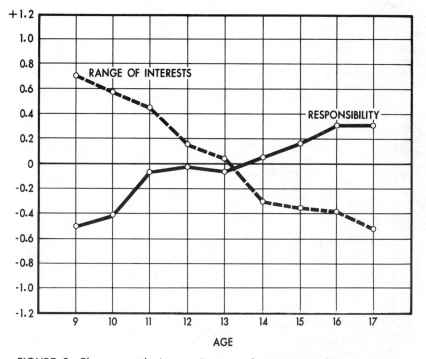

FIGURE 2. Changes with Age in Ranges of Interests and Responsibilities

In some areas and for some measures, however, we found almost no change with age. An example is shown in Figure 3, in which the solid line shows the relation of the child's worries and his concerns about himself to his age. The test is a collection of items having to do with fears, worries, and feelings of inadequacy, and are commonly called "psychoneurotic." Such items are used in many personality measures. When you compare this figure with the others note how little change there is with age. While it is true that the change is upward, the difference with age is so slight as not to be significant.

A somewhat similar finding appears in Figure 4, in which we have plotted for well-adjusted, average-adjusted, and poorly-adjusted children the relation between age and children's liking for and interest in experiences of many types and their favorable attitudes toward such experiences. Note that there is almost no relation to age within the three adjustment categories, which are, however, well separated. Children who are well adjusted seem to be interested in their experiences and to enjoy them to a high degree; while children of average adjustment are less so, and children with poor adjustment seem to be much more negative with respect to their various experiences. Or perhaps it is the other way around—children who enjoy tend to be well adjusted, while children who dislike tend not to be.

When this result was originally obtained, we were quite pleased with it.

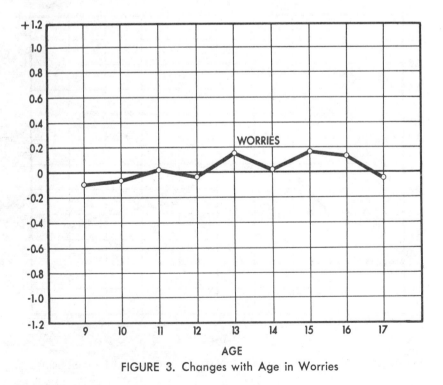

FIGURE 3. Changes with Age in Worries

But when we checked the manner in which these attitudes predicted future adjustment, we did not obtain as good results, as this particular test did not predict well over a long period of time. In much the same way our tests of children's likes and dislikes showed a relation to adjustment at the time they were taken but not to later adjustment. What may be happening is that these tests measure children's immediate emotional reactions to the stimulation in their environment rather than their long-lasting attitudes. Nevertheless, from the practical standpoint in guiding children there is some point in encouraging favorable attitudes toward experiences and a liking for persons and things.

In our data on the age relations of various test scores there is evidence of the principle that growth is not uniform in all areas. In some types of behavior there is a fairly uniform increase throughout the whole of development; in some the increases come mainly in childhood and before puberty, and in some mainly after puberty in the adolescent. In these respects mental growth is uneven, moving more rapidly at one time in one aspect and more rapidly at another time in another aspect. The same principle holds for physical growth. From the practical standpoint, it is important that teachers and parents be aware of these changes and adapt to them. One cannot always expect steady, smooth improvement as children grow older.

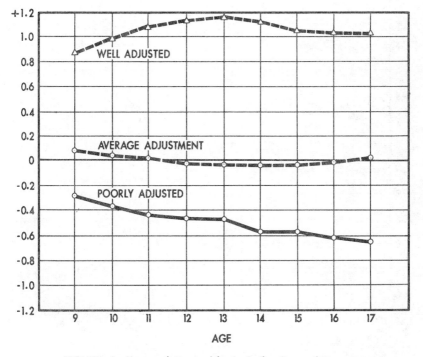

FIGURE 4. Age and Favorable Attitudes Toward Experiences

In the figures presented in this report which relate to measures obtained on pupils, sex differences are not shown. Most of our plots based on the 1950 and the 1954 measures showed insignificant differences between boys and girls of the same age. So much was this true that in the early years of this study, when we were concerned with the Predictors, we felt that we could ignore sex differences, even though they appear as a matter of routine in our statistical analysis. However, when we moved into the study of outcomes and the long-time view of adjustment sex differences became important. It was necessary for us to go back and reanalyze some of our earlier data, with the result that small overlap was found in the items which predicted adjustment for girls over a long time, when compared with those that predicted adjustment for boys over a long time. Here is an area that needs much further examination of item content in terms of its relevance both to sex and to later adjustment.

In one phase of our study, however, marked sex differences were shown in Predictors. This is in teachers ratings. At all ages teachers rate girls as better adjusted and superior to boys, as shown in Figure 5 in which the Teacher Index for boys and girls is plotted against age for the 1950 data. Note that at all ages girls receive much higher ratings than boys. This has also been found in other studies and may be related to the fact that girls are

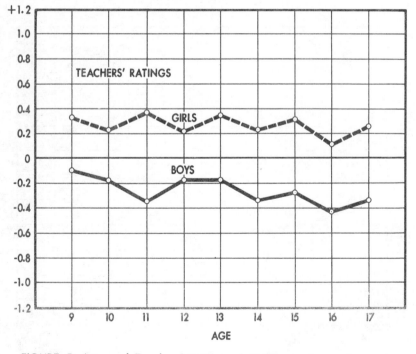

FIGURE 5. Age and Teachers' Ratings of Children's Personality and Adjustment

more responsive to the school environment than boys and hence are easier to control.

Finally, we may say a word about the significance of age-bound and age-free phenomena. In all areas in which we deal with the competence of the individual as measured by skill, knowledge, problem solving, interest, work habits, etc., there seem to be consistent changes with age; whereas in the measures which deal with feelings and emotions, little evidence of change with age appears. Attitude measures change moderately with age and occupy an intermediate position.

The unexpected discovery of measures in which there are no age changes has led to some speculation. It may well be that emotions and feelings change greatly in the early years and have stabilized by the entrance to school or shortly thereafter. Since our youngest children were nine years old, we dealt with children far along in their development. This suggests that studies of emotional behavior be made at earlier ages. It may well be that for feelings and emotions, the home influence is of primary importance in the early years, whereas for skills and knowledge, school experience is of primary importance.

THE PREDICTION OF LATER ADJUSTMENT

We now come to the results obtained with respect to the prediction of later adjustment in the various studies undertaken in Nobles County.

In interpreting the relations obtained in the various parts of the project, some thought must go to the size of the relation that can be expected when we move from a growing child at one age level to the same child some years later, or to him as a young adult. Because such a small number of persons have been studied longitudinally over many years, we do not know very much about these long-time relations in the personality and adjustment areas. Some children change a great deal as they grow older and as they meet new experiences, while others change much less. It may be thought that for physical measurements such as height, good predictions are possible. While tall children tend to become tall adults, nevertheless there are some changes and some reversals. For example, in studies made of various physical measures, a correlation of .88 was found for boys who were measured at 11 years and again at 18 years, and one of .73 for girls measured at 11 years and again at 18 years. For other physical measurements the correlation over a seven year span ranged from .73 to .88 for boys and from .71 to .79 for girls. For strength the correlation between measures at 11 and 18 years were .72 for boys and .70 for girls. These spans have been selected as near in length to those covered in the Nobles County study.

Studies have also been made of the relation between intelligence as measured by tests at one age and by tests at a later age on the same children. Over spans of six and seven years, from 11 to 18 years, these correlations range from .75 to .90 for boys and for girls. The fact that for physical measurements, for strength and for intelligence, all areas in which we have good methods of measurement, we fail to obtain perfect correlations should give us some pause. Because people of all ages change, we cannot expect perfect prediction in areas that are as difficult to measure as personality and adjustment, and children, because of their rapid growth, change more than adults. Moreover, at all ages change is greater the longer the period of time that elapses. With these cautions in mind, we may consider the specific results.

PREDICTORS IN 1950 vs. 1954-56 OUTCOMES

One way of viewing the relations between predictors and outcomes is in terms of the correlation coefficients which we mentioned earlier. In the first column of figures in Table 1 is presented the relation of various predictors to the Adjustment Index (or combined adjustment measure) based on the various aspects of the follow-up.

TABLE 1. 1950-Predictors vs. 1954-56 Follow-up

	Adjust- ment Index	Inter- view	Self- Rating	Morale	Reputa- tion
Boys (n=76)					
1950 IQ	.32**	.39**	.08	.18	.29**
Socio-Economic Status	.25*	.26*	.14	.11	.23*
Pupil Index	.29**	.35**	.02	.15	.29**
Teacher Index	.11	.18	−.18	.05	.41**
IQ+PI+TI	.26*	.30**			.34**
Girls (n=79)					
1950 IQ	.21	.06	.12	.22*	.20
Socio-Economic Status	.31**	.31**	.22*	.30**	.13
Pupil Index	.52**	.36**	.60**	.48**	.17
Teacher Index	.48**	.37**	.52**	.25*	.37**
IQ+PI+TI	.50**	.32**	.54**		

* 5% level, r=.22 up.   ** 1% level, r=.29 up.

Note that for the boys the best predictor of later adjustment is the Intelligence Quotient, next comes the Pupil Index, and next the socio-economic status of the family, while the Teacher Index is poorest and, in fact, is non-significant. For the girls the Pupil Index is the best predictor, the Teacher Index is next, the measure of socio-economic status is next, while the Intelligence Quotient is barely under the 5 per cent significance level. In considering these figures note that for the boys it is a five year follow-up and for the girls a six year follow-up, with the mean age of both sexes at the time of the original measurement in 1950 being 16, and at the time of final assessment of adjustment being 21 for the boys and 22 for the girls.

If we glance for a moment at the pattern of relations for the separate parts of the adjustment inventory, we find that the Predictors for the boys work fairly well in predicting the outcome of the interview, do not predict the boys' self-ratings, or their scores on the morale scale, but do predict their reputation in the community. For the girls the Predictors predict the results on interviews, on the self-ratings, and on the morale scale score, but do not predict community reputation.

In the last line of the table we present the relations obtained when the predictors, that is IQ, socio-economic status, the Pupil Index, and the Teacher Index are combined into a team. The result is a relation of .26 for the boys and .50 for the girls, showing that for this part of the study prediction of outcomes for girls is better than that for boys.

A striking feature of the results that deserves consideration is the quite different pattern of relations obtained for boys and for girls. In considering these sex differences, it should be noted that a man interviewed the boys and a woman interviewed the girls. This may explain the differences. However, the interviewers were both trained psychologists who spent much time in trying to equate their interviewing procedures and who used similar schedules in obtaining their data. There is a real possibility that the adjustment pattern of the girl in the period from 19 to 23 years may be different from that of the boy at the same ages. When we consider the results of the Teacher Index for both sexes, there is also a suggestion that teachers (who are women) are better able to predict the outcomes of their own sex than those of the opposite sex. This is suggested by the correlation of .11 for the boys and .48 for the girls, found in the table. But it is also of some interest that the teachers predicted the community reputation of the boys to the extent of .41, while they failed to predict the interview, the self-rating and the morale score; in other words, they predicted what other people would think of the boys more readily than what boys would think of themselves.

PREDICTIONS FROM 1950 TO 1957 FOR THE 1950-54-57 COHORT

For the children who were followed from 1950 through to 1957 from 11 to 18 years of age, the first column of figures in Table 2 presents the correlations between Intelligence, the Pupil Index, and the Teacher Index, and the combination of the three, and of the combined score of the various measures of adjustment used in 1957. For the boys, each of the measures predicts significantly the adjustment score. When the Intelligence Quotient is combined with the Pupil Index and the Teacher Index, the result gives the highest figure .62, Teacher Index comes next with .53, the Intelligence Quotient follows with .52, and the Pupil Index has the lowest figure, .29. For the girls the Teacher Index with .54 is best, the combined Intelligence Quotient, Pupil Index, and Teacher Index next with .48, the Intelligence Quotient next with .45, and the Pupil Index last with .04. This means that the Pupil Index does not predict for the girls at all.

When the results of this table are compared with those of Table 1, there are some agreements and disagreements. Although the coefficients are, in general, lower for the girls than for the boys, there is not such striking evidence of sex differences as appeared in Table 1. We must, however, remember that the measures of adjustment differ. Some attention should also go to the differences in the life situation that the boy and girl face in adjustment at the age of 18 years when the 1957 Follow-up was done, as compared with that faced at 21 or 22 years, when the 1955-56 Follow-up was done. The 18-year-old is just out of high school, the 21- or 22-year-old is in the early years of marriage. The measures used in 1957 are much more closely tied to the school situation, while those used in 1954-56 are more closely tied to life in the community. This holds, even for the information

TABLE 2. 1950-Predictors vs. 1957 Follow-up of 1950-54-57 Cohort.

	Combination Score	School Score	Informants' Score	Participation
Boys (n=74)				
1950 IQ	.52**	.58**	.37**	.56**
Pupil Index	.29**	.28*	.23*	.17
Teacher Index	.53**	.56**	.40**	.40**
IQ+PI+TI	.62**	.66**	.46**	.55**
Girls (n=65)				
1950 IQ	.45**	.56**	.27*	.43**
Pupil Index	.04	.12	.17	.26*
Teacher Index	.54**	.52**	.44**	.17
IQ+PI+TI	.48**	.60**	.24*	.38**

* 5% level, r=.22 up.   ** 1% level, r=.29 up.

given about the person by informants in 1957, in spite of the fact that school people were not used as informants in order to minimize halo effects.

In the 1957 Follow-up the Intelligence Quotient holds up for both sexes, whereas in 1955-56 it held up for the boys, not the girls, whereas in 1955-56 it held up for both sexes, but especially for the girls. In 1957 the Teacher Index holds up for both sexes, while in 1955-56 it held up for the girls and not for the boys. We feel, however, that the problem of sex differences in adjustment deserves very serious consideration. When this project began we checked against adjustment as of that moment in time and obtained slight differences between the sexes. When later the data on adjustment over longer periods of time began appearing, sex trends became evident.

CONCLUSION

In thinking about the results, we must bear in mind that there are two problems: one of which is the demonstration of relations in the scientific sense and the other of which is the practical problem of prediction for an individual child. Generally, our results show a series of relations between predictors and outcomes over a span of some years. In this sense, our results are positive. But the problem of predicting for an individual is complicated by the presence of change within the person over the years. Hence there are limits to our power to say that Johnny Jones who does poorly on our inventories and tests in 1950 will adjust poorly many years later.

When we look at the lives of some of the children, we see that there are factors operating over a long period of time which affect adjustment and which make too hasty generalizations undesirable. As a person grows, he changes. Likewise, the demands made upon him change. As he moves into new zones of experience, some of his earlier difficulties get straightened out. For example, a fair number of the adolescents who were having difficulties in their homes and difficulties in school when originally examined, seemed to be doing quite well in meeting their obligations six years later when they were accepting the responsibility of their own homes and of their vocations and were out on their own in the community. Giving them responsibility brought out qualities which had not appeared in earlier school and home experience. How much this results from growth and maturity and how much from actual change in the situation it is difficult to say.

Working with the full range of the population rather than with the selected groups that one sees in the behavior clinic or the social agency, we have some feeling that normal persons work out their own ways of adjusting over time and that they possess a kind of resiliency that carries them forward. If our experience in this study does not make us optimistic about the technical aspects of prediction over a long time, at least it makes us hopeful about the capacity of normal, as distinct from clinical, populations to meet problems.

SUMMARY

1. This project examined children and youth between the ages of 9 and 17 years and followed them up five to seven years later in order to study the extent to which later adjustment can be predicted from earlier tests and ratings of the child's personality.

2. Some measures show consistent changes with age, whereas others

show no relation to age. The items related to age are generally found in the cognitive, intellective, skill, and knowledge areas; whereas the items unrelated to age are generally found in the emotional and personality areas.

3. Predictors vary in their effectiveness in forecasting good and poor outcomes. In terms of the various measures of later adjustment, groups of well and poorly adjusted persons are separated on the predictors. But when we examine these relations for individuals, the possibilities of prediction are limited.

4. Throughout much of our results differences are found in the effectiveness with which various measures predict the later adjustment of boys and girls. Our study of later adjustment suggests that the demands for adjustment differ between the sexes and that in planning future studies and in laying out practical programs of care, some attention must go to the differences between the sexes.

5. Factors that present difficulty in interpreting our data arise out of the changes within the person with age and the changes in the life situation the person faces. Some children who were rated low early in life, moved up the scale and achieved satisfactory adjustment when they were on their own and freed from home and school.

54

Long-Term Consistency and Change in Human Behavior[*]

Harold E. Jones

The carefully planned and conscientiously executed longitudinal study is still exceedingly rare in developmental psychology. This type of research, in which the investigator must patiently wait for his subjects to become older between observational periods that may be separated by a decade or more, requires perseverance and a strong conviction that this is the only way that the needed data can be secured. Such studies are infrequently planned and initiated. Of those few that are begun, even fewer are seen to their natural conclusions. It is therefore a high tribute to Dr. Harold E. Jones that during his professional career

[*] Adapted and abridged from Harold E. Jones, "Consistency and Change in Early Maturity," *Vita humana*, 1958, Vol. 1, pp. 43-51. (With permission of the publisher.)

he was associated with three such longitudinal studies conducted at the University of California at Berkeley. Some of the interesting findings of one of these investigations, the Oakland Growth Study, are presented in the accompanying paper. The developmental implications of early and late maturing during the adolescent period and the diagnostic significance of early galvanic-skin-response functioning for predicting later personal-social variables are merely samples of the knowledge yielded by this impressive study. After reading this report one is strongly persuaded to share two of Dr. Jones's beliefs: (1) some questions about developmental processes can be answered only by longitudinal study, and (2) the discovery of invariances transcending a given social period and a particular biological instance will occur earlier and more surely through the cooperative efforts of all the life sciences.

Three longitudinal studies at the University of California have now been in process for more than 25 years. Two of these projects have accumulated research records from birth or early infancy, and one from the preadolescent period. Of about 500 cases in the original samples, nearly two-thirds are still in our active files, at average ages which range from 28 years in two of the groups to 36 years in the third. These investigations, all administered within the Institute of Child Welfare, have published three series of reports under the headings listed below.

BERKELEY GROWTH STUDY

The Berkeley Growth Study has maintained records on the physical, motor, and mental development of a group of Berkeley infants first observed in the neonatal period and at monthly intervals during infancy. Semi-annual or annual contacts were scheduled during childhood and adolescence, and at somewhat longer intervals in early childhood. Dr. Nancy Bayley was the principal staff member of this study for 27 years, beginning in 1928.

GUIDANCE STUDY

The Guidance Study, organized in 1929, was based on a selection of cases from an earlier survey which had sampled births in terms of every third child born in Berkeley during an 18 month period. Under the direction of Dr. Jean Macfarlane (Macfarlane, 1938; Macfarlane, Allen, & Honzik, 1954), developmental records have been carried from 21 months to maturity, with special emphasis upon personality and related developmental variables. The present average age of this group is 28 years.

OAKLAND GROWTH STUDY

Because of space limitations, the principal part of this report will be limited to the third study, initiated in 1932 by Dr. Herbert Stolz and the present writer (H. E. Jones, 1943). Physical growth, physical abilities, and physiological functions (under resting conditions and following exercise) were included in one division of the study, and social behavior (observed in "life situations"), patterns of emotional expression, interests, attitudes, and other personality characteristics in another division.

In defining the general aims of this program, the first point to be made is that we are seeking generalizations about normal populations. We have been concerned with research groups derived through a sampling process which is under our control, rather than under the control of the subjects themselves or of agencies which refer problem cases for treatment. It is for this reason that we consider our cases in the psychological sense as "subjects" rather than in the clinical sense as "patients."

A second principal feature of our program is that we are interested not merely in the characteristics of normal populations, cross-sectioned at a given time, but also in the growth and development of individuals. In the special case of physical growth it is now well understood that growth curves which are based on averages at successive ages give a very misleading picture of the nature and range of growth curves of individuals. In part, this is because the accelerating and decelerating phases of growth occur at different ages in early- and late-maturing individuals, and tend to be obscured or averaged out when means are computed at a given age and compared with means at the next age. Psychological traits, with their great range of individual growth patterns, may suffer even more from the effects of statistical groupings in the study of "average" growth characteristics.

Third, in studying the individual we are vitally concerned with interrelationships and have tried to widen our angle of view of the individual by utilizing data from many diverse sources. This implies the cooperation of physicians, psychologists, physiologists, teachers, and social investigators in the sociobiological study of the individual, but does not imply an exclusive commitment to any single body of doctrine.

Fourth, while emphasizing case studies and qualitative syntheses in "global" terms, we have at the same time found it very necessary to extend the use of quantitative methods. These approaches often involve different purposes and points of view, but are not necessarily incompatible. They imply, on the one hand, an interest in the control and scaling of observations and in the improvement of reliability; and on the other hand an acceptance of various types of records which can be organized in the study of the individual personality.

The Oakland Growth Study sample now under investigation at an average age of 36 consists of approximately 110 men and women who have been observed over a period of 25 years—quite intensively for seven years in the second decade, and now again in the fourth decade after somewhat more limited intermediate contacts.

A recent sample survivorship study has shown that on earlier social and psychological measures those who remain do not differ significantly from the total sample of 25 years ago. I am not certain that a similar statement can be made 25 years from now, but in the study of individual patterns of aging the nature of the surviving selection may be less important than preserving continuity for as many individuals as possible in a group drawn originally from a normal sample.

One of our chief areas of interest is of course in age comparisons, through the study of individual trends, pattern analyses, and various forms of correlation. On the physical side some age changes are already very marked. In visual measurements, for example, Morgan[1] has shown a loss of accommodative amplitude from an average of about 12 diopters at age 13 to 6.9 diopters at age 33. But whereas at the latter age some of our subjects were still at the accommodative level normal for age 25, others were above 40 and one as high as 48. Rapidly increasing heterogeneity is a characteristic of some functions in this age period.

In what follows I shall give a few examples of results which compare measures for the adolescent period with similar measures obtained in early adult life.

Records of physical changes are based both on anthropometric measurements and body photographs (Stolz & Stolz, 1951), recorded on 14 occasions during the adolescent period, and now repeated in the thirties. One approach to the study of consistency in physical pattern has been through estimates of the three Sheldon components of body build, at ages 17 and 33. These were rated independently, so that classification at one age could not influence the other.

For each sex, consistency correlations were between .70 and .80 for mesomorphy and for ectomorphy. But endomorphy, fairly consistent at earlier ages, showed no significant correlations between 17 and 33. The classifications made for a single age level of course pertain to phenotypes at a given time and not necessarily to somatotypes as now conceived by W. H. Sheldon. But the extremely varying manifestation of endomorphy, both in men and women, indicates the difficulty of predicting later body type from assessments made at any single age during adolescence.

Further negative evidence on this point can be found in a comparison of observers' "general impression" ratings at average ages of 13 and 32. Ratings of "fat-thin" and "attractive-unattractive physique" showed no significant degree of stability over this period (Tuddenham, 1959).

Although not predicted by the apparent body build in earlier or later adolescence, differential increases in fat may nevertheless have some constitutional significance, as is suggested by the fact that obesity in the

[1] M. W. Morgan, unpublished paper.

thirties appears to be positively related to physiological aging (accommodative loss).[2]

With regard to physiological functions, a remarkable series of records was obtained for this group by Dr. Nathan Shock during the second decade (Shock, 1942, 1946a, 1946b). Now in the fourth decade Dr. Hardin Jones has recorded approximately 100 different measures for the same individuals, including body composition, blood lipids, and relevant respiratory, circulatory, and metabolic measurements.

Our present task, not yet fulfilled, is to examine the interrelationship of these measures, their relation to earlier data obtained by Dr. Shock, and also their relation to psychological changes in terms of a series of hypotheses concerning mental and physical aging. Differences in personal regime undoubtedly account for some of the adult differences already reported. Thus both among men and women preliminary results indicate that habitual smokers in the group show a higher sedimentation rate in the red blood cells, an elevation of white cells, and disturbances in lipoprotein metabolism, as compared with non-smoking controls. This may be taken to imply differential trends toward vascular disease already apparent in early middle age.

Turning now to another field of measurement, in mental abilities (as measured by the Terman Group Test) I found test-retest correlations of .84 for the men and .90 for the women over a sixteen-year interval, age 17 to 33. This is the same order of correlation as is usually found over much shorter intervals of adolescence. It may be of interest that the greatly widened range of environmental differences to which these subjects have been exposed after graduating from high school, and the cumulative effects of these differences, have had a negligible effect upon consistency in individual test performance.

Ninety-five per cent of the cases showed some gain in total score, but the average amount of gain over this sixteen-year interval amounted to only about one year in mental age months. If we examine the subtests to determine the composition of this gain, we find that more than half was due to improved vocabulary. In line with predictions based on earlier studies with other samples, during this part of the age span little or no gain occurred in functions involving mental ingenuity and problem-solving.

Consistency in aspects of personality is much less easy to determine than in the areas already mentioned. This would be expected in view of the difficulty in achieving comparable measurements at the two ages. As an example of one approach to this problem, we have available a series of adequately reliable measures on what may be termed social acceptance in the adolescent period. The prediction can be made that popularity and social prestige, indicators of easy and effective social relationships, will be

---

[2] H. E. Jones, unpublished paper.

positively related to social measures in adult life. Such measures have been obtained, based both on informal social participation and on structured social activity as represented in membership or leadership in adult organizations.

Among women the prediction was verified for formal but not for informal activities. That is to say, girls who were social successes in high school were not more socially active adults except in clubs or in other structured organizations. Social activity of both kinds was found in a study by Ames (1957) to be related to their husbands' social status.

Among men, a reversed pattern of correlation can be shown. Those who were highly popular social figures in high school tend to excel in maturity in casual and informal activities somewhat like those of the adolescent peer culture. But they do not excel in formal or structured social activity, and their later degree of participation is unrelated to their education or to their parents' social level. These findings lead to the tentative suggestion that the determinants of sociality as we have conceived and measured it lie more in persisting personal traits in the case of men and more in social class and related institutional factors in the case of women.

Among the personal traits which have social prognostic value for men is the rate of maturation as determined from skeletal x-rays. We find that for males early maturing is correlated around .40 to .50 with later measures of social activity and also of occupational status.

The foregoing is just one illustration of the complex interrelationships in age trends and of the difficulty in separating social from biological ontology. Another example is in the relationship of maturity patterns to later personality measures, as recorded through the California Psychological Inventory. Dr. Mary Cover Jones has shown significant relationships, among males, between early maturing in adolescence and a number of personality traits indicative, among adults, of socialization, responsibility, and the ability to make a good impression on others (M. C. Jones, 1957).

The physical differences between early- and late-maturing boys, so marked in the middle period of adolescence, largely disappear in early maturity, but some of the psychological differences which have been generated in response to adolescent physical characteristics tend to persist through the following decades.

These differences have a complex origin. We may think of them as due to environmental impingement, but the environmental differential (consisting of differences in social acceptance, demands, and rewards) is in itself a response to a biological differential in growth characteristics.

Still another illustration of persisting patterns which have both physical and psychological aspects is in the relation of social and emotional adjustment, as classified from observational materials, to autonomic activity as registered in a series of experiments during adolescence. In these experiments we utilized the GSR (galvanic skin response) to ideational stimuli. As previously reported (H. E. Jones, 1950), at successive years in adolescence these measures were positively related to measures of adjustment. The low GSR average of those who were low in adjustment suggests a deficiency in their emotional organization. A patterning in which the response to stress stimuli is only slightly internalized may be relatively inadequate in coping with the social demands to which the maturing organism is exposed.

At the other end of the distribution, adolescents who were strongly responsive in GSR tended to have definitely favorable scores on measures of responsibility and of personal and social adjustment. This emotional organization is marked by reduced overt expressiveness and by autonomic records consistent with a rather marked degree of internalization. When we consider such results with regard to their long-term implications, the question can be raised as to whether these individuals may be paying too great a price for their social adjustment. Although they have achieved a pattern which is favorable for meeting the social demands placed upon the maturing adolescent, in accord with some aspects of mental health theory we might predict that they would be exposing themselves to greater psychosomatic hazards. We might also predict that those individuals who are classed as externalizers in emotional expression would tend, in adult life, to be relatively free from psychosomatic symptoms.

A clinical study of this group by Stewart (1962), utilizing data from both psychological and medical examinations, has not confirmed these predictions. On the contrary, the individuals with a sensitive and labile GSR and with relatively less externalization—an emotional pattern found in our group to be more favorable in adolescence—continued this favorable position in maturity, with a significantly lower registry both in psychosomatic and psychiatric indicators. Conversely, those classified in middle maturity as in a "psychiatric" group, with evidence of more ego damage, greater anxiety, and poorer social adjustment, were (as a group) marked in adolescence by a low average GSR.

In this connection it is interesting to note that in a study of personality traits based on ratings, Tuddenham (1959) found self-assertive, expansive, and expressive characteristics (and their opposites) to be among the most stable and consistent traits for both sexes. The highest degree of consistency for men was in the motivational trait "aggression," and for women in the general trait "social prestige."

When we consider specific organizational aspects of personality, as represented, for example, in our detailed clinical measures of drives, the problem of age trend consistency is a difficult one because we cannot for all variables use the same research approaches with adults as with subjects in schools. We do, however, note numerous instances of consistency between the adolescent measures based on clinical assessments and the adult measures based on the scales of the California Psychological Inventory.

To give a few illustrations: among both men and women social responsibility as measured in adult life is significantly related, at the .01 level or better, to staff ratings (made during adolescence) of the drive for achievement. Impulsivity—poor control of impulses—on the adult scales is significantly related to the drive for aggression and the drive for escape in adolescent ratings. A low degree of socialization on the adult scales is also related to the same drives, and among females to the drive for autonomy (McKee & Turner, 1961).

But in spite of these apparent consistencies it can be noted that our overall measures of adult adjustment show little relation to adolescent drives. Although strong drives, and incompatible drives, are often associated with adolescent maladjustment (Frenkel-Brunswik, 1942), they are not clearly predictive of adult maladjustment.

The problem here may lie partly in the fact that over a long period behavioral consistency, when it occurs, may be countered by changes in the environment. The adaptive significance of a given behavior pattern can thus be interpreted only with reference to changing demands in the life situation.

This is an illustration of the tendency of longitudinal studies to reach beyond a single discipline. Problems of aging in psychological functions require examination not merely through the concepts and methods of the psychologist, but also with reference to the physical person, and the social environment of which he is a part. Sociology as well as human biology must join in this task.

55

Consistency of the Adult Personality[*]

E. Lowell Kelly

How much change will typically occur in the adult personality from the middle twenties to the middle forties of the life span? Dr. Kelly is quick to note in the following report that the answer to this question will always depend in large measure on the rate of social change occurring in the resident culture. The subjects in Dr. Kelly's longitudinal study lived through the stresses of an economic depression and a

* Adapted and abridged from E. Lowell Kelly, "Consistency of the Adult Personality," *The American Psychologist*, 1955, Vol. 10, pp. 659-681. (With permission of the author and the American Psychological Association.)

world-wide war, so one can reasonably assume that they were subjected to shifting social forces well above average for at least the first two-thirds of the twentieth century. Furthermore, the years from 1934 to 1954 saw the harnessing of atomic energy and the electronic implementation of the digital computer—both powerful instruments for social evolution. Despite such strong pressures for personality change, the adults in this research sample were highly selective in modifying their behavior patterns over a twenty-year interval. The changes that did take place in attitudes and values were modest in magnitude. The findings of this study are completely consistent with the conception that the adult personality is basically self-consistent and highly integrated in its adaptations to changing conditions in both its internal and its external environments.

Whether one is an extreme hereditarian, an environmentalist, a constitutionalist, or an orthodox psychoanalyst, he is not likely to anticipate major changes in personality after the first few years of life. Not only do psychologists of different theoretical persuasions tend to agree on this issue, it happens to be one on which the layman and the scientist share a common opinion. Perhaps because of the need to believe in consistency of one's self from moment to moment and from year to year, we tend to infer an unwarranted degree of consistency in others. Yet belief in the possibility of inducing change is implicit in the professional activities of all persons engaged in advertising, public relations, and psychotherapy. While theory underlying these activities is often not explicitly expressed, anyone who attempts to change the attitudes, values, habits, and defense mechanisms of adults may be assumed to hold a position somewhat as follows: "Yes, it is true that the human personality is framed early in life and by late adolescence is quite resistant to change. However, by the skillful application of special techniques it is possible, though admittedly difficult, to effect significant changes in behavior."

The present study reflects an interest on my part in the problem of personality consistency in adulthood and represents an effort to measure such consistency and change over a 20-year period.

SUBJECTS OF THE STUDY

In 1934, I began a program of research designed to answer several questions regarding engagement and marriage. During the years 1935-1938, I enlisted the cooperation of 300 engaged couples. Each of these 600 individuals was assessed with an elaborate battery of techniques including anthropometric measures, blood groupings, a battery of psychological tests, and a 36-variable personality rating scale. In addition, a personally administered questionnaire was used to obtain essential biographical data.

Each of the participating subjects agreed to advise me of the data of his marriage if the engagement eventuated in a marriage, or of the broken engagement if it did not. The original research design called for an annual follow-up questionnaire from each husband and wife for seven years, and retesting at the end of the seven-year period.

Although the follow-up program was initiated on the anniversary of the first marriage and followed until 1941, it was interrupted by the general wartime dislocation of all civilian activities and was not resumed until 1953-54.

As might be expected, the subjects were widely dispersed throughout the United States, and several of them live in foreign countries. It was therefore necessary to plan to collect all data in this follow-up phase of the project by mail. Because we planned to asked for approximately six hours of further participation on the part of each subject, it was decided to mail forms to the subjects in two sets. The first of these, mailed in August, 1954, included the five tests being readministered which provide the data for this report. These materials were sent to 521 subjects. Completed retest forms were returned by 446 of the 521 subjects, or 86%. This return is sufficiently large to encourage us to believe that findings based on an analysis of the data will be reasonably representative of the entire sample.

At the time of original testing, all subjects were members of couples with definite anticipations of marriage. The resulting sample is obviously a select one, in that it is composed of persons who responded positively to an invitation to participate in a long-term scientific study of marriage and were willing to contribute initially six to eight hours of their time as well as enter into an agreement to report annually for seven years on the outcome of their marriage. It is not surprising, therefore, that the resulting sample turned out to be superior to the general population in education and intelligence. Only 1% of the men never went to high school and 75% had at least one year of college; nearly 20% had some sort of graduate or professional training. The females were somewhat less selected on the basis of education; nevertheless, approximately two-thirds of them had attended college for varying lengths of time. The IQ equivalent of the mean score on the Otis Self-Administering Test of Mental Ability was 115 for the males and 112 for the females at the time of the original testing. The mean age of the men at the time of the original testing was 26.7 and that of the women 24.7, with nearly 9 out of 10 of the subjects being between the ages of 21 and 30. With respect to religious affiliation, 82% of the males and 89% of the females indicated membership in some church. Approximately 11% of the sample indicated a preference for the Catholic and 8% for the Jewish faith. In order to facilitate the data analyses, I have excluded all cases for whom there was missing any original or retest score on any one of the 103 scores derived from the five tests. The resulting N's are 176 males and 192 females. As might be expected, a comparison of the retested and nonretested samples revealed differences on many of the original measures. While many of these differences are statistically significant and are of interest in themselves as characterizing groups that did and did not choose to participate in the final phase of the project, they are relatively small in magnitude and do not show a systematic pattern of differences for the two sexes. It appeared defensible, therefore, to carry out our analyses of stability and change on those personality variables using the records of the 176 males and the 192 females for whom complete test-retest data were available. Admittedly, our findings will be generalizable only to a population of adults sufficiently cooperative to provide comparable data.

To the degree that congruent associative mating occurred, that is, to the degree that like tend to marry like, any sex differences in the original test scores will tend to be smaller than might be found for samples of men and women not married to each other. Also, since a man and woman married to each other may be assumed to have shared a large proportion of the life experiences intervening between the two testings, it is possible that sex differences in changes in test scores are smaller than would be found for samples of men and women not married to each other.

THE TEST BATTERY

The assessment battery utilized at both testings included the following standardized instruments: the Allport-Vernon Scale of Values, the Bernreuter Personality Inventory, Strong's Vocational Interest Inventory, two of Remmers' Generalized Attitude Scales, one designed to measure Attitude toward any Institution, the other, Attitude toward any Activity, and a 36-trait graphic personality rating scale which involved ratings for each subject; by self and by partner. These five instruments provided us with scores on 103 variables, 38 of which will be discussed here.

The first set of figures in Table 1 shows the direction and reliability of mean changes after nearly 20 years in scores on the six scales of the Allport-Vernon Scale of Values. This scale is designed to measure the relative prominence of six basic interests or motives in personality: theoretical, economic, aesthetic, social, political, and religious. The direction of these changes has been indicated only if the difference was at least 2.5 times its standard error.

As will be noted, only 5 of the possible 12 changes are significant. By all odds the largest, and in fact the most significant, of all changes to be reported is that for Religious values. Both the men and women score about 5 points higher in their middle years than as young men and women. The change amounts to about one-half sigma of the original score distribution. Since scores derived from the Scale of Values are relative, this shift toward higher Religious values was necessarily accompanied by a downward shift on one or more of the other value scales. For the women, most of this down-

TABLE 1. Means at Time I and Mean Changes After 20 Years.

	Variable	Low 5 10 15 20 25 30	Raw Scores 35 40 45 50	High 55	C.R.
ALLPORT = VERNON SCALE OF VALUES	Theoretical		◀M F		3.7
	Economic	M F			
	Aesthetic	◀M ◀F			4.7 6.9
	Social	M F			
	Political	M F			
	Religious	M▶ F▶			7.5 9.5

0 5 10 15 20 25 30 35 40 45 50 55 60

	Attitude Toward	Con 3	Neutral 6 7 8 9	Pro 10	C.R.
REMMERS' GENERALIZED ATTITUDE SCALES	Marriage			M▶ F ▶	3.8 2.5
	Church			M▬▶ F▬▶	5.8 5.3
	Rearing Children		M▶ F▶		(2.0) 3.6
	Housekeeping		◀M ◀F		2.8 4.9
	Entertaining		M F		
	Gardening		M▶ F		3.0

2 3 6 7 8 9 10 11

	Variable		Percentile Score 20 30 40 50 60 70		C.R.
OTHER PERSONALITY VARIABLES	Bernreuter F1C (Self-Confidence)	Self-Confident	M Self-Conscious ◀▬F		3.58
	Bernreuter F2S (Sociability)	Sociable	M Nonsocial F		
	Strong MF	Feminine	F▶ M▶ Masculine		6.8 4.7
	Strong IM	Low	M High F		
	Strong OL	Low	M High F		

10 20 30 40 50 60 70 80

ward shift occurred in Aesthetic values; for the men, it was about equally divided between Aesthetic and Theoretical values. Quite frankly, I do not know how to interpret this small but significant shift toward higher Religious values. Two alternate interpretations seem equally possible. The shift may merely reflect a cultural change which has taken place in the last 20 years. Perhaps people are generally more religious today than they were during the last part of the great depression. Equally possible and probably a more acceptable interpretation is that in our present-day society people tend to become more religious as they grow older.

One additional aspect of Allport-Vernon findings deserves your attention, again, because it is also characteristic of those which follow. While small sex differences are reflected in the original means of the men and women on certain of the scales, there is but little evidence of sex differences either in the direction or in the magnitude of the changes in scores. In fact, for the 38 variables to be discussed, the direction of the change was the same for men and women on 32 of the 38.

The next set of figures in Table 1 presents the story for 6 attitudes measured. The original scores of both the men and women were favorable toward most of these attitude objects and practices, and the changes tended to be toward the favorable end after 20 years. The one exception is "Housekeeping." Here we find men and women, initially mildly favorable in their attitude toward this practice, both shifting toward the unfavorable end of the continuum. Whether this reflects a cultural change or the effect of 20 years of married life, we are not able to say with any certainty!

The third set of findings in Table 1 presents the data for five other personality variables. The first two were derived from the Bernreuter Personality Inventory. While there was no essential sex difference in the original score for either of these scales, the women show a small but statistically significant shift toward greater self-confidence at Time II.

The other three variables shown on this figure are the three nonvocational interest scales derived from Strong's blank. The first is Masculinity-Femininity. As was to be expected, the original means for the men and women were widely separated on this scale. Not expected on the basis of the evidence reported by Strong and by Terman and Miles was the small but significant shift in the masculine direction for both men and women. In fact, all the evidence reported by these authors would have led to just the opposite prediction. The data of Terman and Miles, all based on cross-sectional comparisons of groups at different ages and with varying amounts of schooling, show that the peak of masculinity in males is reached in the high school period, and that of the females during the college period, after which time both show a trend toward more feminine scores, the trend being more pronounced for men than for women.

Again, the interpretation of this finding is hazardous. It may be that our sample studied longitudinally points to meaningful trends which were masked by cultural differences obtaining in the development periods of the several age groups sampled by Terman and Miles and by Strong. It may also be true that the last 20 years have been accompanied by cultural changes tending to result in more masculine scores for anyone who has lived his first 20 years of adulthood during this period. To the extent that during this period the home has become more mechanized through modern appliances, and on the assumption that women find that they like the mechanical aspects of home appliances, it is understandable that women should become somewhat more masculine in their likes and dislikes. An equally plausible explanation for the shift in masculinity scores in the men for the same period is not readily available. Perhaps our entire culture is becoming more mechanized all the time, and while both men and women react favorably to these changes, men respond a little more than women. This seemingly simple explanation may well be the correct one. As an hypothesis, it fits both our own findings and those reported by Terman and Miles, providing one is willing to assume that this mechanization of the culture is a process which has been going on gradually for several decades.

INTRA-INDIVIDUAL CONSISTENCY OF PERSONALITY VARIABLES OVER LONG TIME INTERVALS

We now turn to an analysis of changes in scores on these same 38 personality variables for individuals. The absence of mean changes could have resulted from either of two states of affairs: for any measure, individuals could have shown little or no change, or, alternately, changes in the score of individuals could have cancelled each other.

In this analysis of change, we shall first compare the retest correlations over the 20-year time span with retest correlations on the same measures for relatively short time intervals.

Figure 1 presents the findings for certain specific tests, both for the 20-year span and for short time intervals which may have been in some cases as long as one year. In all but one instance (strong OL reliability after 20 years) we have combined the data for our men and women subjects, since the values of these correlations for the men and women were generally within sampling errors of each other. The reader may wish to examine the situation for sex differences on specific tests as shown in Table 1, but the general consistency of these traits is demonstrated in summary fashion in Figure 1.

As a further index of long-term consistency of domains of personality variables it seemed appropriate to utilize the coefficient of determination, i.e., the squared values of the median coefficients after correction for attenuation. The resulting values are shown in Figure 2. In view of the considerable evidence for the general constancy of IQ, during the develop-

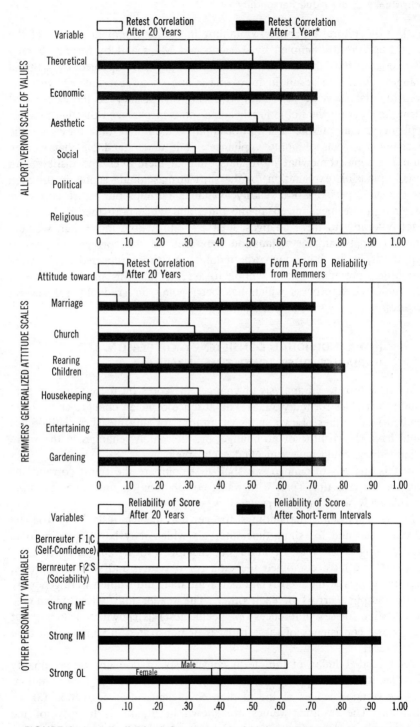

FIGURE 1. Intra-individual Consistency of Values, Attitudes, and Personality Variables over Short and Long Intervals of Time.

mental period, and as reported by Owens (1953) and by Bayley and Oden (1955) for adult groups, it is likely that intelligence would have appeared at the top of this chart, had retest scores been available. Next in order among the personality variables we find values and vocational interests. Apparently these scores are indicative of relatively deeply in-grained motivational patterns that do not change greatly during the period of middle age. Less stable over this long period of time, but as much so as scores based on many test items, are self-ratings on specific personality variables. The relative inconstancy of attitudes during the period of adult-hood came as something of a surprise. While it is possible that this rela-tively low index of constancy is a function of the particular and limited set of attitudes sampled or of the attitude scales utilized, I am inclined to believe that further research will indicate attitudes to be generally less stable than any other group of personality variables. The relative change-ability of attitudes is probably a function of their specificity and the fact that alternative attitude objects can easily be substituted one for the other in the service of maintaining an individual's system of values. Thus a person with high social values as measured by the Allport-Vernon scale might shift his attitudes toward and even his allegiance from one to another of several alternative institutions or organizations, each dedicated to the service of humanity.

Although we have thus far been emphasizing the relative consistencies of personality variables, note in Figure 2 the relatively wide open spaces to the right of each bar. In effect, these are the relative proportions of variance which may be expected to change during the period of life with which we are here concerned. I venture to say that the potentiality, and even the prob-ability, of this amount of change during adulthood is considerably greater

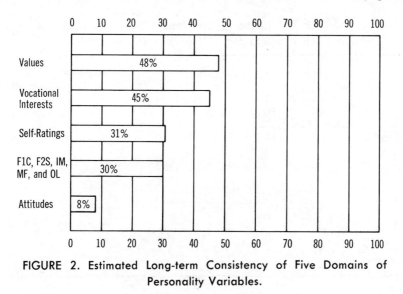

FIGURE 2. Estimated Long-term Consistency of Five Domains of Personality Variables.

than would be assumed from any of the current theories of personality. Similarly I suspect that these changes are larger than would be expected by most laymen.

I find it intriguing to speculate as to whether or not these changes in personality variables in adulthood are sufficiently systematic to be predictable for individuals. Conceivably they result from the interaction of so many varied forces in the lives of individuals that prediction of specific changes for individuals is not possible. To the degree that psychology can develop techniques for predicting the magnitude and direction of change in individual personalities, we should become more effective in the long-term prediction of vocational, marital, and emotional adjustment.

THE RELATION OF CHANGE TO ORIGINAL STATUS

The first question to which we addressed ourselves was: How are these change scores related to original status scores? For each of the measures, correlations were computed between Time I scores and the corresponding change scores. Appropriate analysis must, of course, take into account the phenomenon of statistical regression. Subjects who, because of errors of measurement, originally receive scores higher than their true scores tend on a retest to receive lower scores; similarly, subjects scoring lower than their true scores are likely to score higher on a retest. For each measure, therefore, it was necessary to estimate, on the basis of the known reliability of the score, the probable value of the status-change correlation that would result from statistical regression alone.

The resulting distributions of obtained and estimated status-change correlations for the male subjects are shown in Table 2. These estimates as-

TABLE 2. Distribution of Correlations Between Original
and Change Scores for 37 Variables (N = 176 males)

Minus	Obtained Values	Expected on Basis of Statistical Regression Assuming No Change in Variance of Scores
80-90	/	
70-79	//	
60-69	//// //	
50-59	//// //// //	///
40-49	//// ////	//// ///
30-39	//// /	//// ////
20-29		//// //// //// /
10-19		/
Median	−.54	−.30

sume no change in variance from Time I to Time II scores. As will be noted, the obtained values tend to be considerably larger than those expected on the basis of statistical regression, the medians being —.54 and —.30, respectively. For *each* of the variables, the obtained value was larger than the expected. It appears, therefore, that we are confronted with a general phenomenon which might be called "maturational regression," a tendency for the retest scores of extreme scoring subjects to regress toward the mean of the group.

This phenomenon of maturational regresssion appears to account for as much as half the variance of change for some variables and for as little as 5% of the change variance in other variables.

It is my best guess that these regressive changes of extreme scorers are a function of a variety of social forces operative on the individual. If a person finds himself too deviant from his group on a variable that is subject to change, he apparently finds it easier to shift toward the norm than away from it. Obviously, this statement does not hold for all individuals; strong ego involvement in one's position on the continuum might well lead to "no change" or even to a change in the direction of still greater deviance.

SUMMARY AND CONCLUSIONS

This completes the report of our explorations of personality consistency and change in adulthood. The sample of variables studied was necessarily limited to the techniques available 20 years ago, but the results for the several variables are so consistent that we may accept them as pointing to generalizations that are likely to be confirmed in later research.

With respect to personality consistency, our results can and probably will be used to support very different theoretical positions. Absolute changes in personality scores tended to be small but similar in direction and magnitude for men and women. We found evidence for considerable consistency of several variables, in spite of fallible tools and a time span of nearly 20 years. But we also found evidence for considerable change in all variables measured. These changes were shown to be relatively specific rather than reflecting any over-all tendency to change. While measurable changes occurred on most variables, it appears that correlates of these changes are many and elusive, and hence changes in scores are likely to be difficult to predict for individuals. Finally, we found that the measurable changes showed little or no relation to known forces assumed to be dominant in an individual's immediate social environment; this finding points to the probable difficulty of obtaining firm knowledge concerning the mechanisms of effecting change.

The intensive study of any aspect of growth and development cannot but serve to increase one's respect for the integrative capacities of the human organism. Beginning with the complex structures and functions provided by its unique genetic constitution, each organism, while maintaining its organic integrity and a considerable residue of its original nature, moves through its maturational cycle adapting to and permitting itself to be modified by selected aspects of its immediate environment. These adaptive changes, occurring most rapidly in the years of infancy and childhood, are so appropriately timed that they do not threaten the organism either physiologically or psychologically. Our findings indicate that significant changes in the human personality may continue to occur during the years of adulthood. Such changes, while neither so large nor sudden as to threaten the continuity of the self percept or impair one's day-to-day interpersonal relations, are potentially of sufficient magnitude to offer a basis of fact for those who dare to hope for continued psychological growth during the adult years.

56

Adjustments and Reorientation in the Course of the Life Span[*]

Else Frenkel-Brunswik

When the life span is studied in its entirety it is possible to discern certain significant shifts in motivations and needs and in frustrations and problems. New strivings may result or new orientations may evolve. The present research is notable not only for the broad developmental period studied, but also for its method—the study of biographies and autobiographies. The paper presents an insightful interpretation of what happens psychologically as age increases, as the life span is negotiated. It is suggested that some five major phases can be identified, and that a psychological curve of life paralleling the biological curve, but somewhat retarded as compared with the biological curve, can be discerned. However, it should be kept in mind that these studies were conducted in Austria, and thus the ages at which these investigators put the divisions of the life span are based on data from a culture which in many respects (e.g., age of retirement) differs from what is

* Adapted and abridged from Else Frenkel, "Studies in Biographical Psychology," *Character and Personality*, 1936, Vol. 5, pp. 1-34. (With permission of the publisher, Duke University Press.)

found in the United States. Nonetheless, the present paper is rich in hypotheses relating to the psychological trends and problems during maturity and old age.

Within the past few years there has been developed in Vienna, under the leadership of Professor Charlotte Buhler, a type of empirical research to determine what general principles hold for the human life-span.[1] The aim of the investigation here reported was to describe the psychological development of human beings and to attempt to determine the regularity with which the various phases of life succeed one another in this development.

In order to study our problem it was necessary to become closely acquainted with a great number of life-stories and to compare these lives with one another. In the past few years in Vienna around four hundred biographies of individuals from various nations, social classes, and vocations have been critically studied. Wherever it was possible, letters, diaries, and other documents were also utilized for the purpose of control and also to secure additional information. Furthermore, in order to secure data on living people, of whom no biographies were obtainable, a method of direct questioning, similar to that used in clinical interviews, was introduced. With the help of this method, it became possible to obtain data also on the lives of the working classes, since interviewers went to old peoples' homes, to the poor, and out into the country.

Through these methods, the research material was able to cover the lives of engineers and physicians, politicians and actors, businessmen and industrial magnates, artists and scientists, lawyers and journalists, priests and nuns, officers and soldiers, pilots and mountain climbers, teachers, workers, waiters, farmers, clerks, servants, janitors, etc. The material includes both men and women, and also persons without vocation or employment.

The life-stories were individually analyzed and compared with one another with the help of statistics. In this way an *inventory* was obtained of everything that happened to the individuals concerned, or was experienced inwardly, or accomplished in the various periods of life.

There are three groups of data which were collected in as exact and detailed a manner as possible.

1. The first type is the *external events* of life, everything that a person does, his behavior. Among them, the different fields of activity in which the individual

---

[1] The results to be described in this article are reported and discussed in detail in Charlotte Buhler's comprehensive book, *Der menschliche Lebenslauf als psychologisches Problem* (Leipzig, 1933), and in the more special investigations made before and after the book was published, under the direction of Charlotte Buhler and Else Frenkel at the Psychological Institute of the University of Vienna. The present article was translated from the German by Annette Herzman.

takes an active part are called the *dimensions* of behavior. For instance, practical dimensions would be such as one's study, profession or creations; social dimensions: one's family, friends, or help for others, but also playing cards, etc.; furthermore, sport, travel, hobbies, religious activity, etc., constitute other dimensions. It was possible through our material to set up an approximately complete list of the important activities. We distinguished, in all, ninety-seven such dimensions. We were particularly interested in dividing these activities according to age.

2. The second group of data collected was the *internal reactions* to these events. It is important to know what the individual thinks about his own life. We tried to gather material therefore from letters, diaries, and autobiographical notes, or through direct questioning about these "subjective data." For instance, do the individuals write or tell us that their fate is a happy or an unhappy one (that they have already found the right vocation, their goal in life), or do they mention what they believe to be their wishes and their duties, etc.? All such utterances were also systematically collected and their distribution over the whole course of life was studied.

3. Besides observing the objective behavior and the subjective experiences, we can also study, thirdly, the relation of the course of life to its objective results; namely, the *accomplishments and productions* of man.[2] We gathered material therefore on creative work, its effect on others, and its success, in the individual cases.

THE GENERAL BIOLOGICAL CURVE OF LIFE

In presenting the results obtained, we will begin with a description of biological development because a consideration of these facts was instrumental in giving rise to this study, and because these facts through their exactness and clarity are particularly well suited to serve as a basis for the psychological material.

Many biologists divide the life span into three *growth* phases, the first (lasting until perhaps 25) of progressive growth, the second (lasting until almost 45) of stability of growth, and a third phase of decline or regressive growth. Other biologists divide biological development on the basis of reproductive capacity, designating also three periods marked by the acquisition, the possession, and the loss of reproductive ability.

Let us combine both of these points of view in our consideration of the biological development. The period of progressive growth is divided into two parts through the acquisition of the ability to reproduce around the fifteenth year of life. In the same way the period of restriction or regressive growth is cut in two, through the loss of the reproductive ability at fifty-five (which is the average for men and women). Thus *five biological periods* are formed, all of them marked off by a principal change in direction, such

[2] The analysis of the material on creativity has been omitted from this abbreviated paper.

as an important acquisition or loss. The third and middle period, lasting roughly from twenty-five to forty-five, could be represented schematically by a horizontal line, surrounded symmetrically by the periods of ascent (first and second phase) and descent (fourth and fifth phase) of the "biological curve" of life.

THE BEHAVIOR PATTERN DURING THE DIFFERENT PHASES OF LIFE

Biologically, it is possible to speak of the process of life in terms of rise and decline, ascent and descent. Can we also observe in the distribution of the psychological data a regularity, certain characteristics common to all? Can we find a parallel here to the biological structure? The results show that the changes in the abundance of activity (dimensions) and its distribution are phenomena corresponding to growth and decay. In order to show this it was necessary to use a method of presentation of the material which would allow us to survey the whole behavior of the individual during the course of his life. Since a great deal happened in a person's life we had to summarize in a graphic presentation all the facts about one person, as it is seen in the following sketch, Figure 1.

The diagram shows the life of the mother of Goethe. Up to a certain

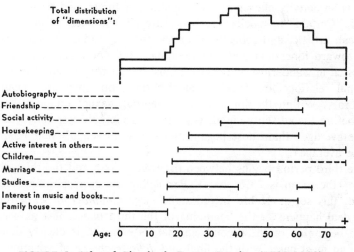

FIGURE 1. Life of Elizabeth Textor-Goethe (1731-1808)

point we can observe that new spheres and new fields of activity are added. In all fields of life, expansion, ascent and increase, can be noticed. The period in the middle of life, called the culmination period, includes the largest and most complete number of dimensions. In this period we find stability also, since losses are replaced by new acquisitions. Beginning with a certain age (around the fiftieth year), certain activities are given up and external losses, such as a case of death, are not compensated for any more. One can observe a decline, a form of retirement from life. If we at first only take those data which relate to the behavior of the individual and present them graphically, we will find here also the ascent and descent in the curve, as it is clearly shown in the upper part of Figure 1. It should be emphasized that other lives, even those of simple working men, would show a very similar general distribution.

Furthermore, we are again able to differentiate *five periods*. The first period is the one in which the child lives at home, and in which his life centers around a narrow group of interests, school and family.

A second period begins between the sixteenth and twentieth year (the average for the cases studied is around seventeen years). The turning point (most of the time quite sharply defined) is characterized by the entrance into a self-chosen and independent activity (in 78.5 per cent of our 140 cases) and by the first independently acquired personal relations (32 per cent). Frequently the turning point can be placed at the time when the youth leaves the home of his family. We find in this period a building up of new activities, an "expansion" of the dimensions. But all the activities in this period (which lasts until the twenty-eighth year of age on the average) are of *preparatory character*. In only 21.5 per cent of the 140 cases is an activity chosen at the beginning of the second period definitive for life. Certain "unspecific" activities are chosen, such as literary, philosophical, artistic, and religious interests, further study, and also the tendency toward loneliness and daydreaming. The motor activities which are expressed in wanderlust and sport are also very strongly represented. Many personal relations are acquired at this time, but they are usually only temporary. Within the limits of our material, sexual relations begun by men before their twenty-eighth year last considerably less time (9.8 years on the average) than those begun after the twenty-eighth year (29.8 years on the average).

The third period begins between the twenty-sixth and the thirtieth years of life (the mean is 28.6 years). Paralleling the corresponding biological period, this sector of life includes the *largest number of dimensions*. A great deal happens at the beginning of the third phase, just as was noted at the beginning of the second, so that its entrance is clearly defined. It begins in most cases with the final and *definite choice* of vocation (in 69 per cent of our 140 cases studied) and, furthermore, with the choice of a definite personal tie together with the establishment of a home (52.5 per cent). This phase (which lasts until approximately fifty years of age) is the *culmination period* of life. It is representative as the most fruitful period in professional and creative work. The social activities reach their high point also, since this is the time of the most numerous personal relations, and the greatest amount of social intercourse. Motor dimensions are represented in the form of travel for professional and personal reasons.

The average beginning of the fourth phase is 48.5 years. The criteria which were decisive in characterizing the first three phases were those which applied to the building up of life, whereas a decrease in the amount of activities and the appearance of "negative dimensions" (such as sickness, loss of associates, etc.) ushers in the fourth and fifth phases, and are the characteristic signs which announce the turning point toward the new period. Cases of death (of relatives and friends) which had less effect in the earlier periods because they were compensated through new acquisitions, acquire now a great deal of importance for the individual (in 34.5 per cent of our cases). Individuals are also strongly affected by other losses of personal or economic nature, or damage to their bodily strength (in 41.1 per cent of our cases such losses were decisive). Furthermore, at this time a change in the type of work is noted, especially in those cases where vital activities (sport, physical labor, etc.) are concerned. The actor becomes a director, the athlete becomes a trainer, the sailor a writer, and so on. In 21.5 per cent of the 140 cases studied we find a complete retirement from work around fifty years of age.

The transition to the fourth phase is marked by psychological crises, just as in the biological development crises also appear at this time (menopause). This will be clearly shown in the treatment of the data on subjective experience. But we can also see here the tendency to change, discontent, and complete negation, as shown objectively through certain events. We find, for instance, the most frequent occurrence of trips taken for rest or recuperation between the ages of forty-five and forty-eight, with a decrease lasting until the age of sixty. This can be looked upon as renewal of unrest, showing itself in an intensified wanderlust, and a frequent change of residence. In the short time between the forty-fifth and forty-eighth years there is further a transitory inclination toward daydreaming and loneliness to be found. Unspecific activities, such as literary interests, a tendency toward retrospection, which otherwise first appear at sixty years, are also to be noticed here as a transitory condition. A high point in the destruction of one's own creative work (according to S. Fischer in about 40 per cent of her fifty cases of creative individuals) is to be found at the beginning of this period. These objective data show us the crisis which takes place at this time, and which we will mention again later. This phase brings with it also a decrease in the number of dimensions, a restriction. However, the factual dimensions, such as the specific activity in one's profession or creative work, are still comparatively numerous. In particular, everything which is related to independent creative work very often first reaches its culmination point in this period. The social activities are shifted somewhat into a new field, since, although the general sociability lessens, the more philanthropic activities begin first at this time. In respect to the motor dimensions, a decrease in participation in sport and an increase in country life are noted.

The decline which we noted in the fourth phase, mostly in connection with the vital processes, becomes much more evident with the beginning of the fifth phase. The average age at which this phase starts is 63.8 years, based again upon the 140 cases studied by Frenkel and Kral. The fifth phase is often introduced by complete retirement from one's profession and from any sort of work in 64.5 per cent of our cases. Sickness constitutes the turning point in 44.5 per cent of the cases, death among close associates in 33 per cent of the cases. Very obvious in this phase is the great decrease in the factual and social dimensions, whereas hobbies, such as collecting stamps, love of animals and flowers, etc., increase in frequency. Retrospection, the writing of memoirs, and the death cult are all very characteristic of this period. Furthermore, the occupation with politics, studying a subject out of interest, and other unspecific activities, as well as the making of various plans, can again be observed. This seems to show a certain similarity to the second phase, a repetition of certain youthful traits. The social dimensions which one finds in this period are various types of active helpfulness, advice, consolation, etc. A strong preference for country life can also be observed. Analogous to the first phase, which seems to stand on the periphery of life but not yet taking place in it, the fifth phase finds the individual more or less "after" life, in that he has loosened the ties, has given up the plan of life which he had built up for himself.

Our results have shown that just as in the biological structure, the psychological structure of the course of life can be divided into phases which are clearly marked off from one another through certain turning points in life. These turning points usher in, in very short time, parallel and permanent changes in many fields of life, all of which allow us to imply that a basic transposition takes place. During the course of each phase one finds in general only a further development of that which was laid out at the beginning of the given phase.

THE BEHAVIORAL PATTERN AS RELATED TO THE BIOLOGICAL CURVE

If we notice the ages at which the respective phases begin, we will see that the phases of the biographical curve *are retarded in comparison to the biological.* We are therefore forced to suppose that some factor is present in the psychological development which influences this deviation and which is independent of the biological function in the narrowest sense of the term. The ability to give the most capable performance in athletics culminates at the same time as the corresponding biological high point, whereas in the manual worker the culmination point is retarded ten years, and in the mental worker still another ten years. We find, therefore, that there are a number of functions—we may call them the vital functions—which are correlated with the biological curve, and, furthermore, a number of psychological functions, such as knowledge, experience, training, which, because they help toward a rise in capability, counteract the biological decline.

The psychological functions are subject to another set of laws, and are therefore responsible for the deviation of the biographical curve from the biological. These factors will be analyzed still better when we bring the subjective data, the inner experiences, under consideration.

As has been done through the study of biographies and through interviews, we are able to differentiate two groups of experiences. The one is closely dependent upon and runs parallel to biological expansion and restriction. We find in the inner life of man, at first, the wish to learn to know a great deal, to try out a number of things, to expand; then, finally, mostly after much struggling, he finds it necessary to give up a great deal. His inner experiences are then of the sort which correspond to his weakened bodily condition, and which point to resignation and restriction.

We also find, however, a second group of experiences, which appear for the first time during adolescence. The young person asks himself for the first time, although in a quite theoretical form, for what purpose he should live at all, or what his design or calling or "objective" in life should be. Actually every person does not only wish to live and exist, but he wishes to have some reason for existing. This reason can be another person, a thing (e.g., money or position), or an idea (e.g., religion or science).

Since the question is first raised during adolescence, we can call this the first step out into life, because in connection with this question the young person begins making decisions about his vocation and his future life. Still, that does not mean that the "purpose" in life is conclusively found at this time. The young person has been given a preliminary answer to his question and he has for the first time made an independent decision about what he wishes to do or study, but we know that he will remain irresolute for a long time, and will make a definite decision as to his vocation and his partner in life only after a lapse of time. And, even if he has made his decisions sooner, these decisions are very often confirmed and accepted through inward conviction much later. Soon the individual is not satisfied simply to know definitely how and for what purpose he is living. He desires now to turn out to "be" someone. This question as to what the results of one's life will be, now becomes very important.

When we now ask how these two groups of experience, the one corresponding to the vital functions, which we call "needs," and the other made up of our aims in life and their realization, are distributed over life, we observe an interesting alternation. In the first half of life, our subjective experience is determined primarily by our needs, in the sense of the expansion of the individual. On the contrary, in the second half of life, the individual regards as more important certain tasks which he has set for himself, or which have been set for him by society, or which have come from some code of values such as religion or science.

In general, we can say that around forty-five years of age a change takes place in that the "needs," which come from the biological nature of man, become less important, and the duties directed by our ideals and our conscience, or laid down by authority and practical demands, play a more dominant role. In connection with this we find at the same time a change in the objects which are of relevancy in life. At first the individual himself plays the important role in his wishes and duties. Later, other more objective interests are placed in the foreground.

Deviations from this general law of development were found only in those subjects who were diagnosed by physicians as *neurotics*. In these cases the wishes strongly outweighed the duties, even in the third and fourth phase. Another type of neurotic personality, the person with a compulsion neurosis, seems to be made up exclusively of duties. The character of these duties, however, corresponds to that of a much earlier phase of development of the individual, since they are of a very general nature out of which no concrete tasks are developed. Another outstanding characteristic of these neurotic personalities is that the subject-matter about which they talk falls into other spheres than does that of the normal person. For instance, some compulsion neurotics, whose emotional life is disturbed, place sexuality in the sphere of duties and not in the field of wishes, as a healthy person does. In this way the sphere of duty has taken over all those individual and social demands which otherwise are guaranteed their realization through the normal biological needs.

We may call the transference from the field of need to the field of duties, which is dictated by society and inner developmental factors, *transference in dominance*. In such changes in dominance a developmental step in early childhood is now repeated, but on a higher level. When we say a child is ripe for school we mean he is capable of giving up the arbitrariness which a four-year-old still evinces, and he is willing to subordinate himself to the group and to accept and perform his tasks.

Still another developmental process which we have observed in the course of life is to be found in early childhood. During the school age the child acquires a maturity in the performance of his tasks; he can now utilize material in a "specific" way. For instance, when the small child is given some blocks, he hits them against his bed. He first begins to build things with these blocks in a later stage of development. We then can say that he uses the material in an adequate way or in the manner for which it was "specified."

This development toward *specification* in the use of materials repeats itself again in the course of life. Namely, in the second phase we find a functional period of activity in mental as well as physical work. This activity is without a goal, being done only for the pleasure in doing it. It is only later that the transition is made to organized, practical, and planned work. Suitable interests are rarely found by the individual during the second phase of his life.

Summarizing, we can say that in the transference of dominance (i.e., a change in stress from needs to duties) and in the gradual specification of interests, the finding of one's calling or objective in life, we have found two important developmental laws.

If, looking back, we consider the inner experiences of man and their arrangement in the course of life, we find that according to our material they are also divided into five phases.

The young person just passed through childhood—the first phase of life —makes the first plans about his life and his first decisions in adolescence or shortly afterwards. Here begins the second phase of experience. It is characterized first through the fact that the young person wishes to acquire contact with reality. He experiments with people and professions. An "expansion" of his person takes place. Also characteristic for him is the temporary nature of his attitudes as to what his life calling will be.

A study, carried out by E. Dichter with fifty-three subjects, dealing with self-criticism of the individual's abilities, which we should like to mention here, showed that the experimental subjects in the second phase of life still were not clear about a great many of their abilities. The average was fourteen abilities in the second phase, about which the individual was subjectively undecided, and in the fourth phase only five abilities. These facts show the tendency toward expansion, and also the uncertainty of this second phase. One does not know which traits can be, and which should be, trained. Chiefly those traits pertaining to character, the body, or social abilities, occupy the mind of the youth of this period.

First, at the end of the second phase (around the twenty-eighth year) the utterances show that the individuals have become clear as to their definite attitude toward life. As has been seen, during the third phase, vitality is still at its high point, while direction and specification are now also present, so that very often this time is found to be the culmination period for subjective experiences.

The transition to the fourth phase very often is introduced by a crisis, since at this point the unfolding of the individual powers has come to a standstill, and much has to be given up which depends upon physical aptitude or was connected with the biological needs. Contrary to the descent of the biological curve and the experiences which are connected with that, we find here an ascending scale by virtue of new interest in the results and productivity of life. If one asks a person in this phase to relate his abilities, he names very few of them and mostly those which are connected with his profession.

Finally, in the fifth phase we find more strongly mentioned age, premonitions of death, complaints of loneliness, and often those persons in this phase are occupied with religious questions. This last period contains experiences of a retrospective nature and considerations about the future, that is, about oncoming death and one's past life. The balance-sheet of life is drawn up, so to speak. This is expressed often through the writing of memoirs and autobiographies. This last phase of life has a certain parallelism queerly enough with the age of adolescence; on the one hand, the adolescent leaves the life of childhood; on the other, he must make the transposition to his future life. The diary is used as a means of helping him clear up his problems in this period of transition.

However, not all types of experience are found to be present in every individual. For instance, in a few cases, only the vital functions have had an influence upon their lives, and therefore only one group of experiences is found. We are thinking in particular of Casanova, or of many women whose life has a short blooming period, and then is completely extinguished. Lives in which sexual experiences play the chief role and in which very little compensatory effects through more sublimated interests are present, and also no productions of any sort, work or children, show an unquestionable subjective decline in the second half of their lives. Physical efficiency is taken as the only measure for the building up or breaking down of their lives. Casanova said in his thirty-eighth year, "The beginning of my end began on this day." Still in most lives, the reduction in vitality is not experienced as a negative affair, since a change from a more physical to a more mental life takes place and the second half of life takes on a more positive form. The ability to transpose oneself, to take on another attitude toward life is a character trait which is almost a necessity for success in life. For the psychology of development it is important that the individual both in personal and in practical fields not only satisfies his needs but that he also at some time accepts certainties and tasks, and works for them.

Part XIII

SOME FACTORS IN PERSONAL AND EMOTIONAL ADJUSTMENT

A SATISFACTORY state of personal-emotional adjustment may be said to exist when an individual's physical and psychological needs can be satisfied by socially acceptable patterns of behavior. Some degree of maladjustment exists whenever the individual's needs are inadequately met, or whenever his behavior deviates significantly from the prevailing social norms. Thus it can be seen that personal-emotional adjustment depends on a combination of individual and social factors.

Healy and Bronner's findings on juvenile delinquency illustrate the essentially *social* nature of this form of maladjustment. The delinquent boy is meeting his needs by indulging in forbidden forms of behavior. As these investigators show, there are many different variables related to an individual's selection of prohibited goals to satisfy his psychological needs. There is no simple explanation for juvenile delinquency, because it is merely one of many possible forms of adjustment—classified as maladjustment on the basis of the prevailing social-cultural codes. Since delinquent acts are responses of a kind that reduce (at least temporarily) the individual's needs (and so in a sense "adjust"), such behavior patterns tend to recur again and again. They may be inhibited by punishment, but are likely to reappear unless some other form of behavior, equally satisfying, becomes available to the offender. In some cases the individual's emotional and intellectual resources are not sufficient to support a change in his manner of seeking adjustment. Guidance and psychotherapy are often employed in an attempt to overcome these readjustment difficulties. The paper by Levitt deals with the effectiveness of psychotherapy and assembles data from a variety of studies suggesting that children who have received therapy improve to no greater degree than do members of a control group, which received no therapy. While such findings may seem discouraging they do not prove that psychotherapy is futile. Rather they stress the need for more systematic and refined studies of the whole question. Such "negative" findings may pave the way for further advances.

The paper by Kutner and his associates deals with adjustment in old age. It stresses the point that good adjustment and relatively high morale in the later years of life is largely a function of the degree to which a person is able to maintain a significant role and the degree to which he has a broad array of "internal resources" (interests, appreciations, hobbies, friendships, etc.) to draw upon as a source of satisfaction. Evidence supporting this last point is derived from the fact that certain factors were related to old age differentially for different economic groups. Those of higher income level and educational level seemed less dependent upon external social supports, such as social contacts with their children, and were less likely to be overwhelmed by illness. But perhaps most important, the findings warn against assuming that any given pattern of living or behavior in old age represents the "good" and appropriate life for everybody, a warning that carries equal force whatever the age group considered. The final paper in this part, by Neugarten, presents evidence that adjustment to old age is simply a continuation of prior methods of adjusting to life's problems. Different personalities find satisfaction and happiness in different, distinctive ways, whatever their ages.

57

Delinquency as a Mode of Adjustment[*]

William Healy and Augusta F. Bronner

Why do youngsters get into trouble, become delinquent? In some cases the answer is clear; their backgrounds are such that it would be amazing, indeed, if delinquency were escaped. But why—and this is the perplexing question—does one child in a family become delinquent while his brothers and sisters do not? Or why do children from apparently highly favorable environments get into difficulty with the law? In the investigation described in this paper, a very careful study was undertaken of the families and of the behavior, developmental history, and emotional and personality make-up of a group of delinquents. The findings were compared with those for a "control" group—carefully studied nondelinquent siblings of the delinquents, who were as far as possible of the same sex and always nearest in age.

The results point to frustration, conflict, and emotional insecurity as the roots of delinquency, with the delinquency turning out to be

* Adapted and abridged from Chapters 5, 6, 8, and 9 of William Healy and Augusta F. Bronner, *New Light on Delinquency and Its Treatment*, 1936, New Haven. (With permission of Dr. Augusta Bronner Healy and the publisher, Yale University Press.)

a psychologically meaningful mode of adjustment, when in the individual case the whole picture is unveiled. This study, one of the most significant investigations of delinquency made so far, thus emphasizes personal psychological factors in the causation of delinquency.

Why in the same family is one child delinquent and another not delinquent? The dissimilar behavior of different children in the same family forces this commonsense query which we have many times put to ourselves. And so why not study the nondelinquent for the purpose of discovering how he escaped being an offender! Now for the first time this research has offered opportunity for delving far enough into the lives of young people so that scientifically ordered comparisons may be made and deductions drawn therefrom. The goal is better understandings of the origins of delinquent tendencies. Whether such understandings will further efficacious preventive treatment is for the future to determine.

POPULATION STUDIED

In summary, we first studied 133 families from which came 152 delinquents. Of the latter 105 had a nondelinquent sibling, in 8 instances a twin, who could be fairly compared. Ninety-two of the delinquents as compared to 81 of the controls were boys. About half were older than their controls and half younger.

In our attempt to study a nondelinquent sibling in every family a good many others were investigated but for various reasons were ruled out. They were not utilized as controls because they could not be compared with the delinquents in all aspects of the research. Not all those selected for controls were available for complete study, some were not fully willing to co-operate, and even after studying them we eliminated several pairs on account of too great disparity in their ages. Then a few, as we came to know them better, proved to have been recently delinquent themselves.

CONTRASTS BETWEEN DELINQUENTS AND NONDELINQUENTS

Detailed inquiry into developmental history and present status brought forth some remarkable contrasts. Information was obtained that can be considered fairly satisfactory and reliable. The enumerated deviations from the ordinarily considered healthy norms for antenatal conditions, birth, and for postnatal development when totaled as separate items show a great difference—170 developmental deviations for the delinquents as compared to 74 for the controls.

It can be seen at once in the top portion of Table 1 that many more

TABLE 1. Contrasts between 105 Delinquents and Their Nondelinquent
Controls from the Same Families

Characteristic	Number of Cases	
	Delinquents	Controls
Developmental History (100)		
Much worried pregnancy	10	3
Very sickly pregnancy	13	6
Premature birth	2	1
Very difficult delivery	12	5
Much underweight in early childhood	12	5
Very early bottle fed	10	8
Very late breast fed	7	4
Very difficult weaning	2	0
Cross fussy babyhood	14	5
Difficult sphincter training	31	13
Many illnesses or severe illness	28	8
Diseases of central nervous system	5	3
Otitis media	3	6
Severe head injury	5	0
Encephalitis	2	1
History of distinctly good health	44	75
Physical Condition at Time of Study		
Weight deviates (more than 10% under or 20% over)	11	10
Very premature sexual development	4	0
Retarded sexual development	5	1
Defective vision—more than slight	17	6
Slight strabismus	3	2
Marked strabismus	0	1
Otitis media	1	5
Moderately defective hearing	1	3
Markedly enlarged or diseased tonsils	20	12
Nasal obstruction	6	2
At least some badly carious teeth	27	19
Endocrine disorder	4	0
Phimosis	4	1
Very poor posture	3	0
Miscellaneous liabilities	7	3

of the delinquents than of the controls had been subject to interference
with healthy normal development. The relationship however between health
conditions and behavior tendencies is not easy to determine. One might
speculate, for example, about the significance of severe illness—as consequent to the disease was there organically caused irritability or restlessness,
or was the child spoiled or overprotected on account of illness, or did he

through illness acquire specially demanding and selfish attitudes? It will also be noted (in the lower portion of Table 1) that currently the non-delinquents reveal a generally better picture as regards health and physical defects.

The importance of abnormal personality, neurosis or early psychosis in relation to delinquency is not to be denied. The great point to be brought

TABLE 2. Contrasts Between 105 Delinquents and 105 Nondelinquent Controls from the Same Families with Respect to Personality and Emotional Characteristics, Mental Capacity and School Performance, and Sociality and Interests

Characteristic	Delinquents	Controls
Personality and Emotional Characteristics and Deviations		
Diagnosed Personality Deviation (neurosis, mild or early psychosis, etc.)	25	2
Individuals showing such nervous habits as food or sleep idiosyncrasies, nail biting, etc.	44	24
Enuresis after 8 years	22	4
Hyperactivity, overrestlessness, etc.	46	0
Control notably quiet, placid, subdued, etc.	..	41
Distinctly submissive tendencies	2	15
Marked feelings of inferiority	38	4
Mental Capacity and School Performance		
IQ 90 or above	69	78
Poor scholarship record	34	18
Strong dislike for school in general	40	4
Repeated, excessive truancy	60	0
Sociality and Interests		
Great urge for crowd membership	31	11
Prior club connections	47	28
Marked interest or activity in sports	73	37
Excessive movie attendance	33	10

out here is the tremendous contrast between the delinquents and controls. As shown in Table 2 the former include 25 instances where a definite diagnosis was made in terms of one of the above categories and among the controls there were only 2 diagnosable by the same criteria. Added to this, such a probable diagnosis was offered for 5 delinquents and no control. Thus the role that personality deviations play in the genesis of delinquent behavior stands out most strongly. When a young individual, abnormal according to any of the above classifications and hence lacking in normal inhibitory powers, encounters the stressful conditions and thwartings that most of our delinquents had to meet through family life, companionship, or school failure and develops from any source ideas of delinquency, evidently delinquent conduct is almost bound to ensue.

Peculiar physical habits were regarded by us as possibly being indicators of internal tensions, whether genetically related to delinquency or the result of it. Counting as separate items food idiosyncracies, sleep disturbances, much nail biting, thumb sucking, and other nervous mannerisms, exhibited at the period when we were making our study, we found the total twice as large for the delinquents as for the controls. However, none of these habits had a frequency rating high enough to be in the least diagnostic for the group and more than one of the items was sometimes scored for the same individual. But the fact that 44 delinquents as against 24 controls exhibited such peculiar habits indicates a tendency for the former to show more signs of nervous tension than the nondelinquent siblings. The same may be said of speech defects—7 delinquents exhibiting this difficulty and only one of the controls. Enuresis, reported by many observers as a habit frequently found among delinquents, shows in great contrast for the two groups.

It appears that the great amount of carefully conducted and intensive psychological testing done in this study resulted, quite unexpectedly, in establishing no signs of differentiation between the mental equipment of the delinquents and the controls in our series. But differences in school behavior and performance were in evidence. We found that almost all the nonattendance of the controls was occasioned by illness or changing residence. But about 60 per cent of the delinquents were out-and-out truants, with evasions of attendance running as high as one year in one case. The scholarship record was of course affected by this but not to the extent that might be surmised. Definitely poor scholarship was registered for only 34 per cent of the delinquents, as against 18 per cent of the controls. So by no means are all delinquents found to be recorded as poor students.

About 40 per cent of the delinquents expressed marked dislike for school in general and 13 per cent marked dislike for some teacher. A mere 4 per cent of the controls evinced any such dislikes. We also discovered that 14 per cent of the delinquents considered themselves unpopular or teased at school—and none of the controls. We are not passing judgment on the causes for any of this but the facts are most striking. While these school attitudes do not seem to show overwhelmingly in scholarship records and less in school achievement tests and in age-grade placement, they must be closely correlated with the great extent of truancy in which the delinquents indulged.

Turning now to comparison of clearly revealed personality characteristics, we begin with dynamic qualities. In an earlier phase of the study it was found that a third of 153 delinquents showed *hyperactivity* or allied manifestations. How do the 105 pairs compare in this respect? We note, in the first place, that 68 of the delinquents were recorded as definitely more active, restless, energetic, or as showing more uninhibited behavior than the controls. Many controls, 41 to be exact, were characterized as being subdued, retiring, quiet, inactive, placid, nonaggressive, not caring for adventure or excitement.

But the difference in the two groups comes out strongest when we consider the exhibition of dynamic characteristics to an extent above the normal. Hyperactivity, overrestlessness, extreme physical aggressiveness, great impulsiveness, or some allied manifestation was recorded for 46 delinquents. *Not one control was so characterized.*

In such display of the emotions as frequently varying moods, often displayed sulkiness, excessive bad temper, etc., divergencies between the two groups are shown but without any large differences if we allow for the peculiar behavior manifestations of the abnormal personalities. The large majority of both delinquents and controls were not recognized as habitually presenting anything but normal emotional poise. So for the most part the delinquents' dissatisfactions, which we know many of them felt, were not manifested by observed outward expressions of emotional disturbance. The frequently hidden emotional difficulties revealed only through psychiatric exploration is a subject dealt with later in the paper. We have enumerated those who overtly exhibited or expressed marked feelings of inferiority. This was found in 38 delinquents and in only 4 controls. We speak of this particularly because in some instances it has come out plainly that the individual engaged in delinquency partly to prove to himself that he could be as daring, courageous, and adequate as others whom he admired. The term "masculine protest" could well be applied to such instances.

The social characteristics of delinquents always appear important to consider because so little delinquency is engaged in without companionship or gang connections. Some 31 of the delinquents were classed as gregarious, but at the other extreme, some 16 had few or no friends, tending markedly to be solitary in both their general interests and in their delinquencies.

Now only 11 of the controls were clearly gregarious, that is, participated in crowd companionship, although the majority had a smaller number of friends. That some 23 controls definitely avoided companionship is not to be wondered at; in their social situation it was part of their defense against getting into trouble. We know that even a greater number were satisfied with quiet home pursuits that would lead them to have very little companionship.

Concerning membership in *clubs,* whether those connected with a settlement house, church, or other supervised organizations such as the scouts, we found that almost twice as many of the delinquents as of the controls had such connections at some time prior to our acquaintance with them. It is not surprising that more of the delinquents had registered club connections, in view of the fact that they on the whole were more outgoing and active. But then we discovered that in many instances clubs had not represented a long-continued interest; attendance was irregular or the activities soon ceased to be attractive.

Participation in active *sports* is often thought of as a preventive of delinquency but our studies show that more of the delinquents than of the controls engaged in swimming and skating or played football, baseball, etc. Indeed 15 of the delinquents were notably good at athletics, almost twice as many as of the controls.

Interest in the *movies* was exhibited much more by the delinquents than the controls. We found that 33 of the former attended excessively, several times a week or whenever they could, sometimes staying to see a performance over and over again—while anything like the same excess of attendance was noted for only 10 controls. Regular attendance once or twice a week was the habit of 88 of the delinquents as against 42 controls. This marked difference between the groups must have its implications though it would require careful study in each and every case to ascertain them: did the movies merely offer a temporary escape from unpleasant situations and unhappiness, or to what extent did the pictures have a specifically pernicious influence? Only a few of the delinquents stated that they had derived ideas from gangster or other crime pictures upon which they definitely patterned their own delinquencies.

Without pretending that we are giving or that we know the whole story, we have positive evidence from accounts given by delinquents themselves that in a full third there had been much loading of the thought-life with ideas of delinquency—and often this had been going on for years. This particular educative process generally began with information received from youthful comrades—two were taught by older criminals. Some said they had learned about delinquency from a mixture of sources, for example, the communications of delinquent companions, perhaps even observations of them in delinquency, plus ideas derived from detective or crime stories and the movies. Some had given really planful thought to possible delinquent exploits—a couple of youthful burglars told of making studies and sketches of the places they entered. Reinforcements of ideas already entertained frequently assailed the individual through further contact with delinquent companions—some gave accounts of much talk about delinquency in detention homes or other institutions. Or further observations of opportunities or of actual delinquencies perpetrated, or further reading or movies gave new suggestions.

DELINQUENTS FROM APPARENTLY FAVORABLE ENVIRONMENTS

One may reasonably ask why *any delinquents* came from family situations which were graded as apparently favorable. Now 19 of these 105 delinquents compared with controls were living under conditions which according to these categories were evaluated as not inimical. Why, then, should these 19 have become delinquent? Was the family life in any way responsible?

In reviewing the characteristics of these delinquents it was remarkable to find that no less than 14 showed marked personality or psycho-physical deviations which certainly are to be regarded as playing a part in determining their behavior. The delinquency of the other 5 represented either strong reactions to family restrictions or to loneliness and boredom, with one case of obsessive urge for reckless automobile driving.

But can we feel altogether satisfied with deriving an explanation of delinquency from physical or personality deviations even when neuroticism is involved? The well-known unstable behavior manifestation of neurotics or of abnormal personalities can hardly be regarded as sole causes of delinquency because we know that some individuals with the same personality disorders are not delinquent. Nor is every restricted, bored, or lonely boy an offender against the law.

As a matter of fact deeper study revealed in nearly every one of these 19 delinquents living under relatively favorable conditions the existence of emotional attitudes that were important factors in the development of the delinquent tendencies. We would have expected that the neurotics had intense affective disturbances but it was not immediately discernible that an endocrine case, coming from a family of the highest integrity, had engaged in various serious offenses because he, in the confusion of adolescence, had a profound feeling of not being understood and of being isolated in the family circle—delinquency appearing to offer compensatory satisfactions. Nor was it at first plain that a boy's desires for the thrills of exciting adventure, expressed in his excursions into shoplifting though he came from a fairly well-to-do family, were reactions to his feelings of loneliness and boredom, and that these in turn were based on his sense of being utterly rejected by his parents and siblings who were all so immersed in their own concerns that they left him almost entirely alone.

TYPES OF EMOTIONAL DISTURBANCES

Some notion of the types of emotional disturbances characterizing the delinquents and a summary of the disturbances of the 96 delinquents suffering from them—not just those from favorable environments—may be appropriate. The types and the enumeration of such emotional disturbances may be presented as follows, but it must be remembered that the same individual may show more than one type or discomfort:

1. Feeling keenly either *rejected, deprived, insecure, not understood* in affectional relationships, unloved, or that love has been withdrawn—46 cases.
2. Deep feeling of being *thwarted* other than affectionally; either (a) in normal impulses or desires for self-expression or other self-satisfactions, (b) in

unusual desires because earlier spoiled, or (c) in adolescent urges and desires—
even when (as in 5 cases) desire for emancipation had been blocked only by the
individual's counteractive pleasure in remaining childishly attached—28 cases.

3. Feeling strongly either real or fancied *inadequacies or inferiorities* in the
home life, in schooling, or in relation to companionship or to sports—46 cases.

4. Intense feelings of *discomfort about family disharmonies,* parental mis-
conduct, the conditions of family life, or parental errors in management and
discipline—34 cases.

5. Bitter feelings of *jealousy* toward one or more siblings, or feelings of
being markedly discriminated against because another in the family circle was
more favored—31 cases.

6. Feelings of confused unhappiness due to some deep-seated, often re-
pressed, *internal mental conflict*—expressed in various kinds of delinquent acts
which often are seemingly unreasonable—17 cases.

7. Conscious or unconscious *sense of guilt* about earlier delinquencies or
about behavior which technically was not delinquency; the guilt sense directly
or indirectly activating delinquency through the individual's feeling of the need
of punishment (in nearly every instance this overlaps with the last category)—
9 cases.

SUMMARY: THE MEANINGFULNESS OF DELINQUENCY

The enumeration of the disturbances of the feeling life characterizing
the delinquents place squarely before us the material for an entirely new
outlook on the activating forces of delinquent behavior. The frustrations
of the fundamental urges, desires, and wishes which belong to the normal
stream of life's activities are plainly to be seen. More explicitly, the desires
for human relationships which are satisfying as they afford affectional acceptance and security, recognition of the individual as a personality, realization of social adequacy, opportunity for satisfactory accomplishment,
for independence, new experience, and for outlets and possessions have
somehow been thwarted. The individual has found himself blocked in any
one or more of these urges or wishes.

We can, in summary, describe the types of reactions represented by
delinquency as follows:

1. Attempt to avoid, even as a temporary measure, the unpleasant situation
by *escape* or *flight* from it.

2. Attempt to achieve substitutive *compensatory satisfactions* through delinquent activities. These satisfactions include the thrill of delinquent adventure
and the gratification at obtaining special recognition or attention, perhaps even
notoriety, as a delinquent. In some instances material gains figure as compensation for deprivation.

3. Attempt to strengthen or *bolster up the ego* wounded by feelings of inadequacy or inferiority. The aim then is to obtain *recognition and status* with
the delinquent crowd; or, if the offender is more solitary in tendencies, by the
individual proving to himself that he really is courageous and can in some way

play a spirited role. This "masculine protest" we found to be a not uncommon reaction with some previously effeminate or feminized boys. Said one such lad, "They thought I was no good so I went out to show a cock-eyed world that I was a regular guy."

4. Attempt to get certain ego-satisfactions through direct and conscious or even unconscious expression of *revenge attitudes*—perhaps through hidden desire to punish parents or others by conduct that will make life difficult for them.

5. Attempt to gain a *maximum of self-satisfaction,* to inflate the ego, by generally aggressive, antisocial attitudes, that is, by the exhibition of definite hostilities and antagonisms to authority.

6. *Response to instinctual urges* felt to be thwarted. While this response may be exhibited in sexual misbehavior, more notably in our delinquents we have discovered the attempt to satisfy the urge for independence and emancipation which normally flares up as an adolescent phenomenon.

7. The wish for punishment was clearly discernible in a few instances and suspected in others. This *seeking punishment*—delinquent behavior possibly offering an opportunity for being punished—was always a response to a conscious or unconscious sense of guilt.

There still remains a question of considerable interest and importance: just why is delinquency selected as a mode of reactive behavior? In almost no instances does delinquency follow upon a simple and conscious mental process—ordinarily the individual does not say to himself, "Through delinquency I will have my revenge," or "By being delinquent I will seize what immediate gratifications I can to make up for deprivations." Usually the act is engaged in by the delinquent without verbalizing to himself, indeed without conscious awareness that he is engaging in an evasive, substitutive, or compensatory form of behavior. It is rather that delinquency offers itself as a vehicle for reactive urges because ideas of delinquency have already been a part of the thought content of the individual.

With all the ideas of delinquency that in our modern world pour in upon the young individual from many sources the acceptance of these ideas as offering a mode of behavior which may be pursued is, as we have shown, dependent upon whether or not there are other sufficient satisfactions. Under the stress of emotional discomforts, even the discomforts of "nothing else to do," the invitation to dwell upon and to accept such ideas is especially great. Then certainly there is more ready acceptance of ideas of delinquency if they accord with what might be termed special needs of the individual, as in the cases of those hyperactive, overrestless boys described earlier, who in their emotional life had found frustrations. Under certain circumstances it may be healthier and more normal to join in with the activities and imbibe the ideas of a delinquent crowd than to be a withdrawing, soft, effeminate "mother's boy" or, as in instances already mentioned, to mope at home and develop an abnormal phantasy life.

58

The Results of Psychotherapy with Children: An Evaluation[*]

Eugene E. Levitt

Many efforts directed toward the improvement of society and the betterment of the individual are assumed to be "good" and effective because their purpose is positive. One reason why this is assumed is that these programs—in education, social welfare, psychotherapy, among others—are frequently not subjected to careful objective scrutiny and evaluation, despite the likelihood that only through such an appraisal is it possible to improve the methods for making things better. In the present paper, Dr. Levitt takes an objective look at the outcomes of psychotherapy in children. He finds little to support the view that psychotherapy is effective. However, he is careful to point out that this does not prove that all psychotherapy is futile. As was pointed out in the introduction to an earlier paper in this volume (by Bonney and Nicholson, in Part X) "negative" findings may pave the way for more refined study of the methods in question, of the particular conditions under which specific types of therapy produce favorable outcomes and with what kinds of children. Clearly we cannot take it for granted that because psychotherapy is designed to help youngsters, it is sure to help them. But, on the positive side, the evidence demonstrates in striking fashion the basic resiliency of the human personality. Three-quarters of the youngsters who were deemed to need help but got none (the control groups) improved over time.

A compendium of results of psychotherapy with adults, published a few years ago by Eysenck (1952), resulted in the conclusion that ". . . roughly two-thirds of a group of neurotic patients will recover or improve to a marked extent within about two years of the onset of their illness, whether they are treated by means of psychotherapy or not." He concludes further

* Adapted and abridged from Eugene E. Levitt, "The Results of Psychotherapy with Children: An Evaluation," *Journal of Consulting Psychology,* 1957, Vol. 21, pp. 189-196. (With permission of the author and the American Psychological Association.)

that "the figures fail to support the hypothesis that psychotherapy facilitates recovery from neurotic disorder."

The purpose of this paper is to summarize available reports of the results of psychotherapy with children using Eysenck's article as a model. Certain departures will be necessitated by the nature of the data, but in the main, the form will follow that of Eysenck.

BASELINE AND UNIT OF MEASUREMENT

As in Eysenck's study, the "Unit of measurement" used here will be evaluations of the degree of improvement of the patient by concerned clinicians. Individuals listed as "much improved, improved, partially improved, successful, partially successful, adjusted, partially adjusted, satisfactory," etc. will be grouped under the general heading of Improved. The Unimproved cases were found in groupings like "slightly improved, unimproved, unadjusted, failure, worse," etc.

Various difficulties arise in the selection of a control group to provide a baseline for comparison. However, a common phenomenon of the child guidance clinic is the patient who is accepted for treatment, but who voluntarily breaks off the clinic relationship without ever being treated. In institutions where the service load is heavy and the waiting period between acceptance and onset of treatment may range up to 6 months, this group of patients is often quite large. Theoretically, they have the characteristics of an adequate control group. So far as is known, they are similar to treated groups in every respect except for the factor of treatment itself.

Nevertheless, the use of this type of group as a control is not common in follow-up evaluations of the efficacy of treatment. Three studies report follow-up data on such groups. Of these, the data of Morris and Soroker (1953) are not suitable for the purposes of this paper. Of their 72 cases, at least 11 had treatment elsewhere between the last formal contact with the clinic and the point of evaluation, while an indeterminate number had problems too minor to warrant clinic treatment.

The samples in the remaining two studies appear satisfactory as sources of baseline data. Witmer and Keller (1942) appraised their group 8 to 13 years after clinic treatment, and reported that 78% were Improved. In the Lehrman study (1949), a one-year follow-up interval found 70% Improved. The overall rate of improvement for 160 cases in both reports is 72.5%. This figure will be used as the baseline for evaluating the results of treatment of children.

THE RESULTS OF PSYCHOTHERAPY

Studies showing outcome at close of treatment are not distinguished from follow-up studies in Eysenck's aggregation. The distinction seems logical, and is also meaningful in the predictive sense, as the analyses of this paper will indicate. Of the reports providing data for the present evaluation, thirteen present data at close, twelve give follow-up results, and five furnish both types, making a total of eighteen evaluations at close and seventeen at follow-up. The data of two reports (Jacobsen, 1948 and Johnson and Reid, 1947) are based on a combined close-follow-up rating. Results for the three kinds of evaluations will be presented separately.

The age range covered by all studies is from preschool to 21 years at the time of original clinic contact, the customary juncture for the determination of age for the descriptive data. However, very few patients were over 18 years at that time, and not many were over 17. The median age, roughly estimated from the ranges, would be about 10 years.

The usual psychiatric classification of mental illnesses is not always appropriate for childhood disorders. The writer has attempted to include only cases which would crudely be termed neuroses, by eliminating the data on delinquents, mental defectives, and psychotics whenever possible. The latter two groups constituted a very small proportion of the clinic cases. The proportion of delinquent cases is also small at some clinics but fairly large at others. Since the data as presented were not always amenable to these excisions, an unknown number of delinquent cases are included. However, the outcomes for the separated delinquents are much the same as those for the entire included group.

The number of categories in which patients were classified varied from study to study. Most used either a three-, four- or five-point scale. A few used only two categories, while one had twelve. Classification systems with more than five points were compressed into smaller scales. The data are presented tabularly in their original form, but the totals are pooled into three categories, Much Improved, Partially Improved, and Unimproved. A summation of the former two categories gives the frequency of Improved Cases.

A summary of results at close is shown in Table 1. Results of follow-up evaluations are summarized in Table 2. In Table 2, the follow-up interval is given as a range of years, the usual form of presentation in the studies. An attempt has been made to compute an average interval per case, using the midpoint of the range as a median when necessary. These averages are tenuous since it cannot be safely assumed that the midpoint actually is the median value. For example, in the Healy-Bronner investigation (1929), the range of intervals is 1 to 20 years, but the median is given as 2½ years. Since the proportion of cases which can be located is likely to vary inversely with the number of years of last clinic contact, the averages of 4.8 years for the follow-up studies and 2.3 years for the close-follow-up studies are probably overestimates.

Table 1 shows that the average percentage of improvement, i.e., the combined percentages in the Much Improved and Partially Improved

TABLE 1. Summary of Results of Psychotherapy with Children at Close

Study	N	Much Improved	Partially Improved	Unimproved	Per cent Improved
Cohen & David (1934)	57	16	18 12	8 3	80.7
Hubbard & Adams (1936)	100	13	18 42	26 1	73.0
Irgens (1936)	70	12	29 19	10	85.7
Reid & Hagan (1952)	250	54	82 46	68	72.8
Lehrman, Sirluck, Black & Glick (1949)	196	76	52	68	65.3
LaMore (1941)	50	15	18	17	66.0
Christianson, Gates & Coleman (1934)	126	25	54	47	62.7
Witmer, et al. (1933)	290	75	154	61	79.0
Barbour (1951)	814	207	398	209	74.3
Newell (1934)	72	26	31	15	79.2
Lee & Kenworthy (1929)	196	93	61	42	78.6
Brown (1947)	27	5	11	11	59.3
Carpenter (1939)	31	13	8	10	67.7
Canaday (1940)	23	2	9	12	47.8
Burlingham (1931)	75	35	22	18	76.0
Albright & Gambrell (1938)	80	31	21	28	65.0
Maas, et al. (1955)	522	225		297	43.1
Cunningham, Westerman & Fischhoff (1955)	420	251		169	59.8
All cases	3,399	1,174	1,105	1,120	67.05
Per cent	100.00	34.54	32.51	32.95	

TABLE 2. Summary of Results of Psychotherapy with Children at Follow-up

Study	Interval in Years	N	Much Improved	Partially Improved		Unimproved		Per-cent Improved
Lee & Kenworthy (1929)	1– 5	197	49	55	39	38	16	72.6
Brown (1931)	2	33	8	11	7	6	1	78.8
Cohen & Davis (1934)	2– 3	57	25	17	6	6	3	84.2
Witmer (1935)[a]	1–10	366	81	78	106	101		72.4
Irgens (1936)	2– 3	70	21	30	13	6		91.4
Walcott (1931)	5– 8	17	7	3		4	3	58.8
Lehrman, Sirluck, Black & Glick (1949)	1	196	99	46		51		74.0
Morris, Soroker & Burress (1954)	16–27	34	22	11		1		97.1
Barbour (1951)	1–20	705	358	225		122		82.7
Bronner (1944)	5–18	650	355	181		114		82.5
Maberly & Sturge (1939)	3–15	484	111	264		109		77.5
Fenton & Ramona (1938)	1– 4	732	179	398		155		78.8
Cunningham, Westerman & Fischhoff (1955)	5	359	228	80		51		85.8
Gollander (1944)	1– 2	25	6	12		7		72.0
Moses (1944)	1– 2	25	10	6		9		64.0
Maas, et al. (1955)	½–1½	191	82			109		42.9
Healy, Bronner, Baylor & Murphy (1929)	1–20	78	71			7		91.0
All cases	4.8[b]	4,219	1,712	1,588		919		
Per cent		100.00	40.58	37.64		21.78		78.22

[a] Data based on 13 studies originally reported in Witmer, Helen L., *et al.* The outcome of treatment in a child guidance clinic: a comparison and an evaluation. *Smith College Stud. soc. Wk*, 1935, 6, 1-98.
[b] Estimated average follow-up interval per case.

categories is 67.05 at close. It is not quite accurate to say that the data are consistent from study to study. A chi-square analysis of improvement and unimprovement yields a value of 230.37, which is significant beyond the .001 level for $17df$. However, as in the case of Eysenck's data, there is a considerable amount of consistency considering the interstudy differences in methodology, definition, etc.

The average percentage of improvement in the follow-up studies is given in Table 2 as 78.22. The percentage for the combined close-follow-up evaluations is 73.98, roughly between the other two. The percentage of improvement in the control studies was 72.5, slightly higher than the improvement at close and slightly lower than at follow-up. It would appear that treated children are no better off at close than untreated children, but that they continue to improve over the years and eventually surpass the untreated group.

This conclusion is probably specious, perhaps unfortunately. One of the two control studies was an evaluation one year after the last clinic contact, the other 8 to 13 years after. The former study reports only 70% improvement while the longer interval provided 78% improvement. The figure for the one-year interval is similar to the results at close, while the percentage of improvement for the control with the 8- to 13-year interval is almost identical with that for the follow-up studies.

The point of the analysis is more easily seen if the results at close and at follow-up are pooled. This combination gives the same sort of estimate as that furnished by the two control groups pooled since one of them is a long-interval follow-up while the other was examined only a short time after clinic contact. The pooled percentage of improvement based on 7,987 cases in both close and follow-up studies is 73.27, which is practically the same as the percentage of 72.5 for the controls.

It now appears that Eysenck's conclusion concerning the data for adult psychotherapy is applicable to children as well; the results do not support the hypothesis that recovery from neurotic disorder is facilitated by psychotherapy.

The discrepancy between results at close and at follow-up suggests that time is a factor in improvement. Denker's report (1946) also indicated the operation of a time factor. He found that 45% of the patients had recovered by the end of one year, 72% had recovered by the end of two years, 82% by three years, 87% by four years, and 91% by five years. The rate of improvement as a function of time in Denker's data is clearly negatively accelerating.

The percentage of improvement as a function of time interval is shown by the data of Table 3. The studies have been grouped at five time-interval points in the table.

The data of Table 3 indicate that most of the correlation between improvement and time-interval is accounted for by the studies with the shortest intervals, and those with the largest. The curve is more or less the same as that of Denker's data, negatively accelerating with most of the improvement accomplished by 2½ years. It is peculiar that the improvement after 1½ years is about 60%, less than the 67% improvement at close. However, the difference is not too great to attribute to variations in methodology and sampling among the concerned studies. Another potential explanation will be offered shortly.

There are a number of different kinds of therapies which have been used in the studies reported here. The therapists have been psychiatrists,

TABLE 3. Improvement as a Function of the Interval Between Last Clinic Contact and Follow-up

Estimated Median Interval in Years	Number of Reports	Total N	N Improved	Per cent Improved
1–1½	4	437	261	59.73
2–2½	6	1,167	929	79.61
5–6½	3	742	583	78.57
10	2	1,189	958	80.57
12	2	684	569	83.19
All cases	17	4,219	3,300	78.22

social workers, and teams of clinicians operating at different points in the patient's milieu. Therapeutic approaches included counseling, guidance, placement, and recommendations to schools and patients, as well as deeper level therapies. In some instances the patient alone was the focus of attention. In others, parents and siblings were also treated. The studies apparently encompassed a variety of theoretical viewpoints, although these are not usually specified. Viewed as a body, the studies providing the data for Tables 1 and 2 are therapeutically eclectic, a plurality, perhaps, reflecting psychoanalytic approaches.

Thus we may say that the therapeutic eclecticism, the number of subjects, the results, and the conclusions of this paper are markedly similar to those of Eysenck's study. Two-thirds of the patients examined at close and about three-quarters seen in follow-up have improved. Approximately the same percentages of improvement are found for comparable groups of untreated children.

As Eysenck pointed out (1955) in a sequel to his evaluation, such appraisal does not *prove* that psychotherapy is futile. The present evaluation of child psychotherapy, like its adult counterpart, fails to support the hypothesis that treatment is effective, but it *does not* force the acceptance of a contrary hypothesis. The distinction is an important one, especially in view of the differences among the concerned studies, and their generally poor caliber of methodology and analysis. Until additional evidence from well-planned investigations becomes available, a cautious, tongue-in-cheek attitude toward child psychotherapy is recommended.

SUMMARY

A survey of eighteen reports of evaluations at close, and seventeen at follow-up, was compared with similar evaluations of untreated children. Two-thirds of the evaluations at close, and three-quarters at follow-up, showed improvement. Roughly the same percentages were found for the respective control groups. A crude analysis indicates that time is a factor in improvement in the follow-up studies; the rate of improvement with time is negatively accelerating. It is concluded that the results of the present study fail to support the view that psychotheraphy with "neurotic" children is effective.

59

Factors Related to Adjustment in Old Age[*]

Bernard Kutner, David Fanshel, Alice M. Togo, and Thomas S. Langner

It is often argued (and with considerable cogency) that civilized societies are essentially unfriendly to old age. Older people, though possessing capabilities, have little opportunity to show their worth, hence are likely to be insecure and feel that they have no real place in society. Are they maladjusted as a group? What factors are related to morale and adjustment? This final paper in the volume indicates that, although morale declines in the later years, a very substantial number of people beyond sixty may be characterized as having high morale. But perhaps most important, is the suggestion that those who

* Adapted and abridged from Bernard Kutner, David Fanshel, Alice M. Togo and Thomas S. Langner, *Five Hundred Over Sixty: A Community Survey on Aging.* New York: Russell Sage Foundation, 1956. (With permission of the senior author and the publisher.)

had more advantages during the course of adult years had developed an array of "internal" resources (interests, appreciations) to draw upon as a means of satisfying their psychological needs. The findings of this study warn against assuming that a single pattern and style of life is most appropriate for old people. Indeed, the evidence suggests that different patterns fit different people, inasmuch as different factors were differentially related to morale in different socioeconomic groups.

If in the later years, the person is beset with personal difficulties that multiply and are generally irreversible, those who manage to make a satisfactory adjustment to life should be found to possess one or more sustaining characteristics. We may speak of external or situational forces, though they may be fortuitous in many instances, that give the individual strength to carry on with minimal stress. Among these may be a pleasant home and surroundings, an emotionally compatible and mutually reinforcing relationship to a life partner, a respected position in the community, a variety of useful activities, companionship of family and friends, an adequate and reliable financial reserve, a sound constitution. These are factors that lend to the patterning and stability of life at any age. They help to inhibit the corrosive and demoralizing influences of retrenchment among any one or more of these forces.

At the same time, there are inner or more personal forces that can make for either good or poor social adjustment. The individual's personality strengths and weaknesses, his emotional needs, the level of his demands for recognition, companionship, comfort, permissiveness are as significant to his ability to bear the brunt of the "insults" of life as are the strength of the insults themselves. Inner resources that are sufficient to offset external stresses may reduce the potency of maladjustive influences.

Sustaining or destroying forces, be they external or internal, operate simultaneously and are reciprocal in their action on the individual. These interlocking effects of internal and external factors influencing adjustment in old age are the central theme of the analysis of data reported here.

THE COMMUNITY SETTING

The survey upon which this report is based was conducted in the Kips Bay-Yorkville Health District of New York City, an area of about two-and-one-half square miles on the East Side of Manhattan Island, lying between Central Park and the East River and bounded roughly by 89th Street to the north and 34th Street to the south. It is one of New York's 30 health districts and houses about 252,000 persons according to the 1950 Census.

Of the total District population, about one-third are foreign born (a somewhat higher proportion than in New York City as a whole) and less than one-half of 1 per cent are nonwhite. Within Kips Bay-Yorkville there are some 50 nonresidential city blocks. Occupying them and some of the blocks adjacent are a variety of public, private, and commercial structures that are part of the renowned character of the city. The United Nations buildings and associated structures, the Chrysler Building, the Empire State Building, the famous Fifth Avenue shops, St. Patrick's Cathedral, and Rockefeller Center are located in Kips Bay and on its fringes. The area is undoubtedly the least homogeneous of all the city's health districts. Kips Bay-Yorkville has aptly been described as follows by one sociologist:

Kips Bay-Yorkville is a congeries of urban contrasts. The world's most luxurious apartments—sub-standard tenement housing; expensive hotels—mean boarding houses; exclusive private schools—outdated, crowded public schools; cathedrals—humble chapels; ranking income tax payers—families on relief for years; "the world's finest stores"—push carts; old American families—newly arrived refugees; all these and others go to make up an urban area with a thousand problems generated by too many people trying to live in too little space.[1]

In 1950 there were about 44,500 persons over sixty living in the District, comprising 17.7 per cent of the population of the area. This proportion is well above the general relation of those over sixty to the total population of the city.

THE SUBJECTS

A total of 500 residents of Kips Bay-Yorkville participated in the survey. This represents a little more than 1 per cent of the population of the area over the age of sixty, the age selected as the baseline of eligibility in the survey. The sample may be described as a stratified sample and is not "representative" of the area in the literal sense of the word. It was felt early in the study that because of the economic distribution of the District, with its great proportion of well-to-do elderly residents, it would be best to weight the relative proportions of each economic group to be included in the survey, in order to lay our greatest stress upon the lower economic and social strata of the area. Although a much larger proportion of well-to-do persons reside in Kips Bay-Yorkville, only 11 per cent of the people are drawn from among them. A little less than 30 per cent come from the middle class, and the bulk, just under 60 per cent, is selected from the lower socioeconomic group. With this limitation incorporated within the sample, our findings tend to overrepresent the lower economic group and to underrepresent the upper economic group in this District. It will be noted, how-

---

[1] Koos, Earl L., editor, *Kips Bay-Yorkville: 1940.* Department of Public Health and Preventive Medicine, Cornell University Medical College, New York, 1942, Introduction.

ever, that the proportions employed for the study are not too far removed from what one would expect to find in almost any large urban complex. The breakdown of the sample into age and socioeconomic level is presented in Table 1.

PROCEDURE

With one or two exceptions, all the respondents in the survey were interviewed in their homes by a corps of 30 trained interviewers. The interviewers followed a prescribed sequence of questions and each required

TABLE 1. Age and Socioeconomic Status of the Sample

Socioeconomic Status	Age (in years)					Number of Cases
	60 to 64	65 to 69	70 to 74	75 to 79	80 and Over	
	(Percentages)					
High	15	8	10	13	8	55
Middle	41	30	25	17	32	148
Low	44	62	65	70	60	297
Total	100	100	100	100	100	
Number of cases	117	139	115	82	47	500

from one to one-and-a-half hours to complete. Areas covered by the questionnaire, in addition to basic personal data, were: the individual's health status with a rather detailed survey of major health problem areas, their knowledge of, attitudes toward, and use of various medical and health services, social activities, extent of contact with peers and relatives, attitudes toward old age, feelings concerning their own aging, areas of satisfaction or dissatisfaction with employment or retirement, specific complaints and problems concerning their style of life, standard of living, housing, leisure time, community participation, and their attitudes toward the use of specialized services for the aged.

In this study we were concerned with the relation of various factors to "adjustment" or "morale" in old age. We shall mean by morale a continuum of responses to life and living problems that reflect the presence or absence of satisfaction, optimism, and expanding life perspectives. It should be clear from this definition that morale and adjustment are part of the same phenomenon. Morale refers to a mental state or a set of dispositions, while adjustment refers to behaviors that stem from these dispositions. Hence, we may assume that an attitude or evaluation scale of morale measures life adjustment.

The morale scale employed is based upon responses to the following items:

1. How often do you feel there's just no point in living?
2. Things just keep getting worse and worse for me as I get older.
3. How much do you regret the chances you missed during your life to do a better job of living?
4. All in all, how much unhappiness would you say you find in life today?
5. On the whole, how satisfied would you say you are with your way of life today?
6. How much do you plan ahead the things you will be doing next week or the week after—would you say you make many plans, a few plans, or almost none?
7. As you get older, would you say things seem to be better or worse than you thought they would be?

For purposes of analysis, the respondents were divided into three groups of approximately equal size. The groups represent high, medium, and low morale scores.

AGE TRENDS IN ADJUSTMENT

It might be assumed that the frustrations and disjunctive factors that afflict older people would result, to an increasing degree, in the reduction in morale in each older age group. As more trying life problems cumulate over the years, the person's efforts to face and overcome them yield diminishing returns. With respect to the women first, it should be noted in Table 2 that morale declines *gradually* with increasing age. The proportion of those having low morale is about the same through the years, and the loss of numbers in the high morale group is absorbed by an increase in the medium morale group. Statistical significance of the differences occurs only between the under sixty-five and the over seventy-five group. We see here that the maladjustments and dislocations of aging include a greater proportion of women in each more advanced age category, but the group shifts slowly. For some women the matter of life adjustment may be affected by the cumulation of the problems of widowhood, declining living standards and health, loss of peers, and the loss of an important life function. Though spread over the years for some, the trend of morale for the group is gradually but continuously downward. Homemaking, housekeeping, a part-time job, involvement in the rearing of grandchildren may make their situation tolerable, and their role in life may continue to be meaningful into the seventh and eighth decades.

Among the men a somewhat different picture appears. Low morale is felt by twice the proportion of the sixty-five to sixty-nine group as in the immediately preceding age group. A mild upturn in morale occurs within the seventy to seventy-four group. It may be anticipated that this increase reflects the balance between those who, having successfully navigated the passage into retirement, are now readjusting adequately to new life conditions and those whose health status and economic position are moving downward and who are suffering some of the other disadvantages of aging. In the group over seventy-five, morale continues downgrade and begins to spread. Unlike the women, morale in the seventh and eighth decades among men is inclined to be good or bad, with a comparatively smaller intermediate group. This undoubtedly reflects the difference in adjustment

TABLE 2. Morale According to Age for 188 Men and 312 Women

| | Age (in years) | | | |
Morale	60 to 64	65 to 69	70 to 74	75 and over
		Men		
		(Percentages)		
High	54	40	48	30
Medium	29	25	26	27
Low	17	35	26	43
Total	100	100	100	100
Number of cases	48	57	43	40
		Women		
		(Percentages)		
High	42	38	32	22
Medium	26	26	33	42
Low	32	36	35	36
Total	100	100	100	100
Number of cases	69	82	72	89

between the married, employed, or successfully retired men and the widowers, single, or poorly retired men. A retired widower or retired single man, as indicated later, seems to make the poorest adjustment of the group as a whole.

FACTORS RELATED TO MORALE AT VARIOUS SOCIOECONOMIC LEVELS

Before turning to a consideration of the relationship between various conditions and morale at contrasting socioeconomic levels, it will be well first to consider the overall relation between economic level and morale.

Table 3 indicates a significant relationship between morale and socioeconomic status, namely, that low status is associated with low morale and vice versa. Since income maintenance, respected social position, and freedom from drudgery are associated with high status, this result is readily understood. With the knowledge that an individual's social and economic position are in themselves important factors, we should want to know more about what types of experiences, conditions of life, and perceptions influence his adjustment at the various socioeconomic levels. The interaction between economic level and various other factors in their relation to morale is clearly shown in Table 4. Some of the results there presented are somewhat unexpected.

HEALTH AND MORALE

First to be noted in Table 4 is the apparent failure of poor health to substantially affect morale among those of high status and the profound

TABLE 3. Morale According to Socioeconomic Status

| | Socioeconomic Status | | Number of |
Morale	High	Low	Cases
	(Percentages)		
High	49	29	185
Medium	29	31	150
Low	22	40	165
Total	100	100	
Number of cases	203	297	500

effect of poor health among those of low status. The importance of these findings cannot be underestimated for a deeper understanding of the relation of adjustment to health in old age. The prevailing optimism and sense of well-being of those holding high social and economic status suggest that possession of the cultural marks of attainment, position in life, and other material evidences of success, may serve to overcome some of the effects of handicapping conditions of the later years. Note that high status usually is associated with a longer history of personal influence, higher educational attainment, and broader cultural background. It is possible that these develop a greater degree of inner strength or personal resourcefulness to deal with the problems of aging. With regard to those of low status: not only are their social and economic circumstances related to lower morale, but, when ill health intervenes, morale is further depressed. At least insofar as this group is concerned, it is clear that a happier old age might be attained if adequate measures were taken to

TABLE 4. Relation to Morale in Old Age of Various Activities and Circumstances by Percentage Distribution of Individuals of High and Low Socioeconomic Status

	No. of Cases	Morale Status (per cent)		
		High	Medium	Low
Health:				
High status, good health	137	50	28	22
High status, poor health	66	44	30	26
Low status, good health	147	39	31	30
Low status, poor health	150	20	30	50
Self-image:				
High status, positive self-image	112	53	32	15
High status, negative self-image	91	43	25	32
Low status, positive self-image	113	40	37	23
Low status, negative self-image	184	23	27	50
Social isolation:				
High status, isolated	85	51	28	21
High status, not isolated	117	47	30	23
Low status, isolated	194	25	28	47
Low status, not isolated	103	37	36	27
Visiting with children (+ or − once a week):				
High status, often	101	47	29	24
High status, less often	29	65	21	14
High status, no children	72	43	35	22
Low status, often	109	28	30	42
Low status, less often	45	36	28	36
Low status, no children	143	27	31	42
Visiting friends (+ or − once a week):				
High status, visit often	88	49	29	22
High status, visit less often	77	48	27	25
High status, no friends	36	47	33	20
Low status, visit often	102	35	37	28
Low status, visit less often	100	29	33	38
Low status, no friends	87	23	20	57
Employment as related to income:				
Employed, less than $25 week	29	31	31	38
Employed, $25-$49 per week	44	49	30	21
Employed, $50 and over per week	80	65	25	10
Retired, less than $25 per week	100	23	33	44
Retired, $25-$49 per week	35	37	29	34
Retired, $50 and over per week	17	35	35	30

assure the maintenance of their health. Low status alone acts as a depressant but when coupled with poor health the outlook becomes still more grim.

SELF-PERCEPTION AND MORALE

A second relationship of interest in Table 4 is that of "self-perception" and morale. Self-perception, the social image of oneself, is of basic importance in understanding the responses of the person to other human beings, as well as to things and situations. The older person who regards himself as relatively young may find himself embittered by the attitude of a prospective employer who regards him as old. The person who perceives himself as middle-aged and attempts to behave accordingly may find himself accepted into social groups that would not admit him if he regarded himself as old. In our society the admission of one's aging and the view of agedness are so distinctly negative that to regard oneself as "old" or "elderly" is considered an aspect of a "negative" self-image. It implies, as used in the following analysis, merely the admission of a disadvantageous or undesirable state. The person who says he is older is therefore regarded as comparatively deprived. It should be noted that this is not a unique position of the authors but is common social usage. The classification of a person as having a positive or negative "self-image" was determined by his answers to questions as to whether he felt younger or older than people of his own age, had better or poorer health than his age peers, had better or poorer living standards than his friends and acquaintances.

Does one's self-image affect adjustment? The effect is pronounced: while 45 per cent of the negative image group are low in morale, only 19 per cent of the positive image group are low. We might be able to explain this result by pointing to the fact that the items comprising the index deal with *relative* deprivation or advantage. Since the high socioeconomic group has most of the advantages, we should expect that those in the high status group have a positive self-image and those in the low group a negative self-image. We find, in fact, that significantly more of those in the higher status group have a positive self-image than do those in the low status group (55 as compared to 38 per cent). However, the size of the difference between the two status groups amounts to no more than 17 per cent. Does this, then, mean that a negative self-image among those of high status is as great a determinant of low morale as we might predict would be the case in the low status group? We see from Table 4 that this is actually the case. Among those of low status, the difference between the positive and negative image groups is obviously large. The difference between the image groups among those of high status, while smaller, is still significant statistically.

In effect, we are saying here that while there is no doubt that high status tends to be associated with higher morale, to an important extent members of both status groups are adversely affected if they believe that their peers are or have been better off than they in certain respects. That those who feel deprived as related to their peers among the low status group show so low a level of morale is dramatic testimony of the inter-relationship of the self-concept and adjustment. At the same time, it should be borne in mind that the relationship between self-image and morale may be mutually reinforcing. Those who do not feel deprived but regard their lot as comparatively good may be influenced by their present state of adjustment. If adjustment is good, their outlook on life may be wholesome even if their objective circumstances are not all desirable.

SOCIAL ACTIVITY AND MORALE

Three of the items in Table 4 relate to social activity—social isolation, visiting with children, visiting with friends. But before examining those findings, what about the general relationship between social and recrea-tional activity (a separate score was computed for this) and morale. Ap-plying our activity scale to our measure of morale, we find that high ac-tivity level and high morale are significantly related. At the same time, nearly a third of the low activity group are rated at high morale and about one-fourth of the active group are rated at low morale.

The relationship between employment and adjustment in old age will be discussed later, but a crucial question at this point is: Do those who are inactive but employed have higher morale than those who are active yet unemployed or retired? This should provide a test of the relative strengths of activity and employment as factors determining the level of morale. Al-though the difference is not statistically significant, we find that there is a greater percentage of cases of high morale as well as a smaller percentage of cases of low morale among the inactive-employed as compared to the active-unemployed or retired. In other words, there is a tendency for employed people who are not otherwise socially active to be better adjusted than those who are active but without gainful employment.

Advocates of activity programs as the solution to problems related to aging will not be especially heartened by these findings. They may draw satisfaction, nevertheless, from the fact that at least a portion of the older group may be subtantially benefited by increasing the individual's general activity. It is important to keep in mind that it may not be the level of one's activity that increases morale but that people whose adjustment is good tend to be more active, and those who are not well-adjusted are less inclined to be active. More fundamental considerations than mere activity are involved in adjustment.

A measure of social isolation was obtained based on frequency of seeing children or relatives, having personal friends, having friends living close, and making new friends. As might be expected, relative social isolation increases with advancing age, although the most marked single increase occurs past the age of seventy-five. Although the downward trend is nearly the same for both men and women, there is an interesting sharp decline in the extent of social interaction among men between sixty-five and sixty-nine, the "retirement years." We have already explored the possibility that the crisis years for men, sixty-five to sixty-nine, bring about a marked withdrawal from participation in social life. There is also a tendency at all age levels, but most marked in the group over seventy-five years of age, for those having had more education to be less isolated. Those who have had a high school or college education are, on the whole, less isolated than those who have had limited education. It is possible that the style of living, interests, and social values of those with more advanced education sustain their ability to continue to seek out others, as well as to place a higher value on social affairs. It is also possible that those with more education have led lives that afford them greater human resources to draw upon in their later years. In line with these findings, it is not surprising to learn that social isolation is a function of socioeconomic status.

Data relating social isolation and visiting children and friends to morale at high and low status levels are presented in Table 4. Although the differences did not reach statistical significance, there is a tendency for morale to be higher among those who see their children less frequently than among those who see them once a week or oftener. This is more striking in the higher than in the lower status group. It is also of interest that the same level of morale is found among those having no children as among those seeing children often in each status group.

Although it might be expected that frequent social relationships with children, relatives, and friends would be conducive to good adjustment, we did not find this *generally* to be the case. Among the low status group, frequency of visiting with family and associates was found to have no relationship to morale. Among those of high status, increased proportions of persons having *low* morale was found to accompany frequent visiting with children and relations. This was not true of frequent contacts with friends. We can only suggest what may enter in here. Involved, perhaps, is friction between generations or about suggestions to the older person for maintaining the youthfulness and health which are highly prized among this group. Or, perhaps, the contrast between the two generations may emphasize for the older person that which he would deny—his own aging.

One further comment should be made. Social isolation does have its negative aspects. It is often accompanied by—sometimes even the result of—failing health. The death of his peers, the circumscription of his social relationships bring home to the older person the fact of his aging. Not to be forgotten, however, is the possibility that some older individuals may prefer the state that we have here termed "isolation." Some are living out cultural traditions and values. To repeat what we have said before, the aged are not a homogeneous group.

WORK AND MORALE

Perhaps the most convincing evidence of the potency of meaningful roles in later life is provided by a comparison of the levels of morale of those employed and retired whose incomes are identical, as shown in the bottom portion of Table 4. It might be assumed that morale would increase with a rising level of income and this would hold regardless of the sources of the person's income. A substantial income may permit the person the freedom and leisure that his available free time provides. He may also maintain a relatively high living standard generally if income is substantial. Our findings, however, are not conducive to so simple a relationship. *How* one derives his income seems to be more importantly related to one's level of morale than *what* the income is itself.

As seen in the table a person who is working but receiving less than $25 per week has a morale rating similar to that of a person who is retired but receiving a higher income. It is also quite clear that as earnings or income increase, morale rises. However, note that while the extent of this rise is great among the employed group (probably reflecting differences in style of living, type of occupation, and satisfaction derived), it is only moderate among the retired group. The social role that provides the greatest degree of gratification for most persons is the employed role, particularly for men. The less desirable role is that of the retiree. Morale responds accordingly.

Statistical analysis does not reveal significant differences between the employed and retired groups at each income level. However, note that the direction of the finding is the same in each instance: whatever the level of income in each income group, the morale rating tends to be higher among those who are employed than among those who are retired.

SUMMARY

This study of factors related to morale in old age has revealed that, with increasing age, social and recreational activity tends to decrease, social isolation to increase, and morale to decline. Although all these factors, in addition to health and having a significant role, were related to morale in the old age group studied, quite different relationships obtained at different social status levels. It appeared that the lack of dependence of higher economic groups upon social interaction was due, in part, to their possessing greater "internal" resources (interests, appreciations) to draw upon as a means of satisfying important psychological needs. The importance of having a significant role is evident in the relationship of *work* to morale when employed and retired individuals of identical incomes are compared. And, finally, the findings suggest that old people are quite heterogeneous, that very different patterns of adjustment and style of life may be appropriate for different people.

60

Personality and Patterns of Aging*

Bernice L. Neugarten

The seventh stage of life, as sketched in Shakespeare's summary of man's total earthly journey, is characterized as a period of sensory and psychomotor erosions, eventuating in a total loss of outer contacts and inner resources. Although this still seems a fair description of one kind of decline into Shakespeare's "nothingness," it is not very helpful in differentiating what appear to be the several different ways that aging individuals face life near its inevitable end. In the following paper Dr. Neugarten shows that the problems of description and prediction during the eighth decade of life are similar to, and continuous with, those encountered during earlier decades. Individuals in their seventies do not suddenly become different people—any more than adolescents suddenly restructure their integrated life patterns. It is Dr. Neugarten's view, supported by convincing research evidence, that "activity" and "disengagement" theories of aging are too simple to encompass the facts. Such conceptions must eventually be replaced by more comprehensive developmental theory that takes into account the essential continuity of the human personality.

In the social-psychological literature of gerontology there have been two general points of view, or two theories, with regard to optimum patterns of aging. Both are based on the observed facts that as people grow older

* From Bernice L. Neugarten, "Personality and Patterns of Aging," *Gawein*, 1965, Vol. 13, pp. 249-256. (With permission of the author and the publisher.)

their behavior changes, the activities that characterized them in middle age become curtailed, and the extent of their social interaction decreases.

The "activity" theory implies that, except for the inevitable changes in biology and in health, older people have the same psychological and social needs as middle-aged people. The decreased social interaction that characterizes old age results from the withdrawal by society from the aging person; and the decrease in interaction proceeds against the desires of most aging men and women. The older person who ages optimally is the person who stays actively engaged in a variety of social roles and who manages to resist the shrinkage of his social world. He maintains the activities of middle age as long as possible, and then finds substitutes for those activities he is forced to relinquish—substitutes for work, when he is forced to retire, substitutes for friends and loved ones whom he loses by death.

The "disengagement" theory, on the other hand, implies that the decrease in social interaction is one in which both society and the aging person withdraw, in a *mutual* process; the decreased interaction of the older person is accompanied by, or even preceded by, increased preoccupation with the self and with decreased emotional investment in the persons and objects of the environment (Cumming & Henry, 1961; Cumming, 1963; Henry, 1963). In this view, the older person who will disengage with a sense of psychological well-being is the one who is relatively disengaged from the social roles of middle age and who has reduced his social involvements.

In a report prepared for the International Congress of Gerontology in 1963, my colleagues and I presented a summary of the data obtained in a large-scale study of aging that has been in progress over the past several years in the United States, a study known as the Kansas City Study of Adult Life (Havighurst, Neugarten, and Tobin, 1964). We said that, in the light of our findings, neither the "activity" nor the "disengagement" theory seemed adequate. Having followed several hundred persons aged 50 to 80 over a six-year interval, we found a positive correlation between the extent of social interaction and psychological well-being, a correlation that is even higher in persons aged 70 and over than in persons aged 50 to 70. In other words, those older persons who are highly engaged in various social roles generally have greater life satisfaction than those who have lower levels of engagement. At the same time, the relationship is not a consistent one. There are some older persons who are low in social role activity and who have high life satisfaction; and vice versa, there are others who are high in activity, but low in satisfaction.

On the basis of these findings, we have moved on to studying differences in personality. Presumably there are certain personality types who, as they age, disengage with relative comfort and who remain highly contented with life. Others disengage with great discomfort and show a drop in life satisfaction. Still others will long have shown low levels of role activity accompanied by high satisfaction, and these latter persons will show relatively little change as they age. In this view, then, personality becomes the important variable—the fulcrum around which the other variables are organized.

We have attempted to order our data in such a way as to describe the *patterns of aging* that characterize the man and woman in our Study. To do so, we have used three sets of data: (1) personality type; (2) extent of social role activity; and (3) degree of life satisfaction.

(1) Our personality types are based on an ego-psychology model, in which individuals were rated on 45 different personality variables reflecting both cognitive and affective personality attributes. The types were established empirically, by methods of factor analysis (Neugarten et al., 1964).

(2) Role-activity measures are made up of ratings of the extent and intensity of activity in eleven different social roles: parent, spouse, grandparent, kin-group member, worker, homemaker, citizen, friend, neighbor, club-and-association member, and church member. For example, with regard to the role of spouse, a man who lives with his wife, but who shares with her few activities other than perfunctory routines such as eating his meals in her company, is rated low in the role of spouse; while a man who plans and carries out most of his day's activities in the company of his wife is rated high in this role. The role-activity score is a sum of ratings in the 11 different roles.

(3) The life satisfaction measure is a sum of ratings on five different components. An individual is regarded as high in psychological well-being to the extent that he (a) takes pleasure from whatever the round of activities that constitutes his everyday life; (b) regards his life as meaningful and accepts resolutely that which life has been; (c) feels he has success in achieving his major goals; (d) holds a positive image of self; and (e) maintains happy and optimistic attitudes and moods (Neugarten, Havighurst, and Tobin, 1961).

These three sets of measures and the assessments of our subjects were carried out by independent teams of investigators.

With respect to the patterns based on these three variables, personality type, role activity, and life-satisfaction, the following report is concerned only with those patterns found in our 70- to 79-year-old men and women. In this age-group almost all the men had retired, and this is the group in which the transition from middle age to old age has presumably been accomplished.

A few words about this sample may be helpful at this point. Of the larger group who formed the original population in the Kansas City Study of Adult Life, about 60 per cent remained after six years. The loss of cases is an important factor; and the overall effect has been to produce a relatively select group over time. Thus the patterns described in this paper do not, by any means, encompass all types of older persons to be found in a community, but only those relatively advantaged 70-year-olds who have better-than-average health, cooperativeness, and general well-being.

There are 59 persons in this age group, 50 of whom fell into one or another of eight patterns of aging.

To help the reader keep these patterns in mind, they are described primarily in terms of the four major personality types. As shown in Table
1, these are the "integrated," the "defended," the "passive-dependent," and
the "disintegrated" personalities. These four groups are then further divided according to role activity score and according to life-satisfaction
ratings, to yield eight patterns.

First, there are 17 in this group of 70-year-olds who are "integrated"
personalities: well-functioning persons who have a complex inner life and,
at the same time, intact cognitive abilities and competent egos. These persons are acceptant of impulse life, over which they maintain a comfortable
degree of control; they are flexible, open to new stimuli; mellow, mature.
All these individuals, it happens, were high in life satisfaction. At the
same time, they were divided with regard to amount of role activity.

There is one pattern whom we call the *re-organizers*, who are the competent
people engaged in a wide variety of activities. (These are marked Group A in
Table 1.) They are the optimum agers in some respects—at least in the American culture, where there is high value placed on "staying young, staying active,
and refusing to grow old." These are persons who substitute new activities for
lost ones; who, when they retire from work, give time to community affairs or to
church or to other associations. They reorganize their patterns of activity.

There is a second pattern which we called the *focussed*. (Group B in Table 1.)
These are integrated personalities, with high life satisfaction, but who show
medium levels of activity. They have become selective in their activities, with
time, and they now devote energy to and gain their major satisfaction from one
or two role areas. One such case, for instance, was a retired man who was now
preoccupied with the roles of homemaker, parent, and husband. He had withdrawn from work and from club-memberships and welcomed the opportunity to
live a happy and full life with his family, seeing his children and grandchildren,
gardening, and helping his wife with homemaking, which he had never done
before.

The next pattern we called the *disengaged* (Group C in Table 1). These are
also integrated personalities with high life satisfaction, but with low activity; persons who have voluntarily moved away from role commitments, not in response
to external losses or physical deficits, but because of preference. These are self-
directed persons, not shallow, with an interest in the world, but an interest that
is not imbedded in a network of social interactions. They have high feelings of
self-regard, just as do the first two groups mentioned, but they have chosen what
might be called a "rocking-chair" approach to old age—a calm, withdrawn, but
contented pattern.

Next we come to the men and women whose personality type was the
"armed" or the "defended." These are the striving, ambitious, achieve-

TABLE 1. Personality Type in Relation to Role Activity and Life Satisfaction (age 70-79) (N = 59).

Personality Type	Role Activity	Life Satisfaction High	Medium	Low
Integrated	High	(9) A	2	
	Medium	(5) B		
	Low	(3) C		
Armored-Defended	High	5 D		
	Medium	6	1 E	
	Low	2	1	1
Passive-Dependent	High		1 F	
	Medium	1	4	
	Low	2	(3	2) G
Unintegrated	High		2	1
	Medium			
	Low	1	(2	5) H
	Total	34	16	9

Name of Pattern

A—Re-organizer
B—Focussed
C—Disengaged
D—Holding on
E—Constricted
F—Succorance-
  seeker
G—Apathetic
H—Disorganized

ment-oriented personalities, with high defenses against anxiety and with the need to maintain tight controls over impulse life. This personality group provided two patterns of aging:

One we called the *holding-on* pattern (Group D in Table 1.) This is the group to whom aging constitutes a threat, and who respond by holding on, as long as possible, to the patterns of their middle age. They are quite successful in their attempts, and thus maintain high life satisfaction with medium-or-high activity levels. These are persons who say, "I'll work until I drop," or "So long as you keep busy, you will get along all right."

The other group of "defended" personalities we called the *constricted* pattern of aging (Group E in Table 1). These are persons busily defending themselves against aging; preoccupied with losses and deficits; dealing with these threats by constricting their social interactions and their energies and by closing themselves off from experience. They seem to structure their worlds to keep off what they regard as imminent collapse; and while this constriction results in low role activity, it works fairly well, given their personality pattern, to keep them high or medium in life satisfaction.

The third group of personalities are the passive-dependent types, among whom there are two patterns of aging:

The *succorance-seeking* (Group F) are those who have strong dependency needs and who seek responsiveness from others. These persons maintain medium levels of activity, and medium levels of life satisfaction, and seem to maintain themselves fairly well so long as they have at least one or two other persons whom they can lean on and who meet their emotional needs.

The *apathetic* pattern (Group G) represents those persons in whom passivity is a striking feature of personality and where there is low role activity and medium or low life satisfaction. These are also "rocking-chair" people, but with very different personality structures from those we have called the disengaged. This apathetic pattern seems to occur in persons in whom aging has probably reinforced long-standing patterns of passivity and apathy. Here, for instance, was a man who, in the interviews, was content to let his wife do his talking for him; and there was a woman whose activities were limited entirely to those of maintaining her physical needs.

Finally, there was a group of unintegrated personalities (Group H) who showed a *disorganized* pattern of aging. These were persons who had gross defects in psychological functions, loss of control over emotions and deterioration in thought processes. They were maintaining themselves in the community, but they were low both in role activity and in life satisfaction.

These eight patterns, in accounting for 50 of the 59 cases, provide considerable coherence in our data on 70- to 79-year-olds. If our original sample had been more representative of the universe of 70-year-olds, perhaps we might have a greater number of discrete patterns, some of them, for example, centered on low physical vitality and poor health. (A larger number of patterns would not necessarily be the case, however, since it may be that persons who survive into the 70's are already a select group, in whom only certain patterns of aging are to be found.)

In any case, it is clear, from this brief description of patterns, that neither the "activity" nor the "disengagement" theory of successful aging accounts for the empirical findings. A "personality-continuity" or "developmental" theory of aging needs to be more formally set forth.

People, as they grow old, seem to be neither at the mercy of the social environment nor at the mercy of some set of intrinsic processes—in either instance, inexorable changes that they cannot influence. On the contrary, the individual seems to continue to make his own "impress" upon the wide range of social and biological changes. He continues to exercise choice and to select from the environment in accordance with his own long-established needs. He ages according to a pattern that has a long history, and that maintains itself, with adaptation, to the end of life.

In summary, then, we regard personality as the pivotal dimension in describing patterns of aging and in predicting relationships between level of social role activity and life satisfaction. There is considerable evidence that, in normal men and women, there is no sharp discontinuity of personality with age, but instead an increasing consistency. Those characteristics that have been central to the personality seem to become even more clearly delineated, and those values the individual has been cherishing become even more salient. In the personality that remains integrated—and in an environment that permits—patterns of overt behavior are likely to become increasingly consonant with the individual's underlying personality needs and his desires.

References

ABOOD, L. G., and GERARD, R. W. A phosphorylation defect in the brains of mice susceptible to audiogenic seizure. In *Biochemistry of the Developing Nervous System.* New York: Academic Press, 1954.

ADORNO, T. W., FRENKEL-BRUNSWIK, E., LEVINSON, D. J., and SANFORD, R. N. *The Authoritarian Personality.* New York: Harper & Row, 1950.

ALBERTS, E., and EHRENFREUND, D. Transposition in children as a function of age. *Journal of Experimental Psychology,* 1951, 41, 30-38.

ALBRIGHT, S., and GAMBRELL, H. Personality traits as criteria for the psychiatric treatment of adolescents. *Smith College Studies in Social Work,* 1938, 9, 1-26.

ALLPORT, G. W. *Becoming: Basic Considerations for a Psychology of Personality.* New Haven: Yale University Press, 1955.

AMES, R. Physical maturing among boys as related to adult social behavior. *California Journal of Educational Research,* 1957, 8, 69-75.

AMSEL, A. The role of frustrative nonreward in noncontinuous reward situations. *Psychological Bulletin,* 1958, 55, 102-119.

ANASTASI, A. *Psychological Testing.* New York: Macmillan, 1954.

ANASTASI, A. *Differential Psychology* (3rd ed.). New York: Macmillan, 1958.

ANASTASI, A., and CORDOVA, F. A. Some effects of bilingualism upon the intelligence test performance of Puerto Rican children in New York City. *Journal of Educational Psychology,* 1953, 44, 1-19.

ANASTASI, A., and FOLEY, J. P., JR. A proposed reorientation in the heredity-environment controversy. *Psychological Review,* 1948, 55, 239-249.

ANDERSON, H. H. The measurement of domination and of socially integrative behavior in teacher's contacts with children. *Child Development,* 1939, 10, 73-89.

ANDERSON, H. H., and BREWER, H. M. Dominative and socially integrative behavior of kindergarten teachers. *Applied Psychology Monograph No. 6.* Stanford, California: Stanford University Press, 1945.

ANDERSON, H. H., and BREWER, J. E. Effects of teachers' dominative and integrative contacts on children's classroom behavior. *Applied Psychology Monograph No. 8.* Stanford, California: Stanford University Press, 1946.

ANDERSON, H. H., BREWER, J. E., and REED, M. F. Studies of teachers' classroom personalities: III. Follow-up studies of the effects of dominative and integrative contacts on children's behavior. *Applied Psychology Monograph No. 11.* Stanford, California: Stanford University Press, 1946.

ANDERSON, J. E. Research in community mental health screening. Paper presented at the meeting of the American Psychological Association, 1952.

ANDERSON, N. H., and GRANT, D. A. A test of a statistical learning theory model for two-choice behavior with double stimulus events. *Journal of Experimental Psychology,* 1957, 54, 305-317.

ANGELL, D. B. Differences in social behavior between elementary school children who have attended nursery school and those who have not attended nursery school. Unpublished master's thesis, North Texas State College, 1954.

ARSENIAN, S. Bilingualism in the post-war world. *Psychological Bulletin,* 1945, 42, 65-86.

ASCH, S. E. *Social Psychology.* New York: Prentice-Hall, 1952.

ATKINSON, J. W. *Motives in Fantasy, Action, and Society.* Princeton: Van No-
strand, 1958.
AUSUBEL, D. P. Negativism as a phase of ego development. *American Journal of
Orthopsychiatry,* 1950, 20, 796-805.
AUSUBEL, D. P. Relationships between shame and guilt in the socializing process.
Psychological Review, 1955, 62, 378-390.

BACH, G. R. Young children's play fantasies. *Psychological Monographs,* 1945,
59, No. 2 (Whole No. 272).
BACH, G. R. Father-fantasies and father-typing in father separated children.
Child Development, 1946, 17, 63-80.
BAGLEY, W. C. *The Educational Process.* New York: Macmillan, 1912.
BAKER, C. T., SONTAG, L. W., and NELSON, V. L. Specific ability in IQ change.
Journal of Consulting Psychology, 1955, 19, 307-310.
BARBOUR, R. F. Selected surveys prepared for the inter-clinic conference. In J. F.
Davidson (Chmn.), Follow-up on child guidance cases. Ninth Child Guidance
Inter-Clinic Conference, London, 1951.
BARKER, R. G., and WRIGHT, H. F. *Midwest and Its Children: The Psychological
Ecology of an American Town.* New York: Harper & Row, 1955.
BARKER, R. G., WRIGHT, B. A., MYERSON, L., and GONICK, M. R. Adjustment to
physical handicap and illness: A survey of the social psychology of physique
and disability. *Social Science Research Council Bulletin,* 1953, No. 55 (Rev.).
BARON, D. Personal-social characteristics and classroom social status. *Sociometry,*
1951, 14, 32-42.
BARRON, D. H. Genetic neurology and the behavior problem. In P. Weiss (Ed.),
Genetic Neurology. Chicago: University of Chicago Press, 1950.
BARTLETT, E. R., and HARRIS, D. B. Personality factors in delinquency. *School
and Society,* 1936, 43, 653-656.
BAYLEY, N. Mental growth in young children. In *Intelligence: Its Nature and
Nurture.* 39th Yearbook, National Society for the Study of Education. Bloom-
ington, Illinois: Public School. Part II, pp. 11-47.
BAYLEY, N. Consistency and variability in the growth in IQ from birth to eighteen
years. *Journal of Genetic Psychology,* 1949, 75, 165-196.
BAYLEY, N. On the growth of intelligence. *American Psychologist,* 1955, 10, 805-
818.
BAYLEY, N., and ODEN, M. H. The maintenance of intellectual ability in gifted
adults. *Journal of Gerontology,* 1955, 10, 91-107.
BEACH, F. A. The neural basis of innate behavior: I. Effects of cortical lesions
upon the maternal behavior pattern in the rat. *Journal of Comparative Psychology,* 1937, 24, 393-436.
BEACH, F. A. *Hormones and Behavior.* New York: Paul B. Hoeber, 1948.
BEACH, F. A., and JAYNES, J. Effects of early experience upon the behavior of
animals. *Psychological Bulletin,* 1954, 51, 239-263.
BELL, H. M. *Matching Youth and Jobs.* Washington, D.C.: American Council
on Education, 1940.
BELLER, E. K. Dependence and independence in young children. Unpublished
doctoral dissertation, State University of Iowa, 1948.
BENDER, I. E. Changes in religious interest: A retest after 15 years. *Journal of
Abnormal and Social Psychology,* 1958, 57, 41-46.
BENDER, L. Anxiety in disturbed children. In P. H. Hoch and J. Zubin (Eds.),
Anxiety. New York: Grune & Stratton, 1950.

BENEDICT, R. *The Chrysanthemum and the Sword*. Boston: Houghton Mifflin, 1946.

BENNETT, C. C. An inquiry into the genesis of poor reading. *Teachers College Contributions to Education*, 1938, No. 442.

BIALICK, I. The relationship between reactions to authority figures on the TAT and overt behavior in an authority situation by hospital patients. Unpublished doctoral dissertation, University of Pittsburgh, 1951.

BIRREN, J. E. (Ed.). *Handbook of Aging and the Individual*. Chicago: University of Chicago Press, 1959.

BOLTON, J. S., and MOYES, J. M. The cyto-architecture of the cerebral cortex of the human fetus of eighteen weeks. *Brain*, 1912, 35, 1-25.

BONNEY, M. E. Popular and unpopular children, a sociometric study. *Sociometry Monographs*, 1947, No. 9.

BONNEY, M. E. A study of social status on the second grade level. *Journal of Genetic Psychology*, 1942, 60, 271-305.

BOTWINICK, J., and SHOCK, N. W. Age differences in performance decrement with continuous work. *Journal of Gerontology*, 1952, 7, 41-46.

BOWLBY, J. In P. H. Hoch and J. Zubin (Eds.), *Anxiety*. New York: Grune & Stratton, 1950.

BRACKBILL, G. A. Studies of brain dysfunction in schizophrenia. *Psychological Bulletin*, 1956, 53, 210-226.

BRADWAY, K. IQ constancy on the Revised Stanford-Binet from the preschool to the junior high school level. *Journal of Genetic Psychology*, 1944, 65, 197-217.

BRAITHWAITE, R. B. *Scientific Explanation*. New York: Cambridge University Press, 1953.

BRAND, H., SAKODA, J. M., and WOODS, P. J. Contingent partial reinforcement and the anticipation of correct alternatives. *Journal of Experimental Psychology*, 1957, 53, 417-424.

BRIDGES, K. M. B. Emotional development in early infancy. *Child Development*, 1932, 3, 324.

BRIDGMAN, C. S., and CARMICHAEL, L. An experimental study of the onset of behavior in the fetal guinea-pig. *Journal of Genetic Psychology*, 1935, 47, 247-267.

BRONNER, A. F. Treatment and what happened afterward. *American Journal of Orthopsychiatry*, 1944, 14, 28-35.

BROWN, A. W., MORRISON, J., and COUCH, G. B. Influence of affectional family relationships on character development. *Journal of Abnormal and Social Psychology*, 1947, 42, 422-428.

BROWN, J. L. The follow-up procedure of an intermittent child guidance clinic. Unpublished master's thesis, Smith College, 1931.

BROWN, M. Adolescents treatable by a family agency. *Smith College Studies in Social Work*, 1947, 18, 37-67.

BROZEK, J., and TIEDE, K. Reliable and questionable significance in a series of statistical tests. *Psychological Bulletin*, 1952, 49, 339-341.

BRUSH, F. R. The effects of shock intensity on the acquisition and extinction of an avoidance response in dogs. *Journal of Comparative and Physiological Psychology*, 1957, 50, 547-552.

BUHLER, C. *Der menschliche Lebenslauf als psychologisches Problem*. Leipzig: Verlag von S. Hirzel, 1933.

BURKS, B. In *Nature and Nurture: Their Influence upon Intelligence*. 27th Yearbook, National Society for the Study of Education. Bloomington, Illinois: Public School, 1928. Part I, p. 219.

BURLINGHAM, S. A quantitative analysis of psychiatric social treatment carried out in seventy-five cases at the Institute for Juvenile Research. Unpublished master's thesis, Smith College, 1931.

BURT, C. Experimental tests of general intelligence. *British Journal of Psychology*, 1909, 3, 94-177.

BURT, C. The inheritance of mental characteristics. *Eugenics Review*, 1912, 4, 168-200.

BURT, C. *Annual reports of the psychologist to the London County Council.* London: London County Council, 1914-1931.

BURT, C. *The distribution and relations of educational abilities.* London: P. S. King & Son, 1917.

BURT, C. Ability and income. *British Journal of Educational Psychology*, 1943, 13, 83-98.

BURT, C. The education of the adolescent: The psychological implications of the Norwood Report. *British Journal of Educational Psychology*, 1943, 13, 126-140.

BURT, C. Is the doctrine of instincts dead? *British Journal of Educational Psychology*, 1941, 11, 155-172; 1943, 13, 1-16.

BURT, C. The differentiation of intellectual ability. *British Journal of Educational Psychology*, 1954, 24, 76-90.

BURT, C. The evidence for the concept of intelligence. *British Journal of Educational Psychology*, 1955, 25, 158-177.

BURT, C., and HOWARD, M. The multifactorial theory of inheritance and its application to intelligence. *British Journal of Statistical Psychology*, 1956, 9, 95-131.

CAMPBELL, D. T. Social attitudes and other acquired behavioral dispositions. In S. Koch (Ed.), *Psychology: A Study of a Science.* Vol. 6. *Investigations of Man as Socius: Their Place in Psychology and the Social Sciences.* New York: McGraw-Hill, 1963.

CAMPBELL, E. H. The social-sex development of children. *Genetic Psychology Monographs*, 1939, 21, 461-552.

CAMPBELL, F. *Eleven Plus and All That.* London: Watts, 1956.

CAMPBELL, N. R. *Physics: the Elements.* New York: Cambridge University Press, 1920.

CANADAY, L. J. A way of predicting the probable outcome of treatment of young children who run away. Unpublished master's thesis, Smith College, 1940.

CANTOR, G. N. The effects of three types of pretraining on discrimination learning in children. *Journal of Experimental Psychology*, 1955, 49, 339-342.

CANTOR, J. H. Amount of pretraining as a factor in stimulus pre-differentiation and performance set. *Journal of Experimental Psychology*, 1955, 50, 180-184.

CARMICHAEL, L. An experimental study in the guinea-pig of the origin and development of reflexes and patterns of behavior in relation to the stimulation of specific receptor areas during the period of active fetal life. *Genetic Psychology Monographs*, 1934, No. 16, 338-491.

CARMICHAEL, L. (Ed.). *Manual of Child Psychology.* New York: Wiley, 1946.

CARNAP, R. Foundations of logic and mathematics. In *International Encyclopedia of Unified Science*, Vol. 1. Chicago: University of Chicago Press, 1955.

CARPENTER, J. A. Some factors relating to the method and outcome of casework treatment with the adolescent girl when the girl herself is the focus of treatment. Unpublished master's thesis, Smith College, 1939.

CASTANEDA, A., McCANDLESS, B. R., and PALERMO, D. S. The children's form of the manifest anxiety scale. *Child Development*, 1956, 27, 317-326.

CASTANEDA, A., PALERMO, D. S., and MCCANDLESS, B. R. Complex learning and performance as a function of anxiety in children and task difficulty. *Child Development*, 1956, 27, 327-332.

CATTELL, R. B. The theory of fluid and crystallized intelligence: A critical experiment. *Journal of Educational Psychology*, 1963, 54, 1-22.

CHARLES, M. S. A developmental study of the electroencephalogram of the puppy. Unpublished master's thesis, University of Maine, 1954.

CHILD, I. L. FRANK, K. F., and STORM, T. Self-ratings and TAT: Their relations to each other and to childhood background. *Journal of Personality*, 1956, 25, 98-114.

CHRISTIANSON, E., GATES, M., and COLEMAN, F. A survey of the intake of a mental hygiene clinic with special reference to the outcome of treatment. *Smith College Studies in Social Work*, 1934, 5, 211-212.

CHURCH, R. M. Transmission of learned behavior between rats. *Journal of Abnormal and Social Psychology*, 1957, 54, 163-165.

COCHRAN, W. G., and COX, G. M. *Experimental Designs*. New York: Wiley, 1950.

COGHILL, G. E. *Anatomy and the Problem of Behavior*. New York: Macmillan, 1929.

COHEN, M., and DAVIS, E. Factors related to the outcome of treatment in a child guidance clinic. *Smith College Studies in Social Work*, 1934, 5, 212-214.

CRAIG, W. The voices of pigeons regarded as a mean of social control. *American Journal of Sociology*, 1908, 14, 86.

CRONBACH, L. J. Correlation between persons as a research tool. In O. H. Mowrer (Ed.), *Psychotherapy: Theory and Research*. New York: Ronald Press, 1953.

CUMMING, E. Further thoughts on the theory of disengagement. *UNESCO International Social Science Journal*, 1963, 15, 337-393.

CUMMING, E., and HENRY, W. E. *Growing Old: The Process of Disengagement*. New York: Basic Books, 1961.

CUNNINGHAM, J. M., WESTERMAN, H. H., and FISCHOFF, J. A follow-up study of children seen in a psychiatric clinic for children. Paper read at the meeting of the American Orthopsychiatry Association, Chicago, March 1955.

D'ABRO, A. *The Rise of the New Physics*. Vol. 1. New York: Dover, 1951.

DANN, R. H. A comparison of four verbal subtests on the Wechsler-Bellevue Form I, and the WAIS. *Journal of Clinical Psychology*, 1957, 13, 70-71.

DARBY, C. L., and RIOPELLE, A. J. Observational learning in the rhesus monkey. *Journal of Comparative and Physiological Psychology*, 1959, 52, 94-98.

DARCY, N. T. A review of the literature on the effects of bilingualism upon the measurement of intelligence. *Journal of Genetic Psychology*, 1953, 82, 21-57.

DARLEY, J. G., and HAGENAH, T. *Vocational Interest Measurement: Theory and Practice*. Minneapolis: University of Minnesota Press, 1955.

DARLING, F. F. *Wild Country*. London: Cambridge University Press, 1938.

DARLINGTON, C. D., and MATHER, K. *The Elements of Genetics*. London: G. Allen, 1949.

DARLINGTON, C. D., and MATHER, K. *Genes, Plants, and People*. London: G. Allen, 1950.

DAVIDS, A., HENRY, A. F., McARTHUR, C. C., and McNAMARA, L. F. Projection, self evaluation, and clinical evaluation of aggression. *Journal of Consulting Psychology*, 1955, 19, 437-440.

DAVIDSON, P. E., and ANDERSON, H. D. *Occupational Mobility in an American Community*. Stanford, California: Stanford University Press, 1937.

DAVIS, A., and HAVIGHURST, R. J. Social class and color differences in child rearing. *American Sociological Review,* 1946, 11, 698-710.

DAVIS, K. B. *Factors in the Sex Life of Twenty-two Hundred Women.* New York: Harper & Row, 1929.

DAVIS, W. A. *Social Class Influences upon Learning.* Cambridge: Harvard University Press, 1948.

DAVIS, W. A., and DOLLARD, J. *Children of Bondage.* Washington, D.C.: American Council on Education, 1940.

DAVIS, W. A., and HAVIGHURST, R. J. *Father of the Man: How Your Child Gets His Personality.* Boston: Houghton Mifflin, 1947.

DeCHARMS, R., and MOELLER, G. H. Values expressed in American children's readers: 1800-1950. *Journal of Abnormal and Social Psychology,* 1962, 64, 136-142.

DeGROAT, A. F., and THOMPSON, G. G. A study of the distribution of teacher approval and disapproval among sixth-grade pupils. *Journal of Experimental Education,* 1949, 18, 57-75.

DEMMING, J. A., and PRESSEY, S. L. Tests "indigenous" to the adult and older years. *Journal of Counseling Psychology,* 1957, 4, 144-148.

DENKER, P. G. Results of treatment of psychoneuroses by the general practitioner. *New York State Medical Journal,* 1946, 46, 2164-2166.

DETAMBEL, M. H. A test of a model for multiple-choice behavior. *Journal of Experimental Psychology,* 1955, 49, 97-104.

DEUTSCH, H. *The Psychology of Women.* Vol. 2. *Motherhood.* New York: Grune & Stratton, 1944.

Dictionary of Occupational Titles: Vol. 2. *Occupational Classification and Industrial Index.* Washington, D.C.: Federal Security Agency, 1949. U.S. Government Printing Office.

DINSMOOR, J. A. Punishment: I. The avoidance hypothesis. *Psychological Review,* 1954, 61, 34-46.

DOBZHANSKY, T. The genetic nature of differences among men. In S. Persons (Ed.), *Evolutionary Thought in America.* New Haven: Yale University Press, 1950-a, 86-155.

DOBZHANSKY, T. Heredity, environment, and evolution. *Science,* 1950-b, 111, 161-166.

DOLLARD, J., and MILLER, N. E. *Personality and Psychotherapy.* New York: McGraw-Hill, 1950.

DOLLARD, J., DOOB, L. W., MILLER, N. E., MOWRER, O. H., and SEARS, R. R. *Frustration and Aggression.* New Haven: Yale University Press, 1939.

DUHEM, P. *The Aim and Structure of Physical Theory.* Princeton: Princeton University Press, 1954.

DUKES, W. F. The psychological study of values. *Psychological Bulletin,* 1955, 52, 24-50.

DUNN, L. C. (Ed.). *Eugenics in the Twentieth Century.* New York: Macmillan, 1921.

DUNNETTE, M. D. Vocational interest differences among engineers employed in different functions. *Journal of Applied Psychology,* 1957, 41, 273-278.

DUREA, M. A. Personality characteristics of juvenile delinquents: I. A method for the selection of differentiating traits. *Child Development,* 1937-a, 8, 115-128.

DUREA, M. A. Personality characteristics of juvenile delinquents: II. Reliability of differentiating traits. *Child Development,* 1937-b, 8, 257-262.

DUREA, M. A., and HESTON, J. C. Differential diagnosis of potential delinquency: Additional suggestions. *American Journal of Orthopsychiatry,* 1941, 11, 338-341.

EDWARDS, A. M. A social reference: Economic grouping of the gainful workers of the United States. *Journal of the American Statistical Association,* 1933, 28, 377-387.

ERIKSON, E. H. *Childhood and Society.* New York: Norton, 1950.

ESTES, W. K. Individual behavior in uncertain situations: An interpretation in terms of statistical association theory. In R. M. Thrall, C. H. Coombs, and R. L. Davis (Eds.), *Decision Processes.* New York: Wiley, 1954.

ESTES, W. K. Stimulus-response theory of drive. In M. R. Jones (Ed.), *Nebraska Symposium on Motivation.* Vol. 6. Lincoln: University of Nebraska Press, 1958.

ESTES, W. K. The statistical approach to learning theory. In S. Koch (Ed.), *Psychology: A Study of a Science.* Vol. 2. New York: McGraw-Hill, 1959.

ESTES, W. K., and STRAUGHN, J. H. Analysis of a verbal conditioning situation in terms of statistical learning theory. *Journal of Experimental Psychology,* 1954, 47, 225-234.

EYSENCK, H. J. The effects of psychotherapy: An evaluation. *Journal of Consulting Psychology,* 1952, 16, 319-324.

EYSENCK, H. J. The effects of psychotherapy: A reply. *Journal of Abnormal and Social Psychology,* 1955, 50, 147-148.

FABRICIUS, E. Zur Ethologie junger Anatiden. *Acta zoologica fennica,* 1951, 68, 1.

FENTON, N., and WALLACE, R. Child guidance in California communities, Part 6. Follow-up study of Bureau cases. *Journal of Juvenile Research,* 1938, 22, 43-60.

FESHBACH, S. The drive-reducing function of fantasy behavior. *Journal of Abnormal and Social Psychology,* 1955, 50, 3-11.

FISHER, R. A. Correlation between relatives on the supposition of Mendelian inheritance. *Transactions of the Royal Society of Edinburgh,* 1918, 52, 399-433.

FISHER, R. A. The causes of human variability. *Eugenics Review,* 1919, 11, 213-220.

FISHER, R. A. *Statistical Methods for Research Workers* (5th ed.). Edinburgh: Oliver & Boyd, 1934.

FISHER, R. A. *The Genetical Theory of Natural Selection.* Oxford: Clarendon Press, 1950.

FLOUD, J. E., HALSEY, A. H., and MARTIN, F. M. *Social Class and Educational Opportunity.* London: Heinemann, 1956.

FORGUS, R. H. The effect of early perceptual learning on the behavioral organization of adult rats. *Journal of Comparative and Physiological Psychology,* 1954, 47, 331-336.

FREEMAN, F. N. *Mental Tests.* New York: Houghton Mifflin, 1926.

FRENKEL, E. Studies in biographical psychology. *Character and Personality,* 1936, 5, 1-34.

FRENKEL-BRUNSWIK, E. Motivation and behavior. *Genetic Psychology Monographs,* 1942, No. 26, 121-265.

FREUD, A. *The Ego and the Mechanisms of Defense.* New York: International Universities Press, Inc., 1946.

FREUD, S. *The Ego and the Id.* London: Hogarth, 1950.

FRIEND, J. G., and HAGGARD, E. A. Work adjustment in relation to family background. *Applied Psychology Monographs,* 1948, No. 16. Stanford, California: Stanford University Press.

FROMM, E. *Escape from Freedom.* New York: Rinehart, 1941.

FULLER, J. L., EASLER, C. A., and BANKS, E. M. Formation of conditioned avoidance responses in young puppies. *American Journal of Physiology,* 1950, 160, 462-466.

FULTON, J. F. *Physiology of the Nervous System.* New York: Oxford University Press, 1943.

GAGNÉ, R. M., and BAKER, K. E. Stimulus predifferentiation as a factor in transfer of training. *Journal of Experimental Psychology,* 1950, 40, 439-451.

GALL, H. S. The development of affiliation motivation. Unpublished doctoral dissertation, University of North Carolina, 1960.

GALTON, F. *Hereditary Genius.* London: Macmillan, 1869.

GARDNER, R. A. Probability learning with two and three choices. *American Journal of Psychology,* 1957, 70, 174-185.

GARNETT, M. *Education and World Citizenship.* Cambridge: Cambridge University Press, 1921.

GERJUOY, I. R. Discrimination learning as a function of the similarity of the stimulus names. Unpublished doctoral dissertation, State University of Iowa, 1953.

GESELL, A. *Wolf Child and Human Child.* London, 1941.

GESELL, A., and ILG, F. L. *Infant and Child in the Culture of Today.* New York: Harper & Row, 1943.

GETZELS, J. W., and JACKSON, P. W. The social context of giftedness: A multidimensional approach to definition and method. Paper read at the meeting of the American Sociological Society, Seattle, Washington, August 1958-a.

GETZELS, J. W., and JACKSON, P. W. The highly creative and the highly intelligent adolescent: An attempt at differentiation. Paper read at the meeting of the American Psychological Association, Washington, September 1958-b.

GETZELS, J. W., and JACKSON, P. W. The meaning of "giftedness": An examination of an expanding concept. *Phi Delta Kappan,* 1958-c, 40, 75-77.

GETZELS, J. W., and JACKSON, P. W. Occupational choice and cognitive functioning: A study of the career aspirations of highly intelligent and of highly creative adolescents. *Journal of Abnormal and Social Psychology,* 1960, 61, 119-123.

GEWIRTZ, J. L. Dependent and aggressive interaction in young children. Unpublished doctoral dissertation, State University of Iowa, 1948.

GIBBS, F. A., and GIBBS, E. L. *Atlas of Electroencephalography.* Cambridge, Massachusetts: Cummings, 1941.

GIBSON, J. J., and GIBSON, E. J. Perceptual learning: Differentiation or enrichment? *Psychological Review,* 1955, 62, 32-41.

GINSBERG, A. Hypothetical constructs and intervening variables. *Psychological Review,* 1954, 61, 119-131.

GINSBERG, B. Genetics and the physiology of the nervous system. *Proceedings of the Association for Research in Nervous and Mental Disease,* 1954, 33, 39-56.

GLASER, D. Dynamics of ethnic identification. *American Sociological Review,* 1958, 23, 31-40.

GLUCK, M. R. The relationship between hostility in the TAT and behavioral hostility. *Journal of Projective Techniques,* 1955, 19, 21-26.

GOLDSCHMIDT, R. B. *Theoretical Genetics.* Berkeley, California: University of California Press, 1955.

GOLLANDER, B. A study of overinhibited and unsocialized aggressive children: III. Later adjustment. Unpublished master's thesis, Smith College, 1944.

GOODENOUGH, F. L. Anger in young children. *Child Welfare Monograph No. 9.* Minneapolis: University of Minnesota Press, 1931.

GOODNOW, J. J. Determinants of choice distribution in two-choice situations. *American Journal of Psychology*, 1955, 68, 106-116.

GOODNOW, J. J., and PETTIGREW, T. F. Effect of prior patterns of experience upon strategies and learning situations. *Journal of Experimental Psychology*, 1955, 49, 381-389.

GOODNOW, J. J., and POSTMAN, L. Probability learning in a problem-solving situation. *Journal of Experimental Psychology*, 1955, 49, 16-22.

GOOLISHIAN, H. A., and RAMSEY, R. The Wechsler-Bellevue Form I and the WAIS: A comparison. *Journal of Clinical Psychology*, 1956, 12, 147-151.

GORER, G. *The American People*. New York: Norton, 1948.

GOSS, A. E. Transfer as a function of type and amount of preliminary experience with task stimuli. *Journal of Experimental Psychology*, 1953, 46, 419-428.

GOUGH, H. G. The C. P. I. Rigidity scale. Unpublished mimeographed manuscript, Institute of Personality Assessment and Research, University of California, 1951.

GOUGH, H. G., McCLOSKEY, H., and MEEHL, P. E. A personality scale for social responsibility. *Journal of Abnormal and Social Psychology*, 1952, 47, 73-80.

GRABOWSKI, U. Prägung eines Jungschafs auf den Menschen. *Zeitschrift für Tierpsychologie*, 1941, 4, 326.

GRANT, D. A. The discrimination of sequences in stimulus events and the transmission of information. *American Psychologist*, 1954, 9, 62-68.

GRANT, D. A., HAKE, H. W., and HORNSETH, J. P. Acquisition and extinction of a verbal conditioned response with differing percentages of reinforcement. *Journal of Experimental Psychology*, 1951, 42, 1-5.

GRANT, D. A., SCHIPPER, L. M., and ROSS, B. M. Effect of intertrial interval during acquisition on extinction of the conditioned eyelid response following partial reinforcement. *Journal of Experimental Psychology*, 1952, 44, 203-210.

GREENBLATT, E. L. Relationship of mental health and social status. *Journal of Educational Research*, 1950, 44, 193-204.

GROSSMAN, B., and WRIGHTER, J. The relationship between selection-rejection and intelligence, social status, and personality among sixth grade children. *Sociometry*, 1948, 11, 346-355.

GUILFORD, J. P. A revised structure of intellect. *Report of the Psychological Laboratory, No. 19*. Los Angeles: University of Southern California, 1957.

GUTTMAN, L. In S. A. Stouffer et al., *Measurement and Prediction*. Princeton: Princeton University Press, 1950.

HAGEN, E. E. How economic growth begins: A general theory applied to Japan. *Public Opinion Quarterly*, 1958, 12, 373-390.

HAGGARD, E. A., DAVIS, A., and HAVIGHURST, R. J. Some factors which influence performance of children on intelligence tests. *American Psychologist*, 1948, 3, 265-266.

HALDANE, J. B. S. *Heredity and Politics*. New York: Norton, 1938.

HARDY, M. G. Social recognition at the elementary school age. *Journal of Social Psychology*, 1937, 8, 365-384.

HARLOW, H. F. Mice, monkeys, men, and motives. *Psychological Review*, 1953, 60, 23-32.

HARMAN, P. J. Private communication, 1952.

HARRELL, R. F., WOODYARD, E., and GATES, A. I. *The Effect of Mothers' Diets on the Intelligence of the Offspring*. New York: Bureau of Publications, Teachers College, Columbia University, 1955.

HARRIS, D., CLARK, K., ROSE, A., and VALASEK, F. The measurement of responsibility in children. *Child Development,* 1954-a, 25, 21-28.

HARRIS, D., CLARK, K. ROSE, A., and VALASEK, F. The relationship of children's home duties to an attitude of responsibility. *Child Development,* 1954-b, 25, 29-33.

HART, H. Changing social attitudes and interests. In *Recent Social Trends in the United States.* New York: McGraw-Hill, 1933. Pp. 382-442.

HARTSHORNE, H., and MAY, M. A. *Studies in the Nature of Character.* Vol. 2. *Studies in Service and Self-Control.* New York: Macmillan, 1929.

HAVIGHURST, R. J., and NEUGARTEN, B. L. *American Indian and White Children.* Chicago: University of Chicago Press, 1955.

HAVIGHURST, R. J., NEUGARTEN, B. L., and TOBIN, S. Disengagement, personality, and life satisfaction. In *Age with a Future.* Copenhagen: Munksgaard, 1964. Proceedings of the Sixth International Congress of Gerontology.

HAYES, M. L. A study of the classroom disturbances of eighth grade boys and girls. *Teachers College Contributions to Education,* 1943, 871, 139.

HEALY, W., BRONNER, A. F., BAYLOR, E. M., and MURPHY, J. P. *Reconstructing Behavior in Youth: A Study of Problem Children in Foster Families.* New York: Knopf, 1929.

HEBB, D. O. *The Organization of Behavior.* New York: Wiley, 1949.

HEDIGER, H. *Wild Animals in Captivity.* London: Butterworth, 1938.

HEINROTH, O. Beiträge zur Biologie, namentlich Ethologie und Psychologie der Anatiden. *Verhandelingen 5th International Kongress,* 1912, 589-702.

HEINROTH, O., and HEINROTH, M. *Die Vögel Mitteleuropas.* Berlin: Lichterfelde, 1924-1933.

HENRY, W. E. The theory of intrinsic disengagement. Paper presented at the International Research Seminar on Social and Psychological Aspects of Aging, Markaryl, Sweden, August 1963.

HESS, E. H. Effects of meprobamate on imprinting in waterfowl. *Annals of the New York Academy of Sciences,* 1957, 67, 724.

HESS, E. H. "Imprinting" in animals. *Scientific American,* 1958, 198, 81-90.

HESS, E. H. Two conditions limiting critical age for imprinting. *Journal of Comparative and Physiological Psychology,* 1959, 52, 515-518.

HESS, E. H., and SCHAEFER, H. H. Innate behavior patterns as indicators of the "Critical Period." *Zeitschrift für Tierpsychologie,* 1959, 16, 155-160.

HILDITCH, T. P. *A Concise History of Chemistry.* New York: Van Nostrand, 1911.

HINDE, R. A., THORPE, M. A., and VINCE, M. A. The following responses of young coots and moorhens. *Behavior,* 1956, 9, 214-242.

HIRSCH, J., and TRYON, R. C. Mass screening and reliable individual measurement in the experimental behavior genetics of lower organisms. *Psychological Bulletin,* 1956, 53, 402-410.

HOLLENBERG, E., and SPERRY, M. Some antecedents of aggression and effects of frustration on doll play. *Personality,* 1951, 1, 32-43.

HOLLINGSHEAD, A. B. *Elmtown's Youth.* New York: Wiley, 1949.

HOOKER, D. Reflex activities in the human fetus. In R. G. Barker, J. S. Kounin, and H. F. Wright (Eds.), *Child Behavior and Development.* New York: McGraw-Hill, 1943.

HOOKER, D. Neural growth and the development of behavior. In P. Weiss (Ed.), *Genetic Neurology.* Chicago: University of Chicago Press, 1950.

HORNEY, K. *Our Inner Conflicts.* New York: Norton, 1945.

HORROCKS, J. E., and THOMPSON, G. G. A study of the friendship fluctuations of rural boys and girls. *Journal of Genetic Psychology,* 1946, 69, 189-198.

HORWITT, M. K. Fact and artifact in the biology of schizophrenia. *Science*, 1956, 124, 429-430

HOWES, D. H., and SOLOMON, R. L. Visual duration threshold as a function of word-probability. *Journal of Experimental Psychology*, 1951, 41, 401-410.

HUBBARD, R. M., and ADAMS, C. F. Factors affecting the success of child guidance treatment. *American Journal of Orthopsychiatry*, 1936, 6, 81-102.

HULL, C. L. *Principles of Behavior*. New York: Appleton-Century-Crofts, 1943.

HULL, C. L. *A Behavior System*. New Haven: Yale University Press, 1952.

HUMPHREYS, L. G. Acquisition and extinction of verbal expectations in a situation analogous to conditioning. *Journal of Experimental Psychology*, 1939-a, 25, 294-301.

HUMPHREYS, L. G. The effect of random alternation of reinforcement on the acquisition and extinction of conditioned eyelid reactions. *Journal of Experimental Psychology*, 1939-b, 25, 141-158.

HUMPHREYS, L. G. Psychogalvanic responses following two conditions of reinforcement. *Journal of Experimental Psychology*, 1940, 27, 71-75.

HURLOCK, E. B. The value of praise and reproof as incentives for children. *Archives of Psychology*, 1924, 11, No. 71.

HURLOCK, E. B. *Child Development* (3rd ed.). New York: McGraw-Hill, 1956.

HUTTEN, E. H. *The Language of Modern Physics*. London: G. Allen, 1956.

International Kindergarten Union. *A Study of the Vocabulary of Children Before Entering the First Grade*. Baltimore: Williams & Wilkins, 1928.

IRGENS, E. M. Must parents' attitudes become modified in order to bring about adjustment in problem children? *Smith College Studies in Social Work*, 1936, 7, 17-45.

IRWIN, O. C., and CHEN, H. Development of speech during infancy: Curve of phonemic types. *Journal of Experimental Psychology*, 1946, 36, 431-436.

JACOBSEN, V. Influential factors in the outcome of treatment of school phobia. *Smith College Studies in Social Work*, 1948, 18, 181-202.

JAMES, H. Flicker: An unconditioned stimulus for imprinting. *Canadian Journal of Psychology*, 1959, 13, 59-67.

JAMES, W. T., and CANNON, D. J. Conditioned avoiding responses in puppies. *American Journal of Physiology*, 1952, 168, 251-253.

JARVIK, L. F., KALLMANN, F. J., and FALK, A. Intellectual changes in aged twins. *Journal of Gerontology*, 1962, 17, 289-294.

JARVIK, M. E. Probability learning and a negative recency effect in the serial anticipation of alternatives. *Journal of Experimental Psychology*, 1951, 41, 291-297.

JAYNES, J. Imprinting: The interaction of learned and innate behavior: I. Development and Generalization. *Journal of Comparative and Physiological Psychology*, 1956, 49, 201-206.

JAYNES, J. Imprinting: The interaction of learned and innate behavior: II. The critical period. *Journal of Comparative and Physiological Psychology*, 1957, 50, 6.

JAYNES, J. Imprinting: The interaction of learned and innate behavior: III. Practice effects on performance, retention and fear. *Journal of Comparative and Physiological Psychology*, 1958-a, 51, 234-237.

JAYNES, J. Imprinting: The interaction of learned and innate behavior: IV. Generalization and emergent discrimination. *Journal of Comparative and Physiological Psychology,* 1958-b, 51, 238-242.

JEANS, SIR J. *An Introduction to the Kinetic Theory of Gases.* Cambridge: Cambridge University Press, 1940.

JENKINS, W. O., and STANLEY, J. C. Partial reinforcement: A review and critique. *Psychological Bulletin,* 1950, 47, 193-234.

JEROME, E. J. Age and learning—experimental studies. In J. E. Birren (Ed.), *Handbook of Aging and the Individual.* Chicago: University of Chicago Press, 1959. Chap. 19, pp. 655-699.

JOHNSON, L. J., and REID, J. H. An evaluation of ten years' work with emotionally disturbed children. *Ryther Child Center Monograph IV,* 1947.

JONES, H. E. *Development in Adolescence.* New York: Appleton-Century-Crofts, 1943.

JONES, H. E. The study of patterns of emotional expression. In M. L. Reymert (Ed.), *Feelings and Emotions: The Moosehart Symposium.* New York: McGraw-Hill, 1950.

JONES, H. E. Age changes in adult mental abilities. In *Old Age in the Modern World.* London: Livingston, 1955. Pp. 267-274.

JONES, H. E. Intelligence and problem-solving. In J. E. Birren (Ed.), *Handbook of Aging and the Individual.* Chicago: University of Chicago Press, 1959.

JONES, H. E., and BAYLEY, N. The Berkeley growth study. *Child Development,* 1941, 12, 167-173.

JONES, H. E., and CONRAD, H. S. The growth and decline of intelligence: A study of a homogeneous group between the ages of ten and sixty. *Genetic Psychology Monographs,* 1933, No. 13, 223-298.

JONES, M. C. The later careers of boys who were early- or late-maturing. *Child Development,* 1957, 28, 113-128.

JUDD, C. H. The relation of special training to general intelligence. *Educational Review,* 1908, 36, 28-42.

KAGAN, J. The measurement of overt aggression from fantasy. *Journal of Abnormal and Social Psychology,* 1956, 52, 390-393.

KAGAN, J. The concept of identification. *Psychological Review,* 1958, 65, 296-305.

KAGAN, J., and MUSSEN, P. H. Dependency themes on the TAT and group conformity. *Journal of Consulting Psychology,* 1956, 20, 29-33.

KALDEGG, A. Responses of German and English secondary school boys to a projection test. *British Journal of Psychology,* 1948, 39, 30-53.

KALLMANN, F. J. *Heredity in Health and Mental Disorder: Principles of Psychiatric Genetics in the Light of Comparative Twin Studies.* New York: Norton, 1953.

KANOUS, L. E., DAUGHERTY, R. A., and COHN, T. S. Relation between heterosexual friendship choices and socioeconomic level. *Child Development,* 1962, 33, 251-255.

KAPLAN, L. The annoyances of elementary school teachers. *Journal of Educational Research,* 1951-1952, 45, 649-665.

KENDLER, H. H. "What is learned?"—A theoretical blind alley. *Psychological Review,* 1952, 59, 269-277.

KENDLER, H. H., and LEVINE, S. Studies on the effects of change of drive: I. From hunger to thirst in a T-maze. *Journal of Experimental Psychology,* 1951, 41, 429-436.

KING, J. A., and GURNEY, N. L. Effect of early social experience on adult aggressive behavior in C57BL10 mice. *Journal of Comparative and Physiological Psychology*, 1954, 47, 326-330.

KLETT, C. J. Performance of high school students on the Edwards Personal Preference Schedule. *Journal of Consulting Psychology*, 1957, 21, 68-72.

KOCH, S., and HULL, C. L. In W. K. Estes et al., *Modern Learning Theory*. New York: Appleton-Century-Crofts, 1954.

KORNER, A. F. *Some Aspects of Hostility in Young Children*. New York: Grune & Stratton, 1949.

KUENNE, M. R. Experimental investigation of the relation of language to transposition behavior in young children. *Journal of Experimental Psychology*, 1946, 36, 471-490.

KUHLEN, R. G., and LEE, B. J. Personality characteristics and social acceptability in adolescence. *Journal of Educational Psychology*, 1943, 34, 321-340.

LA MORE, M. T. An evaluation of a state hospital child guidance clinic. *Smith College Studies in Social Work*, 1941, 12, 137-164.

LASHLEY, K. S., and CLARK, G. The cytoarchitecture of the cerebral cortex of Ateles: A critical examination of architectonic studies. *Journal of Comparative Neurology*, 1946, 85, 223-305.

LASHLEY, K. S., and WADE, M. The Pavlovian theory of generalization. *Psychological Review*, 1946, 53, 72-87.

LAZOWICK, L. On the nature of identification. *Journal of Abnormal and Social Psycholgoy*, 1955, 51, 175-183.

LEE, P. R., and KENWORTHY, M. E. *Mental Hygiene and Social Work*. New York: Commonwealth Fund, 1929.

LEEDS, C., and COOK, W. The construction and differential value of a scale for determining teacher-pupil attitudes. *Journal of Experimental Education*, 1947, 16, 149-159.

LEHMAN, H. C., and WITTY, P. A. *The Psychology of Play Activities*. New York: Barnes, 1927.

LEHRMAN, L. J., SIRLUCK, H., BLACK, B. J., and GLIC, S. J. Success and failure of treatment of children in the child guidance clinics of the Jewish Board of Guardians, New York City. *Jewish Board of Guardians Research Monographs*, 1949, No. 1.

LESSER, G. S. Maternal attitudes and practices and the aggressive behavior of children. Unpublished doctoral dissertation, Yale University, 1952.

LEVY, D. *Maternal Overprotection*. New York: Colombia University Press, 1943.

LEWIN, K. *A Dynamic Theory of Personality*. New York: McGraw-Hill, 1935.

LEWIN, K. *Field Theory in Social Science*. New York: Harper & Row, 1951.

LEWIN, K., DEMBO, T., FESTINGER, L., and SEARS, P. S. Level of aspiration. In J. McV. Hunt (Ed.), *Personality and the Behavior Disorders*. Vol. 1. New York: Ronald Press, 1944. Pp. 333-377.

LEWIS, D. J., and DUNCAN, C. P. Vicarious experience and partial reinforcement. *Journal of Abnormal and Social Psychology*, 1958, 57, 321-326.

LINDEMANN, E. Symptomatology and management of acute grief. *American Journal of Psychiatry*, 1944, 101, 141-148.

LINDZEY, G. Thematic Apperception Test: Interpretive assumptions and related empirical evidence. *Psychological Bulletin*, 1952, 49, 1-25.

LOEVINGER, J. On the proportional contributions of differences in nature and in nurture to differences in intelligence. *Psychological Bulletin*, 1943, 40, 725-756.

LORENZ, K. Der Kumpan in der Umwelt des Vogels. Der Artgenosse als auslo-sendes Moment sozialer Verhaltungsweisen. *Journal of Ornithology,* Leipzig, 1935, 83, 137-213; 289-413.

LOUTTIT, C. M. *Clinical Psychology.* New York: Harper & Row, 1947.

LUCHINS, A. S., and FORGUS, R. H. The effect of differential post-weaning envi-ronment on the ridigity of an animal's behavior. *Journal of Genetic Psychol-ogy,* 1955, 86, 51-58.

LYNN, D. B. A note on sex differences in the development of masculine and feminine identification. *Psychological Review,* 1959, 66, 126-135.

MAAS, H. S. et al. Sociol-cultural factors in psychiatric clinic services for chil-dren: A collaborative study in the New York and San Francisco metropolitan areas. *Smith College Studies in Social Work,* 1955, 25, 1-90.

MABERLY, A., and STURGE, B. After-results of child guidance. *British Medical Journal,* 1939, 1, 1130-1134.

MACFARLANE, J. W. Studies in child guidance: I. Methodology of data collection and organization. *Monographs of the Society for Research in Child Develop-ment,* 1938, 3, 1-254.

MACFARLANE, J. W., ALLEN, L., and HONZIK, M. P. A developmental study of the behavior problems of normal children between 21 months and 14 years. Berkeley: University of California Publications in Child Development, 1954.

MADDOX, H. Nature-nurture balance sheets. *British Journal of Educational Psy-chology,* 1957, 27, 166-175.

MANN, H. B., and WHITNEY, D. R. On a test of whether one of two random variables is stochastically larger than the other. *Annals of Mathematical Sta-tistics,* 1947, 18, 50-60.

MARQUIS, D. P. Learning in the neonate: The modification of behavior under three feeding schedules. *Journal of Experimental Psychology,* 1941, 29, 263-282.

MASSERMAN, J. H. *Principles of Dynamic Psychiatry.* Philadelphia: Saunders, 1946.

McCANDLESS, B. R. Changing relationships between dominance and social ac-ceptability during group democratization. *American Journal of Orthopsychi-atry,* 1942, 12, 529-536.

McCANDLESS, B. R. Motivational and social structure research at pre- and elementary school levels. Presidential address before Division 7, American Psychological Association, San Francisco, September 1955.

McCANDLESS, B. R., and CASTANEDA, A. Anxiety in children, school achievement and intelligence. *Child Development,* 1956, 27, 379-382.

McCARTHY, D. Language development in children. In L. Carmichael (Ed.), *Manual of Child Psychology.* New York: Wiley, 1946. Pp. 427-581.

McCARTHY, D. The psychologist looks at the teaching of English. *Independent School Bulletin,* 1946-1947, No. 5.

McCARTHY, D. Personality and learning. *American Council on Education Stud-ies,* 1949, 35, 93-96.

McCLELLAND, D. C. Some social consequences of achievement motivation. In M. R. Jones (Ed.), *Nebraska Symposium on Motivation.* Vol. 3. Lincoln: University of Nebraska Press, 1955. Pp. 41-65.

McCLELLAND, D. C. The use of measures of human motivation in the study of society. In J. W. Atkinson (Ed.), *Motives in Fantasy, Action, and Society.* Princeton: Van Nostrand, 1958. Pp. 518-552.

McCLELLAND, D. C. *The Achieving Society.* Princeton: Van Nostrand, 1961.

McClelland, D. C., Atkinson, J. W., Clark, R. A., and Lowell, E. L. *The Achievement Motive*. New York: Appleton-Century-Crofts, 1953.

McClelland, D. C., Rindlisbacher, A., and deCharms, R. Religious and other sources of parental attitudes toward independence training. In D. C. McClelland (Ed.), *Studies in Motivation*. New York: Appleton-Century-Crofts, 1955. Pp. 389-397.

McCulloch, T. L. The retarded child grows up: Psychological aspects of aging. *American Journal of Mental Deficiency*, 1957, 62, 201-208.

McGraw, M. B. Maturation of behavior. In L. Carmichael (Ed.), *Manual of Child Psychology*. New York: Wiley, 1946.

McGuffey, W. H. *New Fourth Eclectic Reader*. New York: Wilson, Hinkle, 1857.

McKee, J. B., and Turner, W. S. The relation of "drive" ratings in adolescence to CPI and EPPS scores in adulthood. *Vita humana*, 1961, 4, 1-14.

Mead, M. The application of anthropological techniques to cross-national communication. *Transactions of the New York Academy of Sciences*, 1947, 9, 133-152.

Mead, M. Some anthropological considerations concerning guilt. In M. L. Reymert (Ed.), *Feelings and Emotions: The Moosehart Symposium*. New York: McGraw-Hill, 1950.

Melzack, R. The genesis of emotional behavior: An experimental study of the dog. *Journal of Comparative and Physiological Psychology*, 1954, 47, 166-168.

Messick, S. J., and Solley, C. M. Probability learning in children: Some exploratory studies. *Journal of Genetic Psychology*, 1957, 90, 23-32.

Miles, C. C. Influence of speed and age on intelligence scores of adults. *Journal of General Psychology*, 1934, 10, 208-210.

Miles, C. C., and Miles, W. R. The correlation of intelligence scores and chronological age from early to late maturity. *American Journal of Psychology*, 1932, 44, 44-78.

Miller, D. C., and Form, W. H. *Industrial Sociology*. New York: Harper & Row, 1951.

Miller, N. E. Experimental studies of conflict. In J. McV. Hunt (Ed.), *Personality and the Behavior Disorders*. New York: Ronald Press, 1944. Pp. 431-465.

Miller, N. E. Learnable drives and rewards. In S. S. Stevens (Ed.), *Handbook of Experimental Psychology*. New York: Wiley, 1951. Pp. 435-472.

Miller, N. E., and Dollard, J. *Social Learning and Imitation*. New Haven: Yale University Press, 1941.

Miller, N. E., and Kraeling, D. Displacement: Greater generalization of approach than avoidance in a generalized approach-avoidance conflict. *Journal of Experimental Psychology*, 1952, 43, 217-221.

Miller, N. E., and Murray, E. J. Displacement and conflict: Learnable drive as a basis for the steeper gradient of avoidance than of approach. *Journal of Experimental Psychology*, 1952, 43, 227-231.

Milner, E. A. A study of the relationships between reading readiness in grade one school children and patterns of parent-child interaction. *Child Development*, 1951, 22, 95-112.

Minkowski, M. Über fruhezeitige Bewegungen, Reflexe, und muskulare Reaktionen beim menschlichen Foetus, und inre Beziehungen zum fotalen Nerven und Muskelsystem. *Schweizerische medizinische Wochenschrift*, 1922, 52, 721-724, 751-755.

Mitchell, J. C. A study of teachers' and of mental-hygientists' ratings of certain behavior problems of children. *Journal of Educational Research*, 1942, 36, 292-307.

Moltz, H. Latent extinction and the fractional anticipatory response mechanism. *Psychological Review,* 1957, 64, 229-241.

Moltz, H., and Maddi, S. R. Reduction of secondary reward value as a function of drive strength during latent extinction. *Journal of Experimental Psychology,* 1956, 52, 71-76.

Moltz, H., and Rosenblum, L. A. Imprinting and associative learning: The stability of the following response in Peking ducks. *Journal of Comparative and Physiological Psychology,* 1958, 51, 580.

Morris, D. P., and Soroker, E. A follow-up study of a guidance-clinic waiting list. *Mental Hygiene,* 1953, 37, 84-88.

Morris, D. P., Soroker, E., and Burgess, G. Follow-up studies of shy, withdrawn children: I. Evaluation of later adjustment. *American Journal of Orthopsychiatry,* 1954, 24, 743-754.

Moses, J. A study of overinhibited and unsocialized aggressive children: IV. The later adjustment of unsocialized aggressive children. Unpublished master's thesis, Smith College, 1944.

Mouton, J. S., Blake, R. R., and Fruchter, B. The reliability of sociometric measures. *Sociometry,* 1955, 18, 7-48.

Mouton, J. S., Blake, R. R., and Frutcher, B. The validity of sociometric responses. *Sociometry,* 1955, 18, 181-206.

Mowrer, O. H. *Learning Theory and Personality Dynamics.* New York: Ronald Press, 1950.

Mowrer, O. H. "Q technique"—description, history, and critique. In O. H. Mowrer (Ed.), *Psychotherapy: Theory and Research.* New York: Ronald Press, 1953. Pp. 316-375.

Mowrer, O. H., and Ullman, A. D. Time as a determinant in integrative learning. *Psychological Review,* 1945, 52, 61-90.

Munitz, M. K. *Space, Time and Creation.* Glencoe, Illinois: Free Press, 1957-a.

Munitz, M. K.(Ed.). *Theories of the Universe.* Glencoe, Illinois: Free Press, 1957-b.

Murray, E. J., and Miller, N. E. Displacement: Steeper gradient of generalization of avoidance than of approach with age of habit controlled. *Journal of Experimental Psychology,* 1952, 43, 222-226.

Murray, H. A. *Thematic Apperception Test Manual.* Cambridge: Harvard University Press, 1943.

Mussen, P. H., and Naylor, H. K. The relationships between overt and fantasy aggression. *Journal of Abnormal and Social Psychology,* 1954, 49, 235-240.

Neimark, E. Effects of type of nonreinforcement and number of alternative responses in two verbal conditioning situations. *Journal of Experimental Psychology,* 1956, 52, 209-220.

Nelson, E. N. P. Persistence of attitudes of college students fourteen years later. *Psychological Monographs,* 1954, 68, No. 2.

Neugarten, B. L., Havighurst, R. J., and Tobin, S. S. The measurement of life satisfaction. *Journal of Gerontology,* 1961, 16, 134-143.

Neugarten, B. L. et al. *Personality in Middle and Late Life.* New York: Atherton Press, 1964.

Neuringer, C. The form equivalence between the Wechsler-Bellevue Intelligence Scale, Form I, and the Wechsler Adult Intelligence Scale. *Educational and Psychological Measurement,* 1963, 23, 755-763.

Newell, N. W. The methods of child guidance adapted to a public school system. *Mental Hygiene,* 1934, 18, 362-373.

NEWMAN, H. H. *Twins and Super-Twins*. London: Hutchinson, 1942.

NICE, M. M. Some experiences in imprinting ducklings. *Condor*, 1953, 55, 33.

NICHOLSON, E. L. The relative social development of children with pre-school background as opposed to those who lack such experiences. Unpublished master's thesis, North Texas State College, 1957.

NORTHWAY, M. L. Outsiders: A study of the personality patterns of children least acceptable to their age mates. *Sociometry*, 1944, 7, 10-25.

NORTHWAY, M. L., and WIGDOR, B. T. Rorschach patterns related to sociometric status of school children. *Sociometry*, 1947, 10, 186-199.

OJEMANN, R., and WILKINSON, F. R. The effect on pupil growth of an increase in teacher's understanding of pupil behavior. *Journal of Experimental Education*, 1939, 8, 143-147.

OLSON, W., and WILKINSON, M. Teacher personality as revealed by the amount and kind of verbal direction used in behavior control. *Educational Administration and Supervision*, 1938, 24, 81-93.

OPPENHEIMER, J. M. Functional regulation in fundulus heteroclitus embryos with abnormal central nervous systems. *Journal of Experimental Zoology*, 1950, 115, 461-492.

ORT, R. S. A study of role-conflicts as related to happiness in marriage. *Journal of Abnormal and Social Psychology*, 1950, 45, 691-699.

OSGOOD, C. E. *Method and Theory in Experimental Psychology*. New York: Oxford University Press, 1953.

OWENS, W. A., JR. Age and mental abilities: A longitudinal study. *Genetic Psychology Monographs*, 1953, No. 48, 3-54.

OWENS, W. A., JR. Age and mental abilities: A second phase of a longitudinal study. (Abstract.) *Journal of Gerontology*, 1962, 17, 472.

PALERMO, D. S., CASTANEDA, A., and MCCANDLESS, B. R. The relationship of anxiety in children to performance in a complex learning task. *Child Development*, 1956, 27, 333-337.

PARDUCCI, A. Alternative measures for the discrimination of shift in reinforcement-ratio. *American Journal of Psychology*, 1957, 70, 194-202.

PARSONS, T. Family structure and the socialization of the child. In T. Parsons and R. G. Bales (Eds.), *Family, Socialization and Interaction Process*. Glencoe, Illinois: Free Press, 1955.

PASAMANICK, B., KNOBLOCH, H., and LILIENFELD, A. M. Socioeconomic status and some precursors of neuropsychiatric disorder. *American Journal of Orthopsychiatry*, 1956, 26, 594-601.

PATERSON, D. G., and DARLEY, J. G. *Men, Women, and Jobs*. Minneapolis: University of Minnesota Press, 1936.

PAWLOWSKI, A., and SCOTT, J. P. The development of dominance in different breeds of puppies. *Journal of Comparative and Physiological Psychology*, 1956, 49, 353-358.

PEARSON, K. On a generalized theory of alternative inheritance with special reference to Mendel's laws. *Philosophical Transactions*, 1904, 203, 53-87.

PEARSON, K. Appendix to Dr. Elderton's paper on "The Lanarkshire Milk Experiment." *Annals of Eugenics*, 1932, 5, 337-338.

PHILLIPS, W. S., and GREENE, J. E. A preliminary study of the relationship of age, hobbies, and civil status of neuroticism among women teachers. *Journal of Educational Psychology*, 1939, 30, 440-444.

PIAGET, J. *The Psychology of Intelligence*. London: Kegan Paul, 1950.

PIAGET, J. *Traité de logique*. Paris, 1951-a.

PIAGET, J. *Introduction à l'épistémologie génétique*. Paris, 1951-b.

PIAGET, J. *Essai sur les transformations des opérations logiques*. Paris, 1952.

PIAGET, J., and INHELDER, B. *Le Développement des quantités chez l'enfant. Conservation et atomisme*. Neuchâtel and Paris, 1941.

PIAGET, J., and INHELDER, B. *La Représentation de l'espace chez l'enfant*. Paris, 1948.

PIAGET, J., INHELDER, B., and SZEMINSKA, A. *La Géométrie spontanée chez l'enfant*. Paris, 1948.

PIAGET, J., and SZEMINSKA, A. *La Genèse du nombre chez l'enfant*. Neuchâtel and Paris, 1941.

PITTLUCK, P. The relation between aggressive fantasy and overt behavior. Unpublished doctoral dissertation, Yale University, 1950.

PLENDERLITH, M. Discrimination learning and discrimination reversal learning in normal and feebleminded children. *Journal of Genetic Psychology*, 1956, 88, 107-112.

POTTER, J. H. Dominance relations between different breeds of domestic hens. *Physiological Zoology*, 1949, 22, 261-280.

PRATT, K. C. The neonate. In L. Carmichael (Ed.), *Manual of Child Psychology*. New York: Wiley, 1946.

PRESSEY, S. L. *Manual of the Pressey Interest-Attitude Tests*. New York: The Psychological Corporation, 1933.

PRESSEY, S. L. Changes from 1923 to 1943 in the attitudes of public school and university students. *Journal of Psychology*, 1946, 21, 173-188.

PRESSEY, S. L., and PRESSEY, L. C. Development of the Interest-Attitude Tests. *Journal of Applied Psychology*, 1933, 17, 1-16.

RÄBER, H. An analysis of mating behavior in a domesticated turkey. *Behaviour*, 1948, 1, 237-266.

RADKE, M. J. The relation of parental authority to children's behavior and attitudes. *Child Welfare Monograph No. 22*. Minneapolis: University of Minnesota Press, 1946.

RAMSEY, A. O. Familial recognition in domestic birds. *Auk*, 1951, 68, 1.

RAMSEY, A. O., and HESS, E. H. A laboratory approach to the study of imprinting, *Wilson Bulletin*, 1954, 66, 196.

RAY, W. S. A preliminary report on a study of fetal conditioning. *Child Development*, 1932, 3, 175-177.

REEVE, F. C. R., and WADDINGTON, C. H. (Eds.), *Quantitative Inheritance*. London: H. M. Stationery Office, 1952.

REID, J. H., and HAGAN, H. R. *Residential Treatment of Emotionally Disturbed Children*. New York: Child Welfare League of America, 1952.

RENSHAW, T. Burt's concept of intelligence. *British Psychological Society Bulletin*, 1957.

REYNOLDS, W. F. Acquisition and extinction of the conditioned eyelid response following partial and continuous reinforcement. *Journal of Experimental Psychology*, 1958, 55, 335-341.

RICHARDS, T. W. Mental test performance as a reflection of the child's current life situation: A methodological study. *Child Development*, 1951, 22, 221-233.

RIESEN, A. H. Vision. *Annual Review of Psychology*, 1954, 5, 57-88.

RIESMAN, D., GLAZER, N., and DENNEY, R. *The Lonely Crowd*. New Haven: Yale University Press, 1950.

ROBERTS, J. A. F. *An Introduction to Medical Genetics.* Oxford: Oxford University Press, 1940.

ROE, A. A psychological study of eminent biologists. *Psychological Monographs,* 1951, 65 (Whole No. 331).

ROE, A. A psychological study of physical scientists. *Genetic Psychology Monographs,* 1951, No. 43, 121-235.

ROE, A. A psychological study of eminent psychologists and anthropologists and a comparison with biological and physical scientists. *Psychological Monographs,* 1953, 67 (Whole No. 352).

ROE, A. Early determinants of vocational choice. *Journal of Counseling Psychology,* 1957, 4, 212-217.

ROSSMAN, I. L., and GOSS, A. E. The acquired distinctiveness of cues: The role of discriminative verbal responses in facilitating the acquisition of discriminative motor responses. *Journal of Experimental Psychology,* 1951, 42, 173-182.

ROSTOW, W. W. *The Stages of Economic Growth.* Cambridge: Cambridge University Press, 1960.

ROYCE, J. R. A factorial study of emotionality in the dog. *Psychological Monographs,* 1955, 69, 1-27.

RUCH, F. L. The differentiative effects of age upon human learning. *Journal of General Psychology,* 1934, 11, 261-286.

RUNDQUIST, E. A. The inheritance of spontaneous activity in rats. *Journal of Comparative Psychology,* 1933, 16, 415-438.

RUNDQUIST, E. A. The significance of the form of statement for personality measurement. *Psychological Bulletin,* 1935, 32, 751. (Abstract)

RUSSELL, W. A., and STORMS, L. H. Implicit verbal chaining in paired-associate learning. *Journal of Experimental Psychology,* 1955, 49, 287-293.

SANFORD, N. The dynamics of identification. *Psychological Review,* 1955, 62, 106-118.

SANFORD, N., ADKINS, M. M., MILLER, R. B., COBB, E. A. et al. Physique, personality, and scholarship: A cooperative study of school children. *Monographs of the Society for Research in Child Development,* 1943, 8, No. 1.

SCHAEFER, H. H., and HESS, E. H. Color preferences in imprinting objects. *Zeitschrift für Tierpsychologie,* 1959, 16, 161-172.

SCHWESINGER, G. C. *Heredity and Environment.* New York: Macmillan, 1933.

SCOTT, J. P. The process of socialization in higher animals. In *Interrelations Between the Social Environment and Psychiatric Disorders.* New York: Milbank Memorial Fund, 1953.

SCOTT, J. P., and CHARLES, M. S. Some problems of heredity and social behavior. *Journal of Genetic Psychology,* 1953, 48, 209-230.

SCOTT, J. P., and CHARLES, M. S. Genetic differences in the behavior of dogs: A case of magnification by thresholds and habit formation. *Journal of Genetic Psychology,* 1954, 84, 175-188.

SCOTT, J. P., and FULLER, J. L. Research on genetics and social behavior at the Roscoe B. Jackson Memorial Laboratory, 1946-1951—A progress report. *Journal of Heredity,* 1951, 42, 191-197.

SCOTT, J. P., and GAULT, M. M. Genetic differences in the reactions of dogs to a maze problem. (Abstract.) *Anatomical Record,* 1953, 117, 565.

SCOTT, J. P., and MARSTON, M. V. Critical periods affecting the development of normal and maladjustive social behavior of puppies. *Journal of Genetic Psychology,* 1950, 77, 25-60.

SEARLE, L. V. The organization of hereditary maze-brightness and maze-dullness. *Genetic Psychology Monographs*, 1949, No. 39, 279-325.

SEARS, P. S. Doll play aggression in normal young children: Influence of sex, age, sibling status, father's absence. *Psychological Monographs*, 1951, 65, No. 6.

SEARS, R. R. Ordinal position in the family as a psychological variable. *American Sociological Review*, 1950-a, 15, 397-401.

SEARS, R. R. Relation of fantasy aggression to interpersonal aggression. *Child Development*, 1950-b, 21, 5-6.

SEARS, R. R., MACCOBY, E. E., and LEVIN, H. *Patterns of Child Rearing*. New York: Harper & Row, 1957.

SEARS, R. R., PINTLER, M. H., and SEARS, P. S. Effect of father separation on pre-school children's doll play aggression. *Child Development*, 1946, 17, 219-243.

SEARS, R. R., WHITING, J., NOWLIS, V., and SEARS, P. S. Some child-rearing ante-cedents of aggression and dependency in young children. *Genetic Psychology Monographs*, 1953, No. 47, 135-234.

SENN, M. J. E. (Ed.). *Problems of Early Infancy*. New York: Josiah Macy, Jr., Foundation, 1947.

SEWELL, W. H. A short form of the Farm Family Socio-economic Status Scale. *Rural Sociology*, 1943, 8, 161-170.

SHAW, G. B. Preface to "Androcles and the Lion." In *Nine Plays*. New York: Dodd, Mead, 1948.

SHEPARD, W. O. The effects of verbal pre-training on discrimination learning in preschool children. Unpublished doctoral dissertation, State University of Iowa, 1954.

SHOCK, N. W. Standard values for basal oxygen consumption in adolescents. *American Journal of Diseases of Children*, 1942, 64, 19-32.

SHOCK, N. W. Some physiological aspects of adolescence. *Texas Reports of Bio-logical Medicine*, 1946-a, 4, 289-310.

SHOCK, N. W. Physiological responses of adolescents to exercise. *Texas Reports of Biological Medicine*, 1946-b, 4, 368-386.

SHOLL, D. A. *The Organization of the Cerebral Cortex*. London: Methuen, 1956.

SIDMAN, M. Two temporal parameters of the maintenance of avoidance behavior by the white rat. *Journal of Comparative and Physiological Psychology*, 1953, 46, 253-261.

SINGER, M. B. Shame cultures and guilt cultures. In G. Piers and M. B. Singer (Eds.), *Shame and Guilt*. Springfield, Illinois: Charles C Thomas, 1953.

SKINNER, B. F. Are theories of learning necessary? *Psychological Review*, 1950, 57, 193-216.

SMITH, M. E. An investigation of the development of the sentence and the extent of vocabulary in young children. *University of Iowa Studies in Child Welfare*, 1926, 3, No. 5.

SNYDER, L. H. The genetic approach to human individuality. *Science Mono-graphs*, New York, 1949, 68, 165-171.

SNYDER, L. H., and DAVID, P. R. *The Principles of Heredity* (5th ed.) Boston: Heath, 1957.

SNYDER, W. Do teachers cause maladjustment? *Journal of Exceptional Children*, 1947, 14, 40-46.

SOLLENBERGER, R. T. Some relationships between the urinary excretion of male hormone by maturing boys and their expressed interests and attitudes, *Journal of Psychology*, 1940, 9, 179-189.

SOLOMON, R. L., and BRUSH, E. S. Experimentally derived conceptions of anxiety and aversion. In *Nebraska Symposium on Motivation*. Vol. 4. Lincoln: Uni-versity of Nebraska Press, 1956.

SOLOMON, R. L., and COLES, M. R. A case of failure of generalization of imitation across drives and across situations. *Journal of Abnormal and Social Psychology*, 1954, 49, 7-13.

SONTAG, L. W., BAKER, C. T., and NELSON, V. L. Personality as a determinant of performance. *American Journal of Orthopsychiatry*, 1955, 25, 555-562.

SONTAG, L. W., BAKER, C. T., and NELSON, V. L. Mental growth and personality development. *Monographs of the Society for Research in Child Development*, 1958, 23, No. 2.

SPEARMAN, C. *Abilities of Man*. London: Macmillan, 1927.

SPELT, D. K. The conditioning of the human fetus in utero. *Journal of Experimental Psychology*, 1948, 38, 338-346.

SPENCE, K. W. Theoretical interpretations of learning. In C. P. Stone (Ed.), *Comparative Psychology*. New York: Prentice-Hall, 1951-a.

SPENCE, K. W. Theoretical interpretations of learning. In S. S. Stevens (Ed.), *Handbook of Experimental Psychology*. New York: Wiley, 1951-b.

SPENCE, K. W. *Behavior Theory and Conditioning*. New Haven: Yale University Press, 1956.

SPENCE, K. W. The empirical basis and theoretical structure of psychology. *Philosophy of Science*, 1957, 24, 97-108.

SPENCER, H. *Principles of Psychology*. London: Williams & Norgate, 1870.

SPITZ, R. A., and WOLF, K. M. The smiling response: A contribution to the ontogenesis of social relations. *Genetic Psychology Monographs*, 1946, No. 34, 57-125.

SPOERL, D. T. Bilinguality and emotional adjustment. *Journal of Abnormal and Social Psychology*, 1943, 38, 37-57.

STAATS, C. K., and STAATS, A. W. Meaning established by classical conditioning. *Journal of Experimental Psychology*, 1957, 54, 74-80.

STAATS, A. W., and STAATS, C. K. Attitudes established by classical conditioning. *Journal of Abnormal and Social Psychology*, 1958, 57, 37-40.

STENGEL, E. A clinical and psychological study of echo-reactions. *Journal of Mental Science*, 1947, 93, 598-612.

STERN, C., and STERN, W. *Die Kindersprache*. Leipzig: Barth, 1920.

STEVENSON, H. W., and ZIGLER, E. F. Discrimination learning and rigidity in normal and feebleminded individuals. *Journal of Personality*, 1957, 25, 699-711.

STEWART, L. H. Social and emotional adjustment during adolescence as related to the development of psychosomatic illness in adulthood. *Genetic Psychology Monographs*, 1962, No. 65, 175-215.

STOLZ, H. R., and STOLZ, L. M. *Somatic Development in Boys*. New York: Macmillan, 1951.

STONE, C. P. Methodological resources for the experimental study of innate behaviour as related to environmental factors. *Psychological Review*, 1947, 54, 342-347.

STONE, C. P., and BARKER, R. G. Aspects of personality and intelligence in post menarcheal and pre-menarcheal girls of the same chronological ages. *Journal of Comparative Psychology*, 1937, 23, 439-455.

STRAUGHN, J. H. Human escape learning in relation to reinforcement variables and intertrial conditions. *Journal of Experimental Psychology*, 1956, 52, 1-8.

STRAUSS, M. A., and HOUGHTON, L. J. Achievement, affiliation, and cooperation values as clues to trends in American rural society, 1924-1958. *Rural Sociology*, 1960, 25, 394-403.

SULLIVAN, C. A. Scale for measuring developmental age in girls. *Catholic University of America Studies in Psychology and Psychiatry*, 1934, 3, vii, 65.

SUPER, D. E. Vocational adjustment: Implementing a self-concept. *Occupations,* 1951, 30, 88-92.

SUPER, D. E. A theory of vocational development. *American Psychologist,* 1953, 8, 185-190.

SUPER, D. E. Career patterns as a basis for vocational counseling. *Journal of Counseling Psychology,* 1954, 1, 12-20.

SYMONDS, P. M. *Adolescent Fantasy: An Investigation of the Picture Story Method of Personality Study.* New York: Columbia University Press, 1949.

TANNER, J. M. The inheritance of morphological and physiological traits. Ap. Sorsby, A. *Clinical Genetics.* London: Butterworth, 1953.

TAYLOR, J. A. A personality scale of manifest anxiety. *Journal of Abnormal and Social Psychology,* 1953, 48, 285-290.

TENENBAUM, S. Uncontrolled expression of children's attitudes toward school. *Elementary School Journal,* 1939-1940, 40, 670-768.

TERMAN, L. M. (Ed.). *Genetic Studies of Genius.* Stanford, California: Stanford University Press, 1925, 1947.

TERMAN, L. M. The discovery and encouragement of exceptional talent. *American Psychologist,* 1954-a, 9, 221-230.

TERMAN, L. M. Scientists and nonscientists in a group of 800 gifted men. *Psychological Monographs,* 1954-b, 68, No. 7 (Whole No. 378).

TERMAN, L. M., and MILES, C. C. *Sex and Personality: Studies in Masculinity and Femininity.* New York: McGraw-Hill, 1936.

TERMAN, L. M., and ODEN, M. H. *Genetic Studies of Genius.* Vol. 4. *The Gifted Child Grows Up.* Stanford, California: Stanford University Press, 1947.

TEUBER, H. L., and LIEBERT, R. S. Specific and general effects of brain injury in man. *A.M.A. Archives of Neurology and Psychiatry,* 1958, 80, 403-407.

THOMPSON, D. W. *On Growth and Form* (2nd ed.). Cambridge: Cambridge University Press, 1948.

THOMPSON, G. G. The social and emotional development of preschool children under two separate types of educational program. *Psychological Monographs,* 1944, 56, No. 5.

THOMPSON, G. G., and HORROCKS, J. E. A study of the friendship fluctuations of urban boys and girls. *Journal of Genetic Psychology,* 1947, 70, 53-63.

THOMPSON, W. R., and MELZACK, R. Early environment. *Scientific American,* 1956, 194 (1), 38-42.

THORNDIKE, E. L. *Educational Psychology.* New York: Bureau of Publications, Teachers College, Columbia University, 1914.

THORNDIKE, E. L., and LORGE, I. *The Teacher's Word Book of 30,000 Words.* New York: Bureau of Publications, Teachers College, Columbia University, 1944.

THORPE, J. G. An investigation into some correlates of sociometric status within school classes. *Sociometry,* 1955, 18, 49-61.

THURSTONE, L. L. *The Vectors of Mind.* Chicago: University of Chicago Press, 1935.

THURSTONE, L. L., and THURSTONE, T. G. *Primary Mental Abilities Test.* Chicago: Science Research Associates, 1947.

THURSTONE, L. L., and THURSTONE, T. G. *Examiner Manual for the SRA Primary Mental Abilities.* Chicago: Science Research Associates, 1949.

TIEDEMAN, D. V. Decision and vocational development: A paradigm and its implications. *Personnel and Guidance Journal,* 1961, 40, 15-21.

Tiedeman, S. A study of pupil-teacher relationship. *Journal of Educational Research*, 1942, 35, 657-664.

Tilton, J. W. A measure of improvement in American education over a twenty-five-year period. *School and Society*, 1949, 69, 25-26.

Tolman, E. C. There is more than one kind of learning. *Psychological Review*, 1949, 56, 144-155.

Tomkins, S. S. *The Thematic Apperception Test.* New York: Grune & Stratton, 1947.

Toulmin, S. *The Philosophy of Science.* London: Hutchinson's University Library, 1953.

Tryon, R. C. Genetics of learning ability in rats. *University of California Publications in Psychology*, 1929, 4, 71-89.

Tryon, R. C. Genetic differences in maze-learning ability in rats. In *Intelligence: Its Nature and Nurture.* 39th Yearbook, National Society for the Study of Education. Bloomington, Illinois: Public School. Part I, pp. 111-119.

Tuddenham, R. D. Studies in reputation: I. Sex and grade differences. *Psychological Monographs*, 1952, 66, No. 1.

Tuddenham, R. D. The constancy of personality ratings over two decades. *Genetic Psychology Monographs*, 1959, No. 60, 3-29.

Tyler, L. E. The relationship of interests to abilities and reputation among first-grade children. *Educational and Psychological Measurement*, 1951, 11, 255-264.

Underwood, B. J. *Psychological Research.* New York: Appleton-Century-Crofts, 1957.

Van Alstyne, D. *Play Behavior and Choice of Play Materials of Preschool Children.* Chicago: University of Chicago Press, 1932.

Van Wagenen, G. The monkey. In E. J. Farris, *The Care and Breeding of Laboratory Animals.* New York: Wiley, 1950. Chap. 1.

Wallcott, E. A study of the present adjustment made by solitary children who had withdrawn into an imaginary world. Unpublished master's thesis, Smith College, 1931.

Wapner, S., and Werner, H. *Perceptual Development.* Worcester, Massachusetts: Clark University Press, 1957.

Warner, W. L., Meeker, M., and Eells, K. *Social Class in America.* Chicago: Science Research Associates, 1949.

Watson, J. B. *Behaviourism.* London: Kegan Paul, Trench, Trubner & Co., 1931.

Weber, M. *The Protestant Ethic.* (Trans. by T. Parsons.) New York: Scribner, 1930.

Wechsler, D. *The Measurement of Adult Intelligence* (1st ed.). Baltimore: Williams & Wilkins, 1939.

Wechsler, D. *The Measurement and Appraisal of Adult Intelligence* (4th ed.). Baltimore: Williams & Wilkins, 1958.

Weiss, P. Autonomous versus reflexogenous activity of the central nervous system. *Proceedings of the American Philosophical Society*, 1941, 84, 53-64.

WEISS, P. An introduction to genetic neurology. In P. Weiss (Ed.), *Genetic Neurology*. Chicago: University of Chicago Press, 1950.

WELLMAN, B. L., and McCANDLESS, B. R. Factors associated with Binet IQ changes of preschool children. *Psychological Monographs*, 1946, 60, No. 2 (Whole No. 278).

WENGER, M. A. Conditioned responses in human infants. In R. G. Barker, J. S. Kounin, and H. F. Wright (Eds.), *Child Behavior and Development*. New York: McGraw-Hill, 1943.

WERNER, H. *Comparative Psychology of Mental Development*. Chicago: Follett, 1948.

WHITING, J. W. M. The frustration complex in Kwoma society. *Man*, 1944, 44, 115.

WHITING, J. W. M., and CHILD, I. L. *Child Training and Personality: A Cross-Cultural Study*. New Haven: Yale University Press, 1953.

WHITING, J. W. M. et al. *Field Guide for a Study of Socialization in Five Societies*. Cambridge, Massachusetts: Harvard University, 1954 (mimeographed).

WHITTAKER, E. T. *The Beginning and End of the World*. London: Oxford University Press, 1942.

WHYTE, W. H. *The Organization Man*. Garden City: Doubleday, 1956.

WICKMAN, E. K. *Children's Behavior and Teacher's Attitudes*. New York: Commonwealth Fund, 1928.

WICKMAN, E. K. *Teachers and Behavior Problems*. New York: Commonwealth Fund, 1938.

WIERSMA, W., and KLAUSMEIER, H. J. The effect of age upon speed of concept attainment. *Journal of Gerontology*, 1965, 20, 398-400.

WILLIAMS, J. R., and SCOTT, R. B. Growth and development of Negro infants: IV. Motor development and its relationship to child rearing practices in two groups of Negro infants. *Child Development*, 1953, 24, 103-121.

WILLOUGHBY, R. R. The relationship to emotionality of age, sex, and conjugal condition. *American Journal of Sociology*, 1938, 43, 920-931.

WINCH, R. F. *Mate-selection: A Study of Complementary Needs*. New York: Harper & Row, 1958.

WINDLE, W. F. Reflexes of mammalian embryos and fetuses. In P. Weiss (Ed.), *Genetic Neurology*. Chicago: University of Chicago Press, 1950.

WINTERBOTTOM, M. R. *The relation of childhood training in independence to achievement motivation*. University of Michigan: University Microfilms.

WINTERBOTTOM, M. R. The relation of need for achievement to learning experiences in independence and mastery. In J. W. Atkinson (Ed.), *Motives in Fantasy, Action, and Society*. New York: Van Nostrand, 1958. Pp. 453-478.

WITHALL, J. The development of a technique for the measurement of social-emotional climate in classrooms. *Journal of Experimental Education*, 1949, 17, 347-361.

WITMER, H. L. A comparison of treatment results in various types of child guidance clinics. *American Journal of Orthopsychiatry*, 1935, 5, 351-360.

WITMER, H. L. et al. The outcome of treatment in a child guidance clinic: A comparison and an evaluation. *Smith College Studies in Social Work*, 1933, 3, 339-399.

WITMER, H. L. et al. The later adjustment of problem children. *Smith College Studies in Social Work*, 1935, 6, 1-98.

WITMER, H. L., and KELLER, J. Outgrowing childhood problems: A study in the value of child guidance treatment. *Smith College Studies in Social Work*, 1942, 13, 74-90.

WITRYOL, S. L., and THOMPSON, G. G. A critical review of the stability of social acceptability scores obtained with the partial-rank-order and the paired comparison scales. *Genetic Psychology Monographs,* 1953, No. 48, 221-260.

WITTGENSTEIN, L. *Tractatus logico-philosophicus.* New York: Harcourt, Brace, 1922.

WOLFENSTEIN, M., and LEITES, N. *Movies: A Psychological Study.* Glencoe, Illinois: Free Press, 1950.

WOODWORTH, R. S. Heredity and environment: A critical survey of recently published material on twins and foster children. *Social Science Research Council Bulletin,* 1941, No. 47.

WYATT, G. L. Stammering and language learning in early childhood. *Journal of Abnormal and Social Psychology,* 1949, 44, 75-84.

WYCHOFF, L. B., and SIDOWSKI, J. B. Probability discrimination in a motor task. *Journal of Experimental Psychology,* 1955, 50, 225-231.

YEDINACK, J. G. A study of the linguistic functioning of children with articulation and reading disabilities. *Journal of Genetic Psychology,* 1949, 74, 23-59.

YOUNG, L. L., and COOPER, D. H. Some factors associated with popularity. *Journal of Educational Psychology,* 1944, 35, 513-535.

ZINGG, R. M. *Wolf Children and Feral Man.* New York, 1941.

ZIPF, G. K. *The Psycho-biology of Language.* Boston: Houghton Mifflin, 1935.

Index